Fodor's

ROME

9th Edition

Fodor's Travel Publications   New York, Toronto, London, Sydney, Auckland

www.fodors.com

D1467077

FODOR'S ROME
Editors: Robert I. C. Fisher, Denise Leto

Editorial Contributors: Lynda Albertson, Nicole Arriaga, Martin Wilmot Bennett, Erica Firpo, Dana Klitzberg, Amanda Ruggeri, Margaret Stenhouse

Production Editor: Carolyn Roth
Maps & Illustrations: Mark Stroud, Moon Street Cartography; Henry Colomb; David Lindroth, Inc., *cartographers;* Rebecca Baer, *map editor;* William Wu, *information graphics*
Design: Fabrizio La Rocca, *creative director*; Tina Malaney, Chie Ushio, Jessica Ramirez, *designers*; Melanie Marin, *associate director of photography;* Jennifer Romains, *photo research*
Cover Photo: (Largo dei Librari) SIME/eStock Photo
Production Manager: Angela L. McLean

SPECIAL SALES
This book is available at special discounts for bulk purchases for sales promotions or premiums. Special editions, including personalized covers, excerpts of existing books, and corporate imprints, can be created in large quantities for special needs. For more information, write to Special Markets/Premium Sales, 1745 Broadway, MD 3-1, New York, NY 10019, or e-mail specialmarkets@randomhouse.com.

AN IMPORTANT TIP & AN INVITATION
Although all prices, opening times, and other details in this book are based on information supplied to us at press time, changes occur all the time in the travel world, and Fodor's cannot accept responsibility for facts that become outdated or for inadvertent errors or omissions. So **always confirm information when it matters,** especially if you're making a detour to visit a specific place. Your experiences—positive and negative— matter to us. If we have missed or misstated something, **please write to us.** Share your opinion instantly through our online feedback center at fodors.com/contact-us.

PRINTED IN SINGAPORE

10 9 8 7 6 5 4 3 2 1

CONTENTS

MAPS

ABOUT THIS GUIDE

Fodor's Ratings

Everything in this guide is worth doing—we don't cover what isn't—but exceptional sights, hotels, and restaurants are recognized with additional accolades. **Fodor's**Choice ★ indicates our top recommendations; ★ highlights places we deem highly recommended; and **Best Bets** call attention to notable hotels and restaurants in various categories. Care to nominate a new place? Visit Fodors.com/contact-us.

Trip Costs

We list prices wherever possible to help you budget well. Hotel and restaurant price categories from **$** to **$$$$** are noted alongside each recommendation. For hotels, we include the lowest cost of a standard double room in high season. For restaurants, we cite the average price of a main course at dinner or, if dinner isn't served, at lunch. For attractions, we always list adult admission fees; discounts are usually available for children, students, and senior citizens.

Hotels

Our local writers vet every hotel to recommend the best overnights in each price category, from budget to expensive. Unless otherwise specified, you can expect private bath, phone, and TV in your room. For expanded hotel reviews, facilities, and deals visit Fodors.com.

Restaurants

Unless we state otherwise, restaurants are open for lunch and dinner daily. We mention dress code only when there's a specific requirement and reservations only when they're essential or not accepted. To make restaurant reservations, visit Fodors.com.

Ratings		Hotels & Restaurants	
★	Fodor's Choice	🏨	Hotel
★	Highly recommended	↪	Number of rooms
�ును	Family-friendly	❑	Meal plans
		✕	Restaurant
Listings		☌	Reservations
✉	Address	🏛	Dress code
✉	Branch address	⊟	No credit cards
☎	Telephone	$	Price
⊕	Website		
✍	E-mail	**Other**	
⬙	Admission fee	⇨	See also
◷	Open/closed times	☞	Take note
Ⓜ	Subway	⚐	Golf facilities
⊕	Directions or Map coordinates		

Credit Cards

The hotels and restaurants in this guide typically accept credit cards. If not, we'll say so.

Experience Rome

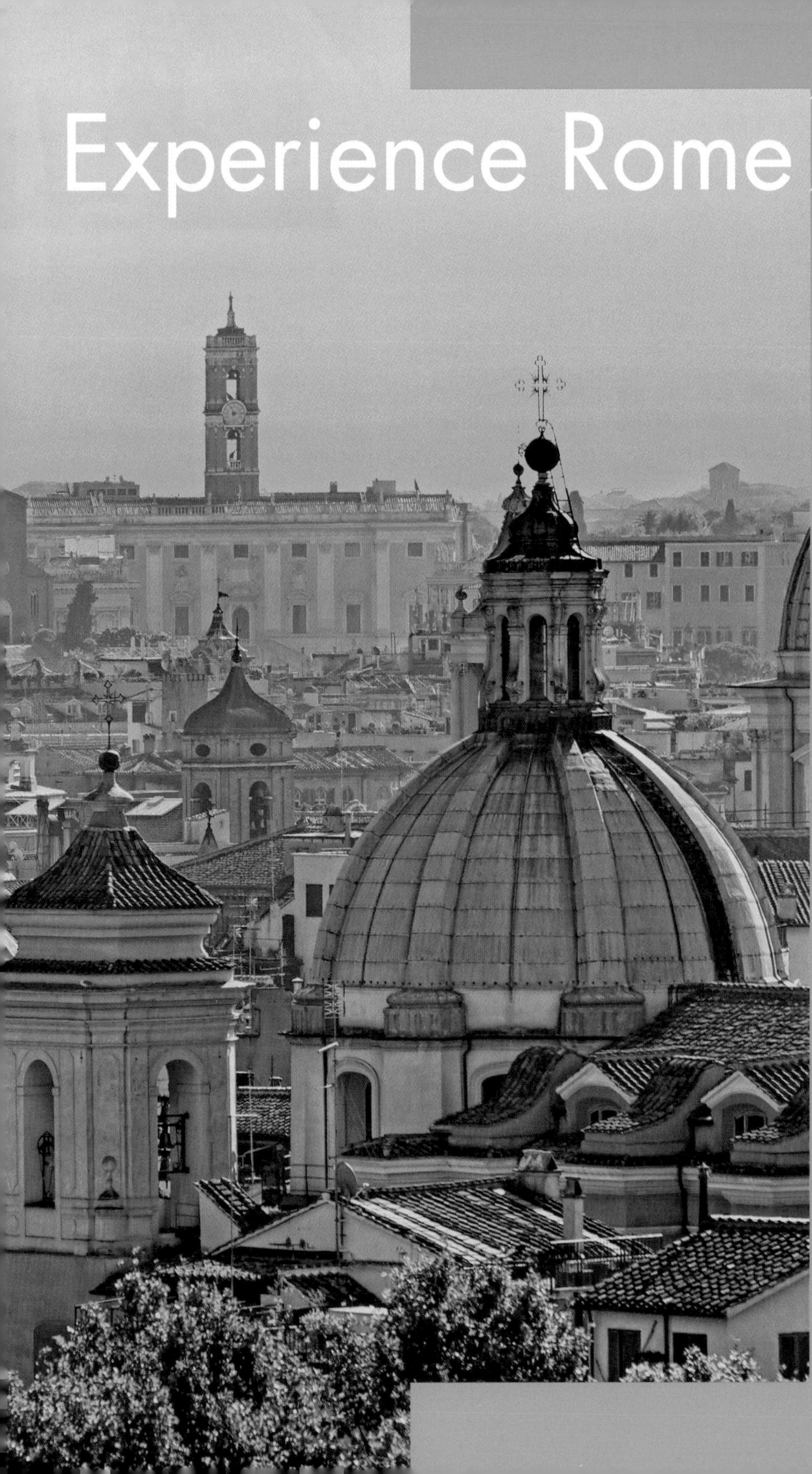

ROME TODAY

Coming off the Autostrada at Roma Nord or Roma Sud, you know by the convergence of heavily trafficked routes that you are entering a grand nexus: All roads lead to Rome. And then the interminable suburbs, the railroad crossings, the intersections—no wonder they call it the Eternal City.

As you enter the city proper, flashbacks of images you saw in fabled films such as *Three Coins in the Fountain* and *Roman Holiday* soon become reality: a bridge with heroic statues along its parapets; a towering cake of frothy marble decorated with allegorical figures in extravagant poses; a piazza and an obelisk under an umbrella of pine trees. Then you spot what looks like a multistory parking lot; with a gasp, you realize it's the Colosseum. That's when you say to yourself, that's right, Dorothy, we're not in Kansas anymore. There's no place like Rome.

You have arrived. You're in the heart of the Città Eterna. As you step down from your excursion bus, you're instantly mesmerized by the sounds of Vespas zipping in and out of traffic. You step onto the broad girdle of tarmac that encircles the great stone arena of the Roman emperors, and scurry out of the way of the passing Fiats—the motorists behind the wheels seem to display the panache of so many Ben-Hurs.

More than Florence, more than Venice, Mamma Roma is Italy's true showstopper. And though the city has one foot forward in the future, its timelessness and pristine preservation of its landmarks continue to captivate millions of visitors each year. Why? Here, the ancient Romans made us heirs-in-law to what we call Western Civilization; where centuries later Michelangelo painted the Sistine Chapel ceiling; where Gian Lorenzo Bernini's Baroque nymphs and naiads still dance in their marble fountains; and where, at Cinecittà Studios, Fellini filmed *La Dolce Vita* and 8½. Today, the city remains a veritable Grand Canyon of culture: Ancient Rome rubs shoulders with the medieval, the modern runs into the Renaissance, and the result is like nothing less than one big open-air museum for the world to marvel at.

Yesterday's Grand Tourists thronged the city for the same reason today's Expedians do. Majestic, complicated, enthralling, romantic, chaotic, monumental Rome is one of the world's great cities—past, present, and, probably, future. While one

. . . IS CREATING NEW "IT" NEIGHBORHOODS

The leader among Rome's "It" nabes is San Lorenzo, with Pigneto trailing just behind.

San Lorenzo is just a stone's throw away from the Termini train station. Rome's new "Left Bank" district is filled with students and a young bohemian crowd, thanks to its close proximity to La Sapienza University.

In fact, if you don't know what you're looking for, you could easily get lost in this maze of dark narrow streets, many now lined with underground cafés, bars, hip restaurants, and locales with live-music venues.

The leading scene-arenas include Formula 1 (✉ *Via degli Equi 13*), for top pizzas; Da Franco ar Vicoletto (✉ *Via dei Falisci 1/b*), just around the corner, for fish lovers; and Arancia Blu (✉ *Via dei Latini 55*), which draws the green crowds thanks to its vegetarian menus.

wouldn't really reckon Rome as "futuristic," the city is taking heartfelt leaps and bounds into the 21st century while flirting with the Facebook generation. In 2013, the Eternal City is outdazzling many of its Italian rivals with a newly unleashed vitality. Move over Milano: Rome is bringing its game up a notch, working its way up to be the next posh metropolitan "It" girl.

Romans are ready to show the world that its old-world ways—slow pace, antique-flair, and everything mini—are ancient history. They're changing gears and starting to live life in the fast lane. For those who had any doubts, Romans can have their *dolce vita*-cake lifestyle and eat it, too.

Mega-shopping malls, tech-savvy sumptuousness, fusion food, and even gas-guzzling SUVs have made their way to the ancient home of the popes. Romans are more "connected" than ever before: even Pope Benedict XVI can't do without his Facebook and Twitter. Though resistance is bound to come with change, Romans seem to be embracing these tumultuous changes with open arms.

TODAY'S ROME . . .

. . . is not the Roma your mother knew.

Home to nearly 3 million residents and a gazillion tourists, Rome is virtually busting at the seams. For decades, the heart and soul of the city was concentrated in its *centro storico*, where a chunk of Rome's legendary museums, monuments, and ancient relics have stood for centuries. Replete with postcard landmarks, Baroque palaces, and hyper-luxury hotels, the "Disneyfication" of the historic center is well underway.

As there was no room to grow upward, Rome has had to stretch outward. To relieve pressure in the city center, officials have focused on building a "new" Rome beyond the historic quarter. In the process, old, economically weaker, satellite districts have been revitalized with the creation of cutting-edge palazzos and museums. Former working-class neighborhoods—San Lorenzo and Pigneto to the north, Ostiense and Testaccio to the south—are also on the fast track of unprecedented change and becoming trendy. This "other" Rome is shabby-chic, alternative, and full of flair.

The likes of bands such as the Cure, U2, and Pearl Jam have been known to play at I Giardini di Adone (✉ *Via dei Reti 38/A*). Or throw down your best moves at Qube Disco (✉ *Viadi Portonaccio 212*), where the vibe ranges from rock to house music and changes its scene and crowd from night to night.

Immortalized as the backdrop for Roberto Rossellini's magnificent Academy Award–nominated *Rome Open City* (*Roma Città Aperta*), Pigneto—set in the northwestern part of the city on the other side of the Porta Maggiore walls—has come a long way since the black-and-white days of the 1950s.

Sixty years ago, you couldn't find much more than old folks playing cards down the Via Fanfulla da Lodi and Via del Pigneto. Fast-forward to 2013 and this hot new *quartiere* has undergone a major transformation into a colorful hub for hipsters who tuck into the many wine bars, *caffè*, and bookshops scattered in and

ROME TODAY

...is going multi-culti.

Spend a day in Rome's Esquilino neighborhood and you'll see just how multicultural the Eternal City is becoming. Once famous for its spice market at Piazza Vittorio, the area neighborhood has fast become a multiethnic stomping ground.

In fact, finding a true Roman restaurant or a local shopkeeper is hard to come by in this area, now that Chinese, Indian, African, and Middle Eastern restaurants have moved in (a typical example: The Syrian restaurant, *Zenobia*, perched on Piazza Dante, even includes a weekend belly-dancing show).

Homegrown and locally produced, the Orchestra di Piazza Vittorio is a perfect picture of the neighborhood's growing ethnic population. Made up of 16 musicians from Brazil, Senegal, Tunisia, Cuba, Argentina, Hungary, Ecuador, and Italy, the troupe was founded in 2002 and got its start in the ramshackle district just steps away from Rome's Termini train station and, by 2006, had a documentary made about them; today, they play at festivals around the world.

...is breaking new ground.

With a big push to modernize parts of Rome particularly lacking in the luster department, visitors will notice some new and novel aspects to the city skyline. First, that former eyesore, the Tiburtina train station, was completely overhauled, to the tune of some €330 million, to become the new avant-garde Tiburtina stazione, the first rail hub in Italy to handle super-high-speed (Alstom AGVs) trains.

Even more buzz has been generated by Rome's first-ever skyscraper, the EuroSky Tower. Located in the distant EUR suburb, the 28-floor building (to be completed in 2013) will be the first to launch Romans into orbit for high-rise luxury apartment living (it's eco-sustainable, replete with solar panels, bio-fuel power, and channels to deliver rainwater to plants and flowers). Feathers were ruffled when Vatican officials worried that the skyscraper would clash with St. Peter's Basilica, Rome's tallest building.

Located by the Tiber River, the grandiose new "Ponte della Musica" bridge has now "bridged the gap" between the worlds of sports and music and arts: it connects the Foro Italico area (home to Rome's stunning Stadio Olimpico and Stadio dei

around main drags like Fanfulla da Lodi and Via del Pigneto.

Definitely on the radar as one of Rome's up-and-coming districts, Pigneto is bohemian in all the good old ways.

Today, the area is now home to many artists, journalists, and designers. And it has even

become the backdrop for a slew of popular Italian TV shows.

Back in the day, Italian film legends Pier Paolo Pasolini and Luchino Visconti spent time here capturing the lives of Pigneto's working-class families. To channel those vibes, head on over to Pigneto's most popular venue, Circolo degli Artisti (⊠ *Via*

Casilina Vecchia 42) where one can rock out to one of the various local bands playing, catch a flick, or savor an art show of homegrown artists. Or enjoy an *aperitivo* at the historic Bar Necci (⊠ *Via Fanfulla da Lodi 68*). It was here at this neighborhood landmark that Pasolini filmed scenes for his award-winning 1961 *Accatone* (an

Marmi) with the Flaminio district (Parco della Musica and the MAXXI museum). Designed by British star-engineer Buro Happold, the eco-friendly ponte can be used by pedestrians, cyclists, and electric buses.

Last but not least, the new convention center of Rome—EUR Congressi Roma—is expected to dazzle when completed in 2013.

Italian starchitect Massimiliano Fuksas whipped up a vast design centered around the "Cloud," an airy futuristic structure that floats in a showcase of steel and glass. City officials have high hopes.

. . . is in political limbo.

After playing a prominent role in politics for nearly two decades, controversial tycoon Silvio Berlusconi stepped down as prime minister at the end of 2011, only after an unprecedented revolt within Parliament, after scandals and continuous market pressures had left Italy in bad shape.

To put a new government into place and turn the country's severe economic crisis around, Mario Monti—a multitasker whose background runs the gamut from professor to economist to president of the prestigious Bocconi University to European commissioner—was appointed not only as the new prime minister but also, due to his formidable expertise, as minister of economy and finance.

He wasted no time and raised taxes, cracked down on tax evaders, and whipped Italy's debt crisis back into shape. He will stay on until major new elections can be held.

. . . is more commuter-connected.

When it comes to train travel in Italy, the competition is growing fierce. Thanks to the introduction of "Italo," Italy's first private railway (owned by NTV and operated by the president of Fiat), rail travelers now have a new alternative to the state-run TrenItalia.

NTV is the first operator in the world to use the new Alstom AGV train, which currently holds the highest speed record for trains.

The new trains are said to be equipped with all sorts of modern amenities and will service various big cities around Italy including Rome, Florence, Venice, Bologna, Naples, and Salerno. In Rome, the high-speed trains will use Rome's new Tiburtina station rather than Termini.

---

unflinching look at how a pimp living in the slums of Rome attempts to go straight).

To catch Pigneto's other celluloid moments of fame, check out Ciak si Mangia (✉ *Via Giovanni Brancaleone 72*), a popular pizzeria with reasonable prices, where walls showcase photos from various movies shot in the neighborhood.

Want a later nightcap? Head to Fanfulla 101 (✉ *Via Fanfulla da Lodi 101*) for some live music with bands ranging from rock to country. Or, for those looking for something a little more laid-back, VI(ci)NO (✉ *Via del Pigneto 25*) is an *enoteca* that serves up a little art and jazz with a glass of wine. Yeah! Music Café (✉ *Via Giovanni de Agostani 41*) is also another hidden gem in Pigneto, busy churning out great vibes, music, and good ol' homey neighborhood ambiente.

A bit bohemian like its next-door neighbor San Lorenzo, Pigneto is definitely getting brighter these days on the traveler's radar screen.

WHAT'S WHERE

1 Ancient Rome. Today, no other archaeological park has so compact a nucleus of fabled history-laden sights. A walk through the Roman Forum—one-time playground for emperors Caesar and Augustus—leads you north to the Campidoglio, the Capitoline Hill, rebuilt by Michelangelo; to the west lies the Palatine Hill; to the east stand the Imperial Forums; and to the south looms the wonder that is the Colosseum.

2 The Vatican. A world in itself, residence of Pope Benedict XVI, and home base for the Catholic Church, the Vatican draws hundreds of thousands of pilgrims and art lovers to St. Peter's Basilica, the Vatican Museums, and the Sistine Chapel.

3 Navona. The *cuore*—heart—of the *centro storico* (historic quarter), this is Baroque Rome at its bravura best, thanks to Piazza Navona, graced with Bernini's most flamboyant fountain, and Caravaggio's paintings at San Luigi dei Francesi. Another showstopper: the ancient Pantheon.

4 Campo. A pop-up Renaissance painting, this nook of Rome is centered around the vibrant piazza of Campo de' Fiori, the 16th-century Via Giulia—"the most beautiful street in Rome"—and the spectacular Farnese and Spada palaces.

5 Corso. Stretching from Piazza Venezia north to Piazza del Popolo, the Corso is Rome's "Broadway" and flaunts monuments of artistic opulence, ranging from Emperor Augustus's Ara Pacis Augustae to the 17th-century Palazzo Doria-Pamphilj and gilded church of Sant'Ignazio.

6 Spagna. Travel back to the days of the Grand Tour in this glamorous area enticingly wrapped around the Piazza de Spagna. After admiring the grandeur of the Spanish Steps, shop like a true VIP along Via dei Condotti, then be sure to throw a coin into the Trevi Fountain.

7 Repubblica. The Piazza del Repubblica is an example of how Rome's history is revealed in layers: The vast Baths of Diocletian here were transformed into a Renaissance church. Westward lie art treasures—like Bernini's *St. Theresa in Ecstasy* at Santa Maria della Vittoria—and Via Veneto, still basking in the afterglow of *La Dolce Vita*.

8 Quirinale. The Quirinale hill has long been crowned by the over-the-top Palazzo del Quirinale, home to Italy's president. Nearby, go for Baroque at two great churches:

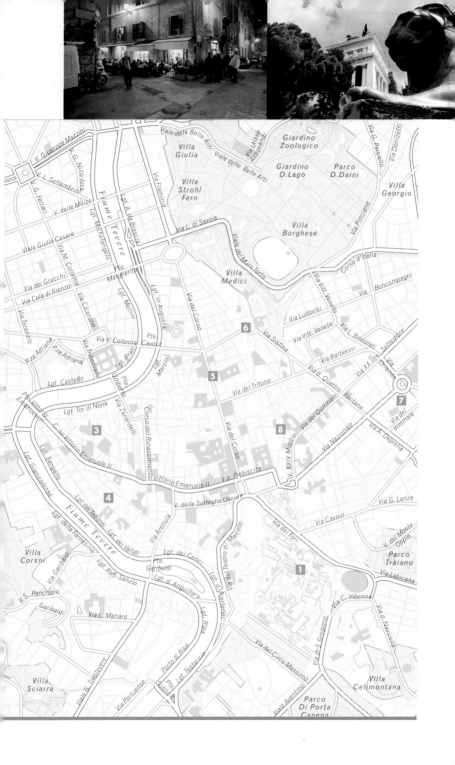

WHAT'S WHERE

Bernini's Sant'Andrea and Borromini's San Carlo alla Quattro Fontane. The two architects called a truce at their grand Palazzo Barberini.

9 Villa Borghese. Rome's "Central Park," the Villa Borghese is home to an array of dazzling museums: Cardinal Scipione Borghese's 17th-century Galleria Borghese is loaded with great Bernini statues; Etruscan treasures fill the eye at Villa Giulia; while the gardens of the Villa Medici remain Edenic as ever.

10 Piazza del Popolo. After touring the Villa Borghese museums, give your less-than-bionic feet a rest at a caffè on the Piazza del Popolo, a prime watch-the-world-go-by spot. Here, Santa Maria del Popolo beckons with Raphaels and Caravaggios.

11 Trastevere. Rome's "Greenwich Village" has kept much of its authéntic roots thanks to mom-and-pop trattorias, winding cobblestone alleyways, and the resplendent church of Santa Maria in Trastevere, stunningly lit at night (when hip new disco-pubs take center stage).

12 The Ghetto. Despite galloping gentrification, the Ghetto—once the home to Rome's Jews during the Middle Ages—still preserves the flavor of Old Rome and

is centered on the ancient Portico d'Ottavia.

13 Aventino. A green and posh residential district, the Aventine Hill is aloof from the bustle of central Rome. At its foot lies Piazza Bocca della Verità and Santa Maria in Cosmedin, a Romanesque masterpiece. To the south, working-class Testaccio becomes party central for hip club-goers.

14 Esquilino. While the multi-culti crowds of the Termini train station set the tone here, the Esqueline Hill has many "islands" of peace and calm: great basilicas (Santa Maria Maggiore), Early Christian wonders (Santa Pudenziana), and noted churches (San Pietro in Vincoli, home to Michelangelo's *Moses*).

15 Celio. Almost entirely given over to parks, churches, and ruins, the peaceful Celian Hill is home to time-travel marvels, including the Early Christian splendors of San Clemente, mystic Santo Stefano Rotondo al Celio, and medieval, magnificent Santi Quattro Coronati.

16 Catacombs and Appian Way. The Via Appia Antica leads past the landmark church of Domine Quo Vadis and walled gardens to the spirit-warm catacombs.

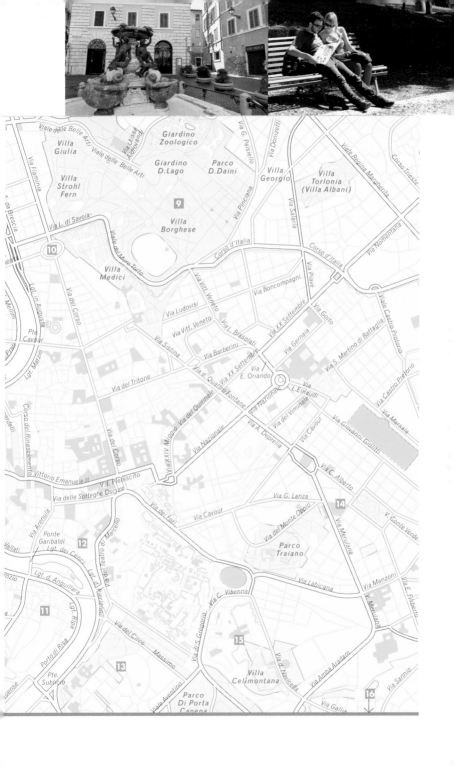

ROME PLANNER

Don't Miss the Metro

Fortunately for tourists, many of Rome's main attractions are concentrated in the *centro storico* (historic center) and can be covered on foot. But not to worry, wherever your feet won't take you, the Metro most probably will. Some sights nearer the border of this quarter can be reached via the Metro Line A, nicknamed the *linea turistica* (tourist line), and include: the Spanish Steps (Spagna stop), the Trevi Fountain (Barberini stop), St. Peter's Square (Ottaviano–San Pietro Musei Vaticani stop), and the Vatican Museums (Cipro stop), to name a few.

Tickets for the bus and Metro cost €1 at any *tabacchi* (tobacco shop) and at most newsstands (the price may go up to €1.50 by 2013). These tickets are good for 75 minutes on buses and trams, or a single Metro ride. Day passes can be purchased for €4, and weekly passes, which allow unlimited use of buses, trams, and the Metro, for €16. For a better explanation of the Metro routes, pick up a free map from information booths around the city: Tech-savvy tourists can navigate Rome on the website of ATAC (Rome's public transport system): ⊕ *www.atac.roma.it.*

Making the Most of Your Time (and Money)

Roma, non basta una vita ("Rome, a lifetime is not enough"): this famous saying should be stamped on the passport of every first-time visitor to the Eternal City. Indeed, the ancient city certainly wasn't built in a day, so you shouldn't expect to see it in one either. Rome is so packed with sights that it is impossible to take them all in; it's easy to run yourself ragged trying to check off the items on your "To Do" list.

At the same time, the saying is a celebration of the city's abundance. There's so much here, you're bound to make discoveries you hadn't anticipated. To conquer Rome, strike a balance between visits to major sights and leisurely neighborhood strolls (and a pit stop for some *gelato*, of course).

In the first category, the Vatican and the remains of ancient Rome loom the largest. Both require at least half a day; a good strategy is to devote your first morning to one and your second to the other. Leave the afternoons for exploring the neighborhoods that comprise Baroque Rome and the shopping district around the Spanish Steps and Via Condotti. Among the sights, Galleria Borghese and the church of San Clemente are particularly worthwhile, and Trastevere and the Ghetto make for great roaming.

Since there's a lot of ground to cover in Rome, it's wise to plan your sightseeing schedule with possible savings in mind, and purchasing the Roma Pass (⊕ *www.romapass.it*) allows you to do just that.

The three-day pass costs €30 and is good for unlimited use of buses, trams, and the Metro. It includes free admission to two of more than 40 participating museums or archaeological sites, including the Colosseum (and bumps you to the head of the long line there, to boot), the Musei Capitolini, and Galleria Borghese, plus discounted tickets to many other museums. The Roma Pass can be purchased at tourist booths across the city, at Termini Station, or between Terminals B and C of the International Arrivals section of Fiumicino Airport.

Hop-On, Hop-Off

Rome has its own "hop-on, hop-off" sightseeing buses. The Trambus Open Roma 110 bus leaves with 10-minute frequencies from Piazza dei Cinquecento (at the main Termini station), with a two-hour loop including the Colosseum, Piazza Navona, St. Peter's, and the Trevi Fountain. Tickets are €18, depending on whether you want to hop on and off or just stay on the whole time. There is also a Tram Open Bus by Night, only on Friday and Saturday and it leaves from Piazza Venezia at 10 pm and 10:30 pm (€12). A variant is the Archeobus (€12), which departs every 20 minutes from the Piazza dei Cinquecento and heads out to the Via Appia Antica, the Colosseum, and the Catacombs. Tickets can also be purchased ahead of time online (⊕ *www.trambusopen.com*).

Roman Hours

On Sunday, Rome virtually shuts down on its official day of rest. Meanwhile, museums, pastry shops, and most restaurants are closed Monday. Daily shop hours generally run from 10 am to 1 pm, then 4 until 7:30 or 8 pm (but on Monday shops usually don't open until around 4 pm). Pharmacies tend to have the same hours as stores unless they advertise *orario notturno* (night hours). As for churches, most open at 8 or 9 in the morning, close from noon to 3 or 4, then reopen until 6:30 or 7. St. Peter's, however, has continuous hours from 7 am to 7 pm (until 6 in the fall and winter) and the Vatican Museums are open on Monday but closed Sunday (except for the last one of the month).

How's the Weather

Spring and fall are the best times to visit, with mild temperatures and many sunny days. Summers are often sweltering. In July and August, come if you like, but learn to do as the Romans do—get up and out early, seek refuge from the afternoon heat, resume activities in early evening, and stay up late to enjoy the nighttime breeze.

Come August, many shops and restaurants close as locals head out for vacation. Remember that air-conditioning is still a relatively rare phenomenon in this city. Roman winters are relatively mild, with persistent rainy spells.

Information Please

The Department of Tourism in Rome, called Roma Capitale, launched a new single phone number that tourists can call for cultural happenings and events, ticket sales, and other visitor information (☎ *06/0608* ⊕ *www.turismo roma.it*). To provide information about cultural events, museums, opening hours, and city transportation, Roma Capitale also staffs green information kiosks (with multilingual personnel) near important sights as well as at Termini Station and Leonardo da Vinci Airport. These kiosks, called Tourist Information Sites (Punti Informativi Turistici, or PIT) can be found at:

Castel S. Angelo, Lungotevere Vaticano; 9:30–7 pm

Cinque Lune, Piazza delle Cinque Lune (Piazza Navona); 9:30–7 pm

Fiumicino, Aeroporto Leonardo Da Vinci–Arrivi Internazionali Terminal C; 9–7:30 pm

Minghetti, Via Marco Minghetti (corner of Via del Corso); 9:30–7 pm

Nazionale, Via Nazionale (Palazzo delle Esposizioni); 9:30–7 pm

Santa Maria Maggiore, at Via dell'Olmata; 9:30–7 pm

Termini, Stazione Termini, at Via Giovanni Giolitti 34; 8–8

Trastevere, on Piazza Sidney Sonnino; 9:30–7 pm

TOP ROME ATTRACTIONS

The Pantheon

Constructed to honor all pagan gods, this best preserved temple of ancient Rome was rebuilt in the 2nd century AD by Emperor Hadrian, and to him much of the credit is due for the perfect dimensions: 141 feet high by 141 feet wide, with a vast dome that was the largest ever designed until the 20th century.

The Vatican

Though its population numbers only in the few hundreds, the Vatican—home base for the Catholic Church and the pope—makes up for them with the millions who visit each year. Embraced by the arms of the colonnades of St. Peter's Square, they attend Papal Mass, marvel at St. Peter's Basilica, and savor Michelangelo's Sistine Chapel ceiling.

The Colosseum

(B) Legend has it that as long as the Colosseum stands, Rome will stand; and when Rome falls, so will the world. One of the Seven Wonders of the World, the mammoth amphitheater was begun by Emperor Vespasian and inaugurated by Titus in the year 80. For "the grandeur that was Rome," this obstinate oval can't be topped.

Piazza Navona

(D) You couldn't concoct a more Roman street scene: caffè and crowded tables at street level, coral- and rust-color houses above, most lined with wrought-iron balconies, street performers and artists and, at the center of this urban "living room," Bernini's spectacular Fountain of the Four Rivers and Borromini's super-theatrical Sant'Agnese.

Roman Forum

(A) This fabled labyrinth of ruins variously served as a political playground, a commerce mart, and a place where justice was dispensed during the days of the emperors (500 BC to AD 400). Today, the Forum is a silent ruin—*sic transit gloria mundi* (so passes away the glory of the world).

The Campidoglio

(C) Catch a bird's-eye view of the Roman Forum from Michelangelo's piazza, atop one of the highest spots in Rome, the Capitoline Hill. Here you'll find the Capitoline Museums and beloved Santa Maria in Aracoeli.

Trevi Fountain

(E) One of the few fountains in Rome that's actually more absorbing than the people crowding around it, the Fontana di Trevi was designed by Nicola Salvi in 1732. Immortalized in *Three Coins in the Fountain* and *La Dolce Vita,* this granddaddy of all fountains may be your ticket back to Rome—that is, if you throw a coin into it.

The Spanish Steps

(F) Byron, Shelley, and Keats all drew inspiration from this magnificent "Scalinata," constructed in 1723. Connecting the ritzy shops at the bottom with the ritzy hotels at the top, this is the place for prime people-watching. The steps face west, so sunsets offer great photo ops.

Castel Sant'Angelo

(G) Originally constructed as a mausoleum for Roman emperor Hadrian, this cylindrical fortress, which towers over the city's skyline, has great views and opulent Renaissance-era salons.

Trastevere

Located just across the Tiber River, this time-stained, charming villagelike neighborhood is a maze of jumbled alleyways, traditional Roman trattorias, cobblestone streets, and medieval houses. Some call it the third smallest country in the world (after the Vatican and Monaco), others dub it Rome's "Greenwich Village." Whatever, it has staunchly resisted the tides of change for centuries. The area also boasts the oldest church of Rome—Santa Maria in Trastevere.

TOP ROME MUSEUMS

Musei Capitolini

(A) None other than the great Michelangelo would suffice to design the master plan for Rome's own collection of art and archaeological museums, which enticingly crown the Capitoline Hill. The museum is divided into two wings: Palazzo Nuovo, devoted to ancient sculpture; and the Palazzo dei Conservatori, with great Old Masters.

Palazzo Doria-Pamphilj

Waltzing through this 17th-century palace may be the closest you ever get to the aristocratic nobles. Fabled Old Master paintings line the walls, with pride of place going to Velàzquez's *Innocent X* (the family pope), perhaps the greatest portrait ever painted.

Palazzo Altemps

Catch a glimpse of exquisite taste in this 15th-century palace, once owned by Cardinal Altemps and today part of the Museo Nazionale Romano—on view are many legendary examples of classic Greek and Roman sculpture, including the Ludovisi Throne.

Galleria Borghese

(D) Only the best could satisfy the aesthetic taste of Cardinal Scipione Borghese, whose holdings evoke the essence of Baroque Rome. Spectacularly frescoed ceilings and multihue marble walls frame great Bernini sculptures and paintings by Titian and Raphael.

Keats-Shelley House

During the 18th century, the Spanish Steps became a gathering place for Grand Tour artists and writers, so here in 1821 the English Romantic poet John Keats came to write—and ultimately die (of tuberculosis)—in the Casina Rossa, a dusty pink house at the base of the steps.

Museo Nazionale Romano

The city's own great collections of ancient Roman sculpture, paintings, and precious relics—salvaged from excavations

completed over several centuries—is so vast that four separate museums at different locations are needed: Palazzo Altemps, Aula Ottagona, Terme di Diocleziano, and Palazzo Massimo alle Terme.

Villa Farnesina
Lifestyles of the Rich and Famous, Renaissance-era version, are on display at this extravagant villa, built around 1511 by banker Agostino Chigi, with loggias decorated by Raphael. After lavish dinners, Chigi would toss his gold plates into the Tiber and slyly retrieve them with a net in the water.

Vatican Museums
(C) The seemingly endless line waiting for entry here can be intimidating, but the reward—a vast collection of masterpieces, including the Raphael Rooms—make it worth it. The rooms here are packed with legendary works, including the *Apollo Belvedere* and the *Laocoön* (from ancient Rome), the *Good Shepherd* (from early

Christian Rome), and great paintings such as Leonardo's *St. Jerome*, Raphael's *Transfiguration*, and Caravaggio's *Deposition*. The agony, not the ecstasy, of it all is summed up in Michelangelo's sublime *Last Judgment* and Sistine ceiling.

Palazzo Barberini
The three fathers of the Baroque—Bernini, Borromini, and Pietro da Cortona—whipped up this imposing 17th-century palace for the Croesus-rich Barberini family. Built around 1625, with the Gran Salone, Rome's largest ballroom, the palazzo is now home to the city's collection of Old Master paintings.

Palazzo Spada
(B) A glorious 17th-century assemblage of stuccowork and statuary, together with the impressive trompe l'oeil "trick" of its courtyard colonnade, inspired by master designer Borromini, is what draws the crowds.

TOP ROME CHURCHES

St. Peter's Basilica

(B) Every year, millions of pilgrims flock to the world's most important Catholic church, as art lovers marvel at Michelangelo's cupola, Bernini's papal altar, and the vast nave. The burial site of its namesake, St. Peter's took such Italian masterminds as Raphael and Bramante more than a century to complete.

Santa Maria in Trastevere

(C) Even locals can't help being mesmerized by the splendors of this church's piazza, chief among them being the incandescent Byzantine mosaics on the basilica's facade and the elegant octagonal fountain. Inside, the vast nave stupefies with its gigantic Roman columns and glittering golden mosaics.

Sant'Ignazio

Studying the dome up high in this fantastically bejeweled 1626 Jesuit church, you may think your eyes are playing tricks on you. But it's not your eyes!

That extraordinarily accurate replica of a Baroque dome was painted in its place after plans for the cupola fell through.

Sant'Agnese in Agone

Prominently positioned in Piazza Navona, this church has some of Rome's most quintessential Baroque architecture. Designed by Borromini (1652), a fervent rival of Bernini's, the church's facade is a stunning symphony of voluminous concave spaces and bell towers.

Santa Maria in Cosmedin

(A) Moody, medieval, and magnificent, this 12th-century Romanesque church draws throngs to its portico where the stone Bocca della Verità (Mouth of Truth) sits in judgment—dare you test the legend that its stone jaws clamp shut on the hands of the untruthful?

San Clemente

Uncover the layers of Medieval Rome here at this half-basilica, half archaeological site. Famed for its mosaics, this

12th-century church actually sits on top of another church that dates back to the 4th century *and* a 2nd-century BC temple to the pagan god, Mithras.

Santa Maria del Popolo

Few other churches in Rome reflect the richness of Renaissance art as does Santa Maria del Popolo, thanks to its nave enlarged by Bramante and the Chigi Chapel, a Raphael masterwork. But equally striking are Baroque treasures like Caravaggio's Cerasi Chapel and Bernini's mosaic-covered dome.

Santa Maria sopra Minerva

Set on a piazza graced by Bernini's famed elephant obelisk, this Gothic-style church—best known for Michelangelo's *Risen Christ* and famed frescoes by Filippino Lippi—gives off a heavenly aura, thanks to arched blue ceilings ashimmer with gold stars.

Santa Maria in Aracoeli

On the Capitoline Hill and atop a towering, 137-step stairway (designed in 1348 to celebrate the passing of the Black Death and the very spot where Gibbon was inspired to write his *Fall and Decline of the Roman Empire*), this Romanesque-Gothic landmark was begun in the 6th century and is home to the famed Santo Bambino, a carved-wood Baby Jesus figure.

San Giovanni in Laterno

It's hard to miss the 15 gargantuan marble statues (including Christ and the 12 Apostles) that tower over the facade of Rome's official cathedral and first church of the popes. The Baroque interior was accomplished by Borromini, but many pilgrims head first to the legendary Scala Santa (Holy Steps).

ROME LIKE A LOCAL

"When in Rome, do as the Romans do." Undoubtedly, the catch phrase may sound a bit clichéd, but locals themselves will even suggest this advice is not to be taken lightly. Romans certainly know how to live life to the fullest, indulging in the simplest pleasures and doing so with style. So put yourself in their shoes (Fendi preferably); try being Roman for a day and you'll learn how *la vita è bella!*

Il Mercato

If you're looking to rub shoulders with real Romans, there's no better place to do it than at your local *mercato all'aperot*—or open-air food market. Ah yes. Exploring the local markets of Rome is indeed the perfect way to experience a true slice of Roman life. Watch vendors take centerstage and turn the practice of selling some of the region's freshest produce into a grand theatrical performance. The most popular mercato is the Campo de' Fiori (⊠ *Piazza Campo de' Fiori*), Rome's oldest food market, situated just south of Rome's Renaissance/Baroque quarter and the Piazza Farnese. Too wide to be called picturesque, the market is nevertheless a favorite photo op, due to the *ombrelloni* (canvas umbrella) food stands. You have to look hard to find the interesting regional foodstuffs, such as Colle Romani strawberries, chestnuts, or the colorful peperoncini piccanti (spicy hot peppers). Other top food markets are the recently renovated Mercato Trionfale (⊠ *Via Tunisi in Prati, north of the Vatican*) and Nuovo Mercato Esquilino (⊠ *Via Filippo Turati*), which is strongly influenced by the multi-culti makeup of the district. Open-air markets typically run Monday through Saturday from 7 am until 2 pm, with Saturday being the busiest shopping day.

La Piazza

For Italians young and old, *la piazza* serves as a *punto d'incontro*—a meeting place—for dinner plans, drinks, people-watching, catching up with friends, and, as Romans would say, exchanging *due chiacchere* (two words). Some of the most popular piazzas in Rome: Piazza di Spagna is not just a postcard-perfect moment for tourists, but is also a favored spot among adolescent Italian boys looking to meet American girls. By day, Piazza Campo de' Fiori is famous for its fresh food and flower market; by night, the piazza turns into a popular hangout for Romans and foreigners lured by its pubs, street caffè, and occasional street performers and magicians. Over the last few years, Campo de' Fiori has even been dubbed "the American college campus of Rome," as pubs in the area now cater to American students by advertising two-for-one drink specials and such. The main attractions of the Piazza Santa Maria in Trastevere are the grand bell tower and marvelous mosaics of its namesake church—a picture-perfect background for some pretty trattorias.

L'Aperitivo

You can thank the Milanesi for inventing it, but it was the Romani who perfected it: *l'aperitivo*. Though l'aperitivo was a custom invented in the north, we have the Romans down south to thank for making the trend *molto, molto moda*. Similar to the concept of "happy hour" (sans the two-for-one drinks), l'aperitivo is a time to meet up with friends and colleagues after work or on weekends—definitely an event at which to see and be seen. Aperitivo hours are usually 7–9 pm, with Sunday being the most popular day. Depending on where you go, the price of a drink often includes an all-you-can-eat

IL GELATO

appetizer buffet of finger foods, sandwiches, and pasta salads. Some aperitivo hot spots on the *trendissimo* list are Fluid (✉ *Via del Governo Vecchio*); Societè Lutece (✉ *Piazza Monte Vecchio*); Gusto (✉ *Piazza Augusto Imperatore*), and Salotto 42 (✉ *Piazza di Pietra*) in the centro storico; and Friends Café (✉ *Piazza Trilussa*) and Freni and Frizioni (✉ *Via del Politeama*) in the Trastevere area.

Il Caffè

If there's something Romans certainly can't live without, it's their cup of java. Caffeine, or *il caffè* (espresso), may be the most important part of their day, and there is no shortage of bars in the Eternal City to help satisfy that coffee craving. A caffè or cappuccino in the morning is typically enjoyed at the counter while debating last night's soccer game or some aspect of local politics. Another espresso or *caffè macchiato* (coffee with a dash of milk) can also be enjoyed after lunch, and again after dinner, especially when dining out. Thinking about ordering that *cappuccino*? Aspetta, hold on a minute. Check the time, for Italians consider it taboo to order one after 11 am. During the summer months, Romans drink a *caffè shakerato* (freshly made espresso shaken briskly with sugar and ice, to form a froth when poured) or a *caffè freddo* (iced espresso). Rome's best coffee? Some say the Tazza D'Oro (✉ *Via degli Orfani*), not far from the Pantheon; others, Il Caffè Sant'Eustachio (✉ *Piazza di Sant'Eustachio*). If you like a dollop of chic along with your caffeine, head to Bar della Pace (✉ *Via della Pace 3*), set on one of the most fashionable piazzas in Rome (but don't forget that outdoor tables sometimes hike up the price).

Il Gelato

You haven't died and gone to food heaven until you've tried some authentic, Italian gelato. A national obsession, the Italian version of ice cream is tastier, less creamy, and traditionally made with only the freshest ingredients. Though many bars and stands purvey it, the best gelatos are found only at *gelaterie*. Small cones cost anywhere from €1.20 to €2.50. Most places allow you up to three flavors (even on a small cone) and portions are usually quite generous. So generous at times, a cone or a cup can almost replace a meal. Typical flavors are *nocciola* (hazelnut), pistachio, chocolate, and anything fruity. Or hunt down the latest and greatest flavors, such as the sweet-with-a-kick *cioccolato con peperoncino* (chocolate with hot pepper) at Millenium (✉ *Piazza Santa Maria delle Grazie 2/a, near the Vatican Museums*). Quality varies: A good sign is a long line at the counter, and two of the longest are at Old Bridge (✉ *Via Bastioni di Michelangelo 5, near St. Peter's Square*), and Giolitti (✉ *Via degli Uffici del Vicario 40, by the Pantheon*).

La Passeggiata

A favorite Roman pastime is the *passeggiata* (literally, the promenade). In the late afternoon and early evening, especially on weekends, couples, families, and packs of teenagers stroll up and down Rome's main streets and piazzas. It's a ritual of exchanged news and gossip, window-shopping, flirting, and gelato eating that adds up to a uniquely Italian experience. You may feel more like an observer than a participant, until you realize that observing is what la passeggiata is all about. Rome's top promenade is Via del Corso, with a grande finale in the Piazza di Spagna shopping district.

ROME WITH KIDS

There's an ancient myth going around that says Rome isn't family-friendly, especially those with small children. Don't be fooled into thinking that the city is one big playground for adults, thanks to its ancient ruins, Baroque churches, and abundance of museums. Rome has an array of child-oriented activities; you just have to know where to look.

Blast from the Past

Hurtle through 3,000 years of Roman history on the four-dimensional flight simulator ride at Time Elevator Roma (✉ *Via S.S. Apostoli 20, near Piazza Venezia* ⊕ *www.timeelevator.it*). Through phenomenal special effects, the one-hour ride takes you on a tour of the city and its monuments as Caesar knew them.

You start with a *Jeopardy!*-style quiz on Rome, then head into a movie theater with roller-coaster seats. Once the safety bar drops, lights dim and you're off to the founding of Rome with Romulus and Remus. Chased by wolves, you dip into a time tunnel to the Ides of March to see Julius Caesar meet his untimely end before your eyes. Then you hurtle on to the gladiator combats in the Colosseum, watch Michelangelo work in the Sistine Chapel, dash on to Bernini's Baroque fountains, and continue right up through Italy's modern history. This ride is air-conditioned—a real plus in the summer—and the narration comes in English and other languages.

Another similar 3-D simulator ride near the Colosseum is the 3-D Rewind Rome Tour (✉ *Via Capo d'Africa 5* ⊕ *www.3d rewind.com*), which takes tourists on a 3-D tour of Ancient Rome in AD 310 that lasts 15 minutes. Visitors can also check out the second-floor museum for all sorts of fun exhibits, including its "Be an Ancient Roman" exhibit, where children can try on togas, armor, and other ancient garb that the ancient Romans once wore.

Say "Cheese," Spartacus

Taking a photo with one of those kitschy gladiators (who aren't Italian by the way) in front of the Colosseum will win some smiles—but maybe some frowns, too. Many of these costumed gladiators pounce on tourists who simply aim a camera at them and then proceed to shake them down for a "photo fee" (usually around €5 a photo). Others have a craftier approach: before you know it, one may envelop your eight-year-old in his red cape and say "*Formaggio*."

Indeed, this may turn out to be the greatest souvenir back home in fourth-grade class, so if interested, step right up, shake hands, and exchange some euros. But pick your Spartacus very carefully: some sloppy guys wear a helmet and cloak but have sweat suits or sneakers on. Others have helmets and swords for tourists to try on. The police try to crack down on these "gladiators" but so far it is caveat emptor.

Playing with the Planets

After roamin' around Rome for a couple of days, your little ones may have had more history than they can handle. If that's the case, you can always switch it up a bit by giving them a bit of science. Taking a trip through outer space is always an easy winner for kids, so head to the Planetarium of Rome (✉ *Piazza G. Agnelli 10*). From Martians to falling stars, the folks there always put on special programs for children on the weekends.

Talk to the Animals

For some fun on wheels, consider renting bikes (✉ *Viale dell'Orologio, on the Pincio hill,* or *Piazzale M. Cervantes*) before

heading over to Rome's zoo, Bioparco, both set in the massive Villa Borghese park. The zoo (⊠ *Piazzale del Giardino Zoologico 1*), which is one of the oldest in Europe, is home to more than 1,000 animals.

For those uniquely Roman critters— *i gatti* (the street cats)—kids can go on a free guided tour of the ancient Largo di Torre Argentina, for it has been made into a sanctuary and home for hundreds of once-homeless Roman cats—Mom and Dad, meanwhile, can ooh-and-aah at the relics and remains of one of the oldest (300 BC) temples in Rome.

Truth or Dare

Long before the advent of lie-detector machines, and even before there were Bibles to swear on, there was the Bocca della Verità—the Mouth of Truth, the famous gaping mouth that so successfully terrified Audrey Hepburn in *Roman Holiday.* Legend has it that people suspected of telling lies would be marched up to the Bocca and have their hand put inside the mouth of this massive stone relief (originally an ancient street drain cover).

If the suspect told the truth, nothing to fear. But if lies were told, the grim unsmiling stone mouth would take its revenge and clamp down on the person's hand. This is a great spot for kids to get the truth out of their brother or sister, so have your camera—and your probing questions!—ready.

Adventures in Learning

Kids love hands-on activities and Rome has one museum that encourages them to do just that. The Explora Children's Museum (⊠ *Via Flaminia 82, near Piazza del Popolo* ☎ 06/3613776 ⊕ *www.mdbr. it*) is a miniature realistic cityscape for children under 12 whose exhibits take

them—and their bodies—through life in the big city. Though the exhibits are mainly in Italian, the visuals, effects, and touchy-feely stuff seem to hold the children's attention whatever their language. Elsewhere, kids learn about the workings of a post office, a bank, and the ABCs of recycling. Also fun for kids are the workshops and readings at the Casina di Raffaello ("Raphael's House") in Villa Borghese (⊠ *Viale della Casina di Raffaello, Piazza di Siena*). Tuesday through Sunday, they offer all sorts of activities from painting to games.

The World on Strings

Looming over Trastevere is the Janiculum Hill (Gianicolo), famed for its panoramic vistas of the Roman skyline and for its colorful, open-air Teatro di Pulcinella puppet theater. Shows here run weekdays from 4 to 7 pm and from 10:30 am to 1 pm on weekends. A small donation is expected.

Over on the Pincio hill in the Villa Borghese park (usually accessed via Piazza del Popolo) is the Teatro Stabile dei Burattini "San Carlino," which puts on live puppet shows on weekends (⊠ *Viale dei Bambini Villa Borghese*).

Don't forget to take a stroll through the pretty park over to the Cinema dei Piccoli, the smallest movie theater in the world— with all of 63 seats (⊠ *Viale della Pineta 15*)—and children's movies shown daily. Shows are in Italian, but most kids are amused by the images. After these puppet shows, the perfect souvenir awaits at Bartolucci (⊠ *Via de' Pastini 99, near the Pantheon*), where you'll meet not one Pinocchio but hundreds, still or animated, from life- to pocket-size, all crafted by artisans.

GREAT ITINERARIES

As Romans would say, these one-day itineraries *basta e avanza* ("are more than enough") to get you started. ⇨ *For other great walks, see The Historic Heart, Across the Tiber, and Postcard Rome on the Rome On-the-Go Pullout Map and also "Roamin' Holiday."*

Rome 101

Rome wasn't built in a day, but if that's all you have to see it in, take a deep breath, strap on some stylish comfy sneakers, and grab a cup of cappuccino to help you get an early start. Think Rome 101, and get ready for a spectacular sunrise-to-sunset spree of the Ancient City.

Begin at 9 by exploring Rome's most beautiful neighborhood—"Vecchia Roma" (the area around Piazza Navona) by starting out on Via del Corso (the big avenue that runs into Piazza Venezia, the traffic hub of the historic center).

A block away from each other are two opulently over-the-top monuments that show off Rome at its Baroque best: the church of Sant'Ignazio and the princely Palazzo Doria-Pamphilj, aglitter with great Old Master paintings. By 10:30, head west a few blocks to find the granddaddy of monuments, the fabled Pantheon, still looking like Emperor Hadrian might arrive. A few blocks north is San Luigi dei Francesi, home to the greatest Caravaggio paintings in the world.

At 11:30, saunter a block or so westward into beyond-beautiful Piazza Navona, studded with Bernini fountains. Then take Via Cucagna (at the piazza's south end) and continue several blocks toward Campo de' Fiori's open-air food market (for some lunch-on-the-run fixings). A great place to stop for a cheap and quick panino or a slice of pizza is the Antico Forno at Campo de' Fiori (⊠ *Campo de' Fiori 22*).

Two more blocks toward the Tiber brings you to one of the most romantic streets of Rome, Via Giulia, laid out by Pope Julius II in the early 16th century. Walk past 10 blocks of Renaissance palazzos and ivy-draped antiques shops to take a bus (from the stop near the Tiber) over to the Vatican.

Arrive around 1 to gape at St. Peter's Basilica, then hit the treasure-filled Vatican Museums (Sistine Chapel) around 1:45—during lunch, the crowds empty out! After two hours, head for the Ottaviano stop near the museum and Metro your way to the Colosseo stop.

Around 4, climb up into the Colosseum and picture it full of screaming toga-clad citizens enjoying the spectacle of gladiators in mortal combat. Striding past the massive Arch of Constantine, enter the back entrance of the Roman Forum around 4:45. Photograph yourself giving a "Friends, Romans, Countrymen" oration (complete with upraised hand) on one of the marble fragments. At sunset, the Forum closes but the floodlights come on.

March down the forum's Via Sacra—people walked here centuries before Christ—and out into Via dei Fori Imperiali where you will head around "the wedding cake"—the looming Vittorio Emanuele Monument (Il Vittoriano)—to the Campidoglio. Here, on the Capitoline Hill, tour the great ancient Roman art treasures of the Musei Capitolini (which is open most nights until 8), and snap the view from the terrace over the spotlit Forum.

After dinner, hail a cab—or take a long passeggiata walk down *La Dolce Vita*

memory lane—to the Trevi Fountain, a gorgeously lit sight at night. Needless to say, toss that coin in to insure your return trip back to the Mother of Us All.

Temples Through Time: Religious Rome

Making a trip to Rome and not going to see the Vatican Museums or St. Peter's Basilica is almost like breaking one of the Ten Commandments. If you head out early enough (yes, 7 am), you might get a jump on the line for the Vatican Museums, where one of the world's grandest and most comprehensive collections of artwork is stored. Even better, book tickets online at ⊕ *biglietteriamusei.vatican.va* beforehand, and you get to skip the line, period (tickets cost slightly more, €19 instead of €15, but it saves you headaches). Once you've conquered both, take the Metro from Ottaviano to Piazza del Popolo (Metro stop: Flaminio) where Santa Maria del Popolo is not to be missed for its famous chapels decorated by Raphael and Caravaggio.

Head south along the Corso for about 10 blocks toward Sant'Ignazio, an eye-popping example of Baroque Rome, with its amazing "Oh, I can't believe my eyes" optical illusion of a dome. Take Via Sant' Ignazio to Via Piè di Marmo, which will lead you to Piazza della Minerva, where Bernini's elephant obelisk monument lies in wait. Take in the adjacent Gothic-style Santa Maria sopra Minerva, best known for Michelangelo's *Risen Christ.*

Then make your way south to Corso Vittorio Emanuele and the bus piazza at Largo Argentina where you'll take Tram No. 8 to picturesque Trastevere, one of Rome's quaintest quarters. Make your way through a series of winding cobblestoned alleyways and piazzas toward the famed Piazza Santa Maria in Trastevere, where one of Rome's oldest churches—Santa Maria in Trastevere—stands. Dedicated to the Virgin Mary, the church has one of the finest displays of glimmering gilded mosaics, which cover the nave, perhaps Rome's most spectacular.

Retail Therapy: Shop-Till-You-Drop Rome

For serious shoppers, there's no better place to treat yourself to some retail therapy than the centro storico. If money is no question, Rome's Via dei Condotti (Metro stop: Spagna) is *paradiso*. VIPs can continue their shopping spree down streets Via del Babuino for fabled antique furniture and fine jewelry, and Via Frattina for exclusive boutiques. Even if you're on a pinch, window-shopping can be just as fun as you make your way down to the more affordable Via del Corso, where department-store-style shopping can be done at La Rinascente.

If vintage is your thing, head toward Piazza Navona and down Via del Governo Vecchio, where there is an assortment of vintage consignment shops featuring high-end clothing, handbags, and accessories.

Now that you've blown your shopping budget, it's time for real bargain-shopping Roman style. For rock-bottom bargains try the city's open air and flea markets. Rome's largest and most famous are markets on Via Sannio in San Giovanni (Monday–Saturday only) and the Porta Portese market (Sunday only) in Trastevere.

The market on Via Sannio specializes in new and used clothing, shoes, and accessories. The Porta Portese market sells everything but the kitchen sink: clothes, souvenirs, antiques, housewares, and knickknacks galore.

FREE AND ALMOST FREE

Rome may be on the fast track to becoming one of the most expensive cities in Europe, however, in compensation, there is a slew of free and inexpensive things to do in the *Città Eterna* that won't break the bank. For a quick look at low-cost activities, check out the Comune di Roma's tourism website (⊕ *www.turismoroma. it*) for great ideas.

Budget Boosters: Art and Archaeological Sites

On Valentine's Day (February 14), the Italian Ministry for Culture hosts its annual *Innamorati dell'Arte*, or "In Love with Art," campaign, where lovers or people in pairs can take advantage of two-for-one admission prices at all state-run museums and archaeological sites. Also sponsored by the Ministry for Culture, during *Settimana della Cultura*, or Cultural Week (typically held in April and May), many of the major archaeological sites and museums in and around Rome waive their entrance fees. Check out ⊕ *www.beniculturali.it* for exact dates and listings. It usually costs €15 to visit the Vatican Museums, but on the last Sunday of nearly every month you can get in free. Make sure to bring comfy shoes, as the wait in line can be a bit overwhelming!

Wallet-Watchers: Movies

If you're up for seeing a flick, head over to the Casa del Cinema (⊠ *Largo Marcello Mastroianni 1, near Villa Borghese*). The movie theater, sponsored by the City of Rome, has free showings daily. See ⊕ *www.casadelcinema.it* for listings.

Looking for a cheap movie night? The Nuovo Olimpia Cinema (⊠ *Via in Lucina 16*) near Piazza di Spagna often shows movies in English and, on Wednesday nights, tickets are just €6. Also on Wednesday nights, the Cinema Alcazar in Trastevere (⊠ *Via Merry del Val 14*) screens movies at €6 a ticket. Monday nights at the Nuovo Sacher Cinema (⊠ *Largo Ascianghi 1*), operated by noted actor Nanni Moretti, movies in English are €7 a person.

Econo-Tips: Music and Performances

Every year on May 1, Italy's Labor Day, hundreds of thousands of people gather for the free concert held in Piazza San Giovanni in Laterano. Headliners are usually Italian rock bands, but occasionally folk troupes perform as well. During the summer (mid-June through August), one of Rome's loveliest parks, Villa Ada, hosts its annual *Roma Incontro il Mondo*–"Rome Meets the World"—concert series. Concerts are held nightly, with ticket prices ranging €5 to €13. Check ⊕ *www.villaada.org* for details.

Euro-Stretchers: Eats

The aperitivo hour allows you to dine out, sort of, in some of Rome's trendiest and finest establishments without breaking the bank. It's like the Italian version of "happy hour," except that the focus is on food and friends, not alcohol. Here's how it works: for the price of a drink (usually €6 to €10), you can feast on an all-you-can-eat buffet. Hipsters and artsy bohemians head to Freni e Frizioni in Trastevere (⊠ *Via del Politeama 4*) or to its sumptuous sister bar Societè Lutecè in the centro storico (⊠ *Vicolo di Montevecchio 17*). A posh scene can be found at Salotto 42 (⊠ *Piazza di Pietra 42*) and Fluid (⊠ *Via Governo Vecchio 46*), where the spread includes veggies, pastas, and finger food. Momart Café in the Piazza Bologna district attracts a young Italian college crowd (⊠ *Viale XXI Aprile 19*) thanks to its wonderful wood-oven pizza.

BEATING THE EURO

It's easy to avoid the scam artists and pickpockets, but finding good value is a little trickier.

We asked travelers on Fodor's Travel Talk Forums (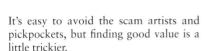 *www.fodors.com*) to reveal some of their insider know-how.

Their response?

When in Rome, spend like a Roman!

Fodorites know that if you live like a local, you'll save like a local as well, and perhaps have a richer traveling experience to boot.

1. "If you aren't hungry and don't want pasta, skip to *secondo*—the second course. Rarely do Italians eat a *primo e secondo* when they go out." —glittergirl

2. "Bars always have two different prices: If you have your coffee at the counter, it's cheaper than when a waiter serves it at a table (*servizio al tavolo*)." —quokka

3. "For the art lover on a budget: Most of the art I saw in Rome is free. Where else can you see countless Caravaggios, two Michelangelos, and even more Berninis for the cost of the wear and tear on the soles of your shoes?" —amyb

4. "Instead of taking the Leonardo Express from Fiumicino to Termini, take the FR1 to whichever station is most convenient for you. The FR1 departs every 15 minutes (instead of every 30 minutes for the Express), costs only €5 (instead of €9.50 for the Express), and avoids the hullabaloo of Termini." —Therese

5. "The boat trip down the Tiber, from the bridge by Castel Sant'Angelo to Isola Tiberina, is only €1 (a great way to get from St. Peter's to Trastevere or the Forum)." —annhig

6. "One way to save on the expense of guided tours is to register online at Sound Guides (*www.sound-guides.com*) and download the various free self-guided tours to your iPod or MP3 player." —monicapileggi

7. "I eat at working-folks places, like the Goose, near the Vatican. Dinner (three courses) runs €20 with wine; if you leave hungry, it's your own fault." —JoanneH

8. "Visit wine fill-up shops in Italy; get table wine from the cask for €2–€3 a liter. In Rome we would get them filled at the Testaccio market. I will usually ask at the local bar where I go for my coffee." —susanna

9. "Go off-season—March or November have better air prices and also accommodations, particularly if you stay in apartments, which you can rent for much less off-season (and plan some meals in-house—make the noon meal your biggest of the day, then have a small dinner in the apartment)." —bobthenavigator

10. "Invest in the bus schedule/map—at any place they sell tickets. Cost is €4. It gives you all the routes, how long between buses, hours they run, where you hop on/off to transfer, etc." —JoanneH

11. "The smaller restaurants in Trastevere also offer better value for money than, say, the ones in the alleys near the Spanish Steps or any of the other tourist areas in central Rome." —friendindelhi

12. "Order your coffee or drinks from the bar before you sit down. Take your coffee, whatever, with you to the table, then return the cup or glass afterwards. That way you'll be charged the much cheaper *al banco* price that the locals pay." —WiseOwl

ROMANTIC ROME

Whether you're looking for love or hoping to rekindle the romance, there's no better place to do so than the Eternal City. Ah yes, it certainly seems that love lurks behind every street corner, park bench, and monument. And if you don't find the abundance of public displays of affection off-putting, you'll be sure to find scores of places to steal both that first and ultimo *bacio*.

The hopeless romantics should start their rendezvous through Rome with a horse-drawn carriage ride that begins at the Spanish Steps (⊠ *Piazza di Spagna*) and continues through the streets of the *centro storico*. Make a stop for some aphrodisiacal treats, such as the decadent, mouth-watering chocolates made by Moriondo e Gariglio (⊠ *Via Piè di Marmo 21*), off the central Corso near Palazzo Doria Pamphilj.

When you're through, ask the driver to drop you off at the famous Villa Borghese park. Whether it's a picnic in the park, a cruise on the lake, or just a hand-in-hand stroll up to the Pincio—the park's terrace that boasts the city's most breathtaking views—you will find *amore* everywhere.

If the hopelessly romantic can spare the time, a trip up to Tivoli's Villa D'Este (a half hour outside Rome via bus) is definitely worth it. Its seductive garden and endless array of fountains (about 500 of them) is the perfect setting to put you in the mood for love, and it won't be long before you hear Frank Sinatra warble "Three Coins in the Fountain" in your head. For extra brownie points, during the summer months, take her or him to the Villa D'Este at night for a spectacular candlelit setting.

That's your cue to return to Rome and make a beeline for the luminous Trevi Fountain, even more enchanting at night than in the daytime. Make sure you and that special someone throw a coin into the fountain, for good luck. For your wish to come true, you must toss the coin over your shoulder with your back to the fountain, left hand over right shoulder (or vice versa). Legend has it that those who do so are guaranteed a return trip back to Rome.

A great way to lift the curtain on a night of romance is a serenaded dinner cruise along the Tiber, where dessert includes views of some of Rome's jewels by night: Castel Sant'Angelo, St. Peter's, and the Janiculum (Gianicolo) hill. See ⊕ *www.battellidiroma.it* for more details.

If you prefer to stay on terra ferma, at sundown head to the Hotel Hassler and its rooftop-garden restaurant, Imàgo, perched just over the Spanish Steps, for unforgettable views of the city's greatest landmarks, best viewed through a glass of Prosecco. Dinner here will set you back a pretty euro-cent, but you may get to rub shoulders with celebs and VIPs at this exclusive locale, whose past visitors included Princess Diana and Hollywood diva Audrey Hepburn.

For an after-dinner stroll, head to north Rome and wander over to the illuminated Ponte Milvio bridge, known as "Lovers Lane" in Roman circles. Inspired by a scene in a popular Italian movie, *Ho Voglia Di Te* (*I Really Want You*), prove your eternal love to your *inammorata* by padlocking him or her to one of the bridge's chains—the city specifically erected 24 columns with chains here so that lovers can do just that. Remember that part of the charm is throwing the key into the river!

2

Roamin' Holiday

THREE STEP-BY-STEP WALKS: BAROQUE ROME, TRASTEVERE, AND THE ROMAN FORUM

WORD OF MOUTH

"I love walking Rome. Keep in mind, though, that estimated times do not include stops for cappuccini, gelati, shopping and/or all those moments where you want to just take all of this amazing city in."

—LucieV

By Martin
Wilmot
Bennett

With more masterpieces per square foot than any other city in the world, Rome presents a particular challenge for visitors: just as they are beginning to feel hopelessly smitten by the spell of the city, they realize they don't have the time—let alone the stamina—to see more than a fraction of its treasures. Rome may not have been built in a day, but neither can it be seen in one day, or even two or three. As the Italian author Silvio Negro once put it: *Roma, non basta una vita* ("Rome, a lifetime is not enough").

It's wise to start out knowing this, and to have a focused itinerary. To provide just that, here are three strolls that introduce you to especially evocative stretches of the city: Vecchia Roma, where Rome's bravura Baroque style sets the city's tone; Trastevere—Rome's Greenwich Village—and the picturesque Tiber Island; and the Roman Forum, where the glory that was (and is) Rome is best captured.

Along the way, terra-cotta-hued palaces, Baroque squares, and time-stained ruins will present an unfolding panorama of color upon color—an endlessly varied palette that makes Rome into one of Europe's most enjoyable cities for walking. Forget about deadly earnest treks through marble miles of museum corridors and get ready to immerse yourself in some of Italy's best "street theater."

In addition, these three tours of clustered sightseeing capture quintessential Rome while allowing roamers to make minidiscoveries of their own. Use these itineraries as suggestions to keep you on track as you explore both the famous sights and those off the beaten path. Remember that people who stop for a caffè get more out of these breaks than those who breathlessly try to make every second count. So be Nero-esque in your rambles and fiddle while you roam.

ENJOYING THE GILT: A STROLL THROUGH THE BAROQUE QUARTER

The most important clue to the Romans is their Baroque art—not its artistic technicalities, but its spirit. When you understand that, you'll no longer be a stranger in Rome. Flagrantly emotional, heavily expressive, and sensuously visual, the 17th-century artistic movement known as the Baroque was born in Rome, the creation of four geniuses, Gian Lorenzo Bernini, Francesco Borromini, Annibale Caracci, and Caravaggio. Ranging from the austere drama found in Caravaggio's painted altarpieces to the jewel-encrusted, gold-on-gold decoration of 17th-century Roman palace decoration, the Baroque sought to both shock and delight by upsetting the placid, "correct" rules of the Renaissance masters. By appealing to the emotions, it became a powerful weapon in the hands of the Counter-Reformation. Although this walk passes such sights as the Pantheon—ancient Rome's most perfectly preserved building—it's mainly an excursion into the 16th and 17th centuries, when Baroque art triumphed in Rome. ⇨ *For a handy introduction to this spectacular style, see "Baroque and Desperate: The Tragic Rivalry between Bernini & Borromini" in Chapter 7.*

We wend our way through one of Rome's most beautiful districts—Vecchia Roma (Old Rome), a romantic nickname given to the areas around Piazza Navona and the Campo de' Fiori. Thick with narrow streets with curious names, airy Baroque piazzas, and picturesque courtyards, and occupying the horn of land that pushes the Tiber westward toward the Vatican, this has been an integral part of the city since ancient times. For centuries, artisans and shopkeepers toiled in the shadow of the huge palaces built to consolidate the power and prestige of the leading figures in the papal court who lived and worked here. The greatest artists flocked here to get commissions. Today, artisans still live hereabouts but their numbers are diminishing as the district has become one of Rome's ritziest.

FROM EARTHLY
TO HEAVENLY
GLORY
We begin just off the main thoroughfare of Rome, the Via del Corso, about four blocks northwest of Piazza Venezia's traffic hub. Heading up the Corso, make a left turn down tiny Via Montecatini to emerge into the delightful proportions of the ocher and stone **Piazza di Sant'Ignazio.** Any lack in size of this square is made up for in theatricality. Indeed, a Rococo theater set was exactly what its architect, Filippo Raguzzini, had in mind when he designed it in 1727. The exits and entrances these days, however, are by carabinieri, not actors, the main building "backstage" being a police station. With perfectly matching concave facades, two other buildings make up "the wings." A rare example of the *barochetto*—that is, the "cute" Baroque—a term that demonstrates how Italian art critics have a name for everything.

At one time the chapel of the gigantic Collegio Romano, the church of **Sant'Ignazio**—on your left—was Rome's largest Jesuit church. Honoring the order's founding saint, it is famous for its over-the-top Baroque spectacle—few churches are as gilt-encrusted, jewel-studded, or stupendously stuccoed. This is the 17th-century Counter-Reformation pulling out all the stops: religion as supreme theater.

Walk down the vast nave and position yourself on the yellow marble disc on the floor and prepare to be transported heavenward. Soaring above you, courtesy of painter-priest Fra Andrea Pozzo, is a frescoed *Allegory of the Missionary Work of the Jesuits* (1691–94). While an angel holding the Jesuit battle motto HIS (*In Hoc Signo*)—"In this sign we conquer"—just below, upward, ever upward, soars Saint Ignatius in triumph, trailed by a cast of thousands. A masterly use of perspective opens giddying vistas where clouds and humans interact until the forces of gravity seem to flounder. *Diavolerie*—"fiendish tricks"—a commentator of the time called such wonders. To rephrase a hopefully not too sacrilegious modern essay: Not until *Superman* comics does anything get close.

Looking back toward the entrance door, notice how the painted columns—continuations more or less of their real marble equivalents below—seem to rise straight into heaven. Now walk 20 yards back toward the door, and gaze again. And experience an optical earthquake: Those straight columns have tilted 60 degrees. Believe it or not, the whole towering edifice of classic arches, columns, and cornices from the windows upward is entirely flat.

Time to walk down the nave and admire the massive dome—although it is anything but. Dome, windows, the golden light, they're all illusion—all that majestic space is in reality flat as the top of a drum, mere paint masterfully applied across a round canvas 17 meters in diameter in trompe l'oeil fashion. Funds for a real dome ran out, so Pozzo created the less costly but arguably no less marvelous "flat" version here. Another disc set in the marble floor marks the spot where his deception takes maximum effect.

GOD'S LITTLE
MASCOT
Head out of the church, turning left to find Via S. Ignazio, then left again to Via Pie' di Marmo, which leads into Piazza Santa Caterina di Siena and the Piazza della Minerva, site of Santa Maria sopra Minerva, the only major church in Rome built in Gothic style, and famous as the home of Michelangelo's *Risen Christ*. But the object of our delight is right on the piazza: the **Obelisk of Santa Maria sopra Minerva,** an astounding conceit of an obelisk astride an elephant, masterfully designed by Gian Lorenzo Bernini. Romans pet-name it *Il Porcino*, or "little pig." The obelisk is a soaring emblem for theology and the vertiginous weight of knowledge, the beast beneath embodying that which is needed to support it—a mind that is both humble and robust, and never, thank heaven, beyond a jest, even when at its own expense.

Straight ahead is the curving, brick-bound mass of the **Pantheon,** the most complete building surviving from antiquity, and a great influence on Baroque architects. Follow Via della Minerva to Piazza della Rotonda and go to the north end of the square to get an overall view of the temple's columned portico: it once bore two Baroque bell towers of Bernini's design but, after being ridiculed for their similarity to "donkey's ears," they were demolished. Enjoy the piazza and side streets, where you will find a busy caffè and shopping scene.

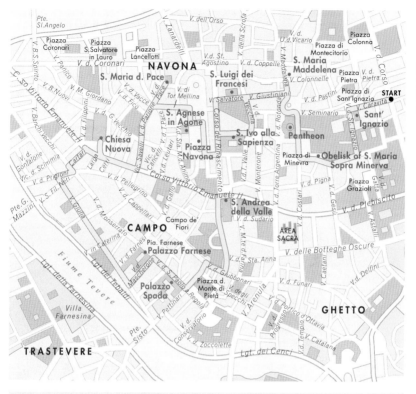

Why Go?:	Rome gave birth to the Baroque—the lavish, eye-popping style that revo-lutionized Europe in the 17th century—and this walk shows off Rome's Baroque at its best.
Good in the 'Hood:	Marveling at Bernini fountains, time-traveling back to the 17th century, watching the world pass by on Piazza Navona, and Rome's best cup of coffee.
Highlights:	Caravaggio paintings at San Luigi dei Francesci, Sant'Ignazio, Via Giulia, Palazzo Farnese, Piazza Navona.
Where to Start:	Piazza di Sant'Ignazio, a few blocks north of Piazza Venezia (turn left off the Corso on Via Montecatina to access the piazza); take Bus 40 or 64 to Piazza Venezia or Bus No. 122 down the Corso to get here.
Where to Stop:	Sant'Andrea della Valle, on the Corso Vittorio Emanuele, a few blocks west of Piazza Venezia.
Time:	Four to six hours, depending on your pace.
Best Time to Go:	Get an early start, around 9 am, and you'll be able to visit most of the churches before they close for their midday siesta at noon.
Worst Time to Go:	If the weather is inclement or gray, wait for a sunnier day.

Returning to the Piazza della Rotunda, continue northward on Via della Maddalena and proceed into Piazza della Maddelena. In the corner is the excellent Gelateria Pasqualetti. Meanwhile, in front is the Rococo facade of the church of **S. Maria Maddelena,** its curly and concave stone appearing as malleable as the ice cream that you may have just eaten, a gelato for the eyes. Inside the church observe how the late-17th-century Baroque twists and meanders into the 18th-century Rococo style. Marble work was seldom given such ornate or sumptuous treatment, and here is often gilded as well, as is the magnificent organ loft.

> ## COUNTING NOSES
>
> For some merriment around the Piazza della Rotonda, head to Via de' Pastini 99, where you'll meet not one Pinocchio but several hundreds, still or animated, from life- to pocket-size. The artisans responsible are the Bartolucci, and this family keeps Pinocchio not just alive and well, but multiplying to a dizzying degree.

Head to Via Pozzo delle Cornacchia, directly opposite the church facade, and take it one block to the looming church across the square, **San Luigi dei Francesi,** the church of Rome's French community. In the left-side chapel closest to the altar are the masterpieces painted by Caravaggio on the life and martyrdom of Saint Matthew—these three gigantic paintings had the same effect on 17th-century art that Picasso's *Demoiselles d'Avignon* had on 20th-century artists. Illuminated in Caravaggio's landmark chiaroscuro (light and shadow) style, these are works unrivaled for emotional spectacle. The artist's warts-and-all drama was a deeply original response to the Counter-Reformation writings by St. Carlo Borromeo and the result is Baroque at its sublime best.

THE STING OF WISDOM — Continue south on Via della Dogana Vecchia to Piazza di Sant'Eustachio. As culture-vulture exhaustion may be setting in, it's time for a coffee. There's no better place than Il Caffè, which, a true Roman will tell you, serves the best coffee in Rome, if not the universe. Inside the bar a cup costs only €1; outside, the price triples, but then, up on your left, the best available view of S. Ivo's dome is thrown in. **Sant'Ivo alla Sapienza** is considered by many to be Francesco Borromini's most astounding building. To get another look at the bizarre pinnacle crowning its dome (the church's rear entrance is on Piazza Sant'Eustachio), head down Via del Salvatore and turn left on Corso del Rinascimento to Number 40. Here a grand courtyard view of the church reveals Borromini—Bernini's great rival—at the dizzying top of his form.

Admire the church's concave facade and follow your gaze upward to see how Borromini mixes concave and convex shapes like a conjurer in stone. This performance is topped first with the many-niched lantern, and then the spiraling, so-called *puntiglione,* or giant stinger. Some suggest Borromini was inspired by that ziggurat of ziggurats—the Tower of Babel, featured in many paintings of the time. A more popular theory cites the sting of a bee, and indeed the nickname means just that. This would also square with the building having been begun under Pope Urban VIII of the Barberini family, whose three-bee'd crest is much in evidence all over Rome. Neatly enough, the bee is also a symbol of wisdom and this palace of Sapienza was once the hoary home of the University of Rome.

THE QUEEN
OF PIAZZAS Leaving the courtyard, follow all the crowds one block to reach that showstopper of Baroque Rome, **Piazza Navona.** The crown jewel of the *centro storico,* this showcases Bernini's extravagant Fontana dei Quattro Fiumi, whose statues represent the four corners of the earth and, in turn, the world's great rivers. Emperor Domitian's stadium once stood on this site, hence the piazza's unusual oval shape. Before someone figured out that the piazza's church of **Sant'Agnese in Agone** was designed prior to the fountain, common belief held that Bernini's fountain-figures were poised as if looking in horror at the inferior creation of Borromini, Bernini's rival. For lunch, grab a ringside caffè seat and take in the piazza spectacle—this is some of the most delicious scenery on view in Europe.

After lunch, escape the madding crowds by exiting the piazza on the little *vicolo* (alleyway) to the right of the church complex, Via di Tor Millina, to turn right on Via di S. Maria dell'Anima. Continue to the soaring bell tower of the church of S. Maria dell'Anima, then make a sharp left up a narrow alley to emerge on pretty Piazza della Pace. The centerpiece of one of the city's cutest streetscapes is the church of **Santa Maria della Pace,** commissioned by the great Chigi-family art patron, Pope Alexander VII. Although there are two great Renaissance treasures inside—Raphael's *Sibyls* and Bramante's cloister—the Baroque masterstroke here is the church facade, designed in 1657 by Pietro da Cortona to fit into the tiny *piazzina,* created to accommodate the 18th-century carriages of fashionable parishioners.

GRAND PALAZ-
ZOS COME
IN THREES Take the street leading to the church, Via della Pace (past the always chic Antico Caffè delle Pace) and continue a few blocks south down to the big avenue, Corso Vittorio Emmanuele II. Turn right for one or two blocks to reach the Chiesa Nuova, another of Rome's great Counter-Reformation churches (with magnificent Rubens paintings inside) and, directly to the left, Borromini's Oratorio dei Filippini. Head across the Corso another two blocks toward the Tiber along Via D. Cartari and turn left on Via Giulia, often called Rome's most beautiful street. While laid out—as a ruler-straight processional to St. Peter's—by Michelangelo's patron, Pope Julius II, it is lined with numerous Baroque palaces (Palazzo Sachetti, at No. 66, is still home to one of Rome's princeliest families). At No. 1 is **Palazzo Falconieri,** probably Borromini's most regal palace and now home to the Hungarian academy—note the architect's rooftop belvedere adorned with the family "falcons."

Looming over everything else is the massive **Palazzo Farnese,** a Renaissance masterpiece topped off by Michelangelo himself. You can tour the palace (today the French Embassy) on Monday and Thursday at 3, 4, and 5 pm, though not from July 24 to September 7. (⇨ *See write-up of palace in Navona section for details*). Inside is the fabled Galleria, with frescoes painted by Annibale Carracci. These florid depictions of gods and goddesses were among the first painted in the Baroque style and were staggeringly influential.

No need to pack bottled Pellegrino on your walks—just savor the refreshing water from city fountains along the way, just as Romans have done for centuries.

If you can't get into the Farnese, no problem. Just a block to the south is the grand **Palazzo Spada.** The rich exterior trim of painted frescoes on the top story hint at the splendors within: grand salons nearly wall-papered with Old Master paintings capture the opulent, 17th-century version of *Lifestyles of the Rich and Famous.*

But don't miss the *colonnato prospettico* in the small courtyard between the library and the palace cortile. While the colonnaded tunnel, with a mythological figure in marble at the far end, seems to extend for 50 feet, it is actually only one-third that length.

Due to anamorphic deformation used as a trick by the designer, once thought to be Borromini himself (now seen as the work of Giovanni Maria da Bitono), the columns at the far end are only two feet high!

PUCCINI'S CHOICE For the finale, head four blocks northward along Via Biscione back to the Corso Vittorio Emmanuele. Landmarking the famous Baroque church of **Sant'Andrea della Valle** is the highest dome in Rome (after St. Peter's).

Designed by Carlo Maderno, the nave is adorned with 17th-century frescoes by Lanfranco, making this one of the earliest ceilings in full Baroque fig.

Richly marbled chapels flank the nave, the setting Puccini chose for Act I of his opera *Tosca.* The arias sung by Floria Tosca and her lover Cavaradossi (load it on your iPod) strike exactly the right note to conclude this tour of Rome.

TRASTEVERE: THE VILLAGE WITHIN THE CITY

Charming, cobblestoned Trastevere might be nicknamed the world's third-smallest nation (after the Vatican, No. 2). Staunchly resisting the tides of change for centuries, the off-the-beaten-path district was known—until the millionaires and chichi real estate agents arrived a decade ago—as "the real Rome." Heavily populated by *romani di Roma*—those born and bred in the Eternal City for at least three generations—these locals called themselves the only true Romans. To brook no arguments, they named their charming July fete the *Festa de Noantri*: the "Festival of We Others," as the people of Trastevere pugnaciously labeled themselves so as to be distinguished from "Voiantri," the "you others" of the rest of Rome or anywhere else.

In fact, the Trasteverini have always been proud and combative, a breed apart. Dating back to republican times when it hosted both Jewish and Syriac communities as well as assorted slaves and sailors, the area was only incorporated into the "Urbs" (or city proper) by Emperor Augustus in 7 BC. By the Middle Ages, Trastevere still wasn't considered truly part of Rome, and the "foreigners" who populated its maze of alleys and piazzas fought bitterly to obtain recognition for the neighborhood as a *rione,* or official district of the city. In the 14th century the Trasteverini won out and became full-fledged Romans, continuing, however, to stoutly maintain their separate identity, however.

It's been the case ever since. Trastevere has always attracted "outsiders," and those have included celebrated artists and artisans. Raphael's model and mistress, the dark-eyed Fornarina (literally, "the baker's daughter"), is believed to have been a Trasteverina. The artist reportedly took time off from painting the *Galatea* in the nearby Villa Farnesina to woo the winsome girl at the tavern now occupied by the district's most toothsome restaurant, Romolo's. Long cocooned from "the strange disease of modern life," the district these days has been colonized with trendy boutiques and discos. Today, the district is newly hip with actors and alternative thinkers. No matter: tourists still love the place, with good reason. Long considered Rome's "Greenwich Village," Trastevere remains a delight for dialecticians, biscuit eaters, winebibbers, and book browsers alike.

TIBER'S ISLAND The best gateway to Trastevere turns out to be one of Rome's most picturesque: the Ponte Fabrizio over the **Isola Tiberina,** the island wedged between Trastevere and the Campo area. As you stride over Rome's

A MIDSUMMER NIGHT'S DREAM

Rome's most charming festival begins on the first Saturday after July 16, when a statue of the Madonna is dressed in precious clothes and jewels and transported from the church of Sant'Agata to the church of San Crisogono. The eight days it remains there signal a local holiday: Trastevere streets are hung with colored lights and lanterns and everyone joins in festive merriment, complete with open-air singing contests, *cocomero* (watermelon) vendors, public dances, and *stornellatori* (quip makers) passing from table to table.

Why Go?:	Frozen-in-amber, this enchanting little nook of Rome has the city's best neighborhood vibe.
Good in the 'Hood:	Chilling out in Piazza Santa Maria in Trastavere, walking in Raphael's footsteps, "Middle-Age"-d alleyways, lunching on Romolo's gorgeous terrace.
Highlights:	Mosaic splendor at Santa Maria in Trastavere, tiny Piazza in Piscinula, picturesque Isola Tiberina, Bernini's Blessed Ludovica Albertoni.
Where to Start:	Isola Tiberina (Tiber Island), accessed via bus from Largo Torre Argentina—get off near the Ghetto area, a few blocks from the Isola.
Where to Stop:	Via della Lungara heads north to the Principe Amadeo bridge, which leads to buses, including No. 64, back to city center.
Time:	Three to five hours, depending on your pace.
Best Time to Go:	The afternoon light here is best, but some churches close for a midday siesta at noon.
Worst Time to Go:	As the sun sets, hipster crowds arrive—Trastavere has a completely different vibe at night.

The Ponte Cestio (above) connects the Isola Tiberina with Trastevere; the Ponte Fabricio (opposite)—Rome's oldest (AD 62)—links the island with the Ghetto.

oldest bridge, let's not forget that Trastevere, literally translated, means "across the Tiber."

In Rome every stone worth its weight has a story attached. The one behind the Tiber Island, writes ancient historian Livy, is that Etruscan leader Tarquin, on his banishment, left behind a crop of grain in the Campo Marzio. For various superstitious reasons this was uprooted, put in baskets, and thrown into the Tiber for good riddance. Mud and sediment did the rest. The resulting island was eventually walled in the shape of a ship, ready to take on board another myth: Allegedly this is where Aesculapius, god of medicine, landed from Greece (or his serpent double did). Whatever, the medical tradition continues to this day in the Hospital of Fratebenefratelli, the large building to your right. For one of Rome's most unique ancient survivals, head (in the opposite direction) down the embankment to the island's southern tip to the **ancient "stone prow"** carved with medicine's serpent. Take in the 18th-century facade of the church of **San Bartolomeo,** built above Aesculapius's Temple. Off to the right is what some call the world's most beautiful movie theater, the open-air Cinema d'Isola di Tiberina (which operates during the summer festival of Estate Romana). Cross the bridge—the Ponte Cestio (dated 26 BC)—to get to Trastevere proper.

MEDIEVAL
NOOKS AND
CRANNIES You're now on the Lungotevere riverside road but continue for another block into the district to hit **Piazza in Piscinula** (from *piscina*, pool), one of Rome's most time-stained squares, home to **S. Benedetto in Piscinula,** a 17th-century church with a much earlier campanile, one of the smallest and cutest in Rome. Here St. Benedict, the founder of Western monasticism, once had a cell. The church has recently been restored by the

Brazilian "Heralds of the Gospel" who, in resplendent uniform, are there on Sunday to greet visitors and worshippers alike. The multicolor 12th-century floor is a wonder in itself. On the opposite flank of the square is the 14th-century **Casa dei Mattei,** replete with cross-mullioned windows and loggias.

History nestles quietly in every nook and cranny off the square, but opt for the charming incline at the northern end, the **Via dell'Arco dei Tolomei,** graced with a medieval house built over an arch. One block north, let history take a rest in Via della Luce at a bakeshop par excellence—just look for the sign "Biscotti." Several blocks farther north, the "Middle-Aged" want to detour up to Piazza Belli, where they'll find one of the largest medieval structures in Trastevere, the **Torre degli Anguillara,** a much-restored mini-fortress whose main tower dates from the 13th century.

Back under the Tolomei arch, this street leads into the Via dei Salumi and one block leftward brings you to **Via dell'Atleta,** with a number of picturesque medieval houses. Via dell'Atleta runs into **Via dei Genovesi,** which commemorates the Genovese sailors who thronged Trastevere when it was the papal harbor in the 15th century: these gents roomed in the vicinity of the 15th-century church of San Giovanni dei Genovesi, which has an extraordinary 15th-century cloister. Whether Christopher Columbus ever stayed here is not recorded, but the dates would fit. Meanwhile, at a ring of the bell (at No. 12 Via Anicia), the cloister is still visitable every afternoon 3–6.

SAINTLY
PORTRAITS
IN STONE

Via dei Genovesi leads directly to one of the district's majestic medieval landmarks, the church of **Santa Cecilia,** which was built above the Roman house of this martyr and patron saint of music. In 1599 her sarcophagus was found, her body inside being miraculously intact. Sculptor Stefano Maderno was summoned to attest in stone to what he saw, and sketched before decomposition set in. In a robe-turned-shroud the saint lies on her side, head turned away and a deep gash across her neck, that she's supposed to have survived for three days after suffocation in a steam bath had left her not only unscathed but singing

(all this sent Marquis de Sade into rather dubious raptures). With its almost mystically white marble, the work has a haunting quality that few statues can match. But the greatest treasure can be seen only if you exit and ring the bell on the left: for €3 a nun will show you to an elevator that ascends to a *Christ in Judgment* by Pietro Cavallini, who art historians believe was Giotto's master. Painted in 1293, the frescoes are remarkably intact.

Leaving the church, turn left and walk down Via Anicia several blocks to Piazza S. Francesco d'Assisi and **San Francesco a Ripa**. The fourth chapel on the left features Bernini's eye-knocking statue of the *Blessed Ludovica Albertoni,* a Franciscan nun whose body is buried beneath the altar. It has been remarked that the Baroque, at its most effective, served not just to educate but to sweep you off your feet. Here's an example. Marble pillow, folds, and drapery in abundance, all set off the deathbed agony and ecstasy of the nun—her provocative gesture of clutching at her breast is actually an allusion to the "milk of charity."

MAJESTIC
SANTA MARIA

We now set off for the walk's northern half by heading upward Via San Francesco a Ripa, one of Trastevere's main shopping strips. But this dreary stretch actually enhances the delight at finding, at the end of the street, **Santa Maria in Trastevere**, famously set on one of Rome's dreamiest piazzas. Noted for its fountain and caffè, it is the photogenic heart of the *rione* (district). Fellini evidently thought the same, making it a supporting star of his film *Roma*.

Staring down at you from the 12th-century church facade are the famed medieval frescoes of the Wise and Foolish Virgins. Dramatically spotlit at night, these young ladies refer to the "miraculous" discovery of oil here in 39 BC. In the mosaic, the Virgin is set between the wise virgins and two foolish ones—the latters' crownless heads bowed with shame at having left their lamps empty, the flame extinguished. In the church's presbytery the *fons olii* marks the spot from whence the oil originally flowed.

Thanks to its gilded ceiling, shimmering mosaics, and vast dimensions, the church nave echoes the spectacle of an ancient Roman basilica—the columns are said to have come from the Baths of Caracalla. The church's main wonder, however, must be the golden mosaics behind the altar. The famous mosaics of Pietro Cavallini depict episodes in the life of the Virgin so often revisited during the Renaissance. With its use of perspective, the work—completed in 1291—is seen as something of a watershed between the old, static Byzantine style and the more modern techniques soon to be taken up by Giotto. This is the very dawn of Western art.

The piazza outside is the very heart of the Trastevere *rione* (district). With its elegant raised fountain and sidewalk caffè, this is one of Rome's most beloved outdoor "living rooms," open to all comers. Through innumerable generations, this piazza has seen the comings and goings of tourists and travelers, intellectuals and artists, who lounge on the steps of the fountain or eat lunch at Sabatini's, whose food has seen much better days but whose real estate, with its tables set up directly in front of the fountain, among Rome's most coveted. Here the paths of Trastevere's residents intersect repeatedly during the day; they pause, gathering in clusters to talk animatedly in the broad accent of Rome or in a score of foreign languages. At night, it's the center of Trastevere's action, with street festivals, musicians, and gamboling dogs vying for attention from the throngs of people taking the evening air.

> ### WHEREFORE ART THOU, ROMOLO?
>
> No visit to Trastevere is complete without a visit to its landmark restaurant, Romolo (✉ *Via di Porta Settimiana 8*), not far from the Villa Farnesina. Haunted by the spirit of Raphael—who wooed his Fornarina here—it has Rome's prettiest garden terrace, menus embellished by Miró, and scrumptious specialties, like the chef's famous artichoke sauce.

RAPHAEL
WAS HERE

Directly north of the church is Piazza di S. Egidio (the small but piquant Museo di Trastevere is here) and then you enter Via della Lungara, where, several blocks along on the right, the **Villa Farnesina** stands (hours are 9–1 daily, except Sunday). Originally built by papal banker and high-roller Agostino "Il Magnifico" Chigi, this is Rome at its High Renaissance best.

Enter the Loggia di Galatea to find, across the ceiling, Peruzzi's 1511 horoscope of the papal banker, presumably not foretelling the family's eventual bankruptcy and the selling off of the same property (and horoscope) to the wealthy Farnese family. Off left, next to the wall, sits Sebastiano di Piombo's depiction of one-eyed giant *Polyphemus* with staff and giant panpipes; this is what, just next door, Raphael's *Galatea* is listening to in her shell-chassis, paddle-wheeled chariot. With the countermovement of its iconic putti, nymphs, sea gods, and dolphins, this legendary image became a hallmark of Renaissance harmony.

In the next room, also—or at least mostly—decorated by Raphael is the *Marriage of Cupid and Psyche*. After provoking the jealousy of Venus, Psyche has to overcome a number of trials before being deemed fit to drink the cup of immortality and marry Cupid. Here, of course is an alter ego for Agostino Chigi. The paintings are made still more wonderful by Giovanni da Udine's depictions of flower and fruit separating one from the other as if it were a giant *pergolato* (or arbor)—gods float at every angle while ornithologists will delight in spotting Raphael's repertoire of bird species. Climbing upstairs one passes through Peruzzi's

Pull up a café seat and settle down to enjoy the daily spectacle that is the Piazza di Santa Maria in Trastevere—one of Rome's favorite "living-rooms."

Hall of Perspectives to Chigi's private rooms. Here, in Il Sodoma's *Alexander's Wedding,* Roxanna is being lovingly undressed by a bevy of cupids. Note the one who is so overexcited he attempts a somersault like a footballer after a winning goal.

QUEEN CHRIS-
TINA AT HOME

Directly across the street from the Villa Farnesina is the **Galleria Corsini** (⏱ *Tuesday through Sunday, 8:30–1:30*), entered via a gigantic stone staircase right out of a Piranesi print. This was formerly the palazzo of pipe-smoking Christina of Sweden, immortalized by Greta Garbo on the silver screen and to whom history, that old gossip, attaches the label, "Queen without a realm, Christian without a faith, and a woman without shame." Her artistic taste is indisputable.

The second room alone contains a magnificent Rubens, Van Dyck's *Madonna of the Straw,* an Andrea del Sarto, and then, courtesy of Hans Hoffman, surely the hare of all hares. Worth the price of admission alone is Caravaggio's *John the Baptist.* In other rooms, for aficionados of high-class gore, there's Salvator Rosa's *Prometheus,* the vulture *in flagrante* and on Prometheus's face a scream to rival Munch. A visit to the **Botanical Gardens** that stretch behind the galleria is well worth a visit, if just to restore a sense of calm after all that Baroque bloodletting.

To get back to central Rome, continue on up Via della Lungara (past the church of Giacomo Apostolo, which has a fine Bernini inside) and cross over the Ponte Principe Amadeo. Taking advantage of one of the bus stops by the Tiber, you can take any number of buses, including the famous No. 64, back to *il centro.*

ROME OF THE EMPERORS:
A ROMAN FORUM WALK

Taking in the famous vista of the Roman Forum from the terraces of the Capitoline Hill, you have probably already cast your eyes down and across two millennia of history in a single glance. Here, in one fabled panorama, are the world's most striking and significant concentrations of historic remains. From this hilltop aerie, however, the erstwhile heart of ancient Rome looks like one gigantic jigsaw puzzle, the last piece being the Colosseum, looming in the distance. Historians soon realized that the Forum's big chunks of weathered marble were the very seeds of our civilization and early-20th-century archaeologists moved in to weed it and reap: in the process, they uncovered the very heart of the ancient Roman Empire. While it is fine to just let your mind contemplate the scattered pieces of the once-impressive whole, it is even better to go exploring to decipher the significance of the Forum's noble fragments. This walk does precisely that.

WORLD'S
MIGHTEST
HEIRLOOM

To kick things off, we start just south of the Forum at ancient Rome's hallmark monument, the **Colosseum** (with its handy Colosseo Metro stop). Convincingly austere, the Colosseum is the Eternal City's yardstick of eternity. Weighing in at 100,000 tons, it must be the world's mightiest heirloom. A special road having been built to transport the Travertine stone from nearby Tivoli—these quarries are still there to this day—the building was begun under the emperor Titus Flavius Vespasianus (aka Vespasian) and named the Flavian Amphitheater after his family. His son Titus, according to his father's will, inherited the task of finishing it in AD 80 while his other son, Domitian, built the gladiatorial schools on the adjacent Colle Oppio.

One rationale for the building was that Rome's only previous amphitheater, the Theater of Taurus, had been destroyed in the great fire of AD 64. Another was that the new version would erase memories of wicked Nero, who had privatized a vast swath of land near the public Forum for his private palace, the so-called Domus Aurea. In fact, the Colosseum was positioned directly over a former lake in Nero's gardens, and nearby would have towered the 110-foot-high, colossal statue of Nero himself. In one of history's ironic twists, the term *Flavian amphitheater* never caught on. Even in its name, the Colosseum serves to publicize the very emperor whose memory it was meant to bury.

A typical day at the Colosseum? The card would usually begin with a wild-beast hunt, then a pause for lunch, during which the sparse crowd was entertained with tamer displays by jugglers, magicians, and acrobats, along with third-tier fights involving "lesser" combatants, such as the Christians. Then, much gorier, would come the main event: the gladiators. The death rates among them have been much debated—30,000 is one estimate.

The building could evidently be filled in as little as 10 minutes, thanks to the 80 entrance archways. Nowadays, you can take one of the elevators upstairs to level one (the uppermost levels are closed for excavation) to spy the extensive subterranean passageways that used to funnel all the unlucky animals and gladiators into the arena.

Leaving the Colosseum behind, admire the **Arch of Constantine,** standing just to the north of the arena. The largest and best preserved of Rome's triumphal arches, it was erected in AD 315 to celebrate the victory of the emperor Constantine (280–337) over Maxentius—it was shortly after this battle that Constantine converted Rome to Christianity. Something of an amalgam historically, it features carved depictions of the triumphs of emperors Trajan, Marcus Aurelius, and Hadrian as well, a cost-cutting recycling that indicates the empire was no longer quite what it once was. Now proceed back westward along the black basalt stones leading to the Via Sacra and into the Forum. Albeit minus the traditional four-horse chariot and Jovian costume, you are treading the same route used by the emperors returning in triumph.

Up there on the mighty pedestal of its hillock stretches the **Temple of Venus and Roma.** In part it was proudly designed by would-be architect Hadrian—at least until the true professional Apollodurus pointed out that with Hadrian's measurements the goddess risked bumping her head on the apse, a piece of advice for which he was repaid with banishment. Off to your left, on the spur of hillside jutting from the Palatine Hill, stands the famed **Arch of Titus.** Completed by his brother and successor, Domitian in AD 81, the arch in one frieze shows the Roman soldiery carrying away booty—Moses's candelabra, silver trumpets, an altar table—from the destruction of the Temple in Jerusalem 10 years earlier. On the other side there is Titus on the same Via Sacra, in this case being charioted toward the Capitol after the campaign in Palestine begun by his father Vespasian. Through the arch, photograph the great vista of the entire Forum as it stretches toward the distant Capitoline Hill.

After carrying on for some hundred yards down the Via Sacra, take a small detour, doubling back to take in the massive **Basilica of Maxentius,** or the third of it left standing. Heavily damaged during Alaric's sack of Rome in 410, it had been founded by Maxentius in 306–310, then completed by Constantine the Great, Maxentius's archenemy at the battle of the Milvian Bridge. The three remaining side vaults give an idea of the building's scale; also to how, through their use of brick and barrel vaulting, the Romans had freed themselves from the tyranny of gravity. Here once stood—or sat rather—the surrealistically large head and other body fragments of Constantine (now in the outside courtyard of the Palazzo dei Conservatori), the first Christian emperor. Rome's first Christian basilica, San Giovanni in Laterano, originated many of the features used in the basilica here. Not surprisingly this most majestic of ruins was much admired and studied by the great Renaissance architects and painters alike—in Raphael's *School of Athens* the background edifice is surely a depiction of what you are seeing here. Today, the basilica is the site of wonderful concerts in summer and the occasional dramatized trial of this or that emperor (i.e., Nero and Tiberius).

Resuming your walk back toward the Capitoline Hill, the next building is the **Temple of Romulus.** The Romulus here is not Rome's founder but the son of Emperor Maxentius. Apart from the Pantheon, this is

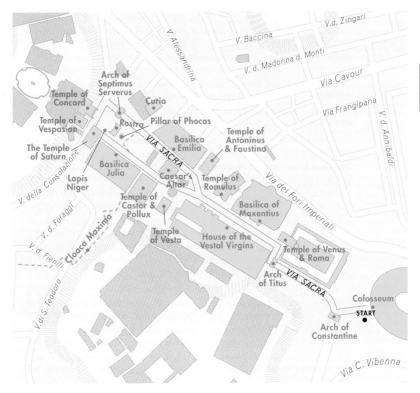

Why Go?:	Ancient Rome's "Times Square," this Forum was the civic core of the city and is the best place to experience the ageless romance of the Eternal City.
Good in the 'Hood:	Walking in the footsteps of Julius Caesar, Mark Antony, St. Paul, and Nero; picnicking in the peaceful gardens of the Palatine, home of the emperors; photographing Colosseum "gladiators."
Highlights:	Arches of Septimus Severus, Titus, and Constantine; the Colosseum; the Via Sacra; the Roman Forum.
Where to Start:	Piazza del Colosseo, with its handy Colosseo Metro stop.
Where to Stop:	Northern edge of the Roman Forum, near the Temple of Vespasian and the exit to Via di San Teodoro, leading to the Capitoline Hill.
Time:	Two to five hours, depending on your pace.
Best Time to Go:	Around 9 am, when you can get a jump on the Colosseum crowds.
Worst Time to Go:	Midday, when the sun is high and merciless—remember, there are no roofs and few trees to shelter under at these archaeological sites.

the only Roman temple to remain entirely intact—so intact even the lock in the original bronze doors is said to still function. This is due to its having subsequently been used, at least until the late 19th century, as the atrium of a Christian church above. The stonework across the lintel is as perfect as when it was made, as are the two porphyry pillars. For an inside view of the same temple and, until a century ago, the attached church atrium, enter the Church of Cosma and Damiano from the Via dei Fori Inperiali side and peer through the glass at the end of the main chapel.

Proof of how deeply buried the Forum was throughout Medieval times can be seen in the wonderful pillars of the next building down, the **Temple of Antoninus and Faustina,** his wife. Those stains reaching halfway up are in fact centuries-old soil marks. Further evidence of the sinking Forum are the doors of the 13th-century church above—note how they seem to hang almost in midair. Now a full 30 feet above the temple's rebuilt steps, originally they would, of course, have been at ground level. Here we see an example of the Christian world not so much supplanting the pagan world as growing out of it. Meanwhile, there against the blue, read the words "Divo Antonino" and "Diva Faustina," proclaiming the couple's self-ordained "divination."

A CAESAR AMONG CAESARS
Continue your walk toward the Capitoline Hill by strolling by the largely vanished **Basilica Emilia.** To the left, however, is the Temple of Caesar, sometimes referred to as **Caesar's Altar,** where, after his assassination from 23 knife wounds, Caesar's body was brought hotfoot for cremation. Peep behind the low wall and now in Caesar's honor there are flowers instead of flames. Now look up and head over, just across the road known as the Vicus Tuscus, to the three wonderfully white pillars of the **Temple of Castor and Pollux.** This was reconstructed by Augustus to pay homage to the twin sons of Jupiter and Leda who helped the Roman army to victory back in the 5th century BC. The emperor Caligula, says Suetonius, "had part of the temple incorporated into his palace as his own vestibule. Often he would stand between the divine brothers displaying himself for worship by those visiting the temple."

To this temple's right sits the **Basilica Julia.** After the death of Julius Caesar, all chaos broke loose in Rome, but a prelude to another long bout of civil war. This ended with the victory of Augustus who, ever the dutiful stepson, had this massive basilica completed in his father's honor. Pitted with column marks, the rectangular piece of ground remains. As with other Roman basilicas, the place was more judicial in nature, swarming, according to Pliny, with 180 judges and a plague of lawyers. Look carefully at the flooring and you might still spy a chessboard carved into the marble, perhaps by a bored litigant.

HAUNT OF THE VESTAL VIRGINS
Backtrack a bit along the Via Sacra past the Temple of Castor and Pollux to the circular **Temple of Vesta.** In a tradition going back to an age when fire was a precious commodity, the famous vestal virgins kept the fire of Rome burning here. Of the original 20 columns only three remain, behind which stretch the vast remains of the **House of the Vestal Virgins.** Privileged in many ways—they had front-row seats in the Colosseum and rights of deciding life and death for poor gladiators,

See you later, gladiator: the Colosseum hosted gladiatorial combats for centuries and up to 30,000 may have tragically perished in its arena.

for example—they were also under a 30-year-long vow of chastity. As everyone knows, the notorious punishment for breaking their vow was being buried alive. But it is time to turn back and press on with our walk. Crossing the central square and walking back toward the towering Capitoline Hill, you are now entering the midsection of the open area of the Forum proper; you can see to your left the **Pillar of Phocas.** The last monument to be built on the by now largely abandoned Forum was this column, erected by an otherwise forgotten Byzantine emperor. In 1813, on the orders of Pope Pius VII, the area was excavated, with the assumption that the column belonged to the Temple of Jove Custode. Then, at the base, surfaced the inscription, describing how it had been erected in 608 to the Christian emperor from the east on his bequeathing the Pantheon to the Roman Church.

A BURIAL TOO SOON

The long stone platform presiding over this area is the famous **Rostra.** *Forum* coming from an old Latin word meaning "to meet," from here Rome's political elite would address the people. Indeed, this is where, with some help from Shakespeare, Mark Antony would have pronounced his rabble-rousing "I come to bury Caesar, not to praise him." The name Rostra dates to the custom of adorning the platform with prows of captured ships following an early naval victory off Antium/Anzio in 338 BC.

Going back even farther is, on the other side of the Via Sacra, the so-called **Lapis Niger,** or Black Stone, which marks the site of a Temple to Romulus. The small sanctuary underneath goes back to the 6th century BC as does a strange column with the oldest Latin inscription yet known, cursing all those who profaned the place—irreverent archaeologists take note!

Altogether mightier in scale is the **Curia**—the Senate house of ancient Rome—nearby. Not the building of the earlier republican period, this is a version rebuilt by Diocletian and in turn rebuilt in 1937. Here sat the 300 members of Senate, then rendered largely powerless by Diocletian. Originally decorating the nearby rostra, the two friezes show the much earlier emperor Trajan. Meanwhile the porphyry statue without a head has been attributed to Trajan also. But there is a neater theory: With the turnover in emperors reaching to as many as six per year and porphyry being almost priceless, the head was replaceable by whatever emperor happened to be in power.

HEADS AND TALES

Continue back down the Via Sacra, where towers one of the Forum's extant spectaculars, the **Arch of Septimus Severus.** Built by his sons, it celebrates Septimus's campaign against the Parthians and the ensuing influx into Rome of booty and slaves. A number of these, their hands tied behind them, are depicted. Also on view is the murderous Caracalla, son number two, though the head of his elder brother Gaeta has, Stalin-fashion, been erased. Sadly, many other heads have also had a Caracalla done on them by the erosive fumes of Roman traffic.

Continuing left and up the Via Sacra, you reach the base of the celebrated **Temple of Saturn.** Now the name of a planet, Saturn was then as close to the earth as you can get, the word originating from *sero*—"to sow." Saturn was originally a corn god, first worshipped in Magna Grecia, then allowed, so goest the patriotic myth, to settle in Rome by the city's presiding deity, Janus. That Saturn was the God of Plenty in more than an agricultural sense is also attested to by the fact that beneath the floor was kept the wealth of the Roman treasury.

Position yourself below the easternmost two of the eight columns of Egyptian marble and peer upward as they reach higher than a rocket at Cape Canaveral and are every bit as majestic.

HAIL AND FAREWELL

Meanwhile, up ahead ascends the last stretch of the Via Sacra—the so-called Clivus Capitolinus. On the left is the **Temple of Vespasian.**

Bowing to the powerful nature of time, now only three splendid columns remain. Next door once stood the **Temple of Concord.**

Built back in Republican times, it celebrated the peace between the often warring patricians and plebs, the two cardinal elements in the winning formula of SPQR—in other words the patrician Senate (S) and the people (PQ). A few stones mark the spot—and the last piece in the Forum's monumental jigsaw.

For a better sense of the whole—a sort of archaeological gestalt—take the steps alongside to ascend to the Campidoglio, the Capitoline Hill, where vistas from the piazza balconies will put your two or three past hours of walking into panoramic context.

You cannot help but ponder on the truth of *sic transit Gloria* ("glory passes away")—a similar view by moonlight inspired Edward Gibbon to embark on his epic *Decline and Fall of the Roman Empire.*

Ancient Rome

CAMPIDOGLIO, ROMAN FORUM, IMPERIAL FORA, COLOSSEUM

WORD OF MOUTH

"Buy tickets at the Forum or Palatine and you can then walk straight . . . when you get to the Colosseum." —Cathies

"I walked to the Colosseum's center, stretched out my arms and yelled, 'Are you not entertained?' There was a small rumble of laughter and a few people chanted 'Maximus! Maximus!' "
—Edward2000

GETTING ORIENTED

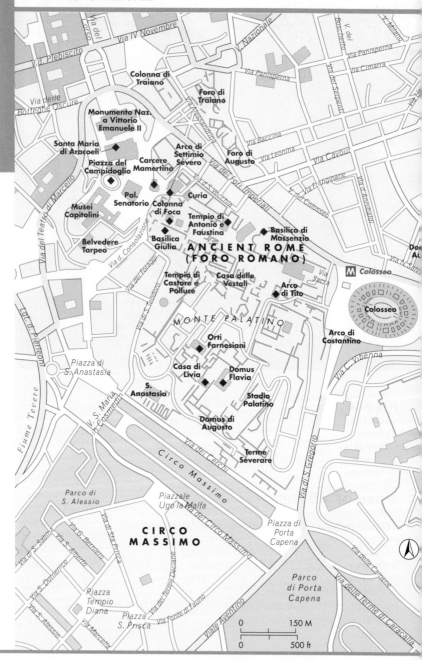

TOP 5 REASONS TO GO

The Colosseum: Clamber up the stands to the emperor's box, and imagine the gory games as Trajan saw them.

The Roman Forum: Walk through the crumbling, romantic ruins, a trip back 2,000 years to the heart of one of the greatest empires the world has ever seen.

Sunset: Watch the sun go down over ancient and Renaissance Rome from the back of the Campidoglio, the best view in town.

Capitoline Museums: Look eye-to-eye with the ancients—the busts of emperors and philosophers are more real than ideal.

Caffè Capitolino: Sip Prosecco on the terrace of the Palazzo Caffarelli—part of the Musei Capitolini complex—while you take in a Cinerama scene of Roman rooftops.

OK, WHERE DO I START?

On the congested Via di Teatro di Marcello, on the spot where emperors once halted their triumphal processions—and Fiats now honk in unison—climb Michelangelo's sloping cordonata walkway up the famed Capitoline Hill. Take in the views over the entire Foro Romano from the piazza terrace, then tour the celebrated museum complex; use the linking terrace to visit Santa Maria in Aracoeli. Use the church's staircase back down to the street (or backtrack to the cordonata to avoid the hundred-plus steps!) and walk past the "eighth hill of Rome"—the Monument to Victor Emmanuel—to find the entrance to the Roman Forum on the Via dei Fori Imperiali. Your ticket also includes entrance to the Palatine Hill and Colosseum, meaning you can jump the lines there. As all these sites are almost entirely outdoors, good weather is ideal; while rain can be cool and keep the crowds away, it also muddies the beaten-earth paths of the Foro Romano and Palatine. In summer, get an early start on touring, as most sites are open to the sun, or take an evening stroll.

GETTING HERE

The Colosseo Metro station is right across from the Colosseum proper and a short walk from both the Roman and imperial forums, as well as the Palatine Hill. Hoofing from the historic center will take about 20 minutes, much of it along the wide and busy Via dei Fori Imperiali. The little electric Bus No. 117 from the center or No. 175 from Termini will also deliver you to the Colosseum's doorstep. Any of the following buses will take you to or near the Roman Forum: Nos. 60, 75, 85, 95, and 175.

BEST TIME-OUTS

Antico Caffè del Brasile. Since 1908, this caffè in the heart of Monti has been a local favorite. Even Pope John Paul II was a fan: As a student, he regularly grabbed coffee here. Come for a pick-me-up—including not only the caffè's own coffee blends, but chocolates and pastries, too. ⊠ *Via dei Serpenti 23, Monti* ☎ *06/4882319.*

Divin Ostilia. Relax over a glass of wine at this *enoteca* (wine bar), just a block from the Colosseum. Sit outside or grab a table in the warm, cozy interior. Although you can find better dinner entrées elsewhere, the wine selection is excellent and the snacks (like the cheese plate or bruschetta) are good bets, too. ⊠ *Via Ostilia 4, Colosseo* ☎ *06/70496526* Ⓜ *Colosseo.*

3

Sightseeing
★★★★★
Nightlife
★★
Dining
★★
Lodging
★★★
Shopping
★

If you ever wanted to feel like the Caesars—with all of ancient Rome (literally) at your feet—simply head to Michelangelo's famed Piazza del Campidoglio. There, make a beeline for the terrace flanking the side of the center building, the Palazzo Senatorio, Rome's ceremonial city hall. From this balcony atop the Capitoline Hill you can take in a panorama that seems like a remnant of some forgotten Cecil B. DeMille movie spectacular.

Looming before you is the entire Roman Forum, the *caput mundi*—the center of the known world for centuries and where many of the world's most important events in the past 2,500 years happened. Here, all Rome shouted as one, "Caesar has been murdered," and crowded to hear Mark Antony's eulogy for the fallen leader. Here, legend has it that St. Paul traversed the Forum en route to his audience with Nero. Here, Roman law and powerful armies were created, keeping the barbarian world at bay for a millennium. And here the Roman emperors staged the biggest blowout extravaganzas ever mounted for the entire population of a city, outdoing even Elizabeth Taylor's Forum entry in *Cleopatra*.

But after a more than 27-century-long parade of pageantry, you'll find that much has changed in this area, known to many locals as the Campitelli (or "Fields"). The rubble-scape of marble fragments scattered over the Forum area makes all but students of archaeology ask: Is this the grandeur that was Rome? It's not surprising that Shelley and Gibbon once reflected on the sense of *sic transit gloria mundi*—"thus pass the glories of the world." Yet spectacular monuments—the Arch of Septimius Severus, the Palatine Hill, and the Colosseum (looming in the background), among them—remind us that this was indeed the birthplace of much of Western civilization.

Before the Christian era, before the emperors, before the powerful republic that ruled the ancient seas, Rome was founded on seven hills. Two of them, the Capitoline and the Palatine, surround the Roman

Forum, where the Romans of the later Republic and Imperial ages worshipped deities, debated politics, and wheeled and dealed. It's all history now (except on the fringes, this area's only residents are lazy lizards and complacent cats), but this remains one of the world's most striking and significant concentrations of ancient remains: an emphatic reminder of the genius and power that made Rome the fountainhead of the Western world.

THE CAMPIDOGLIO

Your first taste of ancient Rome should start from a point that embodies some of Rome's earliest and greatest moments: the Campidoglio. Here, on the Capitoline Hill (which towers over the traffic hub of Piazza Venezia), a meditative Edward Gibbon was inspired to write his 1764 classic, *The History of the Decline and Fall of the Roman Empire*. Of Rome's famous seven hills, the Capitoline is the smallest and most sacred. It has always been the seat of Rome's government, and its Latin name is echoed in the designation of the national and state capitol buildings of every country in the world.

TOP ATTRACTIONS

Fodor'sChoice **Musei Capitolini.** Surpassed in size and richness only by the Musei Vaticani, this immense collection was the first public museum in the world. A greatest-hits collection of Roman art through the ages, from the ancients to the baroque, it is housed in the twin Museo Capitolino and Palazzo dei Conservatori that bookend Michelangelo's famous piazza. Here, you'll find some of antiquity's most famous sculptures, such as the poignant Dying Gaul, the regal Capitoline Venus, the Esquiline Venus (identified as possibly another Mediterranean beauty, Cleopatra herself), and the Lupa Capitolina, the symbol of Rome. Although some pieces in the collection—which was first assembled by Sixtus IV (1414–84), one of the earliest of the Renaissance popes—may excite only archaeologists and art historians, others are unforgettable, including the original bronze statue of Marcus Aurelius whose copy sits in the piazza.

Buy your ticket and enter the museums on the right of the piazza (as you face the center **Palazzo Senatorio**), into the building known as the **Palazzo dei Conservatori.** Before picking up a useful free map from the cloakroom, you cannot miss some of the biggest body parts ever: that giant head, foot, elbow, and imperially raised finger across the courtyard are what remains of the fabled seated statue of Constantine, which once filled the Basilica of Maxentius, his defeated rival (and the other body parts were of wood, lest the figure collapse under its own weight). Constantine believed that Rome's future lay with Christianity and such immense effigies were much in vogue in the latter days of the Roman Empire. Take the stairs up past a series of intricately detailed ancient marble reliefs to the resplendent Salone dei Orazi e Curiazi (Salon of Horatii and Curatii) on the first floor. The ceremonial hall is decorated with a magnificent gilt ceiling, carved wooden doors, and 16th-century frescoes depicting the history of ancient Rome. At both ends of the hall are statues of the baroque era's most charismatic popes: a marble Urban

THE CAMPIDOGLIO

✉ *Piazza dei Campidoglio, incorporating the Palazzo Senatorio and the two Capitoline Museums, the Palazzo Nuovo, and the Palazzo dei Conservatori.*

TIPS

■ The piazza centerpiece is the legendary equestrian statue of Emperor Marcus Aurelius but, as of 1999, a copy took up residence here when the actual 2nd-century AD statue moved to a new wing in the surrounding Musei Capitolini. The Sala Marco Aurelio and its glass room also protect a gold-plated Hercules along with more massive body parts, this time bronze, of what might be Constantine or that of his son Constans II (archaeologists are still undecided).

■ While there are great views of the Roman Forum from the terrace balconies on either side of the Palazzo Senatorio, the best view may be from the Tabularium, the arcade balcony below the Senatorio building and accessed with admission to the Musei Capitolini. The museum also has the Terrazza Caffarelli, featuring a restaurant with a magical view looking toward Trastevere and St. Peter's.

Spectacularly transformed by Michelangelo's late-Renaissance designs, the Campidoglio was once the epicenter of the Roman Empire, the place where the city's first shrines stood, including its most sacred, the Temple of Jupiter.

Originally, the Capitoline Hill consisted of two peaks: the Capitolium and the Arx (where Santa Maria in Aracoeli now stands). The hollow between them was known as the Asylum. Here, prospective settlers once came to seek the protection of Romulus, legendary first king of Rome—hence the term *asylum*. Later, during the Roman Republic, in 78 BC, the Tabularium, or Hall of Records, was erected here.

By the Middle Ages, however, the Capitoline had become an unkempt hill strewn with ancient rubble.

In preparation for the impending visit of Charles V in 1536, triumphant after the empire's victory over the Moors, his host, Pope Paul III Farnese, decided that the Holy Roman Emperor should follow the route of the emperors, climaxing at the Campidoglio.

But the pope was embarrassed by the decrepit goat pasture the hill had become and commanded Michelangelo to restore the site to glory; he added a third palace along with Renaissance-style facades and a grand paved piazza.

Newly excavated ancient sculptures, designed to impress the visiting emperor, were installed in the palaces, and the piazza was ornamented with the giant stone figures of the Discouri and the ancient Roman equestrian statue of Emperor Marcus Aurelius (original now in Musei Capitolini)—the latter a visual reference to the corresponding glory of Charles V and the ancient emperor.

VIII (1568–1644) by Gian Lorenzo Bernini (1598–1680) and a bronze Innocent X (1574–1655) by Bernini's rival, Algardi (1595–1654).

Proceeding to the collection of ancient sculpture, the first room contains the exquisite Spinario: Proving that the most everyday action can be as poetic as any imperial bust, a small boy in the act of removing a thorn becomes unwittingly immortalized. Nearby is the rather eerie glass-eyed bust of Junius Brutus, first Roman consul. Farther along is a separate room devoted to the renowned symbol of Rome, the Capitoline Wolf, a 5th-century BC Etruscan bronze, the Romulus and Remus below being late additions by Antonio Pollaiolo (15th century). Donated by Sixtus IV, the work came to symbolize Roman unity.

MARCUS AURELIUS STATUE The heart of the museum, however, is the Exedra of Marcus Aurelius (Sala Marco Aurelio), a large, airy room with skylights and high windows, which showcases the spectacular original bronze statue of the Roman emperor whose copy sits in the piazza below. Created in the 2nd century AD, the statue should have been melted down like so many other bronze statues of emperors after the decline of Rome, but this one is thought to have survived because it was mistaken for the Christian emperor Constantine. To the right the room segues into the area of the Temple of Jupiter, with its original ruins rising organically into the museum space. A reconstruction of the temple and Capitol Hill from the Bronze Age to present day makes for a fascinating glance through the ages. Some of the pottery and bones on display were dug up from as early as the 12th century BC, recasting Romulus and Remus as Johnny-come-latelies.

Off left are rooms dedicated to statuary from the so-called Horti, or the gardens of ancient Rome's great and mega-rich. From the Horti Lamiani is the Venere Esquilina doing her hair. (Look for the fingers at the back, at the end of the missing arms.) Believe it or not, you might be gazing at the young Cleopatra invited to Rome by Julius Caesar. Or so say some experts—a further clue is the asp. In the same room is an extraordinary bust of the Emperor Commodus, seen here as Hercules and unearthed in the late 1800s during building work for the new capital. On the top floor the museum's *pinacoteca,* or painting gallery, has some noted baroque masterpieces, including Caravaggio's *The Fortune Teller* (1595) and *St. John the Baptist* (1602; albeit, given the ram, some critics see here a representation of Isaac, the pose this time influenced by Michelangelo's *ignudi*), Peter Paul Rubens's (1577–1640) *Romulus and Remus* (1614), and Pietro da Cortona's (1627) sumptuous portrait of Pope Urban VIII. Adjacent to the Palazzo dei Conservatori is **Palazzo Caffarelli,** which holds temporary exhibitions. Here, set on the Piazzale Caffarelli, the new Caffè Capitolino offers a spectacular vista over Rome (looking toward St. Peter's); it is open daily, except Monday, 9 to 7.

To reach the **Palazzo Nuovo** section of the museum (the palace on the left-hand side of the Campidoglio), take the stairs or elevator to the basement of the Palazzo dei Conservatori, where an underground corridor called the Galleria Congiunzione holds a poignant collection of ancient gravestones. But before going up into Palazzo Nuovo, be sure to

A treasure of the Musei Capitolini, this highly ornate ancient Roman sarcophagus proclaimed the wealthy status of the owner, even in death.

take the detour to the right to the Tabularium Gallery with its unparalleled view over the Forum.

ROOM OF THE EMPERORS Inside the Palazzo Nuovo on the stairs you find yourself immediately dwarfed by Mars in full military rig and lion-topped sandals. Upstairs is the noted Sala degli Imperatori, lined with busts of Roman emperors, along with the Sala dei Filosofi, where busts of philosophers sit in judgment—a fascinating who's who of the ancient world, and a must-see of the museum. Although many ancient Roman treasures were merely copies of Greek originals, portraiture was one area in which the Romans took precedence. Within these serried ranks are 48 Roman emperors, ranging from Augustus to Theodosius (AD 346–395). On one console, you'll see the handsomely austere Augustus, who "found Rome a city of brick and left it one of marble." On another rests Claudius "the stutterer," an indefatigable builder brought vividly to life in the history-based novel *I, Claudius*, by Robert Graves. Also in this company is Nero, one of the most notorious emperors, who built for himself the fabled Domus Aurea. And, of course, there are the standout baddies: cruel Caligula (AD 12–41) and Caracalla (AD 186–217), and the dissolute, eerily modern boy-emperor, Heliogabalus (AD 203–222). In the adjacent Great Hall, be sure to take in the 16 resplendently restored marble statues. Nearby are rooms filled with masterpieces, including the legendary *Dying Gaul*, *The Red Faun* from Hadrian's Villa, and a *Cupid and Psyche*—each worth almost a museum to itself. Downstairs near the exit is the gigantic, reclining figure of Oceanus, found in the Roman Forum and later dubbed Marforio, one of Rome's famous "talking statues" to which citizens from the 1500s to the 1900s affixed anonymous satirical verses and notes of political protest. ✉ *Piazza del Campidoglio, Campidoglio* ☎ *06/0608* ⊕ *www.museicapitolini.org* 🎟 *€12; audio guide €5* ⊘ *Tues.–Sun. 9–8* Ⓜ *Bus 44, 63, 64, 81, 95, 85, 492.*

Fodor's Choice ★ **Santa Maria di Aracoeli.** Sitting atop its 124 steps—"the grandest loafing place of mankind," as Henry James put it, and the spot on which Gibbon was inspired to write his great history of the decline and fall of the Roman empire—Santa Maria di Aracoeli perches on the north slope of the Capitoline Hill. You can also access the church using a less challenging staircase from Michelangelo's piazza. The church rests on the site of the temple of Juno Moneta (Admonishing Juno), which also housed the Roman mint (hence the origin of the word "money"). According to legend, it was here that the Sibyl, a prophetess, predicted to Augustus the coming of a redeemer. The emperor supposedly responded by erecting an altar, the Ara Coeli (Altar of Heaven). This was eventually replaced by a Benedictine monastery then church, which passed in 1250 to the Franciscans, who restored and enlarged it in Romanesque-Gothic style. Today, the Aracoeli is best known for the **Santa Bambino,** a much-revered olive-wood figure of the Christ Child (today a copy of the 15th-century original stolen in 1994 and as yet unfound). At Christmas, everyone pays homage to the Bambi Gesù as children recite poems from a miniature pulpit. In true Roman style, the church interior is a historical hodgepodge—classical columns and large marble fragments from pagan buildings, as well as a 13th-century Cosmatesque pavement. The richly gilded Renaissance ceiling commemorates the naval victory at Lepanto in 1571 over the Turks. The first chapel on the right is noteworthy for Pinturicchio's frescoes of San Bernardino of Siena (1486). ✉ *Via del Teatro di Marcello, on top of steep stairway, Campidoglio* ☎ *06/69763838* ⊘ *Oct.–Apr., 7–12:30 and 3–6:30; May–Sept. 7–12:30 and 3–7:30* Ⓜ *Bus 44, 160, 170, 175, 186.*

THAT FACE, THAT FACE!

As a stroll through the Room of the Emperors will reveal, the Romans generally preferred the "warts and all" school of representation (unlike the Greeks, whose portraits were idealized). A prime example is the brutally realistic bust of Commodus (AD 161–192), the emperor-gladiator. Movie lovers will want to search out this bust: he was the inspiration for the character portrayed by Christopher Plummer in *The Fall of the Roman Empire* and by Joaquin Phoenix in *Gladiator.*

WORTH NOTING

Belvedere Tarpeo. In ancient Roman times, traitors were hurled from here to their deaths. In the 18th and 19th centuries, the Tarpeian Rock became a popular stop for people making the Grand Tour, because of the view it gave of the Palatine Hill. Today, the belvedere viewing point has been long shuttered for restoration, but you can proceed a short walk down to Via di Monte Tarpeio, where the view is spectacular enough. It was on this rock that, in the 7th century BC, Tarpeia betrayed the Roman citadel to the early Romans' sworn enemies, the Sabines, only asking in return to be given the heavy gold bracelets the Sabines wore on their left arm. The scornful Sabines did indeed shower her with

An Emperor Cheat Sheet

OCTAVIAN, or Caesar Augustus, was Rome's first emperor (27 BC–AD 14). While it upended the republic once and for all, his rule began a 200-year peace known as the Pax Romana.

The name of **NERO** (AD 54–68) lives in infamy as a violent persecutor of Christians…and as the murderer of his wife, his mother, and countless others. Although it's not certain whether he actually fiddled as Rome burned in AD 64, he was well known as an actor.

DOMITIAN (AD 81–96) declared himself "Dominus et Deus," Lord and God. He stripped away power from the Senate, and as a result after his death he suffered "Damnatio Memoriae"— the Senate had his name and image erased from all public records.

TRAJAN (AD 98–117), the first Roman emperor to be born outside Italy (in southern Spain), enlarged the empire's boundaries to include modern-day Romania, Armenia, and Upper Mesopotamia.

HADRIAN (AD 117–138) designed and rebuilt the Pantheon, constructed a majestic villa at Tivoli, and initiated myriad other constructions, including the famed wall across Britain.

MARCUS AURELIUS (AD 161–180) is remembered as a humanitarian emperor, a Stoic philosopher whose *Meditations* are still read today. Nonetheless, he was devoted to expansion and an aggressive leader of the empire.

CONSTANTINE I (AD 306–337) made his mark by legalizing Christianity, an act that changed the course of history, legitimizing the once-banned religion and paving the way for the papacy in Rome.

their gold…then added the crushing weight of their heavy shields, also carried on their left arms. ⊠ *Via del Tempio di Giove, Campidoglio.*

Palazzo Senatorio. During the Middle Ages this city hall looked like the medieval town halls you can see in Tuscan hill towns, part fortress and part assembly hall. The building was entirely rebuilt in the 1500s as part of Michelangelo's revamping of the Campidoglio for Pope Paul III; the master's design was adapted by later architects, who wisely left the front staircase as the focus of the facade. The ancient statue of Minerva at the center was renamed the Goddess Rome, and the river gods (the River Tigris remodeled to symbolize the Tiber, to the right, and the Nile, to the left) were hauled over from the Terme di Costantino on the Quirinal Hill. Today, it is the regional seat of Rome's commune administration and is not open to the public. ⊠ *Piazza del Campidoglio, Campidoglio.*

THE ROMAN FORUM

Fodor's Choice ★   From the entrance on Via dei Fori Imperiali, descend into the extraordinary archaeological complex that is the Foro Romano. Before the 1st century, when the Roman Republic gave over to hedonistic imperial Rome, this was the heart of the empire. The Forum began life as a marshy valley between the Capitoline and Palatine hills—a valley crossed by a mud track and used as a cemetery by Iron Age settlers.

Over the years a market center and some huts were established here, and after the land was drained in the 6th century BC, the site eventually became a political, religious, and commercial center: the Forum. Hundreds of years of plunder reduced the Forum to its current desolate state. But this enormous area was once Rome's pulsating heart, filled with stately and extrav-

FRIENDS, ROMANS, OR COUNTRYMEN

It's a jumble out there! To make sense of the scattered ruins that cover the Roman Forum floor, ⇨ see our step-by-step tour of the Forum in "Roamin' Holiday" and "Rome Was Not Built in a Day."

3

agant temples, palaces, and shops, and crowded with people from all corners of the empire. Adding to today's confusion is the fact that the Forum developed over many centuries; what you see today are not the ruins from just one period but from a span of almost 900 years, from about 500 BC to AD 400. Nonetheless, the enduring romance of the place, with its lonely columns and great broken fragments of sculpted marble and stone, makes for a quintessential Roman experience. ⊠ *Entrance at Via dei Fori Imperiali, Roman Forum* ☎ *06/39967700* ⊕ *www. pierreci.it* ⊠ *€12 (combined ticket with the Colosseum and Palatine Hill, if used within 2 days); audio guide Forum €5, Forum and Palatine €7* ☉ *Jan.–Feb. 15, daily 8:30–4:30; Feb. 16–Mar. 15, daily 8:30–5; Mar. 16–last Sat. in Mar., daily 8:30–5:30; last Sun. in Mar.–Aug., daily 8:30–7:15; Sept., daily 8:30–7; Oct. 1–last Sat. in Oct., daily 8:30–6:30; last Sun. in Oct.–Dec., daily 8:30–4:30* Ⓜ *Colosseo.*

TOP ATTRACTIONS

Fodor's Choice ★ **Arco di Settimio Severo** (*Arch of Septimius Severus*). One of the grandest triumphal arches erected by a Roman emperor, this richly decorated monument was built in AD 203 to celebrate Severus's victory over the Parthians. It was once topped by a bronze statuary group of a chariot drawn by four or perhaps as many as six life-size horses. Masterpieces of Roman statuary, the stone reliefs on the arch were probably based on huge painted panels depicting the event, a kind of visual report on his foreign campaigns that would have been displayed during the emperor's triumphal parade in Rome to impress his subjects (and, like all statuary back then, were painted in florid, lifelike colors). ⊠ *West end of Foro Romano, Roman Forum.*

★ **Arco di Tito** (*Arch of Titus*). Standing at the northern approach to the Palatine Hill on the Via Sacra, this triumphal arch was erected in AD 81 to celebrate the sack of Jerusalem 10 years earlier, after the great Jewish revolt. The superb view of the Colosseum from the arch reminds us that it was the emperor Titus who helped finish the vast amphitheater, begun earlier by his father, Vespasian. Under the arch are the two great sculpted reliefs, both showing scenes from Titus's triumphal parade along this very Via Sacra. You still can make out the spoils of war plundered from Herod's Temple, including a gigantic seven-branched candelabrum (menorah) and silver trumpets. During his sacking of Jerusalem, Titus killed or deported most of the Jewish population, thus initiating the Jewish Diaspora—an event that would have historical consequences for millennia. ⊠ *East end of Via Sacra, Roman Forum.*

Basilica di Massenzio (*Basilica of Maxentius*). Only about one-third of the original of this gigantic basilica (or meeting hall) remains, so you can imagine what a wonder this building was when erected. Today, its great arched vaults still dominate the north side of the Via Sacra. Begun under the emperor Maxentius about AD 306, the edifice was a center of judicial and commercial activity, the last of its kind to be built in Rome. Over the centuries, like so many Roman monuments, it was exploited as a quarry for building materials and was stripped of its sumptuous marble and stucco decorations. Its coffered vaults, like the coffering inside the Pantheon's dome, later were copied by many Renaissance artists and architects. ⊠ *Via Sacra, Roman Forum.*

Comitium. The open space in front of the Curia was the political hub of ancient Rome. Julius Caesar had rearranged the Comitium, moving the Curia to its current site and transferring the imperial **Rostra,** the podium from which orators spoke to the people (decorated originally with the prows of captured ships, or *rostra,* the source for the term "rostrum"), to a spot just south of the Arch of Septimius Severus. It was from this location that Mark Antony delivered his funeral address in Caesar's honor. On the left of the Rostra stands what remains of the **Tempio di Saturno,** which served as ancient Rome's state treasury. ⊠ *West end of Foro Romano, Roman Forum.*

Curia. This large brick structure next to the Arch of Septimius Severus, built during Diocletian's reign in the late 3rd century AD, is the Forum's best-preserved building—thanks largely to having been turned into a church in the 7th century. By the time the Curia was built, the Senate, which met here, had lost practically all the power and prestige that it had possessed during the Republican era. Still, the Curia appears much as the original Senate house would have looked. Today, the Curia generally is open only if there's an exhibit inside; luckily, that's not infrequent. Definitely peek inside if it's open, and don't miss the original, intricate floor of marble and porphyry, done in *opus sectile*. ⊠ *Via Sacra, northwest corner of Foro Romano, Roman Forum.*

★ **Tempio di Castore e Polluce.** The sole three remaining Corinthian columns of this temple beautifully evoke the former, elegant grandeur of the Forum. This temple was dedicated in 484 BC to Castor and Pollux, the twin brothers of Helen of Troy who carried to Rome the news of

THE RISE AND FALL OF ANCIENT ROME

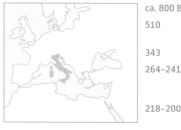

ca. 800 BC	Rise of Etruscan city-states.
510	Foundation of the Roman Republic; expulsion of Etruscans from Roman territory.
343	Roman conquest of Greek colonies in Campania.
264–241	First Punic War (with Carthage): increased naval power helps Rome gain control of southern Italy and then Sicily.
218–200	Second Punic War: Hannibal's attempted conquest of Italy, using elephants, is eventually crushed.

victory at Lake Regillus, southeast of Rome—the definitive defeat of the deposed Tarquin dynasty. The twins flew on their fabulous white steeds 20 km (12 miles) to the city to bring the news to the people before mortal messengers could arrive. Rebuilt over the centuries before Christ, the temple suffered a major fire and was reconstructed by Emperor Tiberius in 12 BC, the date of the three standing columns. ⊠ *West of House of the Vestals, Roman Forum.*

★ **Tempio di Vesta.** While just a fragment of the original building, the remnant of this temple shows the sophisticated elegance that architecture achieved under the later empire. Set off by florid Corinthian columns, the circular tholos was rebuilt by Emperor Septimius Severus when he restored this temple around AD 205. Dedicated to Vesta—the goddess of the hearth—the highly privileged vestal virgins kept the sacred vestal flame alive. Next to the temple, the **Casa delle Vestali**, which reopened after restoration in 2011, gives a glimpse of the splendor in which the women lived out their 30-year vows of chastity. Marble statues of the vestals and fragments of mosaic pavement line the garden courtyard, which once would have been surrounded by lofty colonnades and at least 50 rooms. Chosen when they were between six and 10 years old, the six vestal virgins dedicated the next 30 years of their lives to keeping the sacred fire, a tradition that dated back to the very earliest days of Rome, when guarding the community's precious fire was essential to its well-being. Their standing in Rome was considerable; among women, they were second in rank only to the empress. Their intercession could save a condemned man, and they did, in fact, rescue Julius Caesar from the lethal vengeance of his enemy Sulla. The virgins were handsomely maintained

AIN'T MISBEHAVIN'

Whoever said that bad girls have all the fun? In ancient Rome, the six physically perfect vestal virgins, chosen when they were prepubescent, lived a life of luxury in the sumptuous Casa delle Vestali. As protectors of the empire, the virgins had to keep the sacred fire of Vesta lit (if it went out, the empire would fall). In return, the fortunate femmes were given the best seats in the Colosseum, rode around in special chariots, knew all the imperial gossip, and acted as judges. The catch: if they broke their 30-year vow of chastity, they were buried alive.

3

150 BC	Roman Forum begins to take shape as the principal civic center in Italy.
146	Third Punic War: Rome razes city of Carthage and emerges as the dominant Mediterranean force.
133	Rome rules entire Mediterranean Basin except Egypt.
49	Julius Caesar conquers Gaul.
44	Julius Caesar is assassinated.
27	Rome's Imperial Age begins; Octavian (now named Augustus) becomes the first emperor and is later deified. The Augustan Age is celebrated in the works of Virgil (70 BC– AD 19), Ovid (43 BC– AD 17), Livy (59 BC– AD 17), and Horace (65–8 BC).

by the state, but if they allowed the sacred fire to go out, they were scourged by the high priest, and if they broke their vows of celibacy, they were buried alive (a punishment doled out only a handful of times throughout the cult's 1,000-year history). The vestal virgins were one of the last of ancient Rome's institutions to die out, enduring to the end of the 4th century AD, even after Rome's emperors had become Christian. ⊠ *South side of Via Sacra, Roman Forum.*

Via Sacra. The celebrated basalt-paved road that loops through the Roman Forum, lined with temples and shrines, was also the traditional route of religious and triumphal processions. Pick your way across the paving stones, some rutted with the ironclad wheels of Roman wagons, to walk in the footsteps of Caesar and Anthony. ⊠ *Roman Forum.*

WORTH NOTING

Basilica Giulia. The Basilica Giulia owes its name to Julius Caesar, who ordered its construction; it was later completed by his adopted heir Augustus. One of several such basilicas in the center of Rome, it was where the Centumviri, the hundred-or-so judges forming the civil court, met to hear cases. The open space between the Basilica Emilia and this basilica was the heart of the Forum proper, prototype of Italy's famous piazzas, and the center of civic and social activity in ancient Rome. ⊠ *Via Sacra, Roman Forum.*

Colonna di Foca (*Pillar of Phocas*). The last monument to be added to the Forum was erected in AD 608 in honor of a Byzantine emperor who had donated the Pantheon to Pope Boniface IV. It stands 44 feet high and remains in good condition. ⊠ *West end of Foro Romano, Roman Forum.*

Santa Maria Antiqua. The earliest Christian site in the Forum was originally part of an imperial temple, before it was converted into a church some time in the 5th or 6th century. Within are some exceptional but faded 7th- and 8th-century frescoes of the early church fathers, saints, and popes; the styles vary from typically classical to Oriental, reflecting the empire's expansion eastward. Largely destroyed in a 9th-century earthquake, the church was abandoned only to be rebuilt in 1617, then knocked down again in 1900 following excavation work on the Forum. Its latest incarnation is still off-limits to visitors, along with restored

43 AD	Rome invades Britain.
50	Rome is the largest city in the world, with a population of a million.
65	Emperor Nero begins the persecution of Christians in the Empire; Saints Peter and Paul are executed.
70–80	Vespasian builds the Colosseum.
98–117	Trajan's military successes are celebrated with his Baths (98), Forum (110), and Column (113); the Roman Empire reaches its apogee.

frescoes you can read about but still not see. ⊠ *South of Tempio di Castore and Polluce, at foot of Palatine Hill, Roman Forum.*

Tempio di Antonino e Faustina. Erected by the Senate in honor of Faustina, deified wife of Emperor Antoninus Pius (AD 138–161), Hadrian's successor, this temple was rededicated to the emperor as well upon his death. Because it was transformed into a church, it's one of the best-preserved ancient structures in the Forum. ⊠ *North of Via Sacra, Roman Forum.*

Tempio di Cesare. Built by Augustus, Caesar's successor, the temple stands over the spot where Julius Caesar's body was cremated. A pyre was improvised by grief-crazed citizens who kept the flames going with their own possessions. ⊠ *Between 2 forks of Via Sacra, Roman Forum.*

Tempio di Venere e Roma. Once Rome's largest and possibly cleverest temple (it was dedicated to Venus and Rome or, in Latin, to "amor" and "Roma"), this temple was begun by Hadrian in AD 121 and finished 20 years later. The recent restoration took even longer—some 25 years—and finally ended in 2010, meaning the public can visit the temple once again. ⊠ *East of Arco di Tito, Roman Forum.*

Tempio di Vespasiano. All that remains of Vespasian's temple are three graceful Corinthian columns. They marked the site of the Forum through the centuries while the rest was hidden beneath overgrown rubble. Nearby is the ruined platform that was the **Tempio di Concordia.** ⊠ *West end of Foro Romano, Roman Forum.*

THE PALATINE HILL

Just beyond the Arch of Titus, the Clivus Palatinus gently rises to the heights of the **Colle Palatino** (Palatine Hill)—the oldest inhabited site in Rome. Despite its location overlooking the Forum's traffic and attendant noise, the Palatine was the most coveted address for ancient Rome's rich and famous. More than a few of the 12 Caesars called the Palatine home, including Caligula, who was murdered in the still-standing and unnerving (even today) tunnel, the Cryptoporticus. The palace of Tiberius was the first to be built here; others followed, notably the gigantic extravaganza constructed for Emperor Domitian. But perhaps the most famous lodging goes back to Rome's very beginning. Once

238 AD	The first wave of Germanic invasions penetrates Italy.
293	Diocletian reorganizes the Empire into West and East.
330	Constantine founds a new Imperial capital (Constantinople) in the East.
410	Rome is sacked by Visigoths.
476	The last Roman emperor, Romulus Augustus, is deposed. The western Roman Empire falls.

upon a time, skeptics thought Romulus was a myth. Then, about a century ago, Rome's greatest archaeologist, Rodolfo Lanciani, excavated a site on the hill and uncovered the remains of an Iron Age settlement dating back to the 9th century BC, supporting the belief that Romulus, founder of Rome, lived here. In fall 2007, archaeologists unearthed a sacred sanctuary dedicated to Romulus and Remus set beneath the House of Augustus near the Palatine Hill. This sanctuary is now being renovated.

During the Republican era, the Palatino became the "Beverly Hills" of ancient Rome. Hortensius, Cicero, Catiline, Crassus, and Agrippa all had homes here. Augustus was born on the hill; the House of Livia, reserved for Augustus's wife, is today the hill's best-preserved structure. To visit the ruins of the Palatine (some scholars think this name gave rise to our term "palace") in roughly chronological order, start from the southeast area facing the Aventine. ⊠ *Entrances at Piazza del Colosseo and Via di San Gregorio 30, Roman Forum* ☏ *06/39967700* ⊕ *www. pierreci.it* 💷*€12 (combined ticket with the Colosseum and Roman Forum, if used within 2 days)* ☉ *Daily 8:30 am–one hour before sunset* Ⓜ *Colosseo.*

TOP ATTRACTIONS

★ **Casa di Augustus** (*House of Augustus*). First discovered in the 1970s and only opened in 2006, this was the residence of the great Emperor Augustus (27 BC–14 AD)—before he became great (archaeologists have recently found two courtyards rather than one, though, in the style of Rome's ancient Greek kings, suggesting Augustus maintained this house after his ascension to prominence). The house here dates to the time when Augustus was known merely as Octavian, before the death of, and Octavian's adoption by, his great uncle Julius Caesar. Four rooms have exquisite examples of Roman wall decorative frescoes (so precious that only five people at a time are admitted). Startlingly vivid and detailed are the depictions of a narrow stage with side doors and some striking comic theater masks. ⊠ *Northwest crest of Palatino, Palatine Hill/Ancient Rome* ☏ *06/39967700* ⊕ *www.pierreci.it* ☉ *Mon., Wed., and weekends 11–3:30.*

★ **Casa di Livia** (*House of Livia*). First excavated in 1839, this house was identifiable from the name inscribed on a lead pipe, Iulia Augusta. In other words, it belonged to the notorious Livia that—according to Robert Graves' *I, Claudius*—made a career of dispatching half of the Roman imperial family. (There's actually very little evidence for such claims.) She was the wife of Rome's first, and possibly greatest, emperor, Augustus. He married Livia when she was six months pregnant by her previous husband, whom Augustus "encouraged" to get a divorce. As empress, Livia became a role model for Roman women, serving her husband faithfully, shunning excessive displays of wealth, and managing her household. But she also had real influence: As well as playing politics behind the scenes, she even had the rare honor (for a woman) of being in charge of her own finances. Here, atop the Palatine, is where she made her private retreat and living quarters. The delicate, delightful frescoes reflect the sophisticated taste of wealthy Romans, whose love of beauty and theatrical conception of nature were revived by their

The "Bel Air" of ancient Rome, the Palatine Hill was the address of choice of Cicero, Agrippa, and the emperors Tiberius, Caligula, and Domitian.

descendants in the Renaissance Age. While closed at the time of this writing, the House of Livia will sometimes open for brief periods, so check by phoning or going online at ⊕ *www.pierreci.it*. ✉ *Northwest crest of Palatino, Palatine Hill/Ancient Rome* ☎ *06/39967450* ⊕ *www. pierreci.it* ⊙ *Tues.–Thurs. 9–1.*

Circo Massimo (*Circus Maximus*). From the belvedere of the Domus Flavia, you can see the Circus Maximus, the giant arena where more than 300,000 spectators watched chariot races while the emperor looked on from this very spot. Ancient Rome's oldest and largest racetrack lies in a natural hollow between two hills. The oval course stretches about 650 yards from end to end; on certain occasions, there were as many as 24 chariot races a day and competitions could last for 15 days. The charioteers could amass fortunes rather like the sports stars of today (the Portuguese Diocles—one of many such *miliari*—is said to have totted up winnings of 35 million sesterci). The noise and the excitement of the crowd must have reached astonishing levels as the charioteers competed in teams, each with its own colors—the Reds, the Blues, etc. Betting also provided Rome's majority of unemployed with a potentially lucrative occupation. The central ridge was the site of two Egyptian obelisks (now in Piazza del Popolo and Piazza San Giovanni in Laterano). Picture the great chariot race scene from MGM's *Ben-Hur* and you have an inkling of what this all looked like. ✉ *Valley between Palatine and Aventine hills* Ⓜ *Circo Massimo.*

Domus Augustana. In the Palazzi Imperiali complex, this palace, named for the "August" emperor, consisted of private apartments for Emperor Domitian and his family. Here Domitian—Master and God, as he liked

Continued on page 84

ROME WAS NOT BUILT IN A DAY

by Robert I. C. Fisher

RE-CREATING THE ANCIENT CITY

"All roads lead to Rome" but leave many visitors confused, disoriented, and befuddled. Travelers arrive at the Roman Forum hoping to discover Caesar's World, only to find a picturesque pile of rubble. Could this actually be where Nero once fiddled? Where Mark Antony buried Caesar? To dish the dirt—archaeologically speaking—this guide skillfully interweaves gobs of ancient landmarks to help re-create the ancient city, connecting the dots through time and space. Part atlas, part rendering, part historical tipsheet, it unfolds like a cloak-and-trowel thriller.

Although it has been the capital of the Republic of Italy only since 1946, Rome has been the capital of *something* for more than 2,500 years, and it shows. The magnificent ruins of the Palatine Hill, the ancient complexity of the Forum, the Renaissance harmony of the Campidoglio—all are part of Rome's identity as one of the world's most enduring seats of government.

This is not to say that it's been an easy 2½ millennia. The Vandal hordes of the 3rd century, the Goth sacks of the Middle Ages, the excavations of a modern-day Mussolini, and today's "army"—the motorized Barbarians—all played a part in transforming Rome into a city of fragments. Semi-preserved ruins of ancient forums, basilicas, stadiums, baths, and temples are strewn across the city like remnants of some Cecil B. DeMille movie-set. Even if you walk into the Termini McDonalds, you'll find three chunks of the 4th century BC Servian Wall. No wonder first-time visitors feel the only thing more intimidating than crossing a Roman intersection at rush hour is trying to make sense of the layout of ancient Rome.

Now, to your aid, comes this "ancient atlas." Overlapping the new Rome with the old, it is crammed with details of all the city's ageless walls and ancient sites, even though some of them now lie hidden underneath the earth. Written in these rocks is the story of the emperors, the city's greatest builders. Thanks in large part to their dreams of glory—combined with their architectural megalomania—Imperial Rome became the fountainhead of Western civilization.

Colosseum; (top) Head of Emperor Constantine, Musei Capitolini

THE WAY ROME WAS

Circus Maximus: Atop the Palatine Hill, the emperor's royal box looked down on the races and games of this vast stadium—most Early Christians met their untimely end here, not in the Colosseum.

Capitoline Hill (Campidoglio): Most important of Rome's original seven hills, and home to the Temple of Jupiter, the "capital" hill was strategically located high above the Tiber and became the hub of the Roman Republic.

Palatine Hill (Palatino): The birthplace of Rome, settled by Romulus and Remus, the Palatine ultimately became Rome's

Theater of Pompey

Circus of Domitian

Pantheon

CAMPUS MARTIUS

Temple of Jupiter

Isola Tiberina

Theater of Marcellus

CAMPIDOGLIO

Campus Borum

TRASTEVERE

House of Augustus

A V E N T I N O

P A L A T I N O

Circus Maximus

Rome in the Year 300 AD

"Beverly Hills" for it was home to Cicero, Julius Caesar, and a dozen Emperors.

Roman Forum:
Downtown ancient Rome, this was the political heart of the Republic and Empire—the place for processions, tribunals, law courts, and orations, it was here that Mark Antony buried Caesar and Cleopatra made her triumphant entry.

Colosseum:
Gladiators fought for the chance to live another day on the floor before 50,000 spectators in this giant arena, built in a mere eight years and inaugurated in AD 80.

Domus Aurea:
Nero's "Golden House," a sprawling example of the excesses of Imperial Rome, once comprised 150 rooms, some shimmering with gold.

Via Flaminia

Forum of Trajan

Roman Forum

QUIRINALE

VIMINALE

SUBURRA

Domus Aurea

Basilica of Maxentius

ESQUILINO

Colosseum

Aqueduct of Acqua Claudia

Temple of Claudius

Acqueduct of Acqua Appia

CELIO

3

IN FOCUS ROME WAS NOT BUILT IN A DAY

THEY CAME, THEY SAW, THEY BUILT

Remember the triumphal scene in the 2000 film *Gladiator?* Awesome expanses of pristine marble, a cast of thousands in gold-lavished costumes, and close-ups of Joaquin Phoenix (playing Emperor Commodus) on his way to the Colosseum: Rome à la Hollywood. But behind all the marble splendor seen in the film lies an eight-centuries-long trail that extends back from Imperial Rome to a tiny village of mud-huts along the Tiber river.

Museo della Civiltà Romana's model of Imperial Rome

ROMULUS GOES TO TOWN

Legend has it that Rome was founded by Romulus and Remus, twin sons of the god Mars. Upon being abandoned in infancy by a wicked uncle, they were taken up and suckled by a she-wolf living on a bank of the Tiber. (Ancient gossip says the wolf was actually a woman nicknamed Lupa for her multiple infidelities to her shepherd husband.)

As young men, Romulus and Remus returned in 753 BC to the hallowed spot to found a city but came to blows during its building, ending in the death of Remus—which is how the city became Roma, not Rema.

Where myth ends, archaeology takes over. In 2007, Roman excavators uncovered a cavernous sanctuary dedicated to the brothers situated in the valley between the Palatine and Capitoline (Campidoglio) hills in central Rome. Often transformed into "islands" when the Tiber river overflowed, these two hills soon famously expanded to include seven hills, including the Esquiline, Viminale, Celian, Quirinale, and Aventine.

SIMPLY MARBLE-LOUS

Up to 510 BC, the style of the fledging city had been set by the fun-loving, sophisticated Etruscans—Rome was to adopt their vestal virgins, household gods, and gladiatorial games. Later, when the Republic took over the city (509 BC–27 BC), the austere values promulgated by its democratic Senate eventually fell to the power-mad triumvirate of Crassus, Pompey, and Julius Caesar, who waved away any detractors—including Rome's main power-players, the patrician Senators and the populist Tribunes—by invoking the godlike sovereignty of emperorship.

Republican Rome's city was badly planned, in fact not planned at all, and the great contribution of the Emperor Augustus—who took over when his stepfather Caesar was assassinated in 43 BC—was to commence serious town planning, with results far surpassing even his own claim that he "found Rome brick and left it marble." Which was only fitting, as floridly colored marbles began to flow into Rome from all of the Mediterranean provinces he had conquered (including obelisks transported from Egypt to flaunt his victory over Cleopatra).

Via Sacra in the Roman Forum with the Temple of Saturn in the foreground and the Basilica Julia on the right.

A FUNNY THING HAPPENED ON THE WAY TO THE ROMAN FORUM

It was during Augustus' 40-year-long peaceful reign that Rome began its transition from glorified provincial capital into great city. While excavations have shown that the area of the Roman Forum was in use as a burial ground as far back as the 10th century BC, the importance of the Forum area as the political, commercial, and social center of Rome and, by extension, of the whole ancient world, grew immeasurably during Imperial times. The majestic ruins still extant are remnants of the massive complex of markets, civic buildings, and temples that dominated the city center in its heyday.

After Rome gained "empire" status, however, the original Forum was inadequate to handle the burden of the many trials and meetings required to run Western civilization, so Julius Cae-

sar built a new forum. This apparently started a trend, as over the next 200-plus years (43 BC–AD 180), four different emperors—Augustus, Domitian, Vespasian, and Trajan—did the same. Oddly enough, the Roman Forum became four different Forums. They grew, in part, thanks to the Great Fire of AD 64, which Nero did not set but for which he took credit for laying waste to shabbier districts to build new ones.

For half a millennium, the Roman Forum area became the heart and soul of a worldwide empire, which eventually extended from Britain to Constantinople. Unfortunately, another thousand years of looting, sacking, and decay means you have to use your vivid imagination to see the glory that once was.

■ TIP➔ For a step-by-step tour of the Roman Forum, see the "Roamin' Holiday" chapter.

WHERE ALL ROADS LEAD

Even if you don't dig ruins, a visit to
the Centro Archeologico—the area
in and around the Roman Forum—is
a must. Rome's foundation as a world
capital and crossroads of culture are
to be found here, literally. Over-
lapped with Rome's current streets,
this planimetric map shows the main
monuments of the Foro Romano
(in tan) as they originally stood.

Via IV Novembre
Via C. Battisti

Trajan's Column

V. Alessandrina

TRAJAN'S FORUM

CAMPIDOGLIO

Via del Teatro di Marcello

Palazzo Senatorio

Tabularium

Carcere Mamertino

Arch of Septimus Severus

Curia

Umbilcus Urbis Romae

The Rostra

TEMPLE OF JUPITER

V. L. Petroselli

Temple of Vespasian

Roman Forum

Basilica Julia

Tarpeian Rock

Temple of Saturn

Temple of Castor and Pollux

V. C. Jugario

V. della Consolazione

V. d. Foraggi

V. d. Fienili

V. d. S. Teodoro

Cloaca Maxima

TIBERIAN PALACE

MONTE

House of Livia

V. del Velabro

Circus Maximus

Basilica Julia

Temple of Antoninus and Faustina

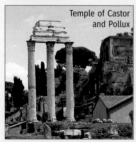
Temple of Castor and Pollux

Domitian's Palace

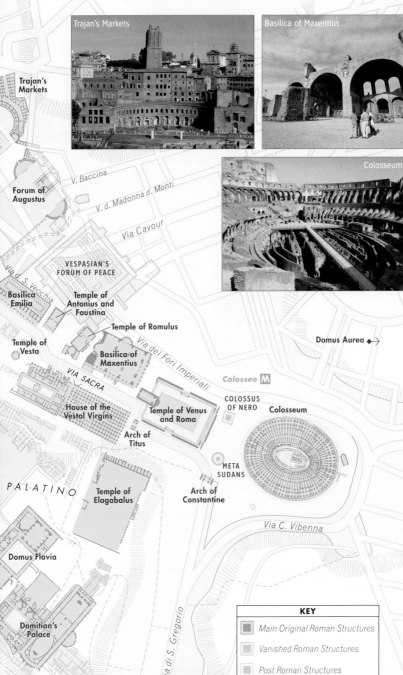

Trajan's Markets

Basilica of Maxentius

Colosseum

Trajan's
Markets

Forum of
Augustus

V. Baccina

V. d. Madonna d. Monti

Via Cavour

VESPASIAN'S
FORUM OF PEACE

Via d. S. Vecchia

Basilica
Emilia

Temple of
Antonius and
Faustina

Temple of Romulus

Domus Aurea ◆→

Temple of
Vesta

Basilica of
Maxentius

Via dei Fori Imperiali

VIA SACRA

Colosseo Ⓜ

COLOSSUS
OF NERO

Colosseum

House of the
Vestal Virgins

Temple of Venus
and Roma

Arch of
Titus

META
SUDANS

PALATINO

Temple of
Elagabalus

Arch of
Constantine

Via C. Vibenna

Domus Flavia

Domitian's
Palace

Via di S. Gregorio

KEY

Main Original Roman Structures

Vanished Roman Structures

Post Roman Structures

URBIS ROMÆ: THE EXPANDING CITY

Pantheon

Today's Campitelli district—the historic area comprising the Forums and the Colosseum—was, in fact, a relatively small part of the ancient city. From the center around the Forum, the old city dramatically grew outwards and in AD 7, the emperor Augustus organized ancient Rome into 14 *regiones*, administrative divisions that were the forerunners of today's historic *rioni* (districts). Rome's first city walls went up in the 6th century BC when King Servius Tullius built an eight-mile ring. As the city's borders greatly expanded, however, the outlaying areas needed extra protection. This became a dire necessity in the 3rd century when Germanic tribes arrived to sack Rome while Emperor Aurelian was fighting wars on the southern border of the empire. Fueled by fear, the emperor commissioned an 11-mile bulwark to be built of brick between 271 and 275. Studding the Aurelian Walls were 380 towers and 18 main gates, the best preserved of which is the Porta di San Sebastiano, at the entrance to the Via Appia Antica. The Porta is now home to the Museo delle Mura (⊠ *Via di Porta San Sebastiano 18* ☎ *06/060608* ⊕ *www.museodellemuraroma.it* ⊠ *Open Tues.–Sun., 9–2*), a small but fascinating museum that allows you to walk the ancient ramparts today; take Bus No. 118 to the Porta. From the walls' lofty perch you can see great vistas of the timeless Appian Way.

KEY

Archeological area of Rome

Hills

Mausoleum of Hadrian (Castel S. Angelo)

CAMPUS MARTIUS

Fiume Tevere

Circus of Domitian (Piazza Navona)

Theater of Pompey (Campo de' Fiori)

TRASTEVERE

Pantheon: Built in 27 BC by Augustus's general Agrippa and totally rebuilt by Hadrian in the 2nd century AD, this temple, dedicated to all the pagan gods, was topped by the largest dome ever built (until the 20th century).

Baths of Caracalla: These gigantic thermal baths, a stunning example of ancient Roman architecture, were more than just a place to bathe—they functioned somewhat like today's swank athletic clubs.

Isola Tiberina: The Temple of Aesculapius once presided over this island—which was shaped by ancient Romans to resemble a ship, complete with obelisk mast and (still visible) marble ship prow—and was Rome's shrine to medicine.

Circus of Domitian: Rome's present Piazza Navona follows the shape of this ancient oval stadium built in 96 AD—houses now stand on top of the *cavea*, the original stone seating, which held 30,000 spectators.

Campus Borum: Today's Piazza della Bocca della Verità was ancient Rome's cattle market and the site of two beautifully preserved 2nd century BC temples, one dedicated to Fortuna Virilis, the other to Hercules.

Porta di San Sebastiano: The largest extant gate of the 3rd-century Aurelian Walls, located near the ancient aqueduct that once brought water to the nearby Baths of Caracalla, showcases the most beautiful stretch of Rome's ancient walls.

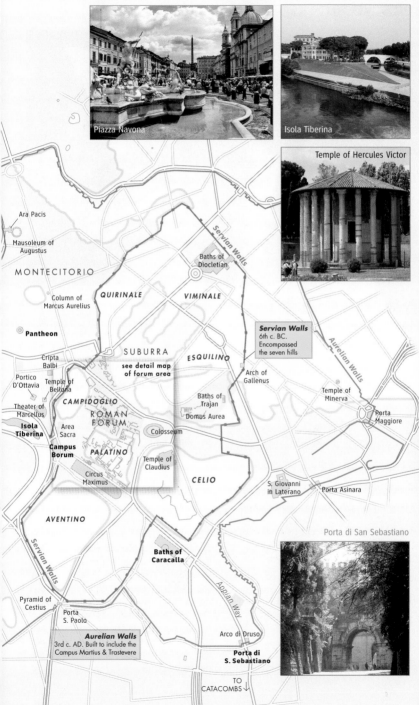

Piazza Navona

Isola Tiberina

Temple of Hercules Victor

Ara Pacis

Mausoleum of Augustus

MONTECITORIO

Baths of Diocletian

Servian Walls

Column of Marcus Aurelius

QUIRINALE

VIMINALE

Pantheon

SUBURRA

ESQUILINO

Servian Walls
6th c. BC.
Encompassed
the seven hills

Cripta Balbi

see detail map of forum area

Arch of Gallenus

Portico D'Ottavia

Temple of Bellona

CAMPIDOGLIO

Baths of Trajan

Domus Aurea

Aurelian Walls

Temple of Minerva

Theater of Marcellus

Isola Tiberina

Area Sacra

ROMAN FORUM

Colosseum

Porta Maggiore

Campus Borum

PALATINO

Temple of Claudius

Circus Maximus

CELIO

S. Giovanni in Laterano

Porta Asinara

AVENTINO

Porta di San Sebastiano

Servian Walls

Baths of Caracalla

Appian Way

Pyramid of Cestius

Porta S. Paolo

Aurelian Walls
3rd c. AD. Built to include the
Campus Martius & Trastevere

Arco di Druso

Porta di S. Sebastiano

TO CATACOMBS ↓

BUILDING BLOCKS OF THE EMPERORS

Vespasian's Colosseum

The oft quoted remark of Augustus, that he found Rome brick and left it marble, omits a vital ingredient of Roman building: concrete. The sheer size and spectacle of ancient Rome's most famous buildings owe everything to this humble building block. Its use was one of the Romans' greatest contributions to the history of architecture, for it ennabled them not only to create vast arches, domes, and vaults—undreamed of before—but also to build at a scale and size never before attempted. The fall of the Roman empire ultimately arrived, but great architectural monuments remain to remind us of its glory.

THE ARCH
VESPASIAN'S COLOSSEUM

Born in Riete, Titus Flavius Vespasian was the first of the new, military emperors. A down-to-earth countryman, with a realistic sense of humor, his dying words "I think I am in the process of becoming a god" have lived on. Along with generally restoring the city, which had burned down under Nero, he started the Colosseum, (his son, Titus, finished it, in AD 80). Erected upon the swampy marsh that once held the *stagnum*, or lake, of Nero's Golden House, the Colosseum was vast; its dimensions underscored how much Romans had come to value audacious size. The main architectural motif was the arch—hundreds of them in four ascending birthday tiers, each tier adorned with a different style of column: Doric, Ionic, Corinthian, Corinthian pilaster. Inside each arch was a statue (all of which have disappeared). Under these arches, called *fornices*, ancient Romans were fond of looking for bedfellows (so famously said the great poet Ovid), so much so that these arches gave a new word to the English language.

Domus Aurea

Hadrian's Pantheon

THE VAULT
NERO'S DOMUS AUREA

Most notorious of the emperors, but by no means the worst, Nero had domestic and foreign policies that were popular at first. However, his increasing megalomania was apparent in the size of his Domus Aurea, the "Golden House," so huge that the cry went up "All Rome has become a villa." Taking advantage of the Great Fire of AD 64, Nero wanted to re-create his seaside villa at Baia (outside Naples) right in the middle of Rome, building a vast palace of polychrome marble with a dining room with perforated ivory ceilings so that diners could be showered with flowers and perfume (designed by Fabullus, Nero's decorator). But the masterstrokes were the gigantic vaulted rooms—the Room of the Owls and the octagonal-shaped center room—designed by Nero's architects, Severus and Celer. Greek post-and-lintel architecture was banished for these highly dramatic spaces created by soaring vaults. You can still tour the ruins of Nero's "villa" but his 120-foot-high colossal bronze statue gave way to make room for the Colosseum.

THE DOME
HADRIAN'S PANTHEON

The concrete Roman dome at its most impressive can be seen in the Pantheon (around AD 125), a massive construction 141 feet across. It is a fascinating feat of both design and engineering, for it is modeled on a sphere, the height of the supporting walls being equal to the radius of the dome. Larger than Saint Peter's, this dome of domes was constructed by the greatest Imperial builder of them all, the Emperor Hadrian. Poised on top of the dome's mighty concrete ring, the five levels of trapezoid-shaped coffers represent the course of the five then-known planets and their concentric spheres. Then, ruling over them, comes the sun, represented symbolically and literally by the so-called oculus—the giant "eye" open to the sky at the top. The heavenly symmetry is further paralleled by the coffers themselves: 28 to each row, the number of lunar cycles. In the center of each would have shone a small bronze star. All of the dome's famous gilt trim was stripped away by the Barberini popes in the 17th century, who melted it down to decorate the Vatican.

to be called—would retire to dismember flies (at least according to Suetonius). ⊠ *Southern crest of Palatino, Palatine Hill/Ancient Rome.*

Domus Flavia. Domitian used this palace in the Palazzi Imperiali complex for official functions and ceremonies. Also called Palazzo dei Flavi, it included a basilica where the emperor could hold judiciary hearings. There were also a large audience hall, a peristyle (a columned courtyard), and the imperial triclinium (dining room), the latter set in a sunken declivity overlooking the Circus Maximus—some of its mosaic floors and stone banquettes are still in place. Domitian had the walls and courtyards of this and the adjoining Domus Augustana covered with the shiniest marble, to act as mirrors to alert him to any knife in the back. They failed in their purpose. He died in a palace plot, engineered, some say, by his wife Domitia. ⊠ *Southern crest of Palatino, Palatine Hill/Ancient Rome.*

IN ROME, DRINK LIKE THE ROMANS DID

There are few more atmospheric places in Rome to wander about in than the Palatine Hill, with its hidden corners and shady lanes. All that strolling, though, can invite serious thirst. Do as the ancients did: Take advantage of the water fountains scattered across Rome, including several in the Forum and on the Palatine. When your water bottle empties, save it and refill it under one of the continuously running streams. The water's fresh, clean, cold, and still comes from the same natural water sources the ancient Romans used.

WORTH NOTING

Museo Palatino. The Palatine Museum charts the history of the hill from Archaic times with quaint models of early villages (ground floor) through to Roman times (ground and upper floors). On display in Room V are painted terra-cotta moldings and sculptural decorations from various temples (notably the Temple of Apollo Actiacus, whose name derives from the god to whom Octavian attributed his victory at Actium; the severed heads of the Medusa in the terra-cotta panels symbolize the defeated Queen of Egypt). Upon request, museum staff will accompany visitors to see the 16th-century frescoes of the Loggia Mattei. Portions of the paintings have been returned here from the Metropolitan Museum of Art in New York City. In the same building are frescoes detached from the Aula Isaica, one of the chambers belonging to the House of Augustus. ⊠ *Northwest crest of Palatino, Palatine Hill/Ancient Rome* 🎫 *€12 (combined ticket with the Colosseum, Roman Forum, and Imperial Forums, if used within 2 days)* ⊙ *Daily 8:30–4* Ⓜ *Colosseo.*

Orti Farnesiani. Alessandro Farnese, a nephew of Pope Paul III, commissioned the 16th-century architect Vignola to lay out this archetypal Italian garden over the ruins of the Palace of Tiberius, up a few steps from the House of Livia. This was yet another example of the Renaissance renewing an ancient Roman tradition. To paraphrase the poet Martial, the statue-studded gardens of the Flavian Palace were such as to make even an Egyptian potentate turn green with envy. ⊠ *Monte Palatino, Palatine Hill/Ancient Rome.*

THE IMPERIAL FORUMS

A complex of five grandly conceived squares flanked with colonnades and temples, the Fori Imperiali (Imperial Fora) formed the magnificent monumental core of ancient Rome, together with the original Roman Forum. Excavations at the start of the 21st century have revealed more of the Imperial Fora than seen in nearly a thousand years.

From Piazza del Colosseo, head northwest on Via dei Fori Imperiali toward Piazza Venezia. On the walls to your left, maps in marble and bronze put up by Benito Mussolini show the extent of the Roman Republic and Empire. The dictator's own dreams of empire led him to construct this avenue, cutting brutally through the Imperial Fora, so that he would have a suitable venue for parades celebrating his expected military triumphs. Among the Fori Imperiali along the avenue, you can see the Foro di Cesare (Forum of Caesar) and the Foro di Augusto (Forum of Augustus). The grandest of all the Imperial Fora was the Foro di Traiano (Forum of Trajan), with its huge semicircular Mercati Traianei and the Colonna di Traiano (Trajan's Column). You can walk through part of Trajan's Markets through the new Museo dei Fori Imperiali, which presents the Imperial Forums and shows how they would have been used, through both ancient fragments and artifacts and modern multimedia. On very rare occasions, guided tours of the Imperial Forums may be offered (check with the tourist office). The fora also are illuminated at night. ⊠ *Via dei Fori Imperiali, Roman Forum* ☎ *06/0608* ⊕ *www.mercatiditraiano.it* ✉ *Museum, €8.50* ⊙ *Museum open Tues.–Sun. 9–7* Ⓜ *Colosseo.*

TOP ATTRACTIONS

★ **Colonna di Traiano** (*Trajan's Column*). The remarkable series of reliefs spiraling up this column celebrate the emperor's victories over the Dacians in today's Romania. It has stood in this spot since AD 113. The scenes on the column are an important primary source for information on the Roman army and its tactics. An inscription on the base declares that the column was erected in Trajan's honor and that its height corresponds to the height of the hill that was razed to create a level area for the grandiose Foro di Traiano. The emperor's ashes, no longer here, were kept in a golden urn in a chamber at the column's base; his statue stood atop the column until 1587, when the pope had it replaced with a statue of St. Peter. ⊠ *Via del Foro di Traiano, Roman Forum.*

Fodor'sChoice **Foro di Traiano** (*Forum of Trajan*). Of all the Imperial Fora complexes,
★   Trajan's was the grandest and most imposing, a veritable city unto itself. Designed by architect Apollodorus of Damascus, it comprised a vast basilica (at the time of writing closed for restoration), two libraries, and a colonnade laid out around the square, all once covered with rich marble ornamentation. Adjoining the forum were the **Mercati Traianei** (Trajan's markets), a huge, multilevel brick complex of shops, walkways, and terraces that was essentially an ancient shopping mall. The **Museo dei Fori Imperiali** (Imperial Forums Museum) opened in 2007, taking advantage of the forum's soaring, vaulted spaces to showcase archaeological fragments and sculptures while presenting a video re-creation of

the original complex. In addition, the series of terraced rooms offers an impressive overview of the entire forum.

To build a complex of this magnitude, Apollodorus and his patron clearly had to have great confidence, not to mention almost unlimited means, and cheap labor at their disposal, this readily provided by captives from Trajans' Dacian wars. Formerly thought to be the Roman equivalent of a multipurpose commercial center, with shops, taverns, and depots, the site is now believed to be more of an administrative complex for storing and regulating Rome's enormous food supplies. They also contained two semicircular lecture halls, one at either end, which were likely associated with the libraries in Trajan's Forum. The markets' architectural centerpiece is the enormous curved wall, or *hexedra,* that shores up the side of the Quirinal Hill exposed by Apollodorus's gangs of laborers. Covered galleries and streets were constructed at various levels, following the hexedra's curves and giving the complex a strikingly modern appearance.

As you enter the markets, a large, vaulted hall stands in front of you. Two stories of shops or offices rise up on either side. It's thought that they were an administrative center for food handouts to the city's poor. Head for the flight of steps at the far end that leads down to Via Biberatica. (*Bibere* is Latin for "to drink," and the shops that open onto the street are believed to have been taverns.) Then head back to the three tiers of shops/offices that line the upper levels of the great hexedra, and look out over the remains of the forum. Empty and bare today, the cubicles were once ancient Rome's busiest market stalls. Though it seems to be part of the market, the **Torre delle Milizie** (Tower of the Militia), the tall brick tower, which is a prominent feature of Rome's skyline, was built in the early 1200s. ⊠ *Entrance: Via IV Novembre 94, Roman Forum* ☎ *06/0608* ⊕ *www.mercatiditraiano.it* ⊠ *€11* ☉ *Tues.–Sun. 9–7 (ticket office closes at 6)* Ⓜ *Bus 85, 175, 186, 810, 850, H, 64, 70.*

Fodor's Choice
★
Santi Cosma e Damiano. Home to one of the most striking Early Christian mosaics in the world, this church was adapted in the 6th century from two ancient buildings: the library in Vespasian's Forum of Peace and a hall of the Temple of Romulus (dedicated to the son of Maxentius and at Christmas the setting for a Christmas crib). In the apse is the famous AD 530 mosaic of Christ in Glory. It reveals how popes at the time strove to re-create the splendor of imperial audience halls into Christian churches: Christ wears a gold, Roman-style toga, and his pose recalls that of an emperor addressing his subjects. He floats on a blue sky streaked with a flaming sunset—a miracle of tesserae mosaic-work. To his side are the figures of Sts. Peter and Paul, who present to him Cosmas and Damian, two Syrian benefactors whose charity was such that they were branded Christians and condemned to death. Beneath this awe-inspiring work is an enchanting mosaic frieze of holy lambs. ⊠ *Via in Miranda 11, Roman Forum* ☎ *06/6920441* ☉ *Daily 9–1 and 3–7* Ⓜ *Bus 85, 850, 87, 571, 3, 117.*

WORTH NOTING

Foro di Augusto (*Forum of Augustus*). These ruins, along with those of the **Foro di Nerva**, on the northeast side of Via dei Fori Imperiali, give only a hint of what must have been impressive edifices. ✉ *Via dei Fori Imperiali, Roman Forum* Ⓜ *Colosseo.*

Foro di Cesare (*Forum of Caesar*). To try to rival the original Roman Forum, Julius Caesar had this forum built in the middle of the 1st century BC. Each year without fail, on the Ides of March, an unknown hand lays a bouquet at the foot of Caesar's statue. ✉ *Via dei Fori Imperiali, Roman Forum* ☎ *06/0608.*

A CLASSY LOOKOUT

The exit of the Palatino leads to the Arch of Titus, where you turn east toward the Colosseum and the Arco di Costantino. Cross Piazza del Colosseo and stroll through the park on the Colle Oppio (Oppian Hill), the site of Trajan's baths and of Nero's Golden House. The park here has some great views over the Colosseum; one of the best vantage points is from Via Nicola Salvi, which climbs uphill from the Colosseum. Around dusk, camera snatchers can appear so keep one eye on your Nikon, one eye on the view.

THE COLOSSEUM AND ENVIRONS

Legend has it that as long as the Colosseum stands, Rome will stand; and when Rome falls, so will the world. No visit to Rome is complete without a trip to the obstinate oval that has been the iconic symbol of the city for centuries. Looming over a group of the Roman Empire's most magnificent monuments to imperial wealth and power, the Colosseo was the gigantic sports arena built by Vespasian and Titus. To its west stands the Arch of Constantine, a majestic, ornate triumphal arch, built solely as a tribute to the emperor Constantine; victorious armies purportedly marched under it on their return from war. On the eastern side of the Colosseum, hidden under the Colle Oppio, is Nero's opulent Domus Aurea, a palace that stands as testimony to the lavish lifestyles of the emperors—unfortunately, closed, once again, for restoration after rainwater caused part of the roof to collapse in 2010.

TOP ATTRACTIONS

Fodor's Choice ★ **Arco di Costantino** (*Arch of Constantine*). This majestic arch was erected in AD 315 to commemorate Constantine's victory over Maxentius at the Milvian Bridge. It was just before this battle, in AD 312, that Constantine—the emperor who converted Rome to Christianity—had a vision of a cross in the heavens and heard the words "In this sign thou shalt conquer." Many of the rich marble decorations for the arch were scavenged from earlier monuments, both saving money and allying Constantine with the greatest emperors of the past. It is easy to picture ranks of Roman legionnaires marching under the great barrel vault. ✉ *Piazza del Colosseo, Colosseo* Ⓜ *Colosseo.*

Fodor's Choice ★ **The Colosseum.** The most spectacular extant edifice of ancient Rome, the Colosseo has a history that is half gore, half glory. Here, before 50,000 spectators, gladiators would salute the emperor and cry *Ave,*

Hollywood got it wrong, historians got it right: plenty of gladiators died in the Colosseum but early Christians only met their tragic fate in the nearby Circus Maximus arena.

imperator, morituri te salutant ("Hail, emperor, men soon to die salute thee"); it is said that when one day they heard the emperor Claudius respond, "or maybe not," they became so offended that they called a strike. Scene of countless Hollywood spectacles—Deborah Kerr besieged by lions in *Quo Vadis*, Victor Mature laying

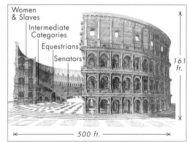

down his arms in *Demetrius and the Gladiators*, and Russell Crowe fighting an emperor in a computer-generated stadium in *Gladiator*, to name just a few—the Colosseum still awes onlookers today with its power and might. And today's sightseers are in luck: for the first time in millennia, the newly restored hypogeum (the basement level of the arena, where gladiators and beasts got ready for battle), along with the third level of the Colosseum, have been newly restored and reopened to the public in fall 2010.

Designed by order of the Flavian emperor Vespasian in AD 72, the Colosseum was inaugurated by Titus eight years later with a program of games lasting 100 days (such shows were a quick way to political popularity—or, to put it another way, a people that yawns is ripe for revolt). The arena has a circumference of 573 yards and was faced with travertine from nearby Tivoli. Its construction was a remarkable feat of engineering, for it stands on marshy terrain reclaimed by draining an artificial lake on the grounds of Nero's Domus Aurea. Originally known as the Flavian amphitheater, it came to be called the Colosseo because it stood on the site of the Colossus of Nero, a 115-foot-tall gilded bronze statue of the emperor that once towered here. Inside, senators had marble seats up front and the vestal virgins took the ringside position, while the plebs sat in wooden tiers at the back, then the masses above on the top tier. Over all was the amazing velarium, an ingenious system of sail-like awnings rigged on ropes and maneuvered by sailors from the imperial fleet, who would unfurl them to protect the arena's occupants from sun or rain.

The Subterranean Hypogeum Once inside, take the steep stairs or elevator up to the second floor, where you can get a birds'-eye view of the hypogeum: the subterranean passageways that were the architectural engine rooms that made the slaughter above proceed like clockwork. In a scene prefiguring something from Dante's *Inferno*, hundreds of beasts would wait to be eventually launched via a series of slave-powered hoists and lifts into the bloodthirsty sand of the arena above. The newly restored hypogeum, along with the third level of the Colosseum, reopened to much acclaim in fall 2010 (visitable only via a prebooked, guided tour). Since then, however, it's open and shut, depending on the season and recent rains. Check the Pierreci website, ⊕ *www.pierreci. it,* for its current state.

Thumbs Down? Although the Colosseum had 80 entrances, it only had one exit named after the Roman goddess of death—the Porta Libitinaria—which was how dead gladiators were trundled out of the arena. Historians state that most of these warriors did survive to fight another day. If the die was cast, however, the rule was that a victorious gladiator was the person to decide to take his opponent's life. He was often spurred on by the audience and the emperor—*pollice verso* meant the downturned thumb. Gladiatorial combat, or *munera*, is now traced back to the funeral rites of the early Etruscans when prisoners of war would sometimes be sacrificed to placate the spirits of the underworld. Rome's city council, in conjunction with Amnesty International, tries to make amends for these horrors by floodlighting the Colosseum by night every time a death sentence is commuted or a country votes to abolish capital punishment.

As well as the sellers pushing tours on the piazza outside the Colosseum, you'll come across costumed men who call themselves the "gladiators." They're actually dressed as Roman centurions, but that doesn't stop them from posing for pictures with tourists—and then insisting on a €5, €10, or even higher price afterwards. If you just have to get that photo op with a sword on your neck, make sure you set the price with the "gladiator" beforehand.

Legend has it that as long as the Colosseum stands, Rome will stand; and when Rome falls, so will the world . . . not that the prophecy deterred Renaissance princes (and even a pope) from using the Colosseum as a quarry. In the 19th century, poets came to view the arena by moonlight; today, mellow golden spotlights make the arena a spectacular sight.

Tips Are there ways to beat the long ticket lines at the Colosseum? Yes and no. First off, if you go to the Roman Forum, a couple of hundred yards down Via dei Fori Imperiali on your left, or to the Palatine, down Via di San Gregorio, the €12 ticket you purchase there includes admission to the Colosseum and, even better, lets you jump to the head of the *looooooong* line. Another way is to buy the Romapass (⊕ *www.romapass.it*) ticket—the Colosseo is covered and you get booted to the front of the line. Or you can book a ticket in advance through ⊕ *www.pierreci.it* (small surcharge)—the main ticket reservation service for many Italian cultural sights. Finally, you can book another tour online with a company (do your research to make sure it's reputable) that lets you "skip the line."

No matter what, however, avoid the tours that are being sold on-the-spot right around the Colosseum, including on the piazza and just outside the Metro. It's all part of a fairly disreputable system that goes on both there and at the Vatican. While the (usually young and English-speaking) "sellers" themselves vary and often work for different companies, their big selling point is always the same: You can skip the line. Although this makes them tempting if you haven't come up with any other game plan, be aware that the tour guides tend to be dry or, due to heavy accents, all but incomprehensible, the tour groups huge, and the tour itself rushed. Plan on an alternative way to get past the line so you don't fall into the last-minute-tour trap.

The exhibition space upstairs often features fascinating temporary exhibitions, included in your ticket price. A bookshop is also on-site. ⊠ *Piazza del Colosseo* ☎ *06/39967700* ⊕ *www.pierreci.it* ✉ *€12 (combined ticket with the Roman Forum, Palatine Hill, and Imperial Forums, if used within 2 days)* ☉ *Daily 8:30–1 hr before sunset* Ⓜ *Colosseo; Bus 117, 87, 186, 85, 850.*

WORTH NOTING

Domus Aurea (*Golden House of Nero*). Legend has it that Nero famously fiddled while Rome burned. Fancying himself a great actor and poet, he played, as it turns out, his harp to accompany his recital of "The Destruction of Troy" while gazing at the flames of Rome's catastrophic fire of AD 64. Anti-Neronian historians propagandized that Nero, in fact, had set the Great Fire to clear out a vast tract of the city center to build his new palace. Today's historians discount this as historical folderol (going so far as to point to the fact that there was a full moon on the evening of July 19, hardly the propitious occasion to commit arson). But legend or not, Nero did get to build his new palace, the extravagant Domus Aurea (Golden House)—a vast "suburban villa" that was inspired by the emperor's pleasure palace at Baia on the Bay of Naples. His new digs were huge and sumptuous, with a facade of pure gold, seawater piped into the baths, decorations of mother-of-pearl, fretted ivory, and other precious materials, and vast gardens. It was said that after completing this gigantic house, Nero exclaimed, "Now I can live like a human being!" Unfortunately, following damage due to flooding in December 2008, the Domus is closed for restorations once again. ⊠ *Via della Domus Aurea, Colle Oppio* ☎ *06/39967700 information about possible future openings* Ⓜ *Colosseo.*

The Vatican

ST. PETER'S BASILICA, SISTINE CHAPEL,
VATICAN MUSEUMS, CASTEL SANT'ANGELO

WORD OF MOUTH

"Like the Vatican Museums, the Sistine Chapel was packed, but you know, you look up and since people still don't fly (yet) the crowd didn't bother me." —Chevre

"Bring a good pair of small binoculars to really see the work on the Sistine ceiling—and enjoy it all from the bench seats along the sides of the chapel . . . ." —Rescue

GETTING ORIENTED

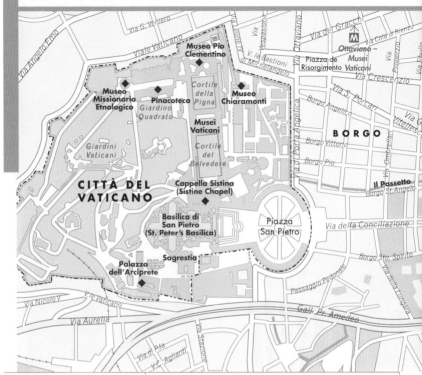

GETTING HERE

From Termini station, hop on the No. 40 Express or the famously crowded No. 64 to deliver you to Piazza San Pietro. On either, as on any bus in Rome, watch out for pickpockets.

Both routes swing past Largo Argentina, where you can also get the 571 or 46. Metro stops Cipro or Ottaviano (Musei Vaticani) will get you within about a 10-minute walk of the entrance to the Vatican Museums.

A leisurely meander from the historic center across the exquisite Ponte Sant'Angelo footbridge will take about a half hour.

HOW TO BEAT THOSE LONG LINES

Home to the Sistine Chapel and the Raphael rooms, the Vatican Museums are among the most congested of all Rome's attractions.

For years, people thought the best way to get a jump on the crowds was to be at the front entrance when it opened at 8:30 am, particularly on the last Sunday of the month when entrance is free (other Sundays the museums are closed).

The problem was that everyone else had the same idea. Result: Rome's version of the Calgary stampede.

Instead, the best way to avoid long lines is to arrive between noon and 2, when lines will be very short or even nonexistent, except Sundays when admissions close at 12:30. Even better is to schedule your visit during the Wednesday Papal Mass, held in the piazza of St. Peter's or at Aula Paolo Sesto. This is usually 10:30 am—to see the pope's calendar, log on to: ⊕ www.vatican.va. Finally, you can purchase your ticket in advance online for an extra €4.

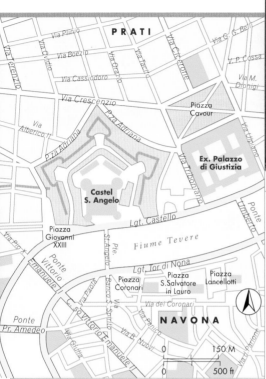

4

Or book a tour, either with the Vatican Museums directly or with a private agency that guarantees a skip-the-line entrance. The Vatican's own guided tour of the museums and Sistine Chapel, which can be booked online, costs €31 and lasts two hours.

All this with the proviso that, traditionally, in July the pope is away on holiday in Val d'Aosta, then in August to mid-September moves to Castel Gandolfo, papal masses being held there instead.

Hours for the Vatican Museums now run 9–4 (last entrance) and exit by 6 (including Saturdays).

The last Sunday of the month, when entrance is free, hours are 9–12:30 (last entrance) and closure by 2.

The Museums close the first three Sundays of every month; other dates of closures include January 1 and 6, February 11, May 1, June 11 and 29, August 14 and 15, November 1, and December 8, 25, and 26.

TOP 5 REASONS TO GO

Michelangelo's Sistine Ceiling: The most sublime example of artistry in the world, this 10,000-square-foot fresco took the artist four long, neck-craning years to finish.

St. Peter's Dome: Climb the claustrophobic and twisting Renaissance stairs to the very top for a view that you will really feel you've earned (or take the elevator on the right of the main church portico).

Papal Blessing: Join the singing, flag-waving throngs from around the world at the Wednesday general audience on St. Peter's Square (October–June only, weather permitting).

Vatican Museums: Savor one of the Western world's best art collections—from the *Apollo Belvedere* to Raphael's *Transfiguration*, this is pure Masterpiece Theater. Taken all together, culture here approaches critical mass.

St. Peter's Basilica: Stand in awe of both the seat of world Catholicism and a Renaissance masterwork.

Sightseeing
★★★★★
Nightlife
★★
Dining
★★★
Lodging
★★★
Shopping
★★

Climbing the steps to St. Peter's Basilica feels monumental, like a journey that has reached its climactic end. Harlequin-costumed Swiss Guards stand at attention, curly spears at their sides, dreaming fiercely of their God and His country as you pass through the gates. Suddenly, all is cool and dark . . . and you are dwarfed by a gargantuan hall and its magnificence.

Like jewels for giants, colored stones stud the floor and walls; above is a ceiling so high it must lead to heaven itself. Great, shining marble figures of saints frozen mid-whirl loom from niches and corners. And at the end, a throne, for an unseen king whose greatness (it is implied) must mirror the greatness of his palace. For this basilica is a palace, the dazzling center of power for a king and a place of supplication for his subjects. Whether his kingdom is earthly or otherwise may be in the eye of the beholder.

For good Catholics and sinners alike, the Vatican is an exercise in spirituality, requiring patience but delivering joy. Some come here to savor a heavenly Michelangelo fresco—others to find their soul. But what all the visitors share, for a few hours, is an awe-inspiring landscape that offers a famous sight for every taste. Rooms decorated by Raphael, antique sculptures like the Apollo Belvedere, famous paintings by Giotto and Bellini, and, perhaps most of all, the Sistine Chapel: For the lover of beauty, few places are as historically important as this epitome of faith and grandeur.

The story of this area's importance dates back to the 1st century, when St. Peter, known (albeit retroactively) as the first pope, was buried here. The first basilica in his honor rose in this spot under Emperor Constantine, the first Christian emperor of Rome, some 250 years later. It wasn't until the Middle Ages, however, that the papacy decided to make this area not only a major spiritual center, but the spot from which they would wield temporal power, as well. Today, it's difficult not to be reminded of that worldly power when you glimpse the massive walls surrounding Vatican City—a sign that you're entering an independent, sovereign state, established by the Lateran Treaty of 1929 between the Holy See and Mussolini's government.

Vatican City covers 108 acres on a hill west of the Tiber and is separated from the city on all sides, except at Piazza di San Pietro, by high walls. Within the walls, about 1,000 people are permanent residents. The Vatican has its own daily newspaper (*L'Osservatore Romano*), issues its own stamps, mints its own coins, and has its own postal system (one run, people say thankfully, by the Swiss). Within its territory are administrative and foreign offices, a pharmacy, banks, an astronomical observatory, a print shop, a mosaic school and art restoration institute, a tiny train station, a supermarket, a small department store, and several gas stations. The sovereign of this little state is the pope, Benedict XVI (elected April 2005). His main role is as spiritual leader to the world's Catholic community.

Today, there are two principal reasons for sightseeing at the Vatican. One is to visit the Basilica di San Pietro, the most overwhelming architectural achievement of the Renaissance; the other is to visit the Vatican Museums, which contain collections of staggering richness and diversity. Here at the Vatican great artists are honored almost as much as any holy power: the paintings, frescoes, sculptures, and buildings are as much monuments to their genius as to the Catholic Church.

Inside the basilica—breathtaking both for its sheer size and for its extravagant interior—are artistic masterpieces including Michelangelo's *Pietà* and Bernini's great bronze *baldacchino* (canopy) over the main altar. The Vatican Museums, their entrance located a 10-minute walk from the piazza, hold endless collections of many of the greatest works of Western art. The Laocoön, Leonardo's *St. Jerome*, and Raphael's *Transfiguration* all are here. The Sistine Chapel, accessible only through the museums, is Michelangelo's magnificent artistic legacy and his ceiling is the High Renaissance in excelsis, in more ways than one. Between the Vatican and the once-moated bulk of Castel Sant'Angelo—erstwhile mausoleum of Emperor Hadrian and now an imposing relic of medieval Rome—the pope's covered passageway flanks an enclave of workers and craftspeople, the old Borgo neighborhood, whose workaday charm has begun to succumb to gentrification (and, right outside the Vatican walls, to a plethora of tourist traps and souvenir shops).

TOP ATTRACTIONS

★ **Basilica di San Pietro.** The world's largest church, built over the tomb of St. Peter, is the most imposing and breathtaking architectural achievement of the Renaissance (although much of the lavish interior dates to the Baroque). The physical statistics are impressive: it covers 18,000 square yards, runs 212 yards in length, and is surmounted by a dome that rises 435 feet and measures 138 feet across its base. Its history is equally impressive. No fewer than five of Italy's greatest artists—Bramante, Raphael, Peruzzi, Antonio Sangallo the Younger, and Michelangelo—died while striving to erect this new St. Peter's.

The history of the original St. Peter's goes back to AD 349, when the emperor Constantine completed a basilica over the site of the tomb of

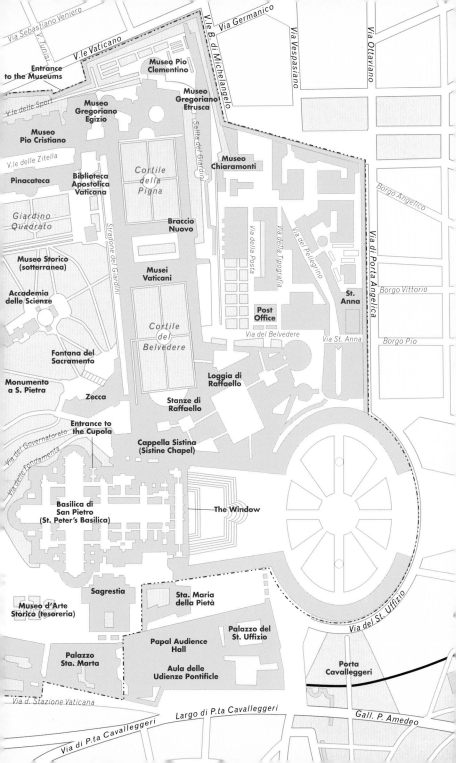

PIAZZA DI SAN PIETRO

✉ *West end of Via della Conciliazione, Vatican*
☎ *06/69881662* ✍ *upt@scv. va* ⊙ *Daily 6:30 am–11 pm (midnight during Christmas)* Ⓜ *Cipro-Musei Vaticani or Ottaviano-San Pietro.*

TIPS

■ Officially called Informazioni per turisti e pellegrini, the Main Information Office is just left of the basilica as you face it, a couple of doors down from the Braccio di Carlo Magno bookshop. On the south side of the Piazza Pio XII square, you'll find another Vatican bookshop, which contains the Libreria Benedetto XVI.

■ As for the famous Vatican post offices (known for fast handling of outgoing mail), they can be found on both sides of St. Peter's Square and inside the Vatican Museums complex. You can also buy Vatican stamps and coins at the shop annexed to the information office. Although postage rates are the same at the Vatican as elsewhere in Italy, the stamps are not interchangeable, so any material stamped with Vatican stamps must be placed into a blue or yellow Posta Vaticana box.

■ Public toilets are near the Information Office, under the colonnade, and outside the exit of the crypt.

Mostly enclosed within high walls that recall the papacy's stormy history, the Vatican opens the spectacular arms of Bernini's colonnade to embrace the world only at St. Peter's Square, scene of the pope's public appearances. One of Bernini's most spectacular masterpieces, the elliptical Piazza di San Pietro was completed in 1667 after only 11 years' work and holds 400,000 people.

Surrounded by a pair of quadruple colonnades, it is gloriously studded with 140 statues of saints and martyrs. Look for the two disks set into the piazza's pavement on either side of the central obelisk. If you stand on either disk, a trick of perspective makes the colonnades look like a single row of columns.

Bernini had an even grander visual effect in mind when he designed the square. By opening up this immense, airy, and luminous space in a neighborhood of narrow, shadowy streets, he created a contrast that would surprise and impress anyone who emerged from the darkness into the light, in a characteristically Baroque metaphor.

At the piazza center, the 85-foot-high Egyptian obelisk was brought to Rome by Caligula in AD 37 and moved here in 1586 by Pope Sixtus V. The emblem at the top of the obelisk is the Chigi star, in honor of Pope Alexander VII, a member of the powerful Chigi family, who commissioned the piazza.

Alexander demanded that Bernini make the pope visible to as many people as possible from the Benediction Loggia and to provide a covered passageway for papal processions.

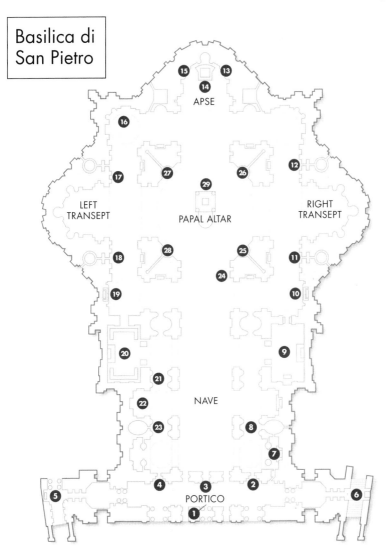

Basilica di San Pietro

APSE

LEFT TRANSEPT

RIGHT TRANSEPT

PAPAL ALTAR

NAVE

PORTICO

St. Peter, the Church's first pope. The original church stood for more than 1,000 years, undergoing a number of restorations and alterations, until toward the middle of the 15th century, it was verging on collapse. In 1452 a reconstruction job began but was quickly abandoned for lack of money. In 1503, Pope Julius II instructed the architect Bramante to raze all the existing buildings and to build a new basilica, one that would surpass even Constantine's for grandeur. It wasn't until 1626 that the basilica was completed and consecrated.

ST. PETER'S CROSSING AND DOME. Though Bramante made little progress in rebuilding St. Peter's, he succeeded in outlining a basic plan for the church. He also, crucially, built the piers of the crossings—the massive pillars supporting the dome.

> ### IT'S ALWAYS WHO YOU KNOW
>
> The story goes that Bernini's Barberini patron, Pope Urban VIII, had no qualms about stripping the bronze from the Pantheon to provide Bernini with the material to create the gigantic bronze *baldacchino* over St. Peter's main altar. (In fact, Bernini already had the bronze he needed; the Pantheon bronze instead went to cannons at Castel Sant'Angelo). Regardless of the bronze's final destination, the Romans reacted with the famous quip: *Quod non fecerunt barbari, fecerunt Barberini* ("What the barbarians didn't do, the Barberini did").

After Bramante's death in 1514, Raphael, the Sangallos, and Peruzzi all proposed, at one time or another, variations on the original plan. In 1546, however, Pope Paul III turned to Michelangelo and forced the aging artist to complete the building. Michelangelo returned to Bramante's first idea of having a centralized Greek-cross plan—that is, with the "arms" of the church all the same length—and completed most of the exterior architecture except for the dome and the facade. His design for the dome, however, was modified after his death by Giacomo della Porta (his dome was much taller in proportion). Pope Paul V wanted a Latin-cross church (a church with one "arm" longer than the rest), so Carlo Maderno lengthened one of the arms to create a longer central nave.

WORKS BY GIOTTO AND FILARETE As you climb the shallow steps up to the great church, flanked by the statues of Sts. Peter and Paul, you'll see the **Loggia delle Benedizioni** (Benediction Loggia) over the central portal. This is the balcony where newly elected popes are proclaimed, and where they stand to give their apostolic blessing on solemn feast days. The vault of the vestibule is encrusted with rich stuccowork, and the mosaic above the central entrance to the portico is a much-restored work by the 14th-century painter Giotto that was in the original basilica. The bronze doors of the main entrance also were salvaged from the old basilica. The sculptor Filarete worked on them for 12 years; they show scenes from the martyrdom of St. Peter and St. Paul, and the life of Pope Eugene IV (1431–47), Filarete's patron.

Pause a moment to appraise the size of the great building. The people near the main altar seem dwarfed by the incredible dimensions of this immense temple. The statues, the pillars, and the holy-water stoups borne by colossal cherubs are all imposing. Walk over to where the cherub clings to a pier and place your arm across the sole of the cherub's foot; you will discover that it's as long as the distance from your fingers to your elbow. It's because the proportions of this giant building are in such perfect harmony that its vastness may escape you at first. Brass inscriptions in the marble pavement down the center of the nave indicate the approximate lengths of the world's other principal Christian churches, all of which fall far short of the 186-meter span of St. Peter's Basilica. In its megascale—inspired by the spatial volumes of ancient Roman ruins—the church reflects Roman *grandiosità* in all its majesty.

As you enter the great nave, immediately to your right, behind a protective glass partition, is **Michelangelo's *Pietà***, sculpted when the artist was only 25. The work was of such genius, some rivals spread rumors it was by someone else, prompting the artist to inscribe his name, unusually for him, across Mary's sash. Farther down, with its heavyweight crown barely denting its marble cushion, is Carlo Fontana's monument to Catholic convert and abdicated Queen Christina of Sweden (who is buried in the Grotte Vaticane below). Just across the way, in the **Cappella di San Sebastiano**, now lies the **tomb of Blessed Pope John Paul II**. The beloved pope's remains were moved into the chapel after his beatification on May 1, 2011. Exquisite bronze grilles and doors by Borromini open into the third chapel in the right aisle, the **Cappella del Santissimo Sacramento** (Chapel of the Most Holy Sacrament, generally open to visitors only from 7 am–8:30 am), with a Baroque fresco of the Trinity by Pietro da Cortona. The lovely carved angels are by Bernini. At the last pillar on the right (the pier with Bernini's statue of St. Longinus) is a bronze statue of St. Peter, whose right foot is ritually touched by lines of pilgrims. In the right transept, over the door to the **Cappella di San Michele** (Chapel of St. Michael), usually closed, Canova created a brooding Neoclassical monument to Pope Clement XIII.

BERNINI'S
BALDACCHINO In the central crossing, Bernini's great bronze *baldacchino*—a huge, spiral-columned canopy—rises high over the *altare papale* (papal altar). At 100,000 pounds, it's said to be the largest, heaviest bronze object in the world. Circling the *baldacchino* are four larger-than-life statues of saints whose relics the Vatican has; the one of St. Longinus, holding the spear that pierced Christ's side, is another Bernini masterpiece. Meanwhile, Bernini designed the splendid gilt-bronze **Cattedra di San Pietro** (throne of St. Peter) in the apse above the main altar to contain a wooden and ivory chair that St. Peter himself is said to have used, though in fact it doesn't date from farther back than medieval times. (You can see a copy of the chair in the treasury.) Above, Bernini placed a window of thin alabaster sheets that diffuses a golden light around the dove, symbol of the Holy Spirit, in the center.

Two of the major papal funeral monuments in St. Peter's Basilica are on either side of the apse and unfortunately are usually only dimly lighted. To the right is the **tomb of Pope Urban VIII**; to the left is the **tomb of Pope Paul III**. Paul's tomb is of an earlier date, designed between 1551 and 1575 by Giacomo della Porta, the architect who completed the dome of St. Peter's Basilica after Michelangelo's death. Many believed the nude figure of Justice to be a portrait of the pope's beautiful sister, Giulia. The charms of this alluring figure were such that in the 19th century, it was thought that she should no longer be allowed to distract worshippers from their prayers, and she was thenceforth clad in marble drapery. It was in emulation of this splendid late-Renaissance work that Urban VIII ordered Bernini to design his tomb. The real star here, however, is *la Bella Morte* ("Beautiful Death") who, all bone and elbows, dispatches the deceased pope above to a register of blue-black marble. The **tomb of Pope Alexander VII**, also designed by Bernini, stands to the left of the altar as you look up the nave, behind the farthest pier of the crossing. This may be the most haunting memorial in the basilica, thanks to another frightening skeletonized figure of Death, holding an hourglass in its upraised hand to tell the pope his time is up. Pope Alexander, however, was well prepared, having kept a coffin (also designed by Bernini) in his bedroom and made a habit of dining off plates embossed with skulls.

SUBSIDIARY
ATTRACTIONS

Vatican Necropolis. With advance notice you can take a 1¼-hour guided tour in English of the Vatican Necropolis, under the basilica, which gives a rare glimpse of Early Christian Roman burial customs and a closer look at the tomb of St. Peter. Apply by fax or email (✎ *scavi@fsp.va*) at least 2–3 weeks in advance, specifying the number of people in the group (all must be age 15 or older), preferred language, preferred time, available dates, and your contact information in Rome. ☎ *06/69885318* 📠 *06/69873017* 💶 *€12* ⏱ *Ufficio Scavi Mon.–Sat. 9–6, visits 9–3:30.*

Museo Storico-Artistico e Tesoro (*Historical-Artistic Museum and Treasury*). Under the Pope Pius V monument, the entrance to the sacristy also leads to the **Museo Storico-Artistico e Tesoro**, a small collection of Vatican treasures. They range from the massive and beautifully sculptured 15th-century tomb of Pope Sixtus IV by Pollaiuolo, which you can view from above, to a jeweled cross dating from the 6th century and a marble tabernacle by Donatello. Continue on down the left nave past Algardi's **tomb of St. Leo.** The handsome bronze grilles in the **Cappella del Coro** (Chapel of the Choir) were designed by Borromini to complement those opposite in the Cappella del Santissimo Sacramento. The next pillar holds a rearrangement of the Pollaiuolo brothers' monument to Pope Innocent VIII, the only major tomb to have been transferred from the old basilica. Lacking in bulk compared to many of its Baroque counterparts, it more than makes up in Renaissance elegance. The next chapel contains the handsome bronze monument to Pope John XXIII by contemporary sculptor Emilio Greco. On the last pier in this nave stands a monument by the late-18th-century Venetian sculptor Canova to the ill-fated Stuarts—the 18th-century Roman Catholic claimants to the British throne, who were long exiled in Rome and some of whom are buried in the crypt below. ☎ *06/69881840* 💶 *€10 (includes audioguide)* ⏱ *Apr. 1–Sept. 30, daily 8 am–7 pm; Oct. 1–Mar. 31, daily 8 am–6:20 pm.*

Dome of St. Peter's. Above, the vast sweep of the basilica's dome is the cynosure of all eyes. Proceed to the right side of the Basilica's vestibule; from here, you can either take the elevator or climb the long flight of shallow stairs to the roof. From here, you'll see a surreal landscape of vast, sloping terraces, punctuated by domes. The roof affords unusual perspectives both on the dome above and the piazza below. The terrace is equipped with the inevitable souvenir shop and restrooms. A short flight of stairs leads to the entrance of the *tamburo* (drum)—the base of the dome—where, appropriately enough, there's a bust of Michelangelo, the dome's principal designer. Within the drum, another short ramp and staircase give access to the **gallery** encircling the base of the dome. (You also have the option of taking an elevator to this point). From here, you have a dove's-eye view of the interior of the church. If you're overly energetic, you can take the stairs that wind around the elevator to reach the roof. Only if you're of stout heart and strong lungs should you then make the taxing climb from the drum of the dome up to the *lanterna* (lantern) at the dome's very apex. A narrow, seemingly interminable staircase follows the curve of the dome between inner and outer shells, finally releasing you into the cramped space of the lantern balcony for an absolutely gorgeous panorama of Rome and the countryside on a clear day. There's also a nearly complete view of the palaces, courtyards, and gardens of the Vatican. Be aware, however, that it's a tiring, slightly claustrophobic climb. There's one stairway for going up and a different one for coming down, so you can't change your mind halfway and turn back. ☎ *06/69883462* 🔲 *Elevator €7, stairs €5* ⊘ *Daily Apr.–Sept., 8 am–6 pm; Oct.–Mar., 8 am–4 pm; on a papal audience Wed., opens after the audience finishes (about 12 pm), closed during ceremonies in piazza.*

Grotte Vaticane (*Vatican Grottoes*). The entrance to the Grotte Vaticane is to the right of the Basilica's main entrance. The crypt, lined with marble-faced chapels and tombs occupying the area of Constantine's basilica, stands over what is believed to be the tomb of St. Peter himself, flanked by two angels and visible through glass. Among the most beautiful tombs leading up to it are that of Borgia pope Calixtus III with its carving of the Risen Christ, and the tomb of Paul II featuring angels carved by Renaissance great Mino da Fiesole 🔲 *Free* ⊘ *Weekdays and Sat., 9–4; Sun. and holidays, 1:30–3:30; closed while the papal audience takes place in St. Peter's Square (until about noon on Wed.)*

✉ *Piazza di San Pietro* ⊘ *Apr.–Sept., daily 7–7; Oct.–Mar., daily 7–6; closed during the papal audience in St. Peter's Square Wed. mornings until about noon* Ⓜ *Ottaviano-San Pietro.*

NEED A BREAK?

Insalata Ricca. Insalata Ricca, about halfway between the Vatican Museums and St. Peter's Basilica, offers no-nonsense light meals: pasta, salads, pizza, and the like. While unremarkable, keep it in mind on a hot day—its air-conditioning is the best in the neighborhood. ✉ *Piazza Risorgimento 6* ☎ *06/39730387.*

Fodor'sChoice ★ **Cappella Sistina** (*Sistine Chapel*). In 1508, the redoubtable Pope Julius II commissioned Michelangelo to fresco the more than 10,000 square feet of the Sistine Chapel's ceiling. (*Sistine*, by the way, is simply the adjective from *Sixtus*, in reference to Pope Sixtus IV, who commissioned the chapel itself.) The task took four years, and it's said that for many years afterward Michelangelo couldn't read anything without holding it over his head. The result, however, was the greatest artwork of the

Meet the Pope

Piazza San Pietro is the scene of large papal audiences as well as special commemorations, masses, and beatification ceremonies. When he's in Rome, the pope makes an appearance every Sunday at noon (call the Vatican Information office to find out if the pope is in town and the exact time) at the window of the Vatican Palace. He addresses the crowd and blesses all present. The pope also holds mass audiences in the square on Wednesday morning about 10:30 am; for a seat, a ticket is necessary. In the winter and inclement circumstances, the audience is held in an indoor audience hall adjacent to the basilica (Aula Paolo Sesto). During summer, while the pope is vacationing at Castel Gandolfo in the Castelli Romani hills outside Rome, he gives a talk and blessing from a balcony of the papal palace there. For admission to an audience, apply for free tickets by phone or fax in advance,

indicating the date you prefer, the language you speak, and the hotel in which you will stay. Contact the Prefettura della Casa Pontefice by telephone (☎ 06/69883114) or fax (🖷 06/69885863). Or apply for tickets before the Wednesday audience in person at the Prefettura, open on Monday 9–1 and Tuesday 9–6, located beyond the Portone di Bronzo (Bronze Door) at the end of the right-hand colonnade. You also can arrange your tickets for free through the Santa Susanna American Church (✉ *Via XX Settembre 15, near Termini,* ☎ *06/69001821*). The best way is to email your request to ✎ *tickets@ santasusanna.org.* You can pick up your tickets on Tuesday between 5 and 6:45 or on Wednesday morning 7–8:15. For a fee, travel agencies make arrangements that include transportation. Arrive early, as security is tight and the best places fill up fast.

Renaissance. A pair of binoculars helps greatly, as does a small mirror—hold the mirror facing the ceiling and look down to study the reflection.

Before the chapel was consecrated in 1483, its lower walls were decorated by famed artists including Botticelli, Ghirlandaio, Perugino, Signorelli, and Pinturicchio. They painted scenes from the life of Moses on one wall and episodes from the life of Christ on the other. Later, Julius II, dissatisfied with the simple vault decoration—stars painted on the ceiling—decided to call in Michelangelo. At the time, Michelangelo was carving Julius II's resplendent tomb, a project that never came near completion. He had no desire to give the project up to paint a ceiling, considering the task unworthy of him. Julius was not, however, a man to be trifled with, and Michelangelo reluctantly began work. ⇨ *See "Heaven's Above: The Sistine Ceiling," for the complete backstory.*

More than 20 years later, Michelangelo was called on again, this time by the Farnese pope Paul III, to add to the chapel's decoration by painting the *Last Judgment* on the wall over the altar. The subject was well suited to the aging and embittered artist, who had been deeply moved by the horrendous Sack of Rome in 1527 and the confusions and disturbances of the Reformation. The painting stirred up controversy even before it was unveiled in 1541, shocking many Vatican officials, especially one

Biagio di Cesena, who criticized its "indecent" nudes. Michelangelo retaliated by painting Biagio's face on Minos, judge of the underworld—the figure with donkey's ears in the lower right-hand corner of the work. Biagio pleaded with Pope Paul to have Michelangelo erase his portrait, but the pontiff replied that while he could intercede for those in purgatory, he had no power over hell. As if to sign this, his late great fresco, Michelangelo painted his own face on the flayed-off human skin in St. Bartholomew's hand. ⊠ *Vatican Palace; entry only through Musei Vaticani.*

ART AND FAITH

Presiding over the great nave of St. Peter's is Michelangelo's legendary *Pietà*. Could you question whether this moving work, sculpted when the artist was only 22, owes more to man's art than to a man's faith? Perhaps as we contemplate this masterpiece we are able to understand a little better that art and faith sometimes partake of the same impulse.

4

Castel Sant'Angelo. Standing between the Tiber and the Vatican, this circular and medieval "castle" has long been one of Rome's most distinctive landmarks. Opera lovers know it well as the setting for the final scene of Puccini's *Tosca;* at the opera's end, the tempestuous diva throws herself from the rampart on the upper terrace. In fact, the structure began life many centuries before as a mausoleum for the emperor Hadrian. Started in AD 135, it was completed by the emperor's successor, Antoninus Pius, about five years later. It initially consisted of a great square base topped by a marble-clad cylinder on which was planted a ring of cypress trees. Above them towered a gigantic statue of Hadrian. From the mid-6th century the building became a fortress, a place of refuge for popes during wars and sieges. Its name dates from 590, when Pope Gregory the Great, during a procession to plead for the end of a plague, saw an angel standing on the summit of the castle, sheathing his sword. Taking this as a sign that the plague was at an end, the pope built a small chapel at the top, placing a statue next to it to celebrate his vision—thus the name, Castel Sant'Angelo.

Enter the building through the original Roman door of Hadrian's tomb. From here, you pass through a courtyard enclosed in the base of the classical monument. You enter a vaulted brick corridor that hints at grim punishments in dank cells. On the right, a spiral ramp leads up to the chamber in which Hadrian's ashes were kept. Where the ramp ends, the Borgia pope Alexander VI's staircase begins. Part of it consisted of a wooden drawbridge, which could isolate the upper part of the castle completely. The staircase ends at the Cortile dell'Angelo, a courtyard that has become the resting place of neatly piled stone cannonballs as well as the marble angel that stood above the castle. (It was replaced by a bronze sculpture in 1753.) In the rooms off the Cortile dell'Angelo, look for the **Cappella di Papa Leone X** (Chapel of Pope Leo X), with a facade by Michelangelo.

In the courtyard named for Pope Alexander VI, a wellhead bears the Borgia coat of arms. The courtyard is surrounded by gloomy cells and huge storerooms that could hold great quantities of oil and grain in case of siege. Benvenuto Cellini, the rowdy 16th-century Florentine

For St. Peter's, Michelangelo originally designed a dome much higher than the one ultimately built and designed by his follower Giacomo della Porta.

goldsmith, sculptor, and boastful autobiographer, spent some time in Castel Sant'Angelo's foul prisons; so did Giordano Bruno, a heretical monk who was later burned at the stake in Campo de' Fiori, and Beatrice Cenci, accused of patricide and incest and executed just across Ponte Sant'Angelo.

Take the stairs at the far end of the courtyard to the open terrace for a view of the Passetto, the fortified corridor connecting Castel Sant'Angelo with the Vatican and recently featured in the book and film *Angels and Demons* (it's possible to request a visit; call for more information). Pope Clement VII used the Passetto to make his way safely to the castle during the Sack of Rome in 1527. Near here is a caffè for refreshments. Continue your walk along the perimeter of the tower and climb the few stairs to the *appartamento papale* (papal apartment). As if times of crisis were no object, the Sala Paolina (Pauline Room), the first you enter, was decorated in the 16th century by Pierino del Vaga and assistants with lavish frescoes of scenes from the Old Testament and the lives of St. Paul and Alexander the Great. Look for the trompe l'oeil door with a figure climbing the stairs. From another false door, a black-clad figure peers into the room. This is believed to be a portrait of an illegitimate son of the powerful Orsini family. Out on to the upper terrace, at the feet of the bronze angel, take in a magnificent view of the city below.

In July and August, the Notti Animate di Castel Sant'Angelo ("Animated Nights") traditionally take place, with the castle and its terraces hosting restaurants, bars, gelaterie, live shows and performances, as well as extended hours. However, the event was called off in both 2010

Vatican Dress Code

To enter the Musei Vaticani (Vatican Museums), the Sistine Chapel, and the Basilica di San Pietro you must comply with the Vatican's dress code, or you may be turned away by the implacable custodians stationed at the doors. (Also no penknives, which will show up under the metal detector.) For both men and women, shorts and tank tops are taboo, as are miniskirts and other revealing clothing. Wear a jacket or shawl over sleeveless tops, and avoid T-shirts with writing or pictures that could risk giving offense. If you opt to start at the Musei Vaticani, note that the entrance on Viale Vaticano (there's a separate exit on the same street) can be reached by Bus No. 49 from Piazza Cavour, which stops right in front; on foot from Piazza del Risorgimento (Bus 81 or Tram 19); or a brief walk from the Via Cipro–Musei Vaticani stop on Metro line A. The collections of the museums are immense, covering about 7 km (4½ mile) of displays. You can rent a taped, if somewhat dry, commentary in English explaining the Sistine Chapel and the Raphael rooms. You cannot take any photographs in the Sistine Chapel. Elsewhere, you're free to photograph what you like, barring use of flash, tripod, or other special equipment, for which permission must be obtained. To economize on time and effort, once you've seen the frescoes in the Raphael rooms, you can skip much of the modern religious art in good conscience, and get on with your tour. With some 20,000 visitors a day, recession notwithstanding, lines at the entrance to the Cappella Sistina (Sistine Chapel) can move slowly, as custodians block further entrance when the room becomes crowded. It may be possible to exit the museums from the Sistine Chapel into St. Peter's, saving further legwork. A sign at the entrance to the museums indicates whether the "For Tour Groups" exit is open. While visitors in the past could use this by following an exiting tour group, lately the guards there have been sterner on this practice. Be aware, too, that the Sistine Chapel is a holy place; loud talking and other excessive noise is frowned upon and can get you shushed.

4

and 2011. Romans are crossing their fingers that it will be back soon. ✉ *Lungotevere Castello 50* ☎ *06/6819111 Central line, 06/6896003 Tickets* ⊕ *www.castelsantangelo.com* 🎟 *€8.50* ⊗ *Tues.–Sun. 9–7:30 (ticket office closes 6:30)* Ⓜ *Ottaviano.*

Fodor's Choice ★ **Musei Vaticani** (*Vatican Museums*). Other than the pope and his papal court, the occupants of the Vatican are some of the most famous artworks in the world. The museums that contain them are part of the **Vatican Palace,** residence of the popes since 1377. The palace consists of an estimated 1,400 rooms, chapels, and galleries. The pope and his household occupy only a small part of the palace; most of the rest is given over to the Vatican Library and Museums. Beyond the glories of the Sistine Chapel, the collection is so extraordinarily rich you may just wish to skim the surface, but few will want to miss out on the great antique sculptures, Raphael Rooms, and the Old Master paintings, such as Leonardo da Vinci's *St. Jerome.*

Subsidiary Museums. Among the collections on the way to the chapel, the **Egyptian Museum** (in which Room II reproduces an underground chamber tomb of the Valley of Kings) is well worth a stop. The **Chiaramonti Museum** was organized by the Neoclassical sculptor Canova and contains almost 1,000 copies of classical sculpture. The gems of the Vatican's sculpture collection are in the **Pio-Clementino Museum,** however. Just off the hall in Room X, you can find the *Apoxyomenos* (Scraper), a beautiful 1st-century AD copy of the famous bronze statue of an athlete. There are other even more famous pieces in the **Octagonal Courtyard,** where Pope Julius II installed the pick of his private collection. On the left stands the celebrated Apollo Belvedere. In the far corner, on the same side of the courtyard, is the Laocoön group. Found on Rome's Esquiline Hill in 1506, this antique sculpture group influenced Renaissance artists perhaps more than any other.

> ### SOMETHING IN PAPAL PURPLE?
>
> If you've come to the Eternal City looking for ecclesiastical garb or religious memorabilia, you'll hit gold in the shops near the Vatican on Via Porta Angelica. A celestial array of pope portraits, postcards, figurines, and even snow globes can be had for low prices. The pious can have their purchases blessed at a papal audience; blasphemers can put pope stickers on their cars. Lay shoppers may want to stick to the windows.

In the **Hall of the Muses,** the Belvedere Torso occupies center stage: This is a fragment of a 1st-century BC statue, probably of Hercules, all rippling muscles and classical dignity, much admired by Michelangelo. The lovely neoclassical room of the **Rotonda** has an ancient mosaic pavement and a huge porphyry basin from Nero's palace.

The room on the Greek-cross plan contains two fine porphyry sarcophagi (burial caskets), one for St. Constantia and one for St. Helena, daughter and mother of the emperor Constantine, respectively.

Upstairs is an **Etruscan Museum,** an **Antiquarium,** with Roman originals; and the domed **Sala della Biga,** with an ancient chariot. In addition, there are the **Candelabra Gallery** and the **Tapestry Gallery,** with tapestries designed by Raphael's students. The incredibly long **Gallery of Maps,** frescoed with 40 maps of Italy and the papal territories, was commissioned by Pope Gregory XIII in 1580. Nearby is the **Apartment of Pius V.**

THE RAPHAEL ROOMS

Rivaling the Sistine Chapel for artistic interest—and for the number of visitors—are the **Stanze di Raffaello** (Raphael Rooms). Pope Julius II moved into this suite in 1507, four years after his election. Reluctant to continue living in the Borgia apartments downstairs, with their memories of his ill-famed predecessor Alexander VI, he called in Raphael to decorate his new quarters. When people talk about the Italian High Renaissance—thought to be the very pinnacle of Western art—it's probably Raphael's frescoes they're thinking about.

The **Stanza della Segnatura,** the first to be frescoed, was painted almost entirely by Raphael himself (his assistants painted much of the other rooms). The theme of the room, which may broadly be said to be "enlightenment," reflects the fact that this was meant to be Julius's private library. Instead, it was used mainly as a room for signing documents, hence *segnatura* (signature). Theology triumphs in the fresco known as the *Disputa,* or *Debate on the Holy Sacrament,* on the wall in front of you as you enter. Opposite, the *School of Athens* glorifies philosophy in its greatest exponents. Plato (likely a portrait of Leonardo da Vinci), in the center, debates a point with Aristotle. The pensive, gloomy figure on the stairs is thought to be modeled after Michelangelo, who was painting the Sistine ceiling at the same time

VATICAN MUSEUMS' TOP 10

Michelangelo's Sistine ceiling

Raphael rooms

Apollo Belvedere

Leonardo's *St. Jerome*

Laocoön

Caravaggio's *Deposition*

Raphael's *Transfiguration*

Aldobrandini Marriage

The Good Shepherd

Belvedere Torso

4

Raphael was working here. Michelangelo does not appear in preparatory drawings, so Raphael may have added his fellow artist's portrait after admiring his work. In the foreground on the right, the figure with the compass is Euclid, depicted as the architect Bramante; on the far right, the handsome youth just behind the white-clad older man is Raphael himself. Over the window on the left is Mt. Parnassus, the abode of the Muses, with Apollo, famous poets (many of them likenesses of Raphael's contemporaries), and the Muses themselves. In the lunette over the window opposite, Raphael painted figures representing and alluding to the Cardinal and Theological Virtues, and subjects showing the establishment of written codes of law. Beautiful personifications of the four subject areas, Theology, Poetry, Philosophy, and Jurisprudence, are painted in circular pictures on the ceiling above.

However, the rooms aren't arranged chronologically. Today, for crowd-management purposes, you head down an outdoor gallery to loop back through them; as you go, look across the way to see, very far away, the Pinecone Courtyard near where you entered the museums. The first Raphael Room is the **Hall of Constantine**—actually decorated by Giulio Romano and Raphael's other assistants after the master's untimely death in 1520. The frescoes represent various scenes from the life of Emperor Constantine, including the epic-sized *Battle of the Milvian Bridge.* Guided by three low-flying angels, Constantine charges to victory as his rival Maxentius drowns in the river below.

The **Room of Heliodorus** is a private antechamber. Working on the theme of Divine Providence's miraculous intervention in defense of the faith, Raphael depicted Leo the Great's encounter with Attila; it's on the wall in front of you as you enter. The *Expulsion of Heliodorus from the Temple of Jerusalem,* opposite, refers to Pope Julius II's attempt to exert papal power to expel the French from Italy. The pope himself appears

CLOSE UP

Tips on Touring the Vatican Museums

Remember that the Vatican's museum complex is humongous—only after walking through what seems miles of galleries do you see the entrance to the Sistine Chapel (which cannot be entered from St. Peter's Basilica directly). Check out the Sistine loca-tion vis-à-vis the main church on their website ⊕ www.stpetersbasilica.org. Most people—especially those who rent an audio guide and must return it to the main desk—tour the complex, see the Sistine, then trudge back to the main museum entrance, itself a 15-minute walk from St. Peter's Square.

That said, there is an "insider" way to exit directly from the Sistine Chapel to St. Peter's Basilica: Look for the "tour groups only" door on the right as you face the rear of the chapel and, when a group exits, go with the flow and follow them. This will deposit you on the porch of St. Peter's Basilica. While this served as a sly trick for years, guards and guides both have gotten

stricter about the practice, meaning you might be the victim of a stern guard or a head count that leaves you in the cold. Also note that if you run to the Sistine Chapel, then do the "short-cut" exit into the basilica, you will have missed the rest of the Vati-can Museum collection.

Plans are afoot to broaden the side-walk leading to the museum, to install electronic information panels, and also to build a streamlined roof to protect queuers from sun or rain (until then, umbrellas are recommended). Another possibility is to visit in the evening. This experiment began in 2009 and has been running intermit-tently ever since, with the Vatican opening on many Friday evenings from 7 to 11. While the major hits, like the Sistine Chapel, are usually open during these special openings, many more off-the-beaten-path rooms and galleries are not. Reservations are essential (and possible over the Internet at ⊕ www.vatican.va).

on the left, watching the scene. On the window wall, the *Liberation of St. Peter* is one of Raphael's best-known and most effective works.

After the Room of the Signature, the last room is the **Room of the Borgo Fire.** The final room painted in Raphael's lifetime, it was executed mainly by Giulio Romano, who worked from Raphael's drawings for the new pope, Leo X. It was used for the meetings of the Segnatura Gratiae et Iustitiae, the Holy See's highest court. The frescoes depict stories of previous popes called Leo, the best of them showing the great fire in the Borgo (the neighborhood between the Vatican and Castel Sant'Angelo) that threatened to destroy the original St. Peter's Basilica in AD 847; miraculously, Pope Leo IV extinguished it with the sign of the cross.

The tiny **Chapel of Nicholas V** is rarely open. But if you can access it, do: One of the Renaissance's greatest gems, it's aglow with Fra Angelico (1395–1455) frescoes of episodes from the life of St. Stephen (above) and St. Lawrence (below). If it weren't under the same roof as Raphael's and Michelangelo's works, it would undoubtedly draw greater attention.

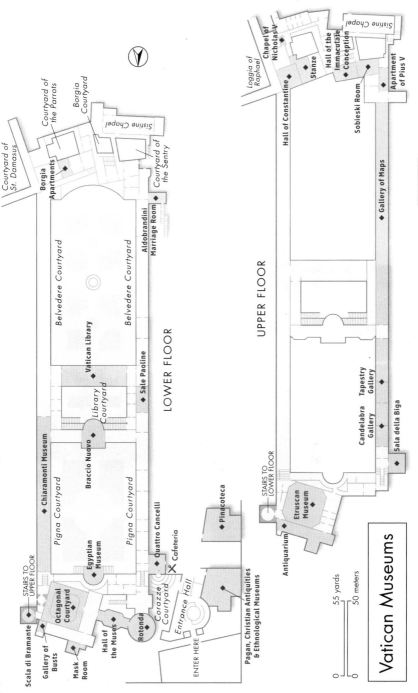

Vatican Museums

DID YOU KNOW?

Designed to be Hadrian's
tomb, the Castel Sant'Angelo
was originally topped by a
marble-sheathed tumulus
and crowned by a gigantic
bronze of the emperor in his
chariot.

Downstairs, enter the recently restored **Borgia apartments,** where some of the Vatican's most fascinating historical figures are depicted on elaborately painted ceilings. Pinturicchio designed the frescoes at the end of the 15th century, though the paintings were greatly retouched in later centuries. It's generally believed that Cesare Borgia murdered his sister Lucrezia's husband, Alphonse of Aragon, in the Room of the Sibyl. In the Room of the Saints, Pinturicchio painted his self-portrait in the figure to the left of the possible portrait of the architect Antonio da Sangallo. (His profession is made clear by the fact that he holds a T-square.) The lovely St. Catherine of Alexandria is said to represent Lucrezia Borgia herself.

> ## LAW AND ORDER, 16TH-CENTURY STYLE
>
> The Raphael room frescoes represent all the revolutionary characteristics of High Renaissance art: naturalism (Raphael's figures lack the awkwardness that pictures painted only a few years earlier still contained); humanism (the idea that man is the most noble and admirable of God's creatures); and a profound interest in the ancient world, the result of the 15th-century rediscovery of archaeology and classical antiquity. The frescoes in this room virtually dared its occupants to aspire to the highest ideas of law and learning—an amazing feat for an artist not yet 30.

In the frescoed exhibition halls, the **Vatican Library** displays precious illuminated manuscripts and documents from its vast collections. The **Aldobrandini Marriage Room** contains beautiful ancient frescoes of a Roman nuptial rite, named for their subsequent owner, Cardinal Aldobrandini. The **Braccio Nuovo** (New Wing) holds an additional collection of ancient Greek and Roman statues, the most famous of which is the *Augustus of Prima Porta*, in the fourth niche from the end on the left. It's considered a faithful likeness of the emperor Augustus, who was 40 years old at the time. Note the workmanship in the reliefs on his armor.

THE VATICAN
PINACOTECA
Equally celebrated are the works on view in the **Pinacoteca** (Picture Gallery). These often world-famous paintings, almost exclusively of religious subjects, are arranged in chronological order, beginning with works of the 12th and 13th centuries. Room II has a marvelous Giotto triptych, painted on both sides, which formerly stood on the high altar in the old St. Peter's. In Room III you'll see Madonnas by the Florentine 15th-century painters Fra Angelico and Filippo Lippi. Room VIII contains some of Raphael's greatest creations, including the exceptional *Transfiguration*, the *Coronation of the Virgin*, and the *Foligno Madonna*, as well as the tapestries that Raphael designed to hang in the Sistine Chapel. The next room contains Leonardo's beautiful (though unfinished) *St. Jerome* and a Bellini *Pietà*. A highlight for many is Caravaggio's gigantic *Deposition*, in Room XII. In the courtyard outside the Pinacoteca you can admire a beautiful view of the dome of St. Peter's, as well the reliefs from the base of the now-destroyed column of Antoninus Pius. A fitting finale to your Vatican visit can be found in the **Museo Pio**

Cristiano (Museum of Christian Antiquities), where the most famous piece is the 3rd-century AD statue called the Good Shepherd, much reproduced as a devotional image.

■ TIP→ To avoid the line into the museums, which can be three hours long in the high season, consider booking your ticket in advance online (w biglietteriamusei.vatican.va); there is a €4 surcharge. For those interested in guided visits to the Vatican Museums, tours are €31 to €36, including entrance tickets, and can also be booked online. One new offering is a regular two-hour guided tour of the Vatican Gardens. Also new are the semiregular Friday night openings, allowing visitors to the museums until 11 pm; call to confirm. For more information, call ☎ *06/69884676* or go to ⊕ *mv.vatican.va.* For information on tours, call ☎ *06/69883145* or *06/69884676*; visually impaired visitors can arrange tactile tours by calling ☎ *06/69884947.* Wheelchairs are free and can be booked in advance by emailing ✎ *accoglienza.musei@scv.va* or by request at the "Special Permits" desk in the entrance hall. Note: Ushers at the entrance of St. Peter's and sometimes the Vatican Museums will bar entry to people with bare knees or bare shoulders. ✉ *Viale Vaticano (near intersection with Via Leone IV)* ⊕ *www.vatican.va* 💶*€15; free last Sun. of the month* ⊙ *Mon.–Sat. 9–6 (last entrance at 4), last Sun. of month 9–12:30* ⊙ *Closed Jan. 1 and 6, Feb. 11, Mar. 19, Easter and Easter Monday, May 1, June 29, Aug. 14 and 15, Nov. 1, and Dec. 8, 25, and 26* Ⓜ *Cipro–Musei Vaticani or Ottaviano–San Pietro. Bus 64, 40.*

■ NEED A BREAK?
Hostaria Dino e Toni. Many of the restaurants near the Vatican are touristy and terrible, so this eatery stands out. It serves typical Roman fare, nice and fresh from the nearby outdoor market on Via Andrea Doria, plus pizza. It's closed Sunday. ✉ *Via Leone IV 60* ☎ *06/39733284.*

WORTH NOTING

Giardini Vaticani (*Vatican Gardens*). Neatly trimmed lawns and flower beds extend over the hills behind St. Peter's Basilica, an area dotted with some interesting constructions and other, duller ones that serve as office buildings. The Vatican Gardens occupy almost 40 acres of land on the Vatican hill. The gardens include a formal Italian garden, a flowering French garden, a romantic English landscape, and a small forest; there's also the little-used Vatican railroad station, which now houses a museum of coins and stamps made in the Vatican. Take a two-hour walking tour with an official Vatican guide (make sure to wear good walking shoes) or, instead, opt for a one-hour RomaCristiana minibus tour of the gardens, done with an audio guide. For either tour, a reservation is necessary. ✉ *For official Vatican tour, Centro Servizi, south side of Piazza San Pietro; for RomaCristiana tour, ORP St. Peter's Office at Piazza Pio XII 9* ☎ *06/69883145 Vatican tour, 06/88816186 minibus tour* ⊕ *www.vatican.va* 💶*€31 for 2-hour tour with Vatican guide (includes €15 entrance ticket to Vatican museums) or €15 for 1-hour bus ride with RomaCristiana* ⊙ *Tours Mon., Tues., and Thurs.–Sat.* Ⓜ *Cipro-Musei Vaticani.*

Continued on page 126

HEAVEN'S ABOVE:
THE SISTINE CEILING

Forming lines that are probably longer than those waiting to pass through the Pearly Gates; hordes of visitors arrive at the Sistine Chapel daily to view what may be the world's most sublime example of artistry:

Michelangelo: *The Creation of Adam*, Sistine Chapel, The Vatican, circa 1511.

Michelangelo's Sistine Ceiling. To paint this 12,000-square-foot barrel vault, it took four years, 343 frescoed figures, and a titanic battle of wits between the artist and Pope Julius II. While in its typical fashion, Hollywood focused on the element of agony, not ecstasy, involved in the saga of creation, a recently completed restoration of the ceiling has revolutionized our appreciation of the masterpiece of masterpieces.

By Martin Wilmot Bennett

MICHELANGELO'S
MISSION IMPOSSIBLE

Designed to match the proportions of Solomon's Temple described in the Old Testament, the Sistine Chapel is named after Pope Sixtus VI, who commissioned it as a place of worship for himself and as the venue where new popes could be elected. Before Michelangelo, the barrel-vaulted ceiling was an expanse of azure fretted with golden stars. Then, in 1504, an ugly crack appeared. Bramante, the architect, managed do some patchwork using iron rods, but when signs of a fissure remained, the new Pope Julius II summoned Michelangelo to cover it with a fresco 135 feet long and 44 feet wide.

Taking in the entire span of the ceiling, the theme connecting the various participants in this painted universe could be said to be mankind's anguished waiting. The majestic panel depicting the Creation of Adam leads, through the stages of the Fall and the expulsion from Eden, to the tragedy of Noah found naked and mocked by his own sons; throughout all runs the underlying need for man's redemption. Witnessing all from the side and end walls, a chorus of ancient Prophets and Sibyls peer anxiously forward, awaiting the Redeemer who will come to save both the Jews and the Gentiles.

APOCALYPSE NOW

The sweetness and pathos of his Pietà, carved by Michelangelo only ten years earlier, have been left behind. The new work foretells an apocalypse, its congregation of doomed sinners facing the wrath of heaven through hanging, beheading, crucifixion, flood, and plague. Michelangelo, by nature a misanthrope, was already filled with visions of doom thanks to the fiery orations of Savonarola, whose thunderous preachments he had heard before leaving his hometown of Florence. Vasari, the 16th-century art historian, coined the word "terrabilità" to describe Michelangelo's tension-ridden style, a rare case of a single word being worth a thousand pictures.

Michelangelo wound up using a *Reader's Digest* condensed version of the stories from Genesis, with the dramatis personae overseen by a punitive and terrifying God. In real life, poor Michelangelo answered to a flesh-and-blood taskmaster who was almost as vengeful: Pope Julius II. Less vicar of Christ than latter-day Caesar, he was intent on uniting Italy under the power of the Vatican, and was eager to do so by any means, including riding into pitched battle. Yet this "warrior pope" considered his most formidable adversary to be Michelangelo. Applying a form of blackmail, Julius threatened to wage war on Michelangelo's Florence, to which the artist had fled after Julius canceled a commission for a grand papal tomb unless Michelangelo agreed to return to Rome and take up the task of painting the Sistine Chapel ceiling.

MICHELANGELO, SCULPTOR

A sculptor first and foremost, however, Michelangelo considered painting an inferior genre—"for rascals and sissies" as he put it. Second, there was the sheer scope of the task, leading Michelangelo to suspect he'd been set up by a rival, Bramante, chief architect of the new St. Peter's Basilica. As Michelangelo was also a master architect, he regarded this fresco commission as a Renaissance mission-impossible. Pope Julius's powerful will prevailed—and six years later the work of the Sistine Ceiling was complete. Irving Stone's famous novel *The Agony and the Ecstasy*—and the granitic 1965 film that followed—chart this epic battle between artist and pope.

THINGS ARE LOOKING UP

To enhance your viewing of the ceiling, bring along opera-glasses, binoculars, or just a mirror (to prevent your neck from becoming bent like Michelangelo's). Note that no photos are permitted. Insiders know the only time to get the chapel to yourself is during the papal blessings and public audiences held in St. Peter's Square. Failing that, get there during lunch hour. Admission and entry to the Sistine Chapel is only through the Musei Vaticani (Vatican Museums).

SCHEMATIC OF THE SISTINE CEILING

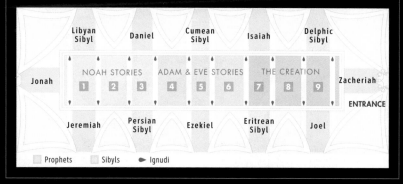

PAINTING
THE BIBLE

The ceiling's biblical symbols were ideated by three Vatican theologians, Cardinal Alidosi, Egidio da Viterbo, and Giovanni Rafanelli, along with Michelangelo.

As for the ceiling's painted "framework," this *quadratura* alludes to Roman triumphal arches because Pope Julius II was fond of mounting "triumphal entries" into his conquered cities (in imitation of Christ's

procession into Jerusalem on Palm Sunday).

THE CENTER PANELS
Prophet turned art-critic or, perhaps doubling as ourselves, the ideal viewer, Jonah the prophet (painted at the altar end) gazes up at the

Creation, or Michelangelo's version of it.

1 The first of three scenes taken from the Book of Genesis: God separates Light from Darkness.

2 God creates the sun and a craterless pre-Galilean moon

while the panel's other half offers an unprecedented rear view of the Almighty creating the vegetable world.

3 In the panel showing God separating the Waters from the Heavens, the Creator

tumbles towards us as in a self-made whirlwind.

4 Pausing for breath, next admire probably Western Art's most famous image—God giving life to Adam.

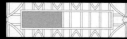

The Creation of Eve from Adam's rib leads to the sixth panel.

6 In a sort of diptych divided by the trunk of the Tree of Knowledge of Good and Evil, Michelangelo retells the Temptation and the Fall.

Illustrating Man's fallen nature, the last three panels narrate, in un-chronological order, the Flood. In the first Noah offers a pre-Flood sacrifice of thanks.

8 Damaged by an explosion in 1794, next comes

Michelangelo's version of Flood itself.

9 Finally, above the monumental Jonah, you can just make out the small, wretched figure of Noah, lying drunk—in pose, the shrunken antitype of the majestic Adam five panels down the wall.

THE CREATION OF ADAM

Michelangelo's Adam was partly inspired by the Creation scenes Michelangelo had studied in the sculpted doors of Jacopo della Quercia in Bologna and Lorenzo Ghiberti's Doors of Paradise in Florence. Yet in Michelangelo's version Adam's hand hangs limp, waiting God's touch to impart the spark of life. Facing his Creation, the Creator—looking a bit like the pagan god Jupiter—is for the first time ever depicted as horizontal, mirroring the Biblical "in his own likeness." Decades after its completion, a crack began to appear, amputating Adam's fingertips. Believe it or not, the most famous fingers in Western art are the handiwork, at least in part, of one Domenico Carnevale.

Ezekiel

Jeremiah

Ignudi

Cumaean Sibyl

Libyan Sibyl

Ignudi

PROPHETS & SIBYLS

Uniting the pagan and pre-Christian worlds of antiquity, below the central painted panels sit seven Prophets and five of their Classical equivalents, the Sibyls, while the lunettes feature Christ's ancestors as listed in Matthew's Gospel.

Ezekiel & the Cumaean Sibyl

Illustrating Hebrew and pagan worlds are Ezekiel, his body and beard straining sideways, full of prophetic tension, and the Cumaean Sibyl, as impressive for her majestic ugliness as the other four sibyls are for their beauty. Look closely at the angels attending the scary prophetess to see how one of them, in Italian-fashion, is "giving the thumb"—then, as today, considered an obcene gesture.

Jeremiah & the Libyan Sibyl

The doomy-faced Jeremiah is taken to be a self portrait of the long-suffering Michelangelo himself while opposite, showing the artist's range, is the almost playful Libyan Sibyl, about on the point of tripping over as her tunic catches on the plinth while she reaches to put her book of prophecy back on its shelf.

THOSE SCANDALOUS "IGNUDI"

The immediate function of the ceiling's naked giants, the "ignudi"—Michelangelo's own coinage—is to carry the shields celebrating famous Israelite victories and so, indi-rectly, those of bellicose Pope Julius. Some refer to them as angels without wings, yet the passion in their faces seem all too human, fear and anxiety of a pagan world awaiting its overthrow in its very redemption. Historians note that the famed ancient sculpture of *Laocoon and His Sons*—a writhing nude grouping—was excavated in Rome recently. The iconographic tradition of the "ascetic athlete"—a figure of virtue—was also known at this time. Other critics see them as an excuse for Michelangelo to paint his favorite male models, discreetly filtered through the homo-erotic optic of Platonic Love, a current trend taken up by Florentine philosophers like Poliziano.

THE SISTINE CEILING REBORN

In 2003, a twenty-year restoration of Michelangelo's frescoes was finally completed. After more than 500 time-stained years of candle-smoke, applied varnishes, and salt mold were removed, the world acclaimed a revolutionary "new" Michelangelo. Gone were the dark shadows and gloomy hues considered so "Michelangelesque." In their place were an array of pink raspberries, sherbet greens, and *changeant* tangerines—a palette even the Impressionist painters might have considered gaudy. Or, as one critic put it, "Michelangelo on Prozac." Some felt there was a gain in definition, but a loss in shadows and underpainting. For the most part, art historians hailed the new look,

proclaiming it the long-lost antecedent for the acidic Mannerist colors that emerged in Italian art in the 1520s. Artists, however, remain scandalized, finding the evocative subtlety of the Renaissance master replaced by a paint-by-numbers version.

But with much of Michelangelo's overpainting removed, it is easier to track his changing artistic style. Halfway through, Michelangelo decided his earlier panels were too busy and, beginning with the *Creation of Adam,* he painted much larger figures and simpler compositions. Another factor was, undoubtedly, the sheer physical difficulty of the execution. Michelangelo left a sonnet describing with stoical humor

the contortions to which his body was subjected daily: for almost four years, he had to stand with aching, bending back just under the ceiling, paint dripping in his face, a worse position in many ways than the false Hollywood image of Michelangelo on his back. Compared to the first executed of the main panels, *The Flood* (which took forty days to paint, just as the biblical flood did), the last of the center panels, *God separating Light from Darkness,* was almost miraculously the work of a single day. Michelangelo's brush had come to obey the same time frame as the Creator himself, a proof of how far the so-called "sculptor" had mastered his technique.

Ponte Sant'Angelo. Angels designed by Baroque master Bernini line the most beautiful of central Rome's 20-odd bridges. Bernini himself carved only two of the angels (those with the scroll and the crown of thorns), both of which were moved to the church of Sant'Andrea delle Fratte shortly afterward due to the wishes of the Bernini family. Though copies, the angels on the bridge today convey forcefully the grace and characteristic sense of movement—a key element of Baroque sculpture—of Bernini's best work. Originally built in AD 133–134, the Ponte Elio, as it was originally called, was a bridge over the Tiber to Hadrian's Mausoleum. Pope Gregory changed the bridge's name after he had a vision of an angel sheathing its sword to signal the ending of the plague of 590. In medieval times, continuing its sacral function, the bridge became an important element in funneling pilgrims toward St. Peter's. As such, in 1667 Pope Clement IX commissioned Bernini to design 10 angels bearing the symbols of the Passion, turning the bridge into a sort of Via Crucis. ✉ *Between Lungotevere Castello and Lungotevere Altoviti, San Pietro* Ⓜ *Ottaviano.*

Navona and Campo

PIAZZA NAVONA, PANTHEON, CAMPO DE' FIORI, VIA GIULIA

WORD OF MOUTH

"The Campo de' Fiori square has a different personality at 9 am than it does at 9 pm, which is different yet than that at 11 pm. I just love that Rome's piazzas are used just as much today as 500 years ago. (Minus the public executions, of course.)"

—Missypie

GETTING ORIENTED

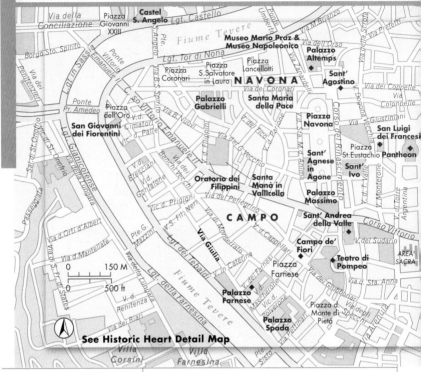

See Historic Heart Detail Map

GETTING HERE	OK, WHERE DO I START?

In the heart of the *centro storico* (historical center), this neighborhood is an easy walk across the river from the Vatican or Trastevere and a half-hour amble from the Spanish Steps neighborhood. Bussing from Termini or the Vatican, take the No. 40 Express or the No. 64 and get off at Largo Torre Argentina, a 10-minute stroll to either Campo de' Fiori or Piazza Navona. Another option is the electric No. 116—tiny enough for narrow streets—that winds its way from Via Veneto past the Spanish Steps to Campo de' Fiori.

Two blocks west of Piazza Venezia—Rome's central transportation hub—sits the grandmother of Rome's 17th-century churches, Il Gesù, whose splendor makes it a fitting overture to this sumptuously Baroque quarter. After this curtain-raiser, cross Corso Vittorio Emanuele and take Via del Gesù, turning left onto Via Piè di Marmo to enter Piazza della Minerva. On the right is Santa Maria sopra Minerva, whose piazza contains Rome's most delightful Baroque conceit, the 17th-century elephant obelisk memorial designed by Bernini. Straight ahead is one of the wonders of the world, the ancient Pantheon, with that postcard icon, Piazza Navona, just a few blocks to the west. As cornucopic with art treasures as any in Rome, this district would take about five hours to explore, not counting breaks—but taking breaks is what this area is all about. Chill out at Campo de' Fiori, a Monday-to-Saturday morning market that becomes a nighttime scene-arena, or hit Piazza Navona in the evening, the ideal time to rest on a bench and revel in the dramatic way the lights hit the fountains and church.

TOP 5 REASONS TO GO

Piazza Navona: Take yourself for the ultimate Roman *passeggiata* (promenade) in the city's most glorious piazza—the showcase for Rome's exuberant Baroque style—and savor how Bernini's fantastic fountain is set off by the curves and steeples of Borromini's church of Sant'Agnese.

Caravaggio: Feel the power of 17th-century Rome's rebel artist in three of his finest paintings, at the church of San Luigi dei Francesi, all dazzling with the chiaroscuro use of light and shadow.

The Pantheon: Gaze up to the heavens through the dome of Rome's best-preserved ancient temple—could this be the world's only architecturally perfect building?

Campo de' Fiori: Stroll through the morning market, basket in hand, for a taste of the sweet life.

Via Giulia: Lined with regal palaces—still home to some of Rome's *princeliest* families—this is a Renaissance-era diorama you can walk through.

BEST TIME-OUTS

Obikà Mozzarella Bar. The first of its kind in the world, this takes the sushi bar concept and instead offers a mouthwatering range of buffalo mozzarella from Naples. The decor is white-wall minimalism, the clientele chic, and the weekend brunch to die for. Grab coffees or salads to go. ⊠ *Via dei Prefetti 26, Navona* ☎ *06/6832630.*

Cul de Sac. Located steps from Piazza Navona, Cul de Sac was one of the first wine bars in Rome. Today, it offers small plates of Italian specialties—as well as a good wine list and outdoor seating. ⊠ *Piazza Pasquino 73, Navona* ☎ *06/68801094.*

Giolitti. The Pantheon area is ice-cream heaven, but this, opened in 1900, is considered the best gelateria. The scene at the counter often looks like the storming of the Bastille. Remember to pay the cashier first, then head to the counter. ⊠ *Via Uffizi del Vicario 40, Pantheon* ☎ *06/6991243* ⊕ *www.giolitti.it* ☉ *Daily 7 am–2 am.*

Sightseeing
★★★★★
Nightlife
★★★★
Dining
★★★
Lodging
★★★★★
Shopping
★★★★

If the Navona quarter doesn't enchant you, nothing in Rome will. Flowered balconies, brilliantly colored palazzi, Bernini's best fountain, friendly sidewalk caffè, priceless Caravaggio altarpieces, and the city's most Baroque squares all make Navona into the crown jewel of the city's historic center. This is not where Rome began (that's the Palatine and Capitoline hills), but it's where all the centuries come together most beautifully. As you wander from the ethereal interior of the ancient Pantheon to explore the Raphaels at Santa Maria della Pace and then discover the gold-on-gold splendor of Il Gesù, you'll quickly learn that this part of Rome supersaturates the senses.

Today, the district's tiny streets brim over with parliamentarians doing deals over plates of *saltimbocca*, fashionistas shopping for shoes, and tourists from every part of the world. Everywhere, caffè, restaurants, and artisan shops line the twisted streets and the lopsided *piazzas*, even as elegant ladies living in apartments upstairs lean out French windows for a breath of air. It's crowded here, and often noisy, but every moment in the *centro* is a slice of Roman life, and you'd be perfectly justified in just strolling the streets and taking it all in.

But it would be a crime to miss out on the cultural treasures this neighborhood holds. The Baroque, Rome's finest artistic moment, was born and raised here, in Bernini's marvelous statuary, in Caravaggio's almost unbearably realistic paintings, in the frippery and froth of its best and most beautiful churches. Piazza Navona is the most theatrical piazza in town, its pedestrian-only oval focused on three of Bernini's fountains, including the sensational Fontana dei Quattro Fiumi (Fountain of the Four Rivers). It's flanked by some of the city's most elegant buildings, first among them Borromini's church of Sant'Agnese in Agone, a masterpiece of the Baroque. Just one street over, the church of San Luigi dei Francesi showcases three of Caravaggio's greatest paintings. The churches of Il Gesù, Sant'Ivo alla Sapienza, and Santa Maria della Pace are each treasures in their own way: Il Gesù grand and imposing, Sant'Ivo eccentric and whimsical, and Santa Maria jewel-like and theatrical.

GILT TRIP

For a full guided itinerary walk through this magical quarter, be sure to see "Roamin' Holiday" and its step-by-step tour, "Enjoying the Gilt: A Stroll Through the Baroque Quarter."

In Piazza Navona, the Baroque rules. However, just across the road is the Pantheon, ancient Rome's best-preserved temple, which escaped destruction due to its consecration in 608 AD as a Christian church, which it remains today. Its dome was until the last century the largest ever built, anywhere; its architectural balance and harmony inspired and informed countless Renaissance artists, Michelangelo and Raphael included. But not all of the area's treasures are of the artistic nature: Campo de' Fiori, the famous market piazza, is a must-see in the morning, when farm and fish stalls bring the square to life with shouting, shopping, and smells. In the evening until past midnight, outdoor bars and restaurants transform this humble square into a hot spot. For Romans, the Navona neighborhood is their downtown—a largely residential area that stretches eastward of the Tiber over to Via del Corso, a main avenue. While locals refer to this district by a number of names—particularly Campo Marzio, Parione, and Regola—we choose the most popular moniker to refer to the northern half of the district set around Piazza Navona.

The southern half we call Campo, referring to its charming hub, the Campo de' Fiori. Occupying the horn of land that pushes the Tiber westward toward the Vatican, the entire area has been an integral part of the city since ancient times. Rome's first emperor and prime scenographer Augustus got things started by transforming the Campo Marzio's military exercise ground into an alternative city-center to the Forum. During the Renaissance the area's proximity to both the Vatican and Lateran palaces drew many of Rome's richest people to settle here and greatest artists to work here. Today, when a busker sings a melancholy song about his *bella città,* chances are he's moved to music by the winding alleys and gentle light of this place: the achingly beautiful heart of the centro storico.

NAVONA

In terms of sheer sensual enjoyment—from a mouthwatering range of restaurants and caffè to the ornate Baroque settings—it's tough to top this area of Rome. Just a few blocks, and some 1,200 years, separate the two main showstoppers: Piazza Navona and the Pantheon. The first is the most beautiful Baroque piazza in the world, which serves as the open-air salon for this quarter of Rome. As if this is not grandeur enough, across Corso di Rinascimento—and more than a millennium

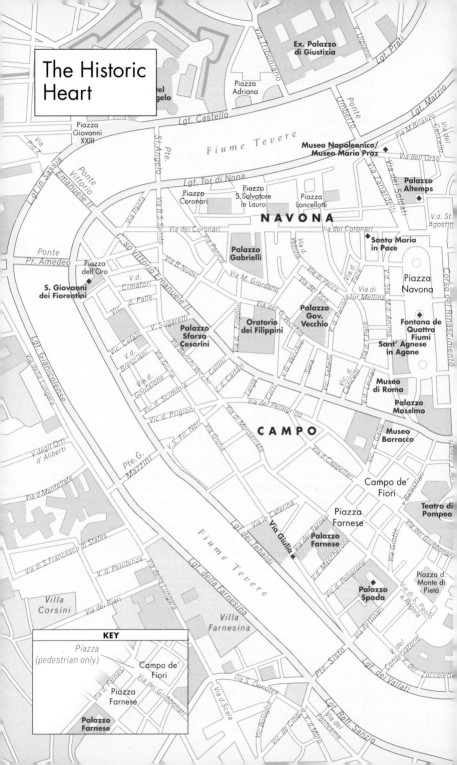

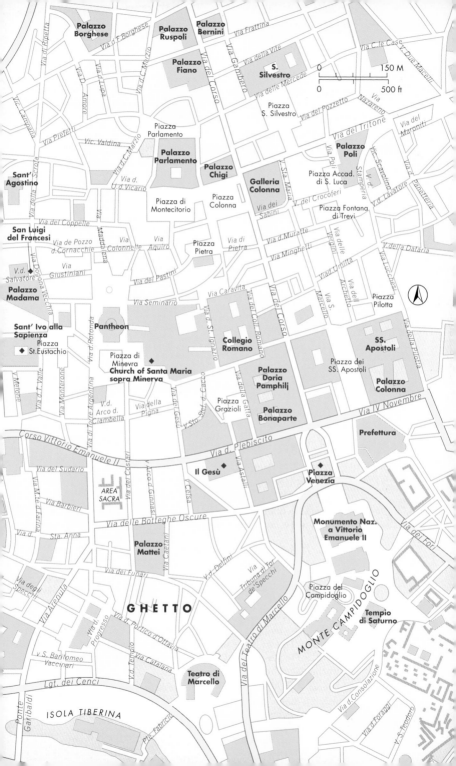

away—is the Pantheon, the grandest extant building still standing from ancient Rome. Even today, it's topped by the world's largest unreinforced concrete dome. Near the same massive hub, Bernini's delightful elephant obelisk shows small can also be beautiful. And beautiful is the word to describe this entire area, one that is packed with Baroque wonders, charming stores, and very happy sightseers.

TOP ATTRACTIONS

Fodor'sChoice ★ **Palazzo Altemps.** Containing some of the finest ancient Roman statues in the world, this collection formerly made up the core of the Museo Nazionale Romano. As of 1995, it was moved to these new, suitably grander digs. The palace's sober exterior belies a magnificence that appears as soon as you walk into the majestic courtyard, studded with statues and covered in part by a retractable awning. The restored interior hints at the Roman lifestyle of the 16th through 18th centuries while showcasing the most illustrious pieces from the Museo Nazionale, including the Ludovisi family collection. In the frescoed salons you can see the Galata, a poignant work portraying a barbarian warrior who chooses death for himself and his wife rather than humiliation by the enemy. Another highlight is the large Ludovisi sarcophagus, magnificently carved from marble. In a place of honor is the Ludovisi Throne, which shows a goddess emerging from the sea and being helped by her acolytes. For centuries this was heralded as one of the most sublime Greek sculptures but, today, at least one authoritative art historian considers it a colossally overrated fake. Look for the framed explanations of the exhibits that detail (in English) how and exactly where Renaissance sculptors, Bernini among them, added missing pieces to the classical works. In the lavishly frescoed Loggia stand busts of the Caesars. In the wing once occupied by early-20th-century poet Gabriele D'Annunzio (who married into the Altemps family), three rooms newly opened in 2009 now host the museum's Egyptian collection. ⊠ *Piazza Sant'Apollinare 46, Navona* ☎ *06/39967700* ⊕ *www.pierreci.it* 🎫 *€10, includes other 3 venues of Museo Nazionale Romano (Crypta Balbi, Palazzo Massimo, Museo Diocleziano)* ⊙ *Tues.–Sun. 9–7:45 (ticket office closes 1 hr before).*

Fodor'sChoice ★ **Pantheon.** One of the wonders of the ancient world, this onetime pagan temple, a marvel of architectural harmony and proportion, is the best-preserved ancient building in Rome. It was entirely rebuilt by the emperor Hadrian around AD 120 on the site of an earlier pantheon (from the Greek *pan,* all, and *theon,* gods) erected in 27 BC by Augustus's general Agrippa. It's thought that the majestic circular building was actually designed *by* Hadrian, as were many of the temples, palaces, and lakes of his enormous villa at Tivoli. Hadrian nonetheless retained the inscription over the entrance from the original building (today, unfortunately, replaced with modern letters) that named Agrippa as the builder. This caused enormous confusion among historians until, in 1892, a French architect discovered that all the bricks used in the Pantheon dated from Hadrian's time.

The most striking thing about the Pantheon is not its size, immense though it is (until 1960 the dome was the largest ever built), nor even the phenomenal technical difficulties posed by so vast a construction; rather,

PIAZZA NAVONA

✉ *Junction of Via della Cuccagna, Corsia Agonale, Via di Sant'Agnese, and Via Agonale*

5

TIPS

■ On the eve of Epiphany (January 5–6), Piazza Navona's toy fair explodes in joyful conclusion, with much noise and rowdiness to encourage Befana, an old woman who brings toys to good children and pieces of coal (represented by similar-looking candy) to the naughty. Dealers also set up before Christmas to sell trinkets and presepio (crèche) figures, while the toy stores of Al Sogno (at No. 53) and Berté (at No. 3) enchant year-round.

■ If you want a caffè with one of the most beautiful, if pricey, views in Rome, grab a seat on Piazza Navona. The sidewalk tables of the Tre Scalini caffè (Piazza Navona 30, 06/6879148) offer a grandstand view of all the action. This is the place that invented the tartufo, a luscious chocolate ice-cream specialty. Piazza Navona is lined with caffè, though, so pick and choose. Just be aware that the restaurants here are food-with-a-view in quality—but what a view!

Here, everything that makes Rome unique is compressed into one beautiful Baroque piazza. Always camera-ready, Piazza Navona has Bernini sculptures, three gorgeous fountains, a magnificently Baroque church (Sant'Agnese in Agone), and, best of all, the excitement of so many people strolling, admiring the fountains, and enjoying the view.

The piazza has been an entertainment venue for Romans ever since being built over Domitian's circus (pieces of the arena are still visible near adjacent Piazza Sant'Apollinare). Although undoubtedly more touristy today, the square still has the carefree air of the days when it was the scene of medieval jousts and 17th-century carnivals. Today, it's the site of a lively Christmas "Befana" fair.

The piazza still looks much as it did during the 17th century, after the Pamphili pope Innocent X decided to make it over into a monument to his family to rival the Barberini's palace at the Quattro Fontane.

At center stage is the Fontana dei Quattro Fiumi, created for Innocent X by Bernini in 1651. Bernini's powerful figures of the four rivers represent the four corners of the world: the Nile; the Ganges; the Danube; and the Plata, with its hand raised. One story has it that the figure of the Nile—the figure closest to Sant' Agnese in Agone—hides its head because it can't bear to look upon the church's "inferior" facade designed by Francesco Borromini, Bernini's rival. In fact, the facade was built after the fountain, and the statue hides its head because it represents a river whose source was then unknown (for more on Bernini and Borromini, see our special photo feature in Chapter 7).

it's the remarkable unity of the building. You don't have to look far to find the reason for this harmony: the diameter described by the dome is exactly equal to its height. It's the use of such simple mathematical balance that gives classical architecture its characteristic sense of proportion and its nobility and why some call it the world's only architecturally perfect building. The great opening at the apex of the dome, the oculus, is nearly 30 feet in diameter and was the temple's only source of light. It was intended to symbolize the "all-seeing eye of heaven."

To do the interior justice defied even Byron. He piles up adjectives, but none seems to fit: "Simple, erect, severe, austere, sublime." Not surprising, perhaps, when describing a dome 141 feet high and the same across. Although little is known for sure about the Pantheon's origins or purpose, it's worth noting that the five levels of trapezoidal coffers represent the course of the five then-known planets and their concentric spheres. Then, ruling over them, comes the sun represented symbolically and literally by the 30-foot-wide eye at the top. The heavenly symmetry is further paralleled by the coffers themselves: 28 to each row, the number of lunar cycles. Note how each coffer takes five planetary steps toward the wall. Then in the center of each would have shone a small bronze star. Down below the seven large niches were occupied not by saints, but, it's thought, by statues of Mars, Venus, the deified Caesar, and the other "astral deities," including the Moon and the Sun, the *sol invictus*.

The Pantheon is by far the best preserved of the major monuments of imperial Rome, a condition that is the result of it being consecrated as a church in AD 608. (It's still a working and Mass-holding church today, and it's the church name, the Basilica of Saint Mary and the Martyrs, that you'll see on the official signs.) No building, church or not, escaped some degree of plundering through the turbulent centuries of Rome's history after the fall of the empire. In 655, for example, the gilded bronze covering the dome was stripped. Similarly, in the early 17th century, Pope Urban VIII removed the bronze beams of the portico. Although the legend holds that the metal went to the *baldacchino* (canopy) over the high altar at St. Peter's Basilica, the reality may be worse—it went to cannons at Castel Sant'Angelo. Most of its interior marble facing has also been stripped and replaced over the centuries. Nonetheless, the Pantheon suffered less than many other ancient structures.

Today, the Pantheon serves as one of the city's important burial places. Its most famous tomb is that of Raphael (between the second and third chapels on the left as you enter). The inscription reads "Here lies Raphael; while he lived, mother Nature feared to be outdone; and when he died, she feared to die with him." Amazingly, the temple's original bronze doors have remained intact (if restored and parts of which were even melted down and recast at one point) for more than 1,800 years. Be sure to ponder them as you leave. One-hour tours (€8) are run regularly in English; check at the information desk on your right as you enter. ⊠ *Piazza della Rotonda, Navona* ☎ *06/68300230* 🖾 *Free; audio guides €5 suggested donation* ⊙ *Mon.–Sat. 8:30–7:30, Sun. 9–6* Ⓜ *Closest bus hub: Argentina (buses 40, 85, 53, 46, 64, 87, 571, tram 8).*

NEED A BREAK?

Tazza d'Oro. On the east corner of the Pantheon's piazza, the Tazza d'Oro coffee bar (no tables, no frills) is the place for serious coffee drinkers. Indulge in their *granita di caffè con panna* (coffee ice with whipped cream). For a classy but gently priced meal, head to Vicolo della Palomba 23, just a corner away from Palazzo Altemps, to find the snazzily named Il Desiderio Preso per la Coda ("Desire Taken by the Tail")—the name comes from a play written by Picasso. ⊠ *Via degli Orfani 86, Pantheon.*

Fodor'sChoice ★ **San Luigi dei Francesi.** A pilgrimage spot for art lovers everywhere, San Luigi's Contarelli Chapel is adorned with three stunningly dramatic works by Caravaggio (1571–1610), the Baroque master of the heightened approach to light and dark. Located at the altar end of the left nave, they were commissioned for San Luigi, the official church of Rome's French colony (San Luigi is St. Louis, patron of France). The inevitable coin machine will light up his *Calling of St. Matthew, Matthew and the Angel,* and *Matthew's Martyrdom,* seen from left to right, and Caravaggio's mastery of light takes it from there. When painted, they caused considerable consternation to the clergy of San Luigi, who thought the artist's dramatically realistic approach was scandalously disrespectful. A first version of the altarpiece was rejected; the priests were not particularly happy with the other two, either. Time has fully vindicated Caravaggio's patron, Cardinal Francesco del Monte, who secured the commission for these works and stoutly defended them. They're now recognized to be among the world's greatest paintings. ⊠ *Piazza San Luigi dei Francesi, Navona* ☎ *06/688271* ⊙ *Weekdays 10–12:30 and 3–7 (closed Thurs. afternoon).*

Fodor'sChoice ★ **Sant'Agnese in Agone.** The quintessence of Baroque architecture, this church has a facade that remains a wonderfully rich mélange of bell towers, concave spaces, and dovetailed stone and marble, the creation of Francesco Borromini (1599–1667), a contemporary and rival of Bernini. Next to his new Pamphilj family palace, Pope Innocent X had the adjacent chapel expanded into this full-fledged church. The work was first assigned to the architect Rainaldi. However, Donna Olimpia, the pope's famously domineering sister, became increasingly impatient with how the work was going and brought in Borromini, whose wonderful concave entrance has the magical effect of making the dome appear much larger than it actually is. The name of this church comes from *agona,* the source of the word *navona* and a corruption of the Latin *agonalis,* describing the type of games held there in Roman times. The saint associated with the church is Agnes, who was martyred here in the piazza's forerunner, the Stadium of Domitian. As she was stripped nude before the crowd, her hair miraculously grew to maintain her modesty before she was killed. The interior is a marvel of modular Baroque space and is ornamented by giant marble reliefs sculpted by Raggi and Ferrata. ⊠ *Piazza Navona, Navona* ☎ *06/68192134* ⊙ *Tues.–Sun. 9:30–12:30 and 3:30–7.*

★ **Santa Maria della Pace.** One of Rome's most delightful little architectural stage sets was created in 1656 when Pietro da Cortona (1596–1669) was commissioned by Pope Alexander VII to enlarge the tiny Piazza della Pace so as to accommodate the carriages of the wealthy parishioners arriving at the church of Santa Maria. His architectural solution was to design a new church facade complete with semicircular portico, add arches to give architectural unity to the piazza, and then complete it with a series of bijou-size palaces (now some of the most coveted addresses in Rome). Within the 15th-century church are two great Renaissance treasures: Raphael's fresco above the first altar on your right depicts the *Four Sibyls*, almost exact, if more relaxed, replicas of Michelangelo's. The fine decorations of the Cesi Chapel, second on

the right, were designed in the mid-16th century by Sangallo. Opposite is Peruzzi's wonderful fresco of the *Madonna and Child*. Meanwhile, the octagon below the dome is something of an art gallery in itself with works by Cavaliere Arpino, Orazio Gentileschi, and others as Cozzo's *Eternity* fills the lantern above. Behind the church proper is its cloister, designed by Bramante (architect of St. Peter's) as the very first expression of High Renaissance style in Rome. ⊠ *Via Arco della Pace 5, Navona* ☎ *06/6861156* ⊘ *Mon., Wed., and Sat. 9–noon.*

Santa Maria sopra Minerva. The name of the church reveals that it was built *sopra* (over) the ruins of a temple of Minerva, ancient goddess of wisdom. Erected in 1280 by the Dominicans on severe Italian Gothic lines, it has undergone a number of more or less happy restorations to the interior. Certainly, as the city's major Gothic church, it provides a refreshing contrast to Baroque flamboyance. Have a €1 coin handy to illuminate the **Cappella Carafa** in the right transept, where Filippino Lippi's (1457–1504) glowing frescoes are well worth the small investment, opening up the deepest azure expanse of sky where musical angels hover around the Virgin. Under the main altar is the tomb of St. Catherine of Siena, one of Italy's patron saints. Left of the altar you'll find Michelangelo's famed *Risen Christ* and the tomb of the gentle artist Fra Angelico. In front of the church, the little obelisk-bearing elephant (under restoration at the time of this printing) carved by Bernini is perhaps the city's most charming sculpture. An inscription on the base of **Bernini's Elephant Obelisk** references the church's ancient patroness, reading something to the effect that it takes a strong mind to sustain solid wisdom. ⊠ *Piazza della Minerva, Navona* ☎ *06/6793926* ⊘ *Weekdays 8–7, weekends 8–12:30 and 3:30–7.*

★ **Sant'Ivo alla Sapienza.** The main facade of this eccentric Baroque church, probably Borromini's best, is on the stately courtyard of an austere building that once housed Rome's university. Sant'Ivo has what must surely be one of the most delightful domes in all of Rome—a golden spiral said to have been inspired by a bee's stinger (⇨ *for more information* on Borromini, see, "Baroque and Desperate: The Tragic Rivalry of Bernini and Borromini"). The bee symbol is a reminder that Borromini built the church on commission from the Barberini pope Urban VIII (a swarm of bees figure on the Barberini family crest). The interior, open only for three hours on Sunday, is worth a look, especially if you share Borromini's taste for complex mathematical architectural idiosyncrasies. "I didn't take up architecture solely to be a copyist," Borromini once said. Sant'Ivo is certainly the proof. ⊠ *Corso Rinascimento 40, Navona* ☏ *06/6864987* ⊙ *Sun. 9–noon* Ⓜ *Bus 130, 116, 186, 492, 30, 70, 81, or 87.*

WORTH NOTING

★ **Museo Mario Praz.** On the top floor of the Palazzo Primoli—the same building (separate entrance) that houses the Museo Napoleonico—is one of Rome's most unusual museums. As if in amber, the apartment in which the famous Italian essayist Mario Praz lived is preserved intact, decorated with a lifetime's accumulation of delightful Baroque and Neoclassical art and antiques arranged and rearranged to create symmetries that take the visitor by surprise like the best trompe d'oeil. As author of *The Romantic Sensibility* and *A History of Interior Decoration*, Praz was fabled for his taste for the arcane and the bizarre; here his reputation for the same lives on. ⊠ *Via Zanardelli 1, Navona* ☏ *06/6861089* ⊕ *www.museopraz.beniculturali.it* ⊡ *Free* ⊙ *Tues.–Sun. 9–2 and 2:30–7:30 (ticket office closes 1 hr before closing)* Ⓜ *Bus 492, 70, 628, 81, 116.*

Fodor'sChoice **Museo Napoleonico.** Housed in an opulent collection of velvet-and-crystal
★ salons that hauntingly capture the fragile charm of early-19th-century Rome, this small museum in the Palazzo Primoli contains a specialized and rich collection of Napoléon memorabilia, including a bust by Canova of the general's sister, Pauline Borghese (as well as a plaster cast of her left bust). You may well ask why this outpost of Napoléon is in Rome, but in 1809 the French emperor had made a grab for Rome, kidnapping Pope Pius VII and proclaiming his young son the King of Rome. All came to naught a few years later, when the emperor was routed off his French throne. Upstairs is the Museo Mario Praz. ⊠ *Museo Napoleonico: Palazzo Primoli, Piazza di Ponte Umberto I, Navona* ☏ *06/68806286* ⊕ *www.museonapoleonico.it* ⊡ *€7* ⊙ *Tues.– Sun. 9 am–7 pm* Ⓜ *Bus lines 70, 30, 81, 628, 492.*

Palazzo Massimo alle Colonne. Following the shape of Emperor Domitian's Odeon arena, a curving, columned portico identifies this otherwise inconspicuous palace on a traffic-swept bend of Corso Vittorio Emanuele. In the 1530s Renaissance architect Baldassare Peruzzi built this new palace for the Massimo family, after their previous dwelling had been destroyed during the sack of Rome. (High in the papal aristocracy, they boasted an ancestor who had been responsible for the defeat of Hannibal.) If you're here on March 16, you'll be able to go upstairs to take part (on an individual basis but not in groups) in commemorations of a miracle performed here in 1583 by Philip Neri, who is said to have recalled a young member of the family, one Paolo Massimo, from the dead. ⊠ *Corso Vittorio Emanuele II 141, Navona.*

Piazza di Pasquino. This tiny piazza takes its name from the figure in the corner, the remnant of an old Roman statue depicting Menelaus. The statue underwent a name change in the 16th century when Pasquino, a cobbler or barber (and part-time satirist), started writing comments around the base. The habit caught on; soon everyone was doing it. The most loquacious of Rome's "talking statues," its lack of arms or face is more than made up for with commentary of any topic of the day. ⊠ *Piazza di Pasquino, Navona.*

Sant'Agostino. Caravaggio's celebrated *Madonna of the Pilgrims*—which scandalized all of Rome because a kneeling pilgrim is pictured, all too realistically for the era's tastes, with dirt on the soles of his feet, with the Madonna standing in a less than majestic pose in a dilapidated doorway—is in the first chapel on the left. At the third column down the nave, admire Raphael's blue-robed *Isaiah*, said to be inspired by Michelangelo's prophets on the Sistine ceiling (Raphael, with the help of Bramante, had taken the odd peek at the master's original against strict orders of secrecy). Directly below is Sansovino's Leonardo-influenced sculpture, *St. Anne and the Madonna with Child.* As you leave, in a niche just inside the door, is the sculpted *Madonna and Child,* known to the Romans as the "Madonna del Parto" (of Childbirth) and piled high with ex-votos. The artist is Jacopo Tatti, also sometimes confusingly known as Sansovino after his master. ⊠ *Piazza Sant'Agostino, Navona* ☎ *06/68801962* ⊙ *Daily 7:45–noon and 4–7:30.*

Santa Maria in Vallicella/Chiesa Nuova. This church, also known as Chiesa Nuova (New Church), was built toward the end of the 16th century at the urging of Philip Neri, and like Il Gesù is a product of the fervor of the Counter-Reformation. It has a sturdy Baroque interior, all white and gold, with ceiling frescoes by Pietro da Cortona depicting a miracle reputed to have occurred during the church's construction: the Virgin and strong-armed angels hold up the broken roof to prevent it crashing down onto the congregation below. The Church is most famed for its three magnificent altarpieces by Rubens. ⊠ *Piazza della Chiesa Nuova, Corso Vittorio Emanuele II, Navona* ☎ *06/6875289* ⊙ *Daily 8–noon and 5:30–7.*

CAMPO

Picture a district as the most charming theater, a cast of gods and godlings, saints and sibyls, tritons and cherubs, with the odd ice-cream seller, acrobat, or clown wandering in-between. Add a backdrop to please an emperor or pope, lowlier caffè-owners and restaurateurs charging for a stage-side view. Such is Campo, which anchors the southern sector of this quarter in the heart of the centro. Campo de' Fiori itself has barely changed from the days of the Renaissance. The area is also studded with other 16th-century treasures like the Palazzo Farnese, a palace Michelangelo helped design; the Palazzo Spada; and Via Giulia, the ruler-straight street laid out by Pope Julius II and long considered Rome's most coveted address.

TOP ATTRACTIONS

Il Gesù. The mother church of the Jesuits in Rome is the prototype of all Counter-Reformation churches. Considered the first fully Baroque church, it has spectacular decor that tells a lot about an era of religious triumph and turmoil. Its architecture (the overall design was by Vignola, the facade by della Porta) influenced ecclesiastical building in Rome for more than a century and was exported by the Jesuits throughout the rest of Europe. Though consecrated as early as 1584, the interior of the church wasn't decorated for another 100 years. It was originally intended that the interior be left plain to the point of austerity—but, when it was finally embellished, no expense was spared. Its interior drips with gold and lapis lazuli, gold and precious marbles, gold and more gold, all covered by a fantastically painted ceiling by Baciccia. Unfortunately, the church is also one of Rome's most crepuscular, so its visual magnificence is considerably dulled by lack of light.

The architectural significance of Il Gesù extends far beyond the splendid interior. The first of the great Counter-Reformation churches, it was put up after the Council of Trent (1545–63) had signaled the determination of the Roman Catholic Church to fight back against the Reformed Protestant heretics of northern Europe. The church decided to do so through the use of overwhelming pomp and majesty, in its effort to woo believers. As a harbinger of ecclesiastical spectacle, Il Gesù spawned imitations throughout Italy and the other Catholic countries of Europe as well as the Americas.

The most striking element is the ceiling, which is covered with frescoes that swirl down from on high to merge with painted stucco figures at the base, the illusion of space in the two-dimensional painting becoming the reality of three dimensions in the sculpted figures. Baciccia, their painter, achieved extraordinary effects in these frescoes, especially in the *Triumph of the Holy Name of Jesus,* over the nave. Here, the figures representing evil cast out of heaven seem to be hurtling down onto the observer. For details, the spectacle is best viewed through a specially tilted mirror in the nave.

The founder of the Jesuit order himself is buried in the Chapel of St. Ignatius, in the left-hand transept. This is surely the most sumptuous Baroque altar in Rome; as is typical, the enormous globe of lapis lazuli that crowns it is really only a shell of lapis over a stucco base—after all, Baroque decoration prides itself on achieving stunning effects and illusions. The heavy bronze altar rail by architect Carlo Fontana is in keeping with the surrounding opulence. ⊠ *Piazza del Gesù, off Via del Plebiscito, Campo* ☎ *06/697001* ⊕ *www.chiesadelgesu.org* ☉ *Daily 7–12:30 and 4–7:30.*

Fodor's Choice
★ **Campo de' Fiori.** A bustling marketplace in the morning (Mon.–Sat. 8 am–1 pm) and a trendy meeting place the rest of the day (and night), this piazza has plenty of earthy charm. By sunset, all the fish, fruit, and flower vendors disappear and this so-called *piazza trasformista* takes on another identity, bar-life bulging out into the street, one person's carousal another's insomnia (⇨ *for the full scoop, see "Life is a Piazza"*). Brooding over the piazza is a hooded statue of the philosopher

Continued on page 148

life is a piazza

A small square with two personalities as
different as day and night, the Campo
de' Fiori is Rome's mecca for people
with a picky purpose—whether it is
picking out food or picking out that
night's amorous *avventura*.

You can explore the Colosseum until your ears ring with roars of wild beasts, and make the rounds of churches until visions of putti dance in your head. But you won't know Rome until you have paused to appreciate the loveliness and vibrancy of the cityscape, perhaps from a table on one of Rome's beautiful squares. The Campo de' Fiori is particularly well endowed with such ringside seats, for here you can enjoy the show 24/7.

The Campo is heavily foot-trafficked at any given hour, whether for its sunlit market stalls or its moon-shadowed cobblestones. If you only have 24 hours in Rome (and especially if the past 20 have been dedicated to sightseeing), take a breather here and inhale a truly Roman social scene, no matter what time of day or night.

In the daytime, the piazza is a buzzing produce market where ancient vendors shout out the day's specialties and caffè-goers gossip behind newspapers while enjoying the morning's cappuccino. In the late afternoon, Campo transforms into the ultimate hangout with overflowing bars, caffès, and restaurants filled with locals and tourists all vying for the perfect '*posto*' to check out passersby.

Campo life is decidedly without pause. The only moment of repose happens in the very wee hours of the morning when the remaining stragglers start the stumble home and just before the produce-filled mini-trucks begin their magnificent march in to the square. At any given hour, you will always find something going on in Campo, the "living room" of today's Rome.

By Erica Firpo

5

IN FOCUS LIFE IS A PIAZZA

24 HOURS IN THE CAMPO DE' FIORI

5–6 am The Flight of the Bumble-Bees: *Ape* ("bee" in Italian) trucks file into Campo to unload the day's goods. These mini-trucks are very cute, no? *Ao! Claudia che sta a fa?!* ("Hey, Claudia how ya doin'"), Daniele yells across to Claudia as market guys and gals joke around. Good lessons in Roman slang.

7–8 am The Calm before the Storm: The only time Campo seems a bit sluggish, as stands have just opened, shoppers have yet to arrive, and everyone is just waking up. Market locals gather before heading off to work and school.

9–10 am The Herd: Tourists arrive, whether on their own or bearing colorful (and matching) t-shirts and hats. The locals take their "Pausa" coffee break while shops and late-opening caffès set up.

11–12 am The Eye of the Storm: Everyone is taking photos—photos of food, market goers, vendors, models, caffè-goers, anything.

1–2 pm Pranzo: Lunchtime in Campo. Everyone is hawking for an outdoor table. Top spots: **1** Magnolia, **2** Obika, **3** Aristo Campo, **4** Roscioli (indoors). Vendors start to pack up.

3–4 pm The Denouement: Campo is officially shutting down, marked by the notable odor of Campo refuse and the loud din of the cleaning trucks. Perhaps the absolute worst time to be in Campo. When the trucks depart, they leave the square to parents and toddlers.

5–6 pm Gelato Time: Shoppers and strollers replace replace marketgoers. The first of Campo's many musicians begin warming up

1PM

3PM

for the evening's concert. Favorites always include: "Guantanamera," "My Way," and "Volare."

7–8 pm Happy Hours: The pre-aperitivi people enjoy the cocktail before the cocktails. Always good for the punctual. By 6 aperitivi have been served. Are you "in" or "out"? Outside means picking any of the umbrella *tavoli* that line the piazza—**5** Baccanale, **2** Okika, **6** Vinera Reggio. If you prefer to be on the sly, try an indoor *enoteca*—**7** Camponeschi, **8** Angolo Divino, **4** Roscioli (three of Rome's best wine bars). Late-comers arrive for a last sip of wine before deciding where to dine.

9–10 pm Dining Hour: Dining in Rome is an all-evening experience. It's common custom to argue for a half-hour about the perfect restaurant.

To make it easy:
9 La Carbonara (on the piazza, Roman cuisine);
10 Osteria ar Gelletto (beautiful view of Piazza Farnese);
11 Cantina Lucifero (good pasta one block north);
4 Roscioli—an inside, cave-like spot for the gourmand.

11 pm–12 am After-dinner Drinks: Everyone moves back to the Campo for a drink (or many). Drunkenness can include catcalls, stiletto falls, volleyed soccer balls, and the cops (polizia or carabinieri, take your pick).

1–2 am Time to Go Home: Bars begin to shut down, with lingering kisses and hugs ("Dude, I love you!"). Clean-up crews come back. The din returns, this time as trucks clean up broken bottles and plastic cups.

3–4 am Some stragglers are still hanging around. For the first time Campo de' Fiori is silent, to the delight of the residents around it. They have to hurry…because the Ape (see 5 am) are pressing to get back in.

Piazza Campo dé Fiori
Via del Baullari
To Via del Giubbonari

CAMPO DE FIORI

11PM

7PM

THE COGNOSCENTI'S CAMPO

WHERE THE POPE BUYS HIS ASPARAGUS

No longer a simple flower market, from Monday through Saturday mornings, Campo is Rome's most famous produce market, with prices that seemingly only the pope can afford. Shopping here is a worthy guilty pleasure as all produce is organic and homegrown, coming directly from the surrounding Lazio countryside and as far away as Sicily. It's here that you find standard Italian favorites (like Pacchino tomatoes, peppers, and eggplant), as well as seasonal delicacies such as *puntarelle* (variety of chicory) and *carciofi romani* (artichokes). For more exotic fruits, visit the stand on the southeast corner—Claudio is reputed to be the pope's *frutti vendolo* (fruit man), thanks to such specialties as star fruit and white asparagus.

Campo's vendors also sell meats (of all beasts), regional cheeses, international spices, and homegrown honeys. On Tuesdays and Fridays, the *penscivendoli* (fish vendors) show off the morning's catch. A recent addition to the market are the several *bancarelle* (tchotchke stands) selling t-shirts, purses, bangles, and cookware. Though less charming than the fruit and flower stands, these bancarelle are great places to find off-beat *ricordi di Roma* (souvenirs) like Bialetti mokas (stovetop espresso-makers) and *"Ciao Roma"* t-shirts.

DRESS TO IMPRESS—OR DIGRESS?

Campo de' Fiori is one of Rome's best people-watching piazzas. Fashion-sense is either right on the money for marketgoers and late-night boozers (fanny packs and heavy metal t-shirts respectively), or else it is short-changed where style makes absolutely no sense. Combining both ends of the spectrum, *nonne* (grandmothers) catwalk in orthopedic shoes, accessorized with training-wheeled, plaid shopping bags, on the very cusp of trendy. If you come to Campo to shop for the perfect tomato, follow their lead—wear sensible shoes and bring a sturdy bag to hold all the day's goodies.

Rather sit stylishly at a caffè? Do like the Romans do: big sunglasses, shot of espresso, and a newspaper. Add a slight twist for the afternoon aperitivo by replacing the coffee and newspaper with a glass of prosecco or wine. Now this is what you came to Italy for!

Fashion Must Have: Umbrella

Fashion No-No: Ladies, leave the stilettos at home—there's nothing quite like watching a tube-topped, twenty-something twist her ankle in the *sampietrini*. Save those heels for the *discoteca*!

HERALD TRIBUNE TO HAUTE COUTURE

Missing some down-home gossip? Campo de' Fiori and the adjacent Piazza Farnese boast two of Rome's best newspaper kiosks that cater to the international set with publications from *Vogue* (French to Russian) to the *Herald Tribune*. On the streets adjacent to the Campo can be found boutiques to delight serious shoppers:

Via dei Giubbonari: standard shops

Via del Pellegrino: stylish boutiques

Via dei Cappellari: artisan craftwork (i.e. furniture restorers, frame makers, art galleries)

Piazza del Paradiso: cupcakes galore at The Perfect Bun Bakery (Piazza del Paradiso 56), morning sweeties such as scones and sticky buns at Nuyorica at Piazza della Pollarola 36.

Dining Al Fresco in the Campo de' Fiori

THE SUN ALSO RISES

Bars and caffès in Campo may look different but all have approximately the same menu, which makes choosing a bar very easy. Mornings mean coffee and pastries while evenings offer wine, beer, and mixed drinks. There is only one requirement for the ideal repast: sunshine. Romans stay away from the shadows. Rule of thumb: Sit on the sunny side of the piazza. FYI: For those who must work while at play, the majority of Campo's bars have Wi-Fi.

Caffè Farnese: a quiet morning cappuccino and newspaper

Obika: mozzarella-centric antipasti

Vineria Reggio: known for its inexpensive wine list

Sloppy Sam's and/or The Drunken Ship: if you are homesick for America

Giordano Bruno, who was burned at the stake here in 1600 for heresy. ✉ *Junction of Via dei Baullari, Via Giubbonari, Via del Pellegrino, and Piazza della Cancelleria, Campo.*

Fodor's Choice ★ **Palazzo Farnese.** The most beautiful Renaissance palace in Rome, the Palazzo Farnese is fabled for the Galleria Carracci, whose ceiling is to the Baroque age what the Sistine ceiling is to the Renaissance. The Farnese family rose to great power and wealth during the Renaissance, in part because of the favor Pope Alexander VI showed to the beautiful Giulia Farnese. The massive palace was begun when, with Alexander's aid, Giulia's brother became cardinal; it was further enlarged on his election as Pope Paul III in 1534. The uppermost frieze decorations and main window overlook-

> **THOSE LUCKY FRENCH**
>
> After completing his massive paintings for the Galleria of the Palazzo Farnese, it is said that Annibale Carracci was so dismayed at the miserly fee he received—the Farnese family was extravagantly rich even by the standards of 15th- and 16th-century Rome's extravagantly rich—that he took to drink and died shortly thereafter. Those who sympathize with the poor man's fate will be further dismayed to learn that the French government pays one euro every 99 years as rent for their sumptuous embassy (the Italian embassy has the same arrangement in Paris).

ing the piazza are the work of Michelangelo, who also designed part of the courtyard, as well as the graceful arch over Via Giulia at the back. The facade on Piazza Farnese has recently been cleaned, further revealing geometrical brick configurations that have long been thought to hold some occult meaning. When looking up at the palace, try to catch a glimpse of the splendid frescoed ceilings, including the **Galleria Carracci** vault painted by Annibale Carracci between 1597 and 1604. The Carracci gallery depicts the loves of the gods, a supremely pagan theme that the artist painted in a swirling style that announced the birth of the Baroque. Other opulent salons are among the largest in Rome, including the Salon of Hercules, which has an overpowering replica of the ancient *Farnese Hercules* front and center. For the first time, the French Embassy, which occupies the palace, now offers weekly tours in English; be sure to book in advance (at least eight days ahead is necessary in any case). Book online at ⊕ *www.inventerrome.com.* ✉ *French Embassy, Servizio Culturale, Piazza Farnese 67, Campo* ☎ *06/686011* ✎ *visite-farnese@inventerrome.it* ✉ *€5* ☉ *Open only to tours. English tour is Wed. at 3.*

★ **Palazzo Spada.** In this neighborhood of huge, austere palaces, Palazzo Spada strikes an almost frivolous note, with its upper stories covered with stuccos and statues and its pretty ornament-encrusted courtyard. While the palazzo houses an impressive collection of Old Master paintings, it is most famous for its trompe l'oeil garden gallery, a delightful example of the sort of architectural games rich Romans of the 17th century found irresistible. Even if you don't go into the gallery, step into the courtyard and look through the glass window of the library to the colonnaded corridor in the adjacent courtyard. See—or seem to see—Borromini's 8-meter-long gallery quadrupled in depth, a sort of optical telescope taking the Renaissance's art of perspective to another level, as it stretches out for a great distance with a large statue at the end. In fact the distance is an illusion: the corridor grows progressively narrower and the columns progressively smaller as they near the statue, which is just 2 feet tall. The Baroque prided itself on special effects, and this is rightly one of the most famous. It long was thought that Borromini was responsible for this ruse; it's now known that it was designed by an Augustinian priest, Giovanni Maria da Bitonto. Upstairs is a seignorial picture gallery with the paintings shown as they would have been, piled on top of each other clear to the ceiling. Outstanding works include Brueghel's *Landscape with Windmills,* Titian's *Musician,* and Andrea del Sarto's *Visitation.* Look for the fact sheets that have descriptive notes about the objects in each room. ⊠ *Piazza Capo di Ferro 13, Campo* ☎ *06/6874893, 06/8555952 guided tours, 06/6832409 information and ticket booking* ⊕ *www.galleriaborghese. it* ⊡ *€5* ☉ *Tues.–Sun. 8:30–7:30.*

Sant'Andrea della Valle. Topped by the highest dome in Rome (designed by Maderno) after St. Peter's, this huge and imposing 17th-century church is remarkably balanced in design. Fortunately, its facade, which had been turned a sooty gray from pollution, has been recently cleaned to a near-sparkling white. Use the handy mirror that's provided to examine the early-17th-century frescoes in the choir vault by Domenichino and those by Lanfranco in the dome. One of the earliest ceilings done in full Baroque style, its upward vortex was influenced by Correggio's dome in Parma, of which Lanfranco was also a citizen. (Bring a few coins to light the paintings, which can be very dim.) The three massive paintings of Saint Andrew's martyrdom are by Maria Preti (1650–51). Richly marbled and decorated chapels flank the nave, and in such a space, Puccini set the first act of *Tosca.* ⊠ *Piazza Vidoni 6, Corso Vittorio Emanuele II, Campo* ☎ *06/6861339* ☉ *Weekdays and Sat. 7:30–noon and 4:30–7:30; Sun. 7:30–12:45 and 4:30–7:45.*

Fodor'sChoice ★ **Via Giulia.** Still a Renaissance-era diorama and one of Rome's most exclusive addresses, Via Giulia was the first street in Rome since ancient times to be laid out in a straight line. Named for Pope Julius II (of Sistine Chapel fame) who commissioned it in the early 1500s as part of a scheme to open up a grandiose approach to St. Peter's Basilica (using funds from the taxation of prostitutes), it became flanked with elegant churches and palaces. Though the pope's plans to change the face of the city were only partially completed, Via Giulia became an important thoroughfare in Renaissance Rome. Today, after more than four centuries, it remains the "salon of Rome," address of choice for Roman aristocrats. A stroll will reveal elegant palaces and old churches (one, **San Eligio,** at No. 18, reputedly designed by Raphael himself). The area around Via Giulia is a wonderful section to wander through and get the feel of daily life as carried on in a centuries-old setting. Among the buildings that merit your attention are **Palazzo Sacchetti** (⊠ *Via Giulia 66*), with an imposing stone portal (inside are some of Rome's grandest state rooms, still, after 300 years, the private quarters of the Marchesi Sacchetti), and the forbidding brick building that housed the **Carceri Nuove,** "New Prison," (⊠ *Via Giulia 52*), Rome's prison for more than two centuries and now the offices of Direzione Nazionale Antimafia. Near the bridge that arches over the southern end of Via Giulia is the church of **Santa Maria dell'Orazione e Morte** (Holy Mary of Prayer and Death), with stone skulls on its door. These are a symbol of a confraternity that was charged with burying the bodies of the unidentified dead found in the city streets. Home since 1927 to the Hungarian Academy, the **Palazzo Falconieri** (⊠ *Via Giulia 1* ☎ *06/6889671*) was designed by

> ## TOSCA'S ROME
>
> Puccini lovers have been known to hire a horse-drawn carriage at night for an evocative journey that traces the course of the opera: from Sant'Andrea della Valle (on Corso Vittorio Emanuele II), then south on Via Biscione to head up Via Giulia past Palazzo Farnese—Scarpia's headquarters—to the locale of the opera's climax, Castel Sant'Angelo.

Borromini—note the architect's roof-top belvedere adorned with statues of the family "falcons," best viewed from around the block along the Tiber embankment. ■TIP➜ **With a prior booking and a €5 fee, you can visit the Borromini-designed salons and loggia.** Remnant of a master plan by Michelangelo, the arch over the street was meant to link massive Palazzo Farnese, on the east side of Via Giulia, with the building across the street and a bridge to the Villa Farnesina, directly across the river. Finally, on the right and rather green with age, dribbles that star of many a postcard, the Fontana del Mascherone. ⊠ *Between Piazza dell'Oro and Piazza San Vincenzo Pallotti, Campo.*

WORTH NOTING

★ **San Giovanni dei Fiorentini.** Imbued with the supreme grace of the Florentine Renaissance, this often-overlooked church dedicated to Florence's patron saint, John the Baptist, stands in what was the heart of the Florentine colony in Rome's *centro storico.* Many of these Florentines were goldsmiths, bankers, and money changers who contributed to the building of the church. Talented goldsmith and sculptor Benvenuto Cellini of Florence, known for his vindictive nature as much as for his genius, lived nearby. While the church was designed by Sansovino, Raphael (yes, he was also an architect) was among those who competed for this commission. Today, the church interior makes you feel you have wandered inside a perfect Renaissance space, one so harmonious it seems to be a Raphael pop-up 3-D painting. Borromini executed a splendid altar for the Falconieri family chapel in the choir. He's buried under the dome, despite the fact that those who committed suicide normally were refused a Christian burial. The late animal-loving pastor allowed well-behaved pets to keep their owners company at services, a tradition that lives on today. ⊠ *Via Accaioli 2, Piazza dell'Oro, Campo* ☎ *06/68892059* ☾ *Daily 7:30–noon and 5–7.*

Corso and Spagna

WORD OF MOUTH

"Lurking around the Trevi fountain, several Fodorites were acting mysteriously: what were they up to?" PalenQ. "They wanted to reenact the famous scene from *La Dolce Vita*?" Kismetchimera. "A modern dance interpretation of *Swan Lake*?" mcnyc. "Trying to figure out if they could get the marble horses in their carry-ons?" MelJ. "Trying to swap Euro coins for U.S.?" cfc. "Clifton Webb's body is buried within the Trevi Fountain," George W.

GETTING ORIENTED

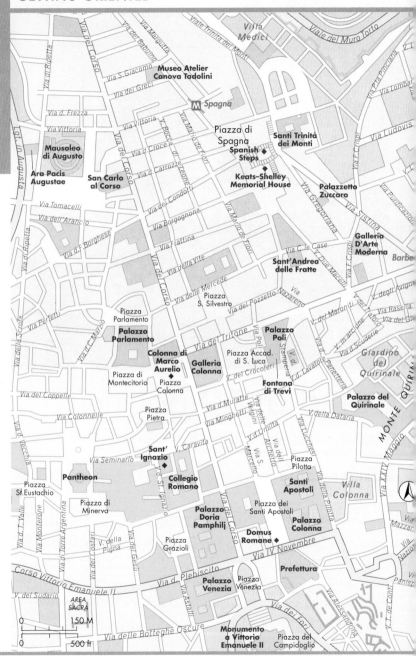

Villa Medici

Viale Trinità dei Monti

Via del Muro Torto

Museo Atelier
Canova Tadolini

M Spagna

Piazza di
Spagna
Spanish
Steps

Santi Trinità
dei Monti

Mausoleo
di Augusto

Ara Pacis
Augustae

San Carlo
al Corso

Keats–Shelley
Memorial House

Palazzetto
Zuccaro

Galleria
D'Arte
Moderna

Barbe

Sant'Andrea
delle Fratte

Piazza
S. Silvestro

Piazza
Parlamento

Palazzo
Parlamento

Palazzo
Poli

Colonna di
Marco
Aurelio

Galleria
Colonna

Piazza Accad.
di S. Luca

Piazza di
Montecitorio

Piazza
Colonna

Fontana
di Trevi

Giardino
del
Quirinale

Palazzo del
Quirinale

Piazza
Pietra

Sant'
Ignazio

Piazza
Pilotta

Pantheon

Piazza
St.Eustachio

Collegio
Romano

Santi
Apostoli

Villa
Colonna

Piazza di
Minerva

Palazzo
Doria
Pamphilj

Piazza dei
Santi Apostoli

Palazzo
Colonna

Domus
Romane

Piazza
Grazioli

Prefettura

Corso Vittorio Emanuele II

V. del Sudario

AREA
SACRA

150 M

500 ft

Palazzo
Venezia

Piazza
Venezia

Via delle Botteghe Oscure

Monumento
a Vittorio
Emanuele II

Piazza del
Campidoglio

TOP 5 REASONS TO GO

Trevi Fountain: In the pantheon of waterworks, this is Elvis—overblown, flashy, and reliably thronged by its legions of fans.

The Spanish Steps: Sprawl seductively on the world's most celebrated stairway—everyone's doing it. If you're able to make it to the top, a Cinerama view awaits you.

See Heaven: Stand beneath the stupendous ceiling of San Ignazio—Rome's most splendiferous Baroque church—and, courtesy of painter-priest Fra Andrea Pozzo, prepare to be transported heavenward.

Lifestyles of the Rich and Famous: Take a peek through the keyhole of two of Rome's grandest palaces, the Palazzo Doria-Pamphilj and the Palazzo Colonna, for an intimate look at the homes of Rome's 17th-century grandees.

Luxe Shopping on Via Condotti: You can get from Bulgari to Gucci to Valentino to Ferragamo with no effort at all, except perhaps that of navigating (and ogling) the crowds of shoppers.

OK, WHERE DO I START?

Begin at Piazza Venezia, the square in front of the gigantic monument to Vittorio Emanuele II. Head north on Via del Corso, Rome's main drag (or, a must if it is Saturday morning, head east one block to the gilded Palazzo Colonna art collection), for a block or so to dazzling Palazzo Doria Pamphilj, loaded with priceless Old Master paintings and one resident prince. Farther up the Corso, Via di Sant'Ignazio leads to the 18th-century stage-set of Piazza di Sant'Ignazio, home to the Church of Sant'Ignazio, where the famous ceiling frescoes hold a surprise or two.

A few blocks farther up the Corso, turn right and you'll soon hear the enchanting Fontana di Trevi. Continuing northwest you'll hit that postcard icon, the Spanish Steps, surrounded by Rome's most glamorous shops.

BEST TIME-OUTS

Caffè Ciampini. Just off the Corso in the jewel of a piazza, San Lorenzo in Lucina, sits this turn-of-the-century tearoom-gelateria-caffè. Stand at the elegant bar for a quick espresso, or pay a bit more to sit outdoors under a big umbrella, lingering over an aperitivo and a plateful of yummy hors d'oeuvres that come with it. ⊠ *Piazza San Lorenzo in Lucina 29, Corso* ☎ *06/6876606.*

La Campana. La Campana, which a document dates way back to 1518, still remains a favorite for its honest Roman cuisine, slightly upmarket feel (white tablecloths! professional servers!), moderate prices, and the best *coda alla vaccinara* (oxtail) in Rome. ⊠ *Vicolo della Campana 18, Navona* ☎ *06/6875273* ⊕ *www.ristorantelacampana. com.*

GETTING HERE

A short walking distance from Piazza del Popolo, the Pantheon, and the Trevi Fountain, the "Spagna" area of the Spanish Steps is nearly impossible to miss. One of Rome's handiest subway stations, Spagna, is tucked just left of the steps (complete with elevator to spare the climb to the top if need be). Buses No. 117 and No. 119 hum through the area (the latter tootles up Via del Balbuino, famed for its shops); the No. 117 from the Colosseum and the No. 119 from Piazza del Popolo.

6

Sightseeing
★ ★ ★ ★ ★

Nightlife
★

Dining
★ ★ ★ ★ ★

Lodging
★ ★ ★ ★ ★

Shopping
★ ★ ★ ★ ★

In spirit, and in fact, this section of Rome is its most grandiose. The overblown Vittoriano monument, the labyrinthine treasure-chest palaces of Rome's surviving aristocracy, even the diamond-draped denizens of Via Condotti: all embody the exuberant ego of a city at the center of its own universe. Here's where you'll see ladies in furs, picking at pastries at *caffè* tables, and walk through a thousand snapshots as you climb the famous Spanish Steps, admired by generations from Byron to Versace. As if to keep up with the area's gilded palaces, the local monuments seem aware that they, too, are expected to put on a show.

Right at the top of everyone's sightseeing list is the great Baroque confection of the Trevi Fountain: the Elton John of hydrants tinkling tirelessly for its droves of fans. Legend has it that a coin in the water guarantees a return. Even the most rational of us may find it hard to resist throwing one in, just in case. Since pickpockets favor this tourist-heavy spot, be particularly aware as you withdraw that wallet to keep your throw from being very expensive indeed. The Trevi is Rome's most celebrated waterwork, and you can rest assured, you are not the only one who knows it. Once you've chucked in your change, follow the crowds and get ready to take some very serious time to explore this neighborhood, which extends along Via del Corso, the ruler-straight avenue that divides central Rome neatly in half.

If Rome has a Main Street, it's Via del Corso, which is often jammed with swarms of Roman teenagers, in from the city's outlying districts for a ritual stroll that resembles a strutting migration of lemmings in blue jeans. Corso begins at noisy, chaotic Piazza Venezia, the imperial-size hub of all this ostentation, presided over by the Vittoriano, also known as the Altare della Patria (Altar of the Nation), or, less piously, as the "typewriter," the "wedding cake," or the Eighth Hill of Rome. Sitting grandly off the avenue are the Palazzo Doria-Pamphilj and the Palazzo Colonna—two of the city's great art collections housed in magnificent family palaces.

Extending just east of Via del Corso, but miles away in style, Piazza di Spagna and its surrounding streets are where the elite meet. Back when, 19th-century artists used to troll the area around the Spanish Steps for models; today, it remains a magnet all day and well into the night for smooching Romans and camera-toting tourists. The density of high-fashion boutiques and trendy little shops leaves little room for any but the richest of residents: the locals are the ladies loaded down with Prada bags and tottering on Gucci stilettos. Lest you think the neighborhood is all Johnny-come-lately frivolity, stop into the Antico Caffè Greco, the one-time haunt of Franz Lizst, Mark Twain, and Hans Christian Andersen. It's been operating since 1760, making it one of the oldest caffè in the world. Prepare to linger.

AROUND VIA DEL CORSO

Because of the 20th-century grime, traffic-ridden Via del Corso appears to be nothing more than a major thoroughfare connecting Piazza Venezia and Piazza del Popolo. In fact, between dodging Vespas, it's easy to forget that the gray and stolid atmosphere comes partially from the enormous palaces lining both sides of the street. Most of them were built over the past 300 years by princely families who wanted to secure front-row seats for the frantic antics of Carnevale. But once you step past entrances here, you'll discover some of Rome's grandest 17th- and 18th- century treasures, including Baroque ballrooms, glittering churches, and great Old Master paintings. And, oh, yes, the god-size and thundering Trevi Fountain. For that, be sure to have your camera—and coins—ready.

TOP ATTRACTIONS

★ **Ara Pacis Augustae** (*Altar of Augustan Peace*). This vibrant monument of the imperial age has been housed in one of Rome's newest architectural landmarks: a gleaming, rectangular glass-and-travertine structure designed by American architect Richard Meier. Overlooking the Tiber on one side and the ruins of the marble-clad **Mausoleo di Augusto** (Mausoleum of Augustus) on the other, the result is a serene, luminous oasis right in Rome's center. Opened in 2006, after a decade of bitter controversy over the monument's relocation, the altar itself dates back to 13 BC; it was commissioned to celebrate the Pax Romana, the era of peace ushered in by Augustus's military victories. It is covered with spectacular and moving relief sculptures. Like all ancient Roman monuments of this type, you have to imagine them painted in vibrant colors, now long gone. The reliefs on the short sides show myths associated with Rome's founding and glory; the long sides display a procession of the imperial family. It's fun to try to play "who's who"—although half of his body is missing, Augustus is identifiable as the first full figure at the procession's head on the south-side frieze—but academics still argue over exact identifications. Notice the poignant presence of several forlorn children; historians now believe they attest to the ambition of Augustus's notorious wife, the Empress Livia, who gained the throne for her son, Tiberius, by dispatching his family rivals with poison, leaving a slew of orphans in her wake. ✉ *Lungotevere in Augusta, around Via del Corso* ☎ *06/0608* ⊕ *www.arapacis.it* ✉ *€7.50* ☉ *Tues.–Sun. 9–7 (last admission 1 hr before closing)* Ⓜ *Flaminio (Piazza del Popolo).*

Fodor'sChoice
★
Le Domus Romane di Palazzo Valentini. If you find your imagination stretching to picture Rome as it was two millennia ago, make sure to check out this "new" ancient site just a stone's throw from Piazza Venezia. As commonly done in Renaissance-era Rome, 16th-century builders filled in the ancient structures with landfill, using them as foundations for Palazzo Valentini. Unwittingly, the builders also preserved the ruins beneath, which archaeologists rediscovered in 2007 excavations. It took another three years for the two opulent, Imperial-era villas to open to the public on a regular basis.

Descending below Palazzo Valentini, which has been the seat of the *Provincia* of Rome since 1873, is like walking into another world. Not only are the villas luxurious and well preserved, still retaining their beautiful mosaics, inlaid marble floors, and staircases, but—unlike any other site in Rome—the ruins have been made to "come alive" through multimedia. Sophisticated light shows re-create what it all would have looked like while a dramatic, automated voiceover accompanies you as you walk through the rooms, pointing out cool finds (the heating system for the private baths, the mysterious fragment of a statue, the porcelain dumped here when part of the site became a dump in the Renaissance) and evidence of tragedy (the burn layer from a fire that ripped through the home). If it sounds corny, hold your skepticism: It's an effectively done, excellent way to actually "experience" the villa as ancient Romans would have—and learn a lot about ancient Rome in the process. A multimedia presentation halfway through also shows you what central Rome would have looked like 2,000 years ago.

The multimedia tour takes about an hour. There are limited spots, so book in advance over the phone, online, or by stopping by in person; make sure you book the English tour. The tour should be enjoyable for older children, but little ones might be afraid of how dark the rooms can be. ✉ *Via IV Novembre 119/A, near Piazza Venezia* ☎ *06/32810,* ⊕ *www.palazzovalentini.it* ✉ *€7.50.*

Monumento a Vittorio Emanuele II, or Altare della Patria (*Victor Emmanuel Monument, or Altar of the Nation*). The huge white mass of the "Vittoriano" is an inescapable landmark—Romans say you can avoid its image only if you're actually standing on it. Some have likened it to a huge wedding cake; others, to an immense typewriter. Though not held in the highest esteem by present-day citizens, it was the source of great civic pride at the time of its construction, at the turn of the 20th century. To create this elaborate marble monster and the vast piazza on which it stands, architects blithely destroyed many ancient and medieval buildings and altered the slope of the Capitoline Hill, which abuts it. Built to honor the unification of Italy and the nation's first king, Victor

Three Coins and a Triton

Who hasn't wanted to emulate Dorothy McGuire, Jean Peters, and Maggie McNamara in *Three Coins in the Fountain*—your Roman fountain fantasy will cost no more than the change in your pocket, and who knows? Your wish might come true.

Anyone who's thrown a coin backward over a shoulder into the Fontana di Trevi to ensure a return to Rome appreciates the magic of the city's fountains.

From the magnificence of the Fontana dei Quattro Fiumi in Piazza Navona to the graceful caprice of the Fontana delle Tartarughe in the Ghetto, the water-spouting sculptures seem as essential to the piazzas they inhabit as the cobblestones and ocher buildings that surround them.

Rome's original fountains date back to ancient times, when they were part of the city's remarkable aqueduct system.

But from AD 537 to 1562 the waterworks were in disrepair and the city's fountains lay dry and crumbling. Romans were left to draw their water from the Tiber and from wells.

During the Renaissance, the popes brought running water back to the city as a means of currying political favor.

To mark the restoration of the Virgin Aqueduct, architect Giacomo della Porta designed 18 unassuming, functional fountains.

Each consisted of a large basin with two or three levels of smaller basins in the center, which were built and placed throughout the city at points along the water line.

Although nearly all of della Porta's fountains remain, their spare Renaissance design is virtually unrecognizable. With the Baroque era, most were elaborately redecorated with dolphins, obelisks, and sea monsters.

Of this next generation of Baroque fountaineers, the most famous is Gian Lorenzo Bernini.

Bernini's writhing, muscular creatures of myth adorn most of Rome's most visible fountains, including the Fontana di Trevi (perhaps named for the three streets—*tre vie*—that converge at its piazza); the Fontana del Nettuno, with its tritons, in Piazza Barberini; and, in Piazza Navona, the Fontana dei Quattro Fiumi, whose hulking figures represent the four great rivers of the known world: the Nile, the Ganges, the Danube, and the Plata.

The most common type of fountain in Rome is a kind rarely noted by visitors: the small, inconspicuous drinking fountains that burble away from side-street walls, old stone niches, and fire hydrant–like installations on street corners.

You can drink this water. Many of these *fontanelle* even have pipes fitted with a little hole from which water shoots up when you hold your hand under the main spout.

To combine the glorious Roman fountain with a drink of water, head to Piazza di Spagna, where the Barcaccia fountain is outfitted with spouts from which you can wet your whistle.

6

Emmanuel II, it also shelters the eternal flame at the tomb of Italy's Unknown Soldier killed during World War I. The flame is guarded day and night by sentinels, while inside the building there is the (rather dry) Institute of the History of the Risorgimento. You can't avoid the *monumento*, so enjoy neo-imperial grandiosity at its most bombastic.

The views from the top are some of Rome's most panoramic. The only way up is by elevator (located to the right as you face the monument); stop at the museum entrances (to the left and right of the structure) to get a pamphlet identifying the sculpture groups on the monument itself and the landmarks you will be able to see once at the top. Opposite the monument, note the enclosed olive-green wooden veranda fronting the palace on the corner of Via del Plebiscito and Via Corso. For the many years that she lived in Rome, Napoléon's mother had a fine view from this spot of the local goings-on. ⊠ *Entrance at Piazza Ara Coeli, next to Piazza Venezia, around Via del Corso* ☎ *06/0608* ⊕ *www.060608. it* ✉ *Monument free, museum free, elevator €7* ☉ *Elevator open Mon–Thurs. 9:30–5:45; Fri. and weekends 9:30–6:45; stairs open winter 9:30–4:30, summer 9:30–5:30.*

Fodor's Choice **Palazzo Colonna.** Rome's grandest family built itself Rome's grandest
★ palazzo in the 18th century—it's so immense, it faces Piazza Santi Apostoli on one side and the Quirinal Hill on the other (a little bridge over Via della Pilotta links the palace with the gardens on the hill). While still home to some Colonna patricians, the palace also holds the family picture gallery, open to the public one day a week. The galleria is itself a setting of aristocratic grandeur; you'll recognize the **Sala Grande** as the site where Audrey Hepburn meets the press in *Roman Holiday*. At one end looms the ancient red marble column (*colonna* in Italian), which is the family's emblem; above the vast room is the spectacular ceiling fresco of the Battle of Lepanto painted by Giovanni Coli and Filippo Gherardi in 1675—the center scene almost puts the computer-generated special effects of Hollywood to shame. Adding redundant luster to the opulently stuccoed and frescoed salons are works by Poussin, Tintoretto, and Veronese, and a number of portraits of illustrious members of the family such as Vittoria Colonna—Michelangelo's muse and longtime friend—and Marcantonio Colonna, who led the papal forces in the great naval victory at Lepanto in 1577. Lost in the array of madonnas, saints, goddesses, popes, and cardinals is, spoon at the ready, with mouth missing some front teeth, Annibale Carracci's lonely *Bean-eater*. As W.H. Auden put it, "Grub first, art later." At 11:45, there's a guided tour in English, included in your entrance fee. ⊠ *Via della Pilotta 17, around Via del Corso* ☎ *06/6784350* ⊕ *www. galleriacolonna.it* ✉ *€10* ☉ *Sat. 9–1:15, English tour 11:45.*

Fodor's Choice **Palazzo Doria Pamphilj.** Along with the Palazzo Colonna and the Gal-
★ leria Borghese, this spectacular family palace provides the best glimpse of aristocratic Rome. Here, the main attractions are the legendary Old Master paintings, including treasures by Velázquez and Caravaggio, the splendor of the main galleries, and a unique suite of private family apartments. The beauty of the graceful 18th-century facade of this patrician palace may escape you unless you take time to step to the

TREVI FOUNTAIN

✉ *Piazza di Trevi, accessed by Via Tritone, Via Poli, Via delle Muratte, Via del Lavatore, and Via di San Vincenzo, Trevi.*

TIPS

■ Everyone knows the famous legend that if you throw a coin into the Trevi Fountain you will ensure a return trip to the Eternal City. But not everyone knows how to do it the right way: You must toss a coin with your right hand over your left shoulder, with your back to the fountain. One coin means you'll return to Rome; two, you'll return and fall in love; three, you'll return, find love, and marry. The fountain grosses some €600,000 a year, and aside from incidences of opportunists fishing coins from the water, all of the money goes to charity.

■ Even though you might like to reenact Anita Ekberg and Marcello Mastroianni's famous Trevi dip in La Dolce Vita, be forewarned that police guard the fountain 24 hours a day to keep out movie buffs and lovebirds alike. Transgressors risk a fine of up to €500.

■ Around the corner, the Gelateria San Crispino (Via della Panetteria 42, 06/6793924) is for discerning palettes, with unusual taste combinations and natural ingredients.

Alive with rushing waters commanded by an imperious Oceanus, the Fontana di Trevi (Trevi Fountain) earned full-fledged iconic status in 1954 when it starred in 20th-Century Fox's *Three Coins in the Fountain.* As the first color film in Cinemascope to be produced on location, it caused practically half of America to pack their bags for the Eternal City.

From the very start, however, the Trevi has been all about theatrical effects. An aquatic marvel in a city filled with them, the fountain's unique drama is largely due to the site: its vast basin is squeezed into the tight meeting of three little streets (the *tre vie*, which may give the fountain its name) with cascades emerging as if from the wall of Palazzo Poli.

The conceit of a fountain emerging full-force from a palace was first envisioned by Bernini and Pietro da Cortona for Pope Urban VIII's plan to rebuild the fountain (which marked the end-point of the ancient Acqua Vergine aqueduct, created in 18 BC by Agrippa).

Only three popes later, under Pope Clement XIII, did Nicolo Salvi finally break ground with his winning design.

Salvi had his cake and ate it, too, for while he dazzles the eye with Baroque pyrotechnics—the sculpted seashells, the roaring seabeasts, the divalike mermaids—he has slyly incorporated them in a stately triumphal arch (in fact, Clement was then restoring Rome's Arch of Constantine).

Salvi, unfortunately, did not live to see his masterpiece completed in 1762: working in the culverts of the aqueduct 11 years earlier, he caught his death of cold and died.

6

opposite side of the street for a good view; it was designed by Gabriele Valvassori in 1730. The foundations of the immense complex of buildings probably date from classical times. The current building dates from the 15th century, with the exception of the facade. It passed through several hands before it became the property of the famous seafaring Doria family of Genoa, who had married into the Roman Pamphilj (also spelled Pamphili) clan. As in most of Rome's older patrician residences, the family still lives in part of the palace.

Housed in four *braccia* (wings) that line the palace's courtyard, the picture gallery contains 550 paintings, including three pictures by Caravaggio—a young *St. John the Baptist, Mary Magdalene,* and the breathtaking *Rest on the Flight to Egypt.* Off the eyepopping **Galleria degli Specchi** (Gallery of Mirrors)—a smaller version of the one at Versailles—are the famous Velázquez *Pope Innocent X,* considered by some historians to be the greatest portrait ever painted, and the Bernini bust of the same Pamphilj pope. Elsewhere you'll find a Titian, a double portrait by Raphael, and some noted 17th-century landscapes by Claude Lorrain and Gaspar Dughet. The audio guide by Prince Jonathan Doria Pamphilj, the current heir (born in England, he was adopted by the late Principessa Orietta), provides an intimate family history well worth listening to. ⊠ *Via del Corso 305, around Via del Corso* ☎ *06/6797323* ⊕ *www.doriapamphilj.it* ⊠ *€10.50* ⊘ *Daily 10–5.*

Fodor's Choice
★
Sant'Ignazio. Rome's largest Jesuit church, this 17th-century landmark harbors some of the most city's magnificent trompe-l'oeil paintings. To get the full effect of the marvelous illusionistic ceiling by priest-artist Andrea Pozzo, stand on the small disk set into the floor of the nave. The heavenly vision above you, seemingly extending upward almost indefinitely, represents the *Allegory of the Missionary Work of the Jesuits* and is part of Pozzo's cycle of works in this church exalting the early history of the Jesuit Order, whose founder was the reformer Ignatius of Loyola. The saint soars heavenward, supported by a cast of thousands; not far behind is Saint Francis Xavier, apostle of the Indies, leading a crowd of Eastern converts; a bare-breasted, spear-wielding America in American Indian headdress rides a jaguar; Europe with crown and scepter sits serene on a heftily rumped horse; while a splendid Africa with gold tiara perches on a lucky crocodile. The artist repeated this illusionist technique, so popular in the late 17th century, in the false dome, which is actually a flat canvas—a trompe l'oeil trick used when the budget drained dry. The overall effect of the frescoes is dazzling (be sure to have coins handy for the machine that switches on the lights) and was fully intended to rival that produced by Baciccia in the nearby mother church of Il Gesù. Scattered around the nave are several awe-inspiring altars; their soaring columns, gold-on-gold decoration, and gilded statues make these the last word in splendor. The church is often host to concerts of sacred music performed by choirs from all over the world. Look for posters at the church doors for more information. ⊠ *Piazza Sant'Ignazio, around Via del Corso* ☎ *06/6794560* ⊘ *Daily 7:30–7.*

WORTH NOTING

Colonna di Marco Aurelio. Inspired by Trajan's Column, this 2nd-century AD column is composed of 27 blocks of marble covered in reliefs recording Marcus Aurelius's victory over the Germans. A bronze statue of St. Paul, which replaced the effigy of Marcus Aurelius in the 16th century, stands at the top. The column is the centerpiece of Piazza Colonna. ⊠ *Piazza Colonna, alongside Via del Corso.*

Palazzo Venezia. Centerpiece of Piazza Venezia, this palace was originally built for Venetian cardinal Pietro Barbo, who became Pope Paul II. It was also the backdrop used by Mussolini to harangue crowds with dreams of empire from the balcony over the main portal. Lights were left on through the night during his reign to suggest that the Fascist leader worked without pause. The palace shows a mixture of Renaissance grace and heavy medieval lines. Generally, however, the only way to see the handsome salons inside is when there is a temporary exhibition on. The caffè on the loggia has a pleasant view over the garden courtyard. ⊠ *Via del Plebiscito 118, around Via del Corso* ☎ *06/69994388* ☙ *Tues.–Sun. 8:30–7:30 during exhibitions.*

Piazza Venezia. The geographic heart of Rome, this is the spot from which all distances from Rome are calculated and the principal crossroads of city traffic. Piazza Venezia stands at what was the beginning of Via Flaminia, the ancient Roman road leading east across Italy to Fano on the Adriatic Sea. The Via Flaminia was, and remains, a vital artery. Its initial tract, from Piazza Venezia to Piazza del Popolo, is now known as Via del Corso, after the horse races (*corse*) that were run here during the wild Roman carnival celebrations of the 17th and 18th centuries. It also happens to be one of Rome's busiest shopping streets. The massive female bust near the church of San Marco in the corner of the piazza, a fragment of the statue of Isis, is known to the Romans as Madama Lucrezia. This was one of the "talking statues" on which anonymous poets hung verses pungent with political satire, a practice that has not entirely disappeared. ⊠ *Junction of Via del Corso, Via Plebiscito, and Via Cesare Battisti, around Via del Corso.*

6

SPAGNA

Piazza di Spagna may be the soul of tourist Rome, but forget the "meet you at the Spanish Steps" thing—it can take hours to find familiar faces in the dense throng. Conversely, heavy crowds mean prime people-watching. Besides the riot of artists and panhandlers, there's an army of travelers, fashion snobs drawn by Rome's most elegant shops, and plenty of young Italians. This entire area also has hosted the grandest of Grand Tourists: Goethe, Lord Byron, the Brownings, and Buffalo Bill frequented the Antico Caffè Greco on Via Condotti. Piazza di Spagna's main draw, however, remains the 18th-century Spanish Steps, which connect ritzy shops at the bottom of the hill with ritzy hotels (and one lovely church) at the top. The reward for climbing the *scalinata* is a dizzying view of central Rome. Because the steps face west, the views are especially good around sunset.

TOP ATTRACTIONS

Keats-Shelley Memorial House. Sent to Rome in a last-ditch attempt to treat his consumption, English Romantic poet John Keats lived—and died—here, in the "Casina Rossa" (the name refers to the blush-pink facade) at the foot of the Spanish Steps. At that point, this was the heart of the colorful bohemian quarter of Rome that was especially favored by the English. Keats had become celebrated through such poems as "Ode to a Nightingale" and "She Walks in Beauty," but his trip to Rome was fruitless. He breathed his last here on February 23, 1821, aged only 25, forevermore the epitome of the doomed poet. In this "Casina di Keats," you can visit his rooms, although all his furnishings were burned after his death as a sanitary measure by the local authorities. You'll also find a rather quaint collection of memorabilia of English literary figures of the period—Lord Byron, Percy Bysshe Shelley, Joseph Severn, and Leigh Hunt as well as Keats—and an exhaustive library of works on the Romantics. ⊠ *Piazza di Spagna 26, Spagna* ☎ *06/6784235* ⊕ *www.keats-shelley-house.org* 🖃 *€4.50* ⊗ *Weekdays 10–1 and 2–6, Sat. 11–2 and 3–6* Ⓜ *Spagna.*

> ### A LITTLE CORNER OF ENGLAND
>
> **Babington's Tea Rooms.** On the left foot of the Spanish Steps is Babington's Tea Rooms, which has catered to the refined cravings of Anglo-Saxon travelers since opening in 1896. The *Inglesi* had long been a mainstay of Grand Tour visitors to Rome, so Anna Maria Babington found her "corner of England" a great success from the start. Inside, it is *molto* charming and you half expect to see Miss Lavish buttering a scone for Lucy Honeychurch, but it's not a budgeteer's cup of tea. ⊠ *Piazza di Spagna 23, Spagna* ☎ *06/6786027* ⊕ *www.babingtons.net* ⊗ *Daily 9–8:15.*

Museo-Atelier Canova Tadolini. A gorgeous remnant of Rome's 19th-century artistic milieu, this is the former atelier of Antonio Canova, Europe's greatest Neoclassic sculptor. Fabled for his frostily perfect statues of antique goddesses and fashionable princesses (sometimes in the same work, as in the Galleria Borghese's nearly naked *Principessa Pauline Borghese* posing as a "Victorious Venus"), he was given commissions by the poshest people. Today, his studio—atmospherically crammed to the gills with models, study sketches, and tools of the trade—has become a caffè and restaurant, so you can ogle Canova's domain for the price of a very expensive meal (or a cheaper coffee at the bar). ⊠ *Via del Babuino 150 A/B, Spagna* ☎ *06/32110702* ⊗ *Closed Sun.* Ⓜ *Spagna.*

Fodor'sChoice
★ **Palazzetto Zuccaro.** The most amusing house in all of Italy, this folly was designed in 1591 by noted painter Federico Zuccaro to form a monster's face. Typical of the outré Mannerist style of the period, the eyes are the house's windows; the entrance portal is through the monster's mouth. Zuccaro (1540–1609)—whose frescoes adorn many Roman churches, including Trinità del Monti just up the block—sank all of his money into his new home, dying in debt before his curious memorial, as it turned out to be, was completed. Today, it is the property of the

Biblioteca Hertziana, Rome's prestigious fine-arts library; unfortunately, at press time, the façade has been sheathed for a long-term renovation project, but when the wraps come off, it will return to its previous claim-to-fame: one of Rome's best photo ops, as many people like to be photographed in front of the main door with their own mouth wide open! Leading up to the quaint Piazza Trinità del Monti, Via Gregoriana is a real charmer and has long been one of Rome's most elegant addresses, home to such residents as 19th-century painter Ingres and writer Hans Christian Andersen, along with famed couturier Valentino's first couture salon. ⊠ *Via Gregoriana 30, Spagna* ☎ *06/69993421 Biblioteca Hertziana* Ⓜ *Spagna.*

Sant'Andrea delle Fratte. Copies have replaced Bernini's original angels on the Ponte Sant'Angelo, but two of the originals are here, on either side of the choir. The door in the right aisle leads into one of Rome's hidden gardens, where orange trees bloom in the cloister. Borromini's fantastic contributions—the dome and a curious bell tower with its droop-winged angels looking out over the city—are best seen from Via Capo le Case, across Via Due Macelli. ⊠ *Via Sant'Andrea delle Fratte 1 (Via della Mercede), Spagna* ☎ *06/6793191* ⊕ *www.santandreadellefratte.it* ⊙ *Apr.–Oct., daily 6:30–noon and 4:30–7:30; Nov.–Mar., daily 6:30–12:30 and 4–7* Ⓜ *Spagna.*

Fodor's Choice
★
Ⓒ

The Spanish Steps. That icon of postcard Rome, the Spanish Steps (often called simply *la scalinata*—"the staircase"—by Italians) and the Piazza di Spagna from which they ascend both get their names from the Spanish Embassy to the Vatican on the piazza—even though the staircase was built with French funds in 1723. In honor of a diplomatic visit by the king of Spain, the hillside was transformed by architect Francesco de Sanctis to link the church of Trinità dei Monti at the top with the Via dei Condotti below. In an allusion to the church, the staircase is divided by three landings (beautifully banked with azaleas from mid-April to mid-May). For centuries, the scalinata and its neighborhood have welcomed tourists, dukes, and writers in search of inspiration—among them Stendhal, Honoré de Balzac, William Makepeace Thackeray, and Byron, along with today's enthusiastic hordes. Bookending the bottom of the steps are two monuments to the 18th-century days when the English colonized the area: to the right, the Keats-Shelley House, to the left, Babington's Tea Rooms, both beautifully redolent of the Grand Tour era. For weary sightseers, there is an elevator at Vicolo del Bottino 8 (next to the adjacent Metro entrance). ■TIP→ In recent years, a low-grade but annoying scam has proliferated in the piazza. This is the "rose scam," where a man comes up to a female tourist with a rose and insists he's giving it to her for free. When she takes it, he waits a couple of beats and then goes to a gentleman in her party, asking for just a few euros for the flower. Often, everyone concerned is too embarrassed not to pay. If this happens to you, simply firmly refuse the rose from the beginning, or hand it back when you're asked for money. Unless you want it, of course! ⊠ *Junction of Via Condotti, Via del Babuino, and Via Due Macelli, Spagna* Ⓜ *Spagna.*

NEED A
BREAK?

Antico Caffè Greco. You may prefer to limit your shopping on Via Condotti to the window variety, but there's one thing here that everybody can afford—a stand-up coffee at the bar at the Antico Caffè Greco, set just off the Piazza di Spagna and the Fontana della Barcaccia. With its tiny marble-top tables and velour settees, this 200-year-old institution has long been the haunt of artists and literati; it's closed Sunday. Johann Wolfgang von Goethe, Byron, and Franz Liszt were habitués. Buffalo Bill stopped in when his road show hit Rome. The caffè is still a haven for writers and artists, along with plenty of Gucci-clad ladies. The tab picks up considerably if you decide to sit down to enjoy table service. ✉ *Via Condotti 86, Spagna* ☎ *06/6791700* ⊕ *www.anticocaffegreco.eu.*

Il Palazzetto. For the ultimate view from atop the Spanish Steps, you can climb up, taking the elevator from inside the Spagna Metro . . . or pay for the privilege at the glamorous wine bar Il Palazzetto, where an interior elevator takes you to the level of the top terrace. ✉ *Vicolo del Bottino 8, Spagna* ☎ *06/699341000* ⊕ *www.ilpalazzettoroma.com.*

WORTH NOTING

Fontana della Barcaccia (*Leaky Boat Fountain*). At the center of Piazza di Spagna and at the bottom of the Spanish Steps, this curious, half-sunken boat gently spills out water rather than cascading it dramatically; it may have been designed that way to make the most of the area's low water pressure. It was thanks to the Barberini pope Urban VIII, who commissioned the fountain, that there was any water at all in this area, which was becoming increasingly built up during the 17th century. He restored one of the ancient Roman aqueducts that once channeled water here. The bees and suns on the boat constitute the Barberini motif. Some insist that the Berninis (Pietro and his more famous son Gian Lorenzo) intended the fountain to be a reminder that this part of town was often flooded by the Tiber; others that it represents the Ship of the Church; and still others that it marks the presumed site of the emperor Domitian's water stadium in which sea battles were reenacted in the glory days of the Roman Empire. ✉ *Piazza del Spagna, Spagna* Ⓜ *Spagna.*

Gagosian Gallery. One of the most prestigious modern art galleries opened this Rome branch in 2007. In a former bank, temporary exhibitions include many mega-stars, including Cy Twombly, Damien Hirst, and Jeff Koons. ✉ *Via Francesco Crispi 16, Spagna* ☎ *06/42086498* ⊕ *www.gagosian.com* ☉ *Tues.–Sat. 10:30–7 and by appointment* Ⓜ *Spagna.*

Galleria d'Arte Moderna. After an 8-year renovation, Rome's modern art gallery reopened in fall 2011. The completely overhauled space—which happens to be the lovely, 18th-century convent of the Discalced Carmelites—perfectly shows off the gem of a collection, which focuses on Roman 19th- and 20th-century paintings, drawings, prints, and sculptures. With more than 3,000 pieces by artists like Giorgio de Chirico,

Gino Severini, Scipione, Antonio Donghi, and Giacomo Manzù, the permanent collection is too large all to be on display at once, so exhibits rotate. Regardless of what the particular exhibit is, stop by to soak in another side of the city: one where, in the near-empty halls, tranquillity and contemplation reign. ⊠ *Via Francesco Crispi 24, Spagna* ☏ *06/0608,* ⊕ *www.galleriaartemodernaroma.it* ☑ *€5.50* ☉ *Tues.–Sun. 10–6* Ⓜ *Spagna.*

Trinità dei Monti. Standing high above the Spanish Steps, this 16th-century church has a rare double-tower facade, suggestive of late-Gothic French style—in fact, the French crown paid for the church's construction. Today, it is beautiful primarily for its dramatic location and magnificent views. ⊠ *Piazza Trinità dei Monti, Spagna* ☏ *06/6794179* ☉ *Tues.–Sun. 8–1 and 3–8* Ⓜ *Spagna.*

Repubblica and Quirinale

PALAZZO DEL QUIRINALE, QUATTRO FONTANE,
PIAZZA DELLA REPUBBLICA, BATHS OF DIOCLETIAN

WORD OF MOUTH

"We were on our way to Santa Maria della Vittoria and another
Bernini masterpiece (man, did this guy ever get to sleep?), the
Ecstasy of St. Theresa. Although 'churched-out,' we still had some
of the biggies left to see before departing Rome, so there would
be no losing my religion today."   —maitaitom

GETTING ORIENTED

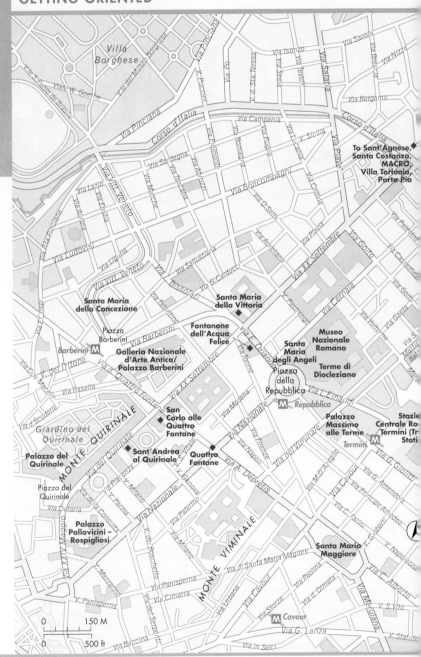

To Sant'Agnese,
Santa Costanza,
MACRO,
Villa Torlonia,
Porta Pia

Santa Maria
della Concezione

Santa Maria
della Vittoria

Piazza
Barberini

Fontanone
dell'Acqua
Felice

Museo
Nazionale
Romano

Barberini **M**

Galleria Nazionale
d'Arte Antica/
Palazzo Barberini

Santa
Maria
degli Angeli

Terme di
Diocleziano

Piazza
della
Repubblica

M Repubblica

Giardino del
Quirinale

San
Carlo alle
Quattro
Fontane

Palazzo
Massimo
alle Terme

Stazie
Centrale Ro
Termini (Tr
Stati

Palazzo del
Quirinale

MONTE QUIRINALE

Sant'Andrea
al Quirinale

Quattro
Fontane

Termini **M**

Piazza del
Quirinale

Palazzo
Pallavicini –
Rospigliosi

MONTE VIMINALE

Santa Maria
Maggiore

0   150 M

0   500 ft

M Cavour

GETTING HERE

Between Termini station and the Spanish Steps, this area is about a 15-minute walk from either. Bus No. 40 will get you from Termini to the Quirinale in two stops; from the Vatican take Bus No. 64. The very busy and convenient Repubblica Metro stop is on the piazza of the same name.

OK, WHERE DO I START?

Coming up from the Metro stop at Piazza della Repubblica, beyond the circular Fountain of the Naiads, you can see the church of Santa Maria degli Angeli, once part of Roman baths. Some of ancient Rome's best art is at the Palazzo Massimo alle Terme at the corner of nearby Piazza Cinquecento, while off another side of the same square stretches its sister museum, Museo di Terme di Diocleziano. To the northwest of Piazza Repubblica, Via Vittorio Emanuele Orlando leads to Piazza San Bernardo, where Santa Maria della Vittoria holds Bernini's famed *Ecstasy of St. Theresa*. Follow Via XX Settembre to Borromini's noted church of San Carlo alle Quattro Fontane—or take Via di Quattro Fontane down the hill to the magnificent Palazzo Barberini.

BEST TIME-OUT

Colline Emiliane. Around the corner from Piazza Barberini, this tiny, family-run trattoria serves up something different: excellent dishes from Emilia-Romagna, which some say is the best food region in Italy. It's a favorite with locals, so make a reservation for dinner. ⊠ *Via degli Avignonesi 22, Barberini* ☎ *06/4817538* Ⓜ *Barberini.*

Cremeria Bar Dagnino. With a wide enough assortment of creamy Sicilian pastries and ice-cream flavors to satisfy a mouthful of sweet tooths, the historic Cremeria Bar Dagnino in the Galleria Esedra on Piazza della Repubblica is the place to go. Enjoy the 1950s feel and the solid selection of dishes for lunch. ⊠ *Via Vittorio Emanuele Orlando 75, Repubblica* ☎ *06/4818660.*

TOP 5 REASONS TO GO

Bernini's Ecstasy of St. Theresa: Admire, or just blush at, the worldly realism of Theresa's allegedly spiritual rapture. Star of the Cappella Cornaro, this sculpture is a climax of Bernini's audacious fusion of architecture, painting, and sculpture.

Palazzo Barberini: Take in five centuries of art at one of Rome's greatest family palaces, where you can gape at Rome's biggest 18th-century ballroom and Raphael's *La Fornarina*.

Changing of the Guard: Snap photos of stony-faced guards as they march in formation at the Quirinale presidential palace, which perches atop the highest of ancient Rome's seven hills.

Santa Maria della Concezione: Contemplate eternity in a creepy, creative, and bizarre crypt "decorated" with the skeletons of 4,000 monks, replete with fluted arches made of collarbones and arabesques of shoulder blades.

On a Clear Day You Can See Forever: Crowning the Quirinale Hill—the loftiest of Rome's seven hills—is the Piazza del Quirinale, offering a spectacular view over the city, with the horizon marked by "Il Cupolino," the dome of St. Peter's. Framing the vista are the enormous ancient statues of Castor and Pollux—the "Discouri" (or Horse-Tamers)—which still give the Quirinale its nickname of Monte Cavallo ("Horse Hill").

7

Sightseeing
★★★★
Nightlife
★★
Dining
★★★★
Lodging
★★★★★
Shopping
★★★

Just west of Rome's modern Termini train station, this area offers an extraordinary Roman blend of old and new. Although ancient artworks, great Bernini sculptures, and Baroque landmarks lure the traveler, this was, for the most part, the "new" Rome of the 19th century: the area owes its broad avenues and dignified palazzos to the city's transformation after 1870, when it became the capital of a newly unified Italy. Toward Via Veneto, the influx of ministries set off a frenzied building boom and distinguished turn-of-the-20th-century architecture became the neighborhood's hallmark. As a gateway, Piazza della Repubblica was laid out to serve as a monumental foyer between the rail station and the rest of the city. And as this square proves, time in Rome comes layered like nowhere else on earth.

Flanking the train station's plate-glass entrance is an elephantine-colored mass of masonry that dates back millennia—a stretch of the so-called Servian Walls, the city boundary built when Rome was still a republic way back in the 6th century BC. Fast-forward about three centuries to find the piazza's main landmark, the vast ruins of the Baths of Diocletian (Terme di Diocleziano). They were subsequently transformed into a Renaissance monastery and, by Michelangelo's own design, to the church of Santa Maria degli Angeli. Following the layout of the ancient baths and the concave entrance to the church (with the nearby 1890s buildings curving likewise as if in tribute), the piazza is a square only in name. At its center lies the turn-of-the-20th-century Fountain of the Naiads, which works wonders with the Roman sunlight. Its busty nymphs and buffed sea tritons announce that beauty awaits at many of the sights in this district.

Off to the right, or west from Via Nazionale, lies the Quirinale, a hill set with various jewels of the Baroque era, including masterpieces by Bernini and Borromini. Nearby stands Palazzo Barberini, a grand and gorgeous 16th-century palace holding five centuries of master-works. For ancient art treasures, head for Palazzo Massimo, famed for the fabulously frescoed rooms of the Empress Livia's summer villa, colorful and vibrant with birds.

Mercifully situated away from traffic is the lofty Quirinale hill.
Crowning the piazza is the enormous Palazzo del Quirinale, built in the 16th century as a summer residence for the popes. It became the presidential palace in 1946; today you can tour its reception rooms, which are as splendid as you might imagine. The changing of the guard (daily at 4), outside on the piazza with its oversize stairway, is an old-fashioned exercise in pomp and circumstance.

> **FULL FRONTAL FASHION**
>
> Outside the gates of the Palazzo del Quirinale, you can see the changing of the military guard at 4pm daily, and occasionally you can glimpse the *corazzieri* (presidential guard). All extra-tall, they are a stirring sight in their magnificent crimson-and-blue uniforms, gleaming knee-high boots, and embossed steel helmets adorned with flowing manes.

While Bernini's work feels omnipresent in much of the city center, the Renaissance-man range of his work is particularly notable here. The artist as architect considered the church of Sant'Andrea al Quirinale one of his best; Bernini the urban designer and waterworker wrought the muscle-bound sea gods who wrestle so provocatively in the fountain at the center of whirling Piazza Barberini. And Bernini the master gives religious passion a joltingly corporeal treatment in what is perhaps his greatest work, the *Ecstasy of St. Theresa,* in the church of Santa Maria della Vittoria. Along with Bernini, this area has big boulevards, big buildings, and big delights.

REPUBBLICA

Climbing the stairs out of the Metro at Piazza della Repubblica feels like stepping into a tornado. The clanging of sirens and car horns, the squeal of brakes, and the roar of mopeds, not to mention the smell of the fast-food joints, may make you want to duck back down underground and get out at another stop. But to do so would be to miss out on a district featuring an array of fascinating attractions. The streets here may not be conducive to wandering but the ancient treasures at Palazzo Massimo, Bernini's spectacular Cornaro Chapel, and, farther afield, the modern MACRO museum will always be vying for your attention.

TOP ATTRACTIONS

Museo delle Terme di Diocleziano (*Baths of Diocletian*). Though part of the ancient structure is now the church of Santa Maria degli Angeli, and other parts were transformed into a Carthusian monastery or razed to make room for later urban development, a visit gives you an idea of the scale and grandeur of this ancient bathing establishment. Upon entering the church you see the major structures of the baths, partly covered by 16th- and 17th-century overlay, some of which is by Michelangelo. The monastery cloister is filled with the lapidary collection of the Museo Nazionale Romano while other rooms have archaeological works, along with a virtual representation of Livia's villa, which you can tour with the help of a joystick. ⊠ *Viale E. De Nicola 79, Repubblica* ☎ *06/39967700* 🎫 *€10, includes entrance to Palazzo Massimo, Palazzo Altemps, and Crypta Balbi* ☉ *Tues.–Sun. 9–7:45 (ticket office closes at 6:45)* Ⓜ *Repubblica.*

Fodor's Choice   **Palazzo Massimo alle Terme.** To get a real feel for ancient Roman art, don't
★   miss the Palazzo Massimo, whose collection rivals even the Vatican's. The Roman National Museum—with a collection ranging from striking classical Roman paintings to marble bric-a-brac—has been organized in four locations: Palazzo Massimo alle Terme, Palazzo Altemps, Crypta Balbi, and the Museo delle Terme di Diocleziano. The vast structure of the Palazzo Massimo holds the great ancient treasures of the archaeological collection and also the coin collection. Highlights include the *Niobid*, the famous bronze *Boxer*, and the *Discobolus Lancelloti*. Pride of place goes, however, to the great ancient frescoes on view, stunningly set up to "re-create" the look of the homes they once decorated. These include stuccos and wall paintings found in the area of the Villa della Farnesina (in Trastevere) and the legendary frescoes from Empress Livia's villa at Prima Porta, delightful depictions of a garden in bloom and an orchard alive with birds. Their colors are remarkably well preserved. These delicate decorations covered the walls of cool, sunken rooms in Livia's summer house outside the city. ■ TIP→ Admission includes entrance to all four national museums, good for three days. ⊠ *Largo Villa Peretti 1, Repubblica* ☎ *06/39967700* ⊕ *www.pierreci. it* 🎫 *€10* ☉ *Tues.–Sun. 9–7:45* Ⓜ *Repubblica.*

Piazza della Repubblica. Often the first view that spells "Rome" to weary travelers walking from the Stazione Termini, this broad square was laid out in the late 1800s and includes the exuberant **Fontana delle Naiadi** (Fountain of the Naiads). This pièce de résistance is draped with voluptuous bronze ladies wrestling happily with marine monsters. The nudes weren't there when the pope unveiled the fountain in 1870, sparing him any embarrassment. But when the figures were added in 1901, they caused a scandal: It's said that the sculptor, Rutelli, modeled them on the ample figures of two musical comedy stars of the day. The piazza owes its curved lines to the structures of the Terme di Diocleziano; the curving, colonnaded Neoclassical buildings on the southwest side trace the underlying form of the ancient baths. Today, one of them is occupied by the superdeluxe Hotel Exedra—which shows you how much the fortunes of the formerly tatterdemalion part of the city have changed. ⊠ *Junction of Via Nazionale, Via Vittorio Emanuele Orlando, and Via delle Terme di Diocleziano, Repubblica* Ⓜ *Repubblica.*

Fodor's Choice   **Santa Maria della Vittoria.** Like the church of Santa Susanna across Piazza
★   San Bernardo, this church was designed by Carlo Maderno, but this one is best known for Bernini's sumptuous Baroque decoration of the **Cappella Cornaro** (Cornaro Chapel), on the left as you face the altar,

where you'll find his interpretation of heavenly ecstasy in his statue of the *Ecstasy of St. Theresa* (⇨ *For more on Bernini, see "Baroque and Desperate: The Tragic Rivalry of Bernini and Borromini"*). Your eye is drawn effortlessly from the frescoes on the ceiling down to the marble figures of the angel and the swooning saint, to the earthly figures of the Cornaro family (who commissioned the chapel), to the two inlays of marble skeletons in the pavement, representing the hope and despair of souls in purgatory.

As evidenced in other works of the period, the theatricality of the chapel is the result of Bernini's masterly fusion of elements. This is one of the key examples of the mature Roman High Baroque. Bernini's audacious conceit was to model the chapel as a theater: Members of the Cornaro family—sculpted in colored marbles—watch from theater boxes as, center stage, the great moment of divine love is played out before them. The swooning saint's robes appear to be on fire, quivering with life, and the white marble group seems suspended in the heavens as golden rays illuminate the scene. An angel assists at the mystical moment of Theresa's vision as the saint abandons herself to the joys of heavenly love. Bernini represented this mystical experience in what, to modern eyes, may seem very earthly terms. Or, as the visiting dignitary President de Brosses put it in the 19th century, "If this is divine love, I know what it is." No matter what your reaction, you'll have to admit it's great theater. ⊠ *Via XX Settembre 17, Largo Santa Susanna, Repubblica* ☎ *06/42740571* ⊕ *www. chiesasmariavittoria.191.it* ⊗ *Daily 7–noon and 3:30–7* Ⓜ *Repubblica.*

★ **Villa Torlonia.** Built for aristocrats-come-lately, the Torlonia family—
Ⓒ the Italian Rockefellers of the 19th century—this villa became Mussolini's residence as prime minister under Italy's king and is now a public park. Long neglected, the park's vegetation and buildings are gradually being refurbished. Newly restored is the **Casina Nobile,** the main palace designed by the great architect Giuseppe Valadier. A grand, Neoclassical edifice, it comes replete with a gigantic ballroom, frescoed salons, and soaring templelike facade. While denuded of nearly all their furnishings and art treasures, some salons have important remnants of decor, including the reliefs once fashioned by the father of Italian Neoclassical sculpture, Antonio Canova. In the park, a complete contrast is offered by the **Casina delle Civette** (Little House of Owls), a hypercharming example of the Liberty (Art Nouveau) style of the early 1900s: the gabled, fairy-tale-like cottage-palace now displays majolica and stained-glass decorations, including windows with owl motifs, and

is a stunning, overlooked find for lovers of 19th-century decorative arts. Temporary exhibits are held in the small and elegant **Il Casino dei Principi** (The House of Princes), designed in part by Valadier. ✉ *Villa Torlonia, Via Nomentana 70, Piazza Bologna* ☎06/0608 ⊕*www. museivillatorlonia.it* ✉*Entrance to Casina delle Civette, Casino Nobile, and Casino dei Principi with temporary exhibit, €10; only Casino Nobile and Casino dei Principi with exhibit, €8* ☉ *Tues.–Sun. 9–7* Ⓜ *Repubblica, Bus 36 or 84.*

WORTH NOTING

Fontanone dell'Acqua Felice (*Fountain of Happy Water*). When Pope Sixtus V completed the restoration of the Acqua Felice aqueduct toward the end of the 16th century, Domenico Fontana was commissioned to design this commemorative fountain. As the story goes, a sculptor named Prospero da Brescia had the unhappy task of executing the central figure, which was to represent Moses (Sixtus liked to think of himself as, like Moses, having provided water for his thirsting population). The comparison with Michelangelo's magnificent *Moses* in the church of San Pietro in Vincoli was inevitable, and the largely disparaging criticism of Prospero's work is said to have driven him to his grave. A full cleaning, however, has left the fountain, whose Moses in recent years had looked as if he were dipped in soot, sparkling white—and uncovered a great deal of its charm. ✉ *Piazza San Bernardo, Repubblica* Ⓜ *Repubblica.*

MACRO. Formerly known as Rome's Modern and Contemporary Art Gallery, and before that formerly known as the Peroni beer factory, this redesigned industrial space has brought new life to the gallery and museum scene of a city formerly known for its then, not its now. The collection here covers Italian contemporary artists from the 1960s through today. Its sister museum, MACRO Testaccio (✉*Piazza O. Giustiniani*) is housed in a renovated slaughterhouse in Testaccio district, Rome's "Left Bank," and features temporary exhibits and installations by current artists. The goal of both spaces is to bring current art to the public in innovative spaces, and, not incidentally, to give support and recognition to Rome's contemporary art scene, which labors in the shadow of the city's artistic heritage. After a few days—or millennia—of dusty marble, it's a breath of fresh air. ✉ *Via Nizza 138, intersection with Via Cagliari, Repubblica* ☎ 06/671070400 ⊕*www.macro. roma.museum* ✉*€11 combined entrance to MACRO and MACRO Testaccio (good for 7 days)* ☉ *Tues.–Sun. 11–10 (ticket office closes at 9); MACRO Testaccio Tues.–Sun. 4–10 (when there's an exhibition)* Ⓜ *Repubblica; Bus 719 or 38.*

Santa Maria degli Angeli. The curving brick facade on the northeast side of Piazza della Repubblica is one small remaining part of the colossal Terme di Diocleziano, the largest and most impressive of the baths of ancient Rome. A gift to the city from Emperor Diocletian, it was erected about AD 300 with the forced labor of 40,000 Christians. In 1561 Michelangelo was commissioned to convert the vast *tepidarium*, the central hall of the baths, into a church. His work was altered by Vanvitelli in the 18th century, but the huge transept, which formed the nave in Michelangelo's plan, has remained as he adapted it. The eight enormous monolithic columns of red granite that support the great beams are the original columns of the tepidarium, 45 feet high and more than 5 feet in diameter. The great hall is 92 feet high. ⊠ *Via Cernaia 9, Repubblica* ☎ *06/4880812* ⊕ *www.santamariadegliangeliroma. it* ⊙ *Daily 7–7* Ⓜ *Repubblica.*

QUIRINALE

Rome's highest hill, the Quirinale has hosted ancient Roman senators, Renaissance popes (it was breezier here than at the Vatican) and, with the end of papal rule, Italy's kings. The latter took up residence in the palace that still diadems the hill, looking down the slope to where lordly families (the Colonna, for one) built palaces to be near all that power. In this district, the triumvirate of Rome's Baroque—Bernini, Borromini, and Pietro di Cortona—vie, even after four centuries, to amaze the visitor. As if Bernini and Borromini could not get away from each other, some of their greatest works are within blocks of each other.

TOP ATTRACTIONS

★ **Capuchin Crypt.** Not for the easily spooked, the crypt under the Church of Santa Maria della Concezione holds the bones of some 4,000 dead Capuchin monks. Arranged in odd decorative designs around the shriveled and decayed skeletons of their kinsmen, a macabre reminder of the impermanence of earthly life, the crypt is strangely touching and beautiful. As one sign proclaims: "What you are, we once were. What we are, you someday will be." Upstairs in the church, the first chapel on the right contains Guido Reni's mid-17th-century *St. Michael Trampling the Devil.* The painting caused great scandal after an astute contemporary observer remarked that the face of the devil bore a surprising resemblance to the Pamphili Pope Innocent X, archenemy of Reni's Barberini patrons. Compare the devil with the bust of the pope that you saw in the Palazzo Doria Pamphilj and judge for yourself. ⊠ *Via Veneto 27, Quirinale* ☎ *06/4871185* ⊕ *www.cappucciniviaveneto.it* ☙ *Donation of at least €1 for crypt* ⊙ *Fri.–Wed. 9–noon and 3–6* Ⓜ *Barberini.*

★ **Palazzo del Quirinale.** Pope Gregory XIII started building this spectacular palace, now the official residence of Italy's president, in 1574. He planned to use it as a summer home. But less than 20 years later, Pope Clement VIII decided to make the palace—safely elevated above the malarial miasmas shrouding the low-lying location of the Vatican—the permanent residence of the papacy. It remained the official papal residence until 1870, in the process undergoing a series of enlargements and alterations. When Italian troops under Garibaldi stormed Rome in 1870, making it the capital of the newly united Italy, the popes moved back to the Vatican; the Quirinale became the official residence of the kings of Italy. After the Italian people voted out the monarchy in 1946, the Quirinal Palace passed to the presidency of the Italian Republic. Visitable only on Sundays, with sometimes a noon concert in the chapel included, the state reception rooms are some of Italy's most majestic. You already get a fair idea of the palace's splendor from the size of the building, especially the interminable flank of the palace on Via del

Continued on page 185

BAROQUE & DESPERATE

By Martin
Wilmot Bennett

ANGELS & DEMONS

Designed by Bernini, the ten angels of the Ponte Sant'Angelo bridge star along with other Berninis in Dan Brown's *Angels & Demons,* the Rome-based prequel to *The Da Vinci Code.* See Chapter 1 ("What's New") for details.

THE TRAGIC RIVALRY OF BERNINI AND BORROMINI

Consider the famous feuding duos of Lennon vs. McCartney, Mozart vs. Salieri, Michelangelo vs. Raphael. None of them match the rivalry of Gian Lorenzo Bernini vs. Francesco Borromini. In a pitched battle of anything-you-can-do-I-can-do-better, these two great geniuses of the Baroque style transformed 17th-century Rome into a city of spectacle, the "theater of the entire world." While it was Bernini who triumphed and Borromini who wound up taking his own life, the real winner was Rome itself—a banquet for the eyes cooked up by these two Baroque masters.

Borromini's dome in San Carlo alle Quattro Fontane

United in genius, the two could not have been more different in fortune and character. Born within a year of each other at the turn of the 1600s, they spent decades laying out majestic squares, building precedent-shattering churches, all the while outdoing each other in Baroque bravado.

AN ARTISTIC THROWDOWN

Compared and contrasted, the pair form the ultimate odd couple: Bernini, perhaps the greatest master showman of all time, exulted in Technicolor-hued theatricality; Borromini, the purist and reclusive genius, pursued the pure light of geometry, although with an artisan's hankering after detail. Bernini grew into the famed lover and solid family man; Borromini seems not to have had any love life at all. Bernini became a smooth mingler with society's great and worthy ranks; Borromini remained the quirky outsider. Bernini triumphed as the all-rounder, he of the so-called *"bel composto,"* as in the Cornaro Chapel where his talents as sculptor/architect/dramatist come stunningly together. Borromini was an architect, pure and simple. Throughout their lives, they had tried to turn the tables—psychologically as well as architecturally—on each other, a struggle that ended with Borromini's tragic suicide.

OPERATION AMAZEMENT

Both, however, fervently believed in the Baroque style and its mission to amaze, as well as edify. Thanks to the Counter-Reformation, the Catholic church discovered, and exploited, the effects on its congregants of such overtly Baroque tricks-of-the-trade as *chiaroscuro* (light-and-dark) and *trompe l'oeil* (fool-the-eye) techniques. Using emotion and motion, Bernini and Borromini learned how to give stone wing. In Bernini's famed *Pluto and Persephone,* the solid stone seems transmuted into living flesh—sculpted effects previously thought possible only in paint. Together transforming the city into a "giant theater," the rivals thus became the principal dramaturges and stage managers of Baroque Rome.

(preceding page) Bernini's *Pluto and Persephone,* (left) Bernini's *Angel* on the Ponte St. Angelo

BERNINI (1598–1680): THE POPE'S FAVORITE

Born: December 7, 1598, in Naples, southern Italy.

Greatest Works: St. Peter's Square, *Ecstasy of St. Theresa*, Piazza Navona's *Fountain of Four Rivers*, *Apollo and Daphne*, Sant'Andrea al Quirinale.

Personality Profile: Extrovert and fully aware of his genius or, to quote his own mother, "He acts as if he were master of the world."

Scandal: Just imagine the headlines: "Brother Attacked with Crowbar/Costanza Slashed with Razor by Jealous Genius." Bernini went ballistic on learning his wife, Costanza Nonarelli, was having an affair with his brother Luigi. Protected by Pope Urban VIII, Bernini was let off with a fine of 3,000 scudi.

Career Low: Largely on Borromini's expert insistence, the two crack-ridden bell-towers Bernini designed for St. Peter's were subsequently pulled down.

"La Bella Morte": Death in Bernini becomes star performer. His tomb for Urban VIII has a skeleton writing the pope's name in a marble registry of death, while his tomb for Alexander VII has a golden skeleton riffling marble drapery (this pope kept a Bernini-designed coffin in his bedroom).

> *"An ignorant Goth who has corrupted architecture...."*
>
> Bernini on Borromini

Considered the "father of the Baroque," Bernini enjoyed almost too many career highs to count, starting from a drawing done as a youth, for which Pope Paul V awarded him a handful of gold ducats, to his being dubbed with the honorarium of "cavaliere" at age 23 (Borromini only received the same honor when he was past fifty). Born "under a happy star," as he himself put it, Bernini had patrons lining up, starting with church potentate and eventual pope, Maffeo Barberini, and Pope Paul's nephew, cardinal and art-dealer, Scipio Borghese, who claimed a bevy of Bernini's sculptures for his new Roman palace.

Bernini was a genius of self-promotion.

Bernini's *David*

Cupola, Sant'Andrea al Quirinale

Trick No. 1: In an early bust of Cardinal Borghese, there was an unsightly crack across the forehead; as cardinal turns away in disappointment, Bernini whips out a perfect copy, no more crack. Trick No. 2: On inaugurating Piazza Navona's River Fountain, Innocent X is distressed upon realizing that the water isn't running; Bernini explains technical hitch; pope steps away; abracadabra, Bernini switches water on. Bravo, Bernini!?

BORROMINI (1599–1667): THE ICONOCLAST

Born: September 27, 1599 in Bissone near Lake Lugano in Italy's far north, but with the name Castelli, the name-change coming later, partly to honor San Carlo Borromeo, whose San Carlo church will be Borromini's first major commission.

Greatest Works: San Carlo alle Quattro Fontane, Sant' Ivo della Sapienza, Sant'Agnese in Piazza Navona, Palazzo Falconieri.

Personality Profile: If Bernini is the "instant hit," Borromini is the "struggling genius," the introspective loner, and the complex, often misunderstood perfectionist.

Scandal: A young man, caught filching marble, was beaten and left for dead in San Giovanni in Lanterno, evidently on Borromini's orders. He avoids murder charges thanks to Pope Innocent's intervention.

Scale: Arguably his greatest work, San Carlo could be fitted into one of the four giant crossing-piers of the dome in St Peter's (in one of which towers Bernini's statue of St. Longinus).

"La Brutta Morte": His messy suicide was anything but "bella," as his brave note written in the hours it took him to expire after he fell on his sword attests.

> *"What I mind is not that the money goes to Bernini but that he should enjoy the honor of my labors."*
>
> Borromini on Bernini

Usually dressed in Spanish black, Borromini evidently had few attachments beyond his art. He not only had great artistic vision but an astounding command of geometry, an impeccable hankering after detail, and an artisan's willingness to get his hands dirty. The main influences on him range from Hiram, the builder of Solomon's temple in Jerusalem (who also died by falling on his sword) to Milan's Gothic cathedral, whose influence has been traced to S. Ivo's spiraled dome. On Urban VIII's death, Borromini's star began to ascend. The new pope, Innocent X, makes him papal architect, responsible for restructuring the S. Giovanni basilica and turning the S. Agnese church into a papal chapel. Bernini, however, is again waiting in the wings, readying himself for a startling come back.

While he had a long run of patrons, Borromini was often overshadowed by Bernini's showmanship. He is done out of designing the *Four Rivers* fountain after Bernini submits a silver model of his own design to the new pope. After Innocent's death, commissions become scarce and depression followed. His suicide note is famously calm: "I've been wounded like this since half past eight this morning and I will tell you how it happened...." Once forgotten and derided, Francesco Borromini is now considered "the architect's architect."

Church of Sant' Agnese

BERNINI & BORROMINI TOP 20 MASTERPIECES

Bernini

1. Apollo and Daphne, Galleria Borghese

2. The Baldacchino, Basilica di San Pietro

3. Ecstasy of Saint Theresa, Santa Maria della Vittoria

4. David, Galleria Borghese

5. Pluto and Persephone, Galleria Borghese

6. Tomb of Pope Urban VIII, Basilica di San Pietro

7. Fountain of the Four Rivers, Piazza Navona

8. Two Angels, Ponte Sant'Angelo

9. Elephant and Obelisk, Piazza Sta Maria sopra Minerva

10. Ludovica Albertoni, San Francesco a Ripa

11. Fontana della Barcaccia, Piazza di Spagna

12. Fontana del Tritone, Piazza Barberini

Borromini

13. San Carlo alla Quattro Fontane, Quirinale

14. Sant' Agnese, Piazza Navona

15. Sant' Ivo alla Sapienza, Piazza Navona

16. Oratory of Saint Phillip Neri, Piazza Chiesa Nuova

17. Palazzo Spada, Piazza Capo di Ferro

18. Palazzo Barberini, Via Barberini

19. Sant'Andrea delle Fratte, Via dell Mercede

20. Palazzo Falconieri, Via Giulia

BERNINI VS. BORROMINI: A MINI-WALK

In Rome, you may become lost looking for the work of one rival, then suddenly find yourself gazing at the work of the other. As though an eerily twinned path was destined for the two giants, several of their greatest works are just a few blocks from each other.

A short street away (Via Orlando) from mammoth Piazza Repubblica stands **Santa Maria della Vittoria,** famed for Bernini's **Cornaro Chapel.** Out of favor with new anti-Barberini Pope Innocent X, Bernini was rescued by a commission from Cardinal Cornaro to build a chapel for his family. Here, as if in a "theater," sculpted figures of family members look down from two marble balconies on the so-called "transverberation" of Carmelite Saint Theresa of Avila being pierced by the arrow of the Angel of Divine Love, eyes shut in agony, mouth open in rapture. Spiritual ecstasy has become shockingly real—to quote the famed comment by President de Brosses, "If this is divine love, I know what it is."

Leave the church and head down Via Barberini to Piazza Barberini where perch three of the largest bees you'll ever see. The **Fountain of the Bees** is Bernini's tribute to his arch-patron from the Barberini family, Pope Urban VIII. The bees were family emblems. Another Bernini masterstroke is the **Triton Fountain** in the center of Piazza Barberini. Turn left up Via delle Quattro Fontane. On your left is spectacular **Palazzo Barberini,** where Bernini and Borromini worked together in an

uneasy partnership. The wonderful winding staircase off to the right is the work of Borromini, while the other more conventionally angled staircase on the left is by Bernini, who also has a self-portrait hanging in the art gallery upstairs.

Borromini's prospects soon took a turn for the better thanks to the Barefoot Spanish Trinitarians, who commissioned him to design **San Carlo alla Quatto Fontane**, set at the crossroads up the road. One of the marvels of architecture, its dome—not much bigger than a down-turned bathtub—is packed immaculately throughout with hexagons, octagons, and crosses. Like jigsaw pieces they diminish upwards until the tiny roof seems anything but: to a space that in another architect might turned out claustrophobic Borromini is able to bring a touch of infinity. In the adjoining cloister, revel in Borromini's rearrangement of columns, which transform what would be a conventional rectangle into an energetic octagon. Don't

forget to stop and admire the church's *movementé* facade.

On the same Via del Quirinale stands a famous Bernini landmark, the Jesuits' **Sant' Andrea al Quirinale**. With steps flowing out into the street, it could be viewed as Bernini's response to his rival's nearby masterpiece.

Ironically, the commission for the Jesuit church was originally earmarked for Borromini (but transferred when Pope Alexander VII took over). Note how the hexagons in Bernini's dome diminish upwards to create an illusion of space—in Borrominiesque fashion.

PALAZZO BARBERINI

✉ *Via Barberini 18, Quirinale, Barberini* ☎ *06/32810*
⊕ *www.galleriaborghese.it*
🎟 *€6* ⊙ *Tues.–Sun. 8:30–7
(ticket office closes at 6)*
Ⓜ *Barberini, Buses 52, 56, 60,
95, 116, 175, 492.*

TIPS

■ Part of the family of muse-
ums that includes the Galleria
Borghese, Palazzo Spada,
Palazzo Venezia, and Palazzo
Corsini, the Palazzo Barberini
has gone into marketing in a
big way—visit the shop here
for some distinctive gifts for
Aunt Ethel back home, includ-
ing tote bags bearing the
beloved visage of Raphael's
La Fornarina, bookmarks with
Caravaggio's Judith slicing off
Holofernes's head, and coffee
mugs bearing the famous
Barberini heraldic bees.

One of Rome's most splendid 17th-century palaces, the
newly renovated Palazzo Barberini is a landmark of the
Roman Baroque style. Pope Urban VIII had acquired
the property and given it to a nephew, who was deter-
mined to build an edifice worthy of his generous uncle
and the ever-more-powerful Barberini clan. The result
was, architecturally, a precedent-shattering affair: a
"villa suburbana" set right in the heart of the urban
city and designed to be strikingly open to the outdoors.
Note how Carlo Maderno's grand facade seems almost
entirely composed of window tiers rising up in proto-
20th-century fashion.

Ascend Bernini's staircase to the Galleria Nazionale
d'Arte Antica, hung with famed paintings including
Raphael's *La Fornarina*, a luminous portrait of the artist's lover (a resident of Trastevere, she was reputedly a
baker's daughter)—study the bracelet on her upper arm
bearing Raphael's name. Also noteworthy are Guido
Reni's portrait of the doomed *Beatrice Cenci* (beheaded
in Rome for parricide in 1599)—Hawthorne called it
"the saddest picture ever painted" in his Rome-based
novel, *The Marble Faun*—and Caravaggio's *Judith and
Holofernes*.

But the showstopper here is the palace's Gran Salone,
a vast ballroom with a ceiling painted in 1630 by the
third (and too-often neglected) master of the Roman
Baroque, Pietro da Cortona. It depicts the *Glorification
of Urban VIII's Reign* and has the spectacular conceit of
glorifying Urban VIII as the agent of Divine Providence
and escorted by a "bomber squadron" (to quote art
historian Sir Michael Levey) of some huge, mutantlike
Barberini bees, the heraldic symbol of the family.

Quirinale. Behind this wall are the palace gardens, which, like the gardens of Villa d'Este in Tivoli, were laid out by Cardinal Ippolito d'Este when he summered here. Unfortunately, they are open to the public only once a year on Republic Day (June 2). ⊠ *Piazza del Quirinale, Quirinale* ☎ *06/46991* ⊕ *www.quirinale.it* ⊠ *€5* ☉ *Sept.–June, Sun. 8:30–noon* Ⓜ *Barberini.*

Piazza del Quirinale. This strategic location atop the Quirinal Hill has long been of great importance. It served as home of the Sabines in the 7th century BC, then deadly enemies of the Romans, who lived on the Capitoline and Palatine Hills (all of 1 km [½ mi] away). Today it's the foreground for the presidential residence, Palazzo del Quirinale, and home to the **Palazzo della Consulta,** where Italy's Constitutional Court sits. The open side of the piazza has an impressive vista of the rooftops and domes of central Rome and St. Peter's. The **Fontana di Montecavallo,** or Fontana dei Dioscuri, is composed of a huge Roman statuary group and an obelisk from the tomb of the emperor Augustus. The group of the Dioscuri trying to tame two massive marble steeds was found in the Baths of Constantine, which occupied part of the summit of the Quirinal Hill. Unlike just about every other ancient statue in Rome, this group survived the Dark Ages intact and accordingly became one of the city's great sights, especially during the Middle Ages. Next to the figures, the ancient obelisk from the Mausoleo di Augusto (Tomb of Augustus) was put here by Pope Pius VI at the end of the 18th century. ⊠ *Junction of Via del Quirinale and Via XXIV Aprile, Quirinale* Ⓜ *Barberini.*

Quattro Fontane (*Four Fountains*). The intersection takes its name from its four Baroque fountains, representing the Tiber (on the San Carlo corner), the Arno, Juno, and Diana. Despite the traffic, it's worthwhile taking in the views from this point in all four directions: to the southwest as far as the obelisk in Piazza del Quirinale; to the northeast along Via XX Settembre to the Porta Pia; to the northwest across Piazza Barberini to the obelisk of Trinità dei Monti; and to the southeast as far as the obelisk and apse of Santa Maria Maggiore. The prospect is a highlight of Pope Sixtus V's campaign of urban beautification and an example of the Baroque influence on city planning. ⊠ *At intersection of Via Quattro Fontane, Via XX Settembre, and Via del Quirinale, Quirinale* Ⓜ *Barberini.*

★ **San Carlo alle Quattro Fontane.** San Carlo (sometimes identified by the diminutive San Carlino because of its tiny size) is one of Borromini's masterpieces. In a space no larger than the base of one of the piers of St. Peter's Basilica, he created a church that is an intricate exercise in geometric perfection, with a coffered dome that seems to float above the curves of the walls. Borromini's work is often bizarre, definitely intellectual, and intensely concerned with pure form. In San Carlo, he invented an original treatment of space that creates an effect of rippling movement, especially evident in the double-S curves of the facade. Characteristically, the interior decoration is subdued, in white stucco with no more than a few touches of gilding, so as not to distract from the form. Don't miss the **cloister,** a tiny, understated Baroque jewel, with a graceful portico and loggia above, echoing the lines of the church.

⇨ *For more on Borromini and this church, see "Baroque and Desperate: The Tragic Rivalry of Bernini and Borromini".* ✉ *Via del Quirinale 23, Quirinale* ☎ *06/4883261* ⊕ *www.sancarlino-borromini.it* ⊙ *Weekdays 10–1 and 3–6, Sat. 10–1, Sun. noon–1* Ⓜ *Barberini.*

★ **Sant'Andrea al Quirinale.** Designed by Bernini, this is an architectural gem of the Baroque. His son wrote that Bernini considered it one of his best works and that he used to come here occasionally just to sit and enjoy it. Bernini's simple oval plan, a classic of Baroque architecture, is given drama and movement by the church's decoration, which carries the story of St. Andrew's martyrdom and ascension into heaven, starting with the painting over the high altar, up past the figure of the saint over the chancel door, to the angels at the base of the lantern and the dove of the Holy Spirit that awaits on high. ✉ *Via del Quirinale 29, Quirinale* ☎ *06/4740807* ⊙ *Mon.–Sat., 8:30–noon and 2:30–6; Sun., 8:30–noon and 3–7* Ⓜ *Barberini.*

WORTH NOTING

Fontana delle Api (*Fountain of the Bees*). Decorated with the famous heraldic bees of the Barberini family, the upper shell and the inscription are from a fountain that Bernini designed for Pope Urban VIII; the rest was lost when the fountain had to be moved to make way for a new street. This inscription was the cause of a considerable scandal when the fountain was first put up in 1644. It said that the fountain had been erected in the 22nd year of the pontiff's reign, although in fact the 21st anniversary of Urban's election to the papacy was still some weeks away. The last numeral was hurriedly erased, but to no avail—Urban died eight days before the beginning of his 22nd year as pope. The superstitious Romans, who had immediately recognized the inscription as a foolhardy tempting of fate, were vindicated. ✉ *Via Veneto at Piazza Barberini, Quirinale* Ⓜ *Barberini.*

Scuderie del Quirinale (*Quirinal Stables*). Directly opposite the main entrance of the Palazzo del Quirinale sits the Scuderie Papale, a grand 18th-century stable strikingly remodeled in the late 1990s by architect Gae Aulenti and now host to big temporary art shows. ✉ *Via XXIV Maggio 16, Quirinale* ☎ *06/39967500* ⊕ *www.scuderiequirinale.it* 🎫 *€10* ⊙ *Sun.–Thurs. 10–8, Fri. and Sat. 10 am–10:30 pm* Ⓜ *Barberini. Buses 16, 36, 60, 62, 136, 175.*

Villa Borghese and Piazza del Popolo

MUSEO BORGHESE, THE PINCIO

WORD OF MOUTH

"We found the Electric Bus No. 119 and rode it to the Galleria Borghese. I loved riding around on this little bus—better than any tour bus could have been. But when I checked online at home there were plenty of open spots for the museum, so I didn't reserve. Big mistake: we couldn't get in."   —nancythenice

GETTING ORIENTED

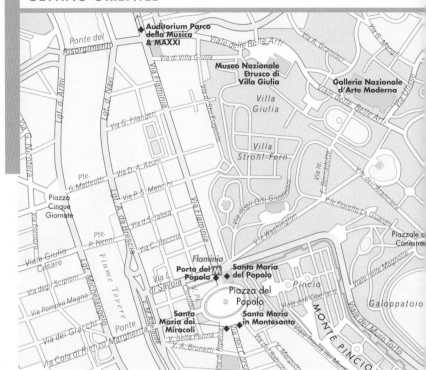

GETTING HERE

Electric Bus No. 119 does a loop that connects Piazza del Popolo to Piazza Venezia. If you're coming from the Colosseum or San Giovanni, take No. 117, which goes to Piazza del Popolo. No. 116, starting near the Museo Borghese, is the only bus that motors through the park and also stops throughout the historic center. The Metro stop for Piazza del Popolo is Line A's Flaminio. The Villa Giulia, the Galleria Nazionale d'Arte Moderna, and Villa Borghese's Biopark are easily accessible from Via Flaminia, 1 km (½ mile) from Piazza del Popolo. Tram 19 and bus No. 3 stop at each.

TOP 5 REASONS TO GO

Piazza del Popolo: At the end of three of the centro storico's most important streets—Via del Babuino, Via del Corso, and Via di Ripetta—the People's Square, as the name translates, offers a ringside seat for some of Rome's best people-watching.

Villa Borghese: Drink in the oxygen in central Rome's largest park—stretches of green and plenty of leafy pathways encourage wandering, biking, or just chilling out.

The Pincio: Stroll through formal gardens in the footsteps of 19th-century fashion plates, aristocrats, and even popes

Santa Maria del Popolo: Marvel at the incredible realism of Caravaggio's gritty paintings in the Cerasi Chapel, then savor Raphael's Chigi Chapel.

Galleria Borghese: Wink at Canova's sexy statue of Pauline Borghese in one of Rome's most spectacularly opulent—and pleasant—museums.

BEST TIME-OUTS

Stravinskij Bar. The Hotel de Russie's luxurious Stravinskij Bar may not be cheap, but it offers a leafy courtyard refuge from Rome's cacophony. This is where visiting Hollywood stars sip martinis and international political movers and shakers clinch deals. Worth the splurge for a vicarious thrill. ✉ *Hotel de la Russie, Via del Babuino 9, Piazza di Spagna* ☎ *06/328881* ⊕ *www.hotelderussie.it.*

Caffè delle Arti. Attached to the Galleria d'Arte Moderna, this spot has a pretty terrace. This is the place to break up your walk with a gelato or lunch. ✉ *Via Gramsci 73, Villa Borghese* ☎ *06/32651236* ⊕ *www.caffedelleartiroma.it.*

Il Margutta. For a meal on the lighter side, head to one of Rome's only vegetarian restaurants (it's also probably the best). A chic, elegant spot—the restaurant is also an art gallery—the food is top-quality and mostly organic. ✉ *Via Margutta 118, Piazza del Popolo* ☎ *06/32650577* ⊕ *www.ilmarguttavegetariano.it* Ⓜ *Flaminio.*

OK, WHERE DO I START?

At the head of famed Via Veneto, the Porta Pinciana is one of the historic city gates in the Aurelian walls, built by Emperor Aurelianus late in the 3rd century AD. Take care—the traffic comes hurtling in here from all directions. Once inside the verdant Villa Borghese park, head north on Viale del Museo Borghese to reach the art-filled Galleria Borghese, probably Rome's most stupendous villa (albeit one that never served as a residence).

Come back to earth with a park stroll along Viale dell'Uccelliera to Rome's once-forlorn zoo, now a "biopark," or alternatively turn left (south) on Viale dei Pupazzi to Piazza dei Cavalli Marini's sea-horse fountain. Continue on Viale dei Pupazzi to Piazza di Siena, then turn left onto Viale Canonica and you'll come to the Giardino del Lago (Lake Garden)—the park's prettiest set piece, replete with lake and a faux "Grecian" temple. Continue south to the famed Pincian gardens, which overlook Rome's vast Piazza del Popolo, home to treasure-filled Santa Maria del Popolo.

Sightseeing
★★★★
Nightlife
★
Dining
★★
Lodging
★★
Shopping
★

If beautiful masterpieces are as common as bricks in Rome, parks are far rarer. Happily, although you'll find few ilex and poplars dotting piazzas and streets, a verdant hoard can be found to the north of central Rome's cobblestoned chaos. Here breathes the city's giant green lung: the Villa Borghese park, where residents love to escape for some serious R&R. But don't think you can completely prevent gallery gout: Three of Rome's most important museums are inside the park, and Piazza del Popolo (which has some art-crammed churches) is close by.

The city's second-largest park started life as a "pleasure garden" for Cardinal Scipione Borghese in the 17th century, but it now serves the democratic pleasure of Rome and its hot and weary visitors. Stretch out under umbrella pines and watch horses trot their riders past, or take in the view from the Pincio, a quiet and shady overlook that's been enchanting visitors since Lucullus hosted his fabulous banquets here back in the days of the Caesars. The heart-shaped park encompasses 19 acres of landscaped plains and formal gardens, adorned with the noseless busts of famous Italians lining paths at the park's southern end. But encircling the park are Renaissance and Baroque palaces, many of which are now museums. The Galleria Borghese, built as an art gallery by Cardinal Borghese, has long been home to the family's great art treasures, with a seemingly endless array of Bernini statuary and paintings by Raphael and Caravaggio to rival the Vatican Museums. (Although one work that belongs squarely in the secular world is Canova's seductive sculptural portrait of Napoléon's sister, the undraped Principessa Pauline Borghese.) A pleasant and green 20-minute walk away on the opposite side of the park, the Museo Etrusco at Villa Giulia offers the world's most comprehensive collection of Etruscan art and artifacts, and next door, the Galleria Nazionale d'Arte Moderna provides a welcome link to the "modern" Italian art of the 19th and 20th centuries.

The formal garden terraces of the Pincio, on the southwestern side of Villa Borghese, give way to a stone staircase down to Piazza del Popolo, a mercifully traffic-free piazza that is one of Rome's best people-watching spots. If you must rest your feet, there are *caffè* and restaurant tables aplenty—but be warned that some would consider the cost of a coffee highway robbery. More improving (and free!) amusement is to be found in the church of Santa Maria del Popolo, on the north side of the square, whose chapels decorated by Raphael and Caravaggio are justly celebrated.

To the southeast of the park is the famed Via Veneto, which, after its 1950s and early '60s heyday as the focus of *dolce vita* excitement, fell out of fashion as the in-crowd headed elsewhere. Basically unchanging, the Via Veneto neighborhood has preserved its solid, bourgeois palaces—many of them now elegant hotels—and enormous ministries. The Romans mostly gone, its caffè still try to woo back tourists, at least, from their counterparts at the Pantheon and Piazza Navona, but with varied success.

VILLA BORGHESE

Central Rome's largest open space is filled with playful fountains, sculptured gardens, and picturesque forests of shady pine trees. But that's not the park's only purpose, for on the perimeter lie three of Rome's most important museums: the Galleria Borghese, for the very best of ancient, Renaissance and Baroque art; the Villa Giulia, for the world's ultimate collection of Etruscan remains; and the Galleria d'Arte Moderna, a reminder that the Italians had their Impressionists, too. For theatergoers, there are summer performances of Shakespeare in a replica of London's Globe. All in all, there's enough here to satisfy the most avid culture vulture. For real vultures, and an excellent day out with the children, head for the new Biopark, Rome's former zoo recently given an ecologically friendly makeover.

TOP ATTRACTIONS

Fodor's Choice ★ **Galleria Borghese.** It's a real toss-up as to which is more magnificent: the villa built for Cardinal Scipione Borghese in 1612, or the art that lies within. Despite its beauty, the villa never was used as a residence. Instead, the luxury-loving cardinal built it as a showcase for his fabulous collection of both antiquities and more "modern" works, including those he commissioned from the masters Caravaggio and Bernini. Today, it's a monument to Roman interior decoration at its most extravagant. With the passage of time, however, the building has become less celebrated than the collections housed within, including one of the finest collections of Baroque sculpture anywhere in the world.

Like the gardens, the casino and its collections have undergone many changes since the 17th century. Much of the building was redecorated in the late 18th century, when the villa received many of its eye-popping ceiling frescoes (although some original decorations also survive). The biggest change to the collection, however, came thanks to Camillo Borghese. After marrying Napoléon's sister Pauline, he sold 154 statues, 170 bas-reliefs, 160 busts, 30 columns, and a number of vases, all ancient pieces, to his new brother-in-law. Today, those sculptures, including the so-called Borghese Gladiator and Borghese Hermaphrodite, are in the Louvre in Paris. At the end of the 19th century, a later member of the family, Francesco Borghese, attempted damage control with his fellow Romans (outraged that many of their art treasures had been shipped off to Paris) with some new acquisitions; he also transferred to the casino the remaining works of art then housed in Palazzo Borghese. In 1902 the casino, its contents, and the estate were sold to the Italian government.

RISQUÉ BUSINESS

Camillo Borghese seems to have been unconcerned that his princess had posed for Canova's erotic masterpiece, ostensibly a sculpted homage to *Venus Victrix*. Principessa Pauline, on the other hand, was supposedly shocked that her husband took pleasure in showing the work to guests. This coyness seems all the more curious given the reply Pauline is supposed to have made to a lady who asked her how she could have posed for the sculpture: "Oh, but the studio was heated." After the couple's divorce, the statue was locked away but Camillo occasionally showed it at night—by the light of a single candle.

One of the most famous works in the collection is Canova's Neoclassical sculpture of Pauline Borghese as Venus Victrix. Scandalously, Pauline reclines on a Roman sofa, bare-bosomed, her hips swathed in classical drapery, the very model of haughty detachment and sly come-hither. You can imagine what the 19th-century gossips were saying!

The next three rooms hold three key early Baroque sculptures: Bernini's *David, Apollo and Daphne*, and *Rape of Proserpina*. All were done when the artist was in his 20s, and all illustrate Bernini's extraordinary skill. They also demonstrate the Baroque desire to invest sculpture with a living quality, to imbue inert marble with a sense of real flesh. Whereas Renaissance sculptors wanted to capture the idealized beauty of the human form that they had admired in ancient Greek and Roman sculptures, later sculptors like Bernini wanted movement and drama as well, capturing not an essence but an instant, infused with theatricality and emotion. The *Apollo and Daphne* shows the moment when, to escape the pursuing Apollo, Daphne is turned into a laurel tree. Leaves and twigs sprout from her fingertips as she stretches agonizingly away from Apollo. In the *Rape of Proserpina,* Pluto has just plucked Persephone (or Proserpina) from her flower-picking—or perhaps he's returning to Hades with his prize. (Don't miss the realistic way his grip causes dimples in Proserpina's flesh.) This is the stuff that makes the Baroque exciting—and moving. Other Berninis on view in the collection include a large, unfinished figure called *Verità,* or Truth. Bernini began work on this brooding figure after the death of his principal patron, Pope Urban VIII. It was meant to form part of a work titled *Truth Revealed by Time.* The next pope, Innocent X, had little love for the ebullient Urban, and, as was the way in Rome, this meant that Bernini would be excluded from the new pope's favors. However, Bernini's towering genius was such that the new pope came around with his patronage with almost indecent haste.

The Caravaggio room holds works by this hotheaded genius, who died of malaria at age 37. All of his paintings, even the charming *Boy with a Basket of Fruit,* seethe with an undercurrent of darkness. The disquieting *Sick Bacchus* is a self-portrait of the artist who, like the god, had a penchant for wine. *David and Goliath,* painted in the last year of Caravaggio's life—while he was on the lam for murder—includes his self-portrait . . . in the head of Goliath. Upstairs, the Pinacoteca (Picture Gallery) boasts paintings by Raphael (including his moving *Deposition*), Pinturicchio, Perugino, Bellini, and Rubens. Probably the gallery's most famous painting is Titian's allegorical *Sacred and Profane Love,* a mysterious and yet-unsolved image with two female figures, one nude, one clothed.

Admission to the Museo is by reservation only. Visitors are admitted in two-hour shifts 9 am to 5 pm. Prime-time slots can sell out days in advance, so in high season reserve by phone or through ⊕ *www.ticketeria.it.* You need to collect your reserved ticket at the museum ticket office a half hour before your entrance. However, when it's not busy you can purchase your ticket at the museum for the next entrance appointment. ⊠ *Piazza Scipione Borghese 5, off Via Pinciana, Villa Borghese* 🕾 *06/32810 information and reservations,* ⊕ *www.galleriaborghese.it* 🎫 *€10.50, including €2 reservation fee; audio guide €5, English tour €6* ⊙ *Tues.–Sun. 9–7, with sessions on hr every 2 hrs (9, 11, 1, 3, 5).* Ⓜ *Bus 910 from Piazza della Repubblica, or Tram 19 orBbus 3 from Policlinico.*

☾ **Pincio.** Redolent of the yesteryears of Henry James and Edith Wharton, the Pincian gardens always have been a favorite spot for strolling. Grand Tourists, and even a pope or two, would head here to see and be seen among the beau monde of Rome. Today, the Pincian terrace remains a favorite spot to cool off overheated locals. The rather formal, early-19th-century style contrasts with the far more elaborate terraced gardens of Lucullus, the Roman gourmand who held legendary banquets here. Today, off-white marble busts of Italian heroes and artists line the pathways. Along with similar busts on the Gianicolo (Janiculum Hill), their noses have been victims of vandalism, perhaps as an attempt to fight ghosts: A belief going back to ancient times held that the nose was the source of breath and therefore of life itself, even after death. By depriving a bust of the same organ, its accompanying spirit would be deprived of oxygen, which evidently spirits need to walk the night.

A stretch of ancient walls separates the Pincio from the southwest corner of Villa Borghese. From the balustraded terrace, you can look down at Piazza del Popolo and beyond, surveying much of Rome. Southeast

Sister of Napoléon, Principessa Pauline Borghese scandalized all Europe by posing as a half-naked Venus for Canova; the statue is on view at the Museo Borghese.

of the Pincian terrace is the **Casina Valadier,** a magnificently decorated Neoclassical building that was reopened to the public in 2007 after a decade-long renovation. It remains one of Rome's most historic restaurants (☎ *06/69922090* ⊕ *casinavaladier.it*). ⊠ *Piazzale Napoleone I and Viale dell'Obelisco, Villa Borghese* Ⓜ *Flaminio (Piazza del Popolo).*

☺ **Villa Borghese.** Rome's "Central Park," the Villa Borghese was originally laid out as a pleasure garden in the early 17th century by Cardinal Scipione Borghese, a worldly and cultivated cleric and nephew of Pope Paul V. The word "villa" was used to mean suburban estate, of the type developed by the ancient Romans and adopted by Renaissance nobles. Today's gardens bear little resemblance to the originals. Not only do they cover a much smaller area—by 1630, the perimeter wall was almost 5 km (3 miles) long—but they also have been almost entirely remodeled. This occurred at the end of the 18th century, when a Scottish painter, Jacob More, was employed to transform them into the style of the "cunningly natural" park so popular in 18th-century England. Until then, the park was probably the finest example of an Italian-style garden in the entire country.

In addition to the gloriously restored Galleria Borghese, the highlights of the park are Piazza di Siena, a graceful amphitheater, and the botanical garden on Via Canonica, where there is a pretty little lake, a Neoclassical faux-Temple of Aesculapius (a favorite photo op), the newly designed Biopark zoo, Rome's own replica of London's Globe Theatre, and the Villa Giulia museum.

The recently opened Carlo Bilotti museum is particularly visitable for De Chirico fans, although there is more modern art in the nearby

Galleria Nazionale d'Arte Moderna. The park is dotted with bike, in-line skating, and electric scooter rental concessions and has a children's movie theater (showing films for adults in the evening), as well as a cinema center, Casa del Cinema, where film buffs can screen films or sit at the slick, cherry red, indoor-outdoor caffè (you can find a schedule of events at ⊕ *www.casa delcinema.it*). ☒ *Main entrances at Porta Pinciana, the Pincio, Piazzale Flaminio (Piazza del Popolo), Viale delle Belle Arti, and Via Mercadante, Villa Borghese* Ⓜ *Flaminio (Piazza del Popolo).*

★ **Villa Medici.** Purchased by Napoléon to create an academy where artists could hone their knowledge of Italian art and so put it to the (French)

> ## ROME'S PRETTIEST RESTAURANT
>
> Ever since it was designed in 1814, the park pavilion restaurant known as the **Casina Valadier** (*Piazza Bucarest,* ☒ *Pincio Gardens* ☎ *06/6992-2090*) has always attracted celebrities like King Farouk of Egypt, Richard Strauss, Gandhi, and Mussolini, all of whom came to see the lavish Empire-style salons and, of course, be seen. In 2007, the elegant pavilion reopened and now has a new array of eateries. Reviews have been decidedly mixed about the food, but the decor is as delicious as it comes.

national good, the villa originally belonged to Cardinal Ferdinando Medici, who also laid out the immaculate Renaissance garden to set off his sculpture collection. Garden tours in English are offered, allowing you to walk in the footsteps of Velázquez, Fragonard, and Ingres, who all worked here (at what is now officially called the French Academy in Rome). The €9 guided tour is also the only way you can see not only the gardens, but the incredibly picturesque garden facade, which is studded with Mannerist and Rococo sculpted reliefs and overlooks a loggia with a beautiful fountain devoted to Mercury. ☒ *Viale Trinità dei Monti 1, Villa Borghese* ☎ *06/67611* ⊕ *www.villamedici.it* ☒ *Entrance including garden tour and exhibit, €9; garden tour when there is no exhibit, €7; exhibit only, €6* ☉ *Tues.–Sun. 10:45–1 and 2–7. Tours of the gardens in English at noon.* Ⓜ *Spagna.*

WORTH NOTING

Biopark. Especially good for a day out with the children, this zoo has been remodeled under eco-friendly lines—more space for the animals, most brought from other zoos or born from animals already in captivity rather than snatched from the wild. There aren't any rhinos, koalas, pandas, or polar bears, but there are local brown bears from Abruzzo and a Reptilarium. Other features are the Biopark train (€1), a picnic area next to the flamingos, and a farm. ☒ *Piazzale del Giardino Zoologico 1, Villa Borghese* ☎ *06/3608211* ⊕ *www.bioparco.it* ☒ *€12.50 adults (€10.50 children)* ☉ *Jan. 1–Mar. 25 and Oct. 24–Dec. 31, daily 9:30–5; Mar. 26–Apr. 1 and Sept. 26–Oct. 23, daily 9:30–6; Apr. 2–Sept. 25, weekdays 9:30–6, weekends 9:30–7. Last admission 1 hr before closing.* Ⓜ *Tram 19 or Bus 3, 88, 95, 490, 495.*

Galleria Nazionale d'Arte Moderna (*National Gallery of Modern Art*). This massive white Beaux Arts building, built for the 1911 World Exposition in Rome, contains one of Italy's leading collections of 19th- and

20th-century works. It's primarily dedicated to the history of Italian modernism, examining the movement's development over the last two centuries, but crowd pleasers Degas, Monet, Courbet, Van Gogh, and Cézanne put in appearances along with an outstanding Dadaist collection. ⊠ *Via delle Belle Arti 131, Villa Borghese* ☎ *06/322981, 06/39967051 guided tours in English* ⊕ *www.gnam.beniculturali.it* 🖱 *Museum only, €8; exhibition only, €10; museum and exhibition, €12* ⊙ *Tues.–Sun. 8:30–7:30 (last entrance 45 mins before closing)* Ⓜ *Tram 19, Bus 3, 88, 95, 490, 495.*

Museo Nazionale Etrusco di Villa Giulia. The world's most outstanding collection of Etruscan art is housed in a grand villa built around 1551 for Pope Julius III (hence its name). Mostly designed by Vignola and Ammannati, the villa has a notable *nymphaeum* (sculpted fountain garden), a superb example of a refined late-Renaissance setting for princely pleasures. The Etruscans are a fascinating civilization, appearing in Italy about 2000 BC as a dazzling prelude to the ancient Romans. But you've never know from this museum, packed with endless rooms stuffed with dusty glass vitrines of objects. Keep your eyes peeled for the masterpieces, such as the serenely beautiful *Sarcophagus of the Wedded Couple* (their Mona Lisa smiles may have influenced Leonardo) and the fabulous Etruscan jewelry, which makes Bulgari look like your village blacksmith. ⊠ *Piazzale Villa Giulia 9, Villa Borghese* ☎ *06/3226571* ⊕ *villagiulia.beniculturali.it* 🖱 *€8* ⊙ *Tues.–Sun. 8:30–7:30 (ticket office closes 1 hr earlier)* Ⓜ *Tram 19, Bus 3.*

PIAZZA DEL POPOLO

Very round, very explicitly defined, and very photogenic, the Piazza del Popolo—the People's Square—is one of Rome's biggest. With twin churches (and two adjacent ritzy caffè) at one end and the Porta del Popolo—Rome's northern city gate—at the other, this square was laid out in its present form by papal architect Giuseppe Valadier (1762–1839). Part of an earlier urban plan, the three streets to the south radiate straight as spokes to other parts of the city, forming the famed "tridente" that nicknames this neighborhood. The center is marked with an obelisk taken from Egypt, one so old it makes the Pantheon look like the Sears Tower: it was carved for Ramses II in the 13th century BC. Today, it is guarded by four water-gushing lions and steps that mark the end of many a sunset *passeggiata*. The most fascinating pieces of art, however, hide within the northeast corner's often-overlooked church of Santa Maria del Popolo, snuggled against the 400-year-old Porta del Popolo). Here you'll find masterpieces by Raphael and Caravaggio.

TOP ATTRACTIONS

★ **MAXXI—Museo Nazionale delle Arti del XXI Secolo** (*National Museum of 21st-Century Arts*). It took 10 years and cost some €150 million, but for lovers of contemporary art and architecture, the MAXXI—Italy's first national museum devoted to contemporary creativity—was worth it. The building alone impresses, as it should: the design, by Anglo-Iraqi starchitect Zaha Hadid, won over 272 other contest entries. The building plays with lots of natural light, curving and angular lines, and big open spaces, all meant to question the division between "within" and "without" (think glass ceilings and steel staircases that twist through the air). While not every critic adored it in its 2010 unveiling, more and more Romans are becoming delighted by this surprisingly playful space. The museum hosts temporary exhibits on art, architecture, film, and more; past shows have showcased Michelangelo Pistoletto and Pietro Nervi. From the permanent collection, rotated through the museum, more than 350 works represent artists including Andy Warhol, Francesco Clemente, and Gerhard Richter. Get to the MAXXI by taking the Metro to Flaminio (near Piazza del Popolo) and then Tram No. 2 two stops to Apollodoro. ⊠ *Via Guido Reni 4, Flaminio* ☎ *06/39967350* ⊕ *www.fondazionemaxxi.it* 🖃 *€11* ⏱ *Tues.–Fri. and Sun. 11–7, Sat. 11–10* Ⓜ *Tram 2 or Bus 53, 217, 280, 910.*

☼ **Piazza del Popolo.** With its obelisk and twin churches, this immense square is a famed Rome landmark. It owes its current appearance to architect Giuseppe Valadier, who designed it about 1820, also laying out the terraced approach to the Pincio and the Pincio's gardens. It marks what was for centuries the northern entrance to the city, where all roads from the north converge and where visitors, many of them pilgrims, would get their first impression of the Eternal City. The desire to make this entrance to Rome something special had been a pet project of popes and their architects for over three centuries. The piazza takes its name from the 15th-century church of Santa Maria del Popolo, huddled on the right side of the Porta del Popolo, or city gate. In the late 17th century, the twin churches of Santa Maria in Montesanto (on the left as you face them) and Santa Maria dei Miracoli (on the right) were added to the piazza at the point where Via del Babuino, Via del Corso, and Via di Ripetta converge. The piazza, crowded with fashionable carriages and carnival revelers in the past, is a pedestrian zone today. At election time, it's the scene of huge political rallies, and on New Year's Eve Rome stages a mammoth alfresco party in the piazza. ⊠ *Junction of Via del Babuino, Via del Corso, and Via di Ripetta, Piazza del Popolo* Ⓜ *Flaminio.*

8

NEED A BREAK?

Buccone. A wineshop serving light snacks at lunchtime, this also offers a handy selection of wine by the glass all day long. ⊠ *Via di Ripetta 19, Piazza del Popolo* ☎ *06/3612154.*

Fodor'sChoice
★

Santa Maria del Popolo. Standing inconspicuously in a corner of the vast Piazza del Popolo, this church often goes unnoticed, but the treasures inside make it a must for art lovers, as they include an entire chapel designed by Raphael and one adorned with striking Caravaggio masterpieces. Bramante enlarged the apse of the church, which had been rebuilt in the 15th century on the site of a much older place of worship. Inside, in the first chapel on the right, you'll see some frescoes by Pinturicchio from the mid-15th century; the adjacent **Cybo Chapel** is a 17th-century exercise in marble decoration. Raphael's famous **Chigi Chapel,** the second on the left, was built around 1513 and commissioned by the banker Agostino Chigi (who also had the artist decorate his home across the Tiber, the Villa Farnesina). Raphael provided the cartoons for the vault mosaic—showing God the Father in benediction—and the designs for the statues of Jonah and Elijah. More than a century later, Bernini added the oval medallions on the tombs and the statues of Daniel and Habakkuk, when, in the mid-17th century another Chigi, Pope Alexander VII, commissioned him to restore and decorate the building.

The organ case of Bernini in the right transept bears the Della Rovere family oak tree, part of the Chigi family's coat of arms. The **choir,** with vault frescoes by Pinturicchio, contains the handsome tombs of Ascanio Sforza and Girolamo delle Rovere, both designed by Andrea Sansovino. The best is for last: The **Cerasi Chapel,** to the left of the high altar, holds two Caravaggios, the *Crucifixion of St. Peter* and *Conversion of St. Paul.* Exuding drama and realism, both are key early Baroque works that show how "modern" 17th-century art can appear. Compare their style with the much more restrained and classically "pure" *Assumption of the Virgin* by Caravaggio's contemporary and rival, Annibale Carracci; it hangs over the altar of the chapel. ⊠ *Piazza del Popolo 12, near Porta Pinciana, Piazza del Popolo* ☎ *06/3610836* ☉ *Mon.–Sat. 7:30–noon and 4–6:30, Sun. 7:30–1:30 and 4:30–7* Ⓜ *Flaminio.*

WORTH NOTING

Porta del Popolo (*City Gate*). The medieval gate in the Aurelian walls was replaced in 1561 by the current one. Bernini further embellished it in 1655 for the much-heralded arrival of Queen Christina of Sweden, who had abdicated her throne to become a Roman Catholic. ⊠ *Piazza del Popolo and Piazzale Flaminio, Piazza del Popolo* Ⓜ *Flaminio.*

Santa Maria dei Miracoli. A twin to Santa Maria in Montesanto, this church was built in the 1670s by Carlo Fontana as an elegant frame for the entrance to Via del Corso from Piazza del Popolo. ⊠ *Via del Corso 528, Piazza del Popolo* ☎ *06/3610250* ☉ *Daily 6:45–12:30 and 4–7:30* Ⓜ *Flaminio.*

Santa Maria in Montesanto. One of the two bookend churches on the eastern side of Piazza del Popolo, this edifice was built by Carlo Fontana, supervised by his brilliant teacher, Bernini (whose other pupils are responsible for the saints topping the facade). ⊠ *Via del Babuino 197, Piazza del Popolo* ☎ *06/3610594* ⊕ *www.chiesadegliartisti.it* ☉ *Weekdays 4:30–8, Sun. 11:15–noon* Ⓜ *Flaminio.*

Trastevere and the Ghetto

ISOLA TIBERINA, SANTA MARIA IN TRASTAVERE, PORTICO D'OTTAVIA

WORD OF MOUTH

"After we took in Santa Maria in Trastevere's stunning mosaics, we walked back having gelati on the way (of course, one gelato a day!). After dinner we returned to the basilica for a concert featuring a beautiful choir before the stroll back—it was lovely crossing the Tiber with Castel Sant'Angelo in the background."   —AmanteDelLimoncello

GETTING ORIENTED

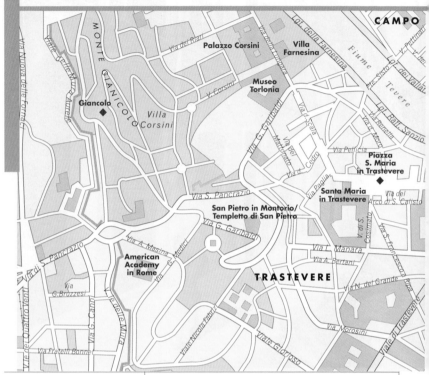

GETTING HERE	TOP 5 REASONS TO GO
From the Vatican or Spanish Steps, expect a 20- to 30-minute walk to reach either the Ghetto or Trastevere.	**Santa Maria in Trastevere:** Tear yourself away from the piazza scene outside to take in the gilded glory of one of the city's oldest and most beautiful churches, fabled for its medieval mosaics.
From Termini, nab the No. 40 Express or the No. 64 bus to Largo Torre Argentina, where you can get off to visit the Ghetto area.	**"Tiber, Father Tiber":** Cross over the river on the Ponte Fabricio—the city's oldest bridge—for a stroll on the paved shores of the adorable Isola Tiberina (and don't forget to detour for the lemon ices at La Gratachecca).
Switch to Tram 8 to get to Trastevere.	**Portico d'Ottavia:** This famed ancient Roman landmark casts a spell over Rome's time-stained Ghetto Ebraico, now getting more gentrified by the minute.
As for ascending the very steep Janiculum Hill, take the No. 41 bus from Ponte Sant'Angelo, then enjoy the stately walk down to the northern reaches of Trastevere.	**I Love the Nightlife:** Trastevere has become one of Rome's hottest nighttime scene-arenas, with hipsterious clubs at nearly every turn.

Get Middle-Aged: With cobblestone alleyways and medieval houses, the area around Trastevere's Piazza di Piscinula offers a magical dip into Rome's Middle Ages. |

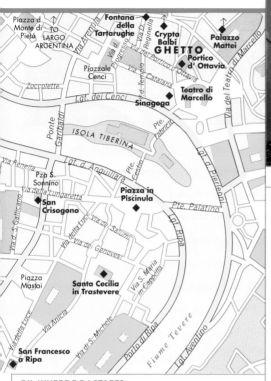

BEST TIME-OUTS

Caffè di Marzio. Over a coffee or a cocktail, sit and gaze upon Santa Maria in Trastevere's glistening golden facade at Caffè di Marzio. Although the outdoor seating is lovely, the interior is warm and welcoming, too. Expect a mix of local regulars and tourists. ✉ *Piazza Santa Maria in Trastevere 15, Trastevere* ☎ *06/5816095.*

La Renella. This no-frills pizzeria and bakery, hidden just off Piazza Trilussa, is a big favorite with the locals. Enough said. ✉ *Via del Moro 15, Trastevere* ☎ *06/5817265.*

Rivendita. The full name is Rivendita: Libri Cioccolata e Vino, and that's exactly what you'll find in this charming, trendy Trastevere hole-in-the-wall: books, chocolate, and wine. With options like Barolo, a fruity cocktail, or coffee served in cups of pure chocolate, this is a place those with a sweet tooth won't want to miss. ✉ *Vicolo del Cinque 11/a, Trastevere* ☎ *06/58301868.*

9

OK, WHERE DO I START?

Piazza Venezia is the starting point for touring the ancient Ghetto quarter of the city. From the piazza, walk to the base of the Campidoglio, take Via del Teatro Marcello, and turn right across the street onto Via Montanara and enter Piazza Campitelli, with its Baroque church and fountain. Take Via dei Funari at the northwest end of the piazza and follow it into Piazza Mattei, where one of Rome's loveliest fountains, the 16th-century Fontana delle Tartarughe (Fountain of the Turtles), is tucked away. A few steps down Via Caetani, off the north side of Piazza Mattei, you'll find a doorway into the courtyard of the venerable Palazzo Mattei—festooned with Baroque sculpture busts, it's a stunner. From Piazza Mattei go south on Via della Reginella onto Via Portico d'Ottavia, heart of the Jewish Ghetto and home to the ancient Portico d'Ottavia (not far away is the even older Teatro di Marcello). Cross Ponte Fabricio over the Isola Tiberina (Tiber Island) to Trastevere. Begin with the medieval little streets around picturesque Piazza in Piscinula. Then make for Bernini's San Francesco a Ripa at the Villa Farnesina.

Sightseeing
★★★★★
Nightlife
★★★★
Dining
★★★★
Lodging
★★★
Shopping
★★★

New York has its Greenwich Village, and Rome has its Trastevere. In Trastevere's case, however, the sense of being a world apart goes back more than two millennia. The inhabitants don't even call themselves Romans but Trasteverini, going on to claim that they, not the citizens north of the river, are the true remaining Romans. No matter: A trip to Trastevere (literally, "across the Tiber") still feels a bit like entering a different time and place. Some call it the world's third-smallest nation (after the Vatican, No. 2). A living chronology, the district remains an enchanting confusion of past and present. With its charming, crumbling streets lined with medieval bell towers and chic *osterie,* this is one big little town where strangers don't remain strangers too long.

Though in the geographic heart of the city, Trastevere and the Ghetto have always been considered outsiders. Trastevere began as a farming settlement for immigrants from the East; until the 14th century, it wasn't even considered part of Rome. Since then, locals regard them as a breed apart, with their own dialect and traditions. The Ghetto—historically known as the Ghetto Ebraico (Jewish Ghetto)—was established by papal decree in the 16th century. It was by definition a closed community, where Roman Jews lived under lock and key until Italian unification in 1870. In 1943–44, the already small Jewish population there was decimated by deportations.

In a city where the past counts at least as much as the present, this history of exclusion endures, and has shaped the present-day neighborhoods in some unexpected ways. Today, Trastevere and the Ghetto are two of the city's hottest real-estate markets, sought after by Italian lefties and bohemian expats, who value their history as much as their earthy, old-fashioned atmosphere. True Trasteverini are now few and far between, most of the older generation having sold their now valuable family apartments, and most of Rome's Jews live outside the Ghetto. But something of them remains. Trastevere's new residents promote a new kind of outsider identity, embodied variously in yoga centers, social outreach programs, and innumerable funky bars. The Ghetto, while undergoing some of the same changes, remains the spiritual and cultural home of Rome's Jews, and that proud heritage permeates its small commercial area of Judaica shops, kosher bakeries, and restaurants.

The heart of Trastevere is the lovely Piazza Santa Maria, presided over by the gilded and floodlit church of the same name. Nearby are a variety of historic churches, set in alleys and sunny piazzas, but the greatest artistic treasures are to be found a short walk to the north, in Raphael's frescoes at the Villa Farnesina, and the Baroque paintings, including a Caravaggio, in the collection at the Palazzo Corsini. The neighborhood's greatest attraction, however, is simply its atmosphere—traditional shops set along crooked streets, peaceful during the day, and alive with throngs of restaurant- and partygoers at night. From here, a steep hike up stairs and the road to the Gianicolo earns you a panoramic view over the whole city.

The turn-of-the-20th-century synagogue, with its museum dedicated to the history of Jewish Rome, is a must for understanding the Ghetto. Tight, teeming alleys lead from there up to Giacomo della Porta's unmistakable Turtle Fountain; nearby is the picture-perfect Palazzo Mattei. Via Portico d'Ottavia is a walk through the olden days. Most businesses in the Ghetto observe the Jewish Sabbath, so it's a ghost town on Saturdays. At its east end, the street leads down to a path past the 1st-century Teatro di Marcello. Separating the Ghetto and Trastevere is the Tiber River, but they are connected by one of the world's prettiest "bridges"—the Isola Tiberina (Tiber Island). Cross over the rushing river by using the Ponte Fabricio, the oldest bridge in Rome.

9

TRASTEVERE

Sometimes futilely resisting the tides of change, Rome has several little communities that have staunchly defended their authenticity over the centuries; the Tiber separates two of them—the Ghetto and Trastevere. Just beyond the charming Tiber Island lies Trastevere, which, despite galloping gentrification, remains about the most tightly knit community in Rome. Perfectly picturesque piazzas, tiny winding medieval alleyways, and time-burnished Romanesque houses all cast a frozen-in-amber spell, while grand art awaits at Santa Maria in Trastevere, San Francesco a Ripa, and the Villa Farnesina. On the northern border of the district looms the Janiculum, Rome's highest hill, with views to prove it.

TOP ATTRACTIONS

♻ **Gianicolo** (*Janiculum Hill*). The Gianicolo is famous for offering panoramic views of the city, a noontime cannon, and statues of Giuseppe and Anita Garibaldi (Garibaldi was the guiding spirit behind the unification of Italy in the 19th century; Anita was his long-suffering wife). The view, backdropped by the first slopes of the Appennine Mountains, attracts Roman lovers, camera-happy tour-

TRASTEVERE STEP-BY-STEP

This enchanting neighborhood was made for walking, *so check out "Roamin' Holiday" for a complete and fascinating tour of Trastevere and the Isola Tiberina, with many more sights outlined in these especially picturesque districts.*

ists, and tchotchke-selling vendors, especially at dusk, although others will point out that Rome's skyline is basically flat and thus the vista singularly undramatic). Small crowd aside, it's fun to pick out Rome's finest buildings, from the Pantheon to St. Peter's—and you'll be surprised at how peaceful and pastel it all looks from up here. At the plaza here there's a free puppet show in Italian on weekends 10:30–noon and 5–7. ⊠ *Via Garibaldi and Passeggiata del Gianicolo, Trastevere.*

Palazzo Corsini. A brooding example of Baroque style, the palace houses part of the 16th- and 17th-century sections of the collection of the Galleria Nazionale d'Arte Antica and is across the road from the Villa Farnesina. Among the most famous paintings in this large, dark collection are Guido Reni's *Beatrice Cenci* and Caravaggio's *St. John the Baptist.* Stop in, if only to climb the 17th-century stone staircase, itself a drama of architectural shadows and sculptural voids. Behind, but separate from, the palazzo is the **Orto Botanico,** Rome's only botanical park, containing 3,500 species of plants. The park is open Monday through Saturday, 9:30 to 6:30 in summer (4:30 in winter); admission is €6. ⊠ *Via della Lungara 10, Trastevere* ☎ *06/68802323 Galleria Corsini, 06/32810 Galleria Corsini tickets booking, 06/49912436 Orto Botanico* ⊕ *www.galleriaborghese.it* ⊠ *€4 (€1 reservations fee)* ⊙ *Tues.–Sun. 8:30–7:30.*

Piazza in Piscinula. One of Trastevere's most historic and time-burnished squares, this piazza takes its name from some ancient Roman baths on the site (*piscina* means "pool"). The tiny church of **San Benedetto** on the piazza is the smallest church in the city and, despite its 18th-century facade, dates back to the 4th century AD. Opposite is the medieval **Casa dei Mattei** (Mattei House). The rich and powerful Mattei family lived here until the 16th century, when, after a series of murders on the premises, they decided to move out of the district entirely, crossing the river to build their magnificent palace in the Ghetto. ⊠ *Via della Lungaretta, Piazza della Gensola, Via in Piscinula, and Via Lungarina, Trastevere.*

★ **Piazza Santa Maria in Trastevere.** At the very heart of the Trastevere *rione*
♻ (district) lies this beautiful piazza, with its elegant raised fountain and sidewalk caffè. The showpiece is the 12th-century church of Santa Maria in Trastevere. The striking mosaics on the church's facade—which add light and color to the piazza, particularly when they're spotlighted at night—are believed to represent the Wise and Foolish Virgins.

ISOLA TIBERINA

✉ *Tiber Island, accessed by the Ponte Fabricio (Lungotevere dei Pierleoni near Via Ponte Quattro Capi) and the Ponte Cestio (Lungotevere degli Anguillara near Piazza San Bartolomeo all'Isola), Trastevere.*

TIPS

■ Sometimes called the world's most beautiful movie theater, the open-air Cinema d'Isola di Tiberina operates from mid-June to early September as part of Rome's big summer festival, Estate Romana (www.estateromana. comune.roma.it). The 450-seat arena unfolds its silver screen against the backdrop of the ancient Ponte Fabricio, while the 50-seat CineLab is set against Ponte Garibaldi facing Trastevere. Screenings usually start at 9:30 pm; admission is €6 for the Arena, €3 CineLab. Call 06/58333113or go to isoladelcinema.com for more information.

■ Line up at the kiosk of La Gratachecca del 1915 (near the Ponte Cestio) for the most yumptious frozen ices in Rome.

It's easy to overlook this tiny island in the Tiber. Don't. In terms of history and sheer loveliness, the charming Isola Tiberina—shaped like a boat about to set sail—gets high marks.

Cross onto the island via Ponte Fabricio, constructed in 62 BC, Rome's oldest remaining bridge; on the north side of the island crumbles the romantic ruin of the Ponte Rotto (Broken Bridge), which dates back to 179 BC. Descend the steps to the lovely river embankment to see the island's claim to fame: a Roman relief of the intertwined-snakes symbol of Aesculapius, the great god of healing. In 291 BC, a temple to Aesculapius was erected on the island. A ship had been sent to Epidaurus in Greece, heart of the cult of Aesculapius, to obtain a statue of the god.

As the ship sailed back up the Tiber, a great serpent was seen escaping from it and swimming to the island—a sign that a temple to Aesculapius should be built here.

In imperial times, Romans sheathed the entire island with marble to make it look like Aesculapius's ship, replete with a towering obelisk as a mast. Amazingly, the ancient sculpted ship's prow still exists. You can marvel at it on the downstream end of the embankment.

Today, medicine still reigns here. The island is home to the hospital of Fatebenefratelli (literally, "Do good, brothers"). Nearby is San Bartolomeo, built at the end of the 10th century by the Holy Roman Emperor Otto III and restored in the 18th century.

9

Through innumerable generations, this square has been the center of Trastevere's action, with street festivals, musicians, and gamboling dogs vying for attention from the throngs of people taking the evening air. ⊠ *Via della Lungaretta, Via della Paglia, and Via San Cosimato, Trastevere.*

★ **San Francesco a Ripa.** Set near Trastevere's southern end, this Baroque church attached to a 13th-century Franciscan monastery holds one of Bernini's last works, a statue of the Blessed Ludovica Albertoni. This is perhaps Bernini's most hallucinatory sculpture, a dramatically lighted figure ecstatic at the prospect of entering heaven as she expires on her deathbed. She clutches her breast as a symbol, art historians say, of the "milk of human kindness" and Christian *caritas* (charity). Gracing the altar is Baciccia's *Madonna and St. Anne.* St. Francis is supposed to have stayed at this monastery when visiting the city; to see his cell, ask the sacristan. ⊠ *Piazza San Francesco d'Assisi 88, Trastevere* ☎ *06/5819020* ⊙ *Daily 7–1 and 2–7.*

> ## ROMOLO'S
>
> Raphael's model and mistress, the dark-eyed Fornarina (literally, "the baker's daughter"), is believed to have been a Trasteverina. The artist reportedly took time off from painting the district's Villa Farnesina to romance—and perhaps marry—the winsome girl. Her family house, legend states, is Trastevere's landmark restaurant, Romolo (Via di Porta Settimiana 8), replete with enchanting, leafy dining garden, menus embellished by Miró, and the city's best artichoke sauces.

★ **San Pietro in Montorio.** Built partly on command of Ferdinand and Isabella of Spain in 1481 near the spot where, tradition says (evidently mistakenly), St. Peter was crucified, this church is a handsome and dignified edifice. It contains a number of well-known works, including, in the first chapel on the right, the *Flagellation* painted by the Venetian Sebastiano del Piombo from a design by Michelangelo, and *St. Francis in Ecstasy,* in the next-to-last chapel on the left, in which Bernini made one of his earliest experiments with concealed lighting effects.

However, the most famous work here is the circular **Tempietto** (Little Temple) in the monastery cloister next door. This sober little building—though tiny, holding only 10 people, it's actually a church in its own right—marks the spot where, legend has it, St. Peter's cross once stood. It remains one of the key Renaissance buildings in Rome. Designed by Bramante (the original architect of the new St. Peter's Basilica) in 1502, it represents one of the earliest and most successful attempts to reproduce an entirely classical building. ⊠ *Piazza San Pietro in Montorio 2 (Via Garibaldi), entrance to cloister and Tempietto at portal next to church, Trastevere* ☎ *06/5813940 San Pietro in Montorio, 06/5812806 Tempietto (Accademia di Spagna)* ⊕ *www.sanpietroinmontorio.it* ⊙ *Church daily 8:30–noon, also weekdays 3–4; Tempietto Tues.–Sat. 9:30–12:30 and 2–4.*

★ **Santa Cecilia in Trastevere.** The basilica commemorates the aristocratic St. Cecilia, patron saint of music. One of ancient Rome's most celebrated Early Christian martyrs, she was put to a supernaturally long death

Dining alfresco in Trastevere—now *this* is what you came to Italy for.

by the emperor Diocletian around the year AD 300. After an abortive attempt to suffocate her in the baths of her own house (a favorite means of quietly disposing of aristocrats in Roman days), she was brought before the executioner. But not even three blows of the executioner's sword could dispatch the young girl. She lingered for several days, converting others to the Christian cause, before finally dying. In 1595, her body was exhumed. It was said to look as fresh as if she still breathed—and the heart-wrenching sculpture by eyewitness Stefano Maderno that lies below the main altar was, the sculptor insisted, exactly how she looked. Time your visit to enter the cloistered convent to see what remains of Pietro Cavallini's *Last Judgment*, dating from 1293. It's the only major fresco in existence known to have been painted by Cavallini, a forerunner of Giotto. ⊠ *Piazza Santa Cecilia in Trastevere 22, Trastevere* ☎ *06/5899289* ⌨ *Church free; frescoes €2.50; underground €2.50* ☉ *Basilica and underground, weekdays 9:30–12:30 and 4–6:30, Sun. 4–6:30; frescoes, weekdays 10 am–12:30 pm.*

Fodor's Choice
★

Santa Maria in Trastevere. Originally built sometime before the 4th century, this spectacular church conjures up the splendor of ancient Rome better than any other in the city. Supposedly Rome's first church dedicated to the Virgin Mary, it was rebuilt in the 12th century by Pope Innocent II (who hailed from Trastevere) with a nave framed by a processional of two rows of 22 gigantic columns taken from ancient Roman temples along with an altar studded with gilded mosaics. Larger Roman naves exist, but none seem as majestic as this one, bathed in a sublime glow from the 12th- and 13th-century mosaics and Domenichino's gilded ceiling (1617). Outside, the 19th-century portico draws attention to the facade's 800-year-old mosaics, which represent the parable of the Wise and Foolish Virgins—magnificent at night when they are illuminated. Back inside, the church's most important mosaics, Pietro Cavallini's six panels of the *Life of the Virgin,* cover the semicircular apse. Their new sense of realism is said to have inspired the great Giotto. Note the little building labeled "Taberna Meritoria" just under the figure of the Virgin in the Nativity scene, with a stream of oil flowing from it. It recalls the legend that on the day Christ was born, a stream of pure oil flowed on the site of the piazza, signifying the coming of the grace of God. Inside, before leaving the nave, take a seat at the back and let the gilded centuries of this place wash over you—unforgettable! ⊠ *Piazza Santa Maria in Trastevere, Trastevere* ☎ *06/5814802* ⊙ *Daily 7:30 am–9 pm.*

NEED A BREAK?

Trattoria Da Augusto. You can find any kind of eatery in Trastevere, from pubs to pizzerias. But for good, honest *cucina romana* at good, honest prices you can't do better than Trattoria Da Augusto, off to the right before you reach Santa Maria in Trastevere. ⊠ *Piazza de Renzi 15, Trastevere* ☎ *06/5803798.*

Fodor'sChoice ★

Villa Farnesina. Money was no object to the extravagant Agostino Chigi, a banker from Siena who financed many a papal project. His munificence is evident in this elegant villa, built for him about 1511. He was especially proud of the delicate fresco decorations in the airy loggias (now glassed in to protect their artistic treasures), for when Raphael could steal a little time from his work on the Vatican Stanze, he came over to execute some of the frescoes himself, notably a luminous *Galatea.* Here, Agostino entertained the popes and princes of 16th-century Rome, delighting in impressing his guests at alfresco suppers held in riverside pavilions by having his servants clear the table by casting the precious silver and gold dinnerware into the Tiber. His extravagance was not quite so boundless as he wished to make it appear, however: he had nets unfurled a foot or two under the water's surface to catch the valuable ware.

In the magnificent **Loggia of Psyche** on the ground floor, Giulio Romano and others worked from Raphael's designs. Raphael's lovely *Galatea* is in the adjacent room. On the floor above you can see the trompe l'oeil effects in the aptly named **Hall of Perspectives** by Peruzzi. Agostino Chigi's bedroom, next door, was frescoed by Sodoma with scenes from the life of Alexander the Great, notably the *Wedding of Alexander and Roxanne,* which is considered to be the artist's best work. The palace also houses the **Gabinetto Nazionale delle Stampe,** a treasure house of old prints and drawings. ⊠ *Via della Lungara 230, Trastevere* ☎ *06/68027268, 06/68027397 to book guided tours* ⊕ *www. villafarnesina.it* 🎟 *€5* ⊙ *Mon.–Sat. 9–1.*

THE GHETTO

The downside of spiritual revival can be religious intolerance. With the Counter-Reformation and its new religious orders also came a papal decree that Trastevere's longstanding Jewish community should be moved north of the river to the so-called Ghetto. A community going back to 180 BC suddenly found itself walled in and subjected to a nightly curfew. With the Italian Unification of 1870 the Ghetto walls were demolished, but less than a century later Vittorio Emanuele III, King of Italy and Emperor of Abyssinia, signed into effect the Race Laws, depriving the Jewish community of the right to education, jobs, and then property. With the coming of the Nazis, worse was to follow, as a visit to this district's synagogue will show. More recently, in 1967, Jewish refugees from Libya found a welcome here. The area now abounds with kosher restaurants—its picturesque atmosphere once more prevailing over the frequent ugliness of history.

TOP ATTRACTIONS

Crypta Balbi. The fourth component of the magnificent collections of the Museo Nazionale Romano and visitable on the same ticket, this museum is unusual in its equitable apportioning of Rome's archaeological cake: a slice of Roman history—the crypt being part of the Balbus Theater complex (13 BC)—but also a slice of the largely vanished medieval Rome that once stood on top. The written explanations accompanying the well-lit exhibits are also excellent, making this museum much visited by teachers and schools. ⊠ *Via delle Botteghe Oscure 31, Largo Argentina* ☎ *06/39967700* 🎟️*€7 (including 3-day access to 3 sister museums)* Ⓜ *Buses 64 and 40, and Tram 8 from Trastevere.*

Fodor'sChoice
★
Palazzo Mattei di Giove. Graceful and opulent, the arcaded, multistory courtyard of this palazzo is a masterpiece of turn-of-the-17th-century style. Designed by Carlo Maderno, it is a veritable panoply of sculpted busts, heroic statues, sculpted reliefs, and Paleo-Christian epigrams, all collected by Marchese Asdrubale Mattei. Have your Nikon ready as Roman and Renaissance heads cross glances across the ages. Inside are various scholarly institutes, including the Centro Studi Americani (Center for American Studies ⊕ *centrostudiamericani.org*), which also contains a library of American books. Various salons are decorated with frescoes by Cortona, Lanfranco, and Domenichino. ⊠ *Via Michelangelo Caetani 32, other entrance in Via dei Funari, Ghetto* ☎ *06/68801613 Centro Studi Americani.*

★ **Portico d'Ottavia.** The Portico d'Ottavia looms over the Ghetto district and comprises one of its most picturesque set pieces, with the time-stained church of Sant'Angelo in Pescheria built right into its ruins. With a few surviving columns, the Portico d'Ottavia is a huge porticoed enclosure, named by Augustus in honor of his sister Octavia. Originally 390 feet wide and 433 feet long, it encompassed two temples, a meeting hall, and a library, and served as a kind of grandiose entrance foyer for the adjacent Teatro di Marcello. The ruins of the portico became Rome's *pescheria* (fish market) during the Middle Ages. A stone plaque on a pillar, a relic of that time, admonishes in Latin that the head of any fish surpassing the length of the plaque was to be cut off "up to the first fin" and given to the city fathers or else the vendor was to pay a fine of 10 gold florins. The heads were used to make fish soup and were considered a great delicacy. After restoration, the lovely medieval church of Sant'Angelo in Pescheria has reopened to the public. It's open 2–5 Wednesday, Saturday, and the first Monday of the month. ⊠ *Via Tribuna di Campitelli 6, Ghetto* ☎ *06/68801819 Church of Sant'Angelo in Pescheria.*

NEED A BREAK?

Dolceroma. Stop in at this bakery to indulge in American and Austrian treats. ⊠ *Via Portico d'Ottavia 20/b, Ghetto* ☎ *06/6892196* ⊕ *www. ladolceroma.com.* **Franco e Cristina.** Franco e Cristina is a stand-up pizza joint with some of the thinnest, crispiest pizza in town. ⊠ *Via Portico d'Ottavia 5, Ghetto.*

★ **Teatro di Marcello.** This theater was begun by Julius Caesar and completed by the emperor Augustus in AD 13. Rome's first permanent building dedicated to drama, it held 20,000 spectators. Like other Roman monuments, it was transformed into a fortress during the Middle Ages. During the Renaissance, it was converted into a residence by the Savelli, one of the city's noble families. The small archaeological zone is used as a summer venue for open-air classical music and lyrical concerts. ⊠ *Via del Teatro di Marcello, Ghetto* ☎ *06/87131590 for concert information* ⊕ *www.tempietto.it.*

WORTH NOTING

★ **Fontana delle Tartarughe.** Designed by Giacomo della Porta in 1581 and sculpted by Taddeo Landini, this 16th-century fountain, set in venerable Piazza Mattei, is Rome's most charming. The focus of the fountain is four bronze boys, each grasping a dolphin spouting water into a marble shell. Bronze turtles held in the boys' hands drink from the upper basin. ⊠ *Piazza Mattei, Ghetto.*

Sinagoga. This aluminum-roof synagogue has been the city's largest Jewish temple and a Roman landmark since its 1904 construction. At the back the Jewish Museum, with its precious ritual objects and other exhibits, documents the uninterrupted presence of a Jewish community for nearly 22 centuries. Until the 13th century the Jews were esteemed citizens of Rome. Among them were the bankers and physicians to the popes, who had themselves given permission for the construction of synagogues. But later, popes of the Counter-Reformation revoked this tolerance, confining the Jews to the Ghetto and imposing a series of restrictions, some of which were enforced as late as 1870. For security reasons, guided visits are mandatory; entrance to the synagogue is through the museum located in Via Catalana (⊠ *Largo 16 Ottobre 1943*). ⊠ *Lungotevere Cenci 15, Ghetto* ☎ *06/68400661* ⊕ *www. museoebraico.roma.it* 🎫 *€10* ⊙ *Mid-Sept.–mid-June, Sun.–Thurs. 10–4:15, Fri. 9–1:15; mid-June–mid-Sept., Sun.–Thurs. 10–6:15, Fri. 10–3:15* Ⓜ *Bus 46, 64, 87; Tram 8.*

Aventino

AVENTINE HILL, PIAZZA BOCCA
DELLA VERITA, TESTACCIO

WORD OF MOUTH

"Walk around Monte Testaccio. A triumph of marketing, this is the world's best trash heap. Hiding a pile of ancient wine amphorae, this huge hill has become a hip neighborhood with great nightlife and restaurants—we loved Checchino dal 1870 where you can have any part of the cow you wish."

—AmanteDelLimoncello

GETTING ORIENTED

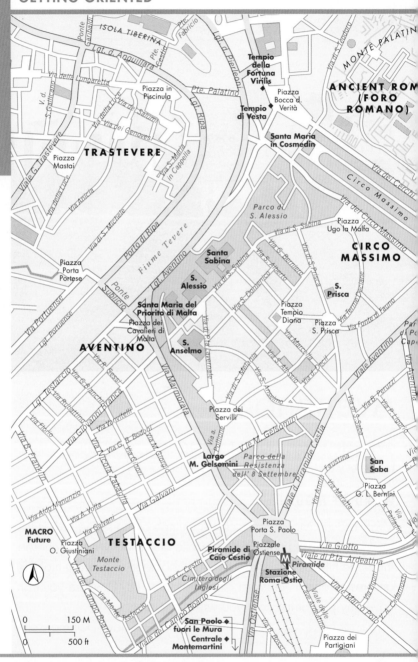

TOP 5 REASONS TO GO

Santa Maria in Cosmedin: Test your truthfulness (or someone else's) at the yawning mouth of the Bocca della Verità.

Cimitero degli Inglesi: Swoon over Keats's body and Shelley's heart in this romantic graveyard.

Piazza Cavalieri di Malta: Peek through the keyhole of the Priorato di Malta for a privileged view—one of Rome's most surprising delights.

Tempting Testaccio: Like New York City's Meatpacking District, this new "It" neighborhood is a sizzling combo of factories and nightclubs.

Roseto Comunale: Overlooking the Circo Massimo (where speeds the ghost of Ben Hur), this rose garden offers a fitting and fragrant vestibule to Rome's most poetic hill.

OK, WHERE DO I START?

After first exploring the two ancient Roman temples and Santa Maria in Cosmedin on Piazza Bocca della Verità, head up the Aventine hill by crossing broad Via della Greca and walk along the street, turning into the first street on the right, Clivo dei Publici. This skirts Valle Murcia, the city's rose garden, open in May and June. Where Clivo dei Publici veers off to the left, continue on Via di Santa Sabina. You'll see Santa Sabina ahead, but just before you reach it, you can take a turn around the delightful walled park, known as the Giardino degli Aranci, famous for its orange trees and wonderful view of the Tiber and St. Peter's Basilica. On the right side of Via di Santa Sabina are two Aventine main attractions: the Early Christian landmark of Santa Sabina and the famous keyhole on Piazza Cavalieri di Malta. Via di Sant'Anselmo winds through quiet residential streets. Cross busy Viale Aventino at Piazza Albania and climb the so-called Piccolo Aventino on Via di San Saba to the medieval church of San Saba. Or from Piazza Cavalieri, head directly down the hill to hip and happening Testaccio.

GETTING HERE

Reaching the Aventine hill on foot from either the Roman Forum or the Campidoglio makes for a spectacular 20-minute walk through ancient ruins like the Circo Massimo. Happily, the subway stop of the same name sits at the foot of the Aventino. Coming from the Colosseum or Trastevere, hop on Bus No. 3. From the Spanish Steps, take Bus No. 160; from Termini, Bus No. 175. For the Testaccio section, use the Piramide (Ostiense) Metro stop. On the Aventine hill, Fodor's Talk Forum poster tomassocroccante notes: "Not far from the famous Priorato di Malta keyhole, walk down the street to the lovely Parco Savelli (great views), near Santa Sabina. At the park's far end is a stone gate leading to a path that descends to the Lungotavere Aventino, not far from famed Piazza Bocca Della Verità."

BEST TIME-OUTS

Cristalli di Zucchero. This chic, Parisian-influenced bakery offers delicious macaroons and cakes so pretty you'll feel bad digging in. Almost. ⊠ *Via di San Teodoro 88, Circo Massimo* ☎ *06/69920945.*

Sicilia e Duci. In the heart of Testaccio, this new Sicilian bakery boasts mouthwatering—and gorgeous—pastries and cannoli. ⊠ *Via Marmorata 87/89, Testaccio* ☎ *06/5743766.*

10

Sightseeing
★★
Nightlife
★★★
Dining
★★
Lodging
★★★
Shopping
★

Rising like a massive headland above the Tiber, the Aventine Hill is the one area in Rome where trills of birdsong win out over the din of traffic. That's highly appropriate, as the hill's name derives from the Latin *avis*, the swallows here having once featured in the bird-watching contest whereby Romulus and Remus decided the best site on which to build their city. As it happened, the Aventine lost out to the Palatine. Still, to Romans, the Aventine is known as the most "poetic" of the city's seven hills, D'Annunzio and other poets long having sung its praises. Scented here with roses (from the Roseto Comunale), there with orange blossom (from the Giardino dei Aranci), and everywhere with pines, it seems the opposite of urban: Rome's most idyllic oasis of calm.

This is a rarefied district, where some houses still have their own bell towers and private gardens are called "parks," without exaggeration. Like the emperors of old on the Palatine, the fortunate residents here look out over the Circus Maximus and the river, winding its way far below. And today's travelers still enjoy the great views, including the famous one spotted through the peculiar keyhole at the gates to the headquarters of the Knights of Malta, which may be the most peered-through in the world—take a look and see why.

At the foot of the Aventine hill to the north, the 1st-century temples to Vesta and Hercules are two of the most complete ancient monuments in the city. They remind us that, under the Republic, this area was home to the "plebs," becoming under the Gracchi a populist stronghold. By Imperial times, however, its tradesman and merchants were displaced by patricians seeking fresh air and space, with grandstand views over the Vallis Murcia, the arena-shaped dip dividing this hill from the Palatine.

Sumptuous villas and gardens sprang up, giving Alaric, when the Goths visited the city in 410 AD, a ready supply of plunder. The Aventine never quite recovered from such depredations.

South of the Aventine, there's an entirely different flavor. Blue-collar Testaccio is flat and homely but as lively as it gets; ancient Rome's dockyard has, in the modern age, an up-and-coming arts scene with music and dance clubs that go all night. You'll know you've reached Testaccio when you see its most incongruous landmark, the Piramide, a large marble pyramid built as a nod to the pharaohs in 12 BC as a tomb for a rich merchant. Behind the monument lie the remains of some of the English poets who put the Rome in *romantic* in the 19th century, in the aptly named, and appropriately scenic, Cimitero degli Inglesi (English Cemetery).

AVENTINO

One of the seven hills on which the city was founded, the Aventine hill enjoys a serenity hard to find elsewhere in Rome. Approach from the Circus Maximus; at the hill's foot, you'll find Piazza Bocca della Verità—the ancient Foro Boario (cattle market)—which is set with both ancient temples and Romanesque churches, making the area one of the most camera-ready in Rome.

TOP ATTRACTIONS

★ **Piazza dei Cavalieri di Malta.** Peek through the keyhole of the **Priorato di Malta,** the walled compound of the Knights of Malta, and you'll get a surprising eyeful: a picture-perfect view of the dome of St. Peter's Basilica, far across the city. This priory landmarks the Piazza dei Cavalieri di Malta. Piranesi—18th-century Rome's foremost engraver—is more famous for drawing architecture than creating it, yet the square is his work along with the priory (1765) within. Stone insignia of the knights notwithstanding, the square's most famed feature is that initially nondescript keyhole in the dark green door of Number 3. Bend slightly and surprise your eyes with a view that is worth walking miles for. As for the Order of the Knights of Malta, it is the world's oldest order of chivalry, founded in the Holy Land during the Crusades, with current headquarters on Rome's Via Condotti. ⊠ *Via Santa Sabina and Via Porta Lavernale, Aventino* 🕾 *06/67581234 to book group tours* ⊙ *Mon.–Sat. 9–noon* Ⓜ *Circo Massimo. Buses 3, 60, 81, 118, 175, 271, 715.*

Roseto Comunale. As signified by the paths shaped like a menorah, this was once a Jewish cemetery (a tombstone is still visible on the side of the garden across from Valle Murcia). The garden is laid out to reflect the history of roses from antiquity to the present day. ⊠ *Viale di Valle Murcia, Aventino* 🕾 *06/5746810* ⊙ *May–June, daily 8–7:30* Ⓜ *Circo Massimo. Buses 3, 60, 81, 118, 160, 271, 628, 715.*

Fodor'sChoice **Santa Maria in Cosmedin.** Though this is one of Rome's oldest churches,
★ with a magical, haunting, almost exotic interior, it plays second fiddle
☾ to the renowned artifact installed in the church portico. The **Bocca della Verità** (Mouth of Truth) is in reality nothing more than an ancient

10

drain cover, unearthed during the Middle Ages. Legend has it, however, that the teeth will clamp down on a liar's hand...and to tell a lie with your hand in the fearsome mouth is to risk losing it. Hordes of tourists line up to take the test every day, with kids especially getting a kick out of it. Few churches, inside or out, are as picturesque as this one. The church was built in the 6th century for the city's burgeoning Greek population. Heavily restored at the end of the 19th century, it has the typical basilica form, and stands across from the **Piazza della Bocca della Verità**, originally the location of the Forum Boarium, ancient Rome's cattle market. ⊠ *Piazza Santa Maria in Cosmedin, Aventino* ☎ *06/6781419* ☉ *May–Sept., daily 9:30–5:50; Oct.–Apr., daily 9:30–4:30* Ⓜ *Circo Massimo. Buses 3, 60, 75, 81, 118, 160, 175, 271, 628.*

★ **Santa Sabina.** This Early Christian basilica demonstrates the severe—but lovely—simplicity common to churches of its era. Although some of the side chapels were added in the 16th and 17th centuries, the essential form is as Rome's Christians knew it in the 5th century. Once bright with mosaics, today the church only has one: that above the entrance door (its gold letters announce how the church was founded by Peter of Illyria, "rich for the poor," under Pope Celestine I). Meanwhile, the mosaics have been partially reproduced in Taddeo Zuccari's Renaissance fresco of Christ and his apostles. Note the beautifully carved, 5th-century cedar doors to the left of the outside entrance: they are the oldest of their kind in existence. ⊠ *Piazza Pietro d'Illiria 1, Via di Santa Sabina, Aventino* ☎ *06/579401* ☉ *Daily 8:30–noon and 3:30–6:30* Ⓜ *Circo Massimo. Buses 3, 60, 75, 81, 118, 160, 175, 715.*

Fodor's Choice ★ **Tempio della Fortuna Virilis.** A picture-perfect, if "dollhouse"-size, Roman temple, this rectangular edifice from the 2nd century BC is built in the Greek style, as was the norm in Rome's early years. It owes its fine state of preservation to the fact that it was consecrated as a Christian church. It was originally built when this giant square was known as the Forum Boarium, ancient Rome's cattle market. ⊠ *Piazza Bocca della Verità, Aventino* Ⓜ *Circo Massimo. Buses 3, 60, 75, 81, 118, 160, 175, 271.*

Fodor's Choice ★ **Tempio di Vesta.** Long called the Temple of Vesta because of its similarity in shape to the building of that name in the Roman Forum, it's now recognized as a temple to Hercules Victor. All but one of the 20 Corinthian columns of this circular temple remain intact. Like its next-door neighbor, the Tempio della Fortuna Virilis, it was built in the 2nd century BC. ⊠ *Piazza Bocca della Verità, Aventino* Ⓜ *Circo Massimo. Buses 3, 60, 75, 81, 118, 160, 175, 271.*

WORTH NOTING

★ **Centrale Montemartini.** After visiting Rome's many old, art-cluttered palaces, the Centrale Montemartini feels like a breath of fresh air. Rome's first electricity plant, repurposed as a museum in 2005, houses the overflow of fabled ancient art from the Capitoline Museum's collection. With Roman sculptures and mosaics set against industrial machinery and pipes, nowhere else in Rome is the contrast between ancient and modern more stark—or enjoyable. A pleasure, too, is the sheer space of the building (and the fact that you're likely to be one of the only visitors here). Unusually, the collection is organized by the district where the ancient pieces were found. Standout pieces include the 4th-century AD mosaic of a hunting scene and two portrait-heads so well preserved that they still retain flakes of the gold that once gilded them. ⊠ *Via Ostiense 106, Aventino* ☎ *06/0608* ⊕ *centralemontemartini.org* ⊠ *€5.50* ⊗ *Tues.–Sun. 9–7* Ⓜ *Garbatella. Bus 23, 271, 769, 770.*

San Saba. Formerly a monastery founded by monks of the order of San Saba after they had fled from Jerusalem following the Arab invasion, this is a major monument of Romanesque Rome. Inside, an almost rustic interior harbors a famed Cosmatesque mosaic pavement. ⊠ *Piazza Gianlorenzo Bernini 20, Via San Saba, Aventino* ☎ *06/64580140* ⊕ *www.sansaba.it* ⊗ *Weekdays and Sat. 8–noon and 4–7:30, Sun. 9:30–1* Ⓜ *Circo Massimo.*

TESTACCIO

Testaccio is perhaps the world's only district built on broken pots: the hill of the same name was born from discarded pottery used to store oil, wine, and other goods loaded from the nearby Ripa, when Rome had a port and the Tiber was once a mighty river to an empire. Quiet during the day, but on Saturday buzzing with the very loud music from rows of discos and clubs (this is sometimes hailed as Rome's new "Left Bank" neighborhood), the area is also a must for those seeking authentic and comparatively cheap Roman cuisine.

TOP ATTRACTIONS

10

★ **Cimitero degli Inglesi** (*Non-Catholic or English Cemetery*). Final resting place of Keats, Shelley's heart, and Goethe's son, this is one of Rome's most picturesque corners. Reminiscent of a country churchyard, this famed cemetery was intended for the interment of non-Catholics. The tomb of John Keats (who tragically died in Rome after succumbing to consumption at age 25 in 1821) is famously inscribed with "Here lies one whose name was writ in water" (the poet said no dates or name should appear). Nearby is the place where Shelley's heart was buried, as well the tombs of Goethe's son, Italian anarchist Antonio Gramsci, and America's famed beat poet Gregory Corso. It is about a 20-minute walk south from the Arch of Constantine along Via San Gregorio and Viale Aventino but the easiest way to get here is to catch the Metro B line from Termini, which deposits you almost directly outside the cemetery. ⊠ *Via Caio Cestio 6, Testaccio* ☎ *06/5741900* ⊕ *www.protestantcemetery. it* ⊗ *Mon.–Sat. 9–5, Sun. 9–1; ring bell for cemetery custodian* Ⓜ *Piramide. Buses 3, 23, 30, 60, 75, 95, 118, 715.*

CLOSE UP

Testaccio: Rome's New "Left Bank'"

After taking in the historic peace and quiet of the Aventine hill, switch lanes and head for the hip-hopping 'hood of Testaccio, especially on Saturday night, when a panoply of clubs and discos rends the air (but is one person's music another's noise pollution?). From the Piazza dei Cavalieri di Malta, take Via di Porta and the Lavernale to Via Marmorata. Testaccio has plain early-1900s housing, a down-to-earth working-class atmosphere, and plenty of good trattorias. And, of course, Monte Testaccio, a grassy knoll about 150 feet high. What makes this otherwise unremarkable-looking hill special is the fact that it's made from pottery shards—pieces of amphorae, large jars used in ancient times to transport oil, wheat, wine, and other goods. Make your way to Piazza Testaccio, dominated by the covered market where you can sample everything from wild strawberries to horsemeat sausage. Move on to the prettier Piazza di Santa Maria Liberatrice. There are some quintessential Roman trattorias along Via Marmorata and near the Mattatoio, the former slaughterhouse. The area sights—the ancient city gate Porta San Paolo, the big white Piramide di Caio Cestio, and the Cimiterio degli Inglesi—are found several blocks to the south around Piazzale Ostiense.

Piramide di Caio Cestio. This monumental tomb was designed in 12 BC for the immensely wealthy praetor Gaius Cestius in the form of a 120-foot-tall pyramid. Though little else is known about him, he clearly had a taste for grandeur—and the then-trendy Egyptian style. On the site of the pyramid is a cat colony run by the famous Roman *gattare* (cat ladies). They look after and try to find homes for some 300 of Rome's thousands of strays (⊕ *www.igattidellapiramide.it*). The pyramid is open to guided tours only (one-hour and in Italian only). ⊠ *Piazzale Ostiense, Testaccio* ☎ *06/39967700 Tour booking and information* ⊕ *www.pierreci.it* ⊠ *€5.50 for tour and visit (in Italian)* Ⓜ *Piramide. Buses 3, 30, 60, 75, 95, 118, 130, 175, 719.*

San Paolo fuori le Mura (*St. Paul's Outside the Walls*). For all its dreary location and dull exterior (19th-century British writer Augustus Hare said the church resembled "a very ugly railway station"), St. Paul's is one of Rome's most important churches. Its size, second only to St. Peter's Basilica, allows ample space for the 272 roundels depicting every pope from St. Peter to Benedict XVI. Built in the 4th century AD by Constantine over the site where St. Paul had been buried, St. Paul's was then destroyed by fire in July 1823. Inside, two great treasures survived: the famous *baldacchino* created by Giotto's contemporary, sculptor Arnolfo di Cambio, along with the Romanesque cloisters. ⊠ *Piazzale San Paolo, Via Ostiense 190, Testaccio* ☎ *06/69880800* ⊠ *€4 for guided tours* ⊕ *www.basilicasanpaolo.org* ☉ *Daily 8–6* Ⓜ *Piramide.*

Esquilino and Celio

CELIAN HILL, BATHS OF CARACALLA, ESQUILINE HILL, THE CATACOMBS

WORD OF MOUTH

"In the Esquilino area, you get a sense of the real Rome, rather than just following the tourist hordesof the Pantheon/Navona area. The frescoes on the Santa Maria Maggiore front are lit up at night: stunning, to sit across the street in a café and stare, in that quiet neighborhood. Nothing like it."

—girlspytravel

GETTING ORIENTED

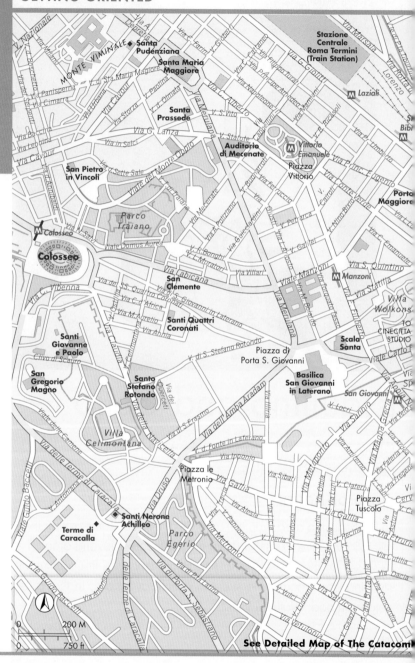

Stazione Centrale Roma Termini (Train Station)

Santa Pudenziana

Santa Maria Maggiore

MONTE VIMINALE

Laziali

Santa Prassede

Auditoria di Mecenate

Vittorio Emanuele

Piazza Vittorio

San Pietro in Vincoli

Porta Maggiore

Parco Traiano

Colosseo

Colosseo

San Clemente

Manzoni

Villa Wolkons

TO CINECITTÀ STUDIO

Santi Quattri Coronati

Scala Santa

Santi Giovanne e Paolo

Piazza di Porta S. Giovanni

San Gregorio Magno

Santo Stefano Rotondo

Basilica San Giovanni in Laterano

San Giovanni

Villa Celimontana

Piazza le Metronio

Piazza Tuscolo

Santi Nerone Achilleo

Terme di Caracalla

Parco Egerio

0   200 M
0   750 ft

See Detailed Map of The Catacomb

TOP 5 REASONS TO GO

San Pietro in Vincoli: Hike uphill past Lucrezia Borgia's palace to visit Michelangelo's magisterial *Moses*.

San Clemente: Hurtle back through three eras—ancient Roman, Early Christian, and medieval—by descending through four excavated levels of this venerated church.

Baths of Caracalla: South of the lovely Villa Celimontana parks tower the Terme di Caracalla, ruins of one of the most spectacular bathing complexes in ancient Rome.

Magnificent Mosaics: In a neighborhood once home to the first Christians, Santa Pudenziana gleams with a stunning 4th-century mosaic of Christ while Santa Prassede shimmers with Byzantine beauty nearby.

Catacomb Country: Be careful exploring the underground graves of the earliest Christians—one wrong turn and you may only surface days later.

BEST TIME-OUT

Enoteca Il Pentagrappolo. With its exposed-brick arches and soft lighting, Il Pentagrappolo offers an ample spread of cheeses and salamis as well as more than 250 wines. On Thursday, Friday, and Saturday nights, there's live jazz, blues, and bossanova. ⊠ *Via Celimontana 21/B, Celio* ☎ *06/7096301* ⊕ *www.ilpentagrappolo.com.*

GETTING HERE

The Esquilino hill can be handily reached with the Piazza Vittorio Emanuele subway stop, about a 10-minute walk from Termini station. The Monti area (running down one side of the Esquilino to the Roman Forum) can be reached by the Cavour Metro stop on Line B. Bus No. 117 runs from Piazza del Popolo and the Corso to both Celio and Monti districts on the Esquilino. Bus No. 3 from Trastevere and Bus No. 75 from Termini reach Celio, about a 5-minute walk from the Colosseo stop.

OK, WHERE DO I START?

If you're tackling the Celian Hill area first, head out from the Arch of Constantine—right by the Colosseum—and walk south along the left side of Via di San Gregorio to the Clivo di Scauro. Ascend this magically picturesque lane to Santi Giovanni e Paolo. Follow the wall lining peaceful Villa Celimontana park and turn right on Via Celimontana to Santo Stefano Rotondo (beware its hyper-gory frescoes).

Backtrack to Piazza Celimontana and head uphill on Via Capo di Africa to the hauntingly medieval church of Santi Quattro Coronati. On the other side of the hill, on Via San Giovanni in Laterano, waits that time machine of a church, San Clemente.

Head back to the Colosseum area and then toward the Esquiline neighborhood by using the Colosseo Metro steps to reach the grandly scenic Largo Agnesi overlook. On the north side of the Colosseum, in the quarter known as Monti, you'll find San Pietro in Vincoli, home to Michelangelo's *Moses.* Walk down Salita dei Borgia, passing under the haunted Torre Borgia palace, to Via Cavour. Cross the street and follow the stairs down to explore Monti, which rivals Trastevere in both age and spirit. Or turn right and head northeast to gigantic Santa Maria Maggiore; nearby are wonderful mosaics in San Prassede and Santa Pudenziana.

Sightseeing
★★★★
Nightlife
★★
Dining
★★★
Lodging
★★★★
Shopping
★★

Rome's most sprawling hill—the Esquiline—lies at the edge of the tourist maps, another Rome. Even Imperial Rome could not have matched this minicosmopolis for sheer internationalism. Right around Termini, sons of the soil, the so-called "romani romani," mingle with Chinese, Sri Lankans, Sikhs, and a hundred nationalities in-between. But not all of this area has the same gritty, graffiti-filled atmosphere you find near the station. Closer to the Colosseum, the Celian Hill area, called "Celio" by locals, is a tranquil, lovely residential area replete with medieval churches and ruins. On the other hand, Monti, a quarter stretching from the Forum to the Basilica of Santa Maria Maggiore, is a *rione* (district) dating back to ancient times, when gladiators, prostitutes, and even Caesar made their homes here. Today, Monti is one of the best-loved neighborhoods in Rome, known for its appealing mix of medieval streets, old-school trattorias, and hip boutiques.

The Esqueline and Celian hills take in some of the city's best sights, including Michelangelo's *Moses*, the Baths of Caracalla, and dazzling Early Christian mosaics at San Clemente and San Pudenziana. Historically speaking, it also took in some of the worst, including the Suburra, Rome's most notorious slum—today, Monti. A dark, warrenlike sector of multistory dwellings populated in part by gladiators from the nearby Colosseum, it lived by its own rules, or lack of them. The empress Messalina would often venture here for illicit pleasures. So mean were the

Suburra's streets that it's thought that the great fire of AD 64, which all but destroyed the neighborhood, may have been ordered by Nero as a public-order measure. But elsewhere on the Esquilino and Celio, Augustus built impressive public markets and the area became the "in" place to be. Palaces of ancient Rome's who's who sprang up with sumptuous gardens to match.

Signs of this remote past are everywhere. The Colosseum's marble-clad walls loom at the end of narrow, shadowy streets with Latin-sounding names: Panisperna, Baccina, Fagutale. Other walls, built for the Caesars, shore up medieval towers. Amid the hints of antiquity, several great churches of the Christian era stand out like islands, connected by broad avenues. The newer streets—laid out by the popes and, later, by city planners at the time of Italy's unification—slice through the meandering byways, providing more direct and navigable routes for pilgrims heading to majestic Santa Maria Maggiore, its interior gleaming with gold from the New World, and San Giovanni in Laterano, with its grand, echoing vastness.

Via Cavour, the area's main drag, extends through the old Suburra to the rough and ready quarter around Termini, Rome's central train station. Predictably gritty, although not unsafe, this area is undergoing a steady transformation as immigration diversifies the face of the city. North of the station, Ethiopian and Eritrean restaurants abound, while just south of the station, Piazza Vittorio and its surrounding streets are an ethnic kaleidoscope, full of Asian and Middle Eastern shops and restaurants. A highlight is the Nuovo Mercato Esquilino, a covered market hall where goods from the four corners of the earth are sold in a multitude of languages. A walk south on Via Merulana leads to San Giovanni, a working-class neighborhood, of late colonized by trendy students, which surrounds Rome's cathedral, San Giovanni in Laterano.

Farther south lies a lovely contrast to the bustle of the Esquiline and San Giovanni quarters: the quiet and green Celio (Celian Hill). Like the Aventino, the Celio seems aloof from the bustle of central Rome. On the slopes of the hill, paths and narrow streets wind through a public park and past walled gardens and some of Rome's earliest churches, such as San Clemente and Santi Quattro Coronati, whose medieval poetry is almost palpable.

Far south of the Celio lies catacomb country—the haunts of the fabled underground graves of Rome's earliest Christians, arrayed to either side of the Queen of Roads, the Appian Way. The gateway to this timeless realm is one of the largest relics of ancient Rome, the Baths of Caracalla. Farther on, the church of Domine Quo Vadis announces you are entering sacred turf, as this is the spot where Jesus is said to have appeared to Peter, causing Peter to ask, *Domine quo vadis?* ("Lord, where are you going?"). As you venture to the catacombs, the countryside is dotted with landmarks like the Tomb of Cecilia Metella that make you feel that the days of the Caesars were not that long ago. Look down from your bus window and you will see chariot ruts.

MONTI AND ESQUILINO

The valley between the Esquiline Hill and the Celian Hill underscores the area's nickname—Monti ("Mounts"). The Esquiline stretches down a hurly-burly slide of the city, from the frantic Termini train station to San Giovanni, a neighborhood long known for its working-class vibe. But if you manage to successfully dodge all the scooters and trucks, you'll find a staggering array of historic churches here, from great pilgrimage basilicas to chapels aglitter with Early Christian mosaics.

TOP ATTRACTIONS

Fodor's Choice ★   **San Clemente.** One of the most impressive archaeological sites in Rome, San Clemente is a historical triple-decker. A 12th-century church was built on top of a 4th-century church, which in turn was built over a 2nd-century pagan temple to the god Mithras and 1st-century Roman apartments. The layers were rediscovered in 1857, when a curious prior, Friar Joseph Mullooly, started excavations beneath the present basilica. Today, you can descend down to explore all three.

The upper church (located at street level) is a gem even on its own. In the apse, a glittering 12th-century mosaic shows Jesus on a cross that turns into a living tree. Green acanthus leaves swirl and teem with small scenes of everyday life. Early Christian symbols, including doves, vines, and fish, decorate the 4th-century marble choir screens. In the left nave, the Castiglioni chapel holds frescoes painted around 1400 by the Florentine artist Masolino da Panicale (1383–1440), a key figure in the introduction of realism and one-point perspective into Renaissance painting. Note the large Crucifixion and scenes from the lives of Sts. Catherine, Ambrose, and Christopher, plus an Annunciation (over the entrance).

To the right of the sacristy (and bookshop), descend the stairs to the 4th-century church, used until 1084, when it was damaged beyond repair during a siege of the area by the Norman prince Robert Guiscard. Still intact are some vibrant 11th-century frescoes depicting stories from the life of St. Clement. Don't miss the last fresco on the left, in what used to be the central nave. It includes a particularly colorful quote—including "Go on, you sons of harlots, pull!"—that's not only unusual for a religious painting, but one of the earliest examples of written vernacular Italian.

Descend an additional set of stairs to the mithraeum, a shrine dedicated to the god Mithras. His cult spread from Persia and gained a hold in Rome during the 2nd and 3rd centuries AD. Mithras was believed to have been born in a cave and was thus worshipped in underground, cavernous chambers, where initiates into the all-male cult would share a meal while reclining on stone couches, some visible here along with the altar block. Most such pagan shrines in Rome were destroyed by Christians, who often built churches over their remains, as happened here. ⊠ *Via San Giovanni in Laterano 108, Monti and Esquilino* ☎ *06/7740021* ⊕ *www.basilicasanclemente.com* ᠍ *Archaeological area €5* ☉ *Mon.–Sat. 9–12:30 and 3–6; Sun. noon–6* Ⓜ *Colosseo.*

San Giovanni in Laterano. The official cathedral of Rome, it's actually San Giovanni in Laterano, not St. Peter's, that serves as the ecclesiastical seat of the bishop of Rome—also known as the pope. San Giovanni dates back to the 4th century, when Emperor Constantine obtained the land from the wealthy Laterani family and donated it to the Church. But thanks to vandals, earthquakes, and fires, today's building owes most of its form to 16th- and 17th-century restorations, including an interior designed by Baroque genius Borromini. Before you go inside, look up: At the top of the towering facade, done for Pope Clement X in 1736, 15 colossal statues (the 12 apostles plus Christ, John the Baptist, and John the Evangelist) stand watch over the suburbs spreading from Porta San Giovanni.

> ### TO MARKET, TO MARKET
>
> For a piece of the new buzzing Esquiline Hill action, try one of Rome's most distinctive luncheon options: the Piazza Vittorio Emanuele, a historic Roman square and its famed food market nearby on Via Principe Amadeo. The surrounding streets are chockablock with international food stores and offer a glimpse at the emerging immigrant scene in the city.

Despite the church's Baroque design, some earlier fragments do remain. Under the portico on the left stands an ancient statue of Constantine, while the central portal's ancient bronze doors were brought here from the Forum's Curia. Inside, the fragment of a fresco on the first pillar is attributed to the 14th-century Florentine painter Giotto; it depicts Pope Boniface VIII proclaiming the first Holy Year in 1300. The altar's rich Gothic tabernacle—holding what the faithful believe are the heads of Sts. Peter and Paul—dates from 1367. Head to the last chapel at the end of the left aisle to check out the **cloister.** Encrusted with 12th-century Cosmatesque mosaics by father-and-son team the Vassallettos, it's a break from Baroque…and from the big tour groups that tend to fill the church's interior. Around the corner, meanwhile, stands one of the oldest Christian structures in Rome. Emperor Constantine built the **Baptistery** in AD 315. While it's certainly changed over time, thanks to several restorations, a 17th-century interior redecoration, and even a Mafia-related car bombing in 1993, the Baptistery remains much like it would have been in ancient times. ⊠ *Piazza di Porta San Giovanni, Monti and Esquilino* ☎ *06/69886433* ⊠ *Church free, cloister €3, museum €4* ⊙ *Church daily 7–6:30. Vassalletto Cloister daily 9–6. Museum daily 9–1. Baptistery daily 7:30–12:30 and 4–6:30.* Ⓜ *San Giovanni.*

★ **San Pietro in Vincoli.** Michelangelo's *Moses*, carved in the early 16th century for the never-completed tomb of Pope Julius II, has put this church on the map. The tomb was to include dozens of statues and stand nearly 40 feet tall when installed in St. Peter's Basilica. But only three statues—*Moses* and the two that flank it here, *Leah* and *Rachel*—had been completed when Julius died. Julius' successor as pope, from a rival family, had other plans for Michelangelo, and the tomb was abandoned unfinished. The fierce power of this remarkable sculpture dominates its setting. People say that you can see the sculptor's profile in the lock of Moses's beard right under his lip, and that the pope's profile is also there somewhere. As for the rest of the church, St. Peter takes second billing to Moses. The reputed chains (*vincoli*) that bound St. Peter during his imprisonment by the Romans in Jerusalem are in a bronze and crystal urn under the main altar. Other treasures in the church include a 7th-century mosaic of St. Sebastian, in front of the second altar to the left of the main altar, and, by the door, the tomb of the Pollaiuolo brothers, two important 15th-century Florentine artists. ⊠ *Piazza San Pietro in Vincoli, Monti and Esquilino* ☎ *06/97844952* ⊘ *Daily 8–12:30 and 3–6* Ⓜ *Cavour.*

Santa Maria Maggiore. The exterior of the church, from the broad sweep of steps on Via Cavour to the more elaborate facade on Piazza Santa Maria Maggiore, is that of a gracefully curving 18th-century building, a fine example of the Baroque architecture of the period. But Santa Maria Maggiore is one of the oldest churches in Rome, built around 440 by Pope Sixtus III. One of the four great pilgrimage churches of Rome, it's also the city center's best example of an Early Christian basilica—one of the immense, hall-like structures derived from ancient Roman civic buildings and divided into thirds by two great rows of columns marching up the nave. The other six major basilicas in Rome (San Giovanni in Laterano and St. Peter's Basilica are the most famous) have been entirely transformed, or even rebuilt. Paradoxically, the major reason why this church is such a striking example of Early Christian design is that the same man who built the incongruous exteriors about 1740, Ferdinando Fuga, also conscientiously restored the interior, throwing out later additions and, crucially, replacing a number of the great columns.

Precious 5th-century mosaics high on the nave walls and on the triumphal arch in front of the main altar are splendid testimony to the basilica's venerable age. Those along the nave show 36 scenes from the Old Testament (unfortunately, tough to see clearly without binoculars), and those on the arch illustrate the Annunciation and the Youth of Christ. The resplendent carved wood ceiling dates from the early 16th century; it's supposed to have been gilded with the first gold brought from the New World. The inlaid marble pavement (called Cosmatesque after the family of master artisans who developed the technique) in the central nave is even older, dating from the 12th century.

The **Cappella Sistina** (Sistine Chapel), which opens onto the right-hand nave, was created by architect Domenico Fontana for Pope Sixtus V in 1585. Elaborately decorated with precious marbles "liberated" from the monuments of ancient Rome, the chapel includes a lower-level museum in which some 13th-century sculptures by Arnolfo da Cambio are all that's left of what was the once richly endowed chapel of the *presepio* (Christmas crèche), looted during the Sack of Rome in 1527.

Directly opposite, on the church's other side, stands the **Cappella Paolina** (Pauline Chapel), a rich Baroque setting for the tombs of the Borghese popes Paul V—who commissioned the chapel in 1611 with the declared intention of outdoing Sixtus's chapel across the nave—and Clement VIII. The **Cappella Sforza** (Sforza Chapel) next door was designed by Michelangelo and completed by della Porta. Just right of the altar, next to his father, lies Gian Lorenzo Bernini; his monument is an engraved slab, as humble as the tombs of his patrons are grand. Above the loggia, the outside mosaic of Christ raising his hand in blessing is, when lit up at night, one of Rome's most beautiful sights. ⊠ *Piazza Santa Maria Maggiore, Monti and Esquilino* ☎ *06/69886802* 🖃 *Free; museum €4* ⊗ *Daily 7–7; museum 9–6* Ⓜ *Termini.*

★ **Santa Prassede.** This small, inconspicuous 9th-century church is known above all for the exquisite **Cappella di San Zenone**, just to the left of the entrance. It gleams with vivid mosaics that reflect their Byzantine inspiration. Though much less classical and naturalistic than the earlier mosaics of Santa Pudenziana, they are no less splendid, and the composition of four angels hovering on the sky-blue vault is one of the masterstrokes of Byzantine art. Note the square halo over the head of Theodora, mother of St. Pasquale I, the pope who built this church. It indicates that she was still alive when she was depicted by the artist. The chapel also contains one curious relic: a miniature pillar, supposedly part of the column at which Christ was flogged during the Passion. It was brought to Rome in the 13th century. Over the main altar, the magnificent mosaics on the arch and apse are also in rigid Byzantine style. In them, Pope Pasquale I wears the square halo of the living and holds a model of his church. ⊠ *Via di Santa Prassede 9/a, Monti and Esquilino* ☎ *06/4882456* ⊗ *Daily 7–noon and 4–6:30* Ⓜ *Cavour.*

Fodor's Choice ★ **Santa Pudenziana.** Outside of Ravenna, Rome has some of the most opulent mosaics in Italy and this church has one of the most striking examples. Commissioned during the papacy of Innocent I, its late 4th-century apse mosaic represents "Christ Teaching the Apostles" and sits high on the wall perched above a Baroque altarpiece surrounded by a bevy of florid 18th-century paintings. Not only is it the largest Early Christian apse mosaic extant, it is remarkable for its iconography. At the center sits Christ Enthroned, looking a bit like a Roman emperor, presiding over his apostles. Each apostle faces the spectator, literally rubs shoulders with his companion (unlike earlier hieratic styles where each figure is isolated), and bears an individualized expression. Above the figures and a landscape that symbolizes the Heavenly Jerusalem float the signs of the four evangelists in a blue sky flecked with an orange sunset, all done in thousands of tesserae. This extraordinary composition seems a sort of paleo-Christian forerunner of Raphael's *School of Athens* in the Vatican.

To either side of Christ, Sts. Praxedes and Pudentia hold wreaths over the heads of Sts. Peter and Paul. These two women were actually daughters of the Roman senator Pudens (probably the one mentioned in 2 Timothy 4:21), whose family befriended both apostles. During the persecutions of Nero, both sisters collected the blood of many martyrs and then suffered the same fate. Pudentia transformed her house into a church, but this namesake church was constructed over a 2nd-century bathhouse. Beyond the sheer beauty of the mosaic work, the size, rich detail, and number of figures make this both the last gasp of ancient Roman art and one of the first monuments of early Christianity. ⊠ *Via Urbana 160, Monti and Esquilino* ☎ *06/4814622* ☉ *Daily 9–noon and 3–6* Ⓜ *Termini.*

WORTH NOTING

Porta Maggiore (*Main Gate*). The massive 1st-century AD monument is not only a *porta* (city gate) but part of the Acqua Claudia aqueduct. It gives you an idea of the grand scale of ancient Roman public works. On the Piazzale Labicano side of the portal, to the east, is the curious **Baker's Tomb,** erected in the 1st century BC by a prosperous baker, shaped like an oven to signal the deceased's trade. ⊠ *Junction of Via Eleniana, Via di Porta Maggiore, and Via Casilina, Monti and Esquilino* Ⓜ *Tram 5, 14, or 19, Bus 3.*

★ **Scala Santa.** According to tradition, the Scala Santa was the staircase from Pilate's palace in Jerusalem—and, therefore, one trodden by Christ himself. St. Helena, Emperor Constantine's mother, brought the 28 marble steps to Rome in 326. As they have for centuries, pilgrims still come to climb the steps on their knees. At the top, they can get a glimpse of the **Sancta Sanctorum** (Holy of Holies), the richly decorated private chapel of the popes containing an image of Christ "not made by human hands." You can sneak a peek, too, by taking one of the (nonsanctified) staircases on either side. ⊠ *Piazza San Giovanni in Laterano, Monti and Esquilino* ☎ *06/69886433* ☉ *Oct.–Mar., weekdays and Sat. 6–noon and 3–6:15, Sun. 7–12:30 and 3–6:30. Apr.–Sept., weekdays and Sat. 6–noon and 3:30–6:45, Sun. 7–12:30 and 3:30–7* Ⓜ *San Giovanni.*

CELIO

As quiet and bucolic as the Esquilino is bustling, the Celian Hill lies across the valley to the south. Celio is like a dip into the Middle Ages. Just off massive Via di S. Gregorio, the most magical gateway to the quarter is the Clivo di Scauro, practically unchanged since medieval times. Picturesquely passing under the Romanesque arches of Santi Giovanni e Paolo, the Clivo was described by author Georgina Masson—in her classic *Companion Guide to Rome*—as one of the few spots in Rome that a medieval pilgrim would easily recognize. And if you continue up the lane to the Villa Celimontana park, you'll find more churches and saintly peace gracing the Celian Hill.

TOP ATTRACTIONS

★ **Case Romane del Celio.** Formerly accessible only through the church of San Giovanni e Paolo, this important ancient Roman excavation was opened in 2002 as a full-fledged museum. An underground honeycomb of rooms, this comprises the lower levels of a so-called *insula,* or

11

apartment tower, the heights of which were a wonder to ancient Roman contemporaries. Through the door on the left of the Clivo di Scauro lane a portico leads to the Room of the Genie, where painted figures grace the walls as if untouched by two millennia. Farther on is the Confessio altar of Sts. John and Paul, officials at Constantine's court who were executed under Julian the Apostate. Still lower is the Antiquarium, where state-of-the-art lighting showcases amphorae, pots, and stamped ancient Roman bricks, the stamps so fresh they might've been imprinted yesterday. ⊠ *Clivus Scauri, Celio* ☎ *06/70454544* ⊕ *www.caseromane. it* 🎫 *€6* ⊗ *Daily 10–1, Tues. and Wed. also 3–6* Ⓜ *Colosseo. Buses 60, 75, 81, 117, 118, 175, Tram 3.*

Fodor'sChoice
★

Santi Giovanni e Paolo. Perched up the incline of the Clivus di Scauro—a magical time machine of a street where the dial seems to be (still!) stuck somewhere in the 13th century—Santi Giovanni e Paolo is an image that would tempt most landscape painters. Landmarked by one of Rome's finest Romanesque bell towers, it looms over a poetic piazza. Underneath, however, are other treasures, whose excavations can be seen in the new Case Romane del Celio museum (⇨ *see above*). A basilica erected on the spot was, like San Clemente, destroyed in 1084 by attacking Normans. Its half-buried columns, near the current church entrance, are visible through misty glass. The current church has its origins at the start of the 12th century, but the interior dates mostly from the 17th century and later. The lovely, incongruous chandeliers are a hand-me-down from New York's Waldorf-Astoria hotel, a gift arranged by the late Cardinal Francis Spellman of New York, whose titular church this was. Spellman also initiated the excavations here in 1949. ⊠ *Piazza Santi Giovanni e Paolo 13, Celio* ☎ *06/772711* ⊗ *Oct.–Apr., 8:30–noon and 3:30–6; May–Sept., 8:30–12:30 and 3:30–6:30* Ⓜ *Colosseo.*

Fodor'sChoice
★

Santi Quattro Coronati. One of those evocative cul-de-sacs in Rome where history seems to be holding its breath, this church is strongly imbued with the sanctity of the Romanesque era. Marvelously redolent of the Middle Ages, this is one of the most unusual and unexpected corners of Rome, a quiet citadel that has resisted the tides of time and traffic. The church, which dates back to the 4th century, honors the Four Crowned Saints—the four brothers Seveus, Severinus, Carpophorus, and Victorius, all Roman officials who were whipped to death for their faith by Emperor Diocletian (284–305). After its 9th century reconstruction, the church was twice as large as it is now. The abbey was partially destroyed during the Normans' sack of Rome in 1084, but reconstructed about 30 years later. This explains the inordinate size of the apse in relation to the small nave. Don't miss the **cloister,** with its well-tended gardens and 12th-century fountain. The entrance is the door in the left nave; ring the bell if it's not open.

There's another medieval gem hidden away off the courtyard at the church entrance: the **Chapel of San Silvestro.** (Enter the door marked "Monache Agostiniane" and ring the bell at the left for the nun; give her the appropriate donation through a grate, and she will press a button to open the chapel door automatically.) The chapel has remained, for the most part, as it was when consecrated in 1246. Some of the best-preserved medieval frescoes in Rome decorate the walls, telling the story of the Christian emperor Constantine's recovery from leprosy thanks to Pope Sylvester I. Note, too, the delightful *Last Judgment* fresco above the door, in which the angel on the left neatly rolls up sky and stars like a backdrop, signaling the end of the world. ⊠ *Via Santi Quattro Coronati 20, Celio* ☎ *06/70475427* 🖥 *Church and cloister free; Chapel of St. Sylvester €1 donation* ⊘ *Basilica, Mon.–Sat. 6:15am–8pm, Sun. 6:45–12:30 and 3–7:30. Cloister and San Silvestro Chapel, Mon.–Sat. 9:30–noon and 4:30–6, Sun. 9–10:40 and 4–5:45* Ⓜ *Colosseo.*

Santo Stefano Rotondo. This 5th-century church likely was inspired by the design of the church of the Holy Sepulchre in Jerusalem. Its unusual round plan and timbered ceiling set it apart from most other Roman churches. So do the frescoes, which lovingly depict the goriest martyrdoms of 34 different Catholic saints. You've been warned: these are not for the fainthearted, cataloging, above the names of different emperors, every type of violent death conceivable. ⊠ *Via Santo Stefano Rotondo 7, Celio* ☎ *06/421199* ⊘ *End of Oct. to Mar., Tues.–Sat. 9:30–12:30 and 3–6, Sun. 9:30–12:30; Apr.–Oct., Tues.–Sat. 9:30–12:30 and 2–5, Sun. 9:30–12:30* Ⓜ *Colosseo.*

★ **Terme di Caracalla** (*Baths of Caracalla*). The Terme di Caracalla are some
🕓 of Rome's most massive—yet least-visited—ruins. They're also a peek into how Romans turned "bathing" into one of the most lavish leisure activities imaginable.

Begun in AD 206 by the emperor Septimius Severus and completed by his son, Caracalla, the 28-acre complex could accommodate 1,600 bathers at a time. Along with an Olympic-size swimming pool and baths, the complex also boasted two different gymnasiums for weight-lifting, boxing, and wrestling, a library with both Latin and Greek texts, and shops, restaurants, and gardens. All the services depended on slaves, who checked clients' robes, rubbed them down, stoked the fires in the basements, and saw to all of their needs.

Taking a bath was a long and complex process—something that makes more sense if you see it, first and foremost, as a social activity. You began in the *sudatoria,* a series of small rooms resembling saunas. Here you sat and sweated. From these you moved to the *caldarium,* a large, circular room that was humid rather than simply hot. This was where the actual business of washing went on. You used a *strigil,* or scraper, to get the dirt off; if you were rich, your slave did this for you. Next stop: the warm(-ish) *tepidarium,* which helped you start cooling down. Finally, you splashed around in the *frigidarium,* a swimming pool filled with cold water.

Today, the complex is a shell of its former self. While some black-and-white mosaic fragments remain, you have to use your imagination to see the interior as it would have been, filled with opulent mosaics, frescoes, and sculptures, including the famous Farnese Bull. But for getting a sense of the sheer size of ancient Rome's ambitions, few places are better. The walls still tower, the spaces still dwarf, and—if you try—you almost can hear the laughs of long-gone bathers, splashing in the pools. If you're here in the summer, don't miss the chance to catch an

Walk in the footsteps of St. Peter along the Via Appia Antica, stretches of which seem barely altered from the days of the Caesars.

open-air opera or ballet in the baths, put on by the Teatro dell'Opera di Roma (€25–€110; 06/48078400). ⊠ *Via delle Terme di Caracalla 52, Aventino* ☎ *06/39967700* ⊕ *www.pierreci.it* 🎟 *€6 (includes Villa dei Quintili and Mausoleo di Cecilia Metella)* ⊙ *Mon. 9–2, Tues.–Sun. 9 until one hr before sunset* Ⓜ *Circo Massimo.*

WORTH NOTING

San Gregorio Magno. Set amid the greenery of the Celian Hill, this church wears its Baroque facade proudly. Dedicated to St. Gregory the Great (who served as pope 590–604), it was built about 750 by Pope Gregory II to commemorate his predecessor and namesake. The church of San Gregorio itself has the appearance of a typical Baroque structure, the result of remodeling in the 17th and 18th centuries. But you can still see what's said to be the stone slab on which the pious Gregory the Great slept; it's in the far right-hand chapel. Outside are three chapels. The right chapel is dedicated to Gregory's mother, St. Sylvia, and contains a Guido Reni fresco of the *Concert of Angels*. The chapel in the center, dedicated to St. Andrew, contains two monumental frescoes showing scenes from the saint's life. They were painted at the beginning of the 17th century by Domenichino (*The Flagellation of St. Andrew*) and Guido Reni (*The Execution of St. Andrew*). It's a striking juxtaposition of the sturdy, if sometimes stiff, classicism of Domenichino with the more flamboyant and heroic Baroque manner of Guido Reni. After being closed for safety reasons, the church has been restored and reopened to the public. ⊠ *Piazza San Gregorio, Celio* ☎ *06/7008227* ⊙ *Daily 8:30–12:30 and 3–6* Ⓜ *Colosseo.*

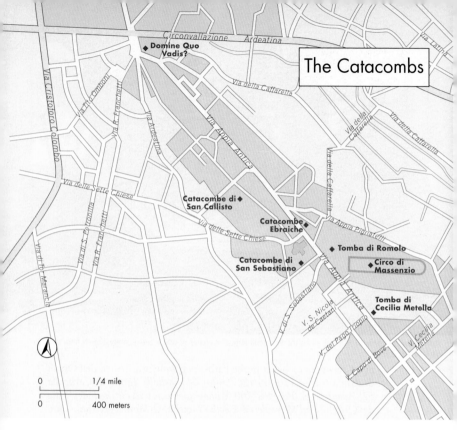

THE CATACOMBS AND VIA APPIA ANTICA

Strewn with classical ruins and dotted with grazing sheep, the Via Appia Antica (Appian Way) stirs images of chariots and legionnaires returning from imperial conquests. It was completed in 312 BC by Appius Claudius, who laid it out to connect Rome with settlements in the south, in the direction of Naples. Here Peter is said to have been stopped by Christ, as commemorated by the Domine Quo Vadis church. Though time and vandals have taken their toll on the ancient relics along the road, the catacombs remain to cast their spirit-warm spell. Although catacombs were used by both Jews and pagans, the Christians expanded the idea of underground burials to a massive scale. Persecution of Christians under pagan emperors made martyrs of many, whose bones, once interred underground, became objects of veneration. Today, the dark, gloomy catacombs contrast strongly with the fresh air, verdant meadows, and evocative classical ruins along the ancient Via Appia Antica, one of Rome's most magical places for a picnic.

The initial stretch of the Via Appia Antica is not pedestrian-friendly—there is fast, heavy traffic and no sidewalk all the way from Porta San Sebastiano to the Catacombe di San Callisto. To reach the catacombs, one route is Bus No. 218 from San Giovanni in Laterano. Alternatively, take Metro line A to Colli Albani and Bus No. 660 to the Tomb of Cecilia Metella. A more expensive option is No. 110 Archeobus from Piazza Venezia; with an open-top deck the big green buses allow you to hop on and off as you please at a price of €12 for two days. An attractive alternative is to hire a bike.

TOP ATTRACTIONS

★ **Catacombe di San Callisto** (*Catacombs of St. Calixtus*). Burial place of many popes of the 3rd century, this is the oldest and best-preserved underground cemetery. One of the (English-speaking) friars who act as custodians of the catacomb will guide you through its crypts and galleries, some adorned with Early Christian frescoes. Watch out for wrong turns: this is a five-story-high catacomb! ⊠ *Via Appia Antica 110/126, Via Appia Antica* ☎ *06/5310151* ⊕ *www.catacombe.roma.it* ⊠ *€8* ⊗ *Thurs.–Tues. 9–noon and 2–5. Closed Feb.* Ⓜ *Bus 118, 218.*

Catacombe di San Sebastiano (*Catacombs of St. Sebastian*). The 4th-century church was named after the saint who was buried in the catacomb, which burrows underground on four different levels. This was the only Early Christian cemetery to remain accessible during the Middle Ages, and it was from here that the term *catacomb* is derived—it's in a spot where the road dips into a hollow, known to the Romans as *catacumbas* (Greek for "near the hollow"). The Romans used the name to refer to the cemetery that had existed here since the 2nd century BC, and it came to be applied to all the underground cemeteries discovered in Rome in later centuries. ⊠ *Via Appia Antica 136, Via Appia Antica* ☎ *06/7850350* ⊕ *www.catacombe.org* ⊠ *€8* ⊗ *Mon.–Sat. 10–4:30, closed the 3rd wk of Nov. and 3rd wk of Dec.* Ⓜ *Bus 118, 218, 660.*

Domine Quo Vadis? (*Church of Lord, Where Goest Thou?*). Domine Quo Vadis? This church was built on the spot where tradition says Christ appeared to St. Peter as the apostle was fleeing Rome and persuaded him to return and face martyrdom. A paving stone in the church bears an imprint said to have been made by the feet of Christ. ⊠ *Via Appia Antica at Via Ardeatina, Via Appia Antica* ☎ *06/5120441* ⊗ *Daily 8–6.*

Fodor's Choice
★ **Tomba di Cecilia Metella.** For centuries, sightseers have flocked to this famous landmark, one of the most complete surviving tombs of ancient Rome. One of the many round mausoleums that once lined the Appian Way, this tumulus-shape tomb is a smaller version of the Mausoleum of Augustus, but impressive nonetheless. It was the burial place of a Roman noblewoman, wife of the son of Crassus, one of Julius Caesar's rivals and known as the richest man in the Roman Empire (infamously entering the English language as "crass"). The original decoration includes a frieze of bulls' skulls near the top. The travertine stone walls were made higher and the medieval-style crenellations added when the tomb was transformed into a fortress by the Caetani family in the 14th century. An adjacent chamber houses a small museum of the area's geological phases. ⊠ *Via Appia Antica 162, Via Appia Antica* ☎ *06/39967700* ⊠ *€6 (also includes entry to Terme di Caracalla and Villa dei Quintili)* ⊗ *Tues.–Sun. 9–1 hr before sunset.*

NEED A BREAK?

Appia Antica Caffè. Placed strategically at the bus stop, the Appia Antica Caffè is a bar rare for its sound of birdsong. It also offers lunch and hires out bikes, which is an economical way of exploring the catacombs and other monuments to the right, spread as they are over several miles (if you're heading leftward, opt for the bus as those bike routes can be blocked off). ⊠ *Via Appia Antica 175, Via Appia Antica* ☎ *3383465440.*

WORTH NOTING

Fodor'sChoice ★ **Cinecittà Studios.** Film lovers will want to make the trip out to Cinecittà Studios, stomping ground of Fellini, Audrey Hepburn, and Elizabeth Taylor and home to such classics as *Roman Holiday*, *Cleopatra*, and *La Dolce Vita*. Another draw is the set built for the recent BBC/HBO series *Rome*, which includes movie versions of ancient homes, temples, and streets. You can take a guided tour of the sets. It also seems likely that the very popular 2011–2012 exhibition *Cinecittà Shows Off*, with its displays of memorabilia like Elizabeth Taylor's *Cleopatra* gown and the dolphin-shaped statue that marked the chariot laps in *Ben-Hur*, may be made permanent (although this had not been announced at press time). Check ⊕ *www.cinecittastudios.it* for more information. Cinecittà is located about 20 minutes southeast on Line B from the Colosseo stop. ⊠ *Via Tuscolana 1055, Cinecittà* ☎ *06/722931* ⊕ *www.cinecittastudios. it* ☑ *€10 exhibition, €20 exhibition and tour* ☉ *Guided tours Mon. and Wed.–Fri. 10:30–2, weekends 10:30–4:30* Ⓜ *Cinecittà.*

Circo di Massenzio. Of the Circus of Maxentius, built in AD 309, remain the towers at the entrance; the *spina*, the wall that divided it down the center; and the vaults that supported the tiers of seating for the spectators. The obelisk now in Piazza Navona was found here. The adjacent **Mausoleo di Romolo** is a huge tomb built by the emperor for his son Romulus, who died young. The tomb and circus were on the grounds of the emperor's villa. ⊠ *Via Appia Antica 153, Via Appia Antica* ☎ *06/0608* ⊕ *www.villadimassenzio.it* ☑ *€4* ☉ *Tues.–Sun. 9–1:30* Ⓜ *Bus: 118.*

★ **Villa dei Quintili.** Even in ruins, this splendid, 52-room villa gives a real sense of ancient Rome's opulence. Even today, two millennia later, it remains clear why Emperor Commodus—the villain in *The Fall of the Roman Empire* and *Gladiator*—coveted the sumptuous property. To get the villa from its owners, the Quintili, he accused the family of plotting against him—and had them executed before moving in himself. He may have used the exedra for training for his fights with ostriches back in the Colosseum. (Note that the villa is best included in a separate itinerary from the catacombs, being 5 km [3 miles] away and accessible by a different route.) ⊠ *Via Appia Nuova 1092, Via Appia Antica* ☎ *06/39967700* ☑ *€6 (includes entrance to Terme di Caracalla and Mausoleo di Cecilia Metella)* ☉ *Tues.–Sun. 9–1 hr before sunset (last entrance 1 hr before closing time)* Ⓜ *Bus 664 from Colli Albani Metro A.*

Where to Eat

WORD OF MOUTH

"We loved La Pergola. After looking through the water menu (it took me a few minutes to realize it was water), I asked for the salt menu. They immediately came with a tray of many small hills of different salts. Yes, it was over the top but [the restaurant] is great for a special occasion."

—Elainee

THE SCENE

Updated by
Dana Klitzberg

In Rome, the Eternal(ly culinarily conservative) City, simple yet joyously traditional cuisine reigns supreme. Most chefs prefer to follow the mantra of freshness over fuss, simplicity of flavor and preparation over complex cooking methods. Here, it's always the old reliables everyone falls back on, the recipes time-tested by centuries of mammas that still manage to put meat on your bones and smiles on your faces.

Rome has been known since ancient times for its grand feasts and banquets, and though the days of the emperor's triclinium and the Saturnalia feasts are long past, dining out is still the Roman's favorite pastime. But even the city's buongustaii (gourmands) will be the first to tell you Rome is distinguished more by its good attitude toward eating out than by a multitude of world-class restaurants; simple, traditional cuisine reigns supreme.

It has been this way ever since the days of the Caesars. Today, you can still dine on a beef-and-citron stew that comes from an ancient recipe of Apicius, probably the first celebrity chef (to Emperor Tiberius) and cookbook author of the Western World. For the most part, today's chefs cling to the traditional and excel at what has taken hundreds, sometimes thousands, of years to perfect. This is why the basic trattoria menu is more or less the same wherever you go. And it's why even the top Roman chefs feature their versions of simple trattoria classics like pasta all'amatriciana (pasta with a tomato, Roman bacon, chili pepper, and pecorino cheese sauce—sometimes with onion, although that's an issue of debate). To a great extent, Rome deliciously is still a town where the Italian equivalent of "what are you in the mood to eat?" translates to "pizza or pasta?"

VATICAN
residential, refined neighborhood favorites

SPAGNA, TREVI & QUIRINALE
celebrity hot spots & shopping-spree respites

BORGHESE & VENETO
former "dolce vita" haunts now overpriced tourist traps

REPUBBLICA & SAN LORENZO
student haunts & innovative regional cuisine

NAVONA
hot young chefs' outposts; traditional pizza joints

PANTHEON
creative assortment of mid-range dining options

MONTI & ESQUILINO
ethnic spots & hip up-and-comers

CAMPO DE' FIORI
trattorias featuring market-fresh ingredients

GHETTO
traditional Roman & Jewish Roman fare among the ruins

TRASTEVERE & GIANICOLO
cheap joints, local favorites

COLOSSEO
local pizzerias & trattorias for tourists & locals alike

AVENTINO & TESTACCIO
old-school Roman eateries meet club/lounge scene

Villa Giulia

Villa Strohl Fern

Parco D.Daini

Giardino D.Lago

Villa Borghese

Villa Medici

Via d. Armi

Lgt. A. da Brescia

Via Flaminia

Lgt. Michelangelo

Via L. di Savoia

Viale del Muro Torto

Corso d'Italia

Via Salaria

Fiume Tevere

Lgt. Prati

Lgt. Marzio

Lgt. Castello

Lgt. Tor di Nona

Via Nazionale

Via A. Depretis

C.so Vittorio Emanuele II

Lgt. Gianicolense

Lgt. Sangallo

Fiume Tevere

Lgt. dei Tebaldi

Lgt. della Farnesina

Lgt. dei Vallati

Lgt. dei Cenci

Lgt. Raff Sanzio

Lgt. d. Anguillara

Lgt. d. Pierleoni

Villa Corsini

Villa Sciarra

Via G. Trastevere

Via di Trastevere

Porto di Risa

Porto di Ripa

Via Marmorata

Fiume Tevere

Via dei Fori

Parco Traiano

Via Labicana

Parco Di Porta Capena

Villa Celimontana

Via delle Terme di Caracalla

Via Druso

Via Aventino

Viale Aventino

V. di. S. Gregorio

Parco Della Resistenza, Dell'8 Sett.

LA CUCINA ROMANA

Hearty, unflinching, and proud, *la cucina romana* originates from all of the various geographic and cultural influences on the city over more than 2,000 years. This has led to an emphasis on meat, since Rome's Testaccio area was once a central zone for the butcher trade in this part of the country, resulting in some tongue-tingling "soul food"—the ubiquity of guanciale (cured pork jowl) in Roman pastas, as well as meat dishes like abacchio (baby lamb) and porchetta (roast pork).

From this grew the famed (or notorious) old-school Roman dishes of the quinto quarto, or "fifth quarter": offal and throw-away parts that were left after the butchers had sold the best cuts to paying customers. This gave birth to coda alla vaccinara (oxtail stewed with celery and tomatoes), pasta with pajata (baby lamb or calf intestines with the mother's milk still inside), coratella (a mix of lamb innards including heart), and trippa alla romana (tripe boiled in a savory tomato sauce).

But Roman cuisine takes as much from the sea as it does from land, as the Mediterranean—Ostia and Fiumicino being the closest towns—is only 25 kilometers (15 mi) from the city center. A variety of fish, including seabass, turbot, and gilthead bream, is served in local restaurants, cooked simply in the oven, on the grill, or baked in a salt crust. And crustaceans, from gamberetti (baby shrimp) to scampi (langoustines) to spiny lobster are served alongside a family of calamari, cuttlefish, octopus, and small and large versions of everything in between.

And the produce! Heading to an outdoor market anywhere in the city will educate you on exactly what is in season at the moment, and what the bounties of Italy, and particularly the Lazio region (where Rome is located) have to offer. Rome has always loved its greens, whether it's chicory or spinach or arugula, or dandelion, beet or broccoli greens. Not to mention beans (string, fava, and broad, to name a few), as well as squash, zucchini, pumpkins, broccoli, and agretti, a staunchly Roman green that resemble sturdy chives and taste more like spinach—if you ask for it outside of Rome, vendors will look at you as if you come from another planet.

Speaking of outside of Rome, the most delicious strawberries (and teeny, fragrant wild strawberries) of the region come from Nemi, a hill town in the Castelli Romani outside of the city. Rome in the summer has an abundance of stone fruits and seasonal treats (fresh plums, apricots, and figs are nothing like their dried counterparts and should be tasted to be believed), and great citrus in cooler months, like the sweet-tasting, beautiful blood oranges arriving daily from Sicily, which are often fresh-squeezed and served in tall glasses at Roman caffè.

EATING LOCAL

Like the Florentines with their cuisine and the Milanese with theirs, Romans go out to eat expecting to "eat local." Forget about Thai stir-frys or Brazilian-style steaks, even the bollito (boiled meats) from Bologna or the cuttlefish risotto from Venice are regarded as "foreign" food. But Rome is the capital city, and the influx of immigrants from other regions of the country is enough to insure there are more variations on the Italian theme in Rome than you'd find anywhere else in the country: Sicilian, Tuscan, Pugliese, Bolognese, Marchegiano, Sardinian, and northern Italian regional cuisines are all represented. And, reflecting the increasingly cosmopolitan nature of the city, you'll find a growing number of good-quality international food here as well, particularly Japanese, Indian, and Ethiopian.

12

DELICIOUS DÉCOR?

Oddly enough for a nation that prides itself on bella figura ("looking good"), most Romans don't care about the background music, other people's personal space, the lighting, or the fanfare of décor. After all, dining al fresco in Rome can place you smack dab in the middle of a glorious Baroque painting.

While the city has some pretty restaurants, and legendary ones that are noted for their historic surrounds—Romolo's, Osteria del Orso, and the Casino Valadier pavilion in the Pincio park—you'll lose count of the osterias that have walls lined with cheap reproductions of Michelangelo's Sistine Chapel ceiling or Raphael's cherubic angels. You'll have to overlook the garish lighting that illuminates pallid skin and every wrinkle and blemish you never knew you had.

The best, most legendary places are almost always overstuffed, with uncomfortable seating and harried service—and there are never enough menus to go around.

But if you can get past this, if you can look beyond the trappings as Romans do, you can eat like an emperor—or at least a well-fed member of the Roman working class—for very little money. Then, the comraderie and friendships and conversations that arise are just a bonus; it's not unusual to share wine with neighbors, or have a forkful of pasta offered to you by the old man sitting on his own at the next table (he probably eats here three times a week). You'll discover there is unmeasurable joy in allowing someone to *fare una scarpetta* (literally "make a little shoe," meaning to sop up sauce with a piece of bread) in your pasta bowl, if only for the satisfied grin on the person's face afterward.

PLANNING

EATING OUT STRATEGY

Where should we eat? With hundreds of eateries competing for your attention, it may seem like a daunting question. But fret not—our expert writers and editors have done the legwork. The 100-plus selections here represent the best the city has to offer, from *caffè* and *gelaterias* to formal *alta cucina* restaurants.

Search our Best Bets feature for top recommendations by price, cuisine, and experience. Sample local flavor in the neighborhood features, or find a review quickly in the listings. They're organized alphabetically within each neighborhood. Delve in and enjoy! Buon Appetito!

RESTAURANT TYPES

Until relatively recently, there was a distinct hierarchy delineated by the names of Rome's eating places. A *ristorante* was typically elegant and expensive; a *trattoria* served more traditional, home-style fare in a relaxed atmosphere; an *osteria* was even more casual, essentially a wine bar and gathering spot that also served food, although the latest species of hip wine bars is now called an *enoteca*. The terms still exist but the distinction has blurred considerably. Now, an osteria in the center of town may be pricier than a ristorante across the street.

HOW TO ORDER: FROM PRIMO TO DOLCE

In a Roman sit-down restaurant, whether a ristorante, trattoria, or osteria, you're expected to order at least a two-course meal. It could be a *primo* (first course, usually pasta or an appetizer) with a *secondo* (second course, which is really a "main course" in English parlance, usually meat or fish); an *antipasto* (starter) followed by a primo or secondo; or a secondo and a *dolce* (dessert). Many people consider a full-rounded meal to consist of a primo, a secondo, and a dolce. If you're in a rush, however, many people only order two of these three courses.

In a pizzeria, it's common to order just one dish. The handiest places for a snack between sights are bars, caffè, and *pizza al taglio* (by the slice) shops. Bars are places for a quick coffee and a sandwich, rather than drinking establishments.

A *caffè* (café) is a bar but usually with more seating. If you place your order at the counter, ask if you can sit down: some places charge more for table service. Often you'll pay a cashier first, then give your *scontrino* (receipt) to the person at the counter who fills your order.

It was not so long ago that the wine you could get in Rome was strictly local; you didn't have to walk far to find a restaurant where you could buy wine straight from the barrel then sit down to drink and nibble a bit. The tradition continues today, as many Roman wine shops also serve food, and are called *enotecas* (wine bars). Behind the bar you'll find serious wine enthusiasts—maybe even a sommelier—with several bottles open to be tasted by the glass. There are often carefully selected cheeses and cured meats, and a short menu of simple dishes and desserts, making a stop in an enoteca an appealing alternative to a three-course restaurant meal.

MEAL TIMES AND CLOSURES

Breakfast (*la colazione*) is usually served from 7 am to 10:30 am, lunch (*il pranzo*) from 12:30 pm to 2:30 pm, dinner (*la cena*) from 7:30 pm to 11 pm. Peak times are around 1:30 pm for lunch and 9 pm for dinner.

Enotecas (wine bars) are sometimes open in the morning and late afternoon for snacks. Most pizzerias open at 8 pm and close around midnight–1 am. Most bars and caffè are open from 7 am to 8 or 9 pm.

Almost all restaurants close one day a week (in most cases Sunday or Monday) and for at least two weeks in August. The city is zoned, however, so that there are always some restaurants in each zone that

12

remain open, to avoid tourists (and residents) getting stuck without any options whatsoever.

Also keep in mind that the laws are in the process of changing in Rome, giving proprietors more leeway in their opening and closing hours. The law is meant to enable places to stay open later, to make more money in a down economy and to offer patrons longer hours and more time to eat, drink, and be merry. It has yet to be seen whether or not Italians will find the law "flexible" and use it as an excuse to also close early when they feel like it. *E' tutto possibile*: anything's possible in Rome.

PRICES

Most restaurants have a "cover" charge, usually listed on the menu as *pane e coperto*. It should be modest (€1–€2.50 per person) except at the most expensive restaurants. Some restaurants instead charge for bread, which should be brought to you (and paid for) only if you order it. When in doubt, ask about the cover policy before ordering. Note that the price of fish dishes is often given by weight (before cooking); the price on the menu will be for 100 grams, not for the whole fish. An average fish portion is about 300 grams. *Note that in our restaurant reviews, the "average cost" of a meal consists of three courses: a primo (pasta or appetizer), a secondo (meat or fish), and a dolce (dessert).*

TIPPING AND TAXES

All prices include tax. Restaurant menu prices include *servizio* (service) unless indicated otherwise. It's customary to leave a small tip (from a euro to 10% of the bill) in appreciation of good service. Tips are always given in cash, and cannot be added to a bill paid for by credit card, as is standard in the United States.

WITH KIDS

In restaurants and trattorias you may find a high chair or a cushion for the child to sit on, but there's rarely a children's menu. Order a *mezza porzione* (half portion) of any dish, or ask the waiter for a *porzione da bambino* (child's portion).

WHAT TO WEAR

We mention dress only when men are required to wear a jacket or a jacket and tie. Keep in mind that Italian men never wear shorts in a restaurant or *enoteca* (wine bar) and infrequently wear sneakers or running shoes, no matter how humble the establishment. The same "rules" apply to ladies' casual shorts, running shoes, and flip-flop sandals. Shorts are acceptable in pizzerias and caffé.

BEST BETS FOR ROME DINING

With thousands of restaurants to choose from, how will you decide where to eat? Fodor's writers and editors have selected their favorite restaurants by price, cuisine, and experience in the Best Bets lists here. In the first column, Fodor's Choice properties represent the "best of the best." You can also search by neighborhood for excellent eats—just peruse the following pages. Or find specific details about a restaurant in the full reviews, *listed later in the chapter.*

Antico Arco, pg. 283
Il Convivio, pg. 261
Il Sanlorenzo, pg. 266
La Pergola, pg. 286
La Rosetta, pg. 262
San Teodoro, pg. 284

Best by Cuisine

CENTRAL ITALIAN

Dal Bolognese, $$$$, pg. 273
Trattoria Monti, $$, pg. 269

MODERN ITALIAN

Agata e Romeo, $$$$, pg. 270
Il Bacaro, $$, pg. 259
Il Convivio, $$$$, pg. 261
Il Pagliaccio, $$$$, pg. 262
La Pergola, $$$$, pg. 286
Osteria dell'Ingegno, $$$, pg. 263
Taverna Angelica, $$$, pg. 278
Uno e Bino, $$$, pg. 272

MEAT

Angelina, $$, p. 284
Dal Toscano, $$$, pg. 278
Il Ciak, $$, pg. 280
Il Simposio di Costantini, $$$$, pg. 278
Maccheroni, $$, pg. 259
Tullio, $$$, pg. 263

Fodor'sChoice ★

Acchiappafantasmi, $, p. 263
Agata e Romeo, $$$$, p. 270
Armando al Pantheon, $$, p. 258
Cul de Sac, $$, p. 260
Da Baffetto, $, pg. 260
Ditirambo, $$, p. 265
Etablì, $$$, pg. 261
Filetti di Baccalà, $, pg. 265
Hostaria dell'Orso, $$$$, p. 259
Il Convivio, $$$$, pg. 261
Il Pagliaccio, $$$$, p. 262
Il Sanlorenzo, $$$$, pg. 266
La Gensola, $$$, pg. 280
La Pergola, $$$$, pg. 286
La Rosetta, $$$$, pg. 262

La Veranda dell'Hotel Columbus, $$$, pg. 276
Nino, $$$, p. 276
Osteria dell'Ingegno, $$$, pg. 263
San Teodoro, $$$$, pg. 284
Taverna Angelica, $$$, pg. 278
Tram Tram, $$, pg. 271
Trattoria Monti, $$, pg. 269
Uno e Bino, $$$, pg. 272
Vecchia Roma, $$$, pg. 269

Best by Price

$

Acchiappafantasmi, p. 263
Da Baffetto, pg. 260
Da Sergio, pg. 265
Dar Poeta, pg. 279
Filetti di Baccalà, pg. 265

Panattoni, pg. 282
Remo, pg. 285

$$

Alle Fratte di Trastevere, pg. 279
Cul de Sac, pg. 260
Ōbikā, pg. 262
Tram Tram, pg. 271
Trattoria Moderna, pg. 267
Trattoria Monti, pg. 269

$$$

Etablì, pg. 261
La Gensola, pg. 280
La Veranda dell'Hotel Columbus, pg. 276
Osteria dell'Ingegno, pg. 263
Taverna Angelica, pg. 278
Uno e Bino, pg. 272

$$$$

Agata e Romeo, pg. 270

12

PIZZA

Acchiappafantasmi, $,
pg. 263

Da Baffetto, $, pg. 260

Dar Poeta, $, pg. 279

Panattoni, $, pg. 282

ROMAN

Armando al Pantheon, $$, p. 258

Checchino dal 1887, $$$$, pg. 284

Da Sergio, $, pg. 265

Piperno, $$$, pg. 268

SEAFOOD

Acquolina, $$$$, pg. 285

F.I.S.H., $$$, pg. 269

Il Sanlorenzo, $$$$, pg. 266

La Rosetta, $$$$, pg. 262

San Teodoro, $$$$, pg. 284

SOUTHERN ITALIAN

La Gensola, $$$, pg. 280

Monte Caruso, $$$, pg. 270

Tram Tram, $$, pg. 271

TUSCAN

Dal Toscano, $$$, pg. 278

Il Ciak, $$, pg. 280

Papá Baccus, $$$, pg. 272

WINE BAR

L'Angolo Divino, $, pg. 266

L'Enoteca Antica di Via della Croce, $, pg. 275

Cavour 313, $, pg. 269

Cul de Sac, $$, pg. 260

Roscioli, $$$, pg. 267

Best by Experience

CHILD-FRIENDLY

Alle Fratte di Trastevere, $$, pg. 279

'Gusto, $$, pg. 275

La Montecarlo, $, pg. 262

Panattoni, $, pg. 282

GOOD FOR GROUPS

Alle Fratte di Trastevere, $$, pg. 279

Dar Poeta, $, pg. 279

Grano, $$$, pg. 258

'Gusto, $$, pg. 275

La Montecarlo, $, pg. 262

Panattoni, $, pg. 282

GORGEOUS SETTING

Hostaria dell'Orso, $$$$, pg. 259

Il Convivio, $$$$, pg. 261

Il Simposio di Costantini, $$$$, pg. 278

La Pergola, $$$$, pg. 286

La Veranda dell'Hotel Columbus, $$$, pg. 276

Osteria dell'Ingegno, $$$, pg. 263

Vecchia Roma, $$$$, pg. 269

OUTDOOR DINING

Boccondivino, $$$, pg. 265

Dal Bolognese, $$$$, pg. 273

Grano, $$$, pg. 258

Osteria della Quercia, $$, pg. 266

Osteria dell'Ingegno, $$$, pg. 263

San Teodoro, $$$$, pg. 284

Z'Imberto, $$, pg. 283

HOT SPOTS

Angelina, $$, pg. 284

Duke's, $$$, pg. 273

Etablì, $$$, 261

Il Sanlorenzo, $$$$, pg. 266

Primo, $$$, pg. 271

Uno e Bino, $$$, pg. 272

LATE-NIGHT

Cul de Sac, $$, pg. 260

'Gusto, $$, pg. 275

Maccheroni, $$, pg. 259

Panattoni, $, pg. 282

MOST ROMANTIC

Antico Arco, $$$$, pg. 283

Hostaria dell'Orso, $$$$, pg. 259

Il Bacaro, $$, pg. 259

Il Convivio, $$$$, pg. 261

Il Simposio di Costantini, $$$$, pg. 278

La Pergola, $$$$, pg. 286

La Veranda dell'Hotel Columbus, $$$, pg. 276

San Teodoro, $$$$, pg. 284

BEST DESSERT

Antico Arco, $$$$, pg. 283

Glass Hostaria, $$$$, pg. 279

La Pergola, $$$$, pg. 286

San Teodoro, $$$$, pg. 284

BUSINESS DINING

Al Ceppo, $$$$, pg. 272

Caffè Romana dell'Hotel Inghilterra, $$$, pg. 273

Il Convivio, $$$$, pg. 261

Papá Baccus, $$$, pg. 272

Sora Lella, $$$, pg. 268

LOTS OF LOCALS

Dar Poeta, $, pg. 279

'Gusto - Osteria, $$$, pg. 275

Panattoni, $, pg. 282

Perilli, $$, pg. 285

Primo, $$$, pg. 271

Tram Tram, $$, pg. 271

Trattoria Monti, $$, pg. 269

HOTEL DINING

Caffè Romana dell'Hotel Inghilterra, $$$, pg. 273

La Pergola, $$$$, pg. 286

La Veranda dell'Hotel Columbus, $$$, pg. 276

PANTHEON, NAVONA, TREVI, AND QUIRINALE

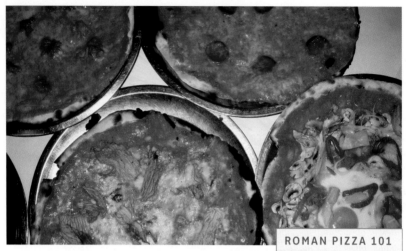

These central areas see as many tourists as they do locals, but the heart of the *centro storico* (historic center) beats here in these narrow *vicoli* (side streets) and grand piazze.

Between the piazzas and cobblestone back streets leading to and from these public gathering spots, you have the widest range of culinary offerings. Here one finds some of Rome's best pizza, in no-frills pizza joints where the waiters scribble the bill on your paper tablecloth. Yet here you also find some of the city's most revered gourmet temples, featuring star chefs, inventive cuisine, and decidedly higher bills placed on the finest high-thread-count damask tablecloths. Quite a range, and yet this coexistence of high- and lowbrow is decidedly Roman.

The Troiani brothers at **Il Convivio** (⊠ *Vicolo dei Soldati 31* ☎ *06/6869432*) have been running what is essentially a high altar to *alta cucina* (haute cuisine) for many years, where revering top-notch ingredients is an art form. Pizzas are the thing at the famed **Da Baffetto** (⊠ *Via Governo Vecchio* 114 ☎ *06/6861617*), where there's always a line.

ROMAN PIZZA 101

The concept is simple: Naples may lay claim to the invention of pizza, but to many pizza purists, Rome perfected the dish. Roman pizza has a thin crust, which makes it important that the crust has the right ratio of crisp-to-chewy. Toppings are spare and of high quality. And, of course, the wood-burning ovens that reach extremely high temperatures are of the utmost importance (look for a sign stating they use wood-burning ovens: *forno a legno*). Since they're so hot, they're usually fired up only in the evenings, which is why Roman pizzerias serving pizza *tonda* (whole rounds) are open exclusively for dinner.

TASTE OF THE CITY

Angelo Troiani
Chef and co-owner of Il Convivio and Acquolina Ristorante

As a dominant force in the capital city's dining scene for two decades, chef and restaurateur Angelo Troiani speaks to us about his cooking style, his adopted home city, and pleasing even the toughest food lovers.

Q: Can you tell us a bit about your cooking style?

A: My cooking is healthy, above all else. It's not about being organic, which it often is, but that's not the focus. Primary materials are paramount, but it's also about letting the food be what it is, and tweaking it as little as possible.

Q: Why did you decide to set up shop in Rome?

A: Though I grew up in Le Marche, my mother's family is from Rome, so it was like coming home in a way. I opened the restaurant with my two brothers, 20 years ago. Back then, Rome was just a beautiful place, a sleeping giant, with so much history. I felt there was a lot of opportunity and potential, and still do.

Q: What was your impetus for opening a second restaurant in Rome?

A: I wanted to create a different dining experience, and to compete with myself, in a way, as a challenge. Acquolina (✉ *Via Antonio Serra 60* ☎ *06/3337629* ✛ *1:G1*)

specializes in seafood, so it's very different from Convivio (✉ *Vicolo dei Soldati 31* ☎ *06/6869432* ✛ *4:D1*). Restaurants are like children: having two is more challenging than having one, but it's also more rewarding. As for Rome, the city has "woken up" and so many entities are reinvesting in Rome; everyone wants to be here.

Q: Who dines at Convivio and Acquolina?

A: Of course we have an international clientele whose first priority is great food. At the same time, we have a very loyal Roman and Italian customer base that we turn to as a measure of our success. If the Italians, who can be tough critics, are happy, we know we're doing something right.

APERITIVO TIME

Head to Via Governo Vecchio, a narrow, medieval street off Piazza Navona, to find charming spots for a pre-dinner aperitivo or an after-dinner cocktail. **Cul de Sac** (✉ *Piazza di Pasquino 73* ☎ *06/68801094* ✛ *4:D3*) serves tasty nibbles—from an enormous cheese and salumi selection to baba ghanouj and patés—with its extensive wine list, which is why its deservedly famous all over Rome. **Il Piccolo** (✉ *Via Governo Vecchio 74* ☎ *06/68801746* ✛ *4:C3*), a diminutive wine bar, named for its teeny space, seats groups of people around tiny marble-topped tables. The **Abbey Theatre Pub** (✉ *Via Governo Vecchio 51* ☎ *06/6861341* ✛ *4:C3*) screens top sports events. **Fluid** (✉ *Via Governo Vecchio 46/47* ☎ *06/6832361*) is a great spot for an aperitivo, like the classic Italian negroni or a glass of prosecco, or a late night mojito or caipiroska. Sitting on glowing glass "ice cubes" ups the kitsch fun factor.

CAMPO DE' FIORI AND GHETTO

Roman cuisine meets Jewish cuisine at the historical crossroads between Campo de' Fiori and the Ghetto.

These two adjacent neighborhoods represent the coming-together of a raucous *carnevale*-like people parade, and the reverential preservation of tradition. Campo de' Fiori has always been the secular crossroads of the city: even in ancient Rome, pilgrims would gather here to eat, drink, and be merry. Across Via Arenula, the Ghetto is home to Europe's oldest Jewish population, living in Rome uninterrupted for more than 2,000 years and, along the way, Jewish cooks helped to create staple dishes that became part of the Roman culinary canon. After centuries, both neighborhoods still define Roman cooking. Campo de' Fiori has always been one of the city's biggest open-air produce markets, and today's shoppers include local chefs who head here to concoct menus based on what looks good at the market that day. The Ghetto, on the other hand, has some great restaurants not just along its main drag, Via del Portico d'Ottavia, but also hidden in the narrow backstreets that wind between the river, Via Arenula, and Piazza Venezia.

GUANCIALE AND ANCHOVIES

Variations on cured pork, such as *guanciale* (pig's cheek), *prosciutto* (smoked ham), and *pancetta* (bacon), are signature flavorings for Roman dishes, found at butchers like **Viola** (⊠ *Campo de' Fiori 43, Campo de' Fiori* ☎ *06/68806114* ✛ *4:C4*) and food shops like **Roscioli** (⊠ *Via del Giubbonari 21-22/A, Campo de' Fiori* ☎ *06/6875287*). When Jewish culinary culture started intermingling with Roman, it was discovered that Jewish cooks used *alici* (anchovies) to flavor dishes the way Romans used cured pork. For great-quality anchovies, check out the Jewish *alimentari* (food shops) in the Ghetto.

IT'S THE LITTLE THINGS

ON THE GO: AT THE FORNO

Sometimes the most satisfying meal you can grab on the go—and on the cheap—is from the *forno*, or bakery.

Il Forno di Campo de' Fiori (✉ *Campo de' Fiori 22, Campo de' Fiori* ☎ *06/68806662* ✚ 4:C4) is easily the most popular bakery in the area, and their outstanding pizzas—*bianca* (white) and *rossa* (red)—leave you happily wondering how something so simple can be so flavorful. For kosher, the 100-year-old **Antico Forno del Ghetto** (✉ *Piazza Costaguti 30, Ghetto* ☎ *06/68803012* ✚ 4:F5) offers tasty bianca and rossa pizzas, as well as a crusty bread that they refer to as *ossi* ("bones").

ARTICHOKES: ALLA ROMANA AND ALLA GIUDIA

If there's one vegetable Rome is known for, it's the artichoke, or *carciofo*. The artichoke itself is a globe artichoke that's larger and leafier than most other, tulip-shaped varieties. In Rome, two preparations are prized. The classic *carciofo alla Romana* is stuffed with wild mint, garlic, and pecorino and then braised in olive oil, white wine, and water. The *carciofo alla Giudia* is deep-fried twice, so it opens like a flower, the outer leaves crisp and golden brown in color, while the thistle's heart remains tender. Either option is unforgettable.

When artichokes are "in season" they're served everywhere. For a good traditional Roman artichoke, go to **Ar Galletto** (✉ *Piazza Farnese 102, Campo de' Fiori* ☎ *06/6861714* ✚ 4:C4) or **Da Sergio** (✉ *Vicolo delle Grotte 27* ☎ *06/6864293*). For the best Giudia, you'll have to try **Da Giggetto** (✉ *Via Portico d'Ottavia 21A-22, Ghetto* ☎ *06/6861105* ✚ 4:F5) or **Piperno** (✉ *Monte Cenci 9, Ghetto* ☎ *06/6833606*) and decide on a winner for yourself, or head to **Sora Margherita** (✉ *Piazza delle Cinque Scole 30, Ghetto* ☎ *06/6874216* ✚ 4:E5), a delicious little hole-in-the-wall, to try them side by side.

FORNO VS. PASTICCERIA

Forno means "oven" in Italian, but it's also the word for a bakery that specializes in bread and simple baked goods, like biscotti and pine nut tarts. The *pasticceria*, on the other hand, specializes in more complicated Italian sweets, like fruit tarts, *montebianco* (a chestnut-cream creation resembling an alpine mountain), and *millefoglie* (puff pastry layered with pastry cream). Straddling the line between the forno and the pasticceria, on the "main drag" of the Ghetto, **Pasticceria Boccioni** (✉ *Via del Portico d'Ottavia 1* ☎ *06/6878637* ✚ 4:F5)—commonly known as *Forno del Ghetto* (aka "The Burnt Bakery," for the dark brown crust most everything here seems to have—is famed for being the only establishment that makes some Roman Jewish specialties. One delight is Rome's most delicious ricotta cheesecake, filled with cherries or chocolate, baked in an almondy crust. (Try to get there early on Friday as they sell out before closing for the Sabbath.)

MONTI, ESQUILINO, REPUBBLICA, AND SAN LORENZO

These distinctly different neighborhoods encompass the best *mischia,* or mix, of traditional Italian and ethnic cuisines in all of Rome.

Monti is a chic, slightly bohemian, boutique-clad neighborhood with the best offerings of ethnic restaurants in the centro—from the Pan-Asian-Mediterranean seafood at **F.I.S.H.** (⌧ *Via dei Serpenti 16* ☎ *06/47824962*) to Punjab Indian at **Maharajah** (⌧ *Via dei Serpenti 124* ☎ *06/4747144* ✛ *2:C5*).

Esquilino is Rome's main ethnic artery, containing many tourist traps, but also some real gems, like the **Italian Bistrò** (⌧ *Via Palestro 40* ☎ *06/44702868* ✛ *2:D3*) and the **Mercato Esquilino** (⌧ *Via Principe Amedeo*), a market for Italian, Asian, and African specialties.

You'll find a lot of hotels (and unremarkable food) in Repubblica, just north of Termini station. Head east of the station, to San Lorenzo, to sample Rome's university quarter and hipster 'hood. It is worth an evening trip for the *burrata* (a creamier mozzarella-like cheese) and puff pastry at the sophisticated **Uno e Bino** (⌧ *Via degli Equi 58* ☎ *06/4466702*) and the *orrechiette* (ear-shaped pasta) with clams and broccoli at **Tram Tram** (⌧ *Via dei Reti 44* ☎ *06/490416*).

PERFECT PIZZA

Pizza is sold on practically every block in Rome, and while hardly any of it is bad, you might be wondering: Where's the best stuff? Here's where: **La Gallina Bianca** (⌧ *Via A. Rosmini 5, Esquilino* ☎ *06/4743777* ✛ *2:F1*) for classic thin-crust Roman pizza; **La Soffitta** (⌧ *Via dei Villini 1/e, Esquilino* ☎ *06/4404642* ✛ *2:F1*) for Neapolitan-certified thick, crispy-crust pizza; **Formula Uno** (⌧ *Via degli Equi 13, San Lorenzo* ☎ *06/4453866*) for thin crusts and a feeding frenzy; **Panella** bakery (⌧ *Via Merulana 54, Esquilino* ☎ *06/4872435* ✛ *2:E5*) for delicious slices to go; **Pizzeria Il Veliero** (⌧ *Via Emanuele Filiberto 199* ☎ *06/77209570*) specializes in Sicilian pizza.

LOCAL FAVES 2 WAYS

	SAVE	SPLURGE
Roman Flavor	**Roman Pommidoro** (✉ Piazza dei Sanniti 44, San Lorenzo ☎ 06/4452692) serves up traditional Roman fare with a focus on grilled meat and fish at fair prices.	One of Rome's most beloved spots, **Agata e Romeo** (✉ Via Carlo Alberto 45, Esquilino ☎ 06/4466115), pleases Roman palates with updated versions of old standards.
Regional Italian	Explore the roasted meats and game of Le Marche region without leaving Rome at **Trattoria Monti** (✉ Via San Vito 13, Monti ☎ 06/4466573).	**Monte Caruso** (✉ Via Farini 12, Esquilino ☎ 06/483549) serves up southern Italian delicacies from Lucania.
Non-Italian	It's not pretty, but **Indian Fast Food** (✉ Via Mamiani 11, Esquilino ☎ 06/4460792 ✛ 2:F5) is mostly a takeout joint anyway. Enjoy your curries for a cheap €6.50.	An art gallery, bookstore, and restaurant, **Doozo** (✉ Via Palermo 51, Monti ☎ 06/4815655 ✛ 2:C4) serves some of the city's best Japanese food for about €20.

TO MARKET, TO MARKET

Long known as the people's market of Rome, the **Mercato Esquilino** (✉ *Via Principe Amedeo* ✛ *2:F5*) has, in recent years, become even more eclectic and egalitarian. This is not your mamma's market, where you see the same Italian ingredients as everywhere else (as beautiful and high-quality as they may be). Here, African vegetable vendors sell yams and okra; Asian vendors sell rice noodles and miso paste, vinegars and lemongrass. Halal butchers abut *macellerie* specializing in pig parts. The seafood hall teems with vendors—Bangladeshi, Chinese, Italian—hawking fish and shellfish; some live, and some already filleted, some gorgeous and some . . . not so gorgeous. And yes, Italian vendors still sell their many varieties of tomato, eggplant, zucchini, pizza and bread, and lots of specialties. A trip to this market is an incredibly energizing experience, allowing shoppers a window onto the daily life of the many diverse locals that make up the Eternal City.

VINI, FORMAGGI, AND ANTIPASTI

Wine, cheese, and assorted cured meats are the star items on the best of the district's *enoteche* (wineshops) menus. **Enoteca Trimani** (✉ *Via Goito 20, San Lorenzo* ☎ *06/4469661*), the oldest wine shop in Rome, dates back to 1821 and stocks more than 4,000 labels from around the world. The Trimani family also owns the highly regarded **Trimani Il Wine Bar** (✉ *Via Cernia 37B, San Lorenzo* ☎ *06/4469630*) around the corner where you can wine and dine with the best selections in town. Closer to the centro, **Cavour 313** (✉ *Via Cavour 313, Monti* ☎ *06/678 5496*) offers more than 25 wines by the glass, plus an array of gourmet cheese and meat plates.

12

VENETO, BORGHESE, AND SPAGNA

The exclusive neighborhoods of Via Veneto, Villa Borghese, and the Tridente encompass an area of Rome densely populated by deluxe hotels and Rome's upscale shopping district.

The area around Via Veneto, the Villa Borghese Park, and Spagna (from Piazza del Popolo down the length of Via di Ripetta, over to Via del Tritone and up to the Spanish Steps) could be considered Rome's downtown, for its business district, though its feeling is much more uptown. It's also the city's fashion epicenter, housing the likes of the Valentino and Fendi headquarters.

Workday lunchtime offerings include classic trattorias and chic caffè like Café Canova-Tadolini (⊠ *Via del Babuino 150A* ☎*06/32110702*), where you can get a nibble, salad, or plate of pasta in a gorgeous sculpture atelier setting. Come sundown, the options increase as modern trattoria-pizzerias like 'Gusto and ReCafé throng with tastemakers and young professionals. Perennial hot spots include Nino and Dal Bolognese. And the upscale hotels in the area—the Hassler, Hotel Eden, and Hotel de Russie—offer great aperitivi in their distinguished bars.

EMPIRE OF "TASTE"

When **'Gusto** (⊠ *Piazza Agusto Imperatore 9* ☎ *06/3226273* ✛ *1:G2*) opened in the late '90s, the concept was new to Rome: a sprawling ground-floor pizzeria, a wine bar with nibbles, and an upstairs upscale restaurant, all in one space. It caught on quickly, and they added on a store selling cookware, cookbooks, and a variety of kitchen tools. The pizzeria offers a popular buffet-style lunch popular with nearby office workers. Or try the always-packed **Gusto–Osteria** (⊠ *Via della Frezza 16* ☎ *06/32111482* ✛ *1:G2*), around the corner, which offers plenty of snack-size tasting portions, even for pastas and secondi.

CELEB HOT SPOTS

12

	WHO'S FREQUENTED	WHY IT'S HOT
Dal Bolognese, Piazza del Popolo 1	Film industry insiders like Martin Scorsese, Gwyneth Paltrow, and Cate Blanchett, along with fashion luminaries like Valentino Garavani.	Hearty food and elegant setting take backseat to ambience. Tables are perfectly spaced for passing headshots and air kisses.
Nino, Via Borgognona 11	Tom Cruise and Katie Holmes hosted their prenuptial feast for friends and guests like Jim Carrey, Posh and Becks, and Brooke Shields.	Old-school waiters in tuxedos and perfect location among the offices of fashion houses and print media make it a shoo-in for the business lunch crowd.
Bar Stravinjsky, Hotel de Russie, Via del Babuino 9	International film stars (George Clooney, Brad Pitt, Julia Roberts, Catherine Zeta-Jones and hubby Michael Douglas, Leo DiCaprio, Cameron Diaz, the list goes on…) to dignitaries and wealthy businesspeople.	Great service, bartenders who mix a great cocktail, and the beautiful outdoor giardino dell'arancio (patio filled with orange trees) makes this a great place to people-watch.

SWEET AND SOUR

As Rome claims the oldest continuous Jewish population in Europe, so Roman cuisine has been influenced by this 2,000-year-old legacy. Keeping the Sabbath and not being able to work (which includes cooking) from sundown Friday to sundown Saturday gave rise to many of the dishes in the Roman Jewish repertoire that are prepared ahead, sometimes marinated, and served at room temperature. Heavily influential on Roman cuisine are the ingredients Jews favored, including eggplant, pumpkin, fennel, and that most Roman of vegetables, *carciofi*, the big, round bulb artichokes, served up fried, *alla giudea* (Jewish style) or braised (Roman style). And when you see the pairing of raisins and pine nuts in Roman food, this is a holdover from the love of *agrodolce*, or sweet-and-sour, brought to the Italian continent from Sicily and originally from the Iberian peninsula by Jews who fled Spain during the Inquisition.

Rome is the city in Italy where the idea of *la bella figura* (the art of looking good) is most often at work—or shall we say, at play. Parioli is considered the neighborhood where many of the posh live, but they work and play in the Spagna, Via Veneto, and Borghese areas. And when celebrities come to town, they frequently reside in the many 5-star luxury hotels in the *zona. Below, we break down who goes where and why.*

VATICAN, BORGO, AND PRATI

The Vatican is the heart of ecclesiastical Rome, and this part of the city has a more serious, less chaotic feel to it.

The massive and awe-striking St. Peter's Basilica dominates the landscape; the streets are teeming with clergy; and despite herds of tourists, it's somehow less chaotic, better organized, and maybe even a little more civilized than classical Rome.

Outside the Vatican walls lies the little nabe of Borgo, a residential zona buzzing with typical Roman life, and home to some genuinely good restaurants off the usual tourist radar.

Prati is a little farther up the river, and known as something of a retail-shopping hot zone for both Romans and foreign visitors—clothes, handbags, shoes, perfume, makeup, and more.

Prati is also known—especially among Romans—for a nice handful of interesting foodie spots, from hidden gems of trattorias to high-quality artisanal gelaterie—so don't omit it from your itinerary, just because you may not have heard anything about it.

FOODIE FINDS

Via Cola di Rienzo is home to two of Rome's best specialty shops.

Franchi (⊠ *Via Cola di Rienzo 204, Prati* ☎ *06/6874651*) is a gastroshop that sells high-quality cured meats, Italian cheeses, wines, pastas, and fresh truffles.

Just next door, **Castroni** (⊠ *Via Cola di Rienzo 196/198, Prati* ☎ *06/6874383* ✛ *1:D2*) is well-known among expats for its imported foreign foods from the United States, Great Britain, Asia, India, and Latin America.

It also well known for its impressive selection of candies, preserves, olive oils, and vinegars.

12

TRADITIONAL FARE WITH FLAIR

Many tourists think the area around the Vatican is rip-off central when it comes to drinking and dining. Despite the overwhelming number of tourist trap-torias, the Borgo and Prati are home to many restaurants revered by Romans in the zona and beyond.

Girarrosto (⌧ *Via Germanico 56, Prati* ☎ *06/39725717* ✛ *1:C2*): The Tuscan region is known for its generous cuts of quality meat, and this Prati restaurant is renowned for grilling up the best Tuscan beef in Rome. Treat yourself to the *Fiorentina* steak.

Velando (⌧ *Borgo Vittorio 26, Borgo* ☎ *06/68809955* ✛ *1:C2*): Departing from the usual Roman fare, the owners of this restaurant serve up traditional dishes from their hometown of Val Camonica in northern Italy. Try the *pizzocheri*, a buckwheat ribbon pasta—you likely won't find it anywhere else in Rome.

Settembrini (⌧ *Via Luigi Settembrini 25, Prati* ☎ *06/3232617* ✛ *1:D1*): Chef Mark Poddi uses Moroccan inspiration to give Italian cuisine a new taste. Try his couscous and tajine, his fresh and affordable Friday fish menu, or the plentiful *aperitivo*, snacks served with an early evening cocktail.

THE SECRET'S IN THE SAUCE

What may appear to the naked eye of a non-Italian as plain, old spaghetti with red sauce, is actually pasta *all'amatriciana* or *matriciana*—a more sophisticated dish with a complexity of flavor owing to an important ingredient: *guanciale*. The English translation—cured pig jowl—is unappetizing, but once you taste a guanciale-flavored sauce, you'll understand why Romans swear by it. You'll find it used in dishes at virtually every trattoria in Rome, but two of the most savory and delicious versions of it are made in Prati at **Dino & Tony** (⌧ *Via Leone IV 60, Prati* ☎ *06/39733284* ✛ *1:B1*) and the 100-year-old **Il Matriciano** (⌧ *Via dei Gracci 55, Prati* ☎ *06/3213040* ✛ *1:D2*), whose signature dish is—you guessed it—the classic pasta alla Matriciana.

ARTIGIANALE

The artisanal food movement, which focuses on craftsmanship and often emphasizes local products, has made its way to Rome, and many Roman specialists are in and around Prati. Pizza expert Gabriele Bonci has breathed new life into the same-old storefront *pizzeria al taglio* (by-the-slice pizza joint) at **Pizzarium** (⌧ *3 Via della Meloria* ☎ *06/39745416* ✛ *1:A2*). Bonci collects yeast from centuries-old sourdough starters from southern Italian villages, and has his flour stone ground by a specialist in Piemonte. The dough is thicker than that of traditional Roman slices, but this Roman rebel thinks the proof is in…well, the pizza.

Gelateria dei Gracchi (⌧ *272 Via dei Gracchi* ☎ *06/3216668* ✛ *1:E1*) is a favorite among Roman foodies. Try the pistachio gelato, which uses Sicilian *pistacchi Bronte* from Mt. Etna. Seasonal flavors also abound, like wild strawberry in late spring, when the nearby hillside town of Nemi is awash in berry red.

TRASTEVERE AND GIANICOLO

The new Trastevere is awash in fantastic foodie haunts. After a long lunch, work off the calories by hiking up the Gianicolo hill for the most breathtaking views of the city.

Trastevere means "across the Tiber river" and is a neighborhood that's always been known for its "otherness." In recent years, however, it has undergone a transformation, trading in its old-school bohemian roots for something trendier and more upscale. The maze of cobbled streets that was once home to working-class people, artists, and foreigners has experienced a real estate boom, and is now lined with so many trattorias and wine bars that it's starting to feel a bit like a Roman gastro-theme park.

While the explosion of hip new places to wine and dine may have had some negative effects on this old village, Trastevere's gritty charm still prevails. The Gianicolo is more subdued, but some of the restaurants at the top are definitely worth hiking all the way up the hill for (of course, you can also go easy on yourself and take a cab or bus).

PEPPERY PASTA

Cacio e pepe is a simple pasta dish from the *cucina povera*, or rustic cooking, tradition.

It's also a favorite Roman primo, usually made with tagliatelle (a long, flat noodle), *tonnarelli* (a narrower squarish noodle), or spaghetti, which is then coated with pecorino cheese and a generous amount of freshly ground black pepper.

Roma Sparita (⊠ *Piazza Santa Cecilia 24* ☎ *06/5800757* ✛ *3:C2*), on the quiet side of Trastevere beyond Viale di Trastevere, makes one of the city's best cacio e pepes, and they serve it in an edible bowl of paper-thin, baked cheese. Mamma mia!

12

SMILE AND SAY "FORMAGGIO": THE BEST CHEESES IN ROME

The "trinity" of cheeses most used in *cucina romana* are mozzarella, ricotta, and pecorino romano. Here's why these varieties can make or break a true Roman dish.

MOZZARELLA

True *mozzarella di bufala*, made from water buffalo milk, comes from the Campania area, between Rome and Naples. You'll know it by its distinctive flavor and its soft consistency. Reverential treatment is given to fresh mozzarella in its many forms at Ōbikā (⊠ *Piazza di Firenze at Via dei Prefetti, Pantheon* ☎ *06/6832630*), which is basically a mozzarella bar based on the sushi bar format. Compare and contrast different mozzarella types from different areas paired with delicious accompanying *salumi* (cured meats) and salads.

RICOTTA

This versatile fresh cheese is used in both sweet and savory dishes. As a savory ingredient, it's used as a filling in ravioli and stuffed pastas and as an accompaniment to various vegetable dishes. The taste varies depending upon the kind of milk it's made from. The famed ricotta cheesecake puts Rome's love of ricotta on the dessert table, and the cheese is even sometimes served with little tampering—a touch of golden honey or some fresh Roman *mentuccia*, wild Roman mint.

PECORINO ROMANO

A *pecora* is a sheep, so technically any cheese made from sheep's milk is a pecorino cheese, and most other regions have their own version of a local pecorino. But *pecorino romano*, the hard, aged cheese grated over Roman pasta dishes, is perhaps the most famous of all pecorinos. With a telltale black rind and pale color, it can be found in most food shops in the city. Some say this most Roman of cheeses is much like the Romans themselves: sharp and salty. But it marries beautifully with the gutsy flavors with which it's often paired.

BOHEMIAN RHAPSODY

Trastevere has always been a bohemian bastion, densely packed with inexpensive Roman pizzerias, trattorias, and countless bars filled with artists and local characters.

Bar San Calisto (⊠ *Piazza di San Calisto 3* ☎ *06/5835869* ✛ *3:B1*) is the classic bohemian Trastevere bar. The drinks are cheap, the tables difficult to snag, and the piazza in front swollen with local pierced and tattooed fringe types. Surprisingly, the hot chocolate and chocolate gelato here are some of the best in the city.

The owners of **Freni e Frizioni** (⊠ *Via del Politeama 4* ☎ *06/58334210* ⊕ *www.freniefrizioni. com* ✛ *3:B1*) know how to capture a bohemian crowd. The aperitivo here is abuzz most nights of the week, with free nibbles to accompany the mojitos and negronis. The locale's grit remains despite the shabby-chic interior: the space is a converted auto garage.

COLOSSEO, AVENTINO, AND TESTACCIO

These neighborhoods are considered the archaeological and the working-class centers of the city, where dining among the ruins takes on a whole new meaning.

Perhaps the most iconic image of Rome since ancient times has been the Colosseum. It's most charming by night. A plate of pasta at **Ai Tre Scalini** (⊠ *Via SS. Quattro Coronati 30* ☎ *06/7096309*), just steps from the Colosseum, or a glass of wine and some nibbles at **Cavour 313** (⊠ *Via Cavour 313* ☎ *06/67855496*), will make you feel unabashedly Roman. For a special Roman evening, head to **San Teodoro** (⊠ *Via dei Fienili 50* ☎ *06/6780933*), where the food is delicious, and descending from the piazza after dinner, one practically stumbles upon the back side of the Roman Forum and Campidoglio.

If you go to the Testaccio neighborhood in the south of the city, dine at **Checchino dal 1887** (⊠ *Via di Monte Testaccio 30* ☎ *06/5746318*). It's an only-in-Rome experience, as the restaurant is carved out of Monte Testaccio, a mountain composed of strata of shards of ancient Roman ceramics.

TAKING HOME A TASTE OF ROME

Volpetti (⊠ *Via Marmorata 153* ☎ *06/5742352* ✛ *3:D4*) is probably Rome's most famous and best-loved *alimentari*, or specialty foods shop. Located on an old passageway between the Tiber River and the Testaccio area, this shop is a family affair. Its jocular owners are highly knowledgeable about their products. They give samples of everything, and will tell you why Sicilian cow's milk cheese is square (round cheeses roll on ships), why aged balsamic vinegar is so delicious, and what makes some chocolates better quality than others. They'll even vacuum-pack and wrap everything you purchase.

THE ANCIENT QUARTIERE AND ITS CUISINE

Testaccio, the neighborhood at the southernmost tip of the city, is the place to go for old Roman cuisine. You'll need to take a cab to this out-of-the-way spot, which once was a center of ancient trade along the Tiber River. It is considered one of the most authentically Roman *zonas*—the *Romani di Roma* (real Romans) hail from this part of town; to wit, the very popular AS Roma soccer team was founded right in this neighborhood.

Head first to Piazza Testaccio to experience an authentic farmers' market, the Mercato di Testaccio, where Italian housewives haggle over the price of vegetables and butchers cut meat to order. (This market will be moving a few blocks down into a spanking new covered market setup—an improvement, or messing with tradition? We'll wait to see…). Appropriately enough, this area once was a major butchering center: the old slaughterhouse nearby has been converted and now houses modern art galleries and live music venues.

In keeping with that tradition, Testaccio is the birthplace of some of the most famous—and infamous—dishes in the *cucina romana* repertoire, those of the *quinto quarto,* or "fifth quarter": offal and throwaway parts.

In Testaccio restaurants, you'll find dishes like *coda alla vaccinara:* a sweet-and-sour stew made of oxtail with tomatoes and celery, and seasoned with garlic, pancetta, and a touch of cocoa (all cooked a day in advance so the flavors can marry). Another favorite is *rigatoni alla pajata*: pasta with baby lamb or calf intestines that still hold the mother's milk. Cooking the intestines coagulates the milk, creating creamy cheese curds, which are then stewed in tomato sauce, *as in the photo below from Checchino dal 1887.* Other common dishes are *coratella,* a mix of lamb innards including heart, with artichokes; and *trippa alla romana,* tripe stewed in a savory tomato sauce. Just a note: Most of these dishes are rarely translated properly on English menus, so forewarned is forearmed.

SUSHI SPOTS

The area in and around Testaccio boasts some particularly popular places for dining with chopsticks and here are just a few of our favorites:
Sushisen (✉ *Via Giuseppe Giuietti 21* ☎ *06/5756945* ✛ *3:D5*) is an authentic Japanese eatery featuring freshly prepared sushi. In the dining room, a conveyor belt carries Asian goodies like tempura shrimp and panko-breaded chicken with a sweet-spicy dipping sauce.
Bishoku Kobo (✉ *Via Ostiense 110b* ☎ *06/5744190* ✛ *3:D6*) is a local favorite, which means it's always crowded. Be prepared to wait if you haven't made a reservation. Sushi "boats" and noodle dishes are on offer.
Trendy **Ketumbar** (✉ *Via Galvani 24* ☎ *06/57305338* ✛ *3:C5*) is many things: bar, restaurant (serving both Italian fare and sushi), and club after dinner hours. Built into Monte Testaccio, the setting is breathtaking.

12

RESTAURANT REVIEWS

Listed alphabetically within neighborhoods. Use the coordinate (⊕ 1:B2) at the end of each listing to locate a property on the Where to Eat and Stay in Rome atlas at the end of this chapter. Remember: "average cost" in these reviews refers to a dinner comprising of a primo, secondo, and a dolce.

USING THE MAPS

Throughout the chapter, you'll see mapping symbols and coordinates (⊕ *4:F4*) after property names or reviews. To locate the property on the map, turn to the Rome Dining and Lodging Atlas at the end of this chapter. The first number after the symbol indicates the map number. Following that is the property's coordinate on the map grid.

PANTHEON, NAVONA, TREVI, AND QUIRINALE

PANTHEON

$$ ROMAN Fodor'sChoice ★

🍴 **Armando al Pantheon.** Right in the shadow of the Pantheon sits this wonderful trattoria, open since 1961. It gets its fair share of tourists, perhaps more at lunch when groups of sightseers need to take a break, and this spot is conveniently located, and highly recommended. But there's always a buzz here and an air of authenticity, witnessed by Roman antique shop owners who have been coming here to dine once a week for 25 years. You can tell these older gentlemen who come here to enjoy a four-course meal... and scold the waitress, by name, when she brings coffee before the profiteroles. This is just the place to try Roman artichokes or *vignarola* (a fava bean, asparagus, pea, and guanciale stew) in the spring, or the wild boar bruschetta in winter. Pastas are filling and great, and secondi deliver all the Roman staples: oxtail, baby lamb chops, tripe, meatballs, and other hearty fare. If you have room, try the blueberry panna cotta for a sweet ending. [$] *Average cost: €35* ✉ *Salita dei Crescenzi 31, Pantheon* ☎ *06/68803034* 🌐 *www.armandoalpantheon.it* 🕒 *Closed Sun. No dinner Sat.* ⊕ *4:E2.*

$ ITALIAN

🍴 **Enoteca Corsi.** Very convenient to the historic center for lunch or an afternoon break, this little hole-in-the-wall looks like it missed the revolution; renovations were done a few years back but it's hard to imagine unless you knew the place *before*. Prices and decor are *come una volta* (like once upon a time) when the shop sold—as the sign says—wine and oil. The genuinely dated feel of the place has its charm: you can still get wine here by the liter, or choose from a good variety of fairly priced alternatives in bottles. The place is packed at lunch, when a few specials—classic pastas and some second dishes like veal roast with peas—are offered. [$] *Average cost: €28* ✉ *Via del Gesù 88, Pantheon* ☎ *06/6790821* 🕒 *Closed Sun. No dinner* ⊕ *4:F4.*

$$$ MODERN ITALIAN

🍴 **Grano.** Light, bright, and happy: that's the setting for this restaurant in a pretty piazza down the street from the Pantheon. The outdoor tables are truly pleasant on a sunny day, and inside, the decor—splashy abstract drawings, high-tech lights, and whitewashed bookcases—lends a Milanese sophistication to the dining rooms. A nice wine from the well-stocked cellar, and you're off, with inventive starters like the *polpetti di brasato* (slow-cooked braised beef made into breaded meatballs topped with a zingy green sauce). And the first courses really shine, mingling meat and seafood and vegetables with aplomb (the gnocchi with clams and sea beans was fresh and delicious). Second courses include tuna steak with caponata and roast chicken, simple and good, but not as interesting as most of the *primi*. Desserts are tasty and the setting calls for slow sipping of dessert wines and post-prandial *digestivi*. [$] *Average cost:* €48 ⊠ *Piazza Rondanini 53, Pantheon* ☎ 06/68192096 ⊕ *www. ristorantegrano.it* ⊹ *4:G3.*

$$$$
MODERN ITALIAN
Fodor's Choice
★

✕ **Hostaria dell'Orso.** Back in the Hollywood-on-the-Tiber 1950s, this was *the* place to be. Everyone from Sophia Loren to Aristotle Onassis reveled in the historic setting: a 15th century palazzo straight out of a Renaissance painting, replete with dark wood-beam ceilings, Gothic fireplaces, terra-cotta floors, and frescoes restored to their original glory. Today, after several fallow decades, a face-lift has brightened the salons with bright orange leather chairs and blue glass goblets. Even more up-to-the-second is the menu fashioned by Italian superchef Gualtiero Marchese. The *alta cucina* deftly utilizes many simple ingredients (like top-quality baby pig or black cod) and just a handful of ingredients—some very Italian, others more esoteric—to tease out as much flavor as possible. One artfully presented dinner included a kidney risotto with Provolone cheese fondue and liquorice dust, a pigeon wth peanut sauce and Java black pepper, and a crème brûlée with coffee parfait, chocolate ice cream, and cotton candy. To further shake things up, there's a piano bar and disco on other floors within the building, so why not dance off this once-in-lifetime feast at Cabala, the club upstairs, with a nightcap? [$] *Average cost:* €95 ⊠ *Via dei Soldati 25c, Piazza Navona* ☎ 06/68301192 ⊕ *www.hdo.it* ⌕ *Reservations essential Jacket required* ☾ *Closed Sun.* ⊹ *4:D1.*

$$
MODERN ITALIAN

✕ **Il Bacaro.** With a handful of choice tables set outside against an ivy-draped wall, this tiny candlelit spot not far from the Pantheon makes for an ideal evening, equally suited for a romantic twosome or close friends and convivial conversation. Pastas—like *orecchiette* (little ear-shaped pasta) with broccoli and sausage, a dish that lip-smacks of Puglia—are star players. As a bonus, the kitchen keeps its clients from picking at each other's plates by offering side dishes of all the pastas ordered among those at the table. The choice main courses are mostly meat—the beef fillet with balsamic vinegar or London broil–style marinated in olive oil and rosemary are winners. [$] *Average cost:* €45 ⊠ *Via degli Spagnoli 27, Pantheon* ☎ 06/6872554 ⊕ *www.ilbacaro.com* ⌕ *Reservations essential* ☾ *Closed Sun. and 1 wk in Aug. No lunch Sat.* ⊹ *4:E2.*

$$
ROMAN

✕ **Maccheroni.** This boisterous, convivial trattoria north of the Pantheon makes for a fun evening out. The decor is basic: white walls with wooden shelves lined with wine bottles, blocky wooden tables covered in white butcher paper—but there's an "open" kitchen (with even the dishwashers in plain view of the diners) and an airy feel that attracts a young clientele as well as visiting celebrities. The menu sticks to Roman basics such as simple pasta with fresh tomatoes and basil, or rigatoni *alla gricia* (with bacon, sheep's-milk cheese, and black pepper). The specialty pasta, *trofie* (short pasta twists) with a black truffle sauce, inspires you to lick your plate. Probably the best choice on the menu is the *tagliata con rughetta*, a juicy, two-inch-thick steak sliced thinly and served on arugula. Ⓢ *Average cost: €45* ✉ *Piazza delle Coppelle 44, Pantheon* ☎ *06/68307895* ⊕ *www.ristorantemaccheroni.com* ⟗ *Reservations essential* ✛ *4:E2.*

NAVONA

$ ✕ **Birreria Peroni.** With its long wooden tables, hard-back booths, and free-flowing beer, this casual restaurant in a palazzo from the 1500s seems to belong more to the genre of Munich beer hall than popular Roman hangout. But let's remember that far to the north of Rome lies a part of Italy in which the people speak as much German as they do Italian, and the simple food seems more *tedesco* than *italiano*. It's from this place that Birreria Peroni draws its inspiration, and the goulash and the many sausage specialties—with sauerkraut and potatoes, of course—certainly provide a nice respite from pasta and tomato sauce. Top tip: this is one of the few places in the historic center where you can eat at very economic prices and fill up on good old-fashioned protein. Ⓢ *Average cost: €25* ✉ *Via di San Marcello 19, Navona* ☎ *06/6795310* ⊕ *www.anticabirreriaperoni.it* ⟗ *Reservations not accepted* ⊘ *Closed Sun. and Aug. No lunch Sat.* ✛ *4:G3.*

NORTHERN
ITALIAN

$$ ✕ **Cul de Sac.** This popular wine bar near Piazza Navona is among the city's oldest enoteche and offers a book-length selection of wines from Italy, France, the Americas, and elsewhere. Food is eclectic, ranging from a huge assortment of Italian meats and cheeses (try the delicious *lonza*, cured pork loin, or *speck*, a northern Italian smoked prosciutto) to various Mediterranean dishes, including delicious baba ghanoush, a tasty Greek salad, and a spectacular wild boar pâté. Outside tables get crowded fast, so arrive early, or come late, as they serve until about 1 am. Ⓢ *Average cost: €35* ✉ *Piazza Pasquino 73, Piazza Navona* ☎ *06/68801094* ⊕ *www.enotecaculdesac.com* ⟗ *Reservations not accepted* ⊘ *Closed 2 wks in Aug.* ✛ *4:D3.*

WINE BAR
Fodor'sChoice
★

$ ✕ **Da Baffetto.** Down a cobblestone street not far from Piazza Navona, this is Rome's most popular pizzeria and a summer favorite for street-side dining. The debate is constant whether or not this spot is massively overrated, but as with all the "great" pizzerias in Rome, it's hard to argue with the line that forms outside here on weekends. Happily, outdoor tables (enclosed and heated in winter) provide much-needed additional seating and turnover is fast (and lingering not encouraged). Baffetto 2, at *Piazza del Teatro di Pompeo 18*, is an extension of the pizzeria with the addition of pasta and *secondi*—and doesn't suffer from the overcrowding of the original location. Ⓢ *Average cost: €22* ✉ *Via*

PIZZA
Fodor'sChoice
★

Who needs an elegantly decorated restaurant when you can dine in the splendor of the Piazza Navona?

del Governo Vecchio 114, Navona ☎ *06/6861617* 💳 *No credit cards* 🕒 *Closed Aug. and Tues. No lunch Mon.–Fri.* ✥ *4:C3.*

$$$ MEDITERRANEAN Fodor's Choice ★ 🍴 **Etablì.** On a narrow vicolo off beloved Piazza del Fico, this multidimensional locale serves as a lounge-bar, and becomes a hot spot by aperitivo hour. Beautifully finished with vaulted wood-beam ceilings, wrought-iron touches, plush leather sofas, and chandeliers, it's all modern Italian farmhouse chic. In the restaurant section (the place is sprawling), it's minimalist Provençal hip (*etabli* is French for the regionally typical tables within). And the food is clean and Mediterranean, with touches of Asia in the raw fish appetizers. Pastas are more traditional Italian, and the *secondi* run the gamut from land to sea. The place fills up by *dopo cena* ("after dinner") when it becomes a popular spot for sipping and posing. [$] *Average cost: €55* ✉ *Vicolo delle Vacche 9/a, Navona* ☎ *06/6871499* 🌐 *www.etabli.it* 🕒 *Closed Sun. in summer, Mon. in winter* ✥ *4:C2.*

$$$$ MODERN ITALIAN Fodor's Choice ★ 🍴 **Il Convivio.** In a tiny, nondescript vicolo north of Piazza Navona, the three Troiani brothers—Angelo in the kitchen, and brothers Giuseppe and Massimo presiding over the dining room and wine cellar—have quietly been redefining the experience of Italian eclectic *alta cucina* (haute cuisine) for many years. Antipasti include a selection of ultra-fresh raw seafood preparations in the mixed *crudi*, while a "carbomare" pasta is a riff on tradition, substituting pancetta with fresh fish roe and house-cured *bottarga* (salted fish roe). Or opt for one of the famed signature dishes, including a fabulous version of a cold-weather pigeon main course prepared four different ways. Service is attentive without being overbearing, and the wine list is exceptional. It is definitely a splurge spot. [$] *Average cost: €110* ✉ *Vicolo dei Soldati 31, Navona*

☎ 06/6869432 ✍ *Reservations essential* ⏲ *Closed Sun., 1 wk in Jan., and 2 wks in Aug. No lunch* ✥ *4:D1.*

$$$$ MODERN ITALIAN Fodor's Choice ★ 🍴 **Il Pagliaccio.** To find some of the latest spins on Roman *alta cucina* (haute cuisine), you might be surprised to head to a hidden back street nestled between the upscale Via Giulia and the popular piazzas of Campo de' Fiori and Navona. But that is where widely traveled chef Anthony Genovese has come to roost, after garnering his first Michelin star at luxe and lavish Palazzo Sasso hotel on the Amalfi Coast. Born in France to Calabrese parents, and having worked in such far-flung places as Japan and Thailand, it's no surprise to note Genovese's love of unusual spices, "foreign" ingredients, and Eastern preparations. These have not only gained him a loyal following but more prized Michelin stars. As a result, prices here are fairly exorbitant, but dishes like pasta bundles filled with onion, tapioca, and red currants in a saffron broth; or duck with black salsify, caramelized pear, and chocolate sauce are well worth it. Desserts are also expertly executed as well, thanks to Alsatian Marion Lichtle. For the full Genovese feast, go for one of his tasting menus. [$] *Average cost: €120* ✉ *near Piazza Navona* ☎ *06/68809595* ✍ *Reservations essential* ⏲ *Closed Sun. and Mon. and 3 wks in Aug. No lunch Tues.*

$ PIZZA 🍴 **La Montecarlo.** Run by the niece of the owner of the pizzeria Da Baffetto, La Montecarlo has a similar menu and is almost as popular as its relative around the corner. Pizzas are super-thin and a little burned around the edges—the sign of a good wood-burning oven. It's one of few pizzerias open for both lunch and dinner. [$] *Average cost: €20* ✉ *Vicolo Savelli 13, Navona* ☎ *06/6861877* 💳 *No credit cards* ⏲ *Closed 2 wks in mid-Aug. and Mon. Nov.–Apr.* ✥ *4:C3.*

$$$$ SEAFOOD Fodor's Choice ★ 🍴 **La Rosetta.** Chef-owner Massimo Riccioli took the nets and fishing gear off the walls of his parents' trattoria to create what is widely known as *the* place to go in Rome for first-rate seafood. But beware: the staff may be friendly and the fish may be of high quality, but the preparation is generally very simple, and the prices can be numbingly high. Start with the justifiably well-known selection of marinated seafood appetizers, like carpaccios of fresh, translucent fish drizzled with olive oil and perhaps a fresh herb. Pastas tend to mix shellfish, usually with a touch of oil, white wine, and lemon. Simple dishes such as the classic *zuppa di pesce* (fish soup) deserve star billing under the title of *secondi*—and command star prices. [$] *Average cost: €120* ✉ *Via della Rosetta 9, Navona* ☎ *06/6861002* 🌐 *www.larosetta.com* ✍ *Reservations essential* 👔 *Jacket required* ⏲ *Closed Sun. and 3 wks in Aug.* ✥ *4:E2.*

$$ ITALIAN 🍴 **Obīkā.** If you've ever wanted to take in a "mozzarella bar," here's your chance. Mozzarella is featured here much like sushi bars showcase fresh fish—even the decor is modern Japanese minimalism–meets–ancient Roman grandeur. The cheese, in all its varieties, is the focus of the dishes: there's the familiar cow's milk, the delectable water buffalo milk varieties from the Campagnia region, and the sinfully rich *burrata* from Puglia (a fresh cow's milk mozzarella encasing a creamy center of unspun mozzarella curds and fresh cream). They're all served with various accompanying cured meats, vegetables, sauces, and breads. An outdoor deck is a great spot for dining alfresco. Also visit the new,

super-central smaller location in Campo de'Fiori (✉ *corner of Via dei Baullari* ☎ *06/68802366*) and the one in posh Parioli (✉ *Via Guido d'Arezzo 49* ☎ *06/685344184*). Indeed, the concept has been such a success that other locations recently opened in cities from Florence and Istanbul to midtown Manhattan and L.A. [$] *Average cost: €45* ✉ *Piazza di Firenze 26, Navona* ☎ *06/6832630* 🌐 *www.obika.it* ✣ *4:E1.*

$$$
MODERN ITALIAN
Fodor's Choice
★

🍴 **Osteria dell'Ingegno.** This casual, yet trendy place is a great spot to enjoy a glass of wine or a gourmet meal in an ancient piazza in the city center. The cheery, modern interior decor—walls made vibrant with modern paintings by local artists and lots of colorful glass bottles—and hip young waiters will bring you back to the present day. So, too, will the simple but innovative menu, including dishes like the panzanella salad, the beef tagliata with red wine reduction and potato tortino, and the perfectly cooked duck breast with a seasonal fruit sauce. Outdoor tables from April to October make you feel as if you're on an opera stage set, for your perch looks out over the Tempio d'Adriano (built in AD 145). If ever there was a place to linger outdoors over limoncello, this is it. [$] *Average cost: €50* ✉ *Piazza di Pietra 45, Pantheon* ☎ *06/6780662* 🕓 *Closed Sun. and 2 wks in Aug.* ✣ *4:F2.*

QUIRINALE

$$$
TUSCAN

🍴 **Tullio.** Just off Piazza Barberini sits this Tuscan-accented upscale trattoria. The decor is basic wood paneling and white linens, with the requisite older—and often grumpy—waiters. The menu is heavy on Tuscan classics such as white beans and the famed *bistecca alla fiorentina,* a carnivore's dream. Meat dishes other than beef, such as lamb and veal, are also dependably good. The homemade pappardelle *al cinghiale* (wide, flat noodles in a tomato and wild boar sauce) are delectable. A few key Roman dishes and greens are offered, like *brocoletti,* sauteéd to perfection with garlic and olive oil. The wine list favors robust Tuscan reds and thick wallets. [$] *Average cost: €60* ✉ *Via San Nicola da Tolentino, near Piazza Barberini, Quirinale* ☎ *06/4745560* 🌐 *www.tullioristorante.it* 🕓 *Closed Sun. and Aug.* ✣ *2:C3.*

CAMPO DE' FIORI AND GHETTO

CAMPO DE' FIORI

$
PIZZA
Fodor's Choice
★
👶

🍴 **Acchiappafantasmi.** This popular pizzeria near Campo de' Fiori offers pizza—and much more. In addition to the traditional margherita and capricciosa, you'll find a spicy pizza with chili peppers and hot salami, and their prizewinning version with buffalo mozzarella and cherry tomatoes, shaped like a ghost (a theme throughout, hence the name, which means "Ghostbusters"). Appetizers are just as delicious—as well as the traditional fried goodies and Calabrese specialties. The menu includes a variety of items not standard to pizzerias, such as a version of eggplant Parmesan with prosciutto and egg, and tongue-tingling spicy nibbles. True to the owners' Calabrian roots, they offer spicy homemade *'nduja,* a spreadable sausage comprised of pork and chili pepper at a ratio of 50/50—not for the weak of constitution! [$] *Average cost: €18* ✉ *Via dei Cappellari 66, Campo de' Fiori* ☎ *06/6873462* 🌐 *www.acchiappafantasmi.it* 🕓 *Closed Mon. and 1 wk in Aug.* ✣ *4:C3.*

CLOSE UP

Gelaterie: A National Obsession

For many travelers, the first taste of *gelato*—Italian ice cream—is one of the most memorable moments of their Italian trip. Almost a cross between regular American ice cream and soft serve, gelato's texture is lighter and fluffier than hard ice cream because of the process by which it's whipped when freezing. Along with the listings here, you can find a number of gelaterias in Via di Tor Millina, a street off the west side of Piazza Navona, where there are also a couple of good places for frozen yogurt and delicious *frullati*—shakes made with milk, crushed ice, and fruit of your choosing.

Il Gelato di San Crispino. Perhaps the most celebrated gelato in all of Italy are created here at San Crispino. Without artificial colors or flavors, these scoops are worth crossing town for—nobody else creates flavors this pure. Flavors like chocolate rum, armagnac, and ginger-cinnamon keep taste buds tap-dancing. And to preserve the "integrity" of the flavor, the ice cream is only served in paper cups. New locations behind the Pantheon (⊠ *Piazza della Maddalena 3*) and San Giovanni (⊠ *Via Acaia 56*) are proof that the word is getting out and the empire is growing. ⊠ *Via della Panetteria 54, Piazza di Trevi* ☎ *06/6793924* ⊕ *www. ilgelatodisancrispino.it* ⊗ *Closed Tues.* ✛ *4:H2.*

Giolitti. For years Giolitti was considered the best gelateria in Rome, and it's still worth a stop if you're near the Pantheon. It's best known for its variety of fresh seasonal fruit flavors, which taste like the essence of the fruits themselves. ⊠ *Via degli Uffici del Vicario 40, Pantheon* ☎ *06/6991243* ✛ *4:F2.*

Della Palma. Close to the Pantheon on a street just north of the Piazza della Rotonda, Della Palma serves 100 flavors of gelato, and for sheer gaudy display and range of choice it's a must. It also offers a colorful selection of bulk candy, as well as several flavors of *granita* on rotation. ⊠ *Via della Maddalena 20/23, Pantheon* ☎ *06/68806752* ✛ *4:E2.*

Cremeria Monteforte. Immediately beside the Pantheon is Cremeria Monteforte, which has won several awards for its flavors. Also worth trying is its chocolate *sorbetto*—it's an icier version of the gelato without the dairy (except, of course, for the whipped cream you'll want them to plop on top)! ⊠ *Via della Rotonda 22, Pantheon* ☎ *06/6867720* ✛ *4:E2.*

Fiocco di Neve. Don't miss the fabulous *granita di caffè* (coffee ice slush) here as well as a big scoop of gelato—the chocolate chip and After Eight (mint chocolate chip) flavors are delicious. ⊠ *Via del Pantheon 51, Pantheon* ☎ *No phone* ✛ *4:F2.*

Gelateria alla Scala. This may be a tiny place but don't let the size fool you. It does a good business offering artisanal gelato prepared in small batches, so when one flavor runs out on any given day, it's finished. ⊠ *Via della Scala 51, Trastevere* ☎ *06/5813174* ⊗ *Closed Dec. and Jan.* ✛ *4:B6.*

Al Settimo Gelo. Located in Prati, this spot has been getting rave reviews for both classic flavors and new-fangled inventions such as cardamom, chestnut, and ginger. ⊠ *Via Vodice 21/a, Prati* ☎ *06/3725567* ⊕ *www. alsettimogelo.it* ✛ *1:A1.*

$ ╳ **Alberto Pica.** This artisan is renowned for his artisanal gelato produc-
CAFÉ tion and selection of seasonal *sorbetti* and *cremolate* (like sorbetto but
made with the fruit pulp, not the juice). An interesting gelato flavor to
try here is the *riso a cannella*, like a cinnamon rice pudding. These are
possibly the grumpiest bar owners in Rome, so remember: in, out, and
nobody gets hurt. Ⓢ *Average cost: €4* ⊠ *Via della Seggiola 12, Campo
de' Fiori* ☎ *06/6868405* ☽ *Closed Sun. and 2 wks in Aug.* ⊹ *4:E5.*

$$$ ╳ **Boccondivino.** The four pillars around which the structure is built are
MODERN ITALIAN ancient Roman, but when you walk through the 16th-century door, it's
clear that Boccondivino ("divine mouthful") is all about the here-and-
now, with the animal-print chairs and glass-fronted dining room. The
outdoor seating in the intimate piazzetta out front is a great summer
spot. This is also the perfect place for a dinner date. Start, perhaps,
with a smoked swordfish served with peppery Roman arugula, candied
citrus, and *parmigiano* cheese, then move on to (or split) the delicious
pasta with pesto, shrimp, and cherry tomatoes. Then go for a *secondo*—
like the perennial sliced beef *tagliata* with veggies and balsamic, or
southern Italian *pezzogna* fish (like a plump snapper) in *acqua pazza*—
a fish broth seasoned with tomato and a pinch of spicy chile pepper.
Kudos for offering a bit more variety in the dessert category beyond
the same-old Italian standards. Ⓢ *Average cost: €55* ⊠ *Piazza Campo
Marzio 6, Campo de' Fiori* ☎ *06/68308626* ⊕ *www.boccondivino.it*
☽ *Closed Sun. and 3 wks in Aug.* ⊹ *4:E2.*

$ ╳ **Da Sergio.** Every neighborhood has at least one old-school Roman
ROMAN trattoria and, for the Campo de' Fiori area, Da Sergio is it. Once you're
seated (there's usually a wait), the red-and-white-check paper table-cov-
ering, bright lights, '50s kitsch, and the stuffed boar's head on the wall
remind you that you're smack in the middle of the genuine article. Go
for the delicious version of pasta *all'amatriciana,* or the generous help-
ing of gnocchi with a tomato sauce and lots of Parmesan cheese, served,
as tradition dictates, on Thursday. Ⓢ *Average cost: €25* ⊠ *Vicolo delle
Grotte 27* ☎ *06/6864293* ☽ *Closed Sun. and 2 wks in Aug.* ⊹ *4:D5.*

$$ ╳ **Ditirambo.** Don't let the country-kitchen ambience fool you. At this
ITALIAN little spot off Campo de' Fiori, the constantly changing selection of
Fodor's Choice offbeat takes on Italian classics is a step beyond ordinary Roman fare.
★ The place is usually packed with diners who appreciate the adventuresome kitchen, though you may overhear complaints about the brusque
service. Antipasti can be delicious and unexpected, like Gorgonzola-
pear soufflé drizzled with aged balsamic vinegar, or a mille-feuille of
eggplant, wild fennel, and anchovies. But people really love this place
for rustic dishes like osso buco, Calabrian eggplant "meatballs," and
hearty pasta with rabbit ragù. Vegetarians will adore the cheesy potato
gratin with truffle shavings. Desserts can be skipped in favor of a *diges-
tivo.* Ⓢ *Average cost: €40* ⊠ *Piazza della Cancelleria 74, Campo de'
Fiori* ☎ *06/6871626* ⊕ *www.ristoranteditirambo.it* ☽ *Closed Aug. No
lunch Mon.* ⊹ *4:D4.*

$ ╳ **Filetti di Baccalà.** For years, Dar Filettaro a Santa Barbara (to use its
ITALIAN official name) has been serving just that—battered, deep-fried fillets of
Fodor's Choice salt cod—and not much else. You'll find no-frills starters such as *brus-
★ chette al pomodoro* (garlic-rubbed toast topped with fresh tomatoes

and olive oil), sautéed zucchini, and, in winter months, the cod is served alongside *puntarelle,* chicory stems tossed with a delicious anchovy-garlic-lemon vinaigrette. The location, down the street from Campo de' Fiori in a little piazza in front of the beautiful Santa Barbara church, begs you to eat at one of the outdoor tables, weather permitting. Long operating hours allow those still on U.S. time to eat as early (how gauche!) as 6 pm. $ *Average cost: €18* ⊠ *Largo dei Librari 88, Campo de' Fiori* ☎ *06/6864018* ⊟ *No credit cards* ☉ *Closed Sun. and Aug. No lunch* ✛ *4:D4.*

$$$$
Fodor's Choice
★
✕ **Il Sanlorenzo.** This revamped, gorgeous space—think chandeliers and soaring original brickwork ceilings—houses one of the better seafood spots in the Eternal City. Tempting tasting menus are on offer, as well as à la carte items like a wonderful series of small plates in their *crudo* (raw fish) appetizer, which can include a perfectly seasoned fish tartare trio, sweet *scampi* (local langoustines), and a wispy-thin carpaccio of red shrimp. The restaurant's version of spaghetti with lobster is an exquisite example of how this dish should look and taste (the secret is cooking the pasta in a lobster stock). Try a main course of a freshly caught seasonal fish prepared to order. Menu items often change based on the chef's whim and the catch of the day. $ *Average cost: €85* ⊠ *Via dei Chiavari 4/5, Campo de' Fiori* ☎ *06/6865097* ⊕ *www.ilsanlorenzo. it* ☉ *No lunch Sat.–Mon.* ✛ *4:D4.*

$
WINE BAR
✕ **L'Angolo Divino.** There's something about this cozy wine bar that feels as if it's in a small university town instead of a bustling metropolis. Serene blue-green walls lined with wood shelves of wines from around the Italian peninsula add to the warm atmosphere. Smoked fish, cured meats, cheeses, and salads make a nice lunch or light dinner, and the kitchen stays open until the wee hours. Ask about tasting evenings dedicated to single grape varieties or regions. $ *Average cost: €25* ⊠ *Via dei Balestrari 12, Campo de' Fiori* ☎ *06/6864413* ☉ *Closed 1 wk in Aug. No dinner Mon.* ✛ *4:D5.*

$$
SEAFOOD
✕ **Monserrato.** In a high-rent area dense with design stores, antiques shops, and jewelers, this simple spot is just a few steps from elegant Piazza Farnese and yet happily devoid of throngs of tourists. Monserrato's signature dishes are its fish specials: carpaccio *di pesce* (fresh fish carpaccio, served with lemon and arugula), *insalatina di seppie* (cuttlefish salad), *bigoli con gamberi e asparagi* (homemade pasta with shrimp and asparagus), and grilled fish that are simple but very satisfying. There's also a nice antipasto assortment so you can eat your share of veggies as well. Select a nice white from the Italo-centric wine list and when the weather heats up, you can enjoy it all with a breeze at umbrella-covered tables on the small, adjacent piazza. $ *Average cost: €45* ⊠ *Via di Monserrato 96, Campo de' Fiori* ☎ *06/6873386* ☉ *Closed Mon. and 1 wk at Christmas* ✛ *4:C4.*

$$
ITALIAN
✕ **Osteria La Quercia.** The beautiful Piazza della Quercia was once devoid of any restaurants, until this casual trattoria opened its doors. Now diners can sit under the gorgeous looming oak tree that lends the square its name. Its menu is simple—the usual suspects include fried starters like stuffed zucchini flowers and baccalà, as well as Roman pasta dishes like spaghetti carbonara and *amatriciana.* Main dishes include

12

baby lamb chops, *involtini* (thinly sliced beef stuffed with herbs and bread crumbs, rolled and baked), and meatballs in tomato sauce. The ubiquitous Roman sautéed *cicoria* (chicory) with olive oil and chili pepper is a good choice for a green side. Service is friendly and allows for lingering on balmy Roman afternoons and evenings—so close, and yet so seemingly far from the chaos of nearby Campo de'Fiori. $ *Average cost: €35* ⊠ *Piazza della Quercia 23, Campo de' Fiori* ☎ *06/68300932* ⊕ *www.laquerciaosteria.com* ✛ *4:C4.*

$$$ ✕ **Roscioli.** More like a Caravaggio painting than a place of business, this
WINE BAR food shop and wine bar is dark and decadent. The shop in front beckons with top-quality comestibles: wild Alaskan smoked salmon, hand-sliced prosciutto from Italy and Spain, more than 300 cheeses, and a dizzying array of wines. Venture farther inside to be seated in a wine cavelike room where you'll be served artisanal cheeses and *salumi*, as well as an extensive selection of unusual menu choices and interesting takes on classics. Try the caprese salad with DOC buffalo milk mozzarella, fresh and roasted tomatoes with bread crumbs and pistachios, or go for pasta with *bottarga* (dried mullet roe) or Sicilian large *fusilli* with swordfish, eggplant, and cherry tomatoes. The menu is further divided among meats, seafood (including a nice selection of tartars and other *crudi* raw fish preparations), and vegetarian-friendly items. ■ TIP→ **Book ahead to reserve a table in the cozy wine cellar beneath the dining room. And afterward head around the corner to their bakery for rightfully famous breads and sweets.** $ *Average cost: €65* ⊠ *Via dei Giubbonari 21/22, Campo de' Fiori* ☎ *06/6875287* ⊕ *www.anticofornoroscioli.com* ☾ *Closed Sun.* ✛ *4:D4.*

$$ ✕ **Trattoria Moderna.** The space is as the name implies—modern, with
ITALIAN high ceilings, and done in shades of beige and gray—and an oversize chalkboard displays daily specials, such as a delicious chickpea and *baccalà* (salt cod) soup. The food runs toward the traditional but with a twist, like a pasta *all'amatriciana* with kosher beef instead of the requisite *guanciale* (cured pork jowl). Main courses are more creative, as well as more hit-or-miss. The jumbo shrimp in a cognac sauce with couscous was tasty, but the scant four shrimp a drawback. The trattoria gets an "A" for effort, with its friendly serving staff and very reasonable prices, and an extra bonus is the outdoor seating—a few tables surrounded by greenery, off the lovely cobblestone street. $ *Average cost: €40* ⊠ *Vicolo dei Chiodaroli 16, Campo de' Fiori* ☎ *06/68803423* ✛ *4:E4.*

GHETTO

$$$ ✕ **Al Pompiere.** The entrance on a narrow side street leads you up a
ROMAN charming staircase and into the main dining room of this neighborhood favorite, all white tablecloths and high arched ceilings. Its Roman Jewish dishes, such as fried zucchini flowers, battered salt cod, and gnocchi, are all consistently good and served without fanfare on white dishes with a simple border. There are also some nice, historic touches like a beef-and-citron stew that comes from an ancient Roman recipe of Apicius. And if you come across the traditional Roman *porchetta* (roasted suckling pig) special, make sure to order it before it runs out—it is truly divine. In 2004, there was a terrible fire in a shop below the restaurant, but the kitchen was soon back in business, though the irony here is

as thick as the chef's tomato sauce: *Al Pompiere* means "the fireman." [$] *Average cost: €55* ✉ *Via Santa Maria dei Calderari 38, Ghetto* ☎ *06/6868377* ⏲ *Closed Sun. and Aug. and 1 wk in Jan.* ⊕ *4:E5.*

WORD OF MOUTH

"From Trastevere it is an easy walk to the Jewish Ghetto neighborhood (over the Isola Tiberina pedestrian island). The Ghetto has a lot of good restaurants with traditional Roman dishes liked fried artichokes." —Vttraveler

$$ ITALIAN 🍴 **Ba' Ghetto.** This hot spot is a welcome addition to the main promenade in the Jewish ghetto. The decor is smart in its black-and-white-with-turquoise-touches look, and outdoor seating in warmer months is a great option in this historic stretch of the district. The kitchen is kosher (many places featuring Roman Jewish fare are not), serves meat dishes, and not only do they feature an assortment of Roman Jewish delights, they also offer a variety of Mediterranean-Middle Eastern Jewish fare. Enjoy starters like phyllo "cigars" stuffed with ground meat and spices, or the *brik*—egg and tomato wrapped in phyllo triangles and briefly fried. There's a nice assortment of pasta dishes, but we advise going for main plates like the assortment of couscous dishes (the spicy seafood is delicious), or baccalà with raisins and pine nuts. Interesting sides like chicory with *bottarga* (cured mullet roe) round out the meal. Note the strictly adhered-to hours: Saturday night, the restaurant posts post-Sabbath/sundown opening times to the minute on a blackboard out front. Check out their latest addition to the ghetto's main drag, with the unfortunate name of **Ba'Ghetto Milky** (✉ *Via del Portico d'Ottavia 2/a*)—it's the kosher dairy version of the original. [$] *Average cost: €45* ✉ *Via del Portico d'Ottavia 57, Ghetto* ☎ *06/68892868* 🌐 *www.kosherinrome.com* ⏲ *No dinner Fri. No lunch Sat.* ⊕ *4:F5.*

$$$ ROMAN 🍴 **Piperno.** *The* place to go for Rome's extraordinary *carciofi alla giudia* (fried whole artichokes), Piperno has been in business for more than a century. The location, up a tiny hill in a piazza tucked away behind the palazzi of the Jewish Ghetto, lends the restaurant a rarefied air. It's a popular location for Sunday brunch. Try the exquisite prosciutto and mozzarella di bufala plate, the *fiori di zucca ripieni e fritti* (fried stuffed zucchini flowers), and *filetti di baccalà* (fillet of cod) to start. The display of fresh local fish is enticing enough to lure diners to try offerings from sea instead of land. Service is in the old-school style of dignified formality. [$] *Average cost: €55* ✉ *Monte dei Cenci 9, Ghetto* ☎ *06/68806629* 🌐 *www.ristorantepiperno.it* ⏲ *Closed Mon. and Aug. No dinner Sun.* ⊕ *4:E5.*

$$$ ROMAN 🍴 **Sora Lella.** It may not be the most original spot in town, but Sora Lella can boast that it's the only restaurant that is open year-round on Isola Tiburina, the wonderously picturesque island set in the middle of the Tiber River between the Jewish ghetto and Trastevere. The dining rooms on two floors are elegant, and service is discreet. As for the food, try the delicious prosciutto and mozzarella to start, and move on to classics like pasta *all'amatriciana,* meatballs in tomato sauce, or Roman baby lamb chops. The stuffed calamari in white wine sauce is worthy of *facendo una scarpetta*—taking a piece of bread to sop up the savory

sauce. [$] *Average cost: €55* ✉ *Via di Ponte Quattro Capi 16, Ghetto* ☎ *06/6861601* 🌐 *www.soralella.com* 🕒 *Closed Sun., Tues. lunch, and 3 wks in Aug.* ✥ *3:D1.*

$$$ SEAFOOD Fodor's Choice ★ 🍴 **Vecchia Roma.** Though the frescoed dining rooms are lovely, the choice place to dine is outside, under the big white umbrellas, with the baroque Piazza Campitelli unrolling before your eyes. After several decades, this is still considered one of the most solid spots on the Roman culinary scene, just the place to experience an intro to Roman cooking, upper-middle-class style. For appetizers, the seafood selection, which may include an assortment of fresh anchovies in vinegary goodness, seafood salad, or baby shrimp, is always fresh and seasonal. Chef Raffaella generally doles out large portions, so select one of her wonderful pasta dishes or skip straight to the *secondi*. Though there are meat and veggie dishes on offer, seafood is a house specialty, and simple southern Italian preparations, such as fresh white flaky fish in a potato crust with cherry tomatoes, are excellent no-fail choices. Sample the house-made fruit desserts for a light(ish) finish to the meal, hopefully accompanied by a dramatic sunset over the 17th-century facade of Santa Maria in Campitelli. [$] *Average cost: €65* ✉ *Piazza Campitelli 18, Ghetto* ☎ *06/6864604* 🌐 *www.ristorantevecchiaroma.com* ✍ *Reservations essential* 🕒 *Closed Wed.* ✥ *4:F5.*

MONTI, ESQUILINO, REPUBBLICA, AND SAN LORENZO

MONTI

$ WINE BAR 🍴 **Cavour 313.** Wine bars are popping up all over the city, but Cavour 313 has been around much longer than most. With a tight seating area in the front, your best bet is to head to the large space in the rear, which is divided into sections with booths that give this bar a rustic feel, halfway to a beer hall. Open for lunch and dinner, it serves an excellent variety of cured meats, cheeses, and salads, with a focus on DOP, organic, and artisanal products. Choose from about 25 wines by the glass or uncork a bottle (there are more than 1,200) and stay a while. [$] *Average cost: €25* ✉ *Via Cavour 313, Monti* ☎ *06/6785496* 🌐 *www.cavour313.it* 🕒 *Closed Aug. No lunch weekends. Closed Sun. and June 15–Sept.* ✥ *2:B5.*

$$$ SEAFOOD 🍴 **F.I.S.H.** The name stands for Fine International Seafood House, which sums up the kitchen's approach. This is fresh, *fresh* fish cooked by capable and creative hands—from Italian fish-based pastas to a Thai mollusk soup with lemongrass and coconut milk that awakens the senses. The menu is divided into sections: appetizers, tapas, Asian, and Mediterranean. Seating is divided into the front aqua lounge, the middle sushi bar, and the back dining room, but it is limited, so book ahead. [$] *Average cost: €60* ✉ *Via dei Serpenti 16, Monti* ☎ *06/47824962* 🌐 *www.f-i-s-h.it* ✍ *Reservations essential* 🕒 *Closed Mon. and 2 wks in Aug. No lunch.* ✥ *2:C5.*

$$ ITALIAN Fodor's Choice ★ 🍴 **Trattoria Monti.** Not far from Santa Maria Maggiore, Monti is one of the most dependable, moderately priced trattorias in the city, featuring the cuisine of the Marches, an area to the northeast of Rome. There are surprisingly few places specializing in this humble fare considering

there are more people hailing from Le Marche in Rome than currently living in the whole region of Le Marche. The fare served up by the Camerucci family is hearty and simple, represented by various roasted meats and game, and a selection of generally vegetarian timbales and soufflés that change seasonally. The region's rabbit dishes are much loved, and here the *timballo di coniglio con patate* (rabbit casserole with potatoes) is no exception. $ *Average cost: €40* ⊠ *Via di San Vito 13a, Monti* ☎ *06/4466573* ⌕ *Reservations essential* ☉ *Closed Aug., 2 wks at Easter, and 10 days at Christmas* ✢ *2:E5.*

ESQUILINO

$$$$

MODERN ITALIAN

Fodor's Choice

★

✕ **Agata e Romeo.** For the perfect marriage of fine dining, creative cuisine, and rustic Roman tradition, the husband-and-wife team of Agata Parisella and Romeo Caraccio is the top. Romeo presides over the dining room and delights in the selection of wine-food pairings. And Chef Agata was perhaps the first in the capital city to put a gourmet spin on Roman ingredients and preparations, elevating dishes of the common folk to new levels, wherein familiar staples like *cacio e pepe* are transformed with the addition of even richer Sicilian aged cheese and saffron. The "baccala' 5 ways" showcases salt cod of the highest quality. From antipasti (try the seafood crudo tasting: it's so artfully presented, it's actually served on a glass plate resembling a painter's palette) to desserts, many dishes are the best versions of classics you can get. The prices here are steep, but for those who appreciate extremely high-quality ingredients, an incredible wine cellar, and warm service, dining here is a real treat. $ *Average cost: €100* ⊠ *Via Carlo Alberto 45, Termini* ☎ *06/4466115* ⊕ *www.agataeromeo.it* ⌕ *Reservations essential* ☉ *Closed weekends, 2 wks in July, and 2 wks in Aug.* ✢ *2:E5.*

$$

PIZZA

✕ **La Gallina Bianca.** This pizzeria's location right down the road from Termini station makes it a perfect place for a welcome-to-Rome meal. A bright, country-cute, noisy locale, La Gallina Bianca attracts a young crowd and serves classic thin-crust pizzas. Try the "full-moon" specialty, perfect for cheese lovers, with ricotta, Parmesan, mozzarella, ham, and tomato. There are other menu items available from the trattoria menu for those who may be trying to stick to a less carb-loaded diet. $ *Average cost: €30* ⊠ *Via A. Rosmini 5, Esquilino* ☎ *06/4743777* ⊕ *www.lagallinabianca.com* ☉ *Closed Aug.* ✢ *2:4D.*

$$$

SOUTHERN ITALIAN

✕ **Monte Caruso.** The regional delicacies of certain areas of Italy are grossly underrepresented in Rome. Monte Caruso is truly a standout, as its menu focuses on food from Lucania, an area of Italy divided between the southern regions of Basilicata and Calabria. Homemade pastas have strange-sounding names, such as *cautarogni* (large cavatelli with Sicilian broccoli) and *cauzuni* (enormous ricotta-stuffed ravioli), but the dishes are generally simple and hearty. $ *Average cost: €50* ⊠ *Via Farini*

12, Esquilino ☎ *06/483549* 🌐 *www.montecaruso.com* ✍ *Reservations essential* ⏲ *Closed Sun. and Aug. No lunch Mon.* ✣ *2:D4.*

$$$ ITALIAN 🍴 **Primo.** A first for this (still) up-and-coming hipster neighborhood, this is a modern Italian restaurant highlighting local ingredients and simplified cooking techniques. But while the name *Primo* may reference the primary ingredients that are the focus of the menu, it could just as easily refer to the *prime* people-watching spot the restaurant enjoys on the 'hood's main drag. The young funky patrons sip from a selection of 250 wines, and nibble on hand-cut prosciutto, anchovy-and-broccoli gratin, and salads with goat cheese and radicchio. Pastas on offer include artichoke tortelli with marjoram and pecorino, and pappardelle with a chicken ragu. Seafood mains, like grilled swordfish with a pistachio sauce are also good choices. Those more carnivorous sink their teeth into the provolone and herb-stuffed veal, or braised beef cheeks with potato puree and artichokes. Desserts are tasty if fairly standard, so why not linger over one of the *digestivi* instead? [$] *Average cost: €55* ✉ *Via del Pigneto 46, Pigneto* ☎ *06/7013827* 🌐 *www.primoalpigneto.it* ⏲ *Closed Mon.* ✣ *2:H6.*

REPUBBLICA

$$ WINE BAR 🍴 **Trimani Il Winebar.** Trimani operates nonstop from 11 am to 12:30 am and serves hot food at lunch and dinner. Decor is minimalist, and the second floor provides a subdued, candlelit space to sip wine. There's always a choice of a soup and pasta plates, as well as second courses and *torte salate* (savory tarts). Around the corner is a wineshop, one of the oldest in Rome, of the same name. Call about wine tastings and classes (in Italian). [$] *Average cost: €30* ✉ *Via Cernaia 37/b, Repubblica* ☎ *06/4469630* ⏲ *Closed Sun. and 2 wks in Aug.* ✣ *2:E2.*

SAN LORENZO

$$ ETHIOPIAN 🍴 **Africa.** Ethiopia was the closest thing Italy ever had to a "colony" at one point. As a result, what Indian food is to London, Ethiopian/Eritrean food is to Rome. Interesting offerings include braised meat main courses, yogurt-based breakfasts, and vegetarian-friendly stews—all under the category of utensil-free dining. [$] *Average cost: €35* ✉ *Via Gaeta 26/28, Termini* ☎ *06/4941077* 💳 *No credit cards* ⏲ *Closed Mon.* ✣ *2:E2.*

$ PIZZA 🍴 **Formula 1.** Its location in the trendy San Lorenzo neighborhood makes this a particularly convenient stop for dinner before checking out some of the area's way-cool bars. The atmosphere here is casual and friendly—posters of Formula 1 cars and drivers past and present attest to the owner's love for auto racing—and draws students from the nearby university as well as pizza lovers from all over the city. [$] *Average cost: €18* ✉ *Via degli Equi 13, San Lorenzo* ☎ *06/4453866* 💳 *No credit cards* ⏲ *Closed Sun. and Aug. No lunch* ✣ *2:G5.*

$$ SOUTHERN ITALIAN Fodor's Choice ★ 🍴 **Tram Tram.** The name refers to its proximity to the tram tracks, but could also describe its size, as it's narrow-narrow and often stuffed to the rafters-rafters (in warmer weather, happily, there's a "side car" of tables enclosed along the sidewalk). The cuisine is derived from cook's hometown region of Puglia. You'll find an emphasis on seafood and vegetables—maybe prawns with saffron-kissed sautéed vegetables—as

well as pastas of very particular shapes. Try the homemade *orecchiette,* ear-shaped pasta, made here with clams and broccoli. Meats tend towards the traditional Roman offerings. No matter where you sit, you'll soon understand why Tram Tram is so snugly packed with satisfied Romans. $ *Average cost: €40* ⊠ *Via dei Reti 44/46, San Lorenzo* ☎ *06/490416* ⊕ *www.ristorantetramtramroma.com* ⊜ *Reservations essential* ☉ *Closed Mon. and 1 wk in mid-Aug.* ✛ *2:H4.*

$$$
MODERN ITALIAN
Fodor'sChoice
★

✕ **Uno e Bino.** The setting is simple: wooden tables and chairs on a stone floor with little more than a few shelves of wine bottles lining the walls for decor. Giampaolo Gravina's restaurant in this artsy corner of the San Lorenzo neighborhood is popular with foodies and locals alike, as the kitchen turns out inventive cuisine inspired by the family's Umbrian and Sicilian roots. Dishes like octopus salad with asparagus and carrots, and spaghetti with swordfish, tomatoes, and capers are specialties. The Parmesan soufflé is a study in lightness, all silky, salty, and absolute perfection. Delicious and simple, yet upscale, desserts cap off the dinner, making this small establishment one of the top dining deals—and pleasurable meals—in Rome. $ *Average cost: €60* ⊠ *Via degli Equi 58, San Lorenzo* ☎ *06/4454105* ☉ *Closed Mon. and Aug. No lunch* ✛ *2:G5.*

VENETO, BORGHESE, AND SPAGNA

VENETO

$$$
TUSCAN

✕ **Papá Baccus.** Italo Cipriani takes his meat as seriously as any Tuscan, using real Chianina beef for the house specialty, the *bistecca alla fiorentina,* a thick grilled steak served on the bone and rare in the center. Cipriani brings many ingredients from his hometown on the border of Emilia-Romagna and Tuscany. Try the sweet and delicate prosciutto from Pratomagno or the *ribollita,* a traditional bread-based minestrone soup. Anything that says "cinta senese" refers to a special breed of pig—and is worth eating. Tuscans are nicknamed "the bean eaters," and after a taste of the *fagioli zolfini* (tender white beans), you'll understand why. The welcome is warm, the service excellent, and the glass of prosecco (gratis) starts the meal on the right foot. $ *Average cost: €65* ⊠ *Via Toscana 36, Veneto* ☎ *06/42742808* ⊕ *www.papabaccus.com* ☉ *Closed Sun. and 2 wks in Aug. No lunch Sat.* ✛ *4:B3.*

BORGHESE

$$$
ITALIAN

✕ **Al Ceppo.** The well-heeled, the business-minded, and those of more refined palate frequent this outpost of tranquillity. Its owners hail from Le Marche, the region north and east of Rome that encompasses inland mountains and the Adriatic coastline. These ladies dote on their customers, as you'd wish a sophisticated Italian *mamma* would. There's always a selection of dishes from their native region, such as *olive ascolane* (green olives stuffed with ground meat, breaded, and fried), various fresh pasta dishes, succulent roast lamb, and a delicious *marchigiano style* rabbit, with sundried tomatoes and mushrooms. Other temptations include a beautiful display of seafood and a wide selection of meats ready to be grilled in the fireplace in the front room. $ *Average cost: €65* ⊠ *Via Panama 2, Parioli* ☎ *06/8419696* ⊕ *www.ristorantealceppo. it* ⊜ *Reservations essential* ☉ *Closed Mon. and 2 wks in Aug.* ✛ *2:C1.*

$$$$ ITALIAN 🍴 **Casina Valadier.** Every Hollywood movie from *Three Coins in the Fountain* to the *Roman Spring of Mrs. Stone* had a scene set here: a splendid pavilion set in the Villa Borghese park and designed by the great neoclassical architect Giuseppe Valadier. Fronted by an Empire-elegant portico and home to grand salons that once welcomed King Farouk of Egypt, Richard Strauss, Gandhi, and Mussolini, "the most beautiful restaurant in Rome" finally underwent a major renovation in 2007, with mixed results. The bar area and terrace are still delightful for sipping an expensive, well-made *aperitivo* but the setting (gorgeous, but even the refurbished interiors could use some upkeep) and magnificent view are not matched by what the kitchen puts out, as quality is inconsistent. Fresh tagliatelle with capon, sweetbreads, and black truffle are truly delicious, but a seafood *fregola* (Sardinian couscous) is fishy and not Mediterranean-fresh. Main courses are simple, so quality is important, but here again: inconsistent. The wine list is surprisingly moderate on cost and offers a nice variety from up and down the peninsula. The best way to enjoy this spot is to see it both in the daylight *and* at night, so coming for sunset *aperitivi* and then gliding into dinner (well lubricated with prosecco?) may be your best bet. [$] *Average cost: €75* ✉ *Piazza Bucarest, Borghese* ☎ *06/69922090* 🌐 *www.casinavaladier.it* ✣ *1:H1.*

$$$ AMERICAN 🍴 **Duke's.** It dubs itself a California-style restaurant and bar, although the California rolls have tuna and carrot in them and they've added mint leaves to the Caesar salad. But the truth is, once you look at Duke's menu after a stretch of Italian-only bingeing, you may actually want it *all.* Perhaps a nice, juicy beef fillet, and the finishing touch of the warm apple pie served with gelato. The decor is Malibu–beach house–minimalist. The outdoor patio in the back is consummately SoCal chic. And up front, opening out onto the street, all the beautiful people from the neighborhood (read: plenty of unnatural blondes) are huddled around the bar, sipping frozen cocktails, the whir of blenders and music blaring in the background. [$] *Average cost: €50* ✉ *Viale Parioli 200, Borghese* ☎ *06/80662455* 🌐 *www.dukes.it* 🕒 *Closed Sat.; June–Sept. closed Sat. and Sun. and 1 wk in Aug.* ✣ *2:C1.*

SPAGNA

$$$ ECLECTIC 🍴 **Caffè Romano dell'Hotel d'Inghilterra.** One of Rome's most soigné hotels, the d'Inghliterra houses this standard-issue symphony in beige marbles, beechwood walls, and Tuscan columns. You can tell that jet-setters like this spot—it's got an *orario continuato,* or nonstop opening hours, from 10 am on, so snacking or having a late lunch is a possibility here. Though its menu claims to be "global," some of the dishes on offer are international misfires, so best bets tend towards the authentic northern Italian meat preparations and southern Italian pasta and seafood dishes. Try interesting selections like the glazed boar with polenta, the guinea hen with stewed chestnuts and bacon, or the seafood soup, as well as a variety of pasta choices. Tables are close together, but perhaps you won't mind eavesdropping on your supermodel neighbor. [$] *Average cost: €60* ✉ *Via Borgongna 4M, Spagna* ☎ *06/69981500* ✣ *1:H2.*

$$$$ EMILIAN 🍴 **Dal Bolognese.** The darling of the media, film, and fashion communities, this classic restaurant on Piazza del Popolo is not only an "in-crowd"

Before dinner, enjoy a glass of wine in one of Spagna's many enotecas, including Il Palazzetto, whose balcony directly overlooks the Spanish Steps.

dinner destination but makes a convenient shopping-spree lunch spot. As the name promises, the cooking adheres to the hearty tradition of Bologna. Start with a plate of sweet *San Daniele* prosciutto with melon, then move on to the traditional egg pastas of Emilia-Romagna. Second plates include the famous Bolognese *bollito misto,* a steaming tray of an assortment of boiled meats (some recognizable, some indecipherable) served with its classic accompaniment, a tangy, herby *salsa verde* (green sauce). During dessert, take in the passing parade of your fellow diners—they love to meet and greet with excessive air kisses. $ *Average cost: €75 ⊠ Piazza del Popolo 1, Spagna* ☎ *06/3611426* ⌕ *Reservations essential* ☉ *Closed Mon. and 3 wks in Aug.* ✛ *1:G1.*

$ ✕ **GiNa.** "Homey minimalism" isn't a contradiction at this whitewashed
CAFÉ cafè with a modern edge. The block seats and sleek booths, the single flowers in Mason jars, white chandeliers, and multiplicity of mirrors make this small but multilevel space a tiny gem tucked away on the street leading from Piazza di Spagna. With a menu ranging from various bruschettas to interesting mixed salads, sandwiches, and pastas, this is a top spot for a light lunch or an aperitivo that won't break the bank in this high-end neighborhood. In fact, the best things here are the sweets: gelato, pastries, fruit with yogurt, and even some American pies and cheesecake, along with the best hot chocolate in Rome during the winter. In warmer months, fully stocked gourmet picnic baskets, complete with checked tablecloth, are ready for pick up on your way to the Villa Borghese park. $ *Average cost: €25 ⊠ Via San Sebastianello 7A, Spagna, Spagna* ☎ *06/6780251* ⊕ *www.ginaroma.com* ☉ *Open daily 11 am–8 pm* ✛ *1:H2.*

$$ ITALIAN 🍴 **'Gusto.** There's an urban-loft feel to this trendy two-story space, a bit like Pottery Barn exploded in Piazza Agusto Imperatore (the name of the restaurant is a play on this location and the Italian word for taste/flavor). The ground floor contains a buzzing pizzeria-trattoria, while upstairs is the more upscale restaurant. We prefer the casual-but-hopping vibe of the ground-floor wine bar in the back, where a rotating selection of wines by the glass and bottle are served up alongside a vast array of cheeses, *salumi*, and bread products. Lunchtime features a great value salad bar. And for the kitchen enthusiast, the 'Gusto "complex" includes a store, selling everything from cookware to cookwear. [$] *Average cost: €45* ✉ *Piazza Augusto Imperatore 9, Spagna* ☎ *06/3226273* ⊕ *1:G2.*

$$$ ITALIAN 🍴 **'Gusto - Osteria.** This is the second sibling in the 'Gusto empire, and they've shifted their focus from *cichetti* (Venetian-style tapas) to hearty traditional Roman fare. And why not? Romans are traditionalists and regionalists, so *When In Rome*.... You may want to begin by choosing from the incredible selection of 400 cheeses in the basement cellar, then from the various *fritti* (fried items), and moving on to pastas such as sheep's milk cheese and pepper spaghetti. Secondi are meats or grilled seafood items, highlighting the simplicity of the *cucina romana*. The atmosphere is predictably buzzy, and the loftlike, airy space is a refreshing change from the trattoria standard. [$] *Average cost: €55* ✉ *Via della Frezza 16, Spagna* ☎ *06/32111482* 🌐 *www.gusto.it* ✍ *Reservations essential* ⊕ *1:G2.*

$ WINE BAR 🍴 **Il Brillo Parlante.** Il Brillo Parlante's location near Piazza del Popolo makes it convenient for lunch or dinner after a bit of shopping in the Via del Corso area. Choose from 20 wines by the glass at the bar or eat downstairs in one of several wood-panel rooms. The menu is extensive for a wine bar; choose from cured meats, *crostini* (toasted bread with various toppings such as pâté or prosciutto), pastas, grilled meats, and even pizzas. [$] *Average cost: €22* ✉ *Via della Fontanella 15, Spagna* ☎ *06/3243334* 🌐 *www.ilbrilloparlante.com* 🕒 *Closed Mon. and 1 wk in mid-Aug.* ⊕ *1:G1.*

$ PIZZA 🍴 **Il Leoncino.** Lines out the door on weekends attest to the popularity of this fluorescent-lighted pizzeria in the otherwise big-ticket neighborhood around Piazza di Spagna. This is one of the few pizzerias open for lunch as well as dinner. [$] *Average cost: €18* ✉ *Via del Leoncino 28, Spagna* ☎ *06/6867757* 🕒 *Closed Wed. and Aug. No lunch Sat. and Sun.* ⊕ *1:G3.*

$ WINE BAR 🍴 **L'Enoteca Antica di Via della Croce.** This wine bar is always crowded, and for good reason. It's long on personality: colorful ceramic-tile tables are always filled with locals and foreigners, as is the half moon–shaped bar where you can order from the large selection of salumi and cheeses on offer. Peruse the chalkboard highlighting the special wines by-the-glass for that day to accompany your nibbles. There's waiter service at the tables in back and out front on the bustling Via della Croce, where people-watching is in high gear. [$] *Average cost: €20* ✉ *Via della Croce 76/b, Spagna* ☎ *06/6790896* 🕒 *Closed 2 wks in Aug.* ⊕ *1:G2.*

$$ VEGETARIAN 🍴 **Margutta Vegetariano.** Parallel to posh Via del Babuino, Via Margutta has long been known as the street where artists have their studios in

Rome. How fitting, then, that the rare Italian vegetarian restaurant, with changing displays of modern art, sits on the far end of this gallery-lined street closest to Piazza del Popolo. Here it takes on a chic and cosmopolitan air, where you'll find meat-free versions of classic Mediterranean dishes as well as more daring tofu concoctions. Lunch is essentially a pasta/salad bar to which you help yourself, while dinner offers à la carte and prix-fixe options. $ *Average cost: €40* ⊠ *Via Margutta 118, Piazza del Popolo* ☎ *06/32650577* ⊕ *www.ilmarguttavegetariano.it* ✢ *1:G1.*

$$$
ITALIAN
Fodor'sChoice
★

✕ **Nino.** A favorite among international journalists and the rich and famous for decades (Tom Cruise and Katie Holmes had their celeb-studded rehearsal dinner here), Nino is Rome's best loved dressed-up trattoria. The decor is country rustic *alla Tuscana*, complete with carved wood wainscoting, dried flowers, old engravings, and a mellow yellow color on the walls that even Botticelli would have adored. Along with its look (and waiters!), Nino sticks to the classics when it comes to its food, which is basically Roman and Tuscan staples. Kick things off with a selection from the fine antipasto spread, or go for the cured meats or warm *crostini* (toasts) spread with liver pâté. Move on to pappardelle *al lepre* (a rich hare sauce) or hearty Tuscan ribollita soup, and go for the gold with a piece of juicy grilled beef. One warning: if you're not Italian, or a regular, or a celebrity, the chance of brusque service multiplies—so insist on good service and you'll win the waiters' respect. $ *Average cost: €55* ⊠ *Via Borgognona 11, Spagna* ☎ *06/6786752, 06/6795676* ⊕ *www.ristorantenino.it* ☉ *Closed Sun. and Aug.* ✢ *1:H2.*

$$$
NORTHERN
ITALIAN

✕ **Tati al 28.** This offshoot of the 'Gusto empire focuses specifically on what can be dubbed Italian brasserie fare: basics, including pizza, with an emphasis on northern Italian fare that leans as heavily on French influence as it does on the rest of the Italian peninsula's tradition. The space is a soaring modern spot, like the rest of the 'Gusto siblings, though here there is a concentration on the interplay between black and white, light and dark, with a vibe of urban smart. A sardine appetizer with fried zucchini is a sophisticated Italian version of fish-and-chips. The *zuppa di pesce* (fish stew) is as packed with flavor as one would hope, and an interesting collection of other northern Italian staple dishes are prettily presented and live up to the visuals with great taste all around. Service can be a bit slow, but hey, the waiters are serious about their *bella figura*—meaning they look good, so important in Rome. $ *Average cost: €50* ⊠ *Piazza Augusto Imperatore 28, Piazza di Spagna* ☎ *06/68134221* ⊕ *www.gusto.it* ✢ *1:G2.*

VATICAN, BORGO, AND PRATI

VATICAN

$$$
ROMAN
Fodor'sChoice
★

✕ **La Veranda dell'Hotel Columbus.** Deciding where to sit at La Veranda is not easy, since both the shady courtyard, torch-lit at night, and the frescoed dining room are among Rome's most spectacular settings. While La Veranda has classic Roman cuisine on tap, the kitchen offers nice, refreshing twists on the familiar with an innovative use of flavor combinations. Try the unusual duck leg confit starter, stuffed with raisins and pinenuts with an onion compote and plum sorbet. Or go for the grilled tuna bites with anchovy-caper dumplings and an eggplant torta. Even

Refueling the Roman Way

12

Staggering under the weight of a succession of three-course meals, you may ask yourself, how do the Romans eat so much, twice a day, every day? The answer is, they don't.

If you want to do as the Romans do, try lunch at a *tavola calda* (literally, hot table), a cross between a caffè and a cafeteria where you'll find fresh food in manageable portions.

There's usually a selection of freshly prepared pastas, cooked vegetables such as *bietola all'agro* (cooked beet greens with lemon), roasted potatoes, and grilled or roasted meat or fish.

Go to the counter to order an assortment and quantity that suits your appetite, and pay by the plate, usually about €5 plus drinks. Tavole calde

aren't hard to find, particularly in the city center, often marked with "tavola calda" or "self-service" signs.

The other ubiquitous options for a light lunch or between-meal snack are pizza *al taglio* (by the slice) shops, bars, and enoteche (wine bars). At bars throughout Italy, coffee is the primary beverage served (drinking establishments are commonly known as pubs or American bars); at them you can curb your appetite with a panino (a simple sandwich) or tramezzino (sandwich on untoasted white bread, usually heavy on the mayonnaise).

Wine bars vary widely in the sophistication and variety of food available. You can count on cheese and cured meats at the very least.

the pastas are unexpected: saffron fettucine with cuttlefish and zucchini flowers is subtle and elegant—much like the surroundings. Call ahead, especially on Saturday, because the hotel often hosts weddings, which close the restaurant, and you don't want to miss passing a few hours of your Roman Holiday in these environs. $ *Average cost: €65* ⊠ *Borgo Santo Spirito 73, Borgo* ☎ *06/6872973* ⊕ *www.hotelcolumbus.net* ⌂ *Reservations essential* ✛ *1:D3.*

PRATI

$$$

ITALIAN

✕ **Cesare.** An old standby in the residential area near the Vatican known as Prati, Cesare is a willing slave to tradition. The refrigerated display of fresh fish of the day is a tip-off of what's on offer. Classic fish dishes, such as fresh marinated anchovies and sardines, and mixed seafood salad dressed in a lemon citronette, quell those seafood cravings. Homemade pasta with meat sauce is the primo to get, and *saltimbocca* (thinly sliced veal with prosciutto and sage) or the thick Florentine steaks are the ultimate meat-lover's dishes. As with any other traditional Roman restaurant, gnocchi are served on Thursday and pasta with chickpeas on Friday. Also try the €38 "menu toscano"—a great, multicourse value. The look of the place is quite clubby, and the menu's tendency toward stick-to-the-ribs comfort food makes it a great place to go in the autumn and winter, when the cooler weather ushers in dishes featuring truffles, game, and heartier fare. $ *Average cost: €50* ⊠ *Via Crescenzio 13, Prati* ☎ *06/6861227* ⊕ *www.ristorantecesare.com* ☾ *Closed Sun., Aug., and Easter wk* ✛ *1:E2.*

$$$ TUSCAN

🍴 **Dal Toscano.** An open wood-fired grill and classic dishes such as *ribollita* (a thick bread and vegetable soup) and *pici* (fresh, thick pasta with wild hare sauce) are the draw at this great family-run Tuscan trattoria near the Vatican. The cuts of beef visible at the entrance tell you right away that the house special is the prized *bistecca alla fiorentina*—a thick grilled steak left rare in the middle and seared on the outside, with its rub of gutsy Tuscan olive oil and sea salt forming a delicious crust to keep in the natural juices of the beef. Seating outside on the sidewalk in warm weather is a nice touch. [$] *Average cost: €55* ✉ *Via Germanico 58/60, Prati* ☎ *06/39725717* 🌐 *www.ristorantedaltoscano.it* ⏲ *Closed Mon., 3 wks in Aug., and 1 wk in Jan.* ✥ *1:C2.*

$$$$ WINE BAR ★

🍴 **Il Simposio di Costantini.** At the most upscale wine bar in town, decorated with wrought-iron vines, wood paneling, and velvet, you come for the wine, but return for the food. Everything here is appropriately *raffinato* (refined): marinated and smoked fish, composed salads, top-quality salami and other cured meats and pâtés. There are plenty of dishes with classic Roman leanings, like the artichoke dish prepared three ways. Main courses favor carnivores, as roast lamb, a fillet with foie gras, or game (like pigeon, in season) complement the vast offering of top-notch red wines. The restaurant boasts 80 assorted cheeses to savor with your dessert wine. [$] *Average cost: €70* ✉ *Piazza Cavour 16, Prati* ☎ *06/3203575* 🌐 *www.pierocostantini.it* ✍ *Reservations essential* ⏲ *Closed Sun. and last 2 wks of Aug. No lunch Sat.* ✥ *1:E2.*

$ PIZZA

🍴 **L'Isola della Pizza.** Right near the Vatican Metro stop, the "Island of Pizza" is also known for its copious antipasti. Simply ask for the house appetizers, and a waiter will swoop down with numerous plates of salad, seafood, bruschetta, prosciutto, and crispy pizza Bianca. Though it's all too easy to fill up on these fun starters, the pizza is dependably good, and meat lovers can get a decent steak. [$] *Average cost: €25* ✉ *Via degli Scipioni 47, Prati* ☎ *06/39733483* 🌐 *www.isoladellapizza.com* ⏲ *Closed Sun., Aug., and Christmas wk. No lunch* ✥ *1:C2.*

$$$ MODERN ITALIAN Fodor's Choice ★

🍴 **Taverna Angelica.** The area surrounding St. Peter's Basilica isn't known for culinary excellence, but Taverna Angelica is an exception. Its tiny size allows the chef to concentrate on each individual dish, and the menu is creative without being pretentious. Dishes such as warm octopus salad on a bed of mashed potatoes with a basil-parsley pesto drizzle are more about taste than presentation. The lentil soup with pigeon breast brought hunter's cuisine to a new level, and spaghetti with crunchy pancetta and leeks is what the Brits call "more-ish" (meaning you want *more* of it). Fresh sliced tuna in a pistachio crust with orange sauce is light and delicious. It may be difficult to find, on a section of the street that's set back and almost subterranean, but Taverna Angelica is worth seeking out. [$] *Average cost: €55* ✉ *Piazza A. Capponi 6, Borgo* ☎ *06/6874514* 🌐 *www.tavernaangelica.it* ✍ *Reservations essential* ✥ *1:D2.*

TRASTEVERE AND GIANICOLO

TRASTEVERE

$$
ROMAN
★
☼

✕ **Alle Fratte di Trastevere.** Here you can find staple Roman trattoria fare as well as dishes with a southern slant. This means that *spaghetti alla carbonara* (with pancetta, eggs, and cheese) shares the menu with the likes of penne *alla Sorrentina* (with tomato, basil, and fresh mozzarella). For starters, the bruschettas here are exemplary, as is the pressed octopus carpaccio on a bed of arugula. As for *secondi,* you can again look south and to the sea for a mixed seafood pasta or a grilled sea bass with oven-roasted potatoes, or go for the meat with a fillet *al pepe verde* (green peppercorns in a brandy cream sauce). Service is always with a smile, as owner Francesco and his trusted staff make you feel at home. $ *Average cost: €35* ✉ *Via delle Fratte di Trastevere 49/50* ☎ *06/5835775* ⊕ *www.allefratteditrastevere.com* ☉ *Closed Wed. and 2 wks in Aug.* ⊕ *3:B2.*

$
PIZZA

✕ **Dar Poeta.** Romans drive across town for great pizza from this neighborhood institution on a small street in Trastevere. Maybe it's the dough—it's made from a secret blend of flours that's reputed to be easier to digest than the competition. They offer both thin-crust pizza and a thick-crust (*alta*) Neapolitan-style pizza with any of the given toppings. For dessert, there's a ridiculously good calzone with Nutella chocolate-hazelnut spread and ricotta cheese, so save some room. Service from the owners and friendly waitstaff is smile-inducing. $ *Average cost: €24* ✉ *Vicolo del Bologna 45, Trastevere* ☎ *06/5880516* ⊕ *www. darpoeta.com* ⊕ *4:B6.*

$$$
ITALIAN

✕ **Ferrara.** What used to be a well-stocked enoteca with a few nibbles has become what locals now know as the "Ferrara block": the enoteca has expanded to become a restaurant, wine bar, and a gastronomic boutique taking over a good section of one of the area's most famous streets. The renovations have resulted in an airy, modernist destination, with the original space as it was, all wooden chairs and ceramic-tiled tables: enoteca chic. Service can be iffy to slow, and, in the end, the results coming out of the kitchen are inconsistent. A fine starter is the ricotta and herb-stuffed zucchini flowers sprinkled with crispy pancetta. Secondi range from seared tuna in a sesame seed crust to roast pork with prunes. But true to its enoteca roots, it's the award-winning wine selection that impresses here. $ *Average cost: €60* ✉ *Piazza Trilussa 41, Trastevere* ☎ *06/58333920* ⊕ *www.enotecaferrara.it* ⌑ *Reservations essential* ⊕ *4:C6.*

$$$$
MODERN ITALIAN

✕ **Glass Hostaria.** After 14 years in Austin, Texas, Glass chef Cristina Bowerman returned to Rome to reconnect with her Italian roots. Her cooking is as innovative as the building she works in—which has received numerous recognitions for its architecture and design since opening in 2004—but Bowerman still abides by some cardinal Italian kitchen rules, such as the use of fresh, local, and seasonal ingredients. With an impassioned sense for detail, taste, and presentation, she serves a delicious pumpkin gnocchi with fontina fondue, black truffle, and toasted almonds. Another favorite dish is the scallops with pistachio cream and seasonal mushrooms. And for dessert: a white truffle crème brûlée. Need help pairing your wine? Glass offers more than 600 labels

12

for the interested oenophiles. $ *Average cost: €85* ⊠ *Vicolo del Cinque 58, Trastevere* ☎ *06/58335903* ⊕ *www.glass-hostaria.com* ☾ *Closed Mon. No lunch* ✛ *4:C6.*

$$ × **Il Ciak.** This Tuscan staple in Trastevere is a carnivore's delight. Spe-
TUSCAN   cializing in the Tuscan *chianina* beef as well as the many game and pork dishes of the region, Il Ciak prepares reliably tasty fare. It's probably best appreciated during the autumn and winter months, when hunter's dishes—such as wild boar sausage or the pasta with wild hare sauce—get accompaniments like porcini mushrooms and truffles with polenta. Be prepared to share the pleasure of your oversize fiorentina steak—prepared *al sangue* (rare), of course. $ *Average cost: €45* ⊠ *Vicolo del Cinque, Trastevere* ☎ *06/5894774* ⌁ *Reservations essential* ☾ *Closed Sun.* ✛ *4:C6.*

$$ × **Jaipur.** Named after the pink city in India, this restaurant meets the
INDIAN   standards of the most discerning Londoners, who know a thing or two about their curries. Here, in this large space just off the main Viale di Trastevere, you'll find a vast, high-ceilinged dining room decked in retina-burning yellow with festive Indian decorations on the huge walls (there's also dining outside when the weather calls for it). Portions are small but made for sharing, so go ahead and get a variety of dishes to "divide and conquer." $ *Average cost: €35* ⊠ *Via di San Francesco a Ripa 56, Trastevere* ☎ *06/5803992* ⊕ *www.ristorantejaipur.it* ☾ *Closed Mon.* ✛ *3:C2.*

$$$ × **La Gensola.** For Italian "mainlanders," going out for Sicilian fare is
SICILIAN   like international dining: it's a culinary adventure involving out-of-the-
Fodor'sChoice ordinary tastes and flavor combinations, many thanks to the island's
★   interesting mix of Arab, African, and Mediterranean influences. La Gensola, tucked away on a back street on the "quiet side" of Viale Trastevere, offers a respite from the Roman standards, and a welcome alternative it is. Start with antipasto, perhaps the fresh tuna "meat-balls" or gratineéd scallops with squid ink. Pastas, like a homemade tagliatelle with sun-dried tomatoes, baby calamari, and spicy peper-oncino, are zippy on the palate. Since Sicily is a Mediterranean island, its cuisine leans heavily on the bounty of the sea, so a fresh fish like tur-bot with tomatoes, red onion, and capers is a wonderful choice. Allow the knowledgeable servers to guide you through the selective wine list featuring some lesser-known southern Italian labels. And for dessert, don't pass up an opportunity to try a cannoli or a piece of cassata cake. *Mmm, buono!* $ *Average cost: €55* ⊠ *Piazza della Gensola 15, Traste-vere* ☎ *06/5816312* ⊕ *www.osterialagensola.it* ✛ *3:C1.*

$ × **Ombre Rosse.** Set on lovely Piazza Sant'Egidio in the heart of Traste-
WINE BAR   vere, this open-day-and-night spot is a great place to pass the time. You can have a morning cappuccino and read one of their international newspapers; have a light lunch (soups and salads are fresh and deli-cious) while taking in some sun or working on your laptop (free Wi-Fi); enjoy an aperitivo and nibbles at an outdoor table; or finish off an evening with friends at the bar. Ombre Rosse bustles with regulars and expats who know the value of a well-made cocktail and an ever-lively atmosphere. $ *Average cost: €25* ⊠ *Piazza Sant'Egidio 12, Trastevere* ☎ *06/5884155* ☾ *No lunch Sun.* ✛ *3:B1.*

CLOSE UP

Caffè: Rome's Best Coffeehouses

Although Rome may not boast the grand caffè of Paris or Vienna, it does have hundreds of small places on pleasant side streets and piazzas to while away the time. Many caffè have tons of personality and are quite friendly to lingering patrons. The coffee is routinely of high quality. Locals usually stop in for a quickie at the bar, where prices are much lower than for the same drink taken at the table.

✕ **Antico Caffè Greco.** A national landmark, this place, once favored by Byron, Shelley, Keats, Goethe, and Casanova, still has enough red-velvet chairs, marble tables, neoclassical sculpted busts, and antique artwork lining the walls to lend it the air of a gorgeously romantic, bygone era. Set in the middle of the shopping madness of Via Condotti, it now gets filled with tourists but locals who love to breathe the air of history—more than 250 years of it—know enough to come here off-hours, the best time to glimpse authenticity. $ *Average cost: €15 ⊠ Via dei Condotti 86, Piazza di Spagna* ☎ *06/6791700* ⊕ *www. anticocaffegreco.eu* ✛ *1:H2.*

✕ **Caffè Sant'Eustachio.** Traditionally frequented by Rome's literati, this has what is generally considered Rome's best cup of coffee. Servers are hidden behind a huge espresso machine, vigorously mixing the sugar and coffee to protect their "secret method" for the perfectly prepared cup. (If you want your *caffè* without sugar here, ask for it *amaro*). $ *Average cost: €2 ⊠ Piazza Sant'Eustachio 82, Pantheon* ☎ *06/68802048* ✛ *4:E3.*

✕ **Tazza d'Oro.** Many admirers contend this is the city's best cup of coffee. The hot chocolate in winter, all thick and gooey goodness, is

a treat. And in warm weather, the coffee granita is the perfect cooling alternative to a regular espresso. $ *Average cost: €4 ⊠ Via degli Orfani, Pantheon* ☎ *06/6789792* ⊕ *www. tazzadorocoffeeshop.com* ✛ *4:E2.*

✕ **Rosati.** You can sit yourself down and watch the world go by at Rosati, one of the closest "institution"-like places that Rome has in its caffè culture, open since 1922. $ *Average cost: €20 ⊠ Piazza del Popolo 5, Spagna* ☎ *06/3225859, 06/3227378* ✛ *1:G1.*

✕ **Caffè della Pace.** With its sidewalk tables taking in Santa Maria della Pace's adorable piazza, this has long been the haunt of Rome's *beau monde*. Set near Piazza Navona, it also has two rooms filled with old-world personality and paparazzi-worthy patrons. The neighborhood, hipper than ever, with newly clogged *vicoli*, means a table here is a very prized commodity. $ *Average cost: €15 ⊠ Via della Pace 3, Navona* ☎ *06/6861216* ⊕ *www.caffedellapace. it* ✛ *4:C2.*

✕ **Bar San Calisto.** Walk toward Viale di Trastevere and discover the wonderfully down-at-the-heels Bar San Calisto, immensely popular with the old local community and expat crowd. The drinks are as inexpensive as the neighborhood gets and the same could be said about the institutional lighting; the crowd waivers between bohemian and just unshowered and drunk. Don't miss the super hot chocolate in winter and the chocolate gelato in summer! $ *Average cost: €4 ⊠ Piazza San Calisto 4, Trastevere* ☎ *06/5895678* ⌂ *Reservations not accepted* ✛ *3:B1.*

$ ✕ **Panattoni.** Nicknamed "the mortuary" for its marble-slab tables, Pan-
PIZZA   attoni is actually about as lively as you can get. Packed every night, it
☾   serves crisp pizzas that come out of the wood-burning ovens at top
speed. The fried starters here, like a nice *baccalà*, are light and tasty.
Panattoni stays open well past midnight, convenient for a late meal after
the theater or a movie nearby. $ *Average cost: €20* ✉ *Viale Trastevere
53–57, Trastevere* ☎ *06/5800919* ⬥ *Reservations not accepted* ⊟ *No
credit cards* ⊙ *Closed Wed. and 3 wks in mid-Aug. No lunch* ✛ *3:C2.*

$$$ ✕ **Rivadestra.** The name is a reference to the right bank of the Tiber
ITALIAN   river—which in Rome encompasses Trastevere, Rome's version of Par-
is's historic "Left Bank" of bohemians and intellectuals. Here, Rivades-
tra stands out among the old-school Roman eateries and amber-lit bars;
walking through the heavy doors of the entrance is like walking into
an oasis. The backlit bar and candelabras create a warm glow, and the
service is quite welcoming. The streamlined menu offers starters like a
pumpkin flan or eggplant stewed with olive oil and herbs, but better to
head straight for well-executed *primi,* like the *gramigna* pasta with a
sea bass and zucchini ragù with shrimp. Main dishes included a delicate
sea bass in a potato crust, and seared tuna steak with a pepper compote.
Finish off with a molten chocolate cake or a cheese plate paired with
their extensive list of digestivi. You won't leave overly stuffed, but you
will leave happily content. $ *Average cost: €55* ✉ *Via della Penitenza
7, Trastevere* ☎ *06/68307053* ⊕ *www.rivadestra.com* ⊙ *Closed Sun.
(summer), Mon. (winter)* ✛ *4:A5.*

$$ ✕ **Romolo.** Nowhere else do the lingering rays of the setting Roman
ROMAN   sun seem more inviting than within the famed tavern garden of this
charming Trastervere haunt—set right by the arch of Porta Settimiana
this was once reputedly the onetime home of Raphael's lady love, La
Fornarina. And though belly-warming winter meals can be enjoyed in
the ancient palazzo, it's the outdoor garden seating that makes this a
truly coveted dining spot in the summer months. Who can resist classic
spaghetti alla carbonara or pasta all'amatriciana in these surroundings?
House specialties include the *mozzarella alla fornarina* (deep-fried mozzarella with ham and anchovies) and anything with the chef's legendary
artichoke sauce. Service is equally warm and the wine list as local as
the staff. $ *Average cost: €50* ✉ *Via di Porta Settimiana 8, Trastevere
06/5818284* ⬥ *Reservations essential* ⊙ *Closed Mon.* ✛ *4:B6.*

$$ ✕ **Spirito di Vino.** At this restaurant on the less-traveled side of Viale
ITALIAN   Trastevere, diners can enjoy an evening of historic and culinary interest.
The restaurant itself was rebuilt on the site of a 12th-century Jewish
synagogue, and as such, the spot is rich with history—several ancient
sculptures, now in the Vatican and Capitoline museums, were unearthed
in the basement. The food ranges from inventive (mini-meatballs sea-
soned with coriander) to traditional (spaghetti with pecorino cheese and
pepper), to historical (braised pork shoulder with apples and leeks, fol-
lowing an ancient Roman recipe). The proud owner is happy to explain
every dish on the menu, and he even offers a postdinner tour of the wine
cellar—and that basement. $ *Average cost: €45* ✉ *Via dei Genovesi 31,
Trastevere* ☎ *06/5896689* ⊕ *www.spiritodivino.com* ⊙ *Closed Sun. and
2 wks in Aug.* ✛ *3:C1.*

12

$$ ✕ **Z'Imberto.** Under a brightly lit awning covering a lively Trastevere
SEAFOOD piazza, you find the kind of casual trattoria one expects to stumble upon in every Italian seaside village: locals waiting for tables, a bustling casual setting, and ebullient servers pushing heaping plates of fresh seafood and pasta. Here, waiters serve with a smile and a wink, joking with clients while dishing out large portions of the house specialty: local seafood. Of course, traditional Roman meat staples are present on the menu, but really, with itsy-bitsy baby calamari the size of a fingertip fried up so perfectly, why stick to the standards? Pastas with all varieties of sea creatures abound, as do main plates of swordfish and grilled calamari. But we think the best plan is to order up the mixed house seafood antipasto for the table, order some salads and a couple of pastas to share, and close the meal with samplings from frosty bottles of *digestivi* planted firmly on your table. *This* is what they meant when they coined the term *la dolce vita.* $ *Average cost: €45* ⊠ *Piazza San Giovanni della Malva, Trastevere* ☎ *06/5816646* ☾ *Closed Mon.* ✛ *3:B1.*

GIANICOLO

$$$$ ✕ **Antico Arco.** Founded by three friends with a passion for wine and fine
MODERN ITALIAN food (the team leader is Patrizia Mattei), Antico Arco attracts foodies from Rome and beyond with its culinary inventiveness and high style. The location up on top of the Janiculum hill provides for a charming setting and a warm ambience difficult to come by elsewhere in the city. Renovations in recent years have updated and transformed the once-dark and cozy dining rooms into plush, modern spaces with whitewashed brick walls, dark floors, and black velvet chairs with fresh lighting. Seating upstairs is still a treat. The menu changes with the season, but you may find delights such as *crudo di ricciola con lime, zenzero, e insalata di puntarelle* (raw amberjack with lime, ginger, and a salad of chicory stems in anchovy vinaigrette), a classic pasta *alla carbonara* made even richer with the addition of black truffles, or a *fillet d'agnello* (fillet of lamb) in a hazelnut crust with a sprout salad in balsamic vinegar. The chocolate soufflé with a molten chocolate center is justly famous among chocoholics all over the city. $ *Average cost: €85* ⊠ *Piazzale Aurelio 7, Gianicolo* ☎ *06/5815274* ⊕ *www.anticoarco. it* ⌂ *Reservations essential* ☾ *Closed Sun. and 2 wks in Aug.* ✛ *3:A1.*

COLOSSEO, AVENTINO, AND TESTACCIO

COLOSSEO

$$ ✕ **Ai Tre Scalini.** A traditional restaurant by the Colosseum, Ai Tre Scal-
ROMAN ini is old-school Roman with touches of the Sicilian. The seating outside in warm weather is pleasant, and some dishes highlight the chef's playfulness, like the unusual radicchio and cheese-stuffed *zagnolotti* (small ravioli) in a lobster sauce. A wide variety of second courses, from gilthead bream topped with paper-thin potato rounds, to simple beef with rosemary, are indeed what they seem, served by waiters who have clearly been around for quite some time. $ *Average cost: €45* ⊠ *Via SS. Quattro 30, Colosseo* ☎ *06/7096309* ✉ *infoai3scalini.com* ⊕ *www. ai3scalini.com* ☾ *Closed Mon. and 10 days in Sept.* ✛ *3:G1.*

$$$$ SEAFOOD Fodor's Choice ★ 🍴 **San Teodoro.** The atmosphere: far removed from the madding crowds. The setting: a pair of enclosed piazzas, walls covered in ivy, nestled by the Roman Forum and the Campidoglio. The specialty: refined Roman cuisine, featuring tastes of Roman Jewish fare and specializing in seafood. In spring and summer there's a lovely outdoor dining deck, and in cooler months, the bright rooms decorated with contemporary art offer pleasant surroundings. The menu includes classic fried artichokes (among the best in the city), homemade ravioli *con cipolla di Tropea* (filled with red onion and tossed in balsamic vinegar), and favorite local fish turbot, barely adorned with perfectly roasted potatoes and extra-virgin olive oil. Everything down to the last bite (make your dessert choice the chocolate medley or the cannoli) is a pleasure, even if it doesn't come cheaply. [$] *Average cost: €80* ✉ *Via dei Fienili 50-51, Ghetto* ☎ *06/6780933* ✍ *Reservations essential* ⏲ *Closed Sun.* ✣ *3:E1.*

WORD OF MOUTH

"One more traditional place, the one with the greatest tradition, and one of Italy's most famous restaurants: Checchino dal 1887. It's in the Testaccio district (the slaughterhouse used to be located here), and in fact, many of those typical Roman entrails dishes were invented in this restaurant—which is still the best place to eat them (restaurants as famous as this are usually living on past glory—but not Checchino!). The famous veal intestine pasta dish's name is *rigatoni alla pajata*; for those who want to venture on trying it, I absolutely recommend it." —franco

TESTACCIO

$$ ITALIAN 🍴 **Angelina.** Via Galvani is prime real estate in the hip Roman nabe of Testaccio, just around the corner from Monte Testaccio where so many bars, restaurants, and discos pulsate into the wee hours. But here at Angelina, you're one or two stories above all the riff-raff, looking out above the soon-to-be new Testaccio market, eating grilled pizzas and steaks, or sipping drinks among the treetops that line the street. Or you're inside, in one of Angelina's whitewashed dining rooms pungently perfumed with the smell of the grill. Starters range from salumi to fried veggies, and first courses are hearty Roman staples like *rigatoni all'amatriciana* or *cacio e pepe*. But the focus here is on meat *alla brace*—anything and everything grilled, from sausages to steaks to lamb. Even *scamorza*, cheese treated almost like a steak and thrown on the grill, is served here with fanfare. It's a bit of a scene here, from aperitivo through *dopocena* (post-dinner), so get ready to enjoy the party, *tesoro* (darling). Another location that's more of a casual bar-café, called Angelina Trevi, is found near the Trevi Fountain at Via Poli 27 (☎ *06/6797274*). [$] *Average cost: €45* ✉ *Via Galvani 24a, Testaccio* ☎ *06/57283840* 🌐 *www.ristoranteangelina.com* ⏲ *No dinner Sun.* ✣ *3:C4.*

$$$$ ROMAN 🍴 **Checchino dal 1887.** Literally carved out of a hill of ancient shards of amphorae, Checchino remains an example of a classic, family-run Roman restaurant, with one of the best wine cellars in the region. Though the slaughterhouses of Testaccio are long gone, an echo of their

past existence lives on in the restaurant's soul food—mostly offal and other less-appealing cuts like *trippa* (tripe), *pajata* (intestine with the mother's milk still inside), and *coratella* (sweetbreads and heart of beef) are all still on the menu for die-hard Roman purists. For the less adventuresome, house specialties include braised milk-fed lamb with seasonal vegetables. Head here for a taste of Old Rome, but note that Checchino is really beginning to show its age. [$] *Average cost: €70* ✉ *Via di Monte Testaccio 30* ☎ *06/5746318* 🌐 *www.checchino-dal-1887.com* 🕒 *Closed Sun., Mon., Aug, and 1 wk at Christmas* ⊕ *3:C5.*

$ ROMAN

🍴 **Da Oio a Casa Mia.** This classic Roman trattoria has all the usual suspects, including locals straight out of central casting and gruff but good-natured service. The Roman classic pastas here are good bets, with delicious versions of *carbonara, amatriciana,* and rigatoni with a *coda alla vaccinara* (stewed oxtail) tomato sauce. Secondi like meatballs, *straccetti* (strips of beef in wine sauce over a bed of arugula), chicken hunter's style, and stewed tripe (for those who enjoy it) are all excellent options. The grilled eggplant preserved in olive oil, vinegar, and with a nice kick from the *peperoncino,* is a killer side dish not to be overlooked. Some critics point their noses in the air when it comes to this place but that is just more room for those of us who appreciate the unrefined finds of Rome. Outdoor seating in warm months is the way to go. [$] *Average cost: €28* ✉ *Via Galvani 43–45, San Lorenzo* ☎ *06/5782680* 🕒 *Closed Sun.* ⊕ *3:C4.*

$$ ITALIAN

🍴 **Perilli.** In this restaurant dating from 1911, the old Testaccio remains, and it has the decor to prove it. A seasonal antipasto table starts things off, offering Roman specialties like stewed Roman artichokes and *puntarelle* (curled chicory stems in a garlicky vinaigrette with lots of lemon and anchovy). The waiters wear crooked bow ties and are just a little bit too hurried—until, that is, you order classics like pasta all'amatriciana and carbonara, which they relish tossing in a big bowl tableside. This is also the place to try rigatoni *con pajata* (with calves' intestines)—if you're into that sort of thing. Secondi plates are for carnivores only, and the house wine is a golden enamel-remover from the Castelli Romani. [$] *Average cost: €40* ✉ *Via Marmorata 39, Testaccio* ☎ *06/5742415* 🕒 *Closed Wed.* ⊕ *3:D4.*

$ PIZZA

🍴 **Remo.** Expect a wait at this perennial favorite in Testaccio frequented by students and locals. You won't find tablecloths or other nonessentials, just classic Roman pizza and boisterous conversation. [$] *Average cost: €18* ✉ *Piazza Santa Maria Liberatrice 44, Testaccio* ☎ *06/5746270* 💳 *No credit cards* 🕒 *Closed Sun., Aug., and Christmas wk. No lunch* ⊕ *3:C4.*

BEYOND THE CITY CENTER

$$$$ SEAFOOD ★

🍴 **Acquolina.** Famed chef Angelo Troiani, chef-proprietor of Il Convivio, has branched out, heading out of the city center to the Flaminio area, and also branched out by now specializing in high-quality seafood. He tapped chef Giulio Terrinoni to head the kitchen, and the results are delicious and understated, with some dishes reflecting the time-honored Italian tradition of letting great seafood speak for itself while others get spiffed-up treatments. The crudo is ultra-fresh, and pastas like the seafood carbonara and the *cacio e pepe* with skate and zucchini flowers are upscale aquatic riffs on Roman classics. Main dishes range from fish stew to a *gran fritto misto*. The owners are concerned about sustainability, and as such, don't serve certain endangered sea creatures (like bluefin tuna carpaccio). Desserts are surprisingly sophisticated. Service is helpful and thorough, which helps to make up for the sometimes slow kitchen. [$] *Average cost: €80* ✉ *Via Antonio Serra 60, Flaminio* ☎ *06/3337192* ⏲ *Closed Sun. No lunch* ✥ *1:G1.*

$$$ ITALIAN

🍴 **L'Archeologia.** In this farmhouse just beyond the catacombs, you dine indoors beside the fireplace in cool weather or in the garden under age-old vines in summer. The atmosphere is friendly and intimate. Specialties include fettuccine *al finocchio salvatico* (with wild fennel), *abbacchio alla scottadito* (grilled lamb), and fresh seafood. But remember that the food here is secondary: you're paying for the view and the setting more than any culinary adventure or excellence with the classics. [$] *Average cost: €55* ✉ *Via Appia Antica 139, Via Appia, south side of Rome* ☎ *06/7880494* 🌐 *www.larcheologia.it* ⏲ *Closed Tues.* ✥ *2:E6.*

$$$$ MODERN ITALIAN Fodor's Choice ★

🍴 **La Pergola.** La Pergola's rooftop location offers a commanding view of the city, and as you're seated in your plush chair, you know you're in for a three–Michelin star experience, and the only one in Rome. First, your waiter will present you with menus: food, wine, and water (you read correctly). Then you must choose between the German Wunderchef Heinz Beck's *alta cucina* specialties, though most everything will prove to be the best version of the dish you've ever tasted. Lobster is oh-so-lightly poached, fish is cooked perfectly, and melt-in-your-mouth lamb in a veggie-accented jus is deceptively simple but earthy and perfect. Each course comes with a flourish of sauces or extra touches that makes it an event in its own right, while the cheese cart is well explained by knowledgeable servers. The dessert course is extravagant, including tiny petits fours and treats tucked away in small drawers that make up the serving "cabinet." The wine list is as thrilling as one might expect with the financial backing of the Waldorf-Astoria, and their investment in one of the top wine cellars in Italy. [$] *Average cost: €150* ✉ *Cavalieri Waldorf-Astoria, Via Cadlolo 101, Monte Mario, Northwest Rome* ☎ *06/3509221* 🌐 *www.romecavalieri.com/lapergola.php* ✍ *Reservations essential* 👔 *Jacket and tie* ⏲ *Closed Sun. and Mon., and 2 wks in Dec. No lunch* ✥ *1:A1.*

Rome Dining and Lodging Atlas

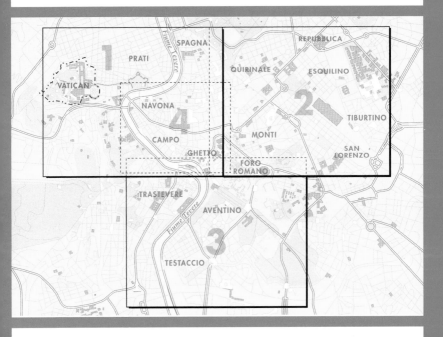

SPAGNA

PRATI

1

Fiume Tevere

VATICAN

NAVONA

4

CAMPO

GHETTO

REPUBBLICA

QUIRINALE

ESQUILINO

2

MONTI

TIBURTINO

FORO
ROMANO

SAN
LORENZO

TRASTEVERE

AVENTINO

Fiume Tevere

3

TESTACCIO

KEY	
☐	Hotels
■	Restaurants
■	Restaurant in Hotel

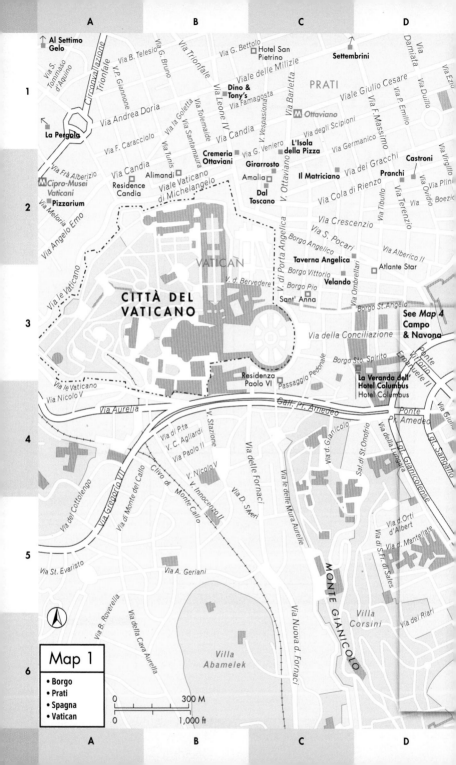

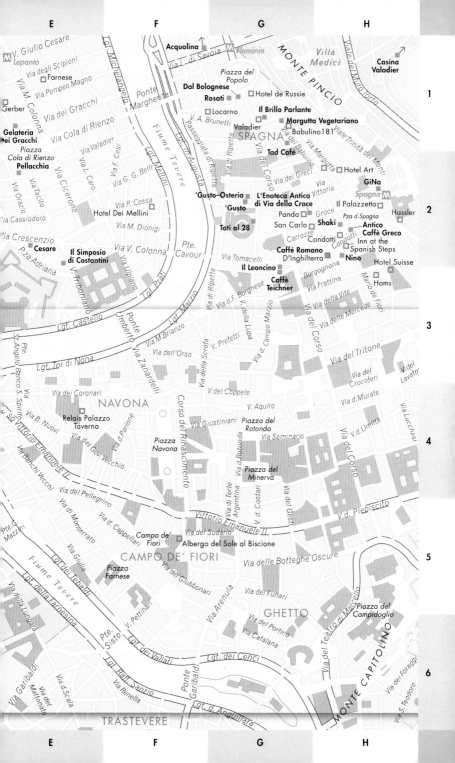

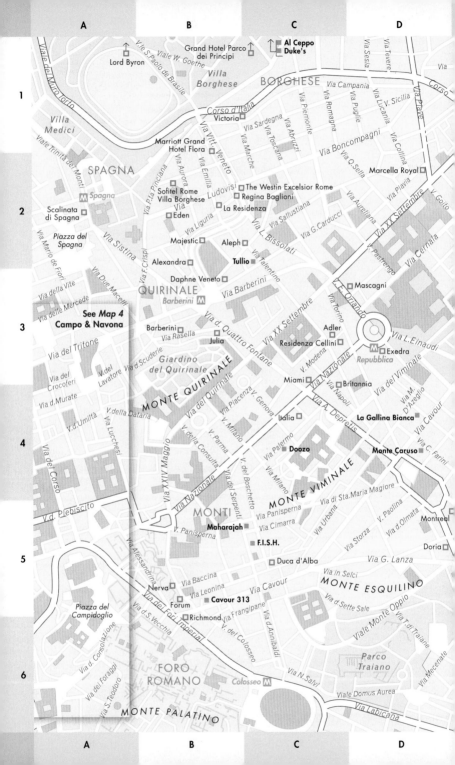

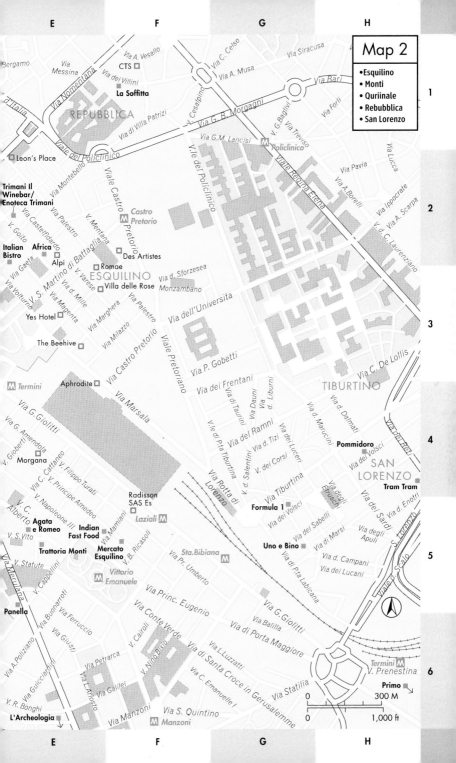

Map 2

- Esquilino
- Monti
- Quriinale
- Rebubblica
- San Lorenzo

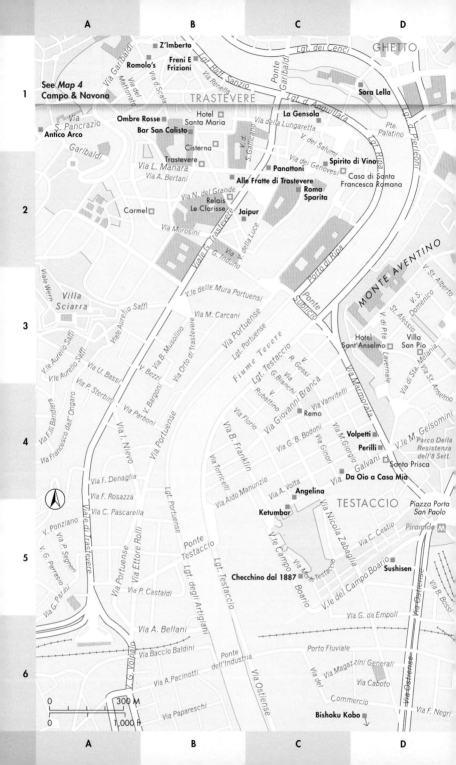

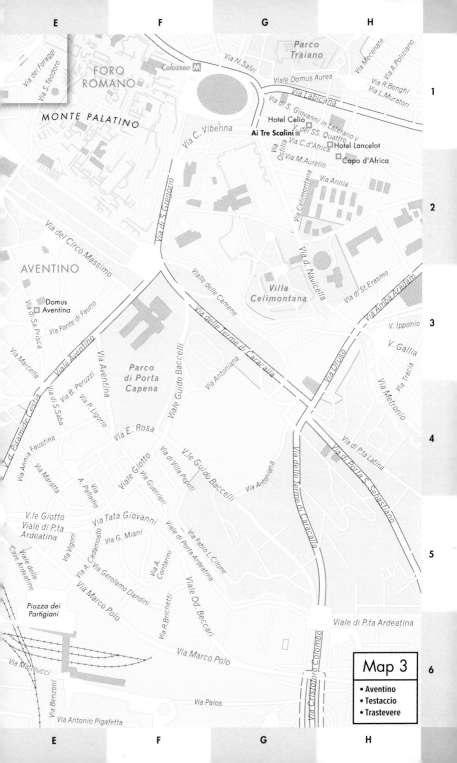

Map 3

- Aventino
- Testaccio
- Trastevere

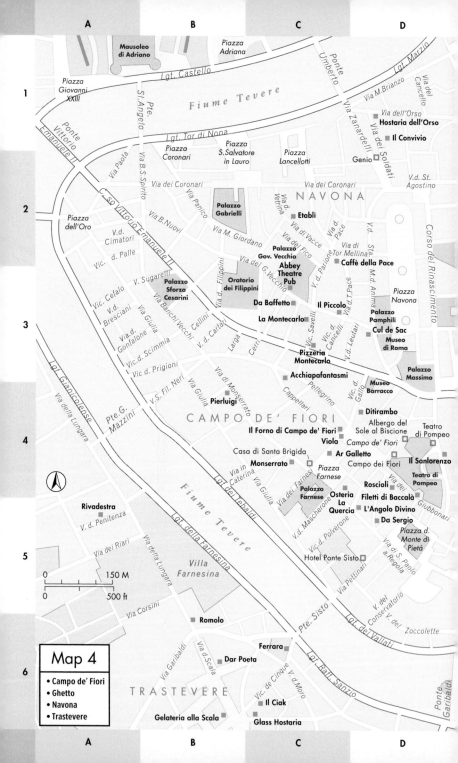

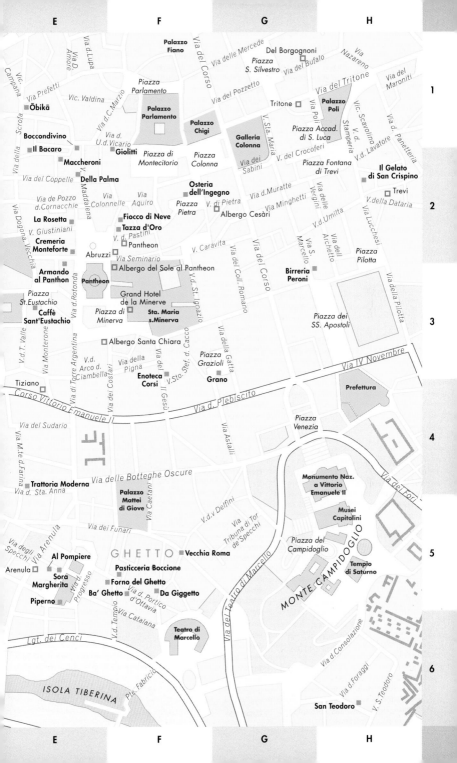

Where to Stay

WORD OF MOUTH

"Trastevere was WONDERFUL!!!! I would totally tell anyone who was going to Rome to stay there. The food was cheap and fantastic, wow! Overall, as someone who's been to Rome many, many times, Trastevere put a new spin on it and gets an A++ in my book. Can't say enough good things about it!"

—GiuliaPiraino

THE SCENE

Updated
by Nicole
Arriaga

It's the click of your heels on inlaid marble, the whisper of 600-thread count Frette sheets, the murmured *buongiorno* of a coat-tailed porter bowing low as you pass. It's a rustic attic room with wood-beamed ceilings, a white umbrella on a roof terrace, a 400-year-old palazzo with Casanova's name in the guest book. Maybe it's the birdsong warbling into your room as you swing open French windows to a sun-kissed view of the Colosseum, a timeworn piazza, a flower-filled marketplace. Obviously, from the moment you saw *Roman Holiday*, your love affair with living *"la dolce vita"* has never been closer to reality than being a guest in some Roman hotels. Audrey Hepburn couldn't have had it better.

Happily, living *la vita bella* doesn't always mean you have to break the bank. There are many midrange and budget hotels and *pensioni* (small, family-run lodgings) available, some with real flair. When it comes to accommodations, Rome offers a wide selection of high-end hotels, bed-and-breakfasts, designer "boutique" hotels, and quiet options that run the gamut from whimsical to luxurious. Whether you want a simple place to rest your head or a complete cache of exclusive amenities, you have plenty to choose from.

WHERE SHOULD I STAY?

	NEIGHBORHOOD VIBE	PROS	CONS
Pantheon, Navona, Trevi, and Quirinale	In the heart of the centro storico, you'll find yourself in a maze of cobblestone streets, surrounded by good restaurants and most of Rome's major attractions.	Everything you need is within walking distance: good eats, shopping, and many of Rome's museums and monuments.	Hotels may set you back a pretty penny and, depending on where your hotel is positioned, street noise may also be an issue. Beware of tourist traps as well.
Campo de' Fiori and Ghetto	Known for its outdoor produce and flower market, by night, Campo turns into a noisy bar and street caffè scene. The Ghetto is much quieter.	Many restaurants, bars, boutiques, and specialty stores. Fresh fruits and veggies at the market. Plenty of Jewish-style fried artichokes.	At night, the Campo is populated by rowdy, bar-hopping American students. Tourist trap restaurants abound.
Monti, Esquilino, Repubblica, and San Lorenzo	Where shabby chic meets the once-sketchy part of town. Home to Rome's hipster crowd and a diverse immigrant neighborhood (with great ethnic food).	Hotels are much cheaper than elsewhere in Rome. Close to the main transportation hub, Termini train station. Great ethnic restaurants and hip bars.	Cheap accommodations are very basic. The area surrounding Termini can be a hit or miss. Public transport in San Lorenzo area is spotty.
Veneto, Borghese, and Spagna	Luxury hotels, renovated palazzos, and 5-star dining that revolve around the Borghese Gardens.	Where all the high rollers and A-listers like to reside.	Everything is expensive. Not exactly close to centro storico hot spots.
Vatican, Borgo, and Prati	A bevy of priests and nuns concentrated in one place. Safe, quiet, residential neighborhood. Prati is an affluent area with chic restaurants and caffè.	For Catholics, this is heaven on earth. The neighborhoods are tranquil when you get away from St. Peter's. Great shopping and eating.	Many tourist traps immediately surrounding the Vatican. Situated away from the other tourist attractions.
Trastevere and Gianicolo	Winding cobbled alleys, beautiful churches, and authentic mom-and-pop trattorias.	Great Roman trattorias, pizzerias, and lovely street caffè, great for people-watching.	At night, Trastevere gets rowdy and rambunctious, especially on the weekends. Full of students.
Aventino, Testaccio, and Palatino	Peace and quiet reign on green Aventine Hill. Hotels tend to be more spacious. Testaccio is the heart of Rome's nightlife.	Tranquillity and amazing views on the Aventino. Party like a rock star in Rome's famous nightlife district, Testaccio.	Transportation is a bit spartan once on the Aventine Hill. Testaccio is insanely crowded on weekend nights.
Colosseo Area	The center of Ancient Rome. Hotels have great views of the Colosseum, ancient ruins, and relics.	Quieter than most of the centro storico. Sightseeing at the Colosseum, the Roman Forum, the Basilica di San Giovanni in Laterano.	Limited accommodations get booked up with tourist groups in spring and summer. Rooms with a view of the Colosseum fetch top dollar.

13

Of course, if you look at the extremes, hotels in Rome are something like the Sistine Chapel: at the top, they're heaven, but at the lower end, they can feel more like *purgatorio*. Palatial settings, cloud-nine comfort, spacious rooms, and high standards of service can be taken for granted in Rome's top establishments. Luxury hotels like the Eden, the Hassler, and the Hotel de Russie are justly renowned for sybaritic comfort: postcard views over Roman rooftops, white linen and silver at a groaning-table breakfast buffet, and the fluffiest, thirstiest, softest towels since cotton was king. Can you hear the angels singing?

But in other categories, especially moderate and inexpensive, standards vary considerably. That's a nice way of saying that very often, Rome's budget hotels are not up to the standards of space, comfort, quiet and service that are taken for granted in the United States: you'll still find places with tiny rooms, lumpy beds, and anemic air-conditioning. Many of the family-run pensions near Termini station and elsewhere suffer from the maladies of budget hotels in major cities everywhere: too little space, too much noise, and chronic, some say fatal, lack of hominess. Happily, the good news is that if you're flexible there are happy mediums aplenty, and the following pages are packed with mid-price-range reviews (*note: the full reviews are available on Fodor's website*).

One thing to figure out before you arrive is which neighborhood do you want to stay in—*check out the "Where Should I Stay" chart*. If a picturesque location is your main concern, stay in one of the small hotels around Piazza Navona or Campo de' Fiori. If luxury is, head for Via Veneto or beyond the city center, where price-to-quality ratios are high and some hotels have swimming pools. Most of Rome's good budget hotels are concentrated around Termini train station, but here accommodations can vary widely, from fine to seedy, and you'll have to use public transportation to get to the historic part of town.

There are obvious advantages to staying in a hotel within easy walking distance of the main sights, particularly because parts of downtown Rome are closed to traffic and are blessedly quieter than they once were. Here, no matter how inexpensive these lodgings may be, they give their guests one priceless perk: a sense of being in the heart of history.

PLANNING

LODGING STRATEGY

Where should we stay? With hundreds of hotels to choose from in Rome, it may seem like a daunting question. But fret not—our expert writers and editors have done most of the legwork. The 90-plus selections here represent the best lodging this city has to offer, from spartan convents to opulent palaces. Scan Best Bets on the following pages for top recommendations by price and experience. Or locate a specific review in the listings. They're organized alphabetically within each neighborhood. Happy hotel hunting!

13

RESERVATIONS

Unless you don't mind flying by the seat of your pants, it's best to book ahead. This is especially true for May and June, when the Eternal City is virtually bursting at the seams; the same goes for major Catholic holidays such as Easter and Christmas. The city is never empty, but July and August and January and February are slower months. These are the best times to find rock-bottom rates as well.

Be as specific as possible about the accommodations you desire. Request the room size (single, double, or triple), type (standard, deluxe, or suite), and whether you want air-conditioning, a no-smoking room, a private bathroom with a shower or tub (or both), a terrace or balcony, or a view of the city (and ask whether there are extra costs associated with any of these). You may be required to leave a deposit; get a statement from the hotel about its refund policy before releasing your credit card number or mailing a money order. Insist on a written confirmation from the hotel stating the duration of your stay, room rate, any extras, location, room size, and type.

CHECKING IN

As soon as you get to Rome, you'll notice the leisurely pace of life here, which extends to hotel check-in times. If you arrive early in the morning (as is often the case with North American flights), you may find that your room is not ready yet (after 2 pm is pretty standard for most hotels, big and small). In which case, most hotels will store your luggage and encourage you to go out sightseeing. If you think you'll arrive later in the day, mention this before booking to make sure someone will be on hand to check you in. Some smaller hotels don't have a round-the-clock staff, and it's best to avoid unpleasant surprises. Checkout times are a little stricter, between 10 am and noon. If you need more time than that, the hotel may try to charge you for an extra night. However, if you just want to store your luggage for a few hours on your last day, most hotels will accommodate this request.

BREAKFAST INCLUDED?

Near the end of each review, we list "Breakfast" if this meal is included in the hotel's room rate.

FACILITIES

The most expensive hotels have all the amenities you would expect at top levels and rates, with full services, spacious lounges, bars, restaurants, and some fitness facilities. Midrange hotels may have refrigerators, in-room safes, and double-glazed windows to keep out street noise. Budget hotels will have in-room direct-dial telephone and TV, and most will have air-conditioning. In less expensive places, you may have to pay extra for air-conditioning, and the shower may be the drain-in-the-floor type that hovers over the toilet and drenches the whole bathroom.

Unless stated in the review, hotels are equipped with elevators, and all guest rooms have air-conditioning, TV, and telephones. The number of rooms listed at the end of each review reflects those with private bathrooms (which means they have a shower or a tub, but not necessarily both). Note that we use "Wi-Fi" when wireless access is available, and "Internet" when any other type of Internet access is available, aside from Wi-Fi.

WITH KIDS

Italians love kids, and many hotels go out of their way to accommodate families, with ideas, special games, and other perks. Although hotels often allow children to stay in their parents' room for free, keep in mind that hotel rooms in Italy tend to be very small by American standards. It's a good idea to inquire about triples, connecting rooms or suites, or consider taking a short-term apartment rental or residence hotel for the duration of your stay.

PRICES

In 2011, the city of Rome implemented a new tax for all overnight stays. Guests in bed-and-breakfasts, vacation apartment rentals, and 1-, 2-, and 3-star hotels will incur an additional €2 surcharge per person per night for a maximum of 10 nights. In 4- and 5-star hotels, the surcharge is €3 per person per night for a maximum of 10 nights. In the off-season months of late January, February, July, and August, prices can be considerably discounted (sometimes up to half off the regular rate). Inquire about specials and weekend deals, and you may be able to get a better rate per night if you are staying a week or longer. Rates are inclusive of service, but it's customary to tip porters, waiters, maids, and concierges. *Prices in the reviews are the lowest cost of a standard double room in high season.*

HOTEL REVIEWS

The following reviews are listed alphabetically within neighborhoods. Throughout, you'll see mapping symbols and coordinates (✥ 3:F2) after property names or reviews. To locate the property on a map, see the Rome Dining and Lodging Atlas at the end of "Where to Eat". The first number after the ✥ symbol indicates the map number. Following that is the property's coordinate on the map grid.

For expanded hotel reviews, visit Fodors.com.

PANTHEON, NAVONA, TREVI, AND QUIRINALE

In this upscale area around spectacular Piazza Navona and the Pantheon and Trevi Fountain to the east, a picture-perfect moment awaits at every turn. The area offers a broad range of accommodations, from pricey digs to rough-around-the-edges *pensioni,* all housed in 17th- and 18th-century palazzos. Much of the area is pedestrian-only, with a lively mix of restaurants and nightlife.

PANTHEON

$$$ HOTEL 🏨 **Abruzzi.** Rarely do magnificent views come with such a relatively gentle price tag: from the windows of this newly updated, comfortable little hotel, the Pantheon is literally in your face. **Pros:** views of the Pantheon; sizeable bathrooms; the piazza is a hot spot. **Cons:** some staff seem to want to avoid running credit cards (though the hotel accepts them). [$] *Rooms from: €250* ✉ *Piazza della Rotonda 69, Pantheon* ☎ *06/97841351* 🌐 *www.hotelabruzzi.it* 🛏 *29 rooms* 🍴 *Breakfast* ✥ *4:F2.*

BEST BETS FOR ROME LODGING

Fodor's offers a selective listing of quality lodging experiences at every price range, from the city's best budget motel to its most sophisticated luxury hotel. Here, we've compiled our top recommendations by price and experience. The very best properties—in other words, those that provide a particularly remarkable experience in their price range—are designated in the listings with the Fodor's Choice logo.

Fodor's Choice ★

Albergo Santa Chiara, $$$, p. 304
Aleph, $$$$, p. 315
The Beehive, $, p. 312
Britannia, $$, p. 311
Casa di Santa Brigida, $$, p. 307
Casa di Santa Francesca Romana, $$, p. 324
Daphne Veneto, $$, p. 315
Eden, $$$$, p. 316
Hassler, $$$$, p. 319
Hotel de Russie, $$$$, p. 319
Hotel Ponte Sisto, $$$, p. 309
Hotel San Pietrino, $, p. 323
Hotel Santa Maria, $$$, p. 324
Il Palazzetto, $$$$, p. 320
Relais Le Clarisse, $$$, p. 325
Residence Paolo VI, $$, p. 322

Scalinata di Spagna, $$$, p. 321
Yes Hotel, $$, p. 314

By Price

$

The Beehive, p. 312
Hotel San Pietrino, p. 323
Hotel Trastevere, p. 324
Santa Prisca, p. 326

$$

Alimandi, p. 322
Casa di Santa Brigida, p. 307
Casa di Santa Francesca Romana, p. 324
Daphne Veneto, p. 315
Hotel Lancelot, p. 327
Italia, p. 310
Yes Hotel, p. 314

$$$

Albergo Santa Chiara, p. 304

Condotti, p. 318
Dei Borgognoni, p. 318
Hotel Campo de' Fiori, p. 309
Hotel Santa Maria, p. 324
Pantheon, p. 305
Relais Le Clarisse, p. 325
Scalinata di Spagna, p. 321

$$$$

Aleph, p. 315
Capo d'Africa, p. 326
Eden, p. 316
Exedra, p. 312
Hassler, p. 319
Hotel de Russie, p. 319

Best by Experience

BEST DESIGN

Aleph, $$$$, p. 315
Capo d'Africa, $$$$, p. 326
Hotel Art, $$$. p. 319

Radisson SAS Es., $$$, p. 311

BEST FOR BUSINESS TRAVEL

Exedra, $$$$, p. 312
Grand Hotel de la Minerve, $$$$, p. 304
Radisson SAS Es., $$$, p. 311
Rome Cavalieri, $$$$, p. 328
Sofitel Rome Villa Borghese, $$$$, p. 317

BEST CONCIERGE

The Beehive, $, p. 312
Daphne Veneto, $$, p. 315
Hotel Lancelot, $$, p. 327
Majestic, $$$$, p. 316
Mascagni, $$$, p. 313

BEST POOL

Exedra, p. 312
Hotel de Russie, p. 319
Grand Hotel Parco dei Principi, p. 318
Radisson SAS Es., p. 311
Rome Cavalieri, p. 328

BEST SPA

Aleph, $$$$, p. 315
Exedra, $$$$, p. 312
Hotel de Russie, $$$$, p. 319
Radisson SAS Es., $$$, p. 311
Westin Excelsior, Rome, $$$$, p. 317

13

$$$ ⊞ **Albergo Cesàri.** On a pedestrian-
HOTEL   only street near the Pantheon, the
exterior of this lovely little hotel
hasn't changed much since Stend-
hal stayed here in the 1800s, and
the restyled interior with soft-green
touches and prints of old Rome has
an air of warmth and serenity, but
perhaps the true gem here is the
hotel's rooftop bar, where guests
can enjoy views of Roman roof-
tops and churches over breakfast
or cocktails. **Pros:** prime location

and soundproofed from the street noise; computer with Internet access
available; friendly staff that provides good service. **Cons:** walls are
paper-thin so noise can be an issue; a/c is not especially strong. *$ Rooms
from: €240 ⊠ Via di Pietra 89/a, Pantheon 📞 06/6749701 ⊕ www.
albergocesari.it ➟ 47 rooms ⃝ Breakfast ✛ 4:F2.*

$$$ ⊞ **Albergo del Sole al Pantheon.** The granddaddy of Roman hotels and
HOTEL   one of the oldest in the world—the doors first opened in 1467—this
charming hotel adjacent to the grand facade of the Pantheon has high
ceilings, terra-cotta floors, and Renaissance-style beds. **Pros:** real Roman
atmosphere and character; a rich breakfast buffet; free Internet point
for guests. **Cons:** rooms are a bit small; despite the double-glazed windows, street noise can be an issue. *$ Rooms from: €275 ⊠ Piazza della
Rotonda 63, Pantheon 📞 06/6780441 ⊕ www.hotelsolealpantheon.
com ➟ 33 rooms ⃝ Breakfast ✛ 4:D4.*

$$$ ⊞ **Albergo Santa Chiara.** If you're looking for a good location (right
HOTEL   behind the Pantheon) and top-notch service at great prices—not to
Fodor's Choice   mention comfortable beds and a quiet stay—look no further than this
★   historic hotel, run by the same family for some 200 years. **Pros:** great
location in the historical center behind the Pantheon; the staff is both
polite and helpful; there is a lovely terrace/sitting area in front of the
hotel that overlooks the piazza. **Cons:** the rooms are small and could
use some restyling. Some rooms don't have a window. *$ Rooms from:
€250 ⊠ Via Santa Chiara 21, Pantheon 📞 06/6872979 ✉ info@alber-
gosantachiara.com ⊕ www.albergosantachiara.com ➟ 96 rooms, 3
suites, 3 apartments ⃝ Breakfast ✛ 4:E3.*

$$$$ ⊞ **Babuino 181.** Named for its street known for high-end boutiques,
HOTEL   antique shops, and upscale inns, this stylish hotel with spacious, loft-
like accommodations offers top-notch amenities, ultimate privacy,
and personalized service. **Pros:** cool amenities in the rooms such as
iPod and iPhone charging docks; Nespresso coffee machines; spacious
suites. **Cons:** the rooms can be a bit noisy; breakfast is nothing special.
*$ Rooms from: €430 ⊠ Via Babuino 181, Borghese 📞 06/69921907
⊕ www.romeluxurysuites.com/babuino ➟ 14 rooms ✛ 1:G1.*

$$$$ ⊞ **Grand Hotel de la Minerve.** Once one of Rome's landmark fixtures, this
HOTEL   17th-century palazzo used to be a favorite address for everyone from
Stendhal to Sartre along with a bevy of crowned (and uncrowned—Car-
lotta, the deposed empress of Mexico resided here for a while) heads

but none would recognize the former grand hotel since its zillion-dollar renovation two decades ago: results were mixed, from the gaudy (that lobby glass ceiling) to the great (the rooftop restaurant, which allows you to almost touch the dome of the Pantheon). **Pros:** only 50 yards from the Pantheon yet set on quiet Piazza della Minerva; staff is friendly and accommodating; some rooms have terraces. **Cons:** not all rooms have the amenities of a 5-star hotel such as a minibar, satellite TV, and safe; Internet connection is spotty and Wi-Fi is expensive. [$] *Rooms from: €400* ✉ *Piazza della Minerva 69, Pantheon* ☎ *06/695201* 🌐 *grandhoteldelaminerve.it* 🛏 *119 rooms, 16 suites* 🍴 *No meals* ✥ *4:F3.*

13

$$$ HOTEL **Pantheon.** A superb little hotel right next to the monument itself, the Pantheon has a typically Roman lobby—warm and cozy yet opulent—and rooms with antique walnut furnishings, fresh flowers, paisley bedspreads, and wood-beam ceilings. **Pros:** proximity to the Pantheon; big, clean bathrooms; friendly staff. **Cons:** rooms are in need of some upgrading; the lighting is low and the rooms can feel a bit stuffy. [$] *Rooms from: €290* ✉ *Via dei Pastini 131, Pantheon* ☎ *06/6787746* 🌐 *www.hotelpantheon.com* 🛏 *13 rooms, 1 suite* 🍴 *Breakfast* ✥ *4:F2.*

NAVONA

$$ HOTEL **Genio.** Located just outside one of Rome's most beautiful piazzas—Piazza Navona—this pleasant hotel has a lovely rooftop terrace where you can sip morning cappuccino and enjoy the view and good-size rooms decorated in warm colors. **Pros:** you can sip wine on the rooftop and take in the view; rooms are a decent size for a Roman hotel; the bathrooms are elegantly designed. **Cons:** Genio is on a busy street so there is often traffic noise; walls are paper-thin; both the decor and the carpet have seen better days. [$] *Rooms from: €170* ✉ *Via Giuseppe Zanardelli 28, Navona* ☎ *06/6832191* 🌐 *www.hotelgenioroma.it* 🛏 *60 rooms* 🍴 *Breakfast* ✥ *4:D2.*

$$ HOTEL ★ **Relais Palazzo Taverna.** This little hidden gem on a side street behind the lovely Via dei Coronari is a pleasant surprise for travelers who happen to stumble upon it, a good compromise for those looking for boutique-style accommodations on a budget: the stylish guest rooms have kitsch wallpaper print that's so cute it looks like someone gift-wrapped them, and it's rare to find lodgings with such cool design at affordable prices like these right around the corner from Piazza Navona. **Pros:** centrally located; boutique-style accommodations at budget prices. **Cons:** breakfast is served in your room; staff is on duty only until midnight. [$] *Rooms from: €150* ✉ *Via dei Gabrielli 92, Navona* ☎ *06/20398064* 🌐 *www.relaispalazzotaverna.com* 🛏 *11 rooms* ✥ 1:E4.

TREVI

$$$ HOTEL **Trevi.** Location, location, location: at this delightful place tucked away down one of Old Rome's quaintest alleys near the Trevi Fountain, the smallish rooms are bright and clean, and you can eat marvelous pasta at the arborlike roof-garden restaurant as you peer at the city below. **Pros:** pass the Trevi Fountain each day as you come and go; comfortable rooms; roof-garden restaurant. **Cons:** breakfast room is cramped; this area can be very noisy due to foot traffic around the Trevi Fountain. [$] *Rooms from: €240* ✉ *Vicolo del Babbuccio 20/21, Trevi*

CLOSE UP

Renting an Apartment in Rome

The saying "Two's company and three's a crowd" definitely holds true in Roman hotel rooms. If you're traveling with a larger group, consider renting a short-term apartment. Apartments are generally rented out the old-fashioned way by their owners, though in some cases a realtor or management company is involved. A three-night minimum is the norm. Prices will vary, but expect them to be higher in the historic city center, the Vaticano/Borgo, the Campo de' Fiori, and Trastevere areas. When seeking a holiday home in Rome, start your research online. Rome's official tourism website (⊕ www.turismoroma.it) offers a search function for a number of different housing options.

Wanted in Rome (⊕ www. wantedinrome.com) is a popular English language expat magazine that features an extensive classifieds section on their website. The Bed & Breakfast Association of Rome (⊕ www.b-b. rm.it) offers an online apartment rental search in addition to their B&B search. They personally inspect all properties on their site. Cross-Pollinate (⊕ www. cross-pollinate.com), an accommodation service owned by the people who run the Beehive Hotel, gives visitors the information to seek out their own accommodations. They personally screen all properties. San Francisco–based Craigslist hosts classifieds for 450 cities worldwide, including Rome. Craigslist Rome lists postings for apartments, houses, swaps, sublets, and other vacation rentals at ⊕ rome. en.craigslist.it.

HOTELS WITH APARTMENTS
More and more hotels in Rome now offer their prospective guests a selection of apartments (either located on the grounds or just nearby), in addition to rooms and suites. **Albergo Santa Chiara.** ⤵ 3 *apartments* ✉ *Via Santa Chiara 21, Pantheon* ☎ *06/6872979* ⊕ *www. albergosantachiara.com* ✛ *4:E3.* **Hotel Campo de' Fiori.** ⤵ *11 apartments* ✉ *Via del Biscione 6, Campo de' Fiori* ☎ *06/68806865* ⊕ *www. hotelcampodefiori.it* ✛ *4:D4.* **Italia.** ⤵ *1 apartment* ✉ *Via Venezia 18, Termini* ☎ *06/4828355* ⊕ *www. hotelitaliaroma.com* ✛ *2:C4.* **Julia.** ⤵ *2 apartments* ✉ *Via Rasella 29, Via Veneto* ☎ *06/4881637* ⊕ *www. hoteljulia.it* ✛ *2:B3.* **Mecenate Palace Hotel.** ⤵ *2 apartments* ✉ *Via Carlo Alberto 3, Termini* ☎ *06/44702024* ⊕ *www.mecenatepalace.com* ✛ *2:D5.* **Hotel Trastevere.** ⤵ *3 apartments* ✉ *Via Luciano Manara 24a–25, Trastevere* ☎ *06/5814713* ⊕ *www. hoteltrastevere.net* ✛ *3:B2.*

RESIDENCE HOTELS
Another alternative to a hotel is a residence. These specialize in apartment-style accommodations and are ideal for longer stays. Residence hotels usually have fully equipped kitchens and offer linens, laundry, and cleaning services. Most are available for weekly or monthly rentals. Costs for an apartment for two range from about €1,300 for a week to €2,600 per month. **Aldrovandi Residence City Suites** ✉ *Via Ulisse Aldrovandi 11, Parioli* ☎ *06/3221430* ⊕ *www.aldrovandiresidence.it.* **Mecenate Palace Hotel.** ⤵ *10 executive "residence" rooms* ✉ *Via Carlo Alberto 3, Termini* ☎ *06/44702024* ⊕ *www.mecenatepalace.com.* **Palazzo al Velabro** ✉ *Via del Velabro 16, Ghetto* ☎ *06/6792758* ⊕ *www. velabro.it.* **Residence Ripetta** ✉ *Via di Ripetta 231, Popolo* ☎ *06/3231144* ⊕ *www.ripetta.it.*

☎ *06/6789563* 🌐 *www.hoteltrevirome.com* 🛏 *29 rooms* 🍴 *Breakfast* ✥ *4:H2.*

$$$ HOTEL **Tritone.** You won't know what to do first—toss your bags in your room or toss a coin in the fountain—so close to the tempting Fontana di Trevi at this trusty hotel, where the rooms have modern decor, plasma-screen TVs, and spacious travertine bathrooms, and breakfast is served in the rooftop garden with panoramic views of the city. **Pros:** walking distance to major attractions; modern decor with flat-screen TVs; friendly staff. **Cons:** cramped reception area; most rooms have twin beds; despite soundproofing, street-side rooms can be noisy; Wi-Fi isn't free. [$] *Rooms from: €210* ✉ *Via del Tritone 210, Piazza di Trevi* ☎ *06/69922575* 🌐 *www.tritonehotel.com* 🛏 *43 rooms* 🍴 *Breakfast* ✥ *4:G1.*

CAMPO DE' FIORI AND GHETTO

There's nothing like being in the heart of stunningly beautiful Vecchia Roma (Old Rome)—a neighborhood that holds two of the most enchanting piazzas of the city: Campo de' Fiori and Piazza Farnese. Just around the corner from here, take a stroll down one of Rome's most romantic streets, Via Giulia, where streams of ivy flow from street corner to street corner, elegantly draping the buildings. Not all the hotels here are as fairy tale–like as the scenery that surrounds them, though. While most are noted for their charm and character, many lack space while others lack style A little to the south in the Ghetto, the impossibly narrow alleyways and deep quiet of most of this small quarter make it easy to imagine its bohemian-chic condos as the teeming tenements they once were.

CAMPO DE' FIORI

$$ HOTEL **Albergo del Sole al Biscione.** This affordable and comfortable hotel, centrally located in the heart of Campo de' Fiori and built atop the ruins of the ancient Theater of Pompey, has warm, cozy decor and a rooftop terrace with a stunning view of Sant'Andrea delle Valle. **Pros:** parking garage in the hotel; reasonable rates for the location; lovely rooftop terrace. **Cons:** some rooms are small and without a/c; no elevator at the entrance of hotel; a bit noisy because of student groups and/or street noise in the area. [$] *Rooms from: €130* ✉ *Via del Biscione 76, Campo de' Fiori* ☎ *06/68806873* 🌐 *www.solealbiscione.it* 🛏 *59 rooms* 💳 *No credit cards* 🍴 *No meals* ✥ *4:D4.*

$$ B&B/INN Fodor's Choice ★ **Casa di Santa Brigida.** The friendly sisters of Santa Brigida oversee simple, straightforward, and centrally located accommodations—right next to Campo de' Fiori—in one of Rome's loveliest convents, with a rooftop terrace overlooking Palazzo Farnese; sometimes the sisters offer guests tickets to the papal audience. **Pros:** no curfew in this historic convent; insider papal tickets; location in the Piazza Farnese. **Cons:** weak a/c; no TVs in the rooms (though there is a common TV room); mediocre breakfast. [$] *Rooms from: €160* ✉ *Piazza Farnese 96, Campo de' Fiori* ☎ *06/68892596* ✍ *piazzafarnese@brigidine.org* 🌐 *www.brigidine.org* 🛏 *2 rooms* 🍴 *Breakfast* ✥ *4:C4.*

| Hassler | Scalinata di Spagna |

| Eden | Relais Le Clarisse |

| Daphne Veneto | Yes Hotel |

$$$
HOTEL

Hotel Campo de' Fiori. Each room in this ivy-draped hotel, perhaps one of Rome's most handsome, is entirely unique in its colors, furnishings, and refined feel, and the views of Roman rooftops from the Campo de' Fiori's terrace certainly don't disappoint. **Pros:** modern amenities such as flat-screen LCD TV with satellite, individual air-conditioning, and free Wi-Fi; rooftop terrace; a 4% discount if you pay in cash. **Cons:** some of the rooms are very small; breakfast works on a voucher system with a nearby caffè; the staff isn't as hospitable as most Italians. *$ Rooms from: €300 ⊠ Via del Biscione 6, Campo de' Fiori ☎ 06/68806865 ⊕ www.hotelcampodefiori.it ⤷ 23 rooms ⦿ Breakfast ✛ 4:D4.*

$$$
HOTEL
Fodor's Choice
★

Hotel Ponte Sisto. With one of the prettiest patio-courtyards in Rome (Europe?), this hotel offers its own blissful definition of Pax Romana: peace, indeed, will be yours, sitting in this enchanting spot, shadowed by gigantic palm trees, set with tables, and adorned with pink and white flowers, all surrounded by the suavely ochre walls of the hotel, gorgeously renovated in 2001 from a palazzo built by the noble Venetian Palottini family. **Pros:** staff is friendly; rooms with views (and some with balconies and terraces); luxury bathrooms; beautiful courtyard garden. **Cons:** street-side rooms can be a bit noisy; some rooms are on the small side; meals at the restaurant can only be planned for groups. *$ Rooms from: €300 ⊠ Via dei Pettinari 64, Campo de' Fiori ☎ 06/686310 ⊕ www.hotelpontesisto.it ⤷ 103 rooms, 4 suites ⦿ Breakfast ✛ 4:D5.*

$$
HOTEL

Teatro di Pompeo. Have breakfast under the ancient stone vaults of Pompey's Theater, the site of Julius Caesar's assassination, and sleep under restored beamed ceilings that date from the days of Michelangelo at this hotel with simple (and perhaps a bit dated) rooms and wonderful, genuinely helpful staff. **Pros:** location is central to the Campo but not right on the market square; helpful staff; an old-school Roman feel. **Cons:** it can be noisy on both the street side and the interior courtyard; rooms are small and some are a bit musty. *$ Rooms from: €200 ⊠ Largo del Pallaro 8, Campo de' Fiori ☎ 06/68300170 ⊕ www.hotelteatrodipompeo.it ⤷ 12 rooms ⦿ Breakfast ✛ 4:D4.*

$$$
HOTEL

Tiziano. With Campo de' Fiori, Piazza Navona, and the Pantheon all at your doorstep, this 18th-century hotel in a former palace—the once grand Palazzo Pacelli—makes an ideal base from which to explore. **Pros:** a very "European" feel; excellent value and location; computer terminal with Internet access at the reception for guests to use. **Cons:** lots of traffic on the Corso, so some rooms are noisy; loud hallways, especially when hosting student university groups; not as glamorous as other 4-star hotels. *$ Rooms from: €210 ⊠ Campo Vittorio Emanuele II 110, Campo de' Fiori ☎ 06/6865019 ⊕ www.tizianohotel.it ⤷ 51 rooms ⦿ Breakfast ✛ 4:E4.*

GHETTO

$$
HOTEL

Arenula. A hefty bargain by Rome standards, Hotel Arenula has an almost unbeatable location (in the Jewish Ghetto just across the river from Trastevere), an imposingly elegant stone exterior, and simple but comfortable rooms with pale-wood furnishings and double-glazed windows, but alas, no elevator. **Pros:** it's a real bargain; conveniently located in the Ghetto (close to Campo de' Fiori and Trastevere), and it's spotless. **Cons:** totally no-frills accommodations; no elevator; can still be a bit

13

noisy despite the double-glazed windows. [$] *Rooms from: €130* ✉ *Via Santa Maria dei Calderari 47, off Via Arenula, Ghetto* ☎ *06/6879454* 🌐 *www.hotelarenula.com* 🛏 *50 rooms* 🍴 *Breakfast* ✥ *4:E5.*

MONTI, ESQUILINO, REPUBBLICA, AND SAN LORENZO

The wide, busy streets around Rome's central train station feel much more urban than the rest of the city center. Traffic is heavier, 19th-century buildings are taller, and the overall feeling is gray and commercial—not the Rome of travel brochure fantasies. But the hotel density here is the highest in the city, and you're assured of finding a room in a pinch. And parts of this area, such as Monti and San Lorenzo, have become popular with the hipster crowd thanks to abundant eateries (both Italian and ethnic) and funky wine bars. Although most travelers choose the area because it's cheap, there are a surprising number of high-end hotels here as well, and if you're looking for a luxurious room, the price-quality ratio here is better than in swankier parts of town.

MONTI

$$ HOTEL 🏨 **Italia.** Just a block from bustling Via Nazionale, this hotel feels like a classic *pensione*: low budget with a lot of heart, with inexpensive rooms with big windows, desks, parquet floors, and baths with faux-marble tiles, and a generous buffet breakfast. **Pros:** free Wi-Fi and Internet access throughout the hotel; Internet point for guests without computers to use; great price; individual attention and personal care. **Cons:** can be a bit noisy; a/c is an extra €10. [$] *Rooms from: €135* ✉ *Via Venezia 18, Monti* ☎ *06/4828355* 🌐 *www.hotelitaliaroma.com* 🛏 *31 rooms, 1 apartment* 🍴 *Breakfast* ✥ *2:C4.*

$ B&B/INN 🏨 **Montreal.** A good choice for budget travelers, this modest hotel on a central avenue across the square from Santa Maria Maggiore, three blocks from Stazione Termini, occupies a totally renovated older building and offers bright, fresh-looking, though small, rooms. **Pros:** informative and helpful staff provides maps and good recommendations; bathrooms are spacious; hotel has a cozy feel. **Cons:** location can be noisy at night; need to take a bus or a Metro to get to most of the sights. [$] *Rooms from: €100* ✉ *Via Carlo Alberto 4, Monti* ☎ *06/4457797* 🌐 *www.hotelmontrealroma.com* 🛏 *27 rooms* 🍴 *Breakfast* ✥ *2:D5.*

$$$ HOTEL 🏨 **Richmond.** Right at the beginning of Via Cavour, this charming little hotel—ideally situated for visits to the Forum, the Colosseum, and all the major sites of Ancient Rome—has an attractive rooftop terrace and modern rooms with hand-painted frescoes. **Pros:** impressive views of the Forum; friendly and courteous staff; modern bathrooms. **Cons:** rooms are small; expect to see some signs of wear; some bathrooms are shared. [$] *Rooms from: €230* ✉ *Largo Corrado Ricci 36, Monti* ☎ *06/69941256* 🌐 *www.hotelrichmond.it* 🛏 *23 rooms* 🍴 *Breakfast* ✥ *2:B6.*

ESQUILINO

$$ B&B/INN 🏨 **Adler.** This tiny pensione, run by the same family for more than three decades, provides a comfortable stay—rooms are basic, but impeccably clean—on a quiet street near the main station for reasonable prices. **Pros:** breakfast on the terrace; free Internet point in the lobby;

strong a/c. **Cons:** some rooms are dark; showers are tiny; no safes in the rooms. $ *Rooms from: €130* ✉ *Via Modena 5, Esquilino* ☎ *06/484466* ⊕ *www.hoteladler-roma.com* ⇋ *8 rooms* ❍| *Breakfast* ✦ *2:C3.*

$$ 🛏 **Britannia.** Originally built as a residence by Prince Philip Don Orsini in 1876, the Britannia is an enticing option for travelers looking for style and comfort—as for the latter, this elegant Art Nouveau building between the Quirinale and Viminale, makes you feel as if you're in a private home furnished with luxury fabrics, original artwork, and handsome marble bathrooms. **Pros:** spacious; comfortable rooms with free Wi-Fi; some pets are allowed; good service. **Cons:** rooms can be noisy for light sleepers; not very close to the city's main attractions. $ *Rooms from: €180* ✉ *Via Napoli 64, Esquilino* ☎ *06/4883153* ⊕ *www.hotelbritannia.it* ⇋ *33 rooms, 1 suite* ❍| *Breakfast* ✦ *2:C4.*
HOTEL
Fodor's Choice
★

$$ 🛏 **Doria.** A convenient location close to the grand Basilica di Santa Maria Maggiore and reasonable rates are the advantages of this diminutive hotel, where space is ingeniously exploited—from the minuscule elevator to the nicely furnished though smallish rooms—and guests take breakfast on the rooftop terrace. **Pros:** smart use of space; breakfast on the rooftop terrace. **Cons:** minuscule elevator; small reception area; despite soundproofing there's still some traffic noise. $ *Rooms from: €130* ✉ *Via Merulana 4, Esquilino* ☎ *06/4465888* ⊕ *www.doriahotel. it* ⇋ *20 rooms* ❍| *Breakfast* ✦ *2:D5.*
HOTEL

$$ 🛏 **Morgana.** A stylish hotel just a stone's throw from Termini sounds like some sort of a miracle, but, complete with unbeatable prices, the Morgan welcomes guests with chic rooms (kitschy striped walls, oversized comfy beds, long flowing drapes), top amenities—Jacuzzi tubs, flat-screen TVs with satellite, and Wi-Fi—and a neighborhood that is super-convenient, if not the best in town. **Pros:** with direct bookings, Morgana offers special packages with free airport transfer or a free guided tour; the hotel is pet-friendly. **Cons:** neighborhood is rundown; removed from most sightseeing (though you can take buses or the Metro). $ *Rooms from: €165* ✉ *Via Filippo Turati 33/37, Esquilino* ☎ *06/4467230* ⊕ *www.hotelmorgana.com* ⇋ *121 rooms, 2 suites* ❍| *Breakfast* ✦ *2:E4.*
HOTEL

$$$ 🛏 **Radisson SAS Es.** Imagine your guest room was at a big-city modern art museum and you'll start to get the picture here: spacious bedrooms with funky fixtures (beds often smack in the middle of the room), windows that light up at night, and plenty of other minimalist and ultra-contemporary design touches, most in complete contrast to what you'll find throughout Rome. **Pros:** distinctive design; convenient, transportation-wise, as it's so close to Termini; friendly and helpful staff, plus a lot of extras (like free Wi-Fi). **Cons:** Termini can be a bit unsavory at night; see-through bathrooms don't allow for much privacy. $ *Rooms from: €240* ✉ *Via Filippo Turati 171, Esquilino* ☎ *06/444841* ⊕ *www.rome. radissonsas.com* ⇋ *232 rooms, 27 suites* ❍| *Breakfast* ✦ *2:F5.*
HOTEL

$ 🛏 **Residence Candia.** Located in the Prati area just behind the Vatican Museums, this place (hotel-style rooms and apartment accommodations both have kitchenettes with refrigerators) is the perfect solution for those looking to be just outside the chaotic *centro* but close enough to all the major sights. **Pros:** Wi-Fi in all rooms; owner sometimes
RENTAL

13

hosts free dinners for his guests and provides free papal mass tickets. **Cons:** the residence can be a bit noisy sometimes when student groups are staying there. [$] *Rooms from: €120* ✉ *Via Candia 135/B, Prati* ☎ *06/39721046* 🌐 *www.residencecandia.it* 🛏 *55* ✣ 1:A2.

REPUBBLICA

$$ HOTEL

🏨 **Alpi.** You'll feel right at home from the moment you waltz into Hotel Alpi, where high ceilings with elegant chandeliers, white walls, and marble floors lend both elegance and warmth and all the guest rooms are tastefully decorated, some with antique furniture. **Pros:** clean and comfortable; lovely terraces for dining and relaxing; numerous common spaces to lounge in. **Cons:** not all rooms are created equal; slow elevator; you'll probably want to take a bus or Metro to most major sights. [$] *Rooms from: €140* ✉ *Via Castelfidardo 84, Repubblica* ☎ *06/4441235* 🌐 *www.hotelalpi.com* 🛏 *48 rooms* 🍴 *Breakfast* ✣ *2:E2.*

$ B&B/INN Fodor's Choice ★

🏨 **The Beehive.** Living the American dream in Italy is exactly what one Los Angeles couple did in 1999, when they opened the Beehive, a hip, alternative budget hotel (bathrooms are shared) near Termini train station where you can take a yoga class, go organic in the on-site caffè, or lounge the afternoon away in the lovely garden or reading lounge. **Pros:** yoga, massage, and other therapies offered on-site; Sunday brunches at their caffè featuring organic pancakes. **Cons:** no TV, a/c, baggage storage, or private bathroom; breakfast is not included in the room rate. [$] *Rooms from: €85* ✉ *Via Marghera 8, San Lorenzo* ☎ *06/44704553* 🌐 *www.the-beehive.com* 🛏 *8 rooms, 1 dormitory, 3 apartments* 🍴 *No meals* ✣ *2:E3.*

$$$$ HOTEL Fodor's Choice ★

🏨 **Exedra.** If Rome's semi-stodgy hotel scene has an It-Girl, it's the hard-to-top Exedra, where high rollers love to host splashy parties by the rooftop swimming pool and magazines love to rave about them; rooms are predictably luscious in an uptown way, with silky linens and handsome nouveau-colonial bedsteads, and many face the spectacular fountain in the piazza outside. **Pros:** spacious and attractive rooms; great spa and pool; terrace with cocktail service; close to Termini station. **Cons:** food and beverages are expensive; beyond the immediate vicinity, parts of the neighborhood can be sketchy. [$] *Rooms from: €360* ✉ *Piazza della Repubblica 47, Repubblica* ☎ *06/489381* 🌐 *www.boscolohotels.com* 🛏 *240 rooms, 18 suites* 🍴 *Breakfast* ✣ *2:D3.*

$$ HOTEL

🏨 **Leon's Place Hotel.** Almost akin to flipping through the pages of Italian *Vogue,* a stroll through this glamorous design hotel (just a short distance from the Piazza Repubblica hub) reveals lots of chic and bling-tastic decor, including Art Deco–inspired furnishings, plush chairs and sofas, sparkling chandeliers sprouting black feathers, a velvety black swing dangling from the ceiling, and streamlined guest rooms done up in gray and black—all this style and you won't even have to splurge for it. **Pros:** several rooms have balconies with panoramic views of the city; free Wi-Fi in the common areas of hotel; top-quality toiletries; affordable prices. **Cons:** not very central; some rooms face the courtyard; no Wi-Fi in the rooms. [$] *Rooms from: €180* ✉ *Via XX Settembre 90/94, Repubblica* ☎ *06/890871* 🌐 *www.leonsplace.net* 🛏 *50 rooms and 4 suites.*

$$ 🛏 **Marcella Royal.** You can do your sightseeing from the rooftop ter-
HOTEL race of the Marcella, a midsize hotel with the feel of a smaller, more
intimate establishment, where all the guest rooms are furnished with
flair. **Pros:** breakfast in the roof garden; aperitivo at the piano bar; light
dinner offered; staff goes the extra mile to help guests with all of their
needs. **Cons:** small rooms; Internet is spotty; not exactly close to the
major attractions. $ *Rooms from: €200* ⊠ *Via Flavia 106, Repubblica*
☎ *06/42014591* ⊕ *www.marcellaroyalhotel.com* ⤳ *85 rooms, 2 suites*
|○| *Breakfast* ⊹ *2:D2.*

$$$ 🛏 **Mascagni.** Situated on a side street around the corner from one of
HOTEL Rome's most impressive piazzas (Piazza della Repubblica), this friendly
⟳ hotel has staff that go out of their way to make you feel at home, public
spaces cleverly styled with contemporary art pieces, and wood fixtures
and furnishings accentuated by warm colors in the guest rooms. **Pros:**
staff is friendly and attentive; evening lounge that serves up cold cuts
or light pasta dishes; great for families with kids. **Cons:** elevator is too
small and takes a while; weak a/c; slow Internet. $ *Rooms from: €250*
⊠ *Via Vittorio Emanuele Orlando 90, Repubblica* ☎ *06/48904040*
⊕ *www.hotelmascagni.com* ⤳ *40 rooms* |○| *Breakfast* ⊹ *2:C3.*

$$ 🛏 **Miami.** Rooms at this low-key hotel, in a dignified 19th-century build-
HOTEL ing on Rome's busy Via Nazionale, are soundproof and tastefully styled
with coordinated curtains, bedspreads, and wallpaper, but the main
draw is the hotel's location on main bus lines and near Termini station
and the Metro, very central for sightseeing and shopping, though not
ideal for eating out. **Pros:** pleasant staff; soundproof windows; strong
a/c. **Cons:** no alarm clock; small breakfast room. $ *Rooms from: €150*
⊠ *Via Nazionale 230, Repubblica* ☎ *06/4817180* ⊕ *www.hotelmiami.
com* ⤳ *42 rooms, 4 suites, 1 apartment* |○| *Breakfast* ⊹ *2:C3.*

$$ 🛏 **Residenza Cellini.** Fresh flowers in the foyer help make this small,
B&B/INN family-run residence close to Termini station feel like a gracious home,
and since there are only six rooms—traditionally furnished and accentuated with fine draperies, stylish furnishings, warm wooden parquet
floors, and authentic decorative stucco ceilings—you're guaranteed personal attention from the eager-to-please staff. **Pros:** it feels like you're
visiting Rome in another era; Jacuzzi bathtubs and hydrojet showers;
personalized care from the staff. **Cons:** not close to the main attractions; the orthopedic mattresses may be too firm for some; breakfast
is the standard Continental fare. $ *Rooms from: €200* ⊠ *Via Modena
5, Repubblica* ☎ *06/47825204* ⊕ *www.residenzacellini.it* ⤳ *6 rooms*
|○| *Breakfast* ⊹ *2:C3.*

$$ 🛏 **Romae.** On the better side of Termini station, the Romae has the advan-
HOTEL tages of a strategic location—it's within walking distance of many sites,
and handy to bus and Metro lines—and attracts guests for its comfort-
able rooms and ample amenities such as satellite TV, in-room safe, and
Internet access. **Pros:** spacious rooms; complimentary beverages offered
throughout the day; international newspapers available; free Internet
access. **Cons:** breakfast is served at the bar across the street; not much
action in the neighborhood at night; showers tend to give problems.
$ *Rooms from: €140* ⊠ *Via Palestro 49, Castro Pretorio* ☎ *06/4463554*
⊕ *www.hotelromae.com* ⤳ *40 rooms* |○| *Breakfast* ⊹ *2:E3.*

13

$ HOTEL **Villa delle Rose.** When the Eternal City becomes too chaotic for you, head to this relaxing retreat in a charming 19th-century palazzo minutes away from Termini station, with its beautiful rose garden where guests typically have breakfast or sip afternoon tea. **Pros:** delightful garden with blooming roses and jasmine; free parking; free Wi-Fi. **Cons:** some of the rooms are small (ask for a larger one); the elevator is also small. [$] *Rooms from: €115* ✉ *Via Vicenza 5, Repubblica* ☎ *06/4451795* 🌐 *www.villadellerose.it* 🛏 *37 rooms* 🍴 *Breakfast* ✣ *2:E3.*

SAN LORENZO

$$ HOTEL **Aphrodite.** Given a recent design makeover, this hotel offers plenty of panache for the money: the mod, minimalist reception area strikes an elegant note (a little off-key since the immediate area here is right next door to Termini Station), and guest rooms are clean and friendly, adorned with soft pastel colors. **Pros:** panache for a low price; big bathrooms with mosaic tiles. **Cons:** not very central location; small rooms. [$] *Rooms from: €130* ✉ *Via Marsala 90, Termini* ☎ *06/491096* 🌐 *www.aphroditehotelrome.com* 🛏 *50 rooms* 🍴 *Breakfast* ✣ *2:E3.*

$$ HOTEL **Des Artistes.** The three Riccioni brothers have put their hearts and souls into running the Des Artistes, making it the crème de la crème of this neighborhood near Termini, and you'll want to book well ahead to reserve your spot in this delightful hotel, decked out with 20th-century paintings, with mahogany furniture and handsome fabrics in the guest rooms. **Pros:** good value; decent-size rooms; relaxing roof garden. **Cons:** breakfast room is small; reception is on the fifth floor; you have to pay for Wi-Fi. [$] *Rooms from: €130* ✉ *Via Villafranca 20, Castro Pretorio* ☎ *06/4454365* 🌐 *www.hoteldesartistes.com* 🛏 *40 rooms, 27 with bath* 🍴 *Breakfast* ✣ *2:F2.*

$$ HOTEL Fodor's Choice ★ **Yes Hotel.** This chic hotel may fool you into thinking these digs are expensive, but the contemporary coolness of Yes Hotel—crisp neutral colors and modern fabrics in the guest rooms and high-end amenities such as flat-screen TVs, top-of-the-line toiletries, and electronic safes—comes at a budget price. **Pros:** flat-screen TVs with satellite TV; doesn't have the feel of a budget hotel; discount if you pay cash; great value. **Cons:** rooms are small; no individual climate control or refrigerators in the rooms. [$] *Rooms from: €140* ✉ *Via Magenta 15, Termini* ☎ *06/44363836* 🌐 *www.yeshotelrome.com* 🛏 *29 rooms, 1 suite* 🍴 *Breakfast* ✣ *2:E3.*

VENETO, BORGHESE, AND SPAGNA

Though the glamorous days of *dolce vita*, when celebs and paparazzi packed the famed Via Veneto, are long gone, this area still houses haute couture shops—Gucci, Prada, Fendi—and loads of fine restaurants and luxury lodgings. It's the absolute best place to do some serious shopping, and its dining scene and street caffè make for great people-watching. The American Embassy is here and so is the Hard Rock Café, and it's convenient to Villa Borghese, the Spanish Steps, and Rome's Metro stop—Barberini is at the bottom of the uphill-winding (and rather steep) street.

VENETO

$$$$ HOTEL Fodor's Choice ★ **Aleph.** If you're wondering where the beautiful people are, look no further than the Aleph, the most unfalteringly fashionable of Rome's design hotels—the just-this-side-of-kitsch theme is Dante's Divine Comedy, and you can walk the line between heaven and hell through the Angelo bar, the red-red-red Sin restaurant, and Paradise spa—where the guest rooms are happily more subdued, in neutral tones with wood furniture, made galleryesque by giant black-and-white photos of Rome. **Pros:** access to the spa facilities is included for all hotel guests without any added cost; award-winning design. **Cons:** rooms are too petite for the price; cocktails are expensive; Internet is costly, too, and Wi-Fi isn't guaranteed. [$] *Rooms from: €500* ✉ *Via San Basilio 15, Veneto* ☎ *06/422901* 🌐 *aleph-roma.boscolohotels.com* 🛏 *96 rooms, 6 suites* 🍴 *No meals* ✣ *2:C2.*

13

$$ HOTEL **Alexandra.** For nearly a century, Hotel Alexandra has been a family affair, and its modest poise and distinguished style—it doesn't feel like a 3-star place—allow it to hold its own against its flashier big brothers and sisters on the Via Veneto. **Pros:** great location near Piazza Barberini for sightseeing, restaurants, and transportation; decorated with authentic antiques; free Wi-Fi. **Cons:** mostly tiny rooms and tinier bathrooms; breakfast is just the standard fare (and no cappuccino). [$] *Rooms from: €160* ✉ *Via Veneto 18, Veneto* ☎ *06/4881943* 🌐 *www.hotelalexandraroma.com* 🛏 *60 rooms* 🍴 *Breakfast* ✣ *2:B2.*

$$$ HOTEL **Barberini.** Here you can find about all you could ask for in a Roman hotel: charm, taste, and the good fortune to look out onto one of the best museums in town, Palazzo Barberini, and its location near the Metro, the Trevi Fountain, and good restaurants is hard to beat. **Pros:** beautiful view from the roof terrace; located on a quiet side street close to several important attractions; facilities for the disabled; spa facilities. **Cons:** breakfast buffet costs €30 extra; some rooms are on the small side; not all rooms have bathtubs; room service is limited. [$] *Rooms from: €270* ✉ *Via Rasella 3, Barberini* ☎ *06/4814993* 🌐 *www.hotelbarberini.com* 🛏 *35 rooms, 4 suites* 🍴 *Breakfast* ✣ *2:B3.*

$$ B&B/INN Fodor's Choice ★ **Daphne Veneto.** Inspired by Baroque artist Gianlorenzo Bernini's exquisite *Apollo and Daphne* sculpture at the Borghese Gallery, the Daphne Inn at Via Veneto is an "urban B&B" run by people who love Rome and will do their best to make sure you love it, too: in addition to an intimate lodging experience, elegantly designed rooms, comfortable beds, and fresh fruit and pastries with your coffee each morning, the staff will help you map out your destinations, schedule itineraries, plan day trips, book tours, choose restaurants, and organize your transportation—it's like having your own personal travel planner. **Pros:** if rooms at Daphne Veneto are booked, inquire about its sister hotel, Daphne Trevi; the opportunity to see Rome "like an insider"; the beds have Simmons mattresses and fluffy comforters. **Cons:** no TVs; some bathrooms are shared; Daphne only accepts Visa or MasterCard to hold bookings (though you can actually pay with an AmEx). [$] *Rooms from: €180* ✉ *Via di San Basilio 55, Veneto* ☎ *06/87450087* 🌐 *www.daphne-rome.com* 🛏 *7 rooms, 2 suites* 🍴 *Breakfast* ✣ *2:B3.*

$$$$
HOTEL
Fodor's Choice
★

🖫 **Eden.** A recent refurbishment of the Hotel Eden has put it back in the running for one of Rome's top luxury lodgings: once a favorite haunt of Hemingway, Ingrid Bergman, and Fellini, this superlative hotel combines dashing elegance, exquisitely lush decor, and stunning vistas of Rome with true Italian hospitality. **Pros:** gorgeous mirrored roof terrace restaurant; you could be rubbing elbows with the stars; 24-hour room service. **Cons:** expensive (unless money is no object for you); no Wi-Fi in the rooms; some say the staff can be hit-or-miss. $ *Rooms from: €440* ⊠ *Via Ludovisi 49, Veneto* 🕾 *06/478121* ⊕ *www.lemeridien.com/eden* ⤳ *121 rooms, 13 suites* ❗❍❘ *No meals* ✛ *2:B2.*

$$
HOTEL

🖫 **Hotel Suisse.** In the same family for more than three generations, this lovely little hotel on the picturesque and fabled Via Gregoriana, minutes away from the Spanish Steps and its famous boutiques (and just steps away from the former residences of Hans Christian Andersen and the painter Ingres), offers rooms that feel more like a friend's elegantly furnished apartment. **Pros:** good value for reasonable price; the rooms are obviously cared for; great location. **Cons:** breakfast is taken in your room; you will need to be buzzed in during certain hours; there are a few stairs to climb before you reach the elevator. $ *Rooms from: €165* ⊠ *Via Gregoriana 54, Veneto* 🕾 *06/6783649* ⊕ *www.hotelsuisserome. com* ⤳ *12 rooms* ❗❍❘ *Breakfast* ✛ *1:H3.*

$
HOTEL

🖫 **Julia.** Tucked away behind Piazza Barberini down a sinuous cobbled lane, this small establishment welcomes you with a reception area that is surprisingly modern and straightforward; and though the more traditional guest rooms are short on character, they're marvelously spacious and clean. **Pros:** safe neighborhood; convenient to sights and transportation; quiet (since it's just off Piazza Barberini on a small side street). **Cons:** no frills; very basic accommodations; some of the rooms are dark. $ *Rooms from: €120* ⊠ *Via Rasella 29, Veneto* 🕾 *06/4881637* ⊕ *www.hoteljulia.it* ⤳ *33 rooms, 30 with bath, 2 suites, 3 apartments* ❗❍❘ *Breakfast* ✛ *2:B3.*

$$$
HOTEL

🖫 **La Residenza.** Mainly Americans frequent this cozy hotel in a converted town house near Via Veneto, where the rooms are basic, comfortable, and tasteful (although single rooms are almost windowless), but the real charm of the hotel is found in its bar, terrace, and lounges, which are adorned with stylish wallpaper and loveseats that invite you to make yourself at home. **Pros:** big American breakfast; spacious; quiet rooms with balconies; friendly staff; cocktail parties. **Cons:** the building's exterior doesn't compare to its interior; located on a street with some "gentleman's" clubs; if you're in Rome for the Vatican, it's a long walk (or a Metro ride) from here. $ *Rooms from: €210* ⊠ *Via Emilia 22, Veneto* 🕾 *06/4880789* ⊕ *www.hotel-la-residenza.com* ⤳ *29 rooms* ❗❍❘ *Breakfast* ✛ *2:B2.*

$$$$
HOTEL

🖫 **Majestic.** The first luxury hotel built on the Via Veneto, in 1889, during the days of the *dolce vita*, the luxurious Majestic was a favorite among Rome's royalty and social climbers and is still a grand, refined hotel lined with luxurious furnishings, spacious, light-filled rooms, up-to-date accessories, and white marble bathrooms. **Pros:** old-world elegance; silky linens on big, plushy beds; some rooms even have their own balconies that overlook the Via Veneto; nice fitness center with personal trainer upon request. **Cons:** pricey; breakfast is especially expensive; not all of the rooms are spacious. $ *Rooms from: €480* ✉ *Via Vittorio Veneto 50, Veneto, Veneto* ☎ *06/421441* ⊕ *www.hotelmajestic.com* ⤵ *85 rooms, 13 suites* ⏏ *No meals* ✛ *2:B2.*

$$$$ 🛏 **Marriott Grand Hotel Flora.** This handsome hotel at the top of Via
HOTEL   Veneto next to the Villa Borghese park is something of a beacon on the Rome landscape, and no expense has been spared in decorating the rooms and suites, among the largest in the Eternal City; each one is unique, and carefully chosen antiques grace them all. **Pros:** convenient location and pleasant staff; spectacular view of the Borghese Gardens and the Roman skyline from the breakfast terrace; free Internet. **Cons:** breakfast finishes fast; sometimes the noise from Via Veneto drifts in; crowded with businessmen and big tour groups. $ *Rooms from: €390* ✉ *Via Veneto 191, Veneto* ☎ *06/489929* ⊕ *www.mariotthotels.com* ⤵ *156 rooms, 24 suites* ⏏ *Breakfast* ✛ *2:B1.*

$$$$ 🛏 **Regina Baglioni.** A former playground of kings and poets, the Regina
HOTEL   Baglioni—royal in its elegance, replete with chandeliers, grand staircases, red carpets, and gigantic statues—enjoys a prime spot on the Via Veneto, which is convenient for the street's dolce vita caffè and the Villa Borghese, but its noisy neighbor, the Hard Rock Café, is too close for comfort for some. **Pros:** over-the-top decor; refurbished rooms; Brunello Lounge and Restaurant. **Cons:** not all the rooms have been refurbished; staff is hit-or-miss; Internet is spotty. $ *Rooms from: €430* ✉ *Via Veneto 72, Veneto* ☎ *06/421111* ⊕ *www.reginabaglioni.com* ⤵ *136 rooms, 7 suites* ⏏ *No meals* ✛ *2:B2.*

$$$$ 🛏 **Sofitel Rome Villa Borghese.** Set in a refurbished 1902 Victorian palace,
HOTEL   the Hotel Sofitel—which has a long-standing reputation with business travelers—is cleverly situated on a quiet street between the hot spots of Via Veneto and the Spanish Steps and exudes old-world elegance, albeit with a modern design sensibility. **Pros:** luxury lodging off the main drag (but not too far from it); first-rate concierge and porter. **Cons:** luxury chain hotel with business clientele that could make it a bit stuffy at times; some say the a/c could be stronger; the showers are a bit leaky. $ *Rooms from: €320* ✉ *Via Lombardia 47, Veneto* ☎ *06/478021* ⊕ *www.sofitel.com* ⤵ *113 rooms, 4 suites* ⏏ *Breakfast* ✛ *2:B2.*

$$$ 🛏 **Victoria.** Oriental rugs, oil paintings, and fresh flowers are scattered
HOTEL   throughout the lobbies and guest rooms at this hotel heavy on traditional-style wallpapers and well furnished with armchairs and other amenities; American businesspeople who prize the hotel's personalized service, restful atmosphere, and elegantly designed restaurant and bar are frequent guests. **Pros:** view of the Borghese Gardens; quiet and comfortable; rooftop bar and restaurant; orthopedic mattresses. **Cons:** it's a schlep to most sights; service is inconsistent; rooms are small. $ *Rooms from: €220* ✉ *Via Campania 41, Veneto* ☎ *06/423701* ⊕ *www.hotelvictoriaroma.com* ⤵ *110 rooms* ⏏ *No meals* ✛ *2:C1.*

$$$$ 🛏 **The Westin Excelsior, Rome.** Ablaze with lights at night, this seven-layer-
HOTEL   cake hotel—topped off by its famous corner cupola, a landmark nearly
🔄   as famous as the American Embassy palazzo across the street—is lavished with mirrors, elegant moldings, Oriental rugs, crystal chandeliers, and huge, Baroque floral arrangements, while guest rooms have elegant

13

drapery, marble baths, top-quality linens, and big, firm beds. **Pros:** elegant period furnishings and decor; potential for star-sightings; health club and indoor pool. **Cons:** not all rooms are created equal; some say the Excelsior's age is starting to show; extras are extra-expensive. [$] *Rooms from: €470* ✉ *Via Veneto 125, Veneto* ☎ *06/47081* 🌐 *excelsior.hotelinroma.com* 🛏 *319 rooms, 32 suites* 🍴 *No meals* ✥ *2:C2.*

BORGHESE

$$$ HOTEL **Grand Hotel Parco dei Principi.** The 1960s-era facade of this large, seven-story hotel contrasts with the turn-of-the-20th-century Italian court decor and the extensive botanical garden, right on the border of the exclusive Parioli district and the Villa Borghese park, resulting in a combination of traditional elegance and contemporary pleasure: picture windows in every room with views over an ocean of green, surmounted by St. Peter's dome; the hotel has a wonderful free-form swimming pool, a piano bar with stained glass and carved walnut appointments, an uber-chic spa, and chamber music in the garden. **Pros:** quiet location on the Borghese Gardens; nice pool; outstanding service. **Cons:** beyond the city center; extras are expensive; a bit of a walk to caffè and restaurants. [$] *Rooms from: €250* ✉ *Via G. Frescobaldi 5, Borghese* ☎ *06/854421* 🌐 *www.parcodeiprincipi.com* 🛏 *160 rooms, 20 suites* 🍴 *Breakfast* ✥ *2:C1.*

SPAGNA

$$$ B&B/INN **Condotti.** Near the most expensive shopping street in Rome, Via dei Condotti, and one block from the Spanish Steps, this delightful little hotel—where all guest rooms are soundproof and many enjoy views of the rooftops of Rome—is all about peace and, comfort, and location. **Pros:** soundproof rooms with terraces; individual climate control; friendly and helpful staff. **Cons:** small rooms; you might have to send your bags up in the elevator and follow them separately—that's how tiny it is. [$] *Rooms from: €215* ✉ *Via Mario de' Fiori 37, Spagna* ☎ *06/6794661* 🌐 *www.hotelcondotti.com* 🛏 *16 rooms, 2 suites* 🍴 *Breakfast* ✥ *1:H2.*

$$$ HOTEL **Dei Borgognoni.** Travelers with shopping on their minds will appreciate the position of this quietly chic hotel near Piazza San Silvestro, a short walk from the Spanish Steps, and set in a centuries-old palazzo that's been remodeled to provide spacious lounges and a glassed-in garden courtyard; a small private art collection is also on view. **Pros:** reasonably priced but still very central; some rooms have private balconies or terraces. **Cons:** some of the rooms are surprisingly small for their price; the breakfast lacks variety; some staff can be a little off-putting. [$] *Rooms from: €300* ✉ *Via del Bufalo 126, Spagna* ☎ *06/69941505* 🌐 *www.hotelborgognoni.it* 🛏 *51 rooms* 🍴 *Breakfast* ✥ *4:G1.*

$$$$ HOTEL Fodor's Choice ★ **D'Inghilterra.** From monarchs and movie moguls to some of the greatest writers of all time (John Keats, Mark Twain, and Hemingway), the D'Inghilterra—with a marvelous residential feel and a staff that is as warm as the surroundings are velvety—has welcomed Rome's most discerning tourists since it opened its doors in 1845, and what they really adore about the hotel are first-floor salons, which seem like old sepia-toned photographs come to life. **Pros:** distinct character and

opulence; turndown service (with chocolates!); a genuinely friendly and attentive staff. **Cons:** the elevator is both small and slow; bathrooms are surprisingly petite; the location—despite soundproofing—is still noisy. [$] *Rooms from: €400* ✉ *Vai Bocca di Leone 14, Spagna* ☎ *06/699811* 🌐 *www.hoteldinghilterraroma.it* 🛏 *97 rooms, 11 suites* 🍴 *No meals* ✥ *1:H2.*

> **WORD OF MOUTH**
>
> "Take a deep breath and go to the Hassler—worth every blessed penny. We had a marvelous room overlooking the Spanish Steps with a small balcony, gorgeous, comfy bed, and huge bathroom. While it's a very lively spot the noise was never an issue up on the 6th floor. Service was extremely good. Public spaces are lovely. Just do it. You'll love it."—laurela

13

$$$$ HOTEL Fodor's Choice ★ **Hassler.** When it comes to million-dollar views, this exclusive hotel has the best seats in the house, which is why movie stars like Tom Cruise and Jennifer Lopez, money shakers, and the nouveaux riche are all willing to pay top dollar to stay at this top address of Rome, perched atop the Spanish Steps; they are indeed lucky, for while the Hassler's exterior is bland, the recently restyled guest rooms are among the world's most extravagant and lavishly decorated. **Pros:** charming old-world feel; prime location and panoramic views at the top of the Spanish Steps; just "steps" away from some of the best shopping in the world. **Cons:** VIP prices; many think the staff is too standoffish; the spa facilities are far from 5-star material. [$] *Rooms from: €650* ✉ *Piazza Trinità dei Monti 6, Spagna* ☎ *06/69934755, 800/223–6800 Toll-free from the U.S.* 🌐 *www.hotelhasslerroma.com* 🛏 *82 rooms, 13 suites* 🍴 *No meals* ✥ *1:H2.*

$$$ HOTEL **Hotel Art.** High Fashion Rome meets Chic Contemporary Gallery at this hotel that sits on Via Margutta, "the street of painters": as you glide your way through the stylish lobby, the smart furnishings and fixtures in the public spaces of the hotel will build up your urge to bid on an item as if you were at an auction at Christie's, but the color-coordinated guest rooms are more standard contemporary style (sleek wood headboards accented by handmade Florentine leather, puffy white comforters, bathrobes, and high-speed Internet). **Pros:** feels like you've checked into an ultra-hip art gallery; helpful and pleasant staff; in between two Metro stops; comfortable beds. **Cons:** the glass floors are noisy at night; the courtyard bar crowd may keep you awake; the a/c can be fussy. [$] *Rooms from: €280* ✉ *Via Margutta 56, Spagna* ☎ *06/328711* 🌐 *www.hotelart.it* 🛏 *44 rooms, 2 suites* 🍴 *Breakfast* ✥ *1:H2.*

$$$$ HOTEL Fodor's Choice ★ 👶 **Hotel de Russie.** A ritzy retreat for government bigwigs and Hollywood high rollers, the de Russie—just steps away from the famed Piazza del Popolo and set in a 19th-century historic hotel that once boasted a clientele that included royalty, Picasso, and Cocteau—got the best money could buy when famed hotelier Sir Rocco Forte gave this dowager a face-lift, replete with that Soho-hip decor (Donghia-style furnishings and a mod minimalism) that seems to depressingly prevail, in cookie-cutter fashion, in Forte hotels New York to Geneva. **Pros:** big potential for celebrity sightings; special activities for children; extensive gardens

(including a butterfly reserve); first-rate luxury spa. **Cons:** hotel is a bit worn around the edges; decor is generic-luxe; breakfast is nothing special; avoid street-side rooms. [$] *Rooms from: €750* ✉ *Via del Babuino 9, Popolo* ☎ *06/328881* 🌐 *www.rfhotels.com* 🛏 *122 rooms, 33 suites* 🍴 *Breakfast* ✥ *1:G1.*

$$ HOTEL **Hotel Homs.** Tucked away on a quiet side street leading to Piazza di Spagna is this midsize hotel with two spectacular rooftop terraces that provide fine views of the whole area and guest rooms furnished in true Roman style: with beautiful antiques, wooden fixtures, rich colored fabrics and bedspreads, and long flowing drapes. **Pros:** walking distance to Piazza di Spagna; steps away from a big bus hub; close to the Metro; helpful staff. **Cons:** no breakfast included in the room rate; small rooms; fee for Internet access. [$] *Rooms from: €190* ✉ *Via della Vite71–72, Spagna* ☎ *06/6792976* 🌐 *www.hotelhoms.it* 🛏 *53 rooms, 5 suites, 1 apartment* 🍴 *No meals* ✥ *1:H3.*

$$$$ Fodor's Choice ★ **Il Palazzetto.** If you have ever fantasized about staying in one of those houses that perch over the Spanish Steps, make that dream your very special reality by checking into one of the four guest rooms here: you'll wind up reclining the day away on Il Palazzetto's gorgeous terrace to watch the never-ending street theater that is the Scalinatella. **Pros:** that address, that view; high-style bar. **Cons:** restaurant here is often rented out for crowded special events; bedrooms do not access the communal terraces; the McDonalds near the hotel entrance. [$] *Rooms from: €350* ✉ *Vicolo del Bottino 8, Spagna* ☎ *06/6993-41000* 🌐 *www.ilpalazzettoroma.com/* 🛏 *4* 🍴 *No meals* ✥ *1:H2.*

$$$$ B&B/INN **Inn at the Spanish Steps.** After a hard day of shopping on Rome's Rodeo Drive, Via dei Condotti, you'll be pleased to see that this quaint yet cushy hotel—which occupies the upper floors of a centuries-old town house it shares with Casanova's old haunt, Antico Caffè Greco—fits right in with its neighbors: the inn wins a gold star for its smart design and sharp decor. **Pros:** some of the world's best shopping at your doorstep; rooms with superb views of the Spanish Steps; afternoon snacks and outstanding breakfast buffets. **Cons:** interior rooms are claustrophobic; the area can be noisy due to crowds at the Spanish Steps; not all rooms are graced with the stunning Spanish Steps view. [$] *Rooms from: €340* ✉ *Via Condotti 85, Spagna* ☎ *06/69925657* 🌐 *www.atspanishsteps.com* 🛏 *22 suites* 🍴 *Breakfast* ✥ *1:H2.*

$$$ HOTEL **Locarno.** The sort of place that inspired a movie (Bernard Weber's 1978 *Hotel Locarno*, to be exact), this has been a longtime choice for art aficionados and people in the cinema, but everyone will appreciate the hotel's fin de siècle charm, intimate feel, and central location off Piazza del Popolo. **Pros:** luxurious feel (it may even seem like you're in a movie); spacious rooms (even by American standards); free bicycles for exploring Rome. **Cons:** some of the rooms are dark; the annex doesn't compare to the main hotel; the regular staff probably won't go out of their way to help you. [$] *Rooms from: €230* ✉ *Via della Penna 22, Spagna* ☎ *06/3610841* 🌐 *www.hotellocarno.com* 🛏 *64 rooms, 2 suites* 🍴 *Breakfast* ✥ *1:G1.*

$ HOTEL **Panda.** You couldn't possibly find a better deal in Rome than here at the Panda—especially given its key location just behind the Spanish

Steps on one of the poshest shopping streets in the centro, Via della Croce—where the smallish guest rooms are outfitted in terra-cotta, wrought iron, and very simple furnishings; spotlessly clean; and quiet, thanks to double-glaze windows. **Pros:** discount if you pay cash; free Wi-Fi; located on a quiet street, but still close to the Spanish Steps. **Cons:** Wi-Fi signal can be a bit weak; not all rooms have private bathrooms; no elevator; no TVs in the rooms. $ *Rooms from: €100* ✉ *Via della Croce 35, Spagna* ☎ *06/6780179* ⊕ *www.hotelpanda.it* ⟿ *20 rooms, 14 with bath* ⦿ *Breakfast* ✛ *1:G2.*

13

$$ ⊡ **San Carlo.** Decidedly classical and refined, this renovated 17th-century

HOTEL mansion–turned–hotel with modern comforts at reasonable prices— right around the corner from the best shopping district in Rome—has bright and comfortable rooms, some with their own terraces overlooking the city's rooftops. **Pros:** rooms with terraces and views of historic Rome; rooftop garden; attentive staff. **Cons:** there are a lot of stairs and no elevator; breakfast is basic Italian fare (great coffee but otherwise just *cornetti* (Italian croissants), cereal, and yogurt); the rooms can be noisy. $ *Rooms from: €195* ✉ *Via delle Carrozze 92–93, Spagna* ☎ *06/6784548* ⊕ *www.hotelsancarloroma.com* ⟿ *50 rooms, 2 suites* ⦿ *Breakfast* ✛ *1:G2.*

$$$ ⊡ **Scalinata di Spagna.** This tiny hotel's prime location at the top of the

B&B/INN Spanish Steps, inconspicuous little entrance, and quiet, sunny charm

Fodor's Choice all add to the character that guests fall in love with over and over

★ again—which explains why it's often booked up for months, even years at a time—but if you're lucky enough to nab a spot here, you'll enjoy stylish rooms accentuated with floral fabrics and Empire-style sofas and the hotel's extravagant rooftop garden: gaze over Rome as you nibble cornetto and sip cappuccino. **Pros:** friendly and helpful concierge; fresh fruit in the lobby; free Wi-Fi throughout. **Cons:** it's a mile up the hill to the hotel; no porter and no elevator; service can be hit-or-miss. $ *Rooms from: €220* ✉ *Piazza Trinità dei Monti 17, Spagna* ☎ *06/6793006* ⊕ *www.hotelscalinata.com* ⟿ *16 rooms* ⦿ *Breakfast* ✛ *2:A2.*

$$$ ⊡ **Valadier.** In the heart of the *centro*, just steps away from the promi-

HOTEL nent Piazza del Popolo and a few minutes' walk from the Spanish Steps, is this luxury hotel—known for comfortable rooms with marble and travertine bathrooms and a superb location—that has captured the hearts of elite travelers over the years. **Pros:** excellent American-style breakfast buffet; piano bar; flat-screen TVs; good water pressure and cool a/c. **Cons:** cocktails are a pretty penny (or, rather, a pretty centesimo); rooms are smaller than you'd expect for a luxury hotel; the lighting in rooms is very dim. $ *Rooms from: €290* ✉ *Via della Fontanella 15, Spagna* ☎ *06/3611998* ⊕ *www.hotelvaladier.com* ⟿ *60 rooms* ⦿ *Breakfast* ✛ *1:G1.*

VATICAN, BORGO, AND PRATI

Since you can't stay in Vatican City itself, the next best thing for those who want a more spiritual stay or something a little more low-key is to stay in the Borgo or Prati areas nearby. These boast a wide range of accommodations ranging from pilgrim plain to cardinal luxe. Borgo, directly outside the Vatican walls, has medieval charm, but can be overrun by tourists. A 10-minute walk to the north lie the residential streets of Prati and many of the hotels listed here.

VATICAN

$$ HOTEL **Alimandi.** A stone's throw away from the Vatican Museums, this family-run hotel offering good service and good prices comes with all sorts of perks: great location, a spiffy lobby, spacious lounges, a tavern, a roof-top terrace, and roof gardens; and while the hotel is a bit out of the center, two nearby Metro stops help you move about. **Pros:** nice family-owned hotel with a friendly staff; a rooftop terrace; a gym; near reasonably priced restaurants and shops. **Cons:** breakfast is a good spread but it goes quickly; rooms are small; not close to much of interest other than the Vatican. [$] *Rooms from: €180* ✉ *Via Tunisi 8, Vatican* ☎ *06/39723948* 🌐 *www.alimandi.it* 🛏 *35 rooms* 🍴 *Breakfast* ✥ *1:B2.*

$$ HOTEL Fodor's Choice ★ **Residenza Paolo VI.** Set in a former monastery that is still an extraterritorial part of the Vatican and magnificently abutting Bernini's colonnade of St. Peter's Square, the Paolo VI (pronounced *Paolo Sesto*, Italian for Pope Paul VI) is unbeatably close to St. Peter's, with guest rooms that are luxurious and comfortable and amazingly quiet. **Pros:** unparalleled views of St. Peter's from the roof terrace; a sound sleep is assured in these quiet rooms; the breakfast spread is huge. **Cons:** the small rooms are really small; bathrooms are small; the atmosphere at night is a little too quiet. [$] *Rooms from: €190* ✉ *Via Paolo VI 29, Vatican* ☎ *06/68134108* 🌐 *www.residenzapaolovi.com* 🛏 *35 rooms* 🍴 *Breakfast* ✥ *1:C4.*

BORGO

$$$ HOTEL **Atlante Star.** The lush rooftop-terrace garden caffè with a stage-front-and-center view of St. Peter's Basilica is one reason guests book their stay here, while others include close proximity to the Vatican, top-notch service, and superb shopping all at your fingertips. **Pros:** close to St. Peter's; impressive view from the restaurant and some of the rooms; Internet points throughout the hotel. **Cons:** some rooms are nicer than others; the area can feel a bit residential. [$] *Rooms from: €260* ✉ *Via Vitelleschi 34, Borgo* ☎ *06/6873233* 🌐 *www.atlantehotels.com* 🛏 *65 rooms, 10 suites* 🍴 *Breakfast* ✥ *1:D3.*

$$ HOTEL **Sant'Anna.** In the picturesque, medieval Borgo neighborhood in the shadow of St. Peter's, this fashionable small hotel has exceedingly stylish ample bedrooms with new wood-beam ceilings, designer fabrics, and comfy beds; the marvelously decorated and spacious attic rooms also have tiny terraces. **Pros:** Borgo Pio is a pedestrian-only zone during the day; beds are comfy; staff is eager-to-please. **Cons:** no bar or restaurant in the hotel; the neighborhood is dead at night. [$] *Rooms from: €130* ✉ *Borgo Pio 133, Borgo* ☎ *06/68801602* 🌐 *www.hotelsantanna.com* 🛏 *20 rooms* 🍴 *Breakfast* ✥ *1:C3.*

PRATI

$$ HOTEL **Amalia.** Convenient to St. Peter's, the Vatican, and Prati's Cola di Rienzo shopping district (and just a block from the Ottaviano stop of Metro line A), this small hotel is crisp and smart with spacious, clean rooms simply furnished, freshly painted, and accented with striped

bedspreads. **Pros:** good location for visiting the Vatican and for shopping; 24-hour turnaround on laundry services; large beds. **Cons:** breakfast is more sweet than savory; sometimes hot water in bathrooms runs out quickly; Wi-Fi is only free when you book the superior rooms. [$] *Rooms from: €140* ✉ *Via Germanico 66, Prati* ☎ *06/39723356* 🌐 *www.hotelamalia.com* 🛏 *33 rooms, 26 with bath, 1 suite* 🍴 *Breakfast* ✥ *1:C2.*

$$ HOTEL 🏨 **Gerber.** Across the river from Piazza del Popolo on a quiet side street in the Prati neighborhood, this intimate, unpretentious hotel offers genuinely friendly service, immaculately maintained facilities including a garden and sun terrace for breakfast or a relaxed moment, and simple rooms with pleasant, neutral-tone, modern furnishings. **Pros:** good value for your money; great service; comfortable beds and big bathrooms. **Cons:** elevator is tiny; some of the rooms are quite small; you'll probably need to take a taxi, bus, or Metro to the other sights around town. [$] *Rooms from: €150* ✉ *Via degli Scipioni 241, Prati* ☎ *06/3221001* 🌐 *www.hotelgerber.it* 🛏 *27 rooms* 🍴 *Breakfast* ✥ *1:E1.*

$$$ HOTEL 🏨 **Hotel Dei Mellini.** On the west bank of the Tiber between the Spanish Steps and St. Peter's Basilica (a three-minute stroll from Piazza del Popolo), this place has style to match its setting: antique prints and fresh flowers give warmth to the light-filled reception rooms, while grand drapes, wood-grain headboards, marble-top sinks, elegant chairs, and framed photos in the sleek and sumptuous guest rooms make for a luxurious stay. **Pros:** spacious and spotless rooms; turndown service; the neighborhood is quiet, so you'll get a good night's rest. **Cons:** if you want to be near the action, this is not the place for you; not a lot of dining options in the immediate vicinity; restaurant in the hotel is used primarily for breakfast and serves light sandwiches upon request. [$] *Rooms from: €280* ✉ *Via Muzio Clementi 81, Prati* ☎ *06/324771* 🌐 *www.hotelmellini.com* 🛏 *80 rooms* 🍴 *Breakfast* ✥ *1:F2.*

$ HOTEL Fodor's Choice ★ 🏨 **Hotel San Pietrino.** The San Pietrino is one secret we just can't keep to ourselves: a cute, simple hotel on the third floor of a 19th-century palazzo a five-minute walk from the Vatican that continues to offer rock-bottom prices even in tough economic times. **Pros:** heavenly prices near the Vatican; TVs with DVD players; high-speed Internet; close to Rome's famous farmers' market, Mercato Trionfale. **Cons:** a couple of Metro stops away from the center of Rome; no breakfast; no bar. [$] *Rooms from: €100* ✉ *Via Giovanni Bettolo 43, Prati* ☎ *06/3700132* 🌐 *www.sanpietrino.it* 🛏 *12 rooms* 🍴 *No meals* ✥ *1:C1.*

TRASTEVERE AND GIANICOLO

With its village-like charm, Trastevere is considered the most characteristic neighborhood in all of Rome, where everyone wants to eat, play, and stay. This former working-class neighborhood, which once hosted artists and artisans, is now the home base of many of Rome's expats and exchange students. Hotels, squeezed into the neighborhood's former denizens' very modest buildings, tend toward the budget pension, although a few midrange hotels set in stylishly converted convents have sprung up in the last few years.

TRASTEVERE

$ HOTEL **Carmel.** Across the Tiber from the main synagogue, Rome's only kosher hotel has back-to-basics furnishings in simple rooms, a very friendly staff, and a charming vine-covered terrace, as well as two kitchens for use by guests keeping kosher (prepared kosher meals can also be arranged). **Pros:** good budget choice; kosher-friendly; short walk to Jewish Ghetto; free Wi-Fi. **Cons:** pay in cash upon check-in; no breakfast served on Sundays; no-frills accommodations; reception closed after 8 pm. [$] *Rooms from: €100* ✉ *Via Goffredo Mameli 11, Trastevere* ☎ *06/5809921* 🌐 *www.hotelcarmel.it* 🛏 *10 rooms, 8 with bath, 1 suite* 💳 *No credit cards* 🍴 *Breakfast* ✥ *3:B2.*

$$ HOTEL Fodor's Choice ★ **Casa di Santa Francesca Romana.** In the heart of Trastevere but tucked away from the hustle and bustle of the medieval quarter, this simply delightful hotel in a former monastery is centered on an impressive ochre-colored courtyard, lined with potted trees and tables, and though there isn't much on the amenities front aside from a TV-room and a reading room and the guest rooms are standard-issue, for the money this is a fabulous location and spectacular buy. **Pros:** the price can't be beat; excellent restaurants nearby; breakfast is delicious; quiet and great location; away from rowdy side of Trastevere. **Cons:** thin walls; decor is a bit bland. [$] *Rooms from: €130* ✉ *Via dei Vasceillari 61, Trastevere* ☎ *06/5812125* 🌐 *www.sfromana.it* 🛏 *36 rooms, 1 suite* 🍴 *Breakfast* ✥ *3:C2.*

$ HOTEL **Cisterna.** On a quiet street in the very heart of medieval Trastevere, this basic but comfortable hotel is ideally located for getting to know Rome's most authentic neighborhood, a favorite of artists and bohemians for decades. **Pros:** simple accommodations for budget travelers; friendly staff; good location in trendy Trastevere. **Cons:** hotel decor does not match the trendiness of the neighborhood; street-side rooms are noisy; the block is popular for just hanging out. [$] *Rooms from: €100* ✉ *Via della Cisterna 7–8–9, Trastevere* ☎ *06/5817212* 🌐 *www.cisternahotel.it* 🛏 *20 rooms* 🍴 *Breakfast* ✥ *2:B1.*

$$$ HOTEL Fodor's Choice ★ **Hotel Santa Maria.** A Trastevere treasure with a pedigree going back four centuries, this ivy-covered, mansard-roofed, rosy-brick-red, erstwhile Renaissance-era convent—just steps away from the glorious Santa Maria in Trastevere church and a few blocks from the Tiber—has sweet and simple guest rooms: a mix of brick walls, "cotto" tile floors, modern oak furniture, and stylishly floral bedspreads and curtains. **Pros:** a quaint and pretty oasis in a central location; relaxing courtyard; stocked wine bar. **Cons:** it might be tricky to find; some of the showers drain slowly; it's not always easy finding a cab in Trastevere. [$] *Rooms from: €220* ✉ *Vicolo del Piede 2, Trastevere* ☎ *06/5894626* 🌐 *www.htlsantamaria.com* 🛏 *18 rooms, 2 suites* 🍴 *Breakfast* ✥ *3:B1.*

$ HOTEL **Hotel Trastevere.** This tiny hotel captures the villagelike charm of the Trastevere district: the entrance hall features a mural of the famous Piazza di Santa Maria, a few blocks away, and hand-painted Art Nouveau wall designs add a touch of graciousness throughout, while open medieval brickwork and a few antiques scattered about complete the mood. **Pros:** cheap with a good location; convenient to transportation; free Wi-Fi; friendly staff. **Cons:** no frills; few amenities. [$] *Rooms from:*

€105 ✉ *Via Luciano Manara 24–25, Trastevere* ☏ *06/5814713* ⊕ *www. hoteltrastevere.net* ⤳ *20 rooms, 3 apartments* ⦿ *Breakfast* ✛ *3:B2.*

$$$
B&B/INN
Fodor's Choice
★

🛏 **Relais Le Clarisse.** Set within the former cloister grounds of the Santa Chiara order, with gardens so beautiful you'll think you were in Sorrento or Capri, Le Clarisse makes travelers feel more like personal guests at a friend's villa rather than at a hotel, thanks to the comfortable size of the accommodations and the personal touches and service extended by the staff. **Pros:** spacious rooms with comfy beds; high-tech showers/ tubs with good water pressure; staff is multilingual, friendly, and at your service. **Cons:** this part of Trastevere can be noisy at night; the rooms here fill up quickly; they only serve American coffee. Ⓢ *Rooms from: €220* ✉ *Via Cardinale Merry del Val 20, Trastevere* ☏ *06/58334437* ⊕ *www.leclarisse.com* ⤳ *5 rooms, 3 suites* ⦿ *Breakfast* ✛ *3:B2.*

13

AVENTINO, TESTACCIO, AND PALATINO

Leafy residential streets, quiet nights, and fresh hilltop breezes are some of the perks of staying in this well-heeled (and relatively unhistoric) neighborhood. Hotels take full advantage of the extra space and the sylvan setting, most with gardens or courtyards where you can enjoy alfresco R & R far from the madding crowds. Bear in mind that public transportation is somewhat limited up here, and allow at least a half hour by foot to major sights. Testaccio, however offers a bountiful surplus of great eateries and a buzzing nightlife for travelers looking for a bit more action after hours.

AVENTINO

$$$
HOTEL

🛏 **Domus Aventina.** The best part of this quaint, friendly hotel is that it's situated between two of Rome's loveliest gardens—a municipal rose garden and Rome's famous Orange Garden, where you might catch a glimpse of brides and grooms taking their wedding pictures—in the heart of the historic Aventine district not far from the Temple to Mithras and the House of Aquila and Priscilla (where St. Peter touched down). **Pros:** quiet location; walking distance to tourist attractions; complimentary Wi-Fi in rooms and public spaces. **Cons:** no elevator in the hotel; small showers; no tubs. Ⓢ *Rooms from: €205* ✉ *Via di Santa Prisca 11/b, Aventino* ☏ *06/5746135* ⊕ *www.domus-aventina.com* ⤳ *26 rooms* ⦿ *Breakfast* ✛ *3:E3.*

$$$
HOTEL

🛏 **Hotel San Anselmo.** Completely refurbished in 2006 and given a sleek metropolitan feel, this 19th-century villa blends bits of Baroque antique-flair (such as period chandeliers) with contemporary pieces (such as the sharp stainless steel fireplace in the public spaces), all within a molto charming garden, where birdsong adds to the charm of this already romantic retreat, set far from the bustle of the city center atop the Aventine Hill. **Pros:** historic building with artful decor; great showers with jets; a garden where you can enjoy your breakfast. **Cons:** some consider it a bit of a hike to sights; limited public transportation; the wireless is pricey. Ⓢ *Rooms from: €210* ✉ *Piazza San Anselmo 2, Aventino* ☏ *06/570057* ⊕ *www.aventinohotels.com* ⤳ *45 rooms* ⦿ *Breakfast* ✛ *3:D3.*

TESTACCIO

$ HOTEL 🏨 **Santa Prisca.** Off the beaten path and on the border of working-class Testaccio, this clean and comfortable hotel has been welcoming guests for more than 50 years, and though the exterior looks like nothing more than your average Roman apartment building, once inside you'll find that rooms are spacious, and if you're lucky you'll get one with a cute little balcony. **Pros:** near public transportation (trams and Metro); complimentary Wi-Fi; outside terrace with chairs and tables for relaxing; Internet point available for guests without computers. **Cons:** some say the breakfast is mediocre; the school next door can be a little noisy on weekdays. [$] *Rooms from: €120* ✉ *Largo M. Gelsomini 25, Testaccio* ☎ *06/5741917* 🌐 *www.hotelsantaprisca.it* 🛏 *49 rooms, 2 suites* 🍴 *Breakfast* ✥ *3:D4.*

COLOSSEO AREA

When Nero fiddled, this neighborhood burned—the lowlands around the Colosseum and the Forum were the Suburra, the Imperial City's most notorious slum. There's nary a trace of evildoing now, and narrow alleys are quaint rather than sinister. This is a fine base for the sights of the ancient city, but area eating and drinking establishments can have a touch of the tourist trap. Waking up to views of the Forum, maybe you won't mind.

$$$$ HOTEL 🏨 **Capo d'Africa.** Many find the modern look and feel of Capo d'Africa—not to mention its plush beds and deep bathtubs—refreshing after a long day's journey through ancient Rome: each room is decorated in warm, muted tones with sleek furniture, stylish accents, and contemporary art. **Pros:** quiet, comfortable rooms; fitness center. **Cons:** despite proximity to Colosseum, there isn't a great view of it from the hotel; not a lot of restaurants in the immediate neighborhood. [$] *Rooms from: €320* ✉ *Via Capo d'Africa 54, Colosseo* ☎ *06/772801* 🌐 *www.hotelcapodafrica.com* 🛏 *64 rooms, 1 suite* 🍴 *Breakfast* ✥ *3:H2.*

$$$ HOTEL 🏨 **Celio.** There's much more to brag about than the Colosseum when it comes to the location of this chic boutique hotel—where the small guest rooms are sumptuously frescoed with "faux" paintings in styles ranging from Pompeiian to Renaissance and have French windows and elegant, marble-tiled bathrooms (some with Jacuzzis)—in the romantic Celian Hill setting; think of them as hidden treasures that are often overlooked by the masses looking to cross everything off their Must-See list: the haunting Santi Quattro Coronati church, the time-capsuled Piazza Santi Giovanni e Paolo, and the verdant slopes of the Villa Celimontana park, all just a stroll away. **Pros:** rooftop garden and gym; mosaic floors and over-the-top decor; comfortable beds. **Cons:** very small bathrooms; breakfast is nothing to brag about. [$] *Rooms from: €220* ✉ *Via dei Santissimi Quattro 35/c, Colosseo* ☎ *06/70495333* 🌐 *www.hotelcelio.com* 🛏 *20 rooms, 2 suites* 🍴 *Breakfast* ✥ *3:G1.*

$$$ HOTEL 🏨 **Duca d'Alba.** In Italy, it's all about the *bella figura* (making a good impression), so when you step into this lovely little boutique hotel near the Colosseum, you'll know you've hit the jackpot: between the marble decor and reproductions of antiquated paintings, the Duca d'Alba

definitively tells the traveler that their stay will be a clean and comfortable one, and the hotel's attentive staff and reasonable rates make it a good value to boot. **Pros:** Ancient Rome is at your doorstep; great cappuccino for your morning pick-me-up; a fitness center with a treadmill and weights; near the Metro. **Cons:** rooms are a bit cramped; late-night revelers from the Irish pub across the way. $ *Rooms from: €220* ⊠ *Via Leonina 14, Colosseo* 🕾 *06/484471* ⊕ *www.hotelducadalba.com* 🗗 *27 rooms, 1 suite* ⍦ *Breakfast* ✛ *2:C5.*

$$$$ 🕾 **Hotel Forum.** A longtime favorite, this converted 18th-century convent
HOTEL has a truly unique setting on one side of the Fori Imperiali with a cinematic view of ancient Rome across the avenue (remember, you can also drink all this in at the rooftop bar/restaurant), while the hotel itself is comfortable though considerably less exciting: the decor is traditional in the extreme, with the requisite gold wall sconces, walnut paneling, red-velvet armchairs, and Asian carpets painting the run-of-the-mill hotel lobby picture. **Pros:** bird's-eye view of ancient Rome; "American" bar on the rooftop terrace. **Cons:** small rooms; noisy pub-crawlers congregate in the street below; food and drinks are expensive. $ *Rooms from: €320* ⊠ *Via Tor de' Conti 25–30, Foro Romano* 🕾 *06/6792446* ⊕ *www. hotelforumrome.com* 🗗 *80 rooms* ⍦ *Breakfast* ✛ *2:B5.*

$$ 🕾 **Hotel Lancelot.** This home away from home in a quiet residential area
HOTEL close to the Colosseum has been run by the same family since 1970
🕭 and is quite popular: its carefully and courteously attentive staff go the extra mile for their guests, and the clean and comfortable rooms tend to have big windows, so they're bright and airy, some have terraces or balconies as well, and they have air-conditioning, en suite bathrooms, TVs, and Wi-Fi. **Pros:** hospitable staff; secluded and quiet; very family-friendly; Wi-Fi included. **Cons:** some of the bathrooms are on the small side; no refrigerators in the rooms; thin walls mean you can sometimes hear your neighbors. $ *Rooms from: €190* ⊠ *Via Capo d'Africa 47, Colosseo* 🕾 *06/70450615* ⊕ *www.lancelothotel.com* 🗗 *60 rooms* ⍦ *Breakfast* ✛ *3:H1.*

$$ 🕾 **Nerva.** Step out of this charming hotel and you'll feel like you're
HOTEL literally in the middle of an ancient imperial stomping ground: strategically located a stone's throw from the Forum, it's surrounded by the breathtaking splendor of ancient ruins and relics, and the hotel itself is clean and well run, with air-conditioning, soundproofed rooms, and orthopedic beds. **Pros:** a stone's throw from the Forum; friendly staff; orthopedic beds; and a great pizzeria (La Base) nearby that's open into the wee hours. **Cons:** showers are tiny; a wall blocks what would otherwise be a fantastic view of Rome's ancient Forum. $ *Rooms from: €180* ⊠ *Via Tor de' Conti 3/4, Foro Romano* 🕾 *06/6781835* ⊕ *www. hotelnerva.com* 🗗 *19 rooms* ⍦ *Breakfast* ✛ *2:B5.*

BEYOND THE CITY CENTER

$$$ 🕾 **Lord Byron.** In the '90s this was a favorite among money movers and
HOTEL shakers, top businesspeople, and yacht brokers, and today, the Art Deco retreat upholds its chicness—it was Rome's first boutique hotel and still retains much of that jewel-like charm inside, where the design is marble meets modern—while serving up a presidential clientele: surrounded by

the twittering of birds in the posh and pricey Parioli district, the Lord Byron feels like a small country hotel, or better, a small country manor where you are the lord. **Pros:** luxury bathrobes and slippers; friendly and helpful staff; free shuttle to some of the major tourist attractions. **Cons:** too far to walk to sights; not many caffè and shops in the area; cabs between the hotel and centro are expensive. ⓢ *Rooms from: €290* ✉ *Via Giuseppe de Notaris 5, Parioli* ☎ *06/3220404* ⊕ *www. lordbyronhotel.com* ⤳ *23 rooms, 9 suites* ⏐⚬⏐ *Breakfast* ✛ *2:A1.*

$$$$
RESORT

🌂 **Rome Cavalieri.** Though the Cavalieri is outside the city center, distance has its advantages, one of them being the magnificent view over Rome (ask for a room facing the city), and another—that elusive element of more central Roman hotels—space: occupying a vast area atop modern Rome's highest hill, this oasis of good taste often feels more like a ritzy resort than a city hotel, with a terraced garden that spreads out from an Olympic-size pool, a smart poolside restaurant and caffè, and legions of white-clothed cushioned lounge chairs scattered throughout the greenery. **Pros:** beautiful bird's-eye view of Rome; shuttle to the city center; three-Michelin-star dining. **Cons:** you definitely pay for the luxury of staying here—everything is expensive; outside the city center; not all rooms have the view. ⓢ *Rooms from: €500* ✉ *Via Cadlolo 101, Monte Mario* ☎ *06/35091* ⊕ *www.romecavalieri.com* ⤳ *357 rooms, 17 suites* ⏐⚬⏐ *Breakfast* ✛ *1:A1.*

Nightlife and the Arts

WORD OF MOUTH

"Take advantage of the Italian tradition of the Passeggiata (evening stroll). Visit the sites in the historical center, particularly Piazza
Navona. There you'll see world-famous fountains, and the people-
watching can't be beat. And in summer, outdoor concerts spring
up everywhere."

—Vicki

By Erica Firpo   Whether it's a romantic rooftop drink, dinner in a boisterous restaurant, or dancing into the wee hours, Roman nightlife has always been a scene set for a movie. Director Federico Fellini immortalized nocturnal Rome in his many films about life in the Eternal City. *Satyricon* showcased Lucullan all-night banquets (and some more naughty entertainments) of the days of the emperors, while *La Dolce Vita* flaunted night-clubs and *paparazzi* of the city's Hollywood-on-the-Tiber era. And as the director lovingly showed in *Fellini's Roma*, the city's streets and piazzas offered the best place for par-ties and alfresco dinners. Many visitors would agree with Fellini: Rome, the city, is entertainment enough.

The city's piazzas, fountains, and delicately colored palazzos make impressive backdrops for Rome's living theater. And Rome is a flirt, taking advantage of its spectacular cityscape, transforming ancient, Renaissance, and contemporary monuments into settings for the per-forming arts, whether outdoors in summer or in splendid palaces and churches in winter. Held at locations such as Villa Celimontana, Teatro dell'Opera, the Baths of Caracalla, or the church of Sant'Ignazio, the venue often steals the show.

Of all the performing arts, music is what Rome does best to entertain people, whether it be opera or jazz or disco. The cinema is also a big draw, particularly for Italian-language speakers, and there's a fantastic array of other options. Toast the sunset with prosecco while overlooking a 1st-century temple. Enjoy an evening reading in the Roman Forum or a live performance of Shakespeare in the Globe theater in the Villa Bor-ghese park. Top off the night in your choice of Rome's many bars and *discoteches*. When all else fails, there's always late-night caffè-sitting, watching the colorful crowds parade by on a gorgeous piazza—it's great fun, even if you don't speak the language. Little wonder Rome inspired Fellini to make people-watching into an art form in his famous films.

PLANNING

HOW DO I FIND OUT WHAT'S GOING ON THIS WEEK?

With its foot firmly in the 21st century, Rome has a pantheon of publications heralding its cultural events. For city-sponsored events, Rome's official website ⊕ *www.comune.roma.it* tries to remain as au courant as any governmental entity can. A broader range of event listings can be found in the *Cronaca* and *Cultura* section of Italian newspapers, as well as in *Metro*, the free newspaper found at Metro stops and on trams.

On the Web, check out ⊕ *inromenow.com*, an events site written exclusively for the English-speaking community, along with expat favorite *The American* (⊕ *www.theamericanmag.com*). Their Italian-language counterpart Roma 2night (⊕ *roma.2night.it*) has an even more robust selection of nightlife, along with food spots. Rome's top cultural, news, and events websites, *06blog* (⊕ *www.06blog.it*) and *RomaToday* (⊕ *www.romatoday.it*), add postings practically hourly. The monthly English-language periodical (with accompanying website) *Wanted in Rome* (⊕ *www.wantedinrome.com*) is available at many newsstands and has good coverage of arts events.

WHEN TO GO?

Discoteche open after 10 pm, but punctuality isn't important. The scene doesn't heat up until later in the evening so never arrive before midnight.

For early evening outings, *enoteche* aperitivi hour, from 6:30 to 9 pm, is the quintessential scene of Roman life where Italians and non-Italians mix together for wine tasting and cocktails.

FEES AND TICKETS

Most clubs charge a cover charge, between €10 and €20, which often includes the first drink.

Depending on the venue, concert tickets can cost between €7 and €50, and as much as several hundred euro for an exclusive, sold-out event.

Often, you can find seating that is unreserved (identified in Italian as *posti non numerati*), or even last-minute tickets. Inquire about this option when ticket shopping; you may have to arrive early to get a good seat.

Procure opera and concert tickets in advance at the box office, or just before the performance.

TicketOne. For blockbuster cultural performances, rock concerts, and sporting events, TicketOne is the major online ticket vendor. ⊕ *www. ticketone.it*.

Hello Ticket. One of Italy's largest ticket vendors (both online and at ticket offices), Hello Ticket covers major musical performances and cultural events in Rome and throughout Italy. ✉ *Viale Alessandro Manzoni 53, San Giovanni* ☎ *06/48078202* ⊕ *www.helloticket.it*.

14

Ticketeria. Ticketeria, the go-to spot for all cultural event listings and the many *punta di vendita* (ticket sellers) in Rome, facilitates online reservations and purchasing. ⊕ *www.ticketeria.it.*

Orbis. An in-person ticket vendor, Orbis stocks a wide array of tickets for music, cultural, and performance events. ⊠ *Piazza dell'Esquilino 37, Repubblica* ☎ *06/4827403.*

THE ARTS

Since the start of the new millennium, Rome has been experiencing a cultural renaissance. In the past, Rome based its value on its vast historical buildings and Renaissance and baroque art, but with the help of international architecture competitions, contemporary art initiatives, and the Internet, the city is embracing the future. Enhanced by new buildings, such as the Auditorium, the MAXXI, MACRO, Museum of the Imperial Forums, and Ara Pacis, Rome has never before looked so good, juxtaposing the classic with the contemporary.

DANCE

Rome is well known for the strength of its visual arts; and though in classical and modern dance the city plays understudy to Milan, Bologna, Florence, and even Cremona, dance is flourishing in Rome. The Auditorium's dance programming has increased to include more performances, many of which showcase international performers. The annual avant-garde RomaEuropa Festival continues to host its fall event, and has extended RomaEuropa with performances throughout the year.

FILM

Andiamo al cinema! Rome has dozens of movie houses, where you'll find both blockbuster and art house films. All films, unless noted "V.O." in the listing, which means *versione originale* (original version or original language), are shown in Italian.

For show times, see the entertainment pages of daily newspapers, *roma c'è,* or Rome's English-language publications. Check out ⊕ *www.inromenow.com* for the most up-to-date reviews of all English-language films or visit ⊕ *www.mymovies.it* or ⊕ *www.cinemadel silenzio.it* for a list of current features and theaters. Tickets range in price from €4.50 for matinees and some weekdays, up to €10 for weekend evenings.

DON'T SEARCH FOR SUBTITLES

Most international films are dubbed in Italian, *grazie a Mussolini,* who insisted on this approach in order to instill pride in the native language. Dubbing has since become an art form—voice-over actors receive recognition and awards, and consistently dub their silver screen counterparts. Unless stated otherwise, non-Italian films are not viewed in the original language.

GALLERIES

Cappuccinos and Carvaggio, and bellinis and Bernini may be what come to mind when you dream of Rome—but provocative contemporary art? Not so much. Remember, Rome is never predictable, and right now, the city is setting ground as the center for contemporary art in southern Europe, with Rome's churches, palazzos, and ancient sites making unique backdrops for contemporary art exhibitions. Rome also has two of Italy's newest contemporary art museums: MAXXI and MACRO. The city's traditional exhibition spaces have joined in and are hosting modern exhibits as well as classical, Renaissance, and baroque shows. Up-to-date exhibition lists can best be found at ⊕ *www. exibart.com.*

Completing the modern and contemporary art scene are the cultural branches of international embassies that have been actively promoting their country's artists with monthly and seasonal shows.

14

MUSIC

CLASSICAL

Since 2002 Rome finally has had its very own state-of-the art auditorium a 10-minute tram ride north of Piazza del Popolo—the Parco della Musica (or Music Park), splashed over the pages of glossy magazines everywhere. However, if you prefer smaller or quirkier venues, Rome does not disappoint. Classical music concerts take place at numerous places throughout the city, and you're likely to see memorable performances in smaller halls and churches, often for free. This is true particularly at Christmas and Easter, especially busy concert seasons in Rome. Some churches that frequently host concerts are Sant'Ivo alla Sapienza, San Francesco a Ripa, and San Paolo entro le Mura. But one of the charming things about Rome is that, with all the little side streets tucked behind quiet piazzas, not to mention the nearly 1,000 churches throughout the Eternal City, it's quite easy to stumble upon a choir rehearsing, or a chorus performing for just a few churchgoers. Sometimes all it takes is some wandering around, and serendipitous luck, to trip over a memorable concert experience.

ROCK, POP, AND JAZZ

Local and smaller-act rock, pop, and jazz concerts are frequent in Rome, although big-name acts come through less frequently—almost exclusively during warmer weather, although even these performances may not be well advertised. Some locales are outside the city center, and sometimes as far as Tivoli, so

> **HALLOWED SOUNDS**
>
> Throughout the year, churches such as Sant'Ivo alla Sapienza, San Francesco a Ripa, and San Paolo entro le Mura have afternoon and evening performances. Look for posters outside churches announcing free concerts, particularly at Sant'Ignazio (✉ Piazza Sant'Ignazio, Pantheon ☎ 06/6794560 ⊕ *www. amicimusicasacra.com*), which hosts concerts in a spectacular setting. Or try the summertime concerts at the ancient Theatre of Marcello (✉ *Via del Teatro Marcello, Ghetto* ☎ *06/488991*).

The City of Eternal Festivals

The City of Eternal Festivals, Rome has gone from "provincial" to "provocative" thanks in large part to its bevy of internationally recognized festivals. In the fall and spring especially, you'll see the best of local and international talent in some of the most beautiful venues in the city.

ART AND DESIGN

RomaContemporary. An annual contemporary art fair where Rome- and Italy-based gallerists and their international colleagues showcase artists, RomaContemporary was created to put Rome on the fair circuit with Basel, Miami, and London. The three-day event is held in late spring, usually May, at MACRO Testaccio (contemporary art center). ⊕ *www. romacontemporary.it.*

RomaEuropa. For three to six weeks in early fall, RomaEuropa is a collective and multivenue avant-garde performing and visual arts program showcasing international artists, installations, film, and performance. ⊕ *www.romaeuropa.net.*

FILM

Da Venezia a Roma Festival. Immediately following the finale of the Venice Film Festival in September, Da Venezia a Roma brings the award-nominated films to Rome for a two-week review. Widely distributed films and art house specials like *Melancholia* make fleeting screen appearances months before international release in Italy. Films are shown in original language with Italian subtitles when necessary. The festival has grown to include lectures and appearances by directors, producers and actors. Check out the local press or the website for more details. ⊕ *www.agisanec.lazio.it/ venezia.html.*

Festival Internazionale del Film di Roma. In October, cinephiles head to Rome for the International Festival of Film, designed to compete with Venice, London, Cannes, and New York. Two dedicated weeks see award-winning and art house films, blockbuster and experimental movies, shorts, celebrity sightings, technical lectures, and awards for best films and silver-screen icons both past and present.

Casa del Cinema. Dedicated to the art of the silver screen, Casa del Cinema is Rome's most modern projection house and film library. Located in Villa Borghese, Casa del Cinema is an oasis for film buffs with its multiple screening rooms and caffè and a resource center with DVD library and laptops for private viewings. Like its indoor counterpart, the outdoor projection screen shows both new and vintage films, sometimes in original languages, though only in the warm months. ⊠ *Largo Marcello Mastroianni 1, Villa Borghese* ☎ *06/423601* ⊕ *www.casadelcinema.it* ⊕ *www. romacinemafest.org.*

MUSIC

In spring and in some summer months, Rome stages fill with internationally recognized musicians of all genres.

Estate Romana. The city-sponsored Estate Romana (Roman Summer) is one of Rome's most anticipated summer series. Starting out as a bunch of low-budget concerts during June and July, Estate Romana now extends through September and draws an audience from all over the peninsula to see music acts and cultural events from around the world. Many events are free and take place outdoors, in and around the city.

Events include cinema, art programs, theater, book fairs, and guided tours of some of Rome's monuments by night. ⊕ *www.estateromana.comune. roma.it.*

Fiesta!. Just as the name suggests, Fiesta! is a huge party—a mega event of more than 4,000 hours of Latin and Caribbean music, jazz, and blues flowing through the Roman summer from mid-June through August. Fiesta! hosts stars of international stature, exhibits related to Latin American culture, and gastro-events with delectables from all over the world. ⊠ *Ippodromo delle Capannelle, Via Appia Nuova 1245, Appia* ☎ *06/66183792* ⊕ *www.fiesta.it.*

I Concerti nel Parco. For more than 10 years, Villa Doria Pamphilj has been organizing *I Concerti nel Parco*, a concert series under the stars and amid the greenery of Rome's largest park on the Janiculum Hill. Running from June through August, the concerts take place at sunset and last late into the evening, showcasing a variety of musical genres. *I Concerti nel Parco* has also added winter events including Christmas concerts to its programming. ⊠ *Piazza Porta di San Pancrazio, Monteverde* ⊕ *www. iconcertinelparco.it.*

Rock in Roma. June through August, the Ippodromo delle Capanelle is the heart of rock and roll with summer concert series Rock in Roma. Past headliners have included Lenny Kravitz, Radiohead, Subsonica, the Cure, and the Killers. ⊠ *Ippodromo delle Capannelle, Via Appia Nuova 1245, Appia* ☎ *06/45496350* ⊕ *www. rockinroma.com.*

Roma Incontra il Mondo. Considered one of Europe's most impressive world-music festivals for its consistently world-class headliners and its beautiful location in Villa Ada, Roma Incontra il Mondo is an evening concert series running from late June to early August. Concerts kick off at 10 pm and are followed by dancing until 2 am. Stands sell handmade goods and ethnic cuisine from around the world. ⊠ *Laghetto di Villa Ada, Parioli* ⊕ *www.villaada.org.*

Villa Celimontana Jazz Festival. From mid-June to early September, the longest-running jazz festival in Europe showcases the broad scope of jazz from contemporary electronic and acid to earlier, more classic styles in a romantic outdoor setting on the the lawns of the restored baroque Villa Celimontana, just behind the Colosseum. ⊠ *Piazza della Navicella, San Giovanni* ☎ *06/5897807* ⊕ *www. villacelimontanajazz.com.*

Il Tempietto. With the the 1st-century Teatro di Marcello as sumptious backdrop, the Tempietto concert series, featuring classical favorites as well as tango, is beautiful evening relaxation in the hot summer season. ⊠ *Teatro di Marcello, Via Teatro di Marcello, Ghetto* ☎ *06/87131590* ⊕ *www. tempietto.it.*

14

it's worth asking about transportation before you buy your tickets. The Estate Romana (Roman Summer) program, organized by the local and regional governments, has been growing every year. The program now includes a diverse offering of well-publicized and well-organized cultural events, most set outdoors and all free or reasonably priced.

Events spread from the center of town to the periphery and run from early June to early September. They include music of every sort, as well as outdoor cinema, theater, and other events, such as book fairs and guided tours of some of Rome's monuments by night. The city administration has really made the push for important music acts to give free concerts, and the crowds at these gigs prove that music is, in fact, an international language. James Taylor gave a heartfelt free performance in lovely Piazza del Popolo, and record crowds once filled the Via dei Fori Imperiali, from Piazza Venezia down to the stage in front of a brightly lighted Colosseum, for free concerts by no less than Paul McCartney and Simon & Garfunkel, respectively.

OPERA

Opera buffs know that the best performances and most exquisite surroundings for opera are to be found at Milan's La Scala, Venice's newly reconstructed La Fenice, and at Verona's Arena (outdoor amphitheater). But Rome is Italy's capital, and so although its opera company does not have the renown of the aforementioned landmarks, it has a healthy following. Rome's opera season runs from November or December to May, and then the summer welcomes open-air concerts, some set amid ancient Roman ruins.

THEATER

Famous Italian film director Federico Fellini's *La Dolce Vita* showed off Rome's nightclubs and paparazzi and introduced the Eternal City as Hollywood-on-the-Tiber. Though its cinematic dominance has diminished since the 1960s, Rome's film industry has undergone a small revival.

Home to Cinecittà—one of the world's largest film studios in one of the most delightful climates—Rome is often the choice location for international film productions, such as Woody Allen's *Nero Fiddled,* Wes Anderson's *Life Aquatic,* JJ Abrams' *Mission Impossible III,* Steven Soderbergh's *Ocean's Twelve,* and Martin Scorsese's *Gangs of New York,* not to mention the HBO/BBC Production's series *Rome.* What's more, the presence of so many actors in the city has also reinvigorated its theater productions.

NIGHTLIFE

E mo'facciamo un giro—(And now let's take a spin). . . To enjoy a night out in Rome, all you need are your feet (or a *motorino*) because you're bound to swing by an *enoteca*—those classic wine bars, which abound in all parts of the city and rarely disappoint. But finding great nightlife is not quite as easy as a walk around the block. Although Rome offers

Opera Alfresco

Opera buffs know that the best performances and most exquisite surroundings for opera are to be found at Milan's La Scala, Venice's newly reconstructed La Fenice, and at Verona's Arena (outdoor amphitheater). But Rome is Italy's capital, and so although its opera company does not have the renown of the aforementioned landmarks, it has a healthy following. Rome's opera season runs from November or December to May, summertime exodus of many of the city's pubs, restaurants, and discos to outdoor venues, opera heads outside for its summer season. Rome's many opera companies commandeer church courtyards, ancient villas, and soccer *campi* (fields) with performances that range from mom-and-poperas to full-scale, large-budget extravaganzas. Quality is generally quite high, even for smaller, low-budget productions. Tickets cost €15 to €40. To find these productions, listen closely or look for the old-fashioned posters advertising classic operas like *Tosca* and *La Traviata*. The weekly *roma c'e*, the monthly *Wanted in Rome*, and the website ⊕ www.inromenow.com also have complete lists of performances.

a cornucopia of evening bacchanalia, from ultrachic to super cheap, all that glitters is not gold. Insiders and visitors alike understand that finding "the scene" in Rome is the proverbial needle in the haystack: it requires patience and pursuit. Word-of-mouth may be the best source, but also look to the entertainment guides like *roma c'è* and ⊕ *www. roma.tonight.eu. Trovaroma* provides up-to-date listings of bars and clubs. Most visitors prefer to head out to one of three locations: between Piazza Navona and the Pantheon; the Campo de' Fiori and Trastevere; or Testaccio. (The Spanish Steps neighborhood is a ghost town by 9 pm.) Remember, Romans love an after-party—after dinner, of course— so plenty of nightlife doesn't start until midnight.

BARS

Leading off the bar scene is the *enoteca*, found (often with outdoor seating) in just about every piazza and on side streets throughout the city. These establishments are mostly small, and offer a smattering of antipasti to accompany a variety of wines and bubblies.

If you're looking for a beer and some telly, peppered around the city are stereotypical English and Irish pubs, complete with a steady stream of Guinness, darts, and footie and rugby on their satellite, flat-screen televisions. Lately, these pubs show American football, baseball, and basketball—ideal for those who don't want to miss a playoff or Super Bowl game.

Last on the list but perhaps the most impressive is the swanky lounge or hotel bar, preferably outdoors and perched on rooftops. These expensive bars have modern designs and creative cocktail lists that would compete with the posh bars of any major metropolis, and everyone dresses to impress.

AUDITORIUM PARCO DELLA MUSICA

✉ *Viale Pietro de Coubertin 30, Flaminia* ☎ *06/80241, 06/6880144 information and tickets* ⊕ *www.auditorium. com.*

TIPS

■ To get to the Auditorium from Rome's Termini train station, take Bus No. 910, which stops directly in front of the complex at Viale Pietro de Coubertin. If you're coming from the city center, walk to Piazzale Flaminio (the other side of Piazza del Popolo) and hop on Tram No. 2 for six stops. Using the Metro, take Line A to Flaminio, and above ground to Tram No. 2, again six stops. Access the Auditorium's underground parking using Viale Maresciallo Pilsudski and Via Giulio Gaudini.

■ To book guided tours, email: visiteguidate@musicaperroma. it. Keep in mind that a summertime visit means outdoor concerts and festivals.

Rome grabbed a front-row seat on the world music scene in 2002 thanks to the futuristic, Renzo Piano–designed Auditorium. Also known as the Parco della Musica, the auditorium is in fact a complex of three enormous pod-shaped concert halls. These halls have become familiar friends of musical greats from Luciano Pavarotti and Philip Glass to Tracy Chapman and Burt Bacharach. The not-just-music programming including specialized festivals, *caffè*, restaurants, a bookstore, outdoor amphitheater, winter skating rink, archaeological site, and children's playground realizes Piano's dream of the space as a "cultural factory."

The Auditorium is in the Flaminio/Villaggio Olimpico neighborhood, 10 minutes from the city center.

Likened to anything from beetles to computer "mice," the musical pods are consistently jammed with people: the Sala Santa Cecilia is a massive hall for grand orchestra and choral concerts; the Sala Sinopoli is more intimately scaled for smaller troupes; and the Sala Petrassi was designed for alternative events. All three are arrayed around the "Cavea," the vast Greco-Roman–style amphitheater. On any given day you might chance upon the Orchestra dell'Accademia di Santa Cecilia in the big hall, the Parco della Musica Jazz Orchestra in Sinopoli, and Peter Gabriel giving a rock "chamber event" in Petrassi. But the calendar here is not just confined to music: Rome's hot new film festival (www. romacinemafest.org) is held during the second half of October, while other festivals—math, science, and philosophy—highlight the spring.

DISCOS AND NIGHTCLUBS

When it comes to clubs, discos, and DJs in Rome, you have two choices: Testaccio—considered mecca for clubs, discotheques, and bars, and perhaps your best choice for disco roulette—and everywhere else, since *discoteche* can be found in any Rome neighborhood. On average, drinks range between €10 and €15, and one is often included with the entrance (€10–€20). In June, July, and August, many clubs relocate to the beach or the Tiber, so call ahead to confirm location and hours. Then there is Via Galvani. Rome's equivalent of the Sunset Strip, this is where hybrid restaurant-clubs largely identical in music and crowd battle for top ranking. People-watchers rejoice: evenings here are a delight, with crowds ranging from romantic twosomes to post-teen "Beliebers" to savant Cassanovas of all ages.

LISTINGS BY NEIGHBORHOOD

BARBERINI

GALLERIES

Gagosian Gallery. Rome is one of the more recent additions to Larry Gagosian's art constellation, an international series of galleries in locations such as New York, Los Angeles, and London. Located in a 19th-century former bank, the gorgeous oval-shaped gallery hosts blockbuster exhibitions every two to three months. Superstars showcased include Damien Hirst, Cy Twombly, and Francesco Vezzoli. ⊠ *Via Francesco Crispi 16* ☎ *06/42086498* ⊕ *www.gagosian.com.*

CAMPO DE' FIORI

BARS

★ **Il Goccetto.** A picturesque wine bar with a fabulous selection of beverages, Il Goccetto specializes in wines from smaller vineyards from Sicily to Venice. Its carefully chosen selection of Italian delicacies (meats and cheeses) represents the entire Italian peninsula. Though primarily an indoor venue, Il Gocetto is a popular meeting place where patrons often overflow into the street. ⊠ *Via dei Banchi Vecchi 14* ☎ *06/6864268* ⊕ *ilgoccetto.com.*

★ **L'Angolo Divino.** Hidden on a back alley, this quiet *enoteca* with wood-paneled walls showing off more than 700 bottles of wine (over 1,000 labels overall), delicious homemade pastas, and local antipasti offers a nice respite from the chaotic, adjacent Campo de' Fiori. ⊠ *Via dei Balestrari 12* ☎ *06/6864413.*

Roof Top Lounge Bar at the St. George Hotel. The latest front-runner in Rome's ever-growing list of rooftop sweet spots has a delicious oyster selection headlining its seafood-based menu and a dizzying drink selection that includes cocktails, beer, and many rosés—from pink champagnes to Italian *rosati*. The St. George's Wine Bar and Cigar Room make an excellent substitute in the non-summer months when the rooftop is closed. ⊠ *Via Giulia 62* ☎ *06/686611* ⊕ *www.stgeorgehotel.it.*

Vineria Reggio. The quintessential Roman wine bar, at the Vineria the first focus is whetting one's whistle and the last is style. The crowd ranges from grandfathers to glitterati. ⊠ *Campo de' Fiori 15* ☎ *06/68803268.*

CONCERTS

★ **Oratorio del Gonfalone.** A small concert hall with an internationally recognized music series of baroque classics, the Oratorio del Gonfalone has highly decorated walls of beautiful mannerist frescoes representing the very best of the mid-16th century. ⊠ *Via del Gonfalone 32/a* ☎ *06/6875952* ⊕ *www.oratoriogonfalone.com.*

THEATER

★ **Teatro Argentina.** The opulence of Rome's beautiful turn-of-the-century theater—burgundy velvet upholstery and large crystal chandeliers—evokes belle epoque glamour. Most productions are in Italian; however, it occasionally showcases some dance performances, which don't require subtitles. ⊠ *Largo di Torre Argentina 52* ☎ *06/68400015* ⊕ *www.teatrodiroma.net.*

IT TAKES A VILLAGE

At the end of May, Roman residents look forward to the cleverly publicized **Gay Village** (⊕ *www. gayvillage.it*), an outdoor megaparty held in a different location each summer from June through August. Along with bars and clubs, the highly sponsored event has international guest stars including DJs and performance artists.

14

CORSO

BARS

★ **Antica Birreria Peroni.** For beer lovers, the art nouveau–style halls of Antica Birreria Peroni will enchant you with their turn-of-the-century atmosphere, not to mention the always-flowing taps. Expect filling canteen-style meals and big steins, with several taps featuring Peroni favorites. Best place for hot dogs in Rome, though presentation may be a bit tasteless. ⊠ *Via di San Marcello 19* ☎ *06/6795310* ⊕ *www. anticabirreriaperoni.net.*

ESQUILINO

BARS

Fiddler's Elbow. Proud of its status as the oldest Irish pub in Rome, Fiddler's Elbow maintains a scruffy appearance in contrast to the fancy pub usurpers that have opened all over town. Singing is encouraged. ⊠ *Via dell'Olmata 43, Esquilino* ☎ *06/4872110* ⊕ *www.thefiddlerselbow. com.*

NIGHTCLUBS

★ **Micca Club.** In a former warehouse, this multi-genre performance venue has DJs spinning in its many rooms and live music that might include anything from swing and easy listening to burlesque and hip-hop. ⊠ *Via Pietro Micca 7a, Termini* ☎ *06/87440079* ⊕ *www.miccaclub.com.*

FLAMINIO

CONCERTS/THEATER

Accademia di Santa Cecilia. The Accademia di Santa Cecilia is part of Rome's amazing and well-versed musical circuit with a program of performances from classical to contemporary and a lineup of world-renowned artists. The futurist Auditorium Parco della Musica hosts Santa Cecilia's concerts. ⇨ *Auditorium Parco della Musica.*

Teatro Eliseo. Hosting musical performances and the work of historical and contemporary playwrights throughout the year, Teatro Eliseo also offers innovative programming for children, including English-language programs. ⊠ *Via Nazionale 183, Repubblica* ☎ *06/488721, 06/48872222* ⊕ *www.teatroeliseo.it* ⊠ *Concert hall and box office, Via Pietro de Coubertin 34* ☎ *06/8082058* ⊕ *www.santacecilia.it.*

Accademia Filarmonica Romana. Nearly two centuries old, the Accademia Filarmonica Romana is one of Rome's historic concert venues featuring classical music. The garden hosts occasional outdoor performances. ⊠ *Via Flaminia 118, Flaminia* ☎ *06/3201752* ⊕ *www. filarmonicaromana.org.*

Fodor's Choice ★ **Auditorium Parco della Musica.** Designed by famous architect Renzo Piano, the Auditorium Parco della Musica is *the* place to perform in Rome. The amazing space features three halls with nearly perfect acoustics, and a large courtyard for outdoor classical, jazz, and pop concerts. In addition, it hosts dance troupes and cultural festivals. The venue is a 10-minute tram ride north of Piazza del Popolo. ⇨ *See the special spotlight "Auditorium Parco della Musica."* ⊠ *Viale Pietro de Coubertin 30* ☎ *06/80241, 06/68801044 information and tickets* ⊕ *www. auditorium.com.*

CULTURAL INSTITUTIONS

Galleria Nazionale di Arte Moderna e Contemporanea. With new renovations, a strong permanent collection and invigorating curatorial programming, Galleria Nazionale di Arte Moderna e Contemporanea (GNAM) is presenting itself as a prominent force on Italy's art scene. The collection includes modern Italian masters from the noted Macchiaioli and Futurists like Severini and Balla to Transavanguardia, Arte Povera, and contemporary with Fontana, Manzoni, Chia, and Clemente. ■TIP➜ Make sure to mix coffee and culture at the art nouveau Caffè delle Arti in the columned alcove of the museum. ⊠ *Viale Belle Arti 131* ☎ *06/322981* ⊕ *www. gnam.beniculturali.it.*

SUMMER LOVIN'

From June through August, many of Rome's bars and clubs shut down to avoid the summer's sweltering heat. Though some close for the summer months, other *locali* open temporary clubs on the beaches of Ostia and Fregene, about 20 minutes outside the city. Though a trip to the beach is always worthwhile, it's not always worth the taxi fare. Happily, *Estate Romana* (Roman Summer) ⊕ *www.estateromana.comune. roma.it* brings the beach nightlife to the banks of the Tiber River, with miniversions of familiar bars, restaurants, and clubs, along with some temporary-and-only-on-the-Tiber-banks original *locali.*

Fodor's Choice ★ **MAXXI** (*Museo Nazionale delle Arte del XXI Secolo, or National Museum of 21st-Century Art*). Finally open, Zahid Hadid's award-winning MAXXI is Rome's latest locale for artsy chic. The permanent collection includes a large range of Italian artists from the mid-20th century to the present, focusing mainly on the contemporary. Major exhibitions of artists and architects encourage temporary outdoor architectural installations. The MAXXI also has strong educational programming for children and occasional concerts. ⊠ *Via Guido Reni 2f* ☎ *06/39967350* ⊕ *www.fondazionemaxxi.it.*

DANCE

Teatro Olimpico. This is the venue for contemporary dance companies, visiting international ballet companies, and touring Broadway shows and Off-Broadway shows like *Stomp.* ⊠ *Piazza Gentile da Fabriano 17* ☎ *06/3265991* ⊕ *www.teatroolimpico.it.*

GHETTO

CONCERTS

★ **Il Tempietto.** Il Tempietto organizes music festivals and concerts throughout the year in otherwise inaccessible sites such as the Teatro di Marcello. Music ranges from classical to contemporary. ⊠ *Piazza Campitelli 9, Ghetto* ☎ *06/87131590* ⊕ *www.tempietto.it.*

MUSIC CLUBS

Rialto. An experimental haven for DJs and artists, Rialto hosts bimonthly "projects" featuring local, national, and international artists in a former warehouse. ⊠ *Via S. Ambrogio 4* ☎ *06/68133640* ⊕ *www.rialto.roma.it.*

MONTEVERDE

CULTURAL INSTITUTIONS

American Academy. The research and artist residency for winners of the Rome Prize, the academy hosts shows and lectures by internationally renowned artists, architects, writers, and photographers, as well as scholars in residence. ⊠ *Via Angelo Masina 5, on the Janiculum Hill* ☎ *06/58461* ⊕ *www.aarome.org.*

MONTI

BARS

Ai Tre Scalini. This rustic hangout—think wooden walls and counters—in Monti, Rome's boho 'hood, serves delicious antipasti and light entrees and has an enticing wine list. ⊠ *Via Panisperna 251* ☎ *06/48907495* ⊕ *www.aitrescalini.org.*

NIGHTCLUBS

Casa Clementina. "There's no place like home" seems to be the motto of Rome's latest concept lounge. Casa Clementina has a truly homey vibe—an ersatz home with kitchen, living room, dining room, and bedroom at your disposal, whether to enjoy live performances or cocktails and the very abundant *aperitivo* hour. ⊠ *Via Clementina 9, Piazza Vittorio* ☎ *39/3927105273.*

14

Charity Café. This small and romantic jazz club has live sessions nightly, hosting local and international jazz musicians in an intimate and relaxed atmosphere. ⊠ *Via Panisperna 68* ☎ *06/47825881* ⊕ *www.charitycafe.it.*

NAVONA

CAFFÈ (ON THE CHIC SIDE)

★ **Antico Caffè della Pace.** It doesn't get any more Roman than this: a cappuccino or cocktail al fresco at a turn-of-the-20th-century-style caffè nestled in the picturesque side streets behind Piazza Navona. Celebrities and literati hang out at the coveted outdoor tables of Antico Caffè della Pace, also known as Bar della Pace, where the atmosphere ranges from peaceful to percolating. La Pace's location is equally enchanting, in the *piazzatina* (tiny piazza) of Santa Maria della Pace, by baroque architect Pietro da Cortona. The only drawbacks: overpriced table service and distracted waiters. ⊠ *Via della Pace 3/7* ☎ *06/6861216* ⊕ *www.caffedellapace.it.*

BARS

Bar del Fico. The once-modest Bar del Fico, where locals reveled in cocktails and chess games, has had a face-lift and is now a fashionable evening coffee and cocktail spot. ⊠ *Piazza del Fico 26* ☎ *06/68892321.*

Chiostro del Bramante. A charming former cloister and art venue/cultural center, the Chiostro has a cocktail room reminiscent of *Mad Men* with equally inspired 1960s cocktails. The Bramante-designed bar hosts smaller shows of modern and contemporary artists like Warhol, Balla, and Basquiat as well as classical works. ⊠ *Via della Pace 5* ☎ *06/68809036* ⊕ *www.chiostrodelbramante.it.*

Fluid. With excellent cocktails and slick design, Fluid lures in passersby with its looking-glass front window where the *aperitivi* crowd likes to be seen. ⊠ *Via del Governo Vecchio 46/47* ☎ *06/6832361* ⊕ *www.fluideventi.com.*

Fodor'sChoice **Les Affiches Baguetterie.** Not just for the itinerant francophile, Les Affiches
★ Baguetterie has French country-chic decor that makes it a charming spot for brunch, but its cocktails bring the crowds. ⊠ *Via dell'Anima 52, Navona* ☎ *06/64760715.*

Terrace Bar of the Hotel Raphael. Noted for its bird's-eye view of the campaniles and palazzos of the Piazza Navona and seemingly floating in the moonlit sky, the Terrace Bar ranks high on Rome's list of romantic views. ⊠ *Largo Febo 2* ☎ *06/682831* ⊕ *www.raphaelhotel.com.*

Fodor'sChoice **Vinoteca Novecento.** A fantastic and tiny enoteca with a very old-fash-
★ ioned feel, the wine bar stocks a vast selection of wines, Proseccos, Vin Santos, and Grappas along with salami-and-cheese tasting menus. Inside is standing-room-only; in good weather, sit outside on one of the oak *barriques* (barrels). ⊠ *Piazza Delle Coppelle 47* ☎ *06/6833078.*

FILM

Nuovo Olimpia. Just off Via del Corso, Nuovo Olimpia shows classic and current films, often in original languages. Wednesday night tickets are often half-price. ⊠ *Via in Lucina 16/b* ☎ *06/6861068* ⊕ *www.circuitocinema.com/roma/nuovo-olimpia.html.*

NIGHTCLUBS

Fodor's Choice ★ **La Cabala.** Atop the medieval palazzo, La Cabala looks over the Eternal City. Rome's version of a supper club, La Cabala is part of the Hostaria dell'Orso trio of restaurant, disco, and piano bar. Dress code is stylish. ✉ *Hostaria dell'Orso, Via dei Soldati 23* ☎ *06/68301192* ⊕ *www. hdo.it.*

★ **La Maison.** At Rome's best after-dinner club the large dance floor plays second fiddle to the VIP room, where wanna-be models lounge in their very best DVF dresses and manicured boys vie for their attention. Depending on the evening, vibe can be chic, hipster, or clubby. Rule of thumb: head straight to the back room and grab a couch. ✉ *Vicolo dei Granari 4* ☎ *06/6833312* ⊕ *www.lamaisonroma.it.*

THEATER

English Theatre of Rome. The oldest English-language theater group in town, English Theatre of Rome has a repertoire of original and celebrated plays. ✉ *Termini, Via Castelfidardo 31 Int. 11* ☎ *06/4441375* ⊕ *www.rometheatre.com.*

PANTHEON

BARS

Fodor's Choice ★ **Roof Garden Bar at Grand Hotel della Minerve.** Open only during the warm season (late spring through summer), the Roof Garden Bar at Grand Hotel della Minerve has perhaps the most inspiring view in Rome—directly to the Pantheon's dome. Though both a restaurant and lounge bar, the cocktail hour is the best time to visit as the sun sets on the dome, the perfect setting for a surprise proposal. ✉ *Grand Hotel della Minerve, Piazza della Minerve 69* ☎ *06/695201* ⊕ *www. grandhoteldelaminerve.com.*

★ **Shari Vari.** One of Rome's hybrid restaurant-clubs, Shari Vari has DJs, but its vibe is more *Breakfast Club* than lounge. ✉ *Via dei Nari 14, Pantheon* ☎ *39/3396325501* ⊕ *www.sharivari.it.*

PARIOLI

CULTURAL INSTITUTIONS

The British School at Rome. The hallowed halls of the British School at Rome host special exhibitions and free, always engaging lectures by visiting professors, whose focus is promoting the humanities while living in Rome. ✉ *Via Gramsci 61* ☎ *06/3264939* ⊕ *www.bsr.ac.uk.*

Istituto Giapponese di Cultura. The Japanese Embassy's cultural branch has programming that includes film screenings, art exhibitions, lectures, conferences, and performances. The modern Heian-style building has a traditional Japanese garden open to the public in spring and summer. ✉ *Via Gramsci 74* ☎ *06/3224794* ⊕ *www.jfroma.it.*

POPOLO

BARS

★ **Stravinskij Bar at the Hotel de Russie.** Rome's *dolce vita* is usually at play here in the restaurant Le Jardin de Russie, in particular the terraced (and glorious) garden of the Stravinskij Bar, where celebrities, blue bloods, and VIPs hang out. Mixed drinks are well above par, as are the prices. ✉ *Hotel de Russie, Via del Babuino 9, Popolo* ☎ *06/328881* ⊕ *www. hotelderussie.it.*

PRATI

BARS

★ **Caffè Propaganda.** The latest entry in the new hybrid bar/restaurant field, where cocktails and style are just as important as dining, this stylish locale is reminiscent of Parisian brasseries of the 1930s, with a complementary cocktail menu along with creative Italian/French cuisine. For a glimpse of Rome's super-stylish, park yourself at Propaganda's bar for a few hours. ✉ *Via Claudia 15/19, Colosseo* ☎ *06/94534255* ⊕ *www. caffepropaganda.it.*

Fonclea. In a cellar close to Castel Sant'Angelo, the publike Fonclea is a live music venue every night of the week—from jazz to Latin American to rhythm and blues. ✉ *Via Crescenzio 82/a* ☎ *06/6896302* ⊕ *www. fonclea.it.*

QUIRINALE

CULTURAL INSTITUTIONS

Scuderie del Quirinale. From papal horse stalls to contemporary exhibition center, the Scuderie del Quirinale hosts shows of every genre from ancient to avant-garde, and its biannual exhibits are notoriously sold-out blockbuster events. ■TIP→ If a Scuderie show piques your interest, book your tickets in advance. ✉ *Via XXIV Maggio 16* ☎ *06/39967500* ⊕ *www.scuderiequirinale.it.*

REPUBBLICA

BARS

Fodor's Choice
★ **Champagnerie Tazio.** A chic Champagne bar named after the original Italian *paparazzo*, Tazio, has a red, black, and white lacquered interior with crystal chandeliers and a distinct '80s feel (think Robert Palmer, "Addicted to Love"). The favorite pastime here is sipping champagne while watching the people parade through the colonnade of the lobby. In summer, the hotel's rooftop Posh bar is the place to be, with its infinity pool and terrace view overlooking downtown. ✉ *Hotel Exedra, Piazza della Repubblica 47* ☎ *06/489381* ⊕ *www.boscolohotels.com.*

Trimani Il Winebar. Perhaps Rome's best-stocked enoteca/wine shop, the never-ending cantina proudly boasts over 4,000 labels. Its elegant, bi-level Trimani Il Winebar is a favorite for wine tasting. Sommeliers frequent Trimani daily to stock up their restaurants. ✉ *Via Cernaia 37/b, Repubblica* ☎ *06/4469661* ⊕ *www.trimani.com.*

CULTURAL INSTITUTIONS

Palazzo delle Esposizioni. Since its 2007 reopening, the Palazzo delle Esposizioni has been bombarding Rome with singularly amazing exhibitions by artists such as Rothko and Calder and about subjects as divergent as Charles Darwin and Bulgari jewelry. The complex also hosts a high-ceiling coffee bar and Open Colonna, one of Rome's nouvelle restaurants with a late evening bar. ⊠ *Via Nazionale 194* ☎ *06/39967500* ⊕ *www.palazzoesposizioni.it.*

DANCE

Corps de Ballet, Teatro dell'Opera. The Corps de Ballet of the Teatro dell'Opera performs throughout the year at the belle epoque opera house. Performances include many of the classics, often with leading international guest stars. During the summer season, the company stages ballets alfresco at the Baths of Caracalla, mixing contemporary set design with the classic structure.

Teatro dell'Opera ⊠ *Piazza Beniamino Gigli 8, Repubblica* ☎ *06/481601, 06/48160255 tickets* ⊕ *www.operaroma.it.* ⊠ *Teatro dell'Opera, Piazza Beniamino Gigli 7, Termini* ☎ *06/48160255* ⊕ *www.operaroma.it.*

14

FILM

The Space Cinema Moderno. Perhaps the most "American" of all Rome's theaters (hint: great concessions, stadium seating, and comfortable, couchlike chairs), the cinema has five screens, occasionally screening English-language and original-language films. Easy to find, the Moderno is located in the porticoes of Piazza Repubblica, next to the classic Exedra Hotel. ⊠ *Piazza della Repubblica 45–46* ☎ *06/47779202* ⊕ *www.thespacecinema.it.*

OPERA

Fodor'sChoice
★

Teatro dell'Opera. Recently Rome has come into the spotlight for opera aficionados thanks to Maestro Riccardo Muti's 2011 *Nabucco* performance and his recent support of Rome's Teatro dell'Opera. Though considered a far younger sibling of Milan's La Scala and Venice's La Fenice, the company does command an audience during its mid-November to May season. Tickets are on sale in advance of the season. In the hot summer months, the company moves to the Baths of Caracalla for its outdoor opera series.

Terme di Caracalla. The 3rd-century AD bath complex Terme di Caracalla doubles as backdrop for the Teatro dell'Opera's summer performance series. As can be expected, the oft-preferred performance is Aida for its spectacle, which has been known to include real elephants. The company has taken a new direction, using projections atop the ancient ruins to create cutting-edge sets. ⊠ *Via Antoniniana 14, Caracalla* ☎ *06/481 601* ⊕ *www.operaroma.it* ⊠ *Piazza Beniamino Gigli 8* ☎ *06/481601, 06/48160255 tickets* ⊕ *www.operaroma.it.*

ROMA NORD

DANCE

Teatro Greco. As part of Rome's rich and intense performance circuit, the Teatro Greco features international contemporary dance performances and often hosts the fall's Festa della Danza. ⊠ *Via Leoncavallo 10* ☎ *06/8607513* ⊕ *www.teatrogreco.it.*

ROMAN FORUM

THEATER

Miracle Players. Looking for a bit of English humor? With an obvious penchant for Monty Python, the Miracle Players are Rome's most vocal English-language comedy troupe performing original plays. Head to the Roman Forum on Friday afternoons in summer for their free, live performances. ⊕ *www.miracleplayers.org.*

SAN GIOVANNI

DANCE

Museo Nazionale degli Strumenti Musicali. A pastoral dance setting, the gardens of the Museo Nazionale degli Strumenti Musicali are the summer stage for a festival of classical and contemporary dance from June through August. ⊠ *Piazza di Santa Croce in Gerusalemme 9/a* ☎ *06/7014796* ⊕ *www.museostrumentimusicali.it.*

SPAGNA

BARS

Antica Enoteca. Piazza di Spagna's most celebrated wine bar literally corners the market on prime people-watching. In addition to a vast selection of wine, Antica Enoteca has delectable antipasti, perfect for a snack or a light lunch. ⊠ *Via della Croce 76/b* ☎ *06/6790896* ⊕ *www. anticaenoteca.com.*

★ **Enoteca Palatium.** Just down the street from the Piazza di Spagna hub is this quiet gem run by Lazio's Regional Food Authority as a chic showcase for the best of Lazio's pantry and wine cellar: from its fine vintages to olive oils, cheese, and meats to a full seasonal menu of Lazio cuisine. Located where famed aesthete and poet Gabriele d'Annunzio once lived, this is not your garden-variety corner wine bar. ■TIP→ **Stop by during aperitivo hour, from 6:30 pm onward (reservations recommended) to enjoy this burst of local flavor.** ⊠ *Via Frattina, 94, Piazza di Spagna.*

Fodor's Choice ★ **5th Floor Terrace at the Palazzetto.** The prize for perfect aperitivo spot goes to the Palazzetto, with excellent drinks and appetizers and a breathtaking view of Rome's domes and rooftops, all from its rooftop overlooking the Spanish Steps. ⊠ *Il Palazzetto, Piazza Trinità di Monti, Spagna* ☎ *06/699341000.*

Gilda. Every year, Gilda reinvents herself to continue the never-ending party near the Spanish Steps. Recent incarnations have added a piano bar and restaurant just off the dance floors. ⊠ *Via Mario de' Fiori 97* ☎ *06/6784838* ⊕ *www.gildabar.it.*

Victoria House. Victoria House, off Via del Corso and a stone's throw from Piazza del Popolo, is Rome's very first English pub. Still considered one of the best for its beer selection and English menu, it has an authentic, worn-in feel—like an old shoe. ⊠ *Via Gesù e Maria 18* ☎ *06/3201698.*

CULTURAL INSTITUTIONS

Fodor'sChoice **Villa Medici.** The 16th-century Villa Medici is the palatial home of the
★ French Academy of Rome, a cultural center where residents are scholars and artists. Modern and contemporary exhibitions of French artists are the focus. However, the palace itself is a permanent exhibition of mannerist architecture, ancient bas-relief, and sculpture. The maze gardens surround a lovely terrace where summertime events include evening music and film series. ⊠ *Viale Trinitá dei Monti 1* ☎ *06/67611* ⊕ *www.villamedici.it.*

14

TESTACCIO

NIGHTCLUBS

Hulala. Still considered a designer discoteca and magnet for fashionistas, Hulala is evolving as the crowd diversifies into a younger generation. Decor is 1960s mod. ⊠ *Via dei Conciatori 7* ☎ *06/57300429.*

Fodor'sChoice **Joia.** Joia has reigned as the gem of Testaccio's Via Galvani for several
★ years now, thanks to its excellent DJs and bartenders. Doors don't open until 11 pm, but lines are always elbow-room-only; try calling ahead to get on the list. ⊠ *Via Galvani 20* ☎ *06/5740802, 39/3290370784.*

Ketum Bar. Excellent for people-watchers, and even better if you want to mix a bit of culture with your clubbing. The glass-covered walls show off shards of 1st-century amphorae to remind you that Ketum Bar was carved out of a mountain of pottery. ⊠ *Via Galvani 24* ☎ *06/57305338* ⊕ *www.ketumbar.it.*

L'Alibi. One of Testaccio's longest-running clubs, L'Alibi hosts parties daily including its much-anticipated Thursday Gloss Party. The crowd crosses all boundaries and the music knows no limits at what is often considered Rome's most famous gay disco. In summer, the open terrace is a large dance space. ⊠ *Via di Monte Testaccio 40, Testaccio* ☎ *06/5743448* ⊕ *www.lalibi.it.*

CULTURAL INSTITUTIONS

MACRO Testaccio. Rome's MACRO (Museum of Contemporary Art in Rome) has converted Testaccio's former slaughterhouse into a multispace venue for visual and performance art. The complex hosts exhibitions, performances, and events including RomaContemporary, the annual contemporary art fair. MACRO Pelanda is the Testaccio complex's exhibition, laboratory, residence, and artist workspace. MACRO Testacctio is open until midnight. ⊠ *Piazza Orazio Giustiniani 4* ☎ *06/671070400* ⊕ *www.macro.roma.museum.*

THEATER

Teatro India. Hosting productions in English as well as Italian, Teatro India occupies a former soap factory—it's funky but does not have the most comfortable seating. ⊠ *Lungotevere Vittorio Gassman 1, Trastevere* ☎ *06/684000314* ⊕ *www.teatrodiroma.net.*

TRASTEVERE

BARS

Artù. The wood-panel walls and fireplace provide a cozy mood at Artù, a popular hangout with an ample selection of beer, wine, and tasty snacks and bar food hidden behind Piazza Santa Maria. ⊠ *Largo F. Biondi 5* ☎ *06/5880398.*

CAFFÈ (ON THE CHIC SIDE)

Fodor's Choice
★
Freni e Frizioni. Hipster hangout Freni e Frizioni's has a cute artist vibe great for coffee, tea, aperitifs, and late-night hanging out. In warmer weather, the crowd overflows the large *terrazzo* overlooking the Tiber and the side streets of Trastevere. ⊠ *Via del Politeama 4* ☎ *06/45497499* ⊕ *www.freniefrizioni.com.*

CONCERTS

Orto Botanico. The historic botanical garden spans over 30 acres at the base of the Janiculum Hill in Trastevere. In this redolent and verdant setting, the spring and summer seasons promote art and summer concert series. ⊠ *Largo Cristina di Svezia 23/a* ☎ *06/49917107* ⊕ *sweb01.dbv.uniroma1.it/orto/index.html.*

FILM

★ **Alcazar.** The small Cinema Alcazar in Trastevere is known for its more international, art house films. Programming includes dubbed and also original language (with Italian subtitles). Best to contact the Alcazar in advance to confirm original language programming. ⊠ *Via Merry del Val 14* ☎ *06/5880099* ⊕ *www.mymovies.it/cinema/roma.*

NIGHTCLUBS

★ **Big Mama.** Recently renovated, Big Mama is a Roman institution of live music including jazz, blues, rhythm and blues, international, and rock. ⊠ *Vicolo San Francesco a Ripa 18* ☎ *06/5812551* ⊕ *www.bigmama.it.*

VATICAN

MUSIC CLUBS

★ **Alexanderplatz.** The black-and-white checkered floors of Alexanderplatz, Rome's most important live jazz and blues club, are reminiscent of Harlem's 1930s jazz halls, and Alexanderplatz loves to promote this image with excellent jazz programming of Italian and international performers. The bar and restaurant are always busy, so reservations are suggested. ⊠ *Via Ostia 9* ☎ *06/39742171* ⊕ *www.alexanderplatz.it.*

The Place. This live music venue has an exceptional and ever-increasing program of funk, Latin, and jazz accompanied by excellent fusion cuisine. ⊠ *Via Alberico II 27–29* ☎ *06/68307137* ⊕ *www.theplace.it.*

VENETO

CAFFÈ (ON THE CHIC SIDE)

h club> doney at the Westin Excelsior. Nattily dressed businesspeople and harried tourists enjoy fresh-fruit aperitifs at the street-side h club> doney, Via Veneto's grand dame of outdoor caffè, in front of the Westin Excelsior. The indoor Orvm bar is a return to the Jazz Age and Roaring Twenties in decor, with excellent cocktails served all day. ⊠ *Westin Excelsior, Via Vittorio Veneto 145* ☎ *06/0647082805* ⊕ *www.restaurantdoney.com.*

CULTURAL INSTITUTIONS

Istituto Svizzero di Roma. The Swiss embassy cultural branch, in the beautiful, turn-of-the-century Villa Maraini, just off Via Veneto, programs innovative art exhibitions, conferences, and film and lecture series throughout the year. ⊠ *Via Ludovisi 48* ☎ *06/420421* ⊕ *www.istitutosvizzero.it.*

NIGHTCLUBS

Fodor'sChoice ★ **Jackie O'.** A dip into Rome's dolce vita is not complete without a visit to the historic Jackie O', a retro-hip disco and restaurant off Via Veneto. The small lounge area is where you want to be, and don't arrive before 11 pm. ⊠ *Via Boncompagni 11, Veneto* ☎ *06/42885457* ⊕ *www.jackieoroma.com.*

VENEZIA

CULTURAL INSTITUTIONS

Palazzo Venezia. A former fortress, Venetian embassy, and fascist headquarters, Palazzo Venezia has a rich history of popes, dictators, and architects (courtyard conceived by Leon Battista Alberti), and thus its incarnation as national museum is not surprising. Its permanent collection includes works by Bernini, Giorgione, and Guercino, and the *piano nobile* (noble floor) hosts private exhibitions of international acclaim. Shows have included Sebastiano del Piombo, Julian Schnabel, and *Caravaggisti* (followers of Caravaggio). ⊠ *Via del Plebiscito 118* ☎ *06/69994284* ⊕ *museopalazzovenezia.beniculturali.it.*

Vittoriano. Part of the Complesso del Vittoriano, incorporated into the Altare della Patria—fondly known as the Wedding Cake—the exhibition hall has showcased world masters including Giotto, Renoir, Gauguin, Picasso, Chagall, and most recently, Mondrian. The complex includes a panoramic rooftop terrace, exhibition hall, and three museums: Risorgimento (post 1870), Italian Immigration, and Armed Forces. ⊠ *Via i San Pietro in Carcere* ☎ *06/6780664.*

VILLA BORGHESE

CULTURAL INSTITUTIONS

Museo Carlo Bilotti. A tiny modern-art collection hidden in Villa Borghese, the museum has a permanent collection comprised of modern and pop art favorites including Giorgio di Chirico and Roy Lichtenstein, while its temporary shows focus on international icons such as Willem de

Kooning, Damien Hirst, Carla Accardi, and Philip Guston. ✉ *Viale Fiorello La Guardia* ☎ *06/82059127* ⊕ *www.museocarlobilotti.it.*

FILM

Fodor's Choice ★ **Casa del Cinema.** Dedicated to the art of the silver screen, Casa del Cinema is Rome's most modern projection house and film library. Located in Villa Borghese, this oasis for film buffs has multiple screening rooms, a caffè, and a resource center with DVD library and laptops for private viewings. They show many new and retro films and often showcase the original language films from the fall's Venice Film Festival and Roma Cinema Fest (⊕ *www.romacinemafest.it*). Like its indoor counterpart, the outdoor projection screen shows both new and vintage films, sometimes in original languages, though only in the warm months. ✉ *Largo Marcello Mastroianni 1, Villa Borghese* ☎ *06/423601* ⊕ *www.casadelcinema.it.*

OUTSIDE THE CITY CENTER

CONCERTS

PalaLottomatica. Built for the 1960 Rome Olympics for basketball and boxing events, the PalaLottamatica now hosts concerts by heavy hitters such as Italian favorites Zucchero and Renato Zero, as well as international superstars like Bruce Springsteen and Elton John. It's in the EUR neighborhood (about 15 minutes out of the city center), which means bring extra cab fare. ✉ *Palazzetto dello Sport, Piazzale dello Sport, EUR* ☎ *06/540901* ⊕ *www.forumnet.it.*

DANCE

Palladium. A historic theater in the Garbatella area of the Ostiense neighborhood, the Palladium has an intense music and performing arts program, especially for contemporary dance. It also participates in the annual RomaEuropa festival in the fall. ✉ *Via dei Magazzini Generali 20, Ostiense* ☎ *06/45553050* ⊕ *www.romaeuropa.net.*

FILM

Cinecittà Studios. Everyone who is anyone has shot or been filmed at Cinecittà. The historic 1960s studio has been home to celluloids stars and their directors from Elizabeth Taylor and Marcello Mastroianni to Martin Scorsese and Woody Allen. Still a functioning studio, Cinecttà also offers organized tours to visitors who wish to walk through pre-skyscraper New York, hang out at the Roman Forum, inside the Sistine Chapel, or in medieval Florence. ✉ *Via Tuscolana 1055, Cinecittà* ☎ *06/58334360* ⊕ *www.cinecittastudios.it.*

Shopping

WORD OF MOUTH

"Ooh, romance! Perhaps you could buy your sweetheart an Italian handbag (Furla maybe, or if you are really flush, Fendi or D&G) and then fill it with surprises for that evening—tickets to the Rome opera or a corkscrew, for the bottle of wine you will purchase to drink on the Spanish Steps after dinner (don't forget plastic cups!)."

—nnolen

By Lynda
Albertson

In Rome shopping is an art form. Perhaps it's the fashionably bespeckled Italian wearing Giorgio Armani as he deftly zips through traffic on his Vespa or all those Anita Ekberg, Audrey Hepburn, and Julia Roberts films that make us want to be Roman for a day. But with limited time and no Hollywood studio backing you, the trick is to find what you're looking for and still not miss out on the city's museums and monuments—and have enough euros left to enjoy the rest of your trip.

These days, many shop-till-you-droppers heading over to the Trevi Fountain may be forgiven for humming that immortal song, "Three Coins in a Cash Register." Yes, the Eternal City is awash in fountains and iconographic Roman rituals: gazing at Saint Peter's Basilica through a secret keyhole on the Aventine; putting your hand inside the Bocca della Verità, the city's ancient lie detector; and tossing that fateful coin over your shoulder into the Fontana di Trevi. All are customs that will buy you a classic photo opportunity, but none will bring you as much pleasure or stay with you longer than the purchases you make in Rome's appealing and overflowing emporia.

There may be no city that takes shopping quite as seriously as Rome, and no district more worthy of your time than Piazza di Spagna, with its abundance of shops and designer powerhouses like Fendi and Armani. The best of them are clumped tightly together along the city's three primary fashion arteries: Via dei Condotti, Via Borgognona, and Via Frattina. From Piazza di Spagna to Piazza Navona and on to Campo de' Fiori, shoppers will find an explosive array of shops within walking distance of one another. A shop for fine handmade Amalfi paper looks out upon the Pantheon, while slick boutiques anchor the corners of 18th-century Piazza di Spagna. Across town in the colorful hive that is Monti, a second-generation mosaic-maker creates Italian masterpieces on a street named for a pope who died before America was even discovered. Even in Trastevere, one can find one of Rome's rising shoe designers creating next-century *nuovo chic* shoes nestled on a side street beside one of the city's oldest churches.

This chapter will help shopaholics choose the perfect souvenir for someone back home, find a vintage poster, choose a boutique for those *molto* chic Versace sandals, or rustle up truffles. When we're done filling your bags with memories of Mamma Roma, you can be sure of two things: that you'll be nostalgic for Caput Mundi long after you arrive back home, and that we will have saved you a few coins—to throw into that fabulous famous fountain.

PLANNING

OPENING HOURS

Store hours in Rome can be frustratingly fickle, so it's best to remain flexible. Small, family-run businesses may close a few hours for lunch and close one day per week so folks can have a day off. Major Rome retailers in the heart of the shopping district open their doors between 9 and 9:30 am and stay open until 7:30 or 8 pm. Most clothing stores adhere to the general operating hours listed above but close Sunday and Monday mornings. Banks are generally open weekdays from 8:30 to 1:30 and from 2:30 to 3:30. Summer travelers should be aware that most small shops close for two to three weeks just before or after August's Ferragosto holiday.

SIZING IT UP

Italian sizes are not uniform, so always try on or measure items. If you wear a size small, you may be surprised to learn that the shirt you like needs to be a medium. Children's sizes are all over the place and though they usually go by age, sizes are calibrated to Italian children. (Average size-per-age standards vary from country to country.) Check washing instruction labels on all garments as many are dry-clean-only or not meant for the dryer. When in doubt about the proper size, ask the shop attendant; most will have an international size chart handy.

COUNTERFEITS

Piracy, in any form, is now considered a serious offense in Italy. This not only applies to citizens, but also to tourists visiting the country. According to Italian law, anyone caught buying counterfeit goods— DVDs, CDs, sunglasses, or those impossibly discounted "Fendi" and "Gucci" bags—sold by sidewalk vendors is subject to a fine of no less than €1,000. While the police in Rome enforce this law to varying degrees, travelers are advised to purchase products only from stores and licensed retailers to avoid unknowingly buying counterfeit goods.

DUTY-FREE SHOPPING

Value-added tax (IVA) is 23% on clothing and luxury goods, but is already included in the amount on the price tag for consumer goods. All non-EU citizens visiting Italy are entitled to a reimbursement of this tax when purchasing nonperishable goods that total more than €180 in a single transaction. If you buy goods in a store that does not

15

PIAZZA DI SPAGNA

Filled with lithe-limbed glamazons looking uber-smart and sporting sun-kissed complexions, the ultrachic zone along Via dei Condotti, Via Borgognona, and Via Frattina gathers up Armani, Bulgari, Fendi, Ferragamo, Gucci, and Valentino into one luxurious, fashionista's Shangri-La.

Rome has been setting fashion trends since the days of the Caesars, so it's little wonder that this is the city that gave us the Gucci "moccasin" loafer, the Fendi bag, and the Valentino dress Jackie O wore when she became Mrs. Onassis. While the famous double-Gs can now be found in boutiques around the world, the mother store is right here on Via Condotti, a "shopping mall" lined with Bulgari diamonds and Pratesi linens. A stroll along this concentrated corridor is as great for people-watching as it is for Italian haute couture and prêt-à-porter. The shops can be as intimidating as they are strikingly beautiful, but plastic is the universal equalizer so go ahead and indulge your inner celebrity.

BEST TIME TO GO

Visitors with a sumptuous sense of *bella figura* will want to time their retail therapy for just after lunch Tuesday through Friday afternoons or during the evening *passeggiata* when Via Condotti becomes one gigantic catwalk.

BEAUTY AND THE BEACH

For candy-apple red polka dots or that bombshell bikini worthy of a pin-up poster, Marisa Padovan (⊠ *Via delle Carrozze 81*) has had the market cornered on one-of-a-kind couture swimwear—ever since Audrey Hepburn and Claudia Cardinale discovered her.

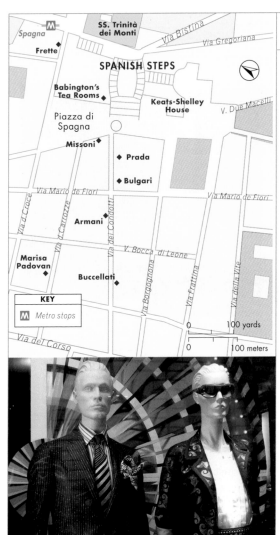

Map labels:
- Spagna (M)
- SS. Trinità dei Monti
- Via Bistina
- Via Gregoriana
- Frette
- **SPANISH STEPS**
- Babington's Tea Rooms
- Keats-Shelley House
- V. Due Macelli
- Piazza di Spagna
- Missoni
- ♦ Prada
- ♦ Bulgari
- Via Mario de Fiori
- Via Mario de Fiori
- Via d. Croce
- Via d. Carrozze
- Via del Condotti
- Armani
- V. Bocca di Leone
- Via Borgognona
- Via Frattina
- Via della Vite
- Marisa Padovan
- Buccellati
- **KEY**
- (M) Metro stops
- Via del Corso
- 0 — 100 yards
- 0 — 100 meters

15

BRUNCH BEFORE BROWSING

Shopping is a great way to work up an appetite, and what better way to satiate your hunger than with a vegetarian brunch at Il **Margutta RistorArte** (✉ *Via Margutta 118, Spagna*, ☎ *06/32650577*). More than just a vegetarian restaurant, Margutta takes a holistic approach to natural, locally sourced vegetarian cuisine that will nourish your body, restore your spirit, and give you a bit of art to look at all in one peaceful sitting. Check out their very original dish called "6 different ways of eating artichokes."

TROPPO ELEGANTE

DADDY WORE BUCKS
If diamonds are your girl's best friend, she need look no further than Via Condotti, where two jewelry barons have breathtaking boutiques: Bulgari and Buccellati.

YARNING FOR THE GOOD OLD DAYS
With knitting in vogue, a stop at Missoni (✉ *Piazza di Spagna 78*) is an absolute must. Their handspun, hand-dyed skirts and sweaters in undulating curves and wild, chevroning colors will have you channeling your inner designer granny. (Psst... find new Missoni patterns in *Vogue Knitting* every year).

THERE ARMANI REASONS
Well-heeled women love Armani for his catwalk couture. Power executives prefer his black-label collection. Recessionistas should check out Armani Jeans, the designer's lovely, lower-priced line with a focus on young urban streetwear.

RESISTANCE IS FUTILE
From Cameron Diaz to Jessica Simpson, nearly every celebrity has been spotted wearing Prada. So why not join them? Can't afford a handbag? Try a strikingly smart pair of sunglasses for your "I'm a celebrity" disguise.

PIAZZA NAVONA

In Rome, shopping and sightseeing are often hard to separate from one another. This is especially *fortissimo* in the Baroque quarter around Piazza Navona, queen of Roman squares. Against a backdrop of street entertainers, mime artists, and brightly lit caffè you'll find the tempting old-world toy shop Al Sogno just down from that Bernini extravaganza, the Fountain of the Four Rivers.

Up and down the length of Via del Governo Vecchio, invitingly small merchants stand shoulder-to-shoulder. On one end of this cobbled street is a string of vintage clothing shops like Maga Morgana, sure to satisfy your retro cravings. If you want world-class denim, head in the opposite direction to SBU (Strategic Business Unit). This is the zone for trendy boutiques you'll never find franchised back home. And don't forget: Via dei Coronari holds some of the best antique shops in the city.

BEST TIME TO GO

For antiques, browse the fair held by the gorgeous stores on pedestrianized Via dei Coronari during the second half of May. In December, Piazza Navona transforms into a magical winter market for Christmas. And remember: during August many smaller shops close for summer holidays.

A SPOON FULL OF MONASTIC SUGAR

Created by Italian monks in the 15th-century, 39-proof Anisetta is stocked by Ai Monasteri, Rome's 120-year-old apothecary, and this aniseed liqueur is tops as a digestif or as a pick-me-up for the jet-lagged.

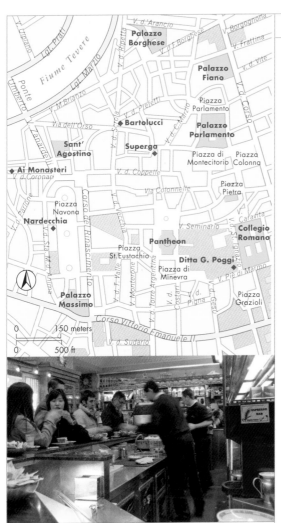

NEIGHBORHOOD NIBBLES

Need an early morning nibble or an afternoon pick-me-up? For 60 years Sant'Eustachio il Caffè has been what Starbucks only dreams of being. At this legendary Piazza Sant'Eustachio coffeehouse, you can have the best cappuccino in town and rub shoulders with an Italian politician or two, drinking at the bar Italian style. Or opt for a cup of black, bitter espresso at Tazzo d'Oro, on Via degli Orfani on the east side of Piazza del Pantheon. If ready for a more daring delight, try the white chocolate basil gelato at little Gelateria del Teatro, just off Via dei Coronari.

ONLY IN ROME

NATURAL BORN THRILLERS

Daring designer Delfina Delettrez successfully joins genius, beauty, and a taste of gothic steam punk to produce some of Rome's most unusual jewelry, complete with totemic fetishes, at her boutique near Piazza Navona.

DEN OF ANTIQUITY

On Piazza Navona, Nardecchia knows that there are three major considerations when it comes to antique prints and etchings: value, aesthetics, and rarity.

A BRUSH WITH CLASS

Behind the Pantheon, Ditta G. Poggi is a mecca for art supplies, brushes, and paints as it was for such artists as Morandi, De Chirico, Guttuso, and Picasso.

SOLE FOOD

Superga has made its iconic 2,750 low-cut sneakers for 100 years. Available in more colors than there are gelato flavors, they are the ubiquitous favorite for casual city-wear and weekends at the beach. They can be found at Piazza Spagna on Via Belsiana.

CRYSTAL CLEAR

For the most *selezionatissima* array of crystal, silver, and china, Roman brides always go to IN.OR. dal 1952.

15

participate in the "Tax-Free Italy" program, ask the cashier to issue you a special invoice known as a *fattura*, which must be made out to you and includes the phrase *Esente IVA ai sensi della legge 38 quater.* The bill should indicate the amount of IVA included in the purchase price. Present this invoice and the goods purchased to the Customs Office on your departure from Italy to obtain your tax reimbursement.

SALES

Saldi (end-of-season sales) can mean real bargains in clothing and accessories and occur twice a year in Italy. Rome's main sale periods run January 7 through February and late July to mid-September. Unlike in many other countries, most stores adopt a no-exchange, all-sales-final policy on sale goods. At other times of year, a *liquidazione* sign indicates a close-out sale, but take a hard look at the goods; they may be bottom-of-the-barrel or may carry stipulations that preclude the shopper from trying them on first.

BARGAINING

If you're a bargain shopper, know that the notice prezzi fissi (fixed prices) posted in some stores means just that. In shops displaying this sign it is a waste of time, and could also be perceived as rude, to ask for discounts. In those increasingly rare shops that do offer discounts, shopkeepers tend to offer discounts only on a sizable quantity of merchandise. You can always try your hand in bargaining at outdoor markets. Remember that Italian stores generally will not give refunds and often cannot exchange goods because of limited stock.

SHOPPING DISTRICTS

CAMPO

Campo de' Fiori is one of Rome's most captivating piazzas and a perfect starting point for exploring the heart of the city. By the 16th century, this neighborhood was already a bustling commercial area as well as a gathering place for the citizens of Rome. The piazza takes center stage early in the morning as an extraordinary spectacle unfolds with the arrival of the *bancarellari* (the moveable cart vendors) just before sunrise. Imbuing the square with a village atmosphere, these hardworking merchants ply their wares six days a week, tables filled to overflowing with a cornucopia of such goods as freshly picked chicory, blood oranges, artichokes, and lavender honey.

Under the billowing white umbrellas, visitors should be sure to take a moment to hunt for an Italian espresso pot or to snap a photo of the pyramids of dried spice where the vendors cheerfully boast—often with exaggerated comedy—the quality of their goods.

Don't forget to explore the labyrinth of narrow streets named for the merchants that once populated the area: Via del Giubbonari (Street of the Jacket Makers), Via dei Cappellari (Street of the Hat Makers), and Via degli Specchi (Street of Mirrors). These meandering lanes have an abundance of shops and boutiques sure to please everyone's budget. Getting here is easy, as many buses pass through Torre Argentina (a short walk away), though the most direct are buses 44, 63, 81, and 95.

MONTI

Nestled beside the Roman Forum is Rome's first and oldest quarter. In ancient times Monti was known as the Suburra, a place filled to overflowing with steamy bordellos and taverns and an atmosphere of naughty risk. Even Nero disguised himself to partake of its plentiful "wares." Today the zone is becoming gentrified, with Armani building designer apartments just up the street.

But Monti has managed to maintain its yesteryear feel, and its narrow streets and picturesque palazzos make it Rome's boho neighborhood of choice. With that popularity, hedonistic pleasures can still be found, though they center mostly on sumptuous food and wine. Everywhere you turn you'll see a plethora of new boutiques, some with patrons still holding celebratory Proseccos at inaugural grand openings. Shops in this area sell chocolate, tea, designer and discount clothing, home interiors, antiques, gourmet and ethnic food, books, artisanal pasta, and more. We won't tell you all of them: some surprises are worth discovering all on your own. To get here, take Metro B to the Cavour Metro stop.

15

BARBERINI

Named after one of Rome's most powerful families, bustling Piazza Barberini is home to Brioni's flagship store. Flanked by noble residences and smaller shops, Brioni dominates not only the piazza but gentlemen's bespoke fashion in general. Step inside and you'll likely drop your entire shopping allowance in one *centro storico* location, but you will walk out smiling. The streets nearby are studded with other great places to shop; just keep in mind that a stroll along the winding tree-lined Via Veneto means putting on the Ritz: this is no place for your casual Friday blue jeans. Immortalized in Fellini's classic *La Dolce Vita*, the boulevard is famous for posh hotels and elite shopping for the rich and famous who want to avoid the Spagna throngs. Can't afford to indulge? Head up Via del Tritone for posh without the dosh (as Brits refer to money) and a great selection of shops offering midprice clothing, shoes, and leather apparel. To get to the area take the Metro (Line A) to Piazza Barberini, or any of a number of buses, including the 116.

VIA DEL CORSO

Someone once said dancing is dreaming with your feet, and a walk along Via del Corso will give you the same effect. Stretching from Piazza Venezia all the way to Piazza del Popolo, this remarkably straight street in a city famous for its winding alleys marks the perfect beginning and end points for a shopping-inspired afternoon stroll. Traditionally home to mainstream, upscale international brands like Levi's, Benetton, H&M, and Zara, the street also has jewels like Yamamay and Frette, as well as fashion giants like the iconic House of Fendi.

Young Romans come here for jeans and inexpensive, trendy wear, some of which is sold in the 17th- and 18th-century mansions that line the street. In the chic area tucked next to Piazza San Lorenzo in Lucina, smart and expensive specialty shops cater to the people who live in the palaces nearby. Piazza della Fontanella Borghese, flanking the palace once inhabited by the uninhibited Pauline Borghese (she posed nude for Canova), has a picturesque street market of permanent stalls selling prints and old books.

Here you will also find the palatial pink-marble Galleria Alberto Sordi at Piazza Colonna, Rome's most elegant shopping mall. Recently restored, and a good place to take a coffee break and enjoy a bit of people-watching under the soaring Stil Liberty (Art Nouveau) glass roof.

Stretching 1½ km (1 mile) with interesting shops along its side streets, knowing which to choose can be tiring as well as time consuming. Opening hours vary enormously and with flagship stores hiring elegant staff to watch you, it can seem a bit daunting. If your trip is truly a shopping holiday or time is of the essence, consider scheduling your own personal shopping assistant through Context Rome (☎ 06/96727371 ⊕ *www.contexttravel.com*).

Via del Corso is the dividing line between the designer-centric fancy shops of the Spagna district and the more reasonably priced emporia near the Pantheon. If you don't feel like walking—though this area is very central—take Bus 62, 63, 117, 199, or 492.

TRASTEVERE

Across the Tiber from the city center is must-see Trastevere, filled with irregular streets and lanes, soaked with atmosphere and character dating back to the Middle Ages. Take in the stark contrast of buildings that have never changed tucked in among newer apartments, creative and funky shops, and the Porta Portese flea market. Open up your senses as you revel in a foodie paradise of old-world open-air markets and wine shops, where you'll likely happen upon a stool-perched owner scribbling daily accounts in an old ledger book. Teenagers and college students flock to this happening part of town full of clubs and pubs. While there are not as many cultural sights in this area, there is a plethora of historical buildings, gorgeous fountains, parts of the old Aurelian wall, statues, and more. Be sure to look up Dermot O'Connell, owner of the Almost Corner Bookshop in Via del Moro 45, who will be happy to chat for a while and share his insights into life here. During the summer months, the area comes alive after sunset. Trastevere can also be reached with Tram 8 three stops from Largo Argentina.

SAN LORENZO

A little off the beaten tourist path, San Lorenzo is most often explored more by visitors staying near Stazione Termini, but its out-of-the-way location is more than made up for by its liveliness and avant-garde vibe. Famous for its youth-friendly shopping, the zone is filled with eateries, pubs, jewelry shops, bookstores, and vintage boutiques, making it the preferred hangout for Italian university students. That said, San Lorenzo's raw earthiness isn't for everyone.

The district has a certain inner-city sophistication that can be lost on those used to Rome's elegant Baroque monuments and statuary and, much like certain neighborhoods in New York or Rio, you have to know where to look. If you are one to go against conventional Roman shopping wisdom, be sure to visit the buzzing L'Anatra all'Arancia, with its captivating prêt-à-porter window displays. Less than a block away, Pifebo is a sensational vintage-clothing emporium where you can rummage like a Roman and come out with a groovy ensemble worthy of any Davy Jones groupie.

DEPARTMENT STORES

BUDGET

Both the Oviesse and Upim department store chains are good places for families to shop for bargain sportswear, bathing suits, underwear, and scarves—where quality doesn't break the bank. Both no-frills franchises have multiple locations throughout Rome where you can also pick up toiletries, makeup, hair-care supplies, and home decor with that Italian sense of style. Some even have invaluable while-you-wait shoe-repair counters. There's a large central Upim store in Stazione Termini and another nearby at Piazza Santa Maria Maggiore. Oviesse has a store at ✉ *Viale Trastevere 62/64.*

15

MARKETS

FLEA MARKETS

Treasure-seekers and bargain-hunters alike will appreciate Rome's open-air markets. Well supplied and oh-so-Roman, these markets are great spots to gain insight into the thrift shopping spirit of the capital. Every Sunday it seems that all of Trastevere comes out for the bustling Porta Portese flea market, where tents overflow with cheap luggage, vintage World War II memorabilia, and old books of Puccini opera lyrics, and folks haggle in the rapid-fire staccato of Roman dialect. Just watch out for pickpockets and tricksters inviting you to play their card games: they *always* win the bets!

FOOD MARKETS

★ Still shadowed by the massive 16th-century Orsini palazzo and a statue of the famed philosopher Giordano Bruno, who was burned at the stake here on accusations of heresy in 1600, the Campo de' Fiori (✉ *near Piazza Navona*) is Rome's oldest food market, situated just south of Rome's Renaissance/Baroque quarter and the Piazza Farnese. If you are staying near the Vatican don't miss the Mercato Trionfale, located at Via La Goletta 1 between the Cipro and Ottaviano (Vatican) Metro stops. In its newly renovated building, this food-lovers' market offers one of the most extensive selections in Rome and like Campo is opened Monday to Saturday. For those looking for high-quality organic and local products and produce, the small Mercato di Campagna Amica del Circo Massimo has a select range of vegetables, meats, honey, and cheese that's to die for; it's open weekends only.

SPECIALTY SHOPS

ANTIQUES AND PRINTS

Rome is one of Italy's happiest hunting grounds for antiques and bric-a-brac. Here you'll find streets lined with shops groaning with gilded Rococo tables, charming Grand Tour memorabilia, fetching 17th-century *veduti* (view) engravings, and curios, perhaps even Lord Byron's snuff spoon. Via dei Coronari is Rome's traditional center of antiques but other top prestigious dealers are concentrated around Via del Babuino. The street's focal point is the time-weathered statue of the "baboon" (actually a satyr) that gave it its name. Right next to the baboon is the charmingly picturesque Museum Atelier Canova-Tadolini, where the great 18th-century Neoclassical sculptor worked. Inside the museum, there's also a coffee bar and restaurant. What better place to stop and have lunch?

BOOKSTORES

English-language books are widely available in Rome. Many of the larger booksellers dedicate at least a few shelves of books for English-speaking patrons, and three English-language-centric bookstores are noteworthy: the Almost Corner Bookstore in Trastevere and the Anglo American and Lion bookstores near Piazza Spagna.

CERAMICS AND DECORATIVE ARTS

Italy has always been beloved for its wonderful craftsmanship and decorative arts. In Rome, where museums can be overwhelming, sometimes the best treasures are found not in its galleries but in artisan shops along twisty alleyways where shoppers can find the perfect collectible, home decor accessory, and gift, hand-painted and made in Italy.

CLOTHING

CHILDREN'S CLOTHING Although consumers may be cutting back, visitors still can't help but indulge when it comes to the little ones. Note that sizes are completely different from U.S. children's sizes, so be sure to take measurements before you leave home and bring along your tape measure, or get a good size-conversion chart.

LEATHER CLOTHING In a country where quality, workmanship, exacting attention to details, and strict manufacturing specifications are standard, customers will find lots to choose from. Leather purses, wallets, jackets, coats, skirts, and pants are carefully constructed from top-quality hides. You can also find small workshops where delicious jackets, coats, and handbags can be made to measure.

VINTAGE CLOTHING Rome has a wide range of vintage shops where you can pick up some great couture from days gone by. With several shops showcased around Piazza Navona, Monti, and San Lorenzo, looking good needn't mean looking like everyone else. A favorite with designers, magazine editors, and Hollywood starlets, vintage is also environmentally friendly, and if you shop carefully you can save money and the planet and still find a suede fringe jacket worthy of Janis Joplin.

HANDBAGS AND LUGGAGE

Really good bags—the classic kind that you can carry for years—are not inexpensive. Almost all the leading fashion houses have their own line of bags, but there are also hundreds of small, lesser-known artisans that still make leather goods the old fashioned way, for each discerning customer.

MUSIC AND FILMS

Most music stores have comprehensive sections of foreign music, heavy metal, retro, and Italian as well as DVD films (just make sure your player back home has the right settings)

Via Condotti Shopping

Castroni is a foodie favorite for most Romans and just the place to pick up the fixings for a gourmand's picnic.

SHOES

When it comes to stylish slingbacks, strappy sandals, and cult-status heels, Rome has a *scarpa* (shoe) to fit every Cinderella. Whet your appetite in the swanky Spagna area, but you may not want to buy the first pair you fall in love with. The city has a sea of shoes for mash-up vintage, skillfully styled ensembles, and incredible, covetable elegance. *Scarpe Diem!*

LISTINGS BY NEIGHBORHOOD

BARBERINI

CERAMICS AND DECORATIVE ARTS

Marmi Line Gifts. For a wide variety of marble and alabaster objets d'art, Marmi Line offers three locations in central Rome. Beautifully worked into familiar shapes, their mesmerizing pieces of fruit make centerpieces that would make Caravaggio proud. If you want something distinctly Roman, choose a practical or whimsical item made from travertine, the stone used to build the Colosseum and Bernini's St. Peter's Colonnade. ✉ *Via del Lavatore 28, Trevi* ☎ *06/6786347.*

LANDMARK STORES

Antica Farmacia Pesci dal 1552. Likely Rome's oldest pharmacy, the Antica Farmacia is run by a family of pharmacists. The shop's 18th-century furnishings, herbs, and vases evoke Harry Potter's Diagon Ally; and while they don't carry Polyjuice Potion, the pharmacists can whip up a just-for-you batch of composite powders, syrups, capsules, gels, and creams to soothe what ails you. ⊠ *Piazza Trevi 89, Trevi* ☎ *06/6792210.*

MEN'S CLOTHING

Brioni. Founded in 1945 and hailed for its impeccable craftsmanship and flawless execution, the Brioni label is known for attracting and keeping the best men's tailors in Italy where the exacting standards require that custom-made suits are designed from scratch and measured to the millimeter. For this personalized line, the menswear icon has 5,000 spectacular fabrics to select from. As thoughtful as expensive, one bespoke suit made from wool will take a minimum of 32 hours to create. Their prêt-à-porter line is also praised for peerless cutting and stitching. Past and present clients include Clark Gable, Donald Trump, Barack Obama and, of course, James Bond. And they say clothing doesn't make the man? ⊠ *Via Barberini 79* ☎ *06/484517* ⊕ *www.brioni.it* ⊠ *Via Condotti 21/A, Piazza di Spagna* ☎ *06/485855.*

15

CAMPO

CHILDREN'S CLOTHING

Rachele. Rachele is a small, charming shop tucked down a small alley not far from the Campo de' Fiori piazza. Most of the items of clothing are handmade by Rachele herself. Choose from whimsical crocheted hats and a cute selection of pants, skirts, and rainbow-colored tops for tykes up to age nine. ⊠ *Vicolo del Bollo 6–7* ☎ *06/6864975.*

CORSO

BOOKSTORES

Ex Libris. Founded in 1931 and one of the oldest antiquarian bookshops in Rome, Ex Libris has a distinctive selection of scholarly and collectible books from the 16th to 21th centuries that will make bookworms drool. The selection includes rare editions on art and architecture, music and theater, and literature and humanities, as well as maps and prints. ⊠ *Via dell' Umiltà 77/a* ☎ *06/6791540* ⊕ *www.exlibrisroma.it.*

Mondadori. Conveniently located close to the Trevi Fountain and pleasantly air-conditioned, Mondadori has a small English-language department on the ground floor near the caffè. The top floor has a generous selection of computer software and accessories, printers, mobile phones, and digital cameras. Mondadori remains one of the most prestigious Italian publishers and carries books of every genre for all readers. ⊠ *Via San Vincenzo 10* ☎ *06/6976501* ⊕ *www.mondadori.it.*

CERAMICS AND DECORATIVE ARTS

Le IV Stagioni. Le IV Stagioni stocks a colorful selection of traditional Italian pottery from well-known manufacturers like Capodimonte, Vietri, Deruta, Caltagirone, and Faenza. If you're looking for something *alla Romana,* opt for the brown glazed pots with a lacy white border and charming flower basket wall ornaments, made in the Rome area. ⊠ *Via dell' Umiltà 30/b* ☎ *06/69941029.*

CHILDREN'S CLOTHING

Bonpoint. Bonpoint brings a little of Paris to Rome in fine French children's wear. The crème de la crème when it comes to styling, refinement, and price, Bonpoint's casual and classic children's clothing are both picture-perfect and fashion-forward. Well-heeled mums will appreciate their soft, cuddly onesies, and hand-stitched party dresses. ⊠ *Piazza San Lorenzo in Lucina 25* ☎ *06/6871548.*

MEN'S CLOTHING

Borsalino Boutique. Borsalino fedoras and Panama hats have donned the heads of many silver screen icons including Humphrey Bogart and Gary Cooper. They may be expensive, but there is a reason for the exorbitant prices. Considered by many to be the Cadillac of fedoras, the dashing Borsolino has been a staple of the fashionable Italian man since 1857. Today, Borsalino retains its unmistakable class, style, and elegance. Few hats are made with such exacting care and attention, and the company's milliners still use machines that are more than 100 years old. ⊠ *Piazza del Popolo 20* ☎ *06/32650838* ⊕ *www.borsalino.it* ⊠ *Piazza Fontana di Trevi 83, Trevi* ☎ *06/6781015* ⊠ *Via Campo Marzio 72/a, Pantheon* ☎ *06/6783945.*

Fodor'sChoice ★ **Fratelli Viganò.** If you are a *Mad Men* wannabe hipster or just maintain a particular fondness for classically styled Italian millinery, this store will have you drooling. Fratelli Viganò was founded in 1873 and has been producing handsome handmade hats ever since. Even if you aren't planning a tribute to Don Draper, the shop is sure to impress with its artisans' painstaking attention to detail. With hundreds of hats arranged in perfect order, you will surely find one to strike your fancy. Roman poet Trilussa and even Mussolini preferred their top hats, but their signature pieces are the sporty fedoras and debonair brown derbies. ⊠ *Via Marco Minghetti 7, Spanga* ☎ *06/6795147.*

MUSIC STORES

Remix. An underground favorite for famous producers and distributors of legendary Roman vinyl labels like Sounds Never Seen, ACV, and many others, Remix specializes in techno. The shop also has a great back catalogue—all at prices that will make new collectors smile. ⊠ *Via del Fiume 8/9* ☎ *06/3216514* ⊕ *www.re-mix.it.*

STATIONERY

★ **Cartoleria Pantheon dal 1910.** An absolute Aladdin's cave for scribblers and those inspired by the blank page, the simply sumptuous Cartoleria Pantheon dal 1910 has unique leather journals and fine handmade paper to write a special letter. Writers and artists can choose from simple, stock paper to artisanal sheets of handcrafted Amalfi paper and from among hand-bound leather journals in an extraordinary array of colors and sizes. ⊠ *Via della Rotonda 15* ☎ *06/6875313* ⊕ *www. pantheon-roma.it.*

ESQUILINO

ANTIQUES

Orologi e Design. Orologi e Design specializes in nostalgic mechanical watches and chronographs from the 1900s through the 1970s. Whether you are looking for a solid gold dress watch or a vintage World War II military pilot's chronograph, chances are you'll find the piece you are looking for here. Have an heirloom piece that has stopped working or that needs a little tuning? Two expert watchmakers have the parts and skilled precision to clean, regulate, and repair your grandfather's vintage timepiece and get it tick-tocking again in no time. ⊠ *Via Urbana 123, Monti* ☎ *06/4742284.*

MONTI

15

FASHION

★ **Anteprima.** Anteprima is filled with revolutionary ready-to-wear separates that make a bold statement. Carrying a large selection of day and evening wear constructed with lustrous fabrics, the style here is offbeat. A deliberate contradiction of colors make the clothing dazzlingly original. Friendly and helpful staff have a unique eye for putting together accessories and shoes from their ever-changing collection. ⊠ *Via delle Quattro Fontane 38–40* ☎ *06/4828445* ⊕ *www.anteprimadimoda.com.*

Hydra. An avant-garde clothing shop for older teens and twentysomethings who believe clothing should make a statement, Hydra has styles that range from voluptuous Betty Boop retro dresses to indie underground to in-your-face T-shirts that would make your grandmother blush. ⊠ *Via Urbana 139* ☎ *06/48907773.*

FOOD, WINE, AND DELICACIES

La Bottega del Cioccolata. At the first shop you'll smell when walking down this picturesque street, master chocolate maker Maurizio Proietti and his father before him have been making chocolates as mouthwatering and beautiful as those seen in the famous film *Chocolat.* ⊠ *Via Leonina 82* ☎ *06/4821473* ⊕ *www.labottegadelcioccolato.it.*

JEWELRY

Art Privé. Just off Monti's principal square is the small jewelry shop where Tiziana Salzano makes multistrand torsade necklaces using the finest silverworks and a combination of boldly hued raw rubies and other semiprecious gemstones. Each piece is unique and cannot be exactly duplicated, so if you see a piece that steals your heart be sure to grab it. ⊠ *Via Leonina 8* ☎ *06/47826347.*

MEN'S CLOTHING

Mimmo Siviglia. Eighty-year-old Mimmo Siviglia is shirtmaking at its apex. The epitome of an old-world master tailor, he has been one of Rome's best-kept secrets for more than 50 years. To achieve a perfectly smooth look, Siviglia knows he has to cut the pattern just right, accounting for the person's shoulder to ensure there are no wrinkles around the collarbone. If you know your fine cloth, you'll enjoy discussing the merits of high-end fabrics such as Alumo, Albini, or Riva. Dress-shirt aficionados will be impressed by his attention to each customer and precise dedication to each order. Once his daughter has your size in the computer, future orders can be shipped anywhere in the world. ⊠ *Via Urbana 14a* ☎ *06/48903310* ⊕ *www.mimmosiviglia.com.*

VINTAGE CLOTHING

★ **Le Gallinelle.** Le Gallinelle is a tiny boutique in a former butcher's shop—hence the large metal hooks. Owner Wilma Silvestri transforms vintage, ethnic, and contemporary fabrics into retro-inspired clothing with a modern edge without smelling like mothballs from your great aunt Suzie's closet. ⊠ *Via del Boschetto 76* ☎ *06/48907175* ⊕ *www. legallinelle.it.*

NAVONA

ACCESSORIES

Spazio IF. In a tiny piazza alongside Rome's historic Via dei Coronari, designers Irene and Carla Ferrara have created a tantalizing hybrid between fashion paradise and art gallery. Working with unconventional designers and artists who emphasize Sicilian design, the shop has more to say about the style of Sicily and the creativity of the island's inhabitants than flat caps, puppets, and rich pastries. Perennial favorites include handbags cut by hand in a *putia* (shop) in Palermo, swimsuits, designer textiles, jewelry, and sportswear. ⊠ *Via dei Coronari 44a, Navona* ☎ *06/64760639* ⊕ *www.spazioif.it.*

ANTIQUES

Galleria Biagiarelli. In a superb setting in the former chapel of the Pre-Renaissance Palazzo Capranica, where the windows still have the cardinal's coat of arms, Rome's leading antiques dealer of 18th- and 19th-century Russian icons and English watercolors has also amassed a collection of Eastern European antique china figurines as well as Soviet-era artwork. ⊠ *Piazza Capranica 97* ☎ *06/6784987* ⊕ *www. biagiarelli.it.*

Fodor's Choice **Nardecchia.** In the heart of Piazza Navona, in front of Bernini's Fountain ★ of the Four Rivers, Nardecchia knows there are three major considerations when it comes to antique prints and etchings: value, aesthetics, and rarity. The shop showcases some of its beautiful 19th-century prints, old photographs, and watercolors, giving browsers a hint at what Rome looked like in centuries past. Can't afford an 18th-century etching? They have refined postcards, too. ⊠ *Piazza Navona 25* ☎ *06/6865318* ⊕ *www.nardecchia.it.*

Quattrocolo. This historic shop dating to 1938 showcases exquisite antique micro-mosaic jewelry painstakingly crafted in the style perfected by the masters at the Vatican mosaic studio. You'll also find 18th- and 19th-century cameos and beautiful engraved stones. Their small works were beloved by cosmopolitan clientele of the Grand Tour age and offer modern-day shoppers a taste of yesteryear's grandeur. If you are a fan of archaeology, don't miss their Etruscan-style jewelry. ⊠ *Via della Scrofa 48* ☎ *06/68801367* ⊕ *www.quattrocolo.com.*

CASUAL CHIC

Replay. A typical example of young Italians' passion for American trends, Replay has jeans and T-shirts with American sports teams emblazoned on them that have that little extra kiss of Italian styling that transforms sloppy hip into fashionable casual chic. Styles range from punk to hip-hop. Strictly for those under 30, with cash to spend. ⊠ *Via della Rotonda 24* ☎ *06/97602555* ⊕ *www.replay.it.*

Taro. Designed by owners Marisa Pignataro and Enrico Natoli, Taro's chic handmade knitwear in unusual yarns and striking colors is handmade in Rome. Selections from their casual, easy-to-wear line include luxuriously textured tunics, loose sleeveless jackets, and shawls and pants. ⊠ *Via della Scrofa 50* ☎ *06/6896476.*

Vestiti Usati Cinzia. There's a fun, unique, and diverse inventory of 1960s- and '70s-style apparel and googly sunglasses at Vestiti Usati Cinzia, beloved by private clients, costume designers, and fashion designers and stylists alike. You'll find lots of flower power, embroidered tops, and psychedelic clothing here, along with trippy boots and dishy bubblegum pink shoes that Twiggy would have loved. ⊠ *Via del Governo Vecchio 45* ☎ *06/6832945.*

CERAMICS AND DECORATIVE ARTS

Arte del Vetro Natolli Murano. Specializing in handblown Venetian art glass pieces, including Murano glass jewelry (necklaces and pendants), tableware, glass vases, and extravagant chandeliers, at Arte del Vetro Natolli Murano every individual piece is handcrafted from the furnaces of master glassmakers using ancient techniques kept alive by the island's artisans since 1291. Some limited-edition designs show not only the craftsman's mastery of the art form but the artisan's love for the vibrant aesthetic of the glassmaking tradition. ⊠ *Corso Rinascimento 53/55* ☎ *06/68301170.*

★ **IN.OR. dal 1952.** For more than 50 years, Romans have registered their bridal china and gifts under the frescoed ceilings of IN.OR. dal 1952, a grand silver and china store occupying the *piano nobile* of an 18th-century palazzo in the characteristic Campo Marzo area, in hopes of receiving something elegant. With seven rooms for browsing, the shop specializes in work handcrafted by the silversmiths of Pampaloni in Florence and Bellotto of Padua. ⊠ *Via della Stelletta 23* ☎ *06/6878579* ⊕ *www.inor.it.*

FASHION

Arsenale. Arsenale has a sleek layout and a low-key elegance that stands out, even in Rome. Rest your feet awhile in an overstuffed chair before sifting through the racks. Whether you are looking for a wedding dress or a seductive bustier, you are bound to find something unconventional here. Designer and owner Patriza Pieroni creates many of the pieces on display, all cleverly cut and decidedly captivating. ⊠ *Via del Pellegrino 172* ☎ *06/6880242* ⊕ *www.patriziapieroni.it.*

Le Tartarughe. Designer Susanna Liso, a Rome native, adds suggestive elements of playful experimentation to her haute couture and ready-to-wear lines, which are much loved by Rome's aristocracy and intelligentsia. With intense and enveloping designs, she mixes raw silks or cashmere and fine merino wool together to form captivating garments that are a mix of seduction and linear form. Le Tartarughe can be found at two locations close to the Pantheon. ⊠ *Via Piè di Marmo 17* ☎ *06/6792240* ⊕ *www.letartarughe.eu.*

★ **Maga Morgana.** Maga Morgana is a family-run business where everyone's nimble fingers contribute to producing the highly original clothes and accessories. From hippie-chick to bridal-chic, designer Luciana Iannace creates lavishly ornate clothes that are as inventive as they are distinguished. In addition to her own designs, she also sources inventive items from Paris and Florence. ⊠ *Via del Governo Vecchio 27* ☎ *06/6879995.*

FOOD, WINE, AND DELICACIES

Enoteca al Parlamento Achilli. The tantalizing smell of truffles from the snack counter, where a sommelier waits to organize your wine-tasting session, is enough alone to lure you into Enoteca al Parlamento Achilli, filled with gastronomic treasures. The proximity of this traditional enoteca to Montecitorio, the Italian Parliament building, makes it a favorite with journalists and politicos, who often stop in for a glass of wine after work, making its prices not for the faint of heart. Ask to take a look at the wine shop's most prized possessions: bottles of the Brunello di Montalcino vintages 1891 and 1925, strictly not for sale. ⊠ *Via dei Prefetti 15* ☎ *06/6873446* ⊕ *www.enotecaalparlamento.it.*

Fodor'sChoice **Moriondo e Gariglio.** The Willy Wonka of Roman chocolate factories ★ opened its doors in 1850. The shop uses the finest cocoa beans and adheres strictly to family recipes passed down from generation to generation. Known for rich, gourmet chocolates, they soon were the favored chocolatier to the House of Savoy. In 2009, the shop partnered with Bulgari and placed 300 pieces of jewelry in their Easter eggs to benefit cancer research. While you may not find diamonds in your bonbons, marrons glacés, or dark-chocolate truffles, you'll still delight in choosing from more than 80 delicacies. ⊠ *Via Piè di Marmo 21* ☎ *06/6990856* ⊕ *www.moriondoegariglio.com.*

HOUSEHOLD ITEMS

Fodor'sChoice **Society.** Have decorator envy? Everything you need for do-it-yourself ★ Italian home couture can be found at Society, the flagship store for Limonta, one of the most prestigious and historic textile brands made in Italy. With a carefully edited collection of inspiring designs, the store sports a free-spirited, lived-in bohemian interior with a multitude of innovations to dress up any area of your home. Centering on the rarest and most sought-after fabrics, their designs give the appearance they come from a different era (the 18th, 19th, and 20th centuries). ⊠ *Piazza di Pasquino 4, Navona* ☎ *06/6832480* ⊕ *www.societylimonta.com.*

Tebro. First opened in 1867 and listed with the Associazione Negozi Storici di Roma (Associaction of Historic Shops of Rome), Tebro is a classic Roman department store that epitomizes quality. It specializes in household linens and sleepwear, and you can even find those 100-percent cotton, Italian waffle-weave bath sheets that are synonymous with Italian hotels. ⊠ *Via dei Prefetti 48–54* ☎ *06/6873441* ⊕ *www.tebro.it.*

JEWELRY

Fodor'sChoice ★ **Delfina Delettrez.** When your great grandmother is Adele Fendi, it's not surprising that creativity runs in your genes. In her early 20s, Delfina Delettrez creates edgy, conceptual collections. Using human body–inspired pieces blending skulls, wild animals, and botanical elements, she daringly merges gold, silver, bone and glass, crystals and diamonds to create gothic, edgy styles worthy of Fritz Lang's *Metropolis* or *Blade Runner*. Don't be put off by her signature goth-glam designs in the window: this dazzling emporium, with its innumerable drawers filled with baubles, has something saucy and refined for everyone's sensibilities. ⊠ *Via Governo Vecchio 67, Navona* ☎ *06/68136362* ⊕ *www. delfinadelettrez.com.*

MMM—Massimo Maria Melis. Drawing heavily on ancient Greek, Roman, and Etruscan designs, Massimo Maria Melis jewelry will carry you back in time. Working with 21-carat gold, he often incorporates antique coins acquired by numismatists or pieces of ancient bronze and polychromatic glass. Some of his pieces are done with an ancient technique much loved by the Etruscans in which tiny gold droplets are soldered together to create intricately patterned designs. ⊠ *Via dell'Orso 57, Navona* ☎ *06/6869188* ⊕ *www.massimomariamelis.com.*

MEN'S CLOTHING

Davide Cenci. For the discerning shopper, Davide Cenci is a Roman classic for high-quality clothing and accessories for every occasion. For most visitors on a short holiday, purchasing custom-fitted clothing is not an option. Cenci's clothiers will adjust and tailor most anything to fit your body like a glove and have it delivered to your hotel within three days. The label is famous for its sinful cashmere, sailing sportswear, and trench coats, and you will appreciate their customer service and attention to detail. ⊠ *Via Campo Marzio 1-7* ☎ *06/6990681* ⊕ *www. davidecenci.com.*

Fodor'sChoice ★ **SBU.** In a city famous for classically sharp suits, it can be a challenge to find hip menswear in Rome, but SBU (Strategic Business Unit) suavely fills the void. In a 19th-century former draper's workshop, it's the place where Rome's VIPS buy their soft and supple vintage low-cut Japanese denims. Behind the old wooden counters, stacked drawer chests, and iron columns, SBU offers a sophisticated range of casual clothing, sportswear, shoes, and upscale accessories. The small hidden garden around back offers a relaxing moment between shopping sprees. ⊠ *Via di San Pantaleo 68–69, Navona* ☎ *06/68802547* ⊕ *www.sbu.it.*

PERFUME AND COSMETICS

★ **Ai Monasteri.** Among dark-wood paneling, choirlike alcoves, and painted angels, at Ai Monasteri you'll find traditional products made by Italy's diligent friars and monks. Following century-old recipes, the herbal decoctions, liqueurs, beauty aids, and toiletries offer a look into the time-honored tradition of monastic trade. The Elixir dell'Amore (love potion) is perfect for any well-deserving valentine, or, if it isn't true love, you can opt for a bottle of the popular Elixir of Happiness. There are myriad products, ranging from colognes for children to quince-apple and Cistercian jams, made exclusively with organic produce and Royal

15

Jelly honey. ⊠ *Corso del Rinascimento 72* ☎ *06/68802783* ⊕ *www. monasteri.it.*

Antica Erboristeria Romana. Complete with hand-labeled wooden drawers holding its more than 200 varieties of herbs, flowers, and tinctures including aper, licorice, and hellbane, Antica Erboristeria Romana has maintained its old-world apothecary feel. The shop stocks an impressive array of herbal teas and infusions, more than 700 essential oils, bud derivatives, and powdered extracts. ⊠ *Via Torre Argentina 15* ☎ *06/6879493* ⊕ *www.anticaerboristeriaromana.it.*

SHOES

Superga. Superga, which celebrated its 100th anniversary in 2011, sells those timeless sneakers that every Italian wears at some point, in classic white or—yum—a rainbow of colors. Their 2750 model has been worn by everyone from Kelly Brook to Katie Holmes. If you are a sneakerhead who has been stuck on Converse, give these Italian brethren a look. Just remember not to wear socks with them. ⊠ *Via della Maddalena 30/a, Navona* ☎ *06/6868737* ⊕ *www.superga.com.*

STATIONERY

Il Papiro. One of Rome's preferred shops for those who appreciate exquisite writing materials and papermaking techniques that are almost extinct, Il Papiro sells hand-decorated marbleized papers made using the 17th-century marbleized technique called *a la cuve*. Their stationery and card stock are printed with great care using exacting standards. Whether you are searching for unique lithography, engraving, or delicate watermarked paper, you'll find some indulgence here. They also carry a fine selection of wax seals, presses for paper embossing, Venetian glass pens, and ink stamps. ⊠ *Via del Pantheon 50* ☎ *06/6795597* ⊕ *www.ilpapirofirenze.it.*

TOYS

Al Sogno. If you're looking for quality toys that encourage imaginative play and learning, look no further than Al Sogno. With an emphasis on the artistic as well as the multisensory, the shop has a selection of toys that are both discerning and individual, making them perfect for children of all ages. Carrying an exquisite collection of fanciful puppets, collectible dolls, masks, stuffed animals, and illustrated books, this Navona jewel is crammed top to bottom with beautiful and well-crafted playthings. If you believe that children's toys don't have to be high-tech, you will adore reliving some of your best childhood memories here. ⊠ *Piazza Navona 53* ☎ *06/6864198* ⊕ *www.alsogno.com.*

★ **Bartolucci.** Bartolucci attracts shoppers with a life-size Pinocchio pedaling furiously on a wooden bike. Inside is a shop that would have warmed Gepetto's heart. For more than 60 years and three generations, this family has been making whimsical, handmade curiosities out of pine, including clocks, bookends, bedside lamps, and wall hangings. You can even buy a child-size vintage car entirely made of wood, including the wheels. ⊠ *Via dei Pastini 98* ☎ *06/69190894* ⊕ *www. bartolucci.com.*

Bertè. One of the oldest toy shops in Rome, Bertè carries a large selection of stuffed animals, dolls, Legos, and other collectibles. It specializes in dolls, both the crying, eating, and talking types, as well as the ribbon-bedecked old-fashioned beauties. ⊠ *Piazza Navona 108* ☎ *06/6875011*.

La Città del Sole. La Città del Sole is the progressive parent's ideal store, chock-full of fair-trade and eco-friendly toys that share shelf space with retro and vintage favorites. With educational toys arranged by age, the store is a child-friendly browser's delight crammed with puzzles, gadgets, books, and toys in safe plastics and sustainable wood. The knowledgeable sales staff can help parents make the right choice. ⊠ *Via della Scrofa 65* ☎ *06/68803805* ⊕ *www.cittadelsole.it.*

VINTAGE CLOTHING

Mado. Still a leader in nostalgia styling, Mado has been vintage cool in Rome since 1969. The shop is funky, glamorous, and often over-the-top wacky. Whether you are looking for a robin's-egg-blue empire-waist dress or a '50s gown evocative of a Lindy Hop, Mado understands the challenges of incorporating vintage pieces into a modern wardrobe. ⊠ *Via del Governo Vecchio 89/a* ☎ *06/6875028.*

15

REPUBBLICA

BOOKSTORES

Mel Bookstore. If you like discounts on remainder stock and secondhand books, come to Mel Bookstore. Browse through the large basement and find a treasure trove of marked-down merchandise as well as a modest selection of English-language paperbacks. Upstairs, shop for books in Italian on a variety of subjects or pick up a DVD of *Roman Holiday*. Afterward, relax with your purchases while you treat yourself to a coffee and dessert in the spacious art deco–style caffè. ⊠ *Via Nazionale 254–255* ☎ *06/4885433* ⊕ *www.melbookstore.it.*

CERAMICS AND DECORATIVE ARTS

Fodor's Choice
★

Il Giardino di Domenico Persiani. Nestled in a cool courtyard garden under the shade of an expansive oak tree is refreshing open-air terra-cotta shop Il Giardino di Domenico Persiani. Whether you're looking for a chubby cherub, a replica of Bacchus, or your very own Bocca della Verità, this is your chance to bring a little piece of Rome home to your garden. With a large selection of handmade Roman masks, busts, flower pots, and vases, there is something here for anyone with a green thumb. ⊠ *Via Torino 92* ☎ *06/4883886.*

FOOD, WINE, AND DELICACIES

Trimani Vinai a Roma dal 1821. For more than 180 years Trimani Vinai a Roma dal 1821, occupying an entire block near the Termini train station, has had the city's largest selection of wines, champagne, spumante, grappa, and other liqueurs. With more than 1,000 bottles to choose from and knowledgeable wine stewards, Trimani will give you the opportunity to explore Europe's diverse wine regions without leaving the city. ⊠ *Via Goito 20* ☎ *06/4469661* ⊕ *www.trimani.com.*

SHOPPING MALLS

Il Forum Termini. Rome's handiest central shopping mall is Il Forum Termini, a cluster of shops that stay open until 10 pm (even on Sunday), conveniently located directly inside Rome's biggest train station,

Stazione Termini. In a city not known for its convenient shopping hours, this "shop before you hop/buy before you fly" hub is a good spot for last-minute goodies or a book for your train or airplane ride. There are more than 50 shops, including the ever-popular United Colors of Benetton, L'Occitane, Sephora, and Optimissimo, which has more than 3,000 super-stylish glasses and sunglasses by top Italian designers. There is even a supermarket for your picnic lunch on the train. ⊠ *Stazione Temini* ⊕ *www.grandistazioni.it.*

SAN GIOVANNI

FLEA MARKETS

Via Sannio. Though not strictly a flea market, the *mercato* Via Sannio is entirely without pretension and open weekdays 8–2 and Saturday 8–5. Here you can find military surplus, leather jackets, cosmetics, and many other bargains. Also expect great deals on shoes—you can buy good-quality name-brand shoes that have served their time only as shop-window displays. ⊠ *Near La Basilica di San Giovanni in Laterano.*

SAN LORENZO

CASUAL CHIC

Fodor'sChoice
★ **L'Anatra all'Arancia.** Repetto ballerinas, roomy handbags, and funky dresses make L'Anatra all'Arancia one of the best local secrets of boho San Lorenzo. Its window display showcases innovative designer clothes from Marina Spadafora, Antik Batik, See by Chloé and Donatella Baroni (the store's owner and buyer). Leaning towards the alternative with an eclectic selection of handpicked Italian and French labels, Donatella carries sinful perfumes from L'Artisan Parfumeur and beautiful jewelry from the line of Serge Thoraval. ⊠ *Via Tiburtina 105* ☎ *06/4456293.*

Red Frame Shop. A small and somewhat hard-to-find boutique that is identified only by its red-brick framed door, Red Frame Shop is open odd hours, so don't be afraid to knock if the door is locked. The shop is filled with wool and cotton sweaters and skirts, each handmade with attention to detail. If you don't find your size or color, let the owner know and they can make it for you. ⊠ *Via degli Equi 70* ☎ *06/4955795.*

CERAMICS AND DECORATIVE ARTS

Le Terre di AT. Le Terre di AT is a modern potters' workshop nestled in the belly of San Lorenzo, Rome's burgeoning university district. Working on the premises, artist Angela Torcivia creates vases, cups, ceramic jewelry, and necklaces. Her pieces have an otherworldly style, combining ancient shapes with fiery contrasting colors, and are modern while still paying homage to the rich history of Roman clay pottery. ⊠ *Via degli Ausoni 13* ☎ *06/491748* ⊕ *www.leterrediat.it.*

VINTAGE CLOTHING

Pifebo. A sensational vintage-clothing emporium packed with thousands of items, fire-engine red Pifebo has a loyal following of university students, offbeat musicians, and even the occasional costume designer. Specializing in '70s, '80s and '90s clothes and shoes, the prices are great, the feel is welcoming, and the merchandise turns over quickly.

La vita è bella, non? Add shopping to the *passeggiata* evening stroll, and who knows what will happen!

✉ *Via dei Volsci 101* ☎ *06/64870813* ✉ *Via dei Serpenti 141, Monti* ☎ *06/64870813.*

SPAGNA

ACCESSORIES

★ **Braccialini.** Founded in 1954 by Florentine stylist Carla Braccialini and her husband, Braccialini—currently managed by their sons—makes bags that are authentic works of art in delightful shapes, such as little gold taxis or Santa Fe stagecoaches. The delightfully quirky beach bags have picture postcard scenes of Italian resorts made of brightly colored appliquéd leather: Be sure to check out their eccentric *Temi* (Theme) creature bags; the opossum-shaped handbag made out of crocodile skin makes a richly whimsical fashion statement. ✉ *Via Mario De' Fiori 73* ☎ *06/6785750* ⊕ *shop.braccialini.com.*

Di Cori. Di Cori packs a lot of gloves into a tiny space, offering a rainbow of color choices. Made of the softest lambskin, and lined with silk, cashmere, rabbit fur, or wool, a pair of these gloves will ensure warm and fashionable hands. They also carry a smaller selection of unlined, washable versions. ✉ *Piazza di Spagna 53* ☎ *06/6784439* ⊕ *www. dicorigloves.it.*

Furla. Furla has 15 franchises in Rome alone. Its flagship store, to the left of the Spanish Steps, sells bags like hot cakes. Be prepared to fight your way through crowds of passionate handbag lovers, all anxious to possess one of the delectable bags, wallets, or watch straps in ice-cream colors. ⊠ *Piazza di Spagna 22, Spagna* ☎ *06/69200363* ⊕ *www. furla.com.*

Gherardini. In business since 1885, Gherardini has taken over a decon-secrated church and slickly transformed it into a showplace for their label, which is known for its retro handbags and logo-stamped syn-thetic materials. Gherardini's leather totes, sling bags, and soft luggage have become classics and are worth the investment. Be sure to take a look at their limited edition Japanese flag bag "Gherardini for Japan"; proceeds will go to the Japanese Red Cross supporting those affected by the 2011 Tōhoku earthquake. ⊠ *Via Belsiana 48/b* ☎ *06/6795501* ⊕ *www.gherardini.it.*

La Coppola Storta. La Coppola Storta describes a type of Sicilian beret and the jaunty way it was worn by Mafiosi. They say the more the hat was twisted to the side, the more connected the wearer was to orga-nized crime. In defiance of Mafia influence across Sicily, activist Guido Agnello helped to open a factory in San Giuseppe specializing in the manufacture of these colorful caps, giving jobs to local sewers, many of whom were previously unemployed or connected to the black market. With the help of some of Italy's best designers, they have created a line of dapper Coppola for adults, children, and even puppies, which have become a sought-after fashion accessory and an unexpected ambas-sador for the anti-mafia struggle all over the world. With every color and fabric imaginable, hat prices start at €55. ⊠ *Via delle Croce 81/a, Piazza di Spagna* ☎ *06/6785824* ⊕ *www.lacoppolastorta.it.*

La Perla. La Perla is the go-to for beautifully crafted lingerie and glam-orous underwear for that special night, a bridal trousseau, or just to spoil yourself on your Roman holiday. In partnership with Jean Paul Gaultier, the brand has just launched a swimwear line alongside his second lingerie collection. If you like decadent finery that is both styl-ish and romantic, you will find something here to make you feel like a goddess. ⊠ *Via Bocca di Leone 24* ☎ *06/69941934* ⊕ *www.laperla.com.*

Mandarina Duck. Mandarina Duck appeared on the Italian design scene in 1997. Their snappy, colored MD20 bags and luggage in durable syn-thetic fabrics were soon a hit. Techno shoppers have begun snapping up their new "unexpected" bag, with a plethora of pockets including two especially for iPads and mobile phones, making it practical in form and design. Working gals will adore their smart business bag made with semirigid material and large pockets for keeping documents organized. ⊠ *Via dei Due Macelli 59/F* ☎ *06/6786414* ⊕ *www.mandarinaduck. com.*

Roxy. Filled with rows of silk ties in every color and pattern, Roxy car-ries a selection bewilderingly large and moderately priced, and the store is usually packed with customers. Be sure to take a look at this season's spotted and checked versions. ⊠ *Via Frattina 115* ☎ *06/6796691* ⊠ *Via Barberini 112, Barberini* ☎ *06/4883931.*

Fodor'sChoice ★ **Saddlers Union.** Reborn on the mythical artisan's street, Via Margutta, across the street from Federico Fellini's old house, Saddlers Union first launched in 1957 and quickly gained a cult following among those who valued Italian artistry and the traditional aesthetic. Jacqueline Kennedy set the trend of classical elegance by sporting Saddlers Union's rich saddle-leather bucket bag. Closed in 2004, one of Italy's finest labels is back, representing everything for which Rome leatherwork has become famous. If you're searching for a sinfully fabulous handbag in a graceful, classic shape or that "I have arrived" attorney's briefcase, you will find something guaranteed to inspire envy. Items are made on-site with true artistry and under the watchful eye of Angelo Zaza, one of Saddlers Union's original master artisans. The prices are high, but so is the quality. ⊠ *Via Margutta 11, Spagna* ☎ *06/32120237* ⊕ *www.saddlersunion. com.*

Schostal. At the end of the 19th century when ladies needed petticoats, corsets, bonnets, or white or colored stockings made of cotton thread, wool, or silk, it was inevitable for them to stop at Schostal. A Piazza di Spagna fixture since 1870, the shop still preserves that genteel ambience. Fine-quality shirts come with spare collars and cuffs. Ultraclassic underwear, handkerchiefs, and pure wool and cashmere are available at affordable prices. ⊠ *Via Fontanella Borghese 29* ☎ *06/6791240* ⊕ *www. schostalroma.com.*

Sermoneta. Sermoneta allures with its stacks of nappa leather, deerskin, and pigskin gloves in all colors. To produce one pair of gloves requires the skill and precision of at least 10 artisans. To satisfy demand, they carry a diverse selection of hand-stitched gloves (lined or unlined) for men and women. You can even find opera-length gloves for those special evenings or you can have your purchases personalized with initials, logos, and other designs. ⊠ *Piazza di Spagna 61* ☎ *06/6791960* ⊕ *www. sermonetagloves.com.*

Fodor's Choice
★
Tod's. With just 30 years under its belt, Tod's has grown from a small family brand into a global powerhouse so wealthy that it has donated €20 million to renovate the Colosseum. Tod's has gathered a cult following among style mavens worldwide, due in large part to owner Diego Della Valle's equally famous other possession: Florence's soccer team. The shoe baron's trademark is his simple, understated designs. Sure to please are his light and flexible slip-on Gommini driving shoes with rubber-bottomed soles for extra driving-pedal grip. Now you just need a Ferrari. ⊠ *Via Fontanella di Borghese 56a/c* ☎ *06/68210066* ⊕ *www.tods.com.*

Yamamay. Specializing in sophisticated lingerie for the fashion-conscious woman, Yamamay designs are a perfect combination of femininity and sexiness. Branches of the store are located throughout the city. ⊠ *Via del Corso 309, Corso* ☎ *06/6991196* ⊕ *www.yamamay.it.*

ANTIQUES

Fratelli Alinari. The gallery store of the world's oldest photography firm, Fratelli Alinari was founded by brothers Leopoldo, Giuseppe, and Romualdo Alinari in 1852. Patrons can browse through a vast archive of prints, books, rare collotypes, and finely detailed reproductions of historical images, drawings, and paintings. Several of the more interesting subjects re-created using this technique are Dante's *Divine Comedy* and both the *Plan de Paris* and *The Origin of New York*, detailed reproductions of the first recorded maps of these two cities. ⊠ *Via Alibert 16/a* ☎ *06/6792923* ⊕ *www.alinari.it.*

Galleria Benucci. With carved and gilded late baroque and Empire period furniture and paintings culled from the noble houses of Italy's past, Galleria Benucci is a treasure trove. An establishment favored by professionals from Europe and abroad, this elegant gallery has a astonishing selection of objects in a hushed atmosphere where connoisseurs will find the proprietors only too happy to discuss their latest finds. ⊠ *Via del Babuino 150/C* ☎ *06/36002190* ⊕ *www.galleriabenucci.it.*

BOOKSTORES

Anglo-American Book Co. A large and friendly English-language bookstore with more than 45,000 books, Anglo-American Book Co. has been a mecca for English-language reading material in Rome for more than 25 years. Whether you are a study-abroad student in need of an art history or archaeology textbook, or a visitor searching for a light read for the train, there is something for everyone here. Among shelves stuffed from floor to ceiling and sometimes several rows deep, book lovers can find British and American editions and easily spend hours just looking. The bilingual staff pampers browsers and does not rush or hover. ⊠ *Via della Vite 102, Spagna* ☎ *06/6795222* ⊕ *www.aab.it.*

La Feltrinelli. As Rome's biggest bookseller, La Feltrinelli's main attraction is the Piazza Colonna flagship store. Ensconced in the elegant 19th-century Galleria Alberto Sordi, this mega-bookstore fills three floors with books, music, postcards, holiday items, and small gifts. A great place to explore Italian-style book shopping, there are 12 branches peppered throughout the city. The Torre Argentina shop also has a ticketing office for music and cultural events and a caffè tucked upstairs with refreshing snacks and good coffee. The Repubblica branch carries a large section of titles in many languages as well as a well-stocked foreign film selection. ⊠ *Piazza Colonna 31/35, Corso* ☎ *06/69755001* ⊕ *www.lafeltrinelli.it* ⊠ *Via Vittorio Emanuele Orlando 84/86, Repubblica* ☎ *06/4827878* ⊠ *Largo Torre Argentina, Campo de' Fiori* ☎ *06/68663001.*

Lion Bookshop. For 50 years Italy's oldest English-language bookstore, with its children's reading corner and small caffè with American snacks and cookies, has been a welcoming haven for moms in search of that special children's book. In addition to books for kids, they also have a broad assortment of contemporary and classic fiction and nonfiction titles, as well as books on Rome and Italy in general, plus art, architecture, and cooking. ⊠ *Via dei Greci 33/36* ☎ *06/32654007.*

CERAMICS AND DECORATIVE ARTS

Musa. Musa is the place to shop if you're looking for decorative ceramic accents. Be sure to pop up to the second floor, where you can find a fine array of extravagant hand-painted ceramic tiles from Vietri, a region renowned for the quality of its clays and artisanal ceramic tradition. Shipping can be arranged. Whether you're planning to tile an entire bathroom or just pick up a few pieces to use in your kitchen as hot plates, your house will have an Italian villa feel when you are done. ⊠ *Via di Campo Marzio 39, Corso* ☎ *06/6871204* ⊕ *www.ceramic hemusa.it.*

CHILDREN'S CLOTHING

La Cicogna. A well-known designer children's clothier found throughout Italy with clothing for little ones from birth to age 14, La Cicogna is one-stop, name-brand shopping for antsy kids and tired parents. The stores carry clothes, shoes, baby carriages, and nursery supplies as well as child-size versions of designer names like Armani, Burberry, Guru, Timberland, Replay, Blumarine, and DKNY. ⊠ *Via Frattina 138* ☎ *06/6791912* ⊠ *Via Cola di Rienzo 268, Vatican* ☎ *06/6896557.*

Pinco Pallino. Founded by Imelde Bronzieri and Stefano Cavalleri in 1980, Pinco Pallino has extraordinary clothing for boys and girls, be it a sedate tulle petal jumper or savvy sailor wear. Moms will find their latest lines for babies and tots absolutely delicious. ⊠ *Via del Babuino 115, Spagna* ☎ *06/69190549* ⊕ *www.pincopallino.it.*

Pùre. The mothership for fashionistas in the making, Pùre carries designer brands that include Fendi, Diesel, Dior, Juicy Couture, Nolita, and Miss Blumarine. The store has plush carpet to crawl on and children's clothes for newborns to age 12. ⊠ *Via Frattina 111* ☎ *06/6794555* ⊕ *www. puresermoneta.it.*

DEPARTMENT STORES

La Rinascente. Italy's best-known department store, La Rinascente is where Italian fashion mogul Giorgio Armani got his start as a window dresser. Recently relocated inside the Galleria Alberto Sordi, the store has a phalanx of ready-to-wear designer sportswear and blockbuster handbags and accessories. The upscale clothing and accessories are a hit with the young and well dressed, while retail turf is geared toward people on lunch breaks and the ubiquitous tourist. The Piazza Fiume location has more floor space and a wider range of goods, including a housewares department. ⊠ *Galleria Alberto Sordi, Piazza Colonna* ☎ *06/6797691* ⊕ *www.rinascente.it* ⊠ *Piazza Fiume, Via Veneto* ☎ *06/8841231* ⊕ *www.rinascente.it.*

FASHION

Brighenti. Brighenti looks like what it is—a traditional Roman shop from a gentler era, replete with a marble floor and a huge crystal chandelier suspended overhead. Sensual silk nightgowns and exquisite peignoirs that have a vintage silver screen feel are displayed downstairs. Upstairs are sumptuous vintage-inspired swimsuits that will make you feel like Marlene Dietrich. ⊠ *Via Frattina 7–10* ☎ *06/6791484* ⊕ *www. brighentiboutique.it.*

Dolce & Gabbana. Dolce and Gabbana met in 1980 when both were assistants at a Milan fashion atelier and opened their first store in 1982. With a modern aesthetic that screams sex appeal, the brand has always thrived on its excesses. The Rome store can be more than a little overwhelming, with its glossy glamazons but at least there is plenty of eye candy, masculine and feminine, with a spring line heavy of stars and sequins as well as enthusiastic fruits, flowers, and veggies. ⊠ *Piazza di Spagna 94* ☎ *06/6782990* ⊕ *www.dolcegabbana.com.*

Elena Mirò. Elena Mirò is an absolutely delectable Italian atelier making its mark designing clothes specifically for those who don't have the proportions of a 14-year-old. If your DNA gave you the curves of *Mad Men*'s Joan Holloway you will love the fact that this designer specializes in beautifully sexy clothes for curvy, European-styled women size 46 (U.S. size 12, UK size 14) and up. ⊠ *Via Frattina 11–12* ☎ *06/6784367* ⊕ *www.elenamiro.com* ⊠ *Via Nazionale 197, Repubblica* ☎ *06/4823881.*

Fodor's Choice   **Fendi.** Fendi has been a fixture of the Roman fashion landscape since
   ★   "Mamma" Fendi first opened shop with her husband in 1925. With an eye for crazy genius, she hired Karl Lagerfeld, who began working with the group at the start of his career. His furs and runway antics have made him one of the world's most influential designers of the 20th century and brought international acclaim to Fendi along the way. Recent Lagerfeld triumphs include new collections marrying innovative textures, fabrics (cashmere, felt, and duchesse satin) with exotic skins like crocodile. Keeping up with technology, they even have an iPad case that will surely win a fashionista's seal of approval. The atelier, now owned by the Louis Vuitton group, continues to symbolize Italian glamour at its finest, though the difference in owners is noticeable. ⊠ *Largo Carlo Goldoni 419–421* ☎ *06/696661* ⊕ *www.fendi.com* ⊠ *Via Borgognona 39.*

Galassia. Galassia has ingenious and avant-garde women's styles by an A-list of designers including Gaultier, Westwood, Issey Miyake, and Yamamoto. If you're the type who dares to be different and in need of some closet therapy, you will love the extravagant selection, which gives the store a look that cannot be found elsewhere. ⊠ *Via Frattina 21* ☎ *06/6797896* ⊕ *www.galassiaroma.com.*

Giorgio Armani. One of the most influential designers of Italian haute couture, Giorgio Armani creates fluid silhouettes and dazzling evening gowns with décolletés so deep they'd make a grown man blush, his signature cuts made with the clever-handedness and flawless technique that you only achieve working with tracing paper and Italy's finest fabrics over the course of a lifetime. His menswear collection uses traditional textiles like wide-ribbed corduroy and stretch jersey in nontraditional ways while staying true to a clean, masculine aesthetic. It's true that exotic runway ideas and glamorous celebrities give Armani saleability, but his staying power is casual Italian elegance with just the right touch of whimsy and sexiness. Want to live *la bella vita* for longer than your Roman holiday? Armani is also selling luxury apartments in Rome at Cavour 220, complete with his personalized interiors. ⊠ *Via Condotti 77* ☎ *06/6991460* ⊕ *www.giorgioarmani.com* ⊠ *Via Del Babuino 71a* ☎ *06/36001848* ⊠ *Via Del Babuino 140* ☎ *06/3221581.*

   ★   **Gucci.** As the glamorous fashion label turns 90, the success of the double-G trademark brand is unquestionable. Survival in luxury fashion depends on defining market share, and creative director Frida Giannini has proven she knows the soul of the House of Gucci. Tom Ford may have made Gucci the sexiest brand in the world, but it's today's reinterpreted horsebit styles and Jackie Kennedy scarves that keep the design house on top. And while Gucci remains a fashion must for virtually every A-list celebrity, their designs have moved from heart-stopping sexy rock star to something classically subdued and retrospectively feminine. ⊠ *Via Condotti 8* ☎ *06/6790405* ⊕ *www.gucci.com.*

Krizia. Designer Mariuccia Mandelli borrowed the name Krizia from the title of Plato's unfinished dialogue on women's vanity to market her designs by. Born in 1933, she began designing dresses for her dolls at age 8. The designer's collections have gone through many top stylists and have recently returned to their original stylized roots. The current prêt-à-porter line emphasizes the use of black and dove grey, mixed with animal prints; it's dramatic, yet classy: wearing Krizia will get you noticed. ⊠ *Piazza di Spagna 87* ☎ *06/6793772* ⊕ *www.krizia.it.*

★ **Laura Biagiotti.** For 40 years Laura Biagiotti has been a worldwide ambassador of Italian fashion. Considered the Queen of Cashmere, her soft-as-velvet pullovers have been worn by Sophia Loren and her snow-white cardigans were said to be a favorite of the late Pope John Paul II. Princess Diana even sported one of Biagiotti's cashmere maternity dresses. Be sure to indulge in her line of his-and-her perfumes. ⊠ *Via Mario de' Fiori 26* ☎ *06/6791205* ⊕ *www.laurabiagiotti.it.*

Fodor's Choice **Marisa Padovan.** The place to go for exclusive, made-to-order lingerie
★ and bathing suits, Marisa Padovan has been sewing for Hollywood starlets like Audrey Hepburn and the well-heeled women of Rome for more than 40 years. Whether you want to purchase a ready-made style trimmed with Swarovski crystals and polished turquoise stones or design your own bespoke bikini or one-piece, their made-to-measure precision will have you looking like Rita Hayworth. ⊠ *Via delle Carrozze 81* ☎ *06/6793946* ⊕ *www.marisapadovan.it.*

Mariella Burani. Highly wearable and never boring, Mariella Burani has classy yet sensual ready-to-wear that borrows judiciously from several of the company's other principal lines. Recently they have begun adding jewelry and accessories to complete their fashion portfolio. ⊠ *Via Borgognona 29, Spagna* ☎ *06/6790630* ⊕ *www.mariellaburani.com.*

Missoni. Notable for its bohemian knitwear designs with now-legendary patterns of zigzags, waves, and stripes (some of which are influenced by folk art), as well as elegant eveningwear and must-have swimsuits, Missoni is unlike other Italian fashion families: in three generations there have been neither vendettas nor buyouts by huge multinational conglomerates to stain their colorful history. And while their eye-popping designs have polarized critics, they continue to deliver exquisite collections, mesmerizing the buying public. ⊠ *Piazza di Spagna 78* ☎ *06/6792555* ⊕ *www.missoni.it.*

Fodor's Choice **Patrizia Pepe.** One of Florence's best-kept secrets for up-and-coming
★ fashions, Patrizia Pepe emerged on the scene in 1993 with designs both minimalist and bold, combining classic styles with low-slung jeans and jackets with oversize lapels that are bound to draw attention. Her line of shoes are hot-hot-hot for those who can walk in stilts. It's still not huge on the fashion scene as a stand-alone brand, but take a look at this shop before the line becomes the next fast-tracked craze. ⊠ *Via Frattina 44* ☎ *06/6781851* ⊕ *www.patriziapepe.com.*

15

★ **Prada.** Not just the devil, but also serious shoppers wear Prada season after season, especially those willing to sell their souls for one of their ubiquitous handbags. If you are looking for that blend of old-world luxury with a touch of fashion-forward finesse, you'll hit pay dirt here. Recent handbag designs have a bit of a 1960s Jackie Kennedy feel, and whether you like them will hinge largely on whether you find Prada's signature retro-modernism enchanting. You'll find the Rome store more service-focused than the New York City branches—a roomy elevator delivers you to a series of thickly carpeted rooms where a flock of discreet assistants will help you pick out dresses, shoes, lingerie, and fashion accessories. ⊠ *Via Condotti 92/95* ☎ *06/6790897* ⊕ *www.prada. com.*

Salvatore Ferragamo. One of the top-10 most-wanted men's footwear brands, Salvatore Ferragamo has been providing Hollywood glitterati and discerning clients with unique handmade designs for years. Ferragamo fans will think they have died and followed the white light when they enter this store. The Florentine design house also specializes in handbags, small leather goods, men's and women's ready-to-wear, and scarves and ties. Men's styles are found at Via Condotti 65, women's at 73/74. Want to sleep in Ferragamo style? Their splendid luxury Portrait Suites Hotel is on the upper floors. ⊠ *Via Condotti 65* ☎ *06/6781130* ⊕ *www.ferragamo.com* ⊠ *Via Condotti 73/74* ☎ *06/6791565.*

Fodor'sChoice
★
Save the Queen!. A hot Florentine design house with exotic and creative pieces for women and girls with artistic and eccentric frills, cut-outs, and textures, Save the Queen! has one of the most beautiful shops in the city, with window displays that are works of art unto themselves. The store is chock-full of Baroque-inspired dresses, shirts, and skirts that are ultrafeminine and not the least bit discreet. Pieces radiate charming excess, presenting a portrait of youthful chic. ⊠ *Via del Babuino 49, Spagna* ☎ *06/36003039* ⊕ *www.savethequeen.com.*

Trussardi. A classic design house moving in a youthful direction, Trussardi has been symbolized by its greyhound logo since 1973. Today, with Gaia Trussardi at the helm and following in her father and brother's footsteps, the line is making use of leather accent pieces like suede tunics and wider belts. Tru Trussardi (in Galleria Alberto Sordi) addresses a modern woman's need for both luxury and comfort in upscale daily wear. ⊠ *Via Condotti 49/50* ☎ *06/6780280* ⊕ *www.trussardi.com.*

Fodor'sChoice
★
Valentino. Since taking the Valentino reins a few years ago, creative directors Maria Grazia Chiuri and Pier Paolo Piccioli have faced numerous challenges, the most basic being keeping Valentino true to Valentino after the designer's retirement in 2008. Both served as accessories designers under Valentino for more than a decade and understand exactly how to make the next generation of Hollywood stars swoon. Spagna's sprawling boutiques showcase designs with a romantic edginess: think kitten heels and or a show-stopping prêt-à-porter evening gown worthy of the Oscars. ⊠ *Via Condotti 12–15, Spagna* ☎ *06/69200618* ⊕ *www. valentino.com* ⊠ *Via del Babuino 61, Spagna* ☎ *06/36001906.*

Versace. Occupying the ground floor of a noble palazzo with wrought-iron gratings on the windows and mosaic pavement, Versace is as imaginative as the store is ostentatious. Here shoppers will find apparel, jewelry, watches, fragrances, cosmetics, and home furnishings. The designs are as flamboyant as Donatella and Allegra (Gianni's niece), drawing heavily on the sexy rocker gothic underground vibe. Be sure to check out the Via Veneto location for pret-à-porter and jewelry. ⊠ *Via Bocca di Leone 23, 26–27, Spagna* ☎ *06/6780521* ⊕ *www.versace.com* ⊠ *Via Vittorio Veneto 104, Veneto* ☎ *06/69925574.*

FLEA MARKETS

Soffitta Sotto i Portici. Held every first and third Sunday of the month from 9 am until sunset, Soffitta Sotto i Portici has more than 100 stands. ⊠ *Piazza Augusto Imperatore* ☎ *06/36005345.*

FOOD, WINE, AND DELICACIES

Buccone. A landmark wine shop inside the former coach house of the Marquesse Cavalcabo, Buccone has 10 layers of shelves packed with quality wines and spirits ranging in price from a few euros to several hundred for rare vintages. The old atmosphere has been preserved with the original wood-beamed ceiling and an antique till. You can also buy sweets, biscuits, and packaged candy perfect for inexpensive gifts. Lunch is available daily and dinner is served Friday and Saturday (reservations essential). Book a week in advance, and they can also give you a guided wine tasting, highlighting vintages from many of Italy's important wine-producing regions. ⊠ *Via di Ripetta 19* ☎ *06/3612154* ⊕ *www.enotecabuccone.com.*

HOUSEHOLD ITEMS

★ **Cesari.** Since 1946 Cesari is where Italian brides traditionally buy their trousseaux. Precious velvets, silks, cottons, damasks, and taffeta abound and are shippable internationally. Famous for their personalized line of bedspreads, tablecloths, lingerie, and embroidered linens, they supply high-end hotels as well as old-fashioned girls of all ages. ⊠ *Via del Babuino 195* ☎ *06/3613456* ⊕ *www.cesari.com.*

Frette. Classic, luxurious, colorful, timeless, and fun, there is nothing like Frette's bed collections. A leader in luxurious linens and towels for the home and hotel industry since 1860, their sophisticated bed linens in cotton satine, percale, and silk are just what the doctor ordered for a great night's sleep. Be sure to look for their Dreamscapes collection, which introduces a romantic, fantastical theme seen in the surreal landscapes of Fellini films, such as *8 1/2* and *Voice of the Moon.* ⊠ *Piazza di Spagna 11, Spagna* ☎ *06/6790673* ⊕ *www.frette.it* ⊠ *Via Nazionale 80, Repubblica* ☎ *06/4882641* ⊕ *www.frette.it* ⊠ *Via del Corso 381, Corso* ☎ *06/6786862.*

JEWELRY

Bulgari. Every capital city has its famous jeweler, and Bulgari is to Rome what Tiffany is to New York and Cartier is to Paris. The jewelry giant has developed a reputation for meticulous craftsmanship melded with noble metals and precious gems. In the middle of the 19th century, the great-grandfather of the current Bulgari brothers began working as a silver jeweler in his native Greece and is said to have moved to Rome with less than 1,000 lire in his pocket. Today the megabrand emphasizes colorful and playful jewelry as the principal cornerstone of its

15

aesthetic. Popular collections include Parentesi, Bulgari-Bulgari and B.zero1. ⊠ *Via Condotti 10, Piazza di Spagna* ☎ 06/6793876 ⊕ *www. bulgari.com* ⊠ *Via Condotti 61, Piazza di Spagna.*

MEN'S CLOTHING

Eddy Monetti. Eddy Monetti is a conservative but upscale men's store featuring jackets, sweaters, slacks, and ties made out of wool, cotton, and cashmere. Sophisticated and pricey, the store carries a range of stylish British- and Italian-made pieces. The women's store is at Via Borgognona 35. ⊠ *Via Borgognona 35* ☎ 06/6794389 ⊕ *www. eddymonetti.com.*

Ermenegildo Zegna. Ermenegildo Zegna, of the unpronounceable name, is a 100-year-old powerhouse of men's clothing. Believing that construction and fabric are the key, Zegna is the master of both. Most of the luxury brand's suits cost in the €1,500–€2,500 range, with the top of the line, known as "Couture," costing considerably more. But don't despair if your pockets aren't that deep: their ready-to-wear dress shirts are suit-defining. ⊠ *Via Condotti 58* ☎ 06/69940678 ⊕ *www.zegna.com.*

MUSIC STORES

Messaggerie Musicali. Central Rome's largest selection of music, DVDs, and concert tickets is at Messaggerie Musicali. Owned by Mondadori, the store also has a limited book section. ⊠ *Via del Corso 472* ☎ 06/684401 ⊕ *www.mondadorishop.it.*

PERFUME AND COSMETICS

Castelli Profumerie. Castelli Profumerie is a straightforward Italian perfume shop with one distinct advantage. Besides being a perfumed paradise offering an array of perfumes like Acqua di Parma, Bois 1920, Bond No. 9, and Comme de Garçons, their precise and courteous staff speaks multiple languages and knows their merchandise, making the experience a lot more pleasant than a dash through duty-free. ⊠ *Via Frattina 18 & 54* ☎ 06/6790339, 06/6780066 beauty salon ⊕ *www. profumeriecastelli.com* ⊠ *Via Condotti 22* ☎ 06/6790998 ⊠ *Via Oslavia 5, Vatican* ☎ 06/3728312.

Pro Fvmvm. The Durante family lives by the motto that a scent can be more memorable than a photograph. Started in 1996 by the grandchildren of Celestino Durante, Pro Fvmvm is fast on its way to becoming a new cult classic in Italian fragrance design. Each of the 20 scents is designed to be unisex and comes complete with a poem that describes the intention of the artisans. Pricey but worth it, some of their top-selling perfumes are Acqva e Zvcchero, Fiore d'Ambra, Thvndra, Volo Az 686 (named after a direct flight from Rome to the Caribbean), and Ichnvsa. ⊠ *Via Ripetta 10, Spagna* ☎ 06/3200306 ⊕ *www.profumum.com.*

SHOES

A. Testoni. Amedeo Testoni was born in 1905 in Bologna, the heart of Italy's shoemaking territory. In 1929 he opened his first shop and began producing shoes as artistic as the Cubist and Art Deco artwork of the period. His shoes have adorned the art-in-motion feet of Fred Astaire and proved that lightweight shoes could be comfortable and luxurious and still make heads turn. Today the Testoni brand includes an extraordinary women's collection and a sports line that is relaxed without losing its artistic heritage. The soft, calfskin sneakers are a dream, as are the matching messenger bags. ⊠ *Via Condotti 80* ☎ *06/6788944* ⊕ *www.testoni.com.*

Bruno Magli. Bruno Magli has high-end, well-crafted, classically styled shoes for both men and women. Magli and his siblings Marino and Maria learned the art of shoemaking from their father and grandfather. From its humble family origins to the corporate design powerhouse it has become today, Bruno Magli footwear always has kept the focus on craftsmanship: it's not uncommon for 30 people to touch each shoe during the course of its manufacture. ⊠ *Via Condotti 6* ☎ *06/69292121* ⊕ *www.brunomagli.it.*

Fausto Santini. Fausto Santini gives a hint of extravagance in minimally decorated shoes that fashion mavens love. For almost 20 years, Santini has successfully attracted an avant-garde clientele of both men and women who flock to his preppy-hipster/nerdy-chic shoes, which are bright and colorful and sport deconstructed forms in plush, supple leathers that scream to be tried on. ■ TIP➔ A second shop at Via Cavour 106 sells last season's shoes at a deep discount. ⊠ *Via Frattina 120* ☎ *06/6784114* ⊕ *www.faustosantini.it.*

15

Fratelli Rossetti. An old-world company with modern aspirations, Fratelli Rossetti is well known to shoe hounds for their captivatingly comfortable Jasper loafers and discreet women's pumps. Their motto has long been sophisticated yet discreet, but while continuing to offer classic power elegance with an emphasis on quality, luxury, and craftsmanship, their new line is a bit more playful. Be sure to check out their new blue suede shoes designed by a Southern California designer. ⊠ *Via Borgognona 5/a* ☎ *06/6782676* ⊕ *www.rossetti.it.*

SPORTWEAR

Renard. A leather boutique that scrupulously selects from superior quality leather hides, Renard carries leathers tanned with natural extracts—not chemicals—a slow and natural process that maintains the hides' original properties. Choose from classic leather blazers, trench coats, and skirts in sporty and sophisticated colors and styles. Be sure to eye their racy motorcycle styles, perfect for windswept and gutsy Ducati rides. ⊠ *Via dei Due Macelli 53* ☎ *06/6797004.*

STATIONERY

Fodor's Choice ★ **Pineider.** Pineider has been making exclusive stationery in Italy since 1774; this is where Rome's aristocratic families have their wedding invitations engraved and their stationery personalized. For stationery and desk accessories, hand-tooled in the best Florentine leather, it has no equal. ⊠ *Via di Fontanella Borghese 22* ☎ *06/6878369* ⊕ *www. pineider.com.*

TESTACCIO

FOOD, WINE, AND DELICACIES

Fodor's Choice ★ **Volpetti.** A Roman institution, Volpetti sells excellent, if pricey, cured meats and salami. Its rich aromas and flavors are captivating from the moment you enter the store. Food selection includes genuine buffalo-milk mozzarella, Roman pecorino, salami, sauces, spreads, oils, balsamic vinegars, desserts, gift baskets, and much more. ⊠ *Via Marmorata 47* ☎ *06/5742352* ⊕ *www.volpetti.com.*

TRASTEVERE

BOOKSTORES

Almost Corner Bookshop. This Trastevere bookstore is a well-loved meeting point for English-speaking residents and visitors to this lively neighborhood. Owner Dermot O'Connell, from Kilkenny, Ireland, stocks an inviting selection ranging from translated Italian classics to today's latest bestsellers. With a reputation for being able to find anything a customer requests, the small shop is a good place to special order books, and it has a wonderful selection of obscura if you've got the time to poke around. ⊠ *Via del Moro 45* ☎ *06/5836942.*

CERAMICS AND DECORATIVE ARTS

Polveri del Tempo. This is the place to go if you are looking for decorative timepieces. At Polveri del Tempo you will find sundials and handcrafted hourglasses—including a giant 18-hour model that is quite memorable. The owner, architect and craftsman Adrian Rodriguez, will tell you how monks once used marked candles, like those on sale here, to note the passage of time. Also on offer is a selection of ancient gizmos that would make any child happy. ⊠ *Via del Moro 59, Trastevere* ☎ *06/05880704* ⊕ *www.polvereditempo.com.*

FLEA MARKETS

Porta Portese. Rome's biggest flea market is at Porta Portese, which welcomes 100,000 visitors every Sunday from 7 am until 2 pm. Larger than the St.Ouen in Paris, this mecca of flea markets is easily accessible with Tram 8. Like one vast yard sale, the market disgorges mountains of new and secondhand clothing, furniture, pictures, old records, used books, vintage clothing, and antiques—all at rock-bottom prices (especially if you're adept at haggling). There is a jovial atmosphere, with an aroma of foods wafting in the air and people crowding around the stalls, hoping to pick up a 1960s Beatles album or a rare Art Deco figurine. Just make sure you bring cash, as stallholders don't accept credit cards and the nearest available cash machine is a hike. ⊠ *Via Portuense and adjacent streets between Porta Portese and Via Ettore Rolli.*

FOOD, WINE, AND DELICACIES

Antica Caciara Trasteverina. The fresh ricotta cheese in the windows of this old-world Trastevere deli catches your eye, enticing you to come inside. Behind the counter you will find heaping helpings of ham, salami, Sicilian anchovies, and burrata cheese from Puglia, as well as Parmigiano-Reggiano and local wines. ⊠ *Via San Francesco a Ripa 140a, Trastevere* ☎ *06/5812815* ⊕ *www.anticacaciara.it.*

SHOES

★ **Joseph DeBach.** The best-kept shoe secret in Rome and open only in the evenings, when Trastevere diners begin to strut their stuff, Joseph DeBach has weird and wonderful creations that are more art than footwear. Entirely handmade from wood, metal, and leather in his small and chaotic studio, his abacus wedge is worthy of a museum. Styles are outrageous "wow" and sometimes finished with hand-painted strings, odd bits of comic books, newspapers, or other unexpected baubles. Individually signed and dated, his shoes are distributed, in very small numbers, in London, Paris, Tokyo, and New York. ⊠ *Vicolo del Cinque 19* ☎ *06/5562756.*

VATICAN

ACCESSORIES

★ **Serafini Ferruccio Pelletteria.** Fifty years ago, there were more than 200 workshops in Rome making handmade leather handbags and shoes. Today only a handful of these saddlers remain, among them Serafini Ferruccio Pelletteria. In this subterranean emporium, both Bobby and Jack Kennedy once ordered loafers and Marlon Brando fancied the maker's doeskin moccasins. Today, the Serafini brand is managed by Francesca, Ferruccio Serafini's youngest daughter, and the laboratory continues to work the leather just as Ferrucio has since beginning his career in the 1940s. Discerning clients adore their lavish retro-styled handbags. Choose from premade stock or, if you have time, select your own style and accompanying leathers. ⊠ *Via Caio Mario 14* ☎ *06/3211719* ⊕ *www.serafinipelletteria.it.*

DEPARTMENT STORES

Coin. A perfect place for upscale merchandise in a proper department store atmosphere, Coin has convenient locations in the center of Rome. Customers can select from trendy merchandise, including clothing separates, lingerie, and sportswear for men, women, and children. Searching for a pressure-driven espresso machine, a simpler stove-top Bialetti model, or a mezzaluna? You can find these and other high-quality, stylish cookware items that are difficult to find back home. If you are hopping a train from Termini station be sure to check out the smaller version of this store, which has a fabulous emphasis on hip fashions. ⊠ *Via Cola di Rienzo 173* ☎ *06/36004298* ⊠ *Piazzale Appio 7, San Giovanni* ☎ *06/7080020* ⊕ *www.coin.it.*

FOOD, WINE, AND DELICACIES

Castroni. The legend over the door reads Castroni Droghe Coloniali, but for years this international food emporium has been known by the single moniker Castroni. Opening its flagship shop near the Vatican in 1932, this gastronomic paradise has long been Rome's port of call for decadent delicacies from around the globe. Jonesing expatriates and study-abroad students pop in for their Fauchon products from Paris, their Twinings teas, or tins of their special smoked Spanish paprika. Travelers will want to stock up on exquisite Italian goodies like Sardinian Bottarga, aromatic Alba white truffles, or their in-house roasted espresso. Just be sure to bring an extra suitcase: you will want to buy everything. ⊠ *Via Cola di Rienzo 196* ☎ *06/6874383* ⊕ *www.castroni. it* ⊠ *Via Nazionale 71, Nazionale* ☎ *06/48947474* ⊠ *Via Frattina 79, Spagna* ☎ *06/69921903.*

15

RELIGIOUS MEMENTOS

Arte Italiana. Arte Italiana stands out among the religious souvenir shops that line the avenue leading to St. Peter's Basilica. Whether you're looking for a unique First Holy Communion gift, rosary bracelets, or Byzantine icons, you will find something meaningful to bestow on your parish back home. The multilingual staff will help you find what you are looking for and mean to be helpful, even if they can seem pushy. The store stocks a wide variety of detailed crèche statuettes, alabaster sculptures, tapestries, saints medals, and crucifixes handmade in Italy. The pieces aren't cheap, but they are of the highest quality and make great mementos to personalize your Vatican experience. ⊠ *Via della Conciliazione 4f* ☎ *06/68806373.*

Savelli Arte e Tradizione. A Roman landmark since 1878, Savelli Arte e Tradizione offers the widest selection of artwork and sacred objects available in Rome. The Savelli name belongs to an old Roman family with four popes among its ancestors: Benedict II, Gregory II, Honorius III, and Honorius IV. The shop is famous for its collection of 18th- and 19th-century–style micromosaics; it's a great spot to watch artists demonstrate this ancient craft. ⊠ *Via Paolo VI, 27–29* ☎ *06/68307017* ⊕ *www.savellireligious.com.*

Side Trips from Rome

WORD OF MOUTH

"In my book Hadrian's Villa should not be considered a villa, not even an estate, this place should be categorized as a mid-sized town! It is amazing. I could not help but marvel at the sheer power the emperor yielded to gather the resources necessary to build an estate of this magnitude."

—marigross

Updated by
Margaret
Stenhouse

All roads may lead to Rome, but today's sightseers should take a cue from imperial emperors and Renaissance popes and head fuori porta—"beyond the gates." In one such locale, the province known as Lazio, those privileged people built spectacular palaces and patrician villas in hopes of exchanging the overheated air of the capitol for a breath of refreshing country air. So why not follow their lead and head to the hills for a change of scenery?

The province surrounding Rome is called Lazio and it remains one of Italy's most fascinating but least known regions. Befitting the former playground of popes, princes, and prelates, it offers a spectacular harvest of sights. At Tivoli, Hadrian's Villa reveals the scale of individual imperial Roman egos-an emperor's dream come true, it was the personal creation of the scholarly ruler, who, with all the resources of the known world at his command, filled his vast retreat with structures inspired by ancient monuments that had impressed him during his world travels. Moving on to Tivoli's Villa d'Este, you can see how a worldly cardinal diverted a river so that he could create a garden stunningly set with hundreds of fountains, demonstrating that the arrival of the Renaissance did not diminish the bent of the ruling classes for self-aggrandizement. To the east lies Ostia Antica, called the "Pompeii" of Rome; to the south, the enchanting Castelli Romani villages, dotted with great castles and lovely lakes. Obviously, if Lazio weren't so obscured by the glare and fame of nearby Rome, it would be one of Italy's star attractions.

OSTIA ANTICA

30 km (19 miles) southwest of Rome.

GETTING HERE

The best way to get to Ostia Antica is by train. The Ostia Lido train leaves every half hour from the station adjacent to Rome's Piramide Metro B subway station, stopping off at Ostia Antica en route. The

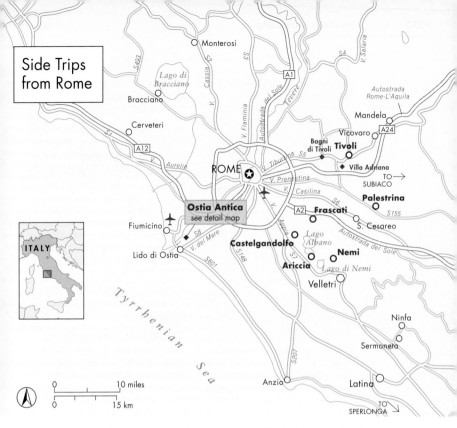

trip takes 35 minutes. By car, take the Via del Mare that leads off from Rome's EUR district. Be prepared for heavy traffic, especially at peak hours, on weekends, and in summer.

EXPLORING

Founded around the 4th century BC, Ostia served as Rome's port city for several centuries until the Tiber changed course, leaving the town high and dry. What has been excavated here is a remarkably intact Roman town in a pretty, parklike setting. Fair weather and good walking shoes are essential. On hot days, be here when the gates open or go late in the afternoon. A visit to the excavations takes two to three hours, including 20 minutes for the museum. Inside the site, there's a snack bar and a bookshop. Ostia Antica is 30 km (19 miles) southwest of Rome.

Castello della Rovere. Before exploring Ostia Antica's ruins, it's worth taking a tour through the medieval *borgo* (town). The distinctive Castello della Rovere, easily spotted as you come off the footbridge from the train station, was built by Pope Julius II when he was the cardinal bishop of Ostia in 1483. Its triangular form is unusual for military architecture. Inside are (badly faded) frescoes by Baldassare Peruzzi and a small museum of ancient Roman and medieval pottery that was found on the site. ⊠ *Piazza della Rocca* ☎ *06/56358013* ⊕ *www.ostiaantica.net* 🎟 *Free* 🕐 *Tues.–Sat. tours at 10 and noon; Sun. tours at 10, noon, and 3.*

A GOOD WALK: OSTIA ANTICA

The **Porta Romana** [2], one of the city's three gates, is where you enter the Ostia Antica excavations. It opens onto the Decumanus Maximus, the main thoroughfare crossing the city from end to end. To your right, a staircase leads to a platform—the remains of the upper floor of the **Terme di Nettuno** [3] (Baths of Neptune)—from which you get a good view of the mosaic pavements showing a marine scene with Neptune and the sea goddess Amphitrite. Behind the baths are the barracks of the fire department. On the north side of the Decumanus Maximus is the beautiful **Teatro** [4] (Theater), built by Agrippa, remodeled by Septimius Severus in the 2nd century AD, and restored by the Rome City Council in the 20th century. In the vast Piazzale delle Corporazioni, where trade organizations had their offices, is the **Tempio di Cerere** [5] (Temple of Ceres)—only appropriate for a town dealing in grain imports, Ceres being the goddess of agriculture. From there you can visit the **Domus di Apuleio** [6] (House of Apuleius), built in Pompeian style, lower to the ground and with fewer windows than was characteristic of Ostia. Next door, the **Mithraeum** [7] has balconies and a hall decorated with symbols of the cult of Mithras, a male-only religion imported from Persia.

On Via Semita dei Cippi, just off Via dei Molini, the **Domus della Fortuna Annonaria** [8] (House of Fortuna Annonaria) is the richly decorated residence of a wealthy Ostian; one of the rooms opens onto a secluded garden. On Via dei Molini you can see a **molino** [9] (mill), where grain was ground with stones that are still here. Along Via di Diana you come upon a **thermopolium** [10] (bar) with a marble counter and a fresco depicting the foods sold here.

At the end of Via dei Dipinti is the **Museo Ostiense** [11] (Ostia Museum), which displays sarcophagi, massive marble columns, and large statuary. (The last entry to the museum is a half hour before the Scavi closes.) The **Forum** [12], on the south side of Decumanus Maximus, holds the monumental remains of the city's most important temple, dedicated to Jupiter, Juno, and Minerva. It's also the site of other ruins of baths, a basilica (which in Roman times was a hall of justice), and smaller temples.

Via Epagathiana leads toward the Tiber, where there are large **horrea** [14] (warehouses) erected during the 2nd century AD for the enormous amounts of grain imported into Rome during the height of the Empire. West of Via Epagathiana, the **Domus di Amore e Psiche** [13] (House of Cupid and Psyche), a residence, was named for a statue found here (now on display in the museum); the house's enclosed garden is decorated with marble and mosaic motifs and has the remains of a large pool. The **Casa di Serapide** [15] (House of Serapis) on Via della Foce is a 2nd-century multilevel dwelling; another apartment building stands a street over on Via degli Aurighi. Nearby, the **Termi dei Sette Sapienti** [16] (Baths of the Seven Wise Men) are named for a group of bawdy frescoes. The **Porta Marina** [17] leads to what used to be the seashore and the **sinagoga** [18], dating from the 4th century AD.

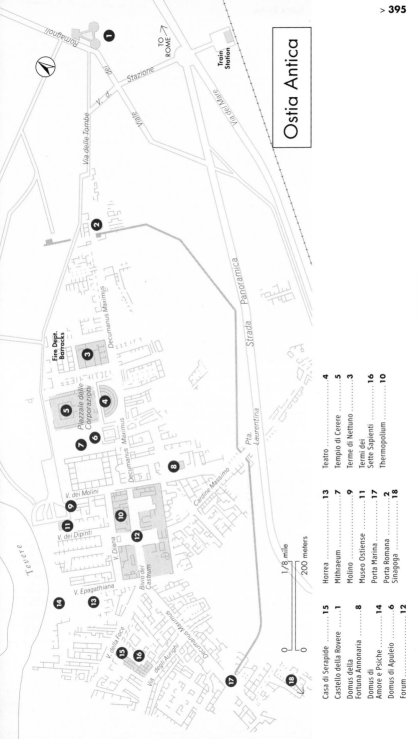

Ostia Antica

1/8 mile

200 meters

16

Fodor's Choice ★ **Scavi di Ostia Antica** (*Ostia Antica excavations*). Tidal mud and wind-blown sand covered the ancient port town, which lay buried until the beginning of the 20th century when it was extensively excavated. The Scavi di Ostia Antica continue to be well maintained today. A cosmopolitan population of rich businessmen, wily merchants, sailors, slaves, and their respective families once populated the city. The great warehouses were built in the 2nd century AD to handle huge shipments of grain from Africa; the *insulae* (forerunners of the modern apartment building) provided housing for the city's growing population. Under the combined assaults of the barbarians and the malaria-carrying mosquito, and after the Tiber changed course, the port was eventually abandoned. ✉ *Viale dei Romagnoli 717* ☎ *06/56350215* 🌐 *www.ostiaantica.net* 🎟 *€6.50 includes Museo Ostiense* 🕒 *Tues.–Sun. 8:30–1 hr before sunset.*

WHERE TO EAT

$$ ITALIAN 🍴 **Cipriani.** Tucked away in the little medieval town under the shadow of the castle, this cozy trattoria is decorated with reproductions of fresco fragments from a Roman palace. The kitchen offers a varied menu of Roman specialties and seasonal fare. Owner Fabrizio Cipriani speaks English and will be happy to guide you in your choice of dishes—and wine from his comprehensive list. [$] *Average cost: €30* ✉ *Via del Forno 11* ☎ *06/56352956* 🌐 *www.ristorantecipriani.com* 🕒 *Closed Wed.*

TIVOLI

In ancient times, just about anybody who was anybody had a villa in Tivoli, including Crassius, Trajan, Hadrian, Horace, and Catullus. Tivoli fell into obscurity in the medieval era until the Renaissance, when popes and cardinals came back to the town and built villas showy enough to rival those of their extravagant predecessors. Nowadays Tivoli is small but vibrant, with winding streets and views over the surrounding countryside, including the deep Aniene river gorge, which runs right through the center of town, and comes replete with a romantically sited bridge, cascading waterfalls, and two jewels of ancient Roman architecture that crown its cliffs-the round Temple of Vesta and the ruins of the rectangular Sanctuary of the Sibyl, probably built earlier. These can be picturesquely viewed across the gorge from the Villa Gregoriana park, named for Pope Gregory XVI, who saved Tivoli from chronic river damage by diverting the river through a tunnel, weakening its flow. An unexpected (but not unappreciated) side effect was the creation of the Grande Cascata (Grand Cascade), which shoots a huge jet of water into the valley below. The Villa Gregoriana is at Largo Sant'Angelo (from the Largo Garibaldi bus stop, follow Via Pacifici—it changes name six times—and veer left on Via Roma to the Largo). There's a small admission charge to the park, which affords a sweaty, steep hike down to the river, so you may prefer to repair to the Antico Ristorante Sibilla, set right by the Temple of Vesta. From its dining terrace, you can drink in one of the most memorably romantic landscape views in Italy, one especially prized by 19th-century painters

TIVOLI

36 km (22 miles) northeast of Rome.

GETTING HERE

Unless you have nerves of steel, it's best not to drive to Tivoli. Hundreds of industries line the Via Tiburtina from Rome and bottleneck traffic is nearly constant. You can avoid some, but not all, of the congestion by taking the Roma–L'Aquila toll road. Luckily, there's abundant public transport. Buses leave every 15 minutes from the Ponte Mammolo stop on the Metro A line. The ride takes an hour. Regional Trenitalia trains connect from both Termini and Tiburtina stations and will have you there in under an hour. Villa d'Este is in the town center, and a frequent bus service from Tivoli's main square goes to Hadrian's Villa.

VISITOR INFORMATION

PIT (Punto Informativo Turistico) (*Tivoli tourist office*). ⊠ *Piazzale Nazioni Unite* ☎ *0774/313536* ⊕ *www.comune.tivoli.rm.it* ☉ *Tues.–Sun. 10–1 and 4–6.*

EXPLORING

Fodor's Choice **Villa Adriana** (*Hadrian's Villa*). The astonishingly grand 2nd-century ★ Villa Adriana, 6 km (4 miles) south of Tivoli, was an emperor's theme park: an exclusive retreat below the ancient settlement of Tibur where the marvels of the classical world were reproduced for a ruler's pleasure. Hadrian, who succeeded Trajan as emperor in AD 117, was a man of genius and intellectual curiosity, fascinated by the accomplishments of the Hellenistic world. From AD 125 to 134, architects, laborers, and artists worked on the villa, periodically spurred on by the emperor himself when he returned from another voyage full of ideas for even more daring constructions (he also gets credit for Rome's Pantheon). After his death in AD 138 the fortunes of his villa declined as it was sacked by barbarians and Romans alike. Many of his statues and decorations ended up in the Vatican Museums, but the expansive ruins are nonetheless compelling. It's not the single elements but the delightful effect of the whole that makes Hadrian's Villa so great. Oleanders, pines, and cypresses growing among the ruins heighten the visual impact. To help you get your bearings, maps are issued free with the audio guides (€5). A visit here takes about two hours, more if you like to savor antiquity slowly. In summer visit early to take advantage of cool mornings. ⊠ *Bivio di Villa Adriana off Via Tiburtina, 6 km (4 mi) southwest of Tivoli* ☎ *0774/382733 reservations* ☑ *€8* ☉ *Daily 9–1 hr before sunset.*

Fodor's Choice **Villa d'Este.** Created by Cardinal Ippolito d'Este in the 16th century, this ★ world-famous villa, set in the center of Tivoli, was the most amazing pleasure garden of its day: it still stuns visitors with its beauty and fabulous fountains. Este (1509–72), a devotee of the Renaissance celebration of human ingenuity over nature, was inspired by the excavation of Villa Adriana. He paid architect Pirro Ligorrio an astronomical sum to create a mythical garden with water as its artistic centerpiece. To console himself for his seesawing fortunes in the political intrigues of his time (he happened to be cousin to Pope Alexander VI), he had his builders tear down part of a Franciscan monastery to clear the site, then divert the Aniene River to water the garden and feed the fountains—and what

16

fountains: big, small, noisy, quiet, rushing, running, and combining to create a late-Renaissance, proto–Busby Berkeley masterpiece in which sunlight, shade, water, gardens, and carved stone create an unforgettable experience. To this day, several hundred fountains cascade, shoot skyward, imitate birdsongs, and simulate rain. The musical **Fontana dell'Organo** has been restored to working order: the organ plays a watery tune every two hours from 10:30 to 6:30 (until 2:30 in winter). Romantics will love the night tour of the gardens and floodlit fountains, available on Friday and Saturday from July until September. Allow at least an hour for the visit, and bear in mind that there are a lot of stairs to climb. There's also a café on the upper terrace leading from the palace entrance, where you can sit and admire the view. ✉ *Piazza Trento 1* ☎ *0774/312070* 🌐 *www.villadestetivoli.info* 🎟 *€8* 🕒 *Tues.–Sun. 8:30–1 hr before sunset.*

WHERE TO EAT AND STAY

For expanded hotel reviews, visit Fodors.com.

$$$ ITALIAN Fodor's Choice ★ 🍴 **Antico Ristorante Sibilla.** This famed restaurant should be included among the most beautiful sights of Tivoli. Built in 1730 beside the circular Roman Temple of Vesta and the Sanctuary of the Sybil, the terrace garden has a spectacular view over the deep gorge of the Aniene River, with the thundering waters of the waterfall in the background. Marble plaques on the walls list the royals who have come here to dine over two centuries. The food, wine, and service standards are all high, and in recent years there's been more and more emphasis placed on seasonal produce and local dishes. Be sure to sample the specialty of the house—a lavish choice of antipasti served on individual triple-tiered trays that resemble old-fashioned cake stands. Dishes for the first course may include *pappardelle* made with spelt and dressed with garlic, olive oil and tiny *datterini* tomatoes. For the second course, local lamb; sucking pig; and a salad with ricotta, herbs, honey, and prunes may all make an appearance. The desserts are equally strong contenders for your attention. [$] *Average cost: €50* ✉ *Via della Sibilla 50* ☎ *0774/335281* 🌐 *www.ristorantesibilla.com.*

$ B&B/INN 🏨 **Adriano.** At the entrance to Hadrian's Villa, this small inn—actually a converted 19th-century mansion—is a modest but comfortable place to overnight and a handy spot to have lunch before or after your trip around the ruins of Hadrian's Villa. **Pros:** wonderful location; peaceful garden; attentive service. **Cons:** busloads of tourists disembark under the windows; restaurant can be crowded. [$] *Rooms from: €120* ✉ *Largo Yourcenar 2, Via di Villa Adriana 194* ☎ *0774/382235* 🌐 *www.hoteladriano.it* 🛏 *10 rooms* 🕒 *Closed Mon. and from Nov–mid-Feb.* 🍴 *Breakfast.*

$ HOTEL 🏨 **Hotel Torre Sant'Angelo.** Only a hotel since 1994, this place began life as a monastery, which, in turn, became the summer residence of the Massimo princes in 1700—but whether noble or today's tourist, all guests at this deluxe hotel 1 km (½ mile) have always enjoyed the magnificent view of Tivoli's "old town," the Aniene Falls, and the gloriously picturesque Temple of the Sybil from this site 1 km (½ mile) outside town. **Pros:** 21st-century comfort in a historic mansion house;

highly competitive rates. **Cons:** isolated location two miles out of town. [$] *Rooms from: €120* ✉ *Via Quintilio Varo* ☎ *0774/332533* 🌐 *www.hoteltorresangelo.it* 🛏 *25 rooms, 10 suites* 🍴 *Breakfast.*

THE CASTELLI ROMANI

The "castelli" aren't really castles, as their name would seem to imply. They're little towns that are scattered on the slopes of the Alban Hills near Rome. And the Alban Hills aren't really hills, but extinct volcanoes. There were castles here in the Middle Ages, however, when each of these towns, fiefs of rival Roman lords, had its own fortress to defend it. Some centuries later, the area became given over to villas and retreats, notably the pope's summer residence at Castelgandolfo, and the 17th- and 18th-century villas that transformed Frascati into the Beverly Hills of Rome. Arrayed around the rim of an extinct volcano that encloses two crater lakes, the string of picturesque towns of the Castelli Romani are today surrounded by vineyards, olive groves, and chestnut woods—no wonder overheated Romans have always loved to escape here.

Ever since Roman times, the Castelli towns have been renowned for their wine. In the narrow, medieval alleyways of the oldest parts, you can still find old-fashioned hostelries where the locals sit on wooden benches, quaffing the golden nectar straight from the barrel. Following the mapped-out **Castelli Wine Route** (🌐 *www.stradadeivinideicastelliromani.it*) around the numerous vineyards and wine cellars is a more sophisticated alternative. Exclusive local gastronomic specialties include the bread of Genzano, baked in traditional wood-fire ovens, the *porchetta* (roast suckling pig) of Ariccia, and the *pupi* biscuits of Frascati, shaped like women or mermaids with three or more breasts (an allusion to ancient fertility goddesses). Each town has its own feasts and saints' days, celebrated with costumed processions and colorful events. Some are quite spectacular, like Marino's annual Wine Festival in October, where the town's fountains flow with wine, or the Flower Festival of Genzano in June, when an entire street is carpeted with millions of flower petals, arranged in elaborate patterns.

FRASCATI

20 km (12 miles) south of Rome.

GETTING HERE

An hourly train service along a single-track line through vineyards and olive groves takes you to Frascati from Termini station. The trip takes 45 minutes. By car, take the Via Tuscolano, which branches off the Appia Nuova road just after St. John Lateran in Rome, and drive straight up.

VISITOR INFORMATION

Frascati Point (tourism office) ✉ *Piazza G. Marconi 5* ☎ *06/94015378* ✉ *frascatipoint@libero.it.*

EXPLORING

It's worth taking a stroll through Frascati's lively old center. Via Battisti, leading from the Belvedere, takes you into Piazza San Pietro with its imposing gray-and-white cathedral. Inside is the cenotaph of Prince Charles Edward, last of the Scottish Stuart dynasty, who tried unsuccessfully to regain the British Crown, and died an exile in Rome in 1788. A little arcade beside the monumental fountain at the back of the piazza leads into Market Square, where the smell of fresh baking will entice you into the Purificato family bakery to see the traditional pupi biscuits, modeled on old pagan fertility symbols.

Take your pick from the cafés and trattorias fronting the central Piazzale Marconi, or do as the locals do—buy fruit from the market gallery at Piazza del Mercato, then get a huge slice of porchetta from one of the stalls, a hunk of *casareccio* bread, and a few *ciambelline frascatane* (ring-shaped cookies made with wine), and take your picnic to any one of the numerous *cantine* (homey wine bars), and settle in for some sips of tasty, inexpensive vino.

★ **Grottaferrata.** Grottaferrata is only a couple of miles from Frascati, but it's quite different in character. The original village has expanded enormously to accommodate a vast army of commuters, and traffic can be very congested at peak hours. In compensation, the town has excellent restaurants and an interesting weekly market. Its main attraction, however, is the **Abbey of San Nilo,** a walled citadel founded by the 90-year-old St. Nilo, who brought his group of Basilian monks here in 1004. The order is unique in that it is Roman Catholic but observes Greek Orthodox rites.

The fortified abbey, considered a masterpiece of martial architecture, was restructured in the 15th century by Antonio da Sangallo for the future Pope Julius II. The abbey church, inside the second courtyard, is a jewel of nearly oriental opulence, with glittering Byzantine mosaics and a revered icon set into a marble tabernacle designed by Bernini. The Farnese chapel, leading from the right nave, contains a series of frescoes by Domenichino.

If you make arrangements in advance you can visit the library, which is one of the oldest in Italy. The abbey also has a famous laboratory for the restoration of antique books and manuscripts, where Leonardo's *Atlantic Code* was restored in 1962 and more than a thousand precious volumes were saved after the disastrous Florence flood in 1966. ✉ *Corso del Popolo 128* ☎ *06/9459309* ⊕ *www.abbaziagreca.it* 🎫 *Free* ⏰ *7:30–12:30 and 4–6.*

Fodor'sChoice **Villa Aldobrandini.** Frascati was a retreat of prelates and princes, who ★ built magnificent villas on the sun-drenched slopes overlooking the Roman plain. The most spectacular of these is Villa Aldobrandini, which dominates Frascati's main square from the top of its steeply sloped park.

Built in the late 16th century and adorned with frescoes by the Zuccari brothers and the Cavalier d'Arpino, the hulking villa is still owned by the Princes Aldobrandini. However, its park, which is open to the public, is a marvel of baroque fountains and majestic box-shaded avenues.

There you can see the magnificent "water theater" that Cardinal Pietro Aldobrandini, Pope Clement VIII's favorite nephew, built to impress his guests, thinking nothing of diverting the water supply that served the entire area in order to make his fountains play. The gigantic central figure of Atlas holding up the world is believed to represent the pope. You can also see another water theater in the grounds of nearby Villa Torlonia, which is now a public park. ✉ *Via Cardinale Massaia* ☎ *06/9421434* 🎟 *Free* ⏲ *Garden: weekdays 10–5.*

WHERE TO EAT AND STAY

For expanded hotel reviews, visit Fodors.com.

$$$ ITALIAN ★ 🍴 **Al Fico Vecchio.** This historic coaching inn, dating to the 16th century, is on an old Roman road a couple of miles outside Frascati. It has a charming garden shaded by the old fig tree that gave the place its name. The dining room has been tastefully renovated, preserving many of the characteristic antique features. The menu offers a wide choice of local dishes, such as gnocchi with cheese and truffles. [$] *Average cost: €50* ✉ *Via Anagnini 257* ☎ *06/9459261* 🌐 *www.alfico.it.*

$$ HOTEL Fodor'sChoice ★ 🏨 **Park Hotel Villa Grazioli.** One of the region's most famous residences, this elegant patrician villa halfway between Frascati and Grottaferrata is now a first-class hotel. **Pros:** wonderful views of the countryside; elegant atmosphere; professional staff. **Cons:** difficult to find. [$] *Rooms from: €150* ✉ *Via Umberto Pavoni 19, Grottaferrata* ☎ *06/9454001* 🌐 *www.villagrazioli.com* 🛏 *56 rooms, 2 suites* 🍽 *Breakfast.*

16

CASTELGANDOLFO

8 km (5 miles) southwest of Frascati, 25 km (15 miles) south of Rome.

GETTING HERE

There's an hourly train service for Castelgandolfo from Termini station (Rome-Albano line). Otherwise, buses leave frequently from the Anagnina terminal of the Metro A subway. The trip takes about 30 minutes. By car, take the Appian Way from San Giovanni in Rome and follow it straight to Albano, where you branch off for Castelgandolfo (about an hour, depending on traffic).

EXPLORING

This little town is well known as the pope's summer retreat. It was the Barberini Pope Urban VIII who first headed here, eager to escape the malarial miasmas that afflicted summertime Rome; before long, the city's princely families also set up country estates around here.

The 17th-century **Villa Pontificia** has a superb position overlooking Lake Albano and is set in one of the most gorgeous gardens in Italy; unfortunately, neither the house nor the park is open to the public (although crowds are admitted into the inner courtyard for papal audiences). On the little square in front of the palace there's a fountain by Bernini, who also designed the nearby Church of San Tommaso da Villanova, which has works by Pietro da Cortona.

The village has a number of interesting craft workshops and food purveyors, in addition to the souvenir shops on the square. On the horizon, the silver astronomical dome belonging to the Specola Vaticana observatory—one of the first in Europe—where the scientific Pope Gregory XIII indulged his interest in stargazing, is visible for miles around.

Lakeside Lido. Lined with restaurants, ice-cream parlors, and cafés, the waterfront stretch of Castelgandolfo is a favorite area for Roman families to relax. No motorized craft are allowed on the lake, but you can rent paddleboats and kayaks. The waters are full of seafowl, such as swans and herons, and nature trails are mapped out along both ends of the shore. All along the central part there are bathing establishments where you can rent deck chairs; you might also want to stop to eat a plate of freshly prepared pasta or a gigantic Roman sandwich at one of the little snack bars under the oak and alder trees. There's also a small, permanent fairground for children.

WHERE TO EAT

$$$$ ITALIAN ★ 🍴 **Antico Ristorante Pagnanelli.** One of most refined restaurants in the Castelli Romani, this has been in the same family since 1882. The present generation—Aurelio Pagnanelli, his Australian wife, Jane, and their four sons—have lovingly restored this old railway inn perched high above Lake Albano. The dining-room windows open onto a breathtaking view across the lake to the conical peak of Monte Cavo. In winter a log fire blazes in a corner; in summer you can dine on the flower-filled terrace. Many of the dishes are prepared with produce from the family's own farm. The wine cellar, carved out of the local tufa rock, boasts more than 3,000 labels. [$] *Average cost: €70* ✉ *Via Gramsci 4* ☎ *06/9361740* 🌐 *www.pagnanelli.it.*

ARICCIA

8 km (5 miles) southwest of Castelgandolfo, 26 km (17 miles) south of Rome.

GETTING HERE

For Ariccia, take the COTRAL bus from the Anagnina terminal of the Metro A underground line. All buses on the Albano-Genzano-Velletri line go through Ariccia. If you take a train to Albano, you can proceed by bus to Ariccia or go on foot (it's just under 3 km [2 miles]). If you are driving, follow the Appian road to Albano and carry on to Ariccia.

EXPLORING

Ariccia is a gem of baroque town planning. When millionaire banker Agostino Chigi became Pope Alexander VII, he commissioned Gian Lorenzo Bernini to redesign his country estate to make it worthy of his new station. Bernini consequently restructured not only the existing 16th-century palace, but also the town gates, the main square with its loggias and graceful twin fountains, and the round church of **Santa Maria dell'Assunzione** (the dome is said to be modeled on the Pantheon). The rest of the village coiled around the apse of the church down into the valley below.

Strangely, Ariccia's splendid heritage has been largely forgotten in the 20th century, and yet it was once one of the highlights of every artist's and writer's Grand Tour. Corot, Ibsen, Turner, Longfellow, and Hans Christian Andersen all came to stay here.

Fodor's Choice ★ **Palazzo Chigi.** This is a true rarity—a baroque residence whose original furniture, paintings, drapes, and decorations are still mostly intact. Italian film director Lucchino Visconti used the villa for most of the interior scenes in his 1963 film *The Leopard*. The rooms contain intricately carved pieces of 17th-century furniture, as well as textiles and costumes from the 16th to the 20th century. See the Room of Beauties, lined with paintings of the loveliest ladies of the day, and the Nuns' Room, with portraits of 10 Chigi sisters, all of whom took the veil. The park stretching behind the palace is a wild wood, the last remnant of the ancient Latium forest, where herds of deer still graze under the trees. Book ahead for tours in English. ✉ *Piazza di Corte 14* ☎ *06/9330053* 🌐 *www.palazzochigiariccia.it* 🎫 *€7* 🕐 *Tours: Apr.–Sept., Tues.–Fri. at 11, 4, and 5:30; weekends at 11:30, 12:30, 3, 4, 5, 6, and 7; Oct.–Mar., Tues.–Fri. at 11, 4, and 5:30; weekends at 11:30, 12:30, 3, 4, 5, and 6.*

WHERE TO EAT

A visit to Ariccia is not complete without tasting the local gastronomic specialty: porchetta, a delicious roasted whole pig stuffed with herbs. The shops on the Piazza di Corte will make up a sandwich for you, or you can do what the Romans do: take a seat at one of the *fraschette* wine cellars that serve cheese, cold cuts, pickles, olives, and sometimes a plate of pasta. Conditions are rather rough and ready—you sit on a wooden bench at a trestle table covered with simple white paper—but there's no better place to make friends and maybe join in a sing-along.

$ ITALIAN 🍴 **L'Ariccíarola.** This is a great place for people-watching while you enjoy the local porchetta (whole roast pig stuffed with herbs), washed down with a carafe of local Castelli wine. It's tucked in a corner under the Galloro bridge. [$] *Average cost: €25* ✉ *Via Borgo S. Rocco 9* ☎ *06/9334103* 🌐 *www.osterialaricciarola.it* 💳 *No credit cards* 🕐 *Closed Mon.*

$ ITALIAN 🍴 **La Locanda del Brigante Gasparone.** The first of the string of informal lodgings you find clustered under the Galloro bridge, on the right-hand side of Palazzo Chigi, this *locanda* (inn) has seats either inside or outside under an awning—a fine place to enjoy simple, robust pasta dishes. [$] *Average cost: €25* ✉ *Via Borgo San Rocco 7* ☎ *06/9333100* 🌐 *www.fraschettabrigantegasperone.com* 💳 *No credit cards* 🕐 *No lunch weekdays.*

16

NEMI

8 km (5 miles) west of Ariccia, 34 km (21 miles) south of Rome.

GETTING HERE

Nemi is a bit difficult to get to unless you come by car. Buses from the Anagnina Metro A station go to the town of Genzano, where a local bus travels to Nemi every two hours. If the times aren't convenient, you can take a taxi or walk the 5 km (3 miles) around Lake Nemi. By car, take the panoramic route known as the Via dei Laghi (Road of the Lakes). Follow the Appia Nuova from St. John Lateran and branch off on the well-signposted route after Ciampino airport. Follow the Via dei Laghi toward Velletri until you see signs for Nemi.

EXPLORING

Nemi is the smallest and prettiest village of the Castelli Romani. Perched on a spur of rock 600 feet above the small crater lake of the same name, it has an eagle's-nest view over the rolling Roman countryside as far as the coast some 18 km (11 miles) away. The one main street, Corso Vittorio Emanuele, takes you to the (now privately owned) baronial Castello Ruspoli, with its 11th-century watchtower, and the quaint little Piazza Umberto 1, lined with outdoor cafés serving the tiny wood strawberries harvested from the crater bowl.

If you continue on through the arch that joins the castle to the former stables, you come to the entrance of the dramatically landscaped public gardens, which curve steeply down to the panoramic **belvedere** terrace. If you enjoy walking, you can follow the road past the garden entrance and go all the way down to the bottom of the crater.

Museo delle Navi Romani (*Roman Ship Museum*). Nemi may be small, but it has a long and fascinating history. In ancient Roman times it was an important sanctuary dedicated to the goddess Diana: it drew thousands of pilgrims from all over the Roman Empire. In the 1930s the Italian government drained the lake in order to recover two magnificent ceremonial ships, loaded with sculptures, bronzes, and art treasures that had been submerged for 2,000 years.

Unfortunately, the ships were burned during World War II. The Museo delle Navi Romani, on the lakeshore, was built to house them. Inside are scale models and photographs of the complex recovery operation, as well as some finds from the sanctuary and the area nearby. ⊠ *Via del Tempio di Diana 9* ☎ *06/9398040* ⊡ *€3* ⊙ *Daily 9–6:30.*

WHERE TO EAT

$$ ✕ **Specchio di Diana.** Halfway down the main street is the town's most
ITALIAN historic inn—Byron reputedly stayed here when visiting the area. A wine bar and café are on street level, while the restaurant proper on the second floor offers marvelous views, especially at sunset. Pizzas are popular, but don't neglect Nemi's regional specialties: *fettucine al sugo di lepre* (fettucine with hare sauce), roasted porcini mushrooms, and the little wood strawberries with whipped cream. $ *Average cost: €40* ⊠ *Corso Vittorio Emanuele 13* ☎ *06/9368805* ⊕ *www.specchiodidiana. it* ⊙ *Closed Mon.*

ITALIAN
VOCABULARY

ITALIAN VOCABULARY

	ENGLISH	ITALIAN	PRONUNCIATION
BASICS			
	Yes/no	Sí/No	see/no
	Please	Per favore	pear fa-**vo**-ray
	Yes, please	Sí grazie	see **grah**-tsee-ay
	Thank you	Grazie	**grah**-tsee-ay
	You're welcome	Prego	**pray**-go
	Excuse me, sorry	Scusi	**skoo**-zee
	Sorry!	Mi dispiace!	mee dis-spee-**ah**-chay
	Good morning/afternoon	Buongiorno	bwohn-**jor**-no
	Good evening	Buona sera	**bwoh**-na **say**-ra
	Good-bye	Arrivederci	a-ree-vah-**dare**-chee
	Mr. (Sir)	Signore	see-**nyo**-ray
	Mrs. (Ma'am)	Signora	see-**nyo**-ra
	Miss	Signorina	see-nyo-**ree**-na
	Pleased to meet you	Piacere	pee-ah-**chair**-ray
	How are you?	Come sta?	**ko**-may **stah**
	Very well, thanks	Bene, grazie	**ben**-ay **grah**-tsee-ay
	Hello (phone)	Pronto?	**proan**-to
NUMBERS			
	one	uno	**oo**-no
	two	due	**doo**-ay
	three	tre	tray
	four	quattro	**kwah**-tro
	five	cinque	**cheen**-kway
	six	sei	say
	seven	sette	**set**-ay
	eight	otto	**oh**-to
	nine	nove	**no**-vay
	ten	dieci	dee-**eh**-chee
	twenty	venti	**vain**-tee

ENGLISH	ITALIAN	PRONUNCIATION
thirty	trenta	**train**-ta
forty	quaranta	kwa-**rahn**-ta
fifty	cinquanta	cheen-**kwahn**-ta
sixty	sessanta	seh-**sahn**-ta
seventy	settanta	seh-**tahn**-ta
eighty	ottanta	o-**tahn**-ta
ninety	novanta	no-**vahn**-ta
one hundred	cento	**chen**-to
one thousand	mille	**mee**-lay
ten thousand	diecimila	dee-eh-chee-**mee**-la

USEFUL PHRASES

Do you speak English?	Parla inglese?	**par**-la een-**glay**-zay
I don't speak Italian.	Non parlo italiano.	non **par**-lo ee-tal-**yah**-no
I don't understand.	Non capisco.	non ka-**peess**-ko
Can you please repeat?	Può ripetere?	pwo ree-**pet**-ay-ray
Slowly!	Lentamente!	**len**-ta-men-tay
I don't know.	Non lo so.	non lo **so**
I'm American.	Sono americano(a).	**so**-no a-may-ree-**kah**-no(a)
I'm British.	Sono inglese.	so-no een-**glay**-zay
What's your name?	Come si chiama?	**ko**-may see kee-**ah**-ma
My name is...	Mi chiamo...	mee kee-**ah**-mo
What time is it?	Che ore sono?	kay **o**-ray **so**-no
How?	Come?	**ko**-may
When?	Quando?	**kwan**-doe
Yesterday/today/tomorrow	Ieri/oggi/domani	**yer**-ee/**o**-jee/do-**mah**-nee
This morning/	Stamattina/Oggi	sta-ma-**tee**-na/**o**-jee
afternoon	pomeriggio	po-mer-**ee**-jo

ENGLISH	ITALIAN	PRONUNCIATION
Tonight	Stasera	sta-**ser**-a
What?	Che cosa?	kay **ko**-za
Why?	Perché?	pear-**kay**
Who?	Chi?	kee
Where is...	Dov'è...	doe-**veh**
the bus stop?	la fermata dell'autobus?	la fer-**mah**-ta del ow-toe-**booss**
the train station?	la stazione?	la sta-tsee-**oh**-nay
the subway	la metropolitana?	la may-tro-po-lee-**tah**-na
the terminal?	il terminale?	eel ter-mee-**nah**-lay
the post office?	l'ufficio postale?	loo-**fee**-cho po-**stah**-lay
the bank?	la banca?	la **bahn**-ka
the...hotel?	l'hotel...?	lo-**tel**
the store?	il negozio?	eel nay-**go**-tsee-o
the cashier?	la cassa?	la **kah**-sa
the...museum?	il museo...?	eel moo-**zay**-o
the hospital?	l'ospedale?	lo-spay-**dah**-lay
the elevator?	l'ascensore?	la-shen-**so**-ray
the restrooms?	Dov'è il bagno?	do-**vay** eel **bahn**-yo
Here/there	Qui/là	kwee/la
Left/right	A sinistra/a destra	a see-**neess**-tra/a **des**-tra
Straight ahead	Avanti dritto	a-**vahn**-tee **dree**-to
Is it near/far?	È vicino/lontano?	ay vee-**chee**-no/ lon-**tah**-no
I'd like...	Vorrei...	vo-**ray**
a room	una camera	**oo**-na **kah**-may-ra
the key	la chiave	la kee-**ah**-vay
a newspaper	un giornale	oon jor-**nah**-lay
a stamp	un francobollo	oon frahn-ko-**bo**-lo
I'd like to buy...	Vorrei comprare...	vo-**ray** kom-**prah**-ray

ENGLISH	ITALIAN	PRONUNCIATION
How much is it?	Quanto costa?	**kwahn**-toe **coast**-a
It's expensive/cheap.	È caro/economico.	ay **car**-o/ ay-ko-**no**-mee-ko
A little/a lot	Poco/tanto	**po**-ko/**tahn**-to
More/less	Più/meno	pee-**oo/may**-no
Enough/too (much)	Abbastanza/troppo	a-bas-**tahn**-sa/tro-po
I am sick.	Sto male.	sto **mah**-lay
Call a doctor.	Chiama un dottore.	kee-**ah**-mah oondoe-**toe**-ray
Help!	Aiuto!	a-**yoo**-toe
Stop!	Alt!	ahlt
Fire!	Al fuoco!	ahl **fwo**-ko
Caution/Look out!	Attenzione!	a-ten-**syon**-ay

DINING OUT

A bottle of . . .	Una bottiglia di . . .	**oo**-na bo-**tee**-lee-ah dee
A cup of . . .	Una tazza di . . .	**oo**-na **tah**-tsa dee
A glass of . . .	Un bicchiere di . . .	oon bee-key-**air**-ay dee
Bill/check	Il conto	eel **cone**-toe
Bread	Il pane	eel **pah**-nay
Breakfast	La prima colazione	la **pree**-ma ko-la-**tsee**-oh-nay
Cocktail/aperitif	L'aperitivo	la-pay-ree-**tee**-vo
Dinner	La cena	la **chen**-a
Fixed-price menu	Menù a prezzo fisso	may-**noo** a **pret**-so **fee**-so
Fork	La forchetta	la for-**ket**-a
I am diabetic.	Ho il diabete.	o eel dee-a-**bay**-tay
I am vegetarian.	Sono vegetariano/a.	**so**-no vay-jay-ta-ree-**ah**-no/a
I'd like . . .	Vorrei . . .	vo-**ray**
I'd like to order.	Vorrei ordinare.	vo-**ray** or-dee-**nah**-ray

ENGLISH	ITALIAN	PRONUNCIATION
Is service included?	Il servizio è incluso?	eel ser-**vee**-tzee-o ay een-**kloo**-zo
It's good/bad.	È buono/cattivo.	ay **bwo**-no/ka-**tee**-vo
It's hot/cold.	È caldo/freddo.	ay **kahl**-doe/**fred**-o
Knife	Il coltello	eel kol-**tel**-o
Lunch	Il pranzo	eel **prahnt**-so
Menu	Il menù	eel may-**noo**
Napkin	Il tovagliolo	eel toe-va-lee-**oh**-lo
Please give me ...	Mi dia ...	mee **dee**-a
Salt	Il sale	eel **sah**-lay
Spoon	Il cucchiaio	eel koo-kee-**ah**-yo
Sugar	Lo zucchero	lo **tsoo**-ker-o
Waiter/Waitress	Cameriere/ cameriera	ka-mare-**yer**-ay/ ka-mare-**yer**-a
Wine list	La lista dei vini	la **lee**-sta **day**-ee **vee**-nee

Travel Smart
Rome

GETTING HERE AND AROUND

Almost all the main attractions in the *centro storico* (historic center) can be covered on foot, or by bus or Metro (subway).

The first thing you should know, especially when moving around the historic city center, is that most street names are posted on ceramiclike plaques on the side of buildings, which can be hard to see. Addresses are fairly straightforward: the street is followed by the street number. It's worth noting that the streets of Rome, even in the newer outskirts, are numbered erratically. Numbers are usually even on one side of the street and odd on the other, but sometimes numbers are in ascending consecutive order on one side of the street and descending order on the other side.

▌ AIR TRAVEL

Flying time to Rome is 7.5–8.5 hours from New York, 10–11 hours from Chicago, 12–13 hours from Los Angeles, and 2.5 hours from London.

Although the trend on international flights is to drop reconfirmation requirements, many airlines still ask you to reconfirm each leg of your international itinerary. Failure to do so may result in your reservations being canceled. When flying out of Italian airports, always check with the airport or tourist agency about upcoming strikes, which are frequent in Italy and often affect air travel.

Airlines and Airports Airline and Airport Links.com. Airline and Airport Links.com has links to many of the world's airlines and airports. ⊕ *www.airlineandairportlinks.com.*

Airline Security Issues Transportation Security Administration. Transportation Security Administration has answers for almost every question that might come up. ☎ 866/289–9673 ✉ *TSA-ContactCenter@dhs. gov* ⊕ *www.tsa.gov.*

AIRPORTS

The principal airport for flights to Rome is Leonardo da Vinci Airport, commonly known by the name of its location, Fiumicino (FCO). It's 30 km (19 miles) southwest of the city, on the coast. It has been enlarged and equipped with computerized baggage handling and has a direct train link with downtown Rome. Rome's other airport is Ciampino (CIA), on Via Appia Nuova, 15 km (9 miles) south of downtown. Ciampino is a civil and military airport now used by most low-cost airlines that fly both nationally and internationally. There are no trains linking the Ciampino airport to downtown Rome but there are a number of shuttle buses running daily.

Airport Information Ciampino ☎ 06/65951 ⊕ *www.adr.it.* **Leonardo da Vinci Airport/ Fiumicino** ☎ 06/65951 ⊕ *www.adr.it.*

TRANSFERS BETWEEN FIUMICINO AND DOWNTOWN

When approaching by car, follow the signs for Rome and the GRA (the ring road that circles Rome). The direction you take on the GRA depends on where your hotel is located. If it's in the Via Veneto area, for instance, you would take the GRA in the direction of the Via Aurelia, turn off the GRA onto the Via Aurelia, and follow it into Rome. Get a map and directions from the car-rental desk at the airport.

A new law implemented by the Comune di Roma requires all Rome taxi drivers to charge a fixed fare of €40, including luggage handling, if your destination is within the Aurelian walls (this covers the centro storico, most of Trastevere, most of the Vatican area, and parts of San Giovanni). To make sure your hotel falls within the Aurelian walls, ask when you book your room. If your hotel is outside of the walls, the cab ride will run you about €60 plus *supplementi* (extra charges) for luggage. (Of course, this also depends on traffic.) The ride from the airport to the city center takes about 30–45 minutes. Private limousines can be booked at booths in the Arrivals hall; they charge a little more than taxis but can carry more passengers. The Comune di Roma now has a representative in place outside the International Arrivals hall (Terminal 2), where the taxi stand is located, to help assist tourists get into a taxi cab safely (hopefully without getting ripped off). Use only licensed white or older yellow taxis. When in doubt, always ask for a receipt and write the cab company and taxi's license number down (it's written on a metal plate on the inside of the passenger door). Avoid drivers who may approach you in the Arrivals hall; they charge exorbitant, unmetered rates and are most often unauthorized taxi drivers.

Airport Shuttle has shuttles that cost €25 (for one person) and €6 for each additional passenger. This fee also includes two bags per person. Airport Connection Services charges €35 (for one person) and €39 (for two people). The fee includes bags and all taxes.

Two trains link downtown Rome with Fiumicino. Inquire at the APT tourist information counter in the International Arrivals hall (Terminal 2) or train information counter near the tracks to determine which takes you closest to your destination in Rome. The 30-minute nonstop Airport-Termini express (called the Leonardo Express) goes directly to Track 25 at Termini station, Rome's main train station, which is well served by taxis and is a hub of Metro and bus lines. The ride to Termini takes about 30 minutes; departures are every half hour beginning at 6:36 am from the airport, with a final departure at 11:36 pm. Trains depart Termini from Tracks 23 and 24 to the airport starting at 5:52 am and the last train leaves at 10:52 pm. Tickets cost €11.

FM1, the other airport train, leaves from the same tracks and runs to Rome and beyond, serving commuters as well as air travelers. The main stops in Rome are at Trastevere (27 minutes), Ostiense (30

NAVIGATING ROME

Remember, Rome wasn't built in a day and no one expects you to see it one either. At the center of a huge city, the historic districts of Rome are quite large. Streets can be quaint and adorable but there are zillions of them, so pace yourself accordingly; as much as visitors feel they can proudly stride across the city in one glorious day, this would leave them in bad need of a week's rest. Happily, if all roads no longer lead to Rome, many streets in the city lead to the Termini, or Stazione Centrale, Rome's main train station and the city's main transportation hub.

Make sure the bus you're waiting for actually runs during that part of the day or on that particular day of the week. For example, notturno buses (late-night buses), which can be distinguished by the "N" sign just above the bus number, don't run until after midnight and only a few times per hour. Oftentimes, tourists get confused while waiting at the bus stop, since the notturno bus schedules are listed side by side with the regular day bus schedules.

Also, be aware that deviata buses run on bus lines that have been rerouted due to road construction or public demonstrations. And festivi buses are ones that only run on Sunday and holidays. Both notturno buses and festivi buses don't run as often as other buses do on weekdays and Saturdays.

Regular buses will either say feriali, which means "daily," or won't have any special distinction.

The Metro A line will take you to a chunk of the main attractions in Rome: Piazza di Spagna, Piazza del Popolo, St. Peter's Square, and the Vatican Museums. The B line will take you to the Colosseum, Circus Maximus, and also lead you to the heart of Testaccio, Rome's nightlife district.

minutes), and Tiburtina (45 minutes); at each you can find taxis and bus and/ or Metro connections to other parts of Rome. FM1 trains run from Fiumicino between 5:57 am and 11:27 pm, with departures every 30 minutes; the schedule is similar going to the airport. Tickets cost €8. For either train, buy your ticket at a vending machine or at ticket counters at the airport and at some stations (Termini, Trastevere, Tiburtina). At the airport, stamp the ticket at the gate. Remember when using the train at other stations to stamp the ticket in the little yellow or red machine near the track before you board. If you fail to stamp your ticket before you board, you could receive a hefty fine, as much as €100.

At night, take COTRAL buses from the airport to Tiburtina station in Rome (45 minutes); they depart from in front of the International Arrivals hall at 1:15, 2:15, 3:30, 5, 10:55 am, noon, and 3:30 pm. Buses leave Tiburtina station for the airport at 12:30, 1:15, 2:30, 3:45, 9:30, 10:30 am, 12:35 pm, and 5:30 pm. Tickets either way cost €4.50 or €7 if bought on board. The two stations are connected by Bus 40N.

TRANSFERS BETWEEN CIAMPINO AND DOWNTOWN

By car, go north on the Via Appia Nuova into downtown Rome.

The new taxi fare law implemented by the Comune di Roma that affects Fiumicino applies to this airport, too. All taxi drivers are supposed to charge a fixed fare of €30, including luggage handling, if your destination is within the Aurelian walls (this covers the centro storico, Trastevere, the Vatican area, and parts of San Giovanni). If your hotel is outside the walls, the cab ride will run you about €60, plus *supplementi* (extra charges) for luggage. The ride takes about 20 minutes. Take only official cabs with the "taxi" sign on top; unofficial cabs often overcharge disoriented travelers.

Airport Connection Services has shuttles that cost €35 for one person and €44 for two people. Airport Shuttle charges €25 for the first person, and €6 for each additional passenger.

A COTRAL bus connects the airport with the Anagnina station of Metro Line A or Ciampino railway station, which takes you into the center of the city. Buses depart from in front of the airport terminal around 25 times a day between 6 am and 11:40 pm. The fare is €1.20 and tickets can be bought on the bus.

TRANSFERS BETWEEN AIRPORTS

It's not easy to move from one airport to another in Rome—the airports aren't connected by a railway system or by the Metro. The only way to make the transfer is by car, taxi, or a combination of bus, Metro, and train. The latter option is not advisable because it would take you at least two to three hours to get from one airport to the other.

A taxi ride from Fiumicino Leonardo Da Vinci Airport to Ciampino Airport will take approximately 45 minutes and could cost roughly €60–€70, plus *supplementi* (extra charges) for luggage.

Contacts **Airport Connection Services** ☎ *06/3383221, 3921540713 emergency phone in case you cannot find the driver., 213/985–3045 from the U.S., 44/2071933062 from the U.K.* ⊕ *www.airportconnection.it.* **Airport Shuttle** ☎ *06/42013469, 06/4740451* ✉ *airportshuttle@airportshuttle.it* ⊕ *www. airportshuttle.it.*

MODE OF TRANSPORT	DURATION	PRICE
Taxi	20 minutes from Ciampino, 30–40 minutes from Fiumicino	€30 from Ciampino, €40 from Fiumicino
Leonardo Express Train	30 minutes	€11
Car	20 minutes from Ciampino, 30–40 minutes from Fiumicino	N/A

FLIGHTS

When flying internationally, you must usually choose between a domestic carrier, the national flag carrier of the country you're visiting, and a foreign carrier from a third country. You may, for example, choose to fly Alitalia to Rome. National flag carriers have the greatest number of nonstops. Domestic carriers may have better connections to your hometown and serve a greater number of gateway cities. Third-party carriers may have a price advantage.

For travel within Italy and around Europe, a number of low-cost airlines can get you where you need to go, often at cheaper rates than by train. Because there are too many of these carriers to name, the best advice is to check out a useful website called Sky Scanner (⊕ *www.skyscanner. net*) which will scan all the major airlines and most of the low-cost airlines for you and give you the dates and companies with the most affordable rates. Keep in mind that low-cost airlines offer no-frills service. Any extras, such as meals, fast check-ins and boarding, extra luggage, and even slightly overweight luggage will cost you. Make sure to read all the fine print when booking a flight with a low-cost airline, especially the rules pertaining to boarding and luggage.

The least expensive airfares to Rome are priced for round-trip travel and must usually be purchased in advance. Airlines generally allow you to change your return date for a fee; most low-fare tickets, however, are nonrefundable.

Airline Contacts Alitalia ☎ *89/2910, 0870/544–8259 in U.K., 06/65643 in Rome, 06/65640 Lost Baggage Claim ⊕ www.alitalia. it.* **American Airlines** ☎ *800/433–7300, 06/66053169 in Rome ⊕ www.aa.com.* **British Airways** ☎ *0845/773–3377 in U.K., 02/69633602 within Italy, 34/91514 1317 Lost Bags ⊕ www.britishairways.com.* **Delta Airlines** ☎ *800/221–1212 for U.S. reservations, 800/241–4141 for international reservations, 02/38591441 within Italy ⊕ www.delta. com.* **easyJet** ☎ *199/201840 within Italy,*

44/8431045454 from abroad, 0843/1045000 from U.K. ⊕ www.easyjet.com. **United Airlines** ☎ *800/864–8331 for U.S. reservations, 800/538–2929 for international reservations, 02/69633707 within Italy ⊕ www.united.com.* **US Airways** ☎ *800/428–4322 for U.S. and Canada reservations, 800/622–1015 for international reservations, 848/813177 within Italy ⊕ www.usairways.com.*

Low-Cost Airlines Blu Express ☎ *199/419777 within Italy, 06/98956677 from abroad ⊕ www.blu-express.com.* **Meridiana** ☎ *892/928 call center, 718/751–4499 from U.S., 0871/222 9319 from U.K. ⊕ www. meridiana.it.* **Ryanair** ☎ *44/8712460002 within the U.K., 899/552589 within Italy ⊕ ryanair.com.* **Wind Jet** ☎ *89/2020 ⊕ www. volawindjet.it.*

■ BUS TRAVEL

An extensive network of bus lines that covers all of the Lazio region is operated by COTRAL (Consorzio Trasporti Lazio). There are several main bus stations. Long-distance and suburban COTRAL bus routes terminate either near Tiburtina station or at outlying Metro stops, such as Rebibbia and Ponte Mammolo (Line B) and Anagnina (Line A).

Fares are reasonable, especially with the BIRG (Bigletto Integrale Regionale Giornali), which allows you to travel on all the lines (and some railroad lines) up to midnight on the day of the ticket's first validation. The cost of a BIRG depends upon the distance to your destination and how many "zones" you travel through. Because of the extent and complexity of the system, it's a good idea to consult with your hotel concierge or to telephone COTRAL's central office when planning a trip. COTRAL buses and other similar bus companies such as SENA are good options for taking short day trips from Rome. There are several buses that leave daily from Rome's Ponte Mammolo (Line B) Metro station for the town of Tivoli, where Hadrian's Villa and Villa D'Este are located. SENA buses leave from Rome's

Tiburtina Metro and train station (Line B) and will take you to Siena and other towns in Tuscany.

While the bus may be an affordable way of moving around, keep in mind that it's also affordable for locals trying to get to and from work. This means certain buses experience heavy commuter traffic and are often very crowded. Just because you've managed to purchase a ticket doesn't mean you're guaranteed a seat. If you don't manage to get a seat, you might have to stand for the entire ride. Hence, what may be more affordable isn't exactly more comfortable.

Bus Information COTRAL ☎ *800/174471*
⊕ *www.cotralspa.it.* **SENA** ☎ *0577/208282*
⊕ *www.sena.it.*

▌ CAR TRAVEL

The main access routes from the north are A1 (Autostrada del Sole) from Milan and Florence and the A12–E80 highway from Genoa. The principal route to or from points south, including Naples, is the A2. All highways connect with the Grande Raccordo Anulare Ring Road (GRA), which channels traffic into the city center. Markings on the GRA are confusing: take time to study the route you need. Be extremely careful of pedestrians and scooters when driving: Romans are casual jaywalkers and pop out frequently from between parked cars. People on scooters tend to be the worst and most careless drivers, as they tend to weave in and out of traffic.

For driving directions, check out ⊕ *www. tuttocitta.it.*

GASOLINE

Only a few gas stations are open on Sunday, and most close for a couple of hours at lunchtime and at 7 pm for the night. Many, however, have self-service pumps that accept both currency and credit cards and are operational 24 hours a day. Most service stations have attendants that pump the gas for you, though self-service pumps are also available. After-hours at self-service stations, it is not uncommon to find someone who will pump your gas for you. While they're not official employees of the gas station, a small tip is usually expected (about €0.30–€0.40 is acceptable). Gas stations on autostrade are open 24 hours. Gas costs about €1.32 per liter. Diesel costs about €1.20 per liter.

PARKING

Be warned: parking in Rome can be a nightmare. The situation is greatly compounded by the fact that private cars are not allowed access to the entire historic center during the day (weekdays 8–6; Saturday 2 pm–6 pm), except for those belonging to residents with resident permits. If you dare enter these restricted areas, also called ZTL zones, without a special permit, video cameras posted on streets that border the centro will photograph your license plate and you will receive a hefty fine. Space is at a premium, and your car may be towed away if it's illegally parked. When you book your hotel, inquire about parking facilities.

There's limited free parking space in the city. Spaces with white lines are free parking, while spaces with yellow lines are for the handicapped only. Make sure to check with your hotel regarding appropriate places to park nearby. Spaces with blue lines are paid parking. All other color-coded spaces are usually reserved for residents, disabled drivers, or carpooling and require special permits. If you park in one of these spaces without a permit, your car could be ticketed or towed. Meter parking costs €1–€1.20 per hour (depending on what area you're in) with limited stopping time allowed in many areas; however, if you pay for four consecutive hours, you will get eight hours of meter time for just €4. Parking facilities near the historic sights exist at the Villa Borghese underground car park (entrance at Viale del Muro Torto) and the Vatican (entrance from Piazza della Rovere).

ROAD CONDITIONS

Italians drive fast and are impatient with those who don't, a tendency that can make driving on the congested streets of Rome a hair-raising experience. Traffic is heaviest during morning and late-afternoon commuter hours, and on weekends. Watch out for mopeds.

ROADSIDE EMERGENCIES

There are phone boxes on highways to report breakdowns. Major rental agencies often provide roadside assistance, so check your rental agreement if a problem arises. Also, ACI (Auto Club of Italy) Service offers 24-hour road service. Dial ☎ 803–116 from any phone, 24 hours a day, to reach the nearest ACI service station. When speaking to ACI, ask and you will be transferred to an English-speaking operator. Be prepared to tell the operator which road you're on, the direction you're going, for example, "*verso* (in the direction of) Pizzo," and the *targa* (license plate number) of your car.

Auto Club of Italy (*ACI*). ☎ *803–116, 39/06491115 from abroad* ✉ *infoturismo@aci. it* ⊕ *www.aci.it.*

RULES OF THE ROAD

Driving is on the right. Regulations are largely similar to those in Britain and the United States, except that the police have the power to levy on-the-spot fines. Although honking abounds, the use of horns is forbidden in many areas; a large sign, "zona di silenzio," indicates where. Speed limits are 50 kph (31 mph) in Rome, 130 kph (80 mph) on autostrade, and 110 kph (70 mph) on state and provincial roads, unless otherwise marked. Talking on a cell phone while driving is strictly prohibited, and if caught, the driver will be issued a fine. Not wearing a seat belt is also against the law. The blood-alcohol content limit for driving is 0.5 gr/l with fines up to €5,000 and the possibility of six months' imprisonment for surpassing the limit. Fines for speeding are uniformly stiff: 10 kph (6 mph) over the speed limit can warrant a fine of up to €500; over 10 kph, and your license could be taken away from you.

Whenever the city decides to implement an "Ecological Day" in order to reduce smog levels, commuters are prohibited from driving their cars during certain hours of the day and in certain areas of the city. These are usually organized and announced ahead of time; however, if you're planning to rent a car during your trip, make sure to ask the rental company and your hotel if there are any planned, because the traffic police won't cut you any breaks, even if you say you're a tourist.

CAR RENTAL

When you reserve a car, ask about cancellation penalties, taxes, drop-off charges (if you're planning to pick up the car in one city and leave it in another), and surcharges (for being under or over a certain age, for additional drivers, or for driving across state or country borders or beyond a specific distance from your point of rental). All these things can add substantially to your costs. Request car seats and extras such as GPS when you book. Make sure to ask the rental car company if they require you to obtain an International Driver's Permit beforehand (most do). These can generally be obtained for a fee through AAA in the United States. Rates are sometimes—but not always—better if you book in advance or reserve through a rental agency's website. There are other reasons to book ahead, though: for popular destinations, during busy times of the year, or to ensure that you get certain types of cars (vans, SUVs, exotic sports cars).

■TIP➜ Make sure that a confirmed reservation guarantees you a car. Agencies sometimes overbook, particularly for busy weekends and holiday periods.

Rates in Rome begin at around $75 a day for an economy car with air-conditioning, a manual transmission, and unlimited mileage. This includes the 20% tax on car rentals. Note that Italian legislation now permits certain rental wholesalers, such as Auto Europe, to drop the value-added tax (V.A.T.). All international car-rental agencies in Rome have a number of locations.

It's usually cheaper to rent a car in advance through your local agency than to rent on location in Italy. Or book ahead online—you can save as much as $10 per day on your car rental. Within Italy, local rental agencies and international ones offer similar rates. Whether you're going with a local or international agency, note that most cars are manual; automatics are hard to find, so inquire about those well in advance.

In Italy your own driver's license is acceptable. An International Driver's Permit is a good idea; it's available from the American or Canadian Automobile Association and, in the United Kingdom, from the Automobile Association or Royal Automobile Club. These international permits are universally recognized, and having one in your wallet may save you a problem with the local authorities.

In Italy you must be 21 years of age to rent an economy or subcompact car, and most companies require customers under the age of 23 to pay by credit card. Upon rental, all companies require credit cards as a warranty; to rent bigger cars (2,000 cc or more), you must often show two credit cards. Debit or check cards are not accepted. Call local agents for details. There are no special restrictions on senior-citizen drivers.

Car seats are required for children under three and must be booked in advance. The rental cost is €5 upward, depending on the type of car.

The cost for an additional driver is about €5–€7 per day.

CAR INSURANCE

Everyone who rents a car wonders whether the insurance that the rental companies offer is worth the expense. No one—including us—has a simple answer. It all depends on how much regular insurance you have, how comfortable you are with risk, and whether or not money is an issue.

If you own a car, your personal auto insurance may cover a rental to some degree, though not all policies protect you abroad; always read your policy's fine print. If you don't have auto insurance, then seriously consider buying the collision- or loss-damage waiver (CDW or LDW) from the car-rental company, which eliminates your liability for damage to the car. If you choose not to purchase the CDW coverage, you could be liable for the first €500 worth of damage. Some credit cards offer CDW coverage, but it's usually supplemental to your own insurance and rarely covers SUVs, minivans, luxury models, and the like. If your coverage is secondary, you may still be liable for loss-of-use costs from the car-rental company. But no credit-card insurance is valid unless you use that card for *all* transactions, from reserving to paying the final bill. All companies exclude car rental in some countries, so be sure to find out about the destination to which you are traveling.

Some rental agencies require you to purchase CDW coverage; many will even include it in quoted rates. All will strongly encourage you to buy CDW—possibly implying that it's required—so be sure to ask about such things before renting. In most cases it's cheaper to add a supplemental CDW plan to your comprehensive travel-insurance policy than to purchase it from a rental company. That said, you don't want to pay for a supplement if you're required to buy insurance from the rental company.

▌ MOPED TRAVEL

As bikes are to Beijing, so mopeds are to Rome; that means they are everywhere. Riders are required to wear helmets, and traffic police are tough in enforcing this law. Producing your country's driver's license should be enough to convince most rental firms that they're not dealing with a complete beginner; but if you're

CAR-RENTAL RESOURCES

Automobile Associations

U.S.: American Automobile Association (AAA)	315/797–5000	www.aaa.com; most contact with the organization is through state and regional members.
National Automobile Club	650/294–7000	www.thenac.com; membership is open to California residents only.
Automobile Association (AA)	0870/600–0371	www.theaa.co.uk
Royal Automobile Club	0800/731–1104	www.rac.co.uk
Local Agencies		
Europcar	06/79340387	www.europcar.it
Major Agencies		
Alamo	800/462–5266	www.alamo.com
Avis	800/331–1084	www.avis.com
Budget	800/472–3325	www.budget.com
Hertz	800/654–3001	www.hertz.com
National Car Rental	800/227–7368	www.nationalcar.com
Wholesalers		
Auto Europe	888/223–5555	www.autoeurope.com
Europe by Car	212/581–3040 in New York, 800/223–1516	www.europebycar.com
Eurovacations	877/471–3876	www.eurovacations.com
Kemwel	877/820–0668	www.kemwel.com

unsure of exactly how to ride a moped, think twice, as driving a scooter in Rome is not like you see it in the movies. It can be very dangerous, and Roman drivers tend to be ruthless; at least ask the assistant for a detailed demonstration. If you don't feel up to braving the Roman traffic on a moped, you can hire an electric car to scoot around the city. The MELEX is a four-seater, golf-cart-style car, with battery power lasting up to eight hours. To rent the MELEX, you need a valid driver's license. Cost: €18 per hour.

Rental Agencies Free Rome (MELEX cars) ✉ *Via Ludovisi 60, Via Veneto* ☏ *335/8357590* ✍ *info@freerome.it* ⊕ *www.freerome.it.* **Scoot-a-Long** ✉ *Via Cavour 302, Colosseo*

☏ *06/6780206.* **Treno e Scooter** ✉ *Piazza dei Cinquecento, in the parking lot in front of the train station, Termini* ☏ *06/48905823* ⊕ *www.trenoescooter.com.*

▌ PUBLIC TRANSPORTATION: BUS, TRAM, AND METROPOLITANA

Although most of Rome's sights are in a relatively circumscribed area, the city is too large to be seen solely on foot. Try to avoid rush hours when taking the Metro (subway) or a bus, as public transport can be extremely crowded. Midmorning or the middle of the day up until early afternoon tends to be less busy. Otherwise, it's best to take a taxi to the area you plan to visit if it is across town. You should always expect to do a lot of walking in Rome (especially considering how little ground the subway actually covers) and so plan on wearing a pair of comfortable, sturdy shoes to cushion the impact of the *sampietrini* (cobblestones). Get away from the noise and polluted air of heavily trafficked streets by taking parallel streets whenever possible. You can get free city and transportation-route maps at municipal information booths.

Rome's integrated transportation system includes buses and trams (ATAC), Metropolitana (subway, often nicknamed the Metro), and suburban trains and buses (COTRAL), and some other suburban trains (Trenitalia) run by the state railways. A ticket (BIT) valid for 75 minutes on any combination of buses and trams and one entrance to the Metro costs €1. Do note, however, that sometime during 2012 or 2013, the fare will rise to €1.50 (the amount of time that your ticket is good for will also be extended to 90 minutes rather than 75 as it is now).

However, once you exit the Metro station even if you get off the wrong stop by mistake, you will be required to purchase and validate another ticket.

Tickets are sold at tobacco shops, newsstands, some coffee bars, automatic ticket machines in Metro stations, some bus stops, and at ATAC ticket booths. You can buy them singly or in quantity; it's always a good idea to have a few tickets handy so you don't have to hunt for a vendor when you need one. Time-stamp your ticket when boarding the first vehicle, and stamp it again when boarding for the last time within 75 minutes. You stamp the ticket at Metro sliding electronic doors, and in the little yellow machines on buses and trams. If you fail to validate your ticket, you could receive a fine of €51 if you pay the ticket controllers on the spot; otherwise, it'll cost you €101 to pay it later.

A BIG ticket—or *Biglietto integrato giornaliero* (integrated daily ticket)—is valid for one day (only for the day it is stamped, not 24 hours) on all public transport and costs €4. A three-day pass (BTI)—or *Biglietto turistico integrato*—costs €11. A weekly ticket (*settimanale*, also known as CIS) costs €16 and gives unlimited travel on ATAC buses, COTRAL urban bus services, trains for the Lido and Viterbo, and subway (Metro). There's an ATAC kiosk at the bus terminal in front of Termini station.

If you're going farther afield, or planning to spend more than a week in Rome, think about getting a BIRG regional ticket or a CIRS (regional weekly ticket) from the railway station. These give you unlimited travel on all state transport throughout the region of Lazio. This can take you as far as the Etruscan city of Tarquinia or medieval Viterbo.

The Metropolitana (or Metro) is the easiest and fastest way to get around Rome *(see our Metro map)*. There are stops near most of the main tourist attractions (street entrances are marked with red "M" signs). The Metro has two lines—A and B—which intersect at Termini station. Line A runs from the eastern part of the city, with stops, among others, at San Giovanni in Laterano, Piazza Barberini, Piazza di Spagna, Piazzale Flaminio (Piazza del Popolo), and Ottaviano/San Pietro, near the Basilica di San Pietro and the Musei Vaticani. Line B has stops near the Colosseum, the Circus Maximus, the Pyramid (Ostiense station and trains for Ostia Antica), and the Basilica di San Paolo Fuori le Mura. The Metro opens at 5:30 am, and the last trains leave the last station at either end at 11:30 pm (on Friday and Saturday nights the last train leaves at 1:30 am).

Although not as fast as the Metropolitana, bus travel is more scenic. With reserved bus lanes and numerous tramlines, surface transportation is surprisingly efficient, given the volume of Roman traffic. At peak times, however, buses can be very crowded. If the distance you have to travel is not too great, walking can be a more comfortable alternative. ATAC city buses are orange, gray-and-red, or blue-and-orange; trams are orange or green. Remember to board at the rear and to exit at the middle: some bus drivers may refuse to let you out the front door, leaving you to scramble through the crowd to exit the middle or rear doors. Don't forget you must buy your ticket before boarding, and stamp it in a machine as soon as you enter. If you find the bus too crowded to get to the ticket machine, write the date and time you boarded on the ticket where you would normally validate it. The ticket is good for a transfer and one Metro trip within the next 75 minutes. Buses and trams run from 5:30 am to midnight, plus there's an extensive network of night buses throughout the city.

The bus system is a bit complicated to navigate due to the number of lines, but ATAC has a website (⊕ *www.atac.roma. it*) that will help you calculate the number of stops and bus route needed, and even give you a map directing you to the appropriate stops. To navigate the site, look for the British flag in the upper right-hand corner to change the website into English.

TICKET/PASS	PRICE
Single Fare	€1
Weekly Pass	€16
Monthly Unlimited Pass	€30

ZONE	PRICE
A	€1
B	€2
C	€3

Information ATAC urban buses ☎ *06/57003* ⊕ *www.atac.roma.it.* **COTRAL** ☎ *800/174471, 06/72057205* ⊕ *www.cotralspa.it.* **Trenitalia suburban trains** ☎ *892021, 06/68475475 from abroad* ⊕ *www.trenitalia.it.*

▌ TAXI TRAVEL

Taxis in Rome do not cruise, but if free they will stop if you flag them down. They wait at stands but can also be called by phone, in which case you're charged a supplement. The various taxi services are considered interchangeable and are referred to by their phone numbers rather than names. Taxicabs can be reserved the night before only if you're traveling to and from the airport or the train station. Only some taxis are equipped to take credit cards. Inquire when you phone to make the booking.

The meter starts at €2.80 during the day, €5.80 after 10 pm, and €4 on Sunday and holidays.

The first piece of luggage is free, then each additional piece will incur a €1 supplement.

There's even a €2 supplement for rides originating from Termini train station. Unfortunately, these charges do not appear on the meter, causing countless misunderstandings. If you take a taxi at night and/or on a Sunday, or if you have baggage or have called the cab by phone, the fare will legitimately be more than the figure shown on the meter. When in doubt, always ask for a receipt (*ricevuta*). This will encourage the taxicab driver to be honest and charge you the correct amount. After 9 pm, women traveling alone in a taxi are entitled to a *sconta rosa*—a special 10% discount for women implemented by the city of Rome. Unfortunately, taxi drivers won't always apply the discount to the fare. You'll have to make sure to ask for it. Use only licensed, metered white or yellow cabs, identified by a numbered shield on the side, an illuminated taxi sign on the roof, and a plaque next to the license plate reading "servizio pubblico." Avoid unmarked, unauthorized, unmetered gypsy cabs (numerous at Rome airports and train stations), whose drivers actively solicit your trade and may demand astronomical fares.

Taxi Companies Cab ☎ *06/6645, 06/3570, 06/8822, 06/5551, 06/4157.*

▌TRAIN TRAVEL

State-owned Trenitalia trains are part of the Metrebus system and also serve some destinations on side trips outside Rome. The main Trenitalia stations in Rome are Termini, Tiburtina, Ostiense, and Trastevere. Suburban trains use all of these stations. The Ferrovie COTRAL line departs from a terminal in Piazzale Flaminio, connecting Rome with Viterbo.

Only Trenitalia trains such as Frecciarossa, Frecciargento, Eurostar, and Intercity Plus have first- and second-class compartments. Local trains can be crowded early morning and evening as many people commute to and from the city, so try to avoid these times. Be ready to stand if you plan to take one of these trains and don't arrive early enough to secure a seat. On long-distance routes (to Florence and Venice, for instance), you can either travel by the cheap (but slow) *regionale* trains, or the fast, but more expensive *Intercity, Eurostar,* Frecciarossa, or Frecciargento, which require seat reservations, available at the station when you buy your ticket, online, or through a travel agent.

For destinations within 200 km (124 miles) of Rome, you can buy a *kilometrico* ticket. Like bus tickets, they can be purchased at some newsstands and in ticketing machines, as well as at Trenitalia ticket windows. Buy them in advance so you won't waste time in line at station ticket booths. Like all train tickets, they must be date-stamped in the little yellow or red machines near the track before you board. Within a range of 200 km (124 miles) they're valid for six hours from the time they're stamped, and you can get on and off at will at stops in between for the duration of the ticket's validity.

The state railways' excellent and user-friendly site at ⊕ *www.trenitalia.it* will help you plan any rail trips in the country. In 2012, a new private railway company called NTV (Nuovo trasporto ferroviario) launched high-speed trains—made by Alstom AGV, whose trains hold the world speed record—that are expected to give Trenitalia some hefty competition. The new trains, called *Italo,* are said to be equipped with satellite TV, Wi-Fi, and even a cinema car. They service various big cities around Italy including Florence, Venice, Naples, and Bologna. In Rome, the trains stop at the newly renovated Tiburtina station.

Information Italo Treno–Nuovo Trasporto Viaggiatori ☎ *06/0708* ⊕ *www.italotreno. it.* **Trenitalia** ☎ *892/2021 within Italy, 199/892021 within Italy, 06/68475475 from abroad* ⊕ *www.trenitalia.it.*

ESSENTIALS

▌COMMUNICATIONS

INTERNET

Getting online in Rome isn't difficult: public Internet stations and Internet *caffè* are common. Prices differ from place to place, so spend some time to find the best deal. This isn't always readily apparent: a place might have higher rates, but because it belongs to a chain you won't be charged an initial flat fee again when you go to a different location of the same chain.

There are several Wi-Fi hotspots around Rome. In fact, many bars and caffè around the city will let you connect to their wireless network for free if you purchase something. Alternatively, if you have an Italian cell phone number you can sign up to access free Wi-Fi in select public spaces and parks such as the MAXXI museum, Piazza di Spagna, Bocca della Verità, Ponte Milvio, Villa Ada, and Villa Borghese. Register in English by accessing ⊕ *https://wasp.provinciawifi. it/owums/account/signup*. Then every time you enter one of Rome's free Wi-Fi hotspots, it should automatically pop up on your smart phone or computer screen. Another service, Roma Wireless (⊕ *www.romawireless.com*) gives visitors free Wi-Fi access for up to one hour a day in various spots such as Campo de' Fiori, Largo Argentina, and the Trevi Fountain. At one of these spots, the Roma Wireless network should pop up on your screen and prompt you to register with the site in order to access the network.

Some hotels have free Wi-Fi or in-room modem lines, but, as with phones, using the hotel's line is relatively expensive. Always check modem rates before plugging in. You may need an adapter for your computer for the European-style plugs. As always, if you're traveling with a laptop, carry a spare battery and an adapter. Never plug your computer into any socket before asking about surge protection. IBM sells a pea-size modem tester that plugs into a telephone jack to check whether the line is safe to use.

Internet Caffè Cybercafes. Cybercafes lists more than 4,000 Internet cafés worldwide. ⊕ *www.cybercafes.com.* **Mail Office** ⊠ *Corso Vittorio Emanuele II 274/a, Navona* ☏ *06/68192051.* **Pantheon Internet Point** ⊠ *Via di Santa Caterina da Siena 40, Pantheon* ☏ *06/69200501.* **TreviNet Place** ⊠ *Via in Arcione 103, Barberini* ☏ *06/69922320.*

Caffè with Wi-Fi Friends Café ⊠ *Piazza Trilussa 34, Trastevere* ☏ *06/5816111* ⊕ *www. cafefriends.it.* **The Library** ⊠ *Vicolo della Cancelleria 7, Piazza Navona* ☏ *333/3517581, 06/97275442* ⊕ *www.thelibrary.it.*

PHONES

The good news is that you can now make a direct-dial telephone call from virtually any point on earth. The bad news? You can't always do so cheaply. Calling from a hotel is almost always the most expensive option; hotels usually add huge surcharges to all calls, particularly international ones. Calling cards usually keep costs to a minimum, but only if you purchase them locally. In Italy, you can also place international calls from call centers. And then there are mobile phones (⇨ *Mobile Phones*)—as expensive as mobile phone calls can be, they are still usually a much cheaper option than calling from your hotel.

The country code for Italy is 39. The area code for Rome is 06. When dialing an Italian number from abroad, do not drop the initial 0 from the local area code.

The country code is 1 for the United States, 61 for Australia, 1 for Canada, 64 for New Zealand, and 44 for the United Kingdom.

CALLING WITHIN ITALY

For general information in English, dial ☏ *176.* To place international telephone calls via operator-assisted service (or for information), dial ☏ *170* or

LOCAL DO'S AND TABOOS

GREETINGS

Italians greet friends with a kiss, usually first on the right cheek, and then on the left. When you meet a new person, shake hands.

SIGHTSEEING

Italy is teeming with churches, many with significant works of art in them. Because they are places of worship, care should be taken with appropriate dress. Shorts, cropped tops, miniskirts, and bare midriffs are taboo at St. Peter's in Rome, and in many other churches throughout Italy. So, too, are short shorts anywhere. When touring churches—especially in summer when it's hot and no sleeves are desirable—it's wise to carry a sweater, or scarf, to wrap around your shoulders before entering the church. Do not enter a church with food, and do not drink from your water bottle while inside. Do not go in if a service is in progress. And if you have a cell phone, turn it off before entering.

OUT ON THE TOWN

In Italy, almost nothing starts on time except for maybe a theater, opera, or movie showing. Italians even joke about a "15-minute window" before actually being late somewhere.

LANGUAGE

You can always find someone who speaks at least a little English in Rome, albeit with a heavy accent. When you do encounter someone who speaks English, it's polite to speak slowly and phonetically so the person can understand you better. Remember that the Italian language is pronounced exactly as it's written—many Italians try to speak English as it's written, with bewildering results.

You may run into a language barrier in the countryside, but a phrase book and close attention to the Italians' astonishing use of pantomime and expressive gestures will go a long way.

Try to master a few phrases for daily use, and familiarize yourself with the terms you'll need to decipher signs and museum labels. Some museums have exhibits labeled in both English and Italian, but this is the exception rather than the rule.

Most exhibitions have multi-language headphones you can rent, and English-language guidebooks are generally available at museum shops.

Many newsstands and bookstores stock a useful guide called *Rome, Past & Present*. It has photos of the most famous ancient monuments, together with drawings of what they originally looked like, and is particularly useful to get children interested in what seems (to them) just heaps of old stones.

A phrase book and language-CD set can help get you started.

Fodor's *Italian for Travelers* (available at bookstores everywhere) is excellent.

Private language schools and U.S.- and U.K.-affiliated educational institutions offer a host of Italian language study programs in Rome.

Language Schools American University of Rome ⊠ *Via Pietro Rosselli 4, Monteverde* ☎ *06/58330919* ⊕ *www.aur. edu.* **Arco di Druso** ⊠ *Via Otranto 12, San Pietro* ☎ *06/39750984* ⊕ *www.arcodidruso. com.* **Berlitz** ⊠ *Via Fabio Massimo 95, Prati* ☎ *06/6872561* ⊕ *www.berlitz.com.* **Centro Linguistico Italiano Dante Alighieri** ⊠ *Piazza Bologna 1* ☎ *06/44231490* ⊕ *www. clidante.it.* **Ciao Italia** ⊠ *Via delle Frasche 5, Repubblica* ☎ *06/4814084* ⊕ *www.ciao-italia.it.* **Dilit International House** ⊠ *Via Marghera 22, Termini* ☎ *06/4462593* ⊕ *www. dilit.it.* **Scuola Leonardo da Vinci** ⊠ *Piazza dell'Orologio 7, Navona* ☎ *06/68892513* ⊕ *www.scuolaleonardo.com.*

long-distance access numbers (⇨ *Long Distance Services*).

Phone numbers in Rome, and throughout Italy, don't have a set number of digits. All calls (except for cell phones) in Rome are preceded by the city code 06, with the exception of three-digit numbers (113 is for general emergencies). Emergency numbers can be called for free from pay phones (if you can find one).

Throughout Italy, long-distance calls are dialed in the same manner as local calls: the city code plus the number. Rates vary, depending on the time of day, with the lowest late at night and early in the morning.

CALLING OUTSIDE ITALY

Hotels tend to overcharge, sometimes exorbitantly, for long-distance and international calls. Use your AT&T, MCI, or Sprint card or buy an international phone card, which supplies a local number to call and gives a low rate. Or make your calls from Telefoni offices, designated "telecom," where operators will assign you a booth, sell you an international telephone card, and help you place your call. You can make collect calls from any phone by dialing ☎ *800/172444*, which will get you an English-speaking AT&T operator. Rates to the United States are lowest round the clock on Sunday and 10 pm–8 am, Italian time, on weekdays.

Access Codes AT&T Direct ☎ *800/172444.* **MCI WorldPhone** ☎ *800/905825.* **Sprint International Access.** From cell phones, call 892–176. ☎ *800/172–405, 800/787–986.*

CALLING CARDS

When you do run into a pay phone in the city, you'll find that many no longer accept only coins. Most require *schede telefoniche* (phone cards). You buy the card (values vary—€2.50, €5, and so on) at post offices, newsstands (called *edicole*), and tobacconists. Tear off the corner of the card and insert it in the slot. When you dial, its value appears in the window. After you hang up, the card is returned so you can use it until its value

runs out. The best cards for calling North America or Europe are the €5 or €10 Eurocity, Eurotel, and Editel cards, which give you a local number to dial and a pin number, and roughly 180 minutes and 360 minutes, respectively, of calling time.

MOBILE PHONES

If you have a multiband phone (some countries use different frequencies from those used in the United States) and your service provider uses the world-standard GSM network (as do T-Mobile, AT&T, and Verizon), you can probably use your phone abroad. Roaming fees can be steep, however: 99¢ a minute is considered reasonable. And overseas you normally pay the toll charges for incoming calls. It's almost always cheaper to send a text message than to make a call, since text messages have a very low set fee (often less than 10¢).

If you just want to make local calls, consider buying a new SIM card (note that your provider may have to unlock your phone for you to use a different SIM card) and a prepaid service plan in the destination. You'll then have a local number and can make local calls at local rates. If your trip is extensive, you could also simply buy a new cell phone in your destination, as the initial cost will be offset over time.

Renting phones may seem like an inexpensive way to go, but in the end it could cost you more than using your own cell phone from home. The per-minute rates tend to be higher, and a lot of times there are hidden costs. Usually, companies ask you to leave a credit card number when renting the phone, which can be iffy, as hidden costs sneak up onto your bill at the end of the month after you've left the country, making it harder to dispute the charges.

Contacts Cellular Abroad. Cellular Abroad rents and sells GMS phones and sells SIM cards that work in many countries. ☎ *800/287–5072, 310/862-7100, 800/3623-3333 toll-free within Italy* ⊕ *www.cellularabroad.com.* **Mobal.** Mobal rents mobiles and sells GSM phones (starting at $29) that will operate in 140 countries. Per-call rates vary throughout the world. ☎ *888/888–9162* ⊕ *www.mobalrental.com*. **Planet Fone**. Planet Fone rents cell phones, but the per-minute rates are expensive. ☎ *888/988–4777* ⊕ *www.planetfone.com*.

▌ CUSTOMS AND DUTIES

You're always allowed to bring goods of a certain value back home without having to pay any duty or import tax. But there's a limit on the amount of tobacco and liquor you can bring back duty-free, and some countries have separate limits for perfumes; for exact figures, check with your customs department. The values of so-called "duty-free" goods are included in these amounts. When you shop abroad, save all your receipts, as customs inspectors may ask to see them as well as the items you purchased. If the total value of your goods is more than the duty-free limit, you'll have to pay a tax (most often a flat percentage) on the value of everything beyond that limit.

Of goods obtained anywhere outside the European Union or goods purchased in a duty-free shop within an EU country, the allowances are as follows: (1) 200 cigarettes or 100 cigarillos or 50 cigars or 250 grams of tobacco; (2) 2 liters of still table wine or 1 liter of spirits over 22% volume or 2 liters of spirits under 22% volume or 2 liters of fortified and sparkling wines; and (3) 50 ml of perfume and 250 ml of toilet water.

Of goods obtained (duty and tax paid) within another EU country, the allowances are (1) 800 cigarettes or 400 cigarillos (under 3 grams) or 200 cigars or 1 kilogram of tobacco; (2) 90 liters of still table wine or 10 liters of spirits over 22% volume or 20 liters of spirits under 22% volume or 110 liters of beer.

Information in Rome Italian Customs, Fiumicino Airport ✉ *Via Bragadin, Fiumicino* ☎ *06/65956366, 06/65956949*.

U.S. Information U.S. Customs and Border Protection ☎ *877/227–5511 from the U.S., 703/526–4200 from abroad* ⊕ *www.cbp.gov*.

▌ ELECTRICITY

The electrical current in Italy is 220 volts, 50 cycles alternating current (AC); wall outlets take Continental-type plugs, with two or three round prongs.

Consider making a small investment in a universal adapter, which has several types of plugs in one lightweight, compact unit. Most laptops and mobile phone chargers are dual voltage (i.e., they operate equally well on 110 and 220 volts), so require only an adapter. These days the same is true of small appliances such as hair dryers. Always check labels and manufacturer instructions to be sure. Don't use 110-volt outlets marked "for shavers only" for high-wattage appliances such as hair dryers.

Note that straightening irons from the United States don't heat up very well and tend to blow a fuse even with correct adapters—as do American hair dryers.

Contacts Help for World Travelers. Steve Kropla's Help for World Travelers has information on electrical and telephone plugs around the world. ⊕ *www.kropla.com*. **Walkabout Travel Gear**. Walkabout Travel Gear has good coverage of electricity under "adapters." ☎ *800/852–7085 U.S. toll-free number* ⊕ *www. walkabouttravelgear.com*.

▌ EMERGENCIES

No matter where you are in Italy, dial ☎ *113* for all emergencies, or find somebody (your concierge, a passerby) who will call for you, as not all 113 operators speak English; the Italian word to use to draw people's attention in an emergency is *Aiuto!* (Help!, pronounced ah-*you*-toh). *Pronto soccorso* means "first aid." When confronted with a health emergency, head straight for the Pronto Soccorso department of the nearest hospital or dial ☎ *118*. To call a Red Cross ambulance (*ambulanza*), dial ☎ *06/5510*. If you just need a doctor, you should ask for *un medico*; most hotels will be able to refer you to a local doctor (*medico*). Don't forget to ask the doctor for *una ricevuta* (an invoice) to show to your insurance company to get a reimbursement. Alternatively, the city of Rome has recently opened a medical clinic dedicated to tourists suffering from symptoms (flu, fever, minor aches and pains, etc.) that would probably have them waiting into the wee hours of the night at the emergency room. The Nuovo Regina Margherita Hospital offers a 24-hour tourist medical service and is staffed by one medical doctor and two nurses. The tourist medical service is free of charge every night 8–8 and on weekends. On weekdays (8–8), there is a charge of €20.66. Patients under six years old or over 65 are always free. The tourist service is located at the Nuovo Regina Margherita Hospital on Via Morosini 30 (Trastevere); the phone number is ☎ *06/58441*.

Other useful Italian words to use are *Al fuoco!* (Fire!, pronounced ahl fuh-*woe*-co) and *Al ladro!* (Follow the thief!, pronounced ahl *lah*-droh).

Italy has a national military police force (*carabinieri*) as well as local police (*polizia*). Both are armed and have the power to arrest and investigate crimes. Always report any theft or the loss of your passport to either the carabinieri or the police, as well as to your embassy. Local traffic officers are known as *vigili* (though their official name is *polizia municipale*)—they are responsible for, among other things, giving out parking tickets and clamping cars, so before you even consider parking the Italian way, make sure you are at least able to spot their white (in summer) or black uniforms (many are women). Should you find yourself involved in a minor car accident, you should contact the vigili. Call the countrywide toll-free number 113 if you need the police.

Most pharmacies are open Monday–Saturday 8:30–1 and 4–8; some are open all night. A schedule posted outside each pharmacy indicates the nearest pharmacy open during off-hours (afternoons, through the night, and Sunday). Farmacia Internazionale Capranica, Farmacia Internazionale Barberini (open 24 hours), and Farmacia Cola di Rienzo are pharmacies that have some English-speaking staff. The hospitals listed here have English-speaking doctors. Rome American Hospital is about 30 minutes by cab from the center of town.

For a full listing of doctors and dentists in Rome who speak English, consult the English Yellow Pages at ⊕ *www.english yellowpages.it* or pick up a copy at any English-language bookstore. Your embassy will also have a list of recommended medical professionals.

Doctors and Dentists Aventino Medical Group ✉ *Via Sant'Alberto Magno 5, Aventino* ☎ *06/57288349, 06/57288329* ⊕ *www.aventinomedicalgroup.com*. **Pro Dent Medica** ✉ *Via Bisagno 5, Piazza Fiume* ☎ *06/8605056, 339/3602158* ⊕ *prodentmedica.blogspot.com*. **Roma Medica (weekends, house calls)** ☎ *338/6224832 24-hour service* ⊕ *www.romamedica.com*.

General Emergency Contacts Emergencies ☎ *113*. **Police** ☎ *113*. **Ambulance** ☎ *118*.

Hospitals and Clinics Rome American Hospital ✉ *Via Emilio Longoni 69, Tor Sapienza* ☎ *06/22551* ⊕ *www.rah.it*. **Salvator Mundi International Hospital** ✉ *Viale delle Mura Gianicolensi 67, Monteverde* ☎ *06/588961, 800/402323 toll-free within Italy* ⊕ *www.salvatormundi.it*.

Hotlines Highway Police ☎ *06/22101*. **Road Breakdown** ☎ *116*. **Women's Rights and Abuse Prevention** ☎ *06/4882832, 800/001122*.

Pharmacies Farmacia Cola di Rienzo ✉ *Via Cola di Rienzo 213/215, San Pietro* ☎ *06/3243130, 06/3244476*. **Farmacia Internazionale Barberini** ✉ *Piazza Barberini 49, Barberini* ☎ *06/4825456, 06/4871195*.

Farmacia Internazionale Capranica ⊠ *Piazza Capranica 96, Pantheon* ☎ *06/6794680.*

▌ HEALTH

Smoking has been banned in Italy in all public places. This includes trains, buses, offices, and waiting rooms, as well as restaurants, pubs, and discotheques (unless the latter have separate smoking rooms). If you're an unrepentant smoker, you would be advised to check with restaurants before making a booking, as very few can offer smokers' facilities. Fines for breaking the law are so stiff that they have succeeded (for the moment) in curbing the Italians' propensity to light up everywhere. Outside dining is exempt from the rule, so if smoking annoys you, you may find it better to eat indoors even in warm weather. Many restaurants are now equipped with air-conditioning. There are no smoking cars on any FS (Italian state railway) trains.

It's always best to travel with your own tried and true medicines. The regulations regarding what medicines require a prescription are not likely to be exactly the same in Italy and in your home country—all the more reason to bring what you need with you. Aspirin (*l'aspirina*) can be purchased at any pharmacy, as can over-the-counter medicines such as ibuprofen and Aleve. Other over-the-counter remedies, including cough syrup, antiseptic creams, and headache pills, are only sold in pharmacies.

▌ HOURS OF OPERATION

Banks are typically open weekdays 8:30–1:30 and 2:45–3:45 or 3–4. Exchange offices are open all day, usually 8:30–8.

Post offices are open Monday–Saturday 8–2; central and main district post offices stay open until 8 on weekdays for some operations. You can buy stamps (*francobolli*) at tobacconists.

Only a few gas stations are open on Sunday, and most close during weekday lunch hours and at 7 pm for the night. Many, however, have self-service pumps that are operational 24 hours a day, and gas stations on autostrade are open 24 hours.

Museum hours vary and may change with the seasons. Many important national museums are closed one day a week, often on Monday. The Roman Forum, other sites, and some museums may be open until late in the evening during the summer. Always check locally.

Most churches are open from early morning until noon or 12:30, when they close for two hours or more; they open again in the afternoon, generally around 4 pm, closing about 7 pm or later. Major cathedrals and basilicas, such as the Basilica di San Pietro, are open all day. Note that sightseeing in churches during religious rites is usually discouraged. Be sure to have some coins handy for the *luce* (light) machines that illuminate the works of art in the perpetual dusk of ecclesiastical interiors. A pair of binoculars will help you get a good look at painted ceilings and domes. Many churches do not allow you to take pictures inside. When permitted, use of flash is prohibited.

A tip for pilgrims and tourists keen to get a glimpse of the pope: avoid the weekly general audience on Wednesday morning in Piazza di San Pietro, and go to his Sunday angelus instead. This midday prayer service tends to be far less crowded (unless beatifications or canonizations are taking place) and is also mercifully shorter, which makes a difference when you're standing.

Most pharmacies are open Monday–Saturday 8:30–1 and 4–8; some are open all night. A schedule posted outside each pharmacy indicates the nearest pharmacy open during off-hours (afternoons, through the night, and Sunday).

Shop hours vary. Many shops in downtown Rome are open all day during the week and also on Sunday, as are some department stores and supermarkets. Alternating city neighborhoods also have general once-a-month Sunday opening days. Otherwise, most shops throughout the city are closed on Sunday. Shops that take a lengthy lunch break are open 9:30–1 and 3:30 or 4–7:30 or 8. Many shops close for one half day during the week: Monday morning in winter and Saturday afternoon in summer.

Food shops are open 8–2 and 5–7:30, some until 8, and most are closed on Sunday. They also close for one half day during the week, usually Thursday afternoon from September to June and Saturday afternoon in July and August.

Termini station has a large, modern shopping mall with more than a hundred stores, many of which are open late in the evening. Pharmacies, bookstores, and boutiques, as well as caffè, bathrooms, ATMs, and money-exchange services, a first-aid station, and an art gallery and exhibition center can all be found here. The Drug Store here (which oddly doesn't sell medicines) is open every day between 6 am and midnight. It sells sandwiches, fresh fruit, gourmet snacks, toiletries, gifts, and things like cameras, electric razors, and bouquets of fresh flowers (useful if you get an unexpected invitation to someone's home).

Traditionally the worst days to arrive in Rome, or do anything that hasn't been preplanned, are Easter Sunday, May 1 (Labor Day), Christmas Day, and New Year's Day. Expect to find many shops and businesses closed, and only a skeleton transport system working. Ferragosto (the middle weekend of August) will also be very challenging.

HOLIDAYS

If you can avoid it, don't travel at all in Italy in August, when much of the population is on the move, especially around Ferragosto, the August 15 national holiday, when cities such as Rome are deserted and many restaurants and shops are closed.

National holidays are New Year's Day; January 6 (Epiphany); Easter Sunday and Monday; April 25 (Liberation Day); May 1 (Labor Day or May Day); June 29 (Sts. Peter and Paul, Rome's patron saints); August 15 (Assumption of Mary, also known as Ferragosto); November 1 (All Saints' Day); December 8 (Immaculate Conception); Christmas Day and the feast of Saint Stephen (December 25 and 26).

▌ MAIL

The Italian mail system has improved tremendously with the introduction of a two-tier postal system. A *posta prioritaria* stamp (first-class stamp) costs €0.85 and usually guarantees delivery to EEC destinations within three days. Mailing a letter or a postcard from Italy to the United States requires two of these posta prioritaria stamps. A posta prioritaria stamp within Italy costs €0.60. When you mail letters, pay attention to the mail slot on the mailbox. The red mailboxes have two slots: the slot on the left is for Rome mail, and the slot on the right is for all other destinations, including abroad. Blue mailboxes are for foreign (*estero*) mail only.

The Vatican postal service has a reputation for efficiency and many foreigners prefer to send their mail from there, with Vatican stamps. You can buy these in the post offices on either side of Piazza di San Pietro, one next to the information office and the other under the colonnade opposite. During peak tourist seasons a Vatican Post Office mobile unit is set up in Piazza di San Pietro. All letters with Vatican stamps can only be mailed from the Vatican Post Office or Vatican mailboxes located near San Pietro.

Letters and postcards to the United States and Canada cost €1.60 for up to 20 grams and automatically go airmail. Letters and postcards to the United Kingdom cost €0.65. You can buy stamps at tobacco shops.

American Express also has a general-delivery service. There's no charge for cardholders, holders of American Express traveler's checks, or anyone who booked a vacation with American Express.

If you can avoid it, try not to have packages sent to you while you're in Rome or in Italy. Packages sent from abroad are notorious for being stopped by the Italian Customs Office or "Ufficio Dogonale." If your package gets stuck in customs, not only will you likely have to pay hefty customs fees but it could also take weeks for you to receive it. Sending medicine and even vitamins through the mail is highly unadvisable, and if discovered it will definitely be held up in customs for inspection.

Main Branches Main Rome post office ✉ *Piazza San Silvestro 19, Spagna* ☎ *06/6797398* 🌐 *www.poste.it.*

▌ MONEY

Rome's prices are comparable to those in other major capitals, such as Paris and London. Unless you dine in the swankiest places, you'll still find Rome one of the cheapest European capitals in which to eat. Clothes and leather goods are also generally less expensive than in northern Europe. Public transport is relatively cheap.

A Rome 2-km (1-mile) taxi ride costs €6. An inexpensive hotel room for two, including breakfast, is about €100; an inexpensive dinner for two is €45. A simple pasta item on the menu is about €8, and a ½-liter carafe of house wine €3.50. A McDonald's Big Mac is about €4. A pint of beer in a pub is around €4.

Admission to the Musei Vaticani is €15. The cheapest seat at Rome's Opera House runs €17; a movie ticket is €7.50. A daily English-language newspaper is €2.50.

Though more and more places are starting to accept credit cards as method of payment, cash is still king in Rome. This holds especially true for street markets and small mom-and-pop stores and restaurants.

ITEM	AVERAGE COST
Cup of Coffee	€0.80–€1
Glass of Wine	€3–€5
Glass of Beer	€4
Sandwich	€2.50–€4
One-Mile Taxi Ride	€6–€8
Museum Admission	€8–€12

Prices throughout this guide are given for adults. Substantially reduced fees are almost always available for children, students, and senior citizens when it comes to entrances to monuments and museums.

▌TIP➜ Banks never have every foreign currency on hand, and it may take as long as a week to order. If you're planning to exchange funds before leaving home, don't wait until the last minute.

ATMS AND BANKS

Your own bank will probably charge a fee for using ATMs abroad; the foreign bank you use may also charge a fee. Some banks, such as Citibank, which has a branch in Rome (near Via Veneto), don't charge extra fees to customers who use the Citibank ATM. Other banks may have similar agreements with Italian or foreign banks in Rome where customers won't get charged a transaction fee. Check with your bank to see if they have any agreements before your trip. Nevertheless, you'll usually get a better rate of exchange at an ATM than you will at a currency-exchange office or even when changing money in a bank. And extracting funds as you need them is a safer option than carrying around a large amount of cash.

▌TIP➜ PIN numbers with more than four digits are not recognized at ATMs in many countries. If yours has five or more, remember to change it before you leave.

ATMs are common in Rome and are the easiest way to get euros. The word for ATM in Italian is *bancomat*, for PIN, *codice segreto.* Four-digit PINs are the standard, though in some machines longer numbers will work. When using an ATM or *bancomat,* always use extra caution when punching in your PIN and collecting your money.

CREDIT CARDS

Always make your credit card company and bank aware that you'll be traveling or spending some time abroad, especially if don't travel internationally very often. Otherwise, the credit-card company or even your bank might put a hold on your card owing to unusual activity—not a good thing halfway through your trip. Record all your credit-card numbers—as well as the phone numbers to call if your cards are lost or stolen—in a safe place, so you're prepared should something go wrong. Both MasterCard and Visa have general numbers you can call (collect if you're abroad) if your card is lost, but you're better off calling the number of your issuing bank, since Master-Card and Visa usually just transfer you to your bank; your bank's number is usually printed on your card.

If you plan to use your credit card for cash advances, you'll need to apply for a PIN at least two weeks before your trip. Although it's usually cheaper (and safer) to use a credit card abroad for large purchases (so you can cancel payments or be reimbursed if there's a problem), note that some credit-card companies *and* the banks that issue them add substantial percentages to all foreign transactions, whether they're in a foreign currency or not. Check on these fees before leaving home, so there won't be any surprises when you get the bill.

Although increasingly common, credit cards aren't accepted at all establishments, and some require a minimum expenditure. If you want to pay with a card in a small hotel, store, or restaurant, it's a good idea to ask before conducting your business. Visa and MasterCard are preferred to American Express, but in tourist areas American Express is usually accepted. Acceptance of Diners Club is rare.

Some credit card companies require that you obtain a police report if your credit card was lost or stolen. In this case, you should go to the police station at Termini train station or at Rome's central police station on Via San Vitale 15.

Reporting Lost Cards American Express

☎ *800/528–4800 in U.S., 06/72282 within Italy ⊕ www.americanexpress.com.* **Diners Club** ☎ *800/234–6377 in U.S., 514/877–1577 collect from abroad, 800/393939 toll-free in Italy ⊕ www.dinersclub.com.* **MasterCard** ☎ *800/627–8372 in U.S., 636/722–7111 collect from abroad, 800/870866 toll-free in Italy ⊕ www.mastercard.com.* **Visa** ☎ *800/847–2911 in U.S., 303/967–1096 collect from abroad, 800/819014 toll-free in Italy ⊕ www.visa.com.*

CURRENCY AND EXCHANGE

The euro is the main unit of currency in Italy, as well as in 12 other European countries. Under the euro system, there are eight coins: 1, 2, 5, 10, 20, and 50 *centesimi* (at 100 centesimi to the euro), and 1 and 2 euros. Note: The 1 and 2 euro coins look very similar. Therefore, pay close attention when using these so that you don't overpay. There are seven notes: 5, 10, 20, 50, 100, 200, and 500 euros.

At this writing, the exchange rate was about €0.76 to the U.S. dollar; €0.76 to the Canadian dollar; €.83 to the pound sterling; €.80 to the Australian dollar; and €.62 to the New Zealand dollar.

■ TIP➔ Even if a currency-exchange booth has a sign promising no commission, rest assured that there's some kind of huge, hidden fee. (Oh ... that's right. The sign didn't say no fee.) And as for rates, you're almost always better off getting foreign currency at an ATM or exchanging money at a bank.

Currency Conversion Google. Google does currency conversion. Just type in the amount you want to convert and an explanation of how you want it converted (e.g., "14 Euro"), and then voilà. ⊕ *www.google.com.* **Oanda. com.** Oanda.com also allows you to print out a handy table with the current day's conversion rates. ⊕ *www.oanda.com.* **XE.com.** XE.com is a good currency conversion website. ⊕ *www. xe.com.*

PACKING

Plan your wardrobe in layers, no matter what the season. Rome generally has mild winters and hot, sticky summers. Heavy rain showers are common in spring and late fall, so bring some fashionable rain boots. Take a medium-weight coat for winter; a lightweight all-weather coat for spring and fall; and a lightweight jacket or sweater for summer evenings, which may be cool. Brief summer thunderstorms are common, so take a folding umbrella, and keep in mind that anything more than light cotton clothes is unbearable in the humid heat. Few public buildings in Rome, including museums, restaurants, and shops, are air-conditioned. Interiors can be cold and sometimes damp in the cooler months, so take woolens or flannels.

Dress codes are strict for visits to the Basilica di San Pietro, the Musei Vaticani, and some churches: for both men and women, shorts, scanty tops, bare midriffs, and sometimes even flip-flops are taboo. Shoulders must be covered. Women should carry a scarf or shawl to cover bare arms if the custodians insist. Those who do not comply with the dress code are refused admittance. Although there are no specific dress rules for the huge outdoor papal audiences, you'll be turned away if you're in shorts or a revealing outfit. The Vatican Information Office in Piazza di San Pietro will tell you the dress requirements for smaller audiences.

Most public and private bathrooms are often short on toilet paper. Therefore, it's best to always carry a small packet of tissues with you.

■ PASSPORTS AND VISAS

All U.S., Canadian, U.K., Australian, and New Zealand citizens, even infants, need a valid passport to enter Italy for stays of up to 90 days. Visas are not required for stays under 90 days.

■ TIP→ Before your trip, make two copies of your passport's data page (one for someone at home and another for you to carry separately). Or scan the page and email it to someone at home and/or yourself.

U.S. Passport Information U.S. Department of State ☎ 877/487–2778 ⊕ *travel.state.gov/ passport.*

U.S. Passport and Visa Expediters A. Briggs Passport & Visa Expediters ☎ 800/806– 0581, 202/338–0111 ⊕ *www.abriggs.com.* **American Passport Express** ☎ 800/455– 5166, 800/841–6778 ⊕ *americanpassport.com.* **Passport Express** ☎ 800/362–8196 ⊕ *www. passportexpress.com.* **Travel Document Systems** ☎ 800/874–5100, 877/874–5104 ⊕ *www.traveldocs.com.* **Travel the World Visas** ☎ 866/886–8472, 202/223–8822 ⊕ *www.world-visa.com.*

■ RESTROOMS

Public restrooms are a rare commodity in Rome. Although there are public toilets in Piazza di San Pietro, Piazza San Silvestro, Piazza di Spagna, at the Roman Forum, and in a few other strategic locations (all with a charge of €0.50–€0.70), the locals seem to make do primarily with well-timed pit stops and rely on the local bar. Most bars will allow you to use the restroom if you ask politely, though it's courteous to buy a little something—such as a bottle of water or espresso—in exchange for access to the facilities. Standards of cleanliness and comfort vary greatly. Restaurants, hotels, department stores like La Rinascente and Coin, and McDonald's restaurants tend to have the cleanest restrooms. Pubs and bars rank among the worst. It's a good idea to carry a packet of tissues with you, as you can't rely on most places having any toilet paper at all. There are bathrooms in all airports, train stations, and in most subway stations. In major train stations you'll also find well-kept pay toilets for €0.70 and in most museums. Carry a selection of coins, as some turnstiles do not give change. There are also free facilities at highway rest stops and gas stations: a small tip to the cleaning person is always appreciated. There are no bathrooms in churches, post offices, and public beaches.

▌ SAFETY

Wear a bag or camera slung across your body bandolier style, and don't rest your bag or camera on a table or underneath your chair at a sidewalk caffè or restaurant. If you have to bring a purse, make sure to keep it within sight by wearing it toward the front. Women should avoid wearing purses that don't have a zipper or that don't snap shut. Men should always keep their wallet in one of their front pockets with their hand in the same pocket. In Rome, beware of pickpockets on buses, especially Line 64 (Termini–St. Peter's train station); the Line 40 Express, which takes a faster route, and Bus 46 which takes you closer to St. Peter's Basilica; and subways—and when making your way through the corridors of crowded trains. Pickpockets often work in teams and zero in on tourists who look distracted or are in large groups. Pickpockets may be active wherever tourists gather, including the Roman Forum, the Spanish Steps, Piazza Navona, and Piazza di San Pietro. Purse snatchers work in teams on a single motor scooter or motorcycle: one drives and the other grabs.

Groups of gypsy children and young women (often with babies in arms and a scarf or a shawl wrapped around their shoulders) are present around sights popular with tourists and on buses and are adept pickpockets. One well-tried method is to approach a tourist and proffer a piece of cardboard with writing on it. While the unsuspecting victim attempts to read the message *on* it, the children's hands are busy *under* it, trying to make off with wallets and valuables. If you see such a group, do not even allow them near you—they are quick and know more tricks than you do. The phrases *Vai via!* (Go away!) and *Chiamo la polizia* (I'll call the police) usually keep them at bay. The colorful characters dressed as Roman legionaries, who hover around the Colosseum and other monuments, expect a tip if you photograph them. A €5 tip is quite sufficient.

The difficulties encountered by women traveling alone in Italy are often overstated. Younger women have to put up with much male attention, but it's rarely dangerous or hostile. Ignoring whistling and questions is the best way to get rid of unwanted attention. Women who care to avoid uncomfortable eye contact with strangers tend to wear big sunglasses. Women should also be aware that smiling at others can sometimes be viewed as a sign of flirtation in Italy. Do be careful of gropers on the Metro and on Buses 64 and 46 (Vatican buses) and 218 and 660 (Catacombs). They're known to take advantage of the cramped space. React like the locals: forcefully and loudly. ▌ **TIP→ Distribute your cash, credit cards, IDs, and other valuables between a deep front pocket, an inside jacket or vest pocket, and a hidden money pouch. Don't reach for the money pouch once you're in public.**

Transportation Security Administration (*TSA*). ⊕ *www.tsa.gov.*

▌ TAXES

The service charge and IVA, or value-added tax (V.A.T.), are included in the rate except in five-star deluxe hotels, where the IVA (15% on luxury hotels) may be a separate item added to the bill at departure.

Many, but not all, Rome restaurants have eliminated extra charges for service and for *pane e coperto* (a cover charge that includes bread, whether you eat it or not). If it is an extra, the service charge may be 12%–15%. Only part, if any, of this amount goes to the waiter, so an additional tip is customary (⇨ *Tipping*).

Always ask for an itemized bill and a *scontrino*, or receipt. Officially you have to keep this receipt with you for 600 feet from the restaurant, bar, or store and be able to produce it if asked by the tax police. Sound absurd? It's something of a desperate measure for the country with the highest taxes in Europe and the highest levels of tax evasion/avoidance, and there have been cases of unwitting customers falling foul of the law, even though this practice is meant to catch noncompliant restaurants.

Be advised that the vendors selling imitation knock-off purses, sunglasses, and other accessories are unauthorized street vendors. If caught buying from any of these street vendors, you could be served with a hefty fine by Italy's tax police (Guardia di Finanza). Value-added tax (IVA in Italy, V.A.T. to English-speakers) is 23% on luxury goods, clothing, and wine. On most consumer goods, it's already included in the amount shown on the price tag; on services, such as car rentals, it's an extra item. If a store you shop in has a "euro tax free" sign outside and you make a purchase above €155 (before tax), present your passport and request a "Tax Free Shopping Check" when paying, or at least an invoice itemizing the article(s), price(s), and the amount of tax.

To get an IVA refund when you're leaving Italy, take the goods and the invoice to the customs office at the airport or other point of departure and have the invoice stamped. (If you return to the United States or Canada directly from Italy, go through the procedure at Italian customs; if your return is, say, via Britain, take the Italian goods and invoice to British customs.) Once back home—and within 90 days of the date of purchase—mail the stamped invoice to the store, which will forward the IVA rebate to you.

V.A.T. Refunds Global Blue ☎ 800/566-9828, 0331/1778 000 within Italy ⊕ www.global-blue.com.

▌TIME

Rome is one hour ahead of London, six ahead of New York, seven ahead of Chicago, and nine ahead of Los Angeles. Rome is nine hours behind Sydney and 11 behind Auckland. Like the rest of Europe, Italy uses the 24-hour (or "military") clock, which means that after 12 noon you continue counting forward: 13:00 is 1 pm, 23:30 is 11:30 pm.

Time Zones Timeanddate.com. Timeanddate.com can help you figure out the correct time anywhere. ⊕ www.timeanddate.com/worldclock.

▌TIPPING

Many Rome restaurants have done away with the service charge of about 12%–15% that used to appear as a separate item on your check—now service is almost always included in the menu prices. It's customary to leave an additional 5% tip, or a couple of euros, for the waiter, depending on the quality of service. Tip checkroom attendants €1 per person, restroom attendants €0.50. In both cases tip more in expensive hotels and restaurants. Tip €0.05–€0.10 for whatever you drink standing up at a coffee bar, €0.25 or more for table service in a caffè. At a hotel bar, tip €1 and up for a round or two of cocktails, more in the grander hotels.

For tipping taxi drivers, it is acceptable if you round up to the nearest euro. Railway and airport porters charge a fixed rate per bag. Tip an additional €0.50, more if the porter is very helpful. Not all theater ushers expect a tip; if they do, tip €0.25 per person, more for very expensive seats. Give a barber €1–€1.50 and a hairdresser's assistant €1.50–€4 for a shampoo or cut, depending on the type of establishment and the final bill; 5%–10% is a fair guideline.

On sightseeing tours, tip guides about €1.50 per person for a half-day group tour, more if they're very good. In museums and other places of interest where admission is free, a contribution is expected; give anything from €0.50 to €1 for one or two people, more if the guardian has been especially helpful. Service station attendants are tipped only for special services.

In hotels, give the *portiere* (concierge) about 15% of his bill for services, or €2.50–€5 if he has been generally helpful. For two people in a double room, leave the chambermaid about €1 per day, or about €4–€6 a week, in a moderately priced hotel; tip a minimum of €1 for valet or room service. Increase these amounts by one half in an expensive hotel, and double them in a very expensive hotel. In very expensive hotels, tip doormen €0.50 for calling a cab and €1 for carrying bags to the check-in desk, bellhops €1.50–€2.50 for carrying your bags to the room, and €2–€2.50 for room service.

▌ TOURS AND GUIDES

ORIENTATION TOURS

Some might consider them campy and kitschy, but guided bus tours can prove a blissfully easy way to enjoy a quick introduction to the city's top sights—if you don't feel like being on your feet all day. Sitting in a bus, with friendly tour guide commentary (and even friendlier fellow sightseers, many of whom will be from every country under the sun), can make for a delightful and fun experience—so give one a whirl *even* if you're an old Rome hand. Of course, you'll want to savor these incredible sights at your own leisure later on.

Appian Line, Carrani, Vastours (in collaboration with American Express), and other operators offer half-day and full-day tours in air-conditioned buses with English-speaking guides. The four main itineraries are: "Ancient Rome," "Classic Rome," "Christian Rome," and "The Vatican Museums and Sistine Chapel." Half-day tours cost around €35 and full-day tours (including lunch and entrance fees) are between €100 and €137. The Musei Vaticani tour costs €60, but offers the advantage of not having to queue (sometimes for an hour or more) at the museum doors, awaiting your turn for admission. All the companies pick you up at centrally located hotels.

All operators can provide a luxury car for up to three people, a limousine for up to seven, or a minibus for up to nine, all with an English-speaking driver, but guide service is extra. Almost all operators offer "Rome by Night" tours, with or without dinner and entertainment. You can book tours through travel agents.

Various sightseeing buses following a continuous circle route through the center of town operate daily. Stop-'n'-Go has eight daily departures and makes 14 scheduled stops at important sites, where you can get on and off at will. Check with the Rome tourist information kiosks or inquire at your hotel for prices and further information.

The least expensive organized sightseeing tour of Rome is that run by ATAC, the municipal bus company. Double-decker Bus 110 leaves from Piazza dei Cinquecento, in front of Termini station, but you can pick it up at any of its 10 stopover points. A day ticket costs about €18 and allows you to stop off and get on as often as you like. The price includes an audio guide system in six languages. The total tour takes about two hours and covers the Colosseum, Piazza Navona, St. Peter's, the Trevi Fountain, and Via Veneto. Tickets can be bought on board. Two-day and three-day tickets are also available. Tours leave from Termini station every 20 minutes between 9 am and 8:30 pm.

The Archeobus, which takes you to the Old Appian Way, the Catacombs, and the new Park of the Aqueducts in the open countryside, also operates with the stop 'n' go formula. Little 15-seater buses leave from Piazza della Cinquecento every hour between 10 am and 4 pm. Tickets cost €12 and are valid all day. A combined 110 and Archeobus ticket costs €25 and is valid for one day.

Of course, you get a real bargain if you do your sightseeing "tours" of Rome by public transport. Many buses and trams pass major sights. With a single €1 ticket you can get in 75 minutes of sightseeing (or an entire day, with a €4 *giornaliero* ticket). Time your ride to avoid rush hours. The little electric Bus 116 scoots through the heart of Old Rome, with stops near the Pantheon, the Spanish Steps, and Piazza del Popolo, among others. The route of Bus 117 takes in San Giovanni in Laterano, the Colosseum, and the Spanish Steps.

Since certain parts of the historic center are open to pedestrians only, some walking is involved in most escorted bus tours of the city. Don't forget to dress appropriately for visits to churches *(⇨ Local Dos and Taboos)*. Tour operators can also organize minibus tours for small parties.

Bus Line ATAC ☎ *06/57003* ⊕ *www.atac. roma.it.*

Tour Operators American Express
☎ *06/67642250* ⊕ *www.americanexpress.com/ italy.* **Appian Line** ☎ *06/48786601* ⊕ *www. appianline.it.***Carrani** ✉ *Via Vittorio Emanuele Orlando 95, Repubblica* ☎ *06/4742501* ⊕ *www.carrani.com.* **Ciao Roma Trolley Tour** ☎ *06/47824580* ⊕ *ciaoromaopenbus.com.* **Segway Roma Tours** ☎ *380/3012913* ⊕ *www. segwayroma.net.* **Stop-'n'-go City Tours** ☎ *06/48905729.* **Vastours** ☎ *06/4814309* ⊕ *www.vastours.it.*

SPECIAL-INTEREST TOURS

You can make your own arrangements (at no cost) to attend a public papal audience at the Vatican or at the pope's summer residence at Castel Gandolfo. The easiest way is to request them online through the Santa Susanna Church, the American Catholic Church of Rome (⊕ *www. santasusanna.org/popevatican/tickets.*

html). You can also book through a travel agency for a package that includes coach transportation to the Vatican for the audience and some sightseeing along the way, returning you to your hotel, for about €35. The excursion outside Rome to Castel Gandolfo on summer Sundays for the pope's blessing costs about €45. Agencies that arrange these tours include Appian Line and Carrani.

Tourvisa Italia organizes lunch and dinner boat trips on the Tiber, departing and returning to Ponte Sant'Angelo. Boats leave four times daily for a cruise that covers all of the main historical bridges of Rome and other important sights. Tickets cost approximately €35 for lunch and €55 for dinner. The company also does combined bus and boat tours lasting 2½ hours.

A ride in a horse-drawn carriage is the Rome equivalent of a gondola ride in Venice. Coachmen can be contacted directly at popular sights like St. Peter's Square and the Colosseum. An hour's ride for four passengers to view the fountains of Rome will cost around €150, depending on your bargaining skills.

Centro Studi Cassia organizes courses in Italian cooking, art, music, and current events in simple Italian. This is an enjoyable way to learn to speak some of the language and, at the same time, find out more about the culture and traditions of the country.

Tour Operators Appian Line ☎ *06/487861* ⊕ *www.appianline.it.* **Carrani** ✉ *Via Vittorio Emanuele Orlando 95, Repubblica* ☎ *06/4742501* ⊕ *www.carrani.com.* **Centro Studi Cassia** ☎ *06/33253852* ⊕ *www. centrostudicassia.it.***Tourvisa Italia** ☎ *06/448741* ⊕ *www.tourvisa.it.*

WALKING TOURS

In Rome, there are tours and there are *tours.* Why pay to be led around by someone who just memorizes some lines and gives you the run-of-the-mill tour, when you can learn firsthand from the experts? Context Rome is an organization formed by a group of architects, archaeologists, art historians, sommeliers, and professors that give specialized walking seminars to small intimate groups (no more than six people) in and around Rome. Every day of the week offers five or six theme walks, which might include Imperial Rome: Architecture and History of the Archaeological Center; Underground Rome: The Hidden City; Baroque Rome: The Age of Bernini; Vatican Collections, and even Rome Shopping. Prices range from €55–€75 per person. If you want to get graduate "summa cum laude" as a serious Rome tourist and aficionado, the walking tours of Context Rome—with 26 PhDs and 25 Masters docents in its ranks—can't be beat. Similar to Context, Walks of Italy focuses on sustainable travel and also gives specialized tours of Rome in small, intimate groups.

All About Rome, Enjoy Rome, Through Eternity, and Argiletum Tour also offer some fascinating walking tours of the city and its sights. Argiletum and the cultural association Genti e Paesi offer regular walking tours and museum visits in English, including private tours of the Sistine Chapel before all the hordes arrive. Book at least one day in advance. For a popular food tour that's off-the-beaten path, check out Eating Italy Food Tours, in Testaccio. Owner Kenny Dunn takes you behind the scenes at the Testaccio open-air food market, various mom-and-pop restaurants, and specialty food shops and explains the history of this working-class neighborhood and the "slow food" movement in Italy. If you have a reasonable knowledge of Italian, you can take advantage of the free guided visits and walking tours organized by Rome's cultural associations and the city council for museums and monuments. These usually take place on weekends. Programs are announced in the daily papers and in the weekly magazine *roma c'è*.

Those who want to see everything during their trip to Rome without eliminating their daily run or workout might consider

hiring a guide from Sight Jogging Tours. The company consists of highly experienced trainers that give tours of Rome based on the level of difficulty chosen by the client. Routes may take in Villa Borghese, Imperial Forum and Colloseum, St. Peter's Basilica, and many other sights. Trainers meet tourists at their hotel and take them back after the run is over. Most tours take 45–60 minutes and cost about €85 per person per hour.

Tour Operators Argiletum Tour ✉ *Via Madonna dei Monti 49, Monti* ☎ *06/45438906* ⊕ *www.argiletumtour.com.* **Context Rome** ✉ *Via Santa Maria Maggiore 145, Santa Maria Maggiore* ☎ *06/97625204 within Italy, 800/691–6036 within the U.S.* ⊕ *www. contexttravel.com.* **Eating Italy Food Tours** ☎ *800/838–3006 from the U.S. or Canada, 800/4118881 within Europe* ⊕ *www. eatingitalyfoodtours.com.* **Enjoy Rome** ✉ *Via Marghera 8/A, Termini* ☎ *06/4451843* ⊕ *www.enjoyrome.com.* **Genti e Paesi** ✉ *Via Adda 111, Parioli* ☎ *06/85301755* ⊕ *www. gentiepaesi.it.* **Sightjogging** ☎ *347/3353185* ⊕ *www.sightjogging.it.* **Through Eternity** ☎ *06/7009336* ⊕ *www.througheternity. com.* **Walks of Italy** ☎ *334/9744274 within Italy, 202/684–6916 within the U.S.* ⊕ *www. walksofitaly.com.*

EXCURSIONS

Most operators offer half-day excursions to Tivoli to see the fountains and gardens of Villa D'Este. Appian Line's afternoon tour to Tivoli includes a visit to Hadrian's Villa, with its impressive ancient ruins, as well as the many-fountained Villa D'Este. Most operators also have full-day excursions to Assisi, to Pompeii and/or Capri, and to Florence.

Tour Operator Appian Line ✉ *Piazza Esquilino 6/7, Esquilino* ☎ *06/48786601* ⊕ *www. appianline.it.*

PERSONAL GUIDES

You can arrange for a personal guide through the main APT (Azienda Per Turismo) Tourist Information Office.

Tour Operator APT ⊠ *Via Parigi 11, Repubblica* ☎ *06/51687240.*

∎ TRIP INSURANCE

Comprehensive trip insurance is valuable if you're booking a very expensive or complicated trip (particularly to an isolated region) or if you're booking far in advance. Comprehensive policies typically cover trip cancellation and interruption, letting you cancel or cut your trip short because of illness, or, in some cases, acts of terrorism in your destination. Such policies might also cover evacuation and medical care. Some also cover you for trip delays because of bad weather or mechanical problems as well as for lost or delayed luggage.

Another type of coverage to consider is financial default—that is, when your trip is disrupted because a tour operator, airline, or cruise line goes out of business. Generally you must buy this when you book your trip or shortly thereafter, and it's available to you only if your operator isn't on a list of excluded companies.

Always read the fine print of your policy to make sure that you're covered for the risks that most concern you. Compare several policies to be sure you're getting the best price and range of coverage available.

Insurance Comparison Info **Insure My Trip** ☎ *800/487–4722* ⊕ *www.insuremytrip.com.* **Square Mouth** ☎ *800/240–0369, 727/564–9203* ⊕ *www.squaremouth.com.*

Comprehensive Insurers **Allianz Global Assistance** ☎ *800/284–8300* ⊕ *www.allianztravelinsurance.com.* **Travel Guard Chartis** ☎ *800/826–4919* ⊕ *www.travelguard.com.* **CSA Travel Protection** ☎ *800/348–9505* ⊕ *www.csatravelprotection.com.* **Travelex Insurance** ☎ *888/228–9792* ⊕ *www.travelexinsurance.com.* **Travel Insured International** ☎ *800/243–3174, 603/328–1707 emergency travel assistance* ⊕ *www.travelinsured.com.*

∎ VISITOR INFORMATION

Rome has an APT (Azienda Per Turismo) Tourist Information Office in the city center. Green APT information kiosks called Punti Informativi Turistici (P.I.T.), with multilingual personnel, are near the most important sights and squares, as well as at Termini station and Leonardo da Vinci and Ciampino airports. They're open 9–1 and 3–7:30 and provide information about cultural events, museums, opening hours, city transportation, and so on. You can also pick up free tourist maps and brochures.

In Rome **APT Tourist Information Office** ⊠ *Via Parigi 11, Termini* ☎ *06/51687240.* **Call Center–Comune di Roma Ufficio Turismo** ☎ *06/0608* ⊕ *www.060608.it.* **ENIT (Italian Government Tourist Board).** ⊠ *Via Marghera 2–6, Termini* ☎ *06/49711, 039/039039* ⊕ *www.italiantourism.com.*

ONLINE RESOURCES

The Turismo Roma website is ⊕ *www.turismoroma.it* and is packed with information about events and places to visit. For more information specifically on Italy, visit ⊕ *www.italiantourism.com,* ⊕ *www.initaly.com,* and ⊕ *www.wel.it.* Other particularly useful sites are ⊕ *www.romeguide.it* and ⊕ *www.unospitearoma.it,* both of which have English versions. You may also want to consult ⊕ *www.ahotelinitaly.com.* Particularly provocative, fascinating, and up-to-date are the monthly Web issues of *The American,* a popular English magazine based in Rome; their website is ⊕ *www.theamericanmag.*

com. Magnificent is the only word to describe this passionate writer's ode to the city's treasures of art and architecture, replete with hundreds of photos and little-known facts: ⊕ *www.romeartlover. it.* An official website for many of Rome's most famous sights, and a place to make ticket reservations, is ⊕ *www.pierreci.it.* If you're particularly curious about the history of food and where to get the best of it in Rome, check out this comprehensive blog ⊕ *www.parlafood.com.* One example of a top website devoted to one sight in Rome is ⊕ *www.capitolium.org.* A dynamic organization offering unusual tours and news about what's happening in Rome is ⊕ *www.nerone.cc,* and ⊕ *www. museionline.it* has invaluable links to almost all the city's many museums and galleries together with news of the latest exhibitions, opening hours, and prices. A handy guide to the bus lines threading Rome and its surrounding areas is ⊕ *www.cotralspa.it.*

INDEX

PHOTO CREDITS

ABOUT OUR WRITERS

Perpetual traveler, adventurer, and champion of worthy artistic causes, Lynda Albertson is a writer, editor, and founding member of the Café.Blue list-serve. Today, she lives in Rome where she serves as CEO for the Association for Research into Crimes Against Art (ARCA), an international nonprofit that examines contemporary issues in art crime and cultural heritage protection. In addition, she serves as copy editor and writer for the Journal of Art Crime and the Art Crime Blog (⊕ http://art-crime.blogspot.it). For this edition, she updated our Shopping chapter.

After her first Italian coffee and her first Italian bacio in 1999, Nicole Arriaga just knew she'd have to find a way to make it back to Rome and moved to the Eternal City in 2003 to earn her Master's in political science. There Nicole freelances for several publications including Romeing, 10Best, and The American. When not writing, Nicole works as a programs coordinator for an American Study Abroad organization based in Rome. For this edition, she updated our Experience Rome chapter (which she wrote for our last edition), and also updated our Where to Stay chapter and Travel Smart section.

Happy not to have a car, Rome resident (and teacher at the city's University of Tor Vergata) Martin Wilmot Bennett spends much of his time walking around, an ideal activity which has paid off royally in our "Roamin' Holiday" chapter. In addition, his vast background in Italian art led to his writing our special features on Michelangelo's Sistine Ceiling and the Bernini/Borromini rivalry.

Erica Firpo writes for an array of publications including New York Times, Huffington Post, Fathom, Oryx, and Insight Guides. In addition, she has penned a series of restaurant guide books starting with Rome Little Black Book, and is author of Rome Select. She also covers fashion, art and life-style issues in her blog (⊕ moscerina.com). For this edition, she updated our Nightlife/Arts chapter and wrote our photo-feature on the Campo de' Fiori.

Dana Klitzberg is a chef and culinary expert from New York City. After studying in Florence and traveling to Italy for a decade, she moved to Rome in 2000, after completing culinary school in Manhattan (and cooking in top Italian eatery San Domenico NY). Once top toque in various Roman restaurants, she now works in several "foodie" areas through her company Blu Aubergine (⊕ www.bluaubergine.com): catering, private chef services, restaurant consultant, cooking class teacher, and a leader of culinary tours around Rome. A food and travel writer, this University of Virginia grad updated our Where to Eat chapter, which she originally penned years back.

Journalist, traveler, and blogger, Amanda Ruggeri lives just down the street from the Colosseum. After graduating from Yale, getting a master's in international relations from Cambridge, and working as a reporter in Washington, D.C., she made her way to Rome—and has never looked back. Today, she writes for the New York Times, Guardian, New York Magazine, National Geographic Traveller, and AFAR. She's also appeared on the History Channel as a documentary host, provided travel consulting sessions to Italy-bound travelers, and filmed a series of news clips for Vocativ. Her blog (⊕ www.revealedrome.com) features tips, tricks, and things not to miss in the Eternal City.

An award-winning travel writer, Margaret Stenhouse has written for The Herald and the International Herald Tribune's "Italy Daily" supplement, is author of The Goddess of the Lake: Legends and Mysteries of Nemi, and updated our Side Trips from Rome chapter.

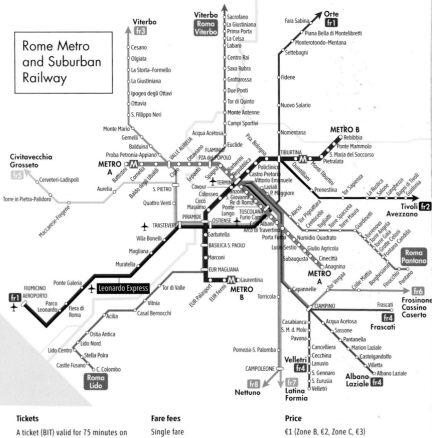

Rome Metro and Suburban Railway

Tickets

A ticket (BIT) valid for 75 minutes on any combination of buses and trams and one entrance to the metro costs €1. Tickets are sold at newsstands, some coffee bars, ticket machines in metro stations, and ATAC and COTRAL ticket booths. Time-stamp your ticket when boarding the first vehicle, and stamp it again when boarding for the last time within 75 minutes. You stamp the ticket at Metro sliding electronic doors, and in the little yellow machines on buses and trams.

Fare fees	Price
Single fare	€1 (Zone B, €2, Zone C, €3)
Weekly pass	€16
Monthly unlimited pass	€30
Biglietto integrato giornaliero (Integrated Daily Ticket)	€4
Biglietto turistico integrato (Three-Day Pass)	€11
Settimanale (Weekly Ticket)	€16